用心雕刻每一本……
http://site.douban.com/110283/
http://weibo.com/nccpub

用心字里行间　雕刻名著经典

ORGANIZATIONAL BEHAVIOR

Improving Performance and Commitment in the Workplace

Third Edition

JASON A. COLQUITT
University of Georgia

JEFFERY A. LEPINE
Arizona State University

MICHAEL J. WESSON
Texas A&M University

组织行为学

第3版

双语教学通用版

贾森·科尔基特
〔美〕杰弗里·勒平　著
迈克尔·韦森

苏晓艳　译注

人民邮电出版社
北　京

图书在版编目（CIP）数据

组织行为学：第3版：双语教学通用版：汉英对照 /（美）科尔基特等 著；苏晓艳 译．
—北京：人民邮电出版社，2016.4（2019.12 重印）
ISBN 978-7-115-41520-2

I. ①组… II. ①科… ②苏… III. ①组织行为学 - 双语教学 - 研究生 - 教材 - 汉、英 IV. ① C936

中国版本图书馆 CIP 数据核字（2016）第 023521 号

Jason A. Colquitt, Jeffery A.Lepine, Michael J. Wesson
Organizational Behavior, 3rd Edition
ISBN 0-07-802935-X

北京市版权局著作权合同登记号：01-2014-8594

组织行为学（第3版，双语教学通用版）

◆ 著　　　[美] 贾森·科尔基特　杰弗里·勒平　迈克尔·韦森
　译　注　苏晓艳
　策　划　刘　力　陆　瑜
　责任编辑　刘冰云
　装帧设计　陶建胜

◆ 人民邮电出版社出版发行　北京市丰台区成寿寺路 11 号
　邮编　100164　电子邮件　315@ptpress.com.cn
　网址　http://www.ptpress.com.cn
　电话（编辑部）010-84931398　（市场部）010-84937152
　三河市少明印务有限公司印刷
　新华书店经销

◆ 开本：850 × 1092　1/16
　印张：23.25
　字数：510 千字　2016 年 4 月第 1 版　2019 年 12 月第 2 次印刷
　著作权合同登记号　图字：01-2014-8594

ISBN 978-7-115-41520-2

定价：68.00 元

本书如有印装质量问题，请与本社联系　电话：（010）84937153

内容提要

本教材由美国佐治亚大学贾森·科尔基特、亚利桑那州立大学杰弗里·勒平与得克萨斯 A&M 大学迈克尔·韦森精心编写，凝聚了三位教授多年的科研成果和教学经验之精华，在美国以及世界多个国家和地区拥有广大的读者，被百余所院校采用作为工商管理或人力资源管理专业学习的教材。

本教材在编写上主题清晰、内容完整、结构严谨、体例规范、形式统一、难易适度，既适合学生的学习，也易于教师安排教学。全书围绕组织行为学的两个成果，即工作绩效和组织承诺，从影响变量的个体机制、个人特征、团体机制和组织机制等方面进行了系统论述，做到了由表及里、深入浅出。另外，在内容安排上，不仅专业术语明确、图表清晰，而且还从学生生活、电影剧情、体育运动、跨国公司等案例中分别论述组织行为学的实践应用，更有利于学生对教材内容的理解。

本书适用于经济管理类专业本科生、MBA、EMBA、MPA，既可作为相关双语课程的教材，还可作为研究人员及各类组织尤其是企业经营管理人员的参考用书。

Dedication

To Catherine, Cameron, Riley, and Connor, and also to Mom, Dad, Alan, and Shawn. The most wonderful family I could imagine, two times over.

–J.A.C.

To my parents who made me, and to Marcie, Izzy, and Eli, who made my life complete.

–J.A.L.

To Liesl and Dylan: Their support in all I do is incomparable. They are my life and I love them both. To my parents: They provide a foundation that never wavers.

–M.J.W.

About the Authors
作者简介

贾森・科尔基特

JASON A. COLQUITT

Jason A. Colquitt is the William H. Willson Distinguished Chair in the Department of Management at the University of Georgia's Terry College of Business. He received his PhD from Michigan State University's Eli Broad Graduate School of Management, and earned his BS in Psychology from Indiana University. He has taught organizational behavior and human resource management at the undergraduate, masters, and executive levels and has also taught research methods at the doctoral level. He has received awards for teaching excellence at both the undergraduate and executive levels.

Jason's research interests include organizational justice, trust, team effectiveness, and personality influences on task and learning performance. He has published more than 20 articles on these and other topics in *Academy of Management Journal, Academy of Management Review, Journal of Applied Psychology, Organizational Behavior and Human Decision Processes, and Personnel Psychology.* He is currently serving as the Editor-in-Chief for *Academy of Management Journal and has served on a number of editorial boards, including Academy of Management Journal, Journal of Applied Psychology, Organizational Behavior and Human Decision Processes, Personnel Psychology, Journal of Management,* and *International Journal of Conflict Management.* He is a recipient of the Society for Industrial and Organizational Psychology's Distinguished Early Career Contributions Award and the Cummings Scholar Award for early to mid-career achievement, sponsored by the Organizational Behavior division of the Academy of Management. He was also elected to be a Representative-at-Large for the Organizational Behavior division.

Jason enjoys spending time with his wife, Catherine, and three sons, Cameron, Riley, and Connor. His hobbies include playing basketball, playing the trumpet, watching movies, and rooting on (in no particular order) the Pacers, Colts, Cubs, Hoosiers, Spartans, Gators, and Bulldogs.

杰弗里・勒平

JEFFERY A. LEPINE

Is the PetSmart Chair in Leadership in the Department of Management at Arizona State University's W.P. Carey School of Business. He received his PhD in Organizational Behavior from the Eli Broad Graduate School of Management at Michigan State University. He also earned an MS in Management from Florida State University and a BS in Finance from the University of Connecticut. He has taught organizational behavior, human resource management, and management of groups and teams at undergraduate and graduate levels.

Jeff's research interests include team functioning and effectiveness, individual and team adaptation, citizenship behavior, voice, engagement, and occupational stress. He has published more than 20 articles on these and other topics in *Academy of Management Journal, Academy of Management Review, Journal of Applied Psychology, Organizational Behavior and Human Decision Processes,* and *Personnel Psychology.* He has served as Associate Editor of *Academy of Management Review,* and has served (or is currently serving) on the editorial boards of *Academy of Management Journal, Journal of Applied Psychology, Organizational Behavior and Human Decision Processes, Personnel Psychology, Journal of Management, Journal of Organizational Behavior, and Journal of Occupational and Organizational Psychology.* He is a recipient of the Society for Industrial and Organizational

Psychology's Distinguished Early Career Contributions Award and the Cummings Scholar Award for early to mid-career achievement, sponsored by the Organizational Behavior division of the Academy of Management. He was also elected to the Executive Committee of the Human Resource Division of the Academy of Management. Prior to earning his PhD, Jeff was an officer in the U.S. Air Force.

Jeff spends most of his free time with his wife Marcie, daughter Izzy, and son Eli. He also enjoys playing guitar, hiking in the desert, and restoring his GTO.

MICHAEL J. WESSON

迈克尔・韦森

Is an associate professor in the Management Department at Texas A&M University's Mays Business School. He received his PhD from Michigan State University's Eli Broad Graduate School of Management. He also holds an MS in human resource management from Texas A&M University and a BBA from Baylor University. He has taught organizational behavior and human resource management–based classes at all levels but currently spends most of his time teaching Mays MBAs, EMBAs, and executive development at Texas A&M. He was awarded Texas A&M's Montague Center for Teaching Excellence Award.

Michael's research interests include organizational justice, goal-setting, organizational entry (employee recruitment, selection, and socialization), person–organization fit, and compensation and benefits. His articles have been published in journals such as *Journal of Applied Psychology, Personnel Psychology, Academy of Management Review,* and *Organizational Behavior and Human Decision Processes.* He currently serves on the editorial boards of the *Journal of Applied Psychology* and the *Journal of Organizational Behavior* and is an ad hoc reviewer for many others. He is active in the Academy of Management and the Society for Industrial and Organizational Psychology. Prior to returning to school, Michael worked as a human resources manager for a *Fortune* 500 firm. He has served as a consultant to the automotive supplier, healthcare, oil and gas, and technology industries in areas dealing with recruiting, selection, onboarding, compensation, and turnover.

Michael spends most of his time trying to keep up with his wife Liesl and son Dylan. He is a self-admitted food and wine snob, home theater aficionado, and college sports addict. (Gig 'em Aggies!)

Preface
前言

Why did we decide to write this textbook? Well, for starters, organizational behavior (OB) remains a fascinating topic that everyone can relate to (because everyone either has worked or is going to work in the future). What makes people effective at their job? What makes them want to stay with their employer? What makes work enjoyable? Those are all fundamental questions that organizational behavior research can help answer. However, our desire to write this book also grew out of our own experiences (and frustrations) teaching OB courses using other textbooks. We found that students would end the semester with a common set of questions that we felt we could answer if given the chance to write our own book. With that in mind, *Organizational Behavior: Improving Performance and Commitment in the Workplace,* was written to answer the following questions.

DOES ANY OF THIS STUFF REALLY MATTER?

Organizational behavior might be the most relevant class any student ever takes, but that doesn't always shine through in OB texts. The introductory section of our book contains two chapters not included in other books: *Job Performance* and *Organizational Commitment.* Being good at one's job and wanting to stay with one's employer are obviously critical concerns for employees and managers alike. After describing these topics in detail, every remaining chapter in the book links that chapter's content to performance and commitment. Students can then better appreciate the practical relevance of organizational behavior concepts.

IF THAT THEORY DOESN'T WORK, THEN WHY IS IT IN THE BOOK?

In putting together this book, we were guided by the question, "What would OB texts look like if all of them were first written now, rather than decades ago?" We found that many of the organizational behavior texts on the market include outdated (and indeed, scientifically disproven!) models or theories, presenting them sometimes as fact or possibly for the sake of completeness or historical context. Our students were always frustrated by the fact that they had to read about, learn, and potentially be tested on material that we knew to be wrong. Although historical context can be important at times, we believe that focusing on so-called "evidence-based management" is paramount in today's fast-paced classes. Thus, this textbook includes new and emerging topics that others leave out and excludes flawed and outdated topics that some other books leave in.

HOW DOES ALL THIS STUFF FIT TOGETHER?

Organizational behavior is a diverse and multidisciplinary field, and it's not always easy to see how all its topics fit together. Our book deals with this issue in two ways. First, all of the chapters in our book are organized around an integrative model that opens each chapter (see the back of the book). That model provides students with a road map of the course, showing them where they've been and where they're going. Second, our chapters are tightly focused around specific topics and aren't "grab bag–ish" in nature. Our hope is that students (and instructors) won't ever come across a topic and think, "Why is this topic being discussed in this chapter?"

DOES THIS STUFF HAVE TO BE SO DRY?

Research on motivation to learn shows that students learn more when they have an intrinsic interest in the topic, but many OB texts do little to stimulate that interest. Put simply, we wanted to create a book that students enjoy reading. To do that, we used a more informal, conversational style when writing the book. We also tried to use company examples that students will be familiar with and find compelling. Finally, we included insert boxes, self-assessments, and exercises that students should find engaging (and sometimes even entertaining!).

NEW AND IMPROVED COVERAGE

- *Chapter 1: What is Organizational Behavior?*—This chapter now opens with a wraparound case on Facebook. The case describes Facebook's emphasis on hiring talented people with an entrepreneurial mindset while attempting to maintain the start-up culture in the company. The case also describes some of the ethical issues at play in Facebook's core products and new initiatives. The discussion of the resource-based view now uses Apple as an example, describing how Apple's history, status, and "numerous small decisions" conspire to create an inimitable advantage in the consumer electronics space. The OB on Screen feature has been revised to focus on *The Social Network,* illustrating how Facebook's initial exclusivity created an inimitable advantage relative to MySpace and Friendster. The OB at the Bookstore feature now focuses on *SuperFreakonomics,* which is used to illustrate the scientific method and the use of data to describe human behavior. Finally, the chapter concludes with an expanded discussion of evidence-based management.
- *Chapter 2: Job Performance*—This chapter features a new wraparound case on Frito-Lay, which overviews the company's concern with the alignment of employee job performance with its corporate vision. The case describes how Frito-Lay sought to better understand the job performance of route sales representatives in an attempt to manage their performance more effectively. The book now uses an example of women's college basketball to illustrate the distinction between results-based and behavior-based job performance perspectives. The OB on Screen feature now centers on the movie *Despicable Me* to illustrate how dimensions of job performance may be related in ways that are somewhat counterintuitive. The concept of "bullying" is now discussed as an example of abusive counterproductive behavior. Our OB at the Bookstore feature has been changed to *Helping People Win at Work.* This best-selling book provides an outlook on performance management that contrast sharply with forced ranking practices, which are also discussed.
- *Chapter 3: Organizational Commitment*—NASA serves as the wraparound case in this edition, spotlighting the agency's challenge of maintaining commitment after the end of the space shuttle program. The case also describes similar challenges faced by NASA suppliers, and how some of those suppliers are using technology to identify employee "flight risks." The discussion of the three types of organizational commitment includes all new company examples, including spotlights on SAS and Comcast. The OB on Screen feature now uses *Up in the Air* to illustrate the concept of embeddedness–of how links to one's organization and community can create a sense of anxiety about leaving a company. OB at the Bookstore has been revised to focus on *The War for Late Night,* chronicling how Conan O'Brien's commitment to NBC (and *The Tonight Show*) affected his reactions to NBC's decision to bump the show back to 12:05. The chapter also includes an expanded discussion of organizational attempts to combat absenteeism, including the hiring of private investigators to tail employees on "sick days."

- *Chapter 4: Job Satisfaction*—The chapter's wraparound case now higlights Hasbro. The discussion focuses on the meaningfulness that Hasbro employees derive from their jobs, as well as the steps taken to inject variety into their work, and the company's product portfolio. The case also discusses the satisfaction issues at play in traditional manufacturing environments vs. more knowledge-based work contexts. The discussion of the five facets of job satisfaction draws on a revised set of company examples, including Nordstrom, General Mills, and DreamWorks Animation. The section on satisfaction with the work itself now covers job crafting, where employees shape, mold, and redefine their jobs in some proactive fashion. Lastly, the OB at the Bookstore feature now spotlights *The Pleasures and Sorrows of Work,* which is used to illustrate the positive and negative moods and emotions that the work context is capable of inspiring in employees.
- *Chapter 5: Stress*—Google is the focus of a new wraparound case that illustrates the importance of stress and stress management to organizations today. The case highlights the practices that help Google manage the stress of its employees. The case also illustrates how certain practices, such as the use of sleeping pods, may have unintended consequences and pose additional managerial challenges. The chapter includes several new and revised examples to illustrate the stress process. For example, the stress experienced by call center operators is described in a way that reflects a more complete set of stressful demands. There are also new examples of companies that approach stress management in innovative ways. For example, there is an example of a large relocation service company that prohibits employees from working during lunch, eating at their desks, or leaving at the end of the day with any work hanging over their heads. Other new company examples, such as L.L. Bean, describe the return on investment of practices such as wellness programs.
- *Chapter 6: Motivation*—This chapter now opens with a wraparound case on American Express–in particular, employees in their card services call center. The case describes the extrinsic and intrinsic incentives that impact the motivation levels of call center employees, and how the company seeks to provide meaning to the work. The case also describes, in some detail, the specific compensation policies that shape the extrinsic rewards of call center employees. The discussion of equity theory and CEO pay has been revised to include 2010 salaries and listings for the top-paid executives. The OB on Screen feature has been revised to focus on *Wall Street: Money Never Sleeps,* illustrating how greed shapes the "meaning of money" and the unique way in which money motivates. *Drive* is now the focus of the OB at the Bookstore feature, illustrating how autonomy, mastery, and purpose can create a brand of motivation that is uniquely powerful in jobs that demand creative and "nonprogrammed" action.
- *Chapter 7: Personality and Cultural Values*—The chapter's wraparound case is now Panda Express. The case describes the personality traits and cultural values that characterize the company's CEO, as well as its customer service employees. The case also describes the CEO's affinity for "self-help" programs and workshops that encourage employees to grow and nurture their personality traits. The OB on Screen feature has been revised to focus on *The Adjustment Bureau,* illustrating the importance of an internal locus of control, where individuals see themselves as master of their own destiny and fate. Finally, the discussion of integrity testing now offers more information on Kronos, one of the leading vendors in the personality testing industry.
- *Chapter 8: Ability*—This chapter's new wraparound case focuses on Johnson & Johnson, and how recent events and new competitive pressures have caused the company to focus on enhancing the employee abilities. The case overviews research within the company that highlighted the importance of emotional intelligence, and discusses initiatives the company undertook in response to this finding. To give students a better feel for the practical implications of ability, as well as some of the controversies, the chapter now includes discussion of associations with a wider array of variables. For

example, the chapter discusses relationships between IQ and variables such as life satisfaction, accidents, disease and life span. The new OB on Screen insert box features the movie *Sherlock Holmes.* The discussion of this movie provides vivid examples of certain types of cognitive and emotional abilities, and it illuminates how these abilities are related to each other in non-obvious ways.

- *Chapter 9: Teams: Characteristics and Diversity*—Automobile parts manufacturer TRW is featured in this chapter's wraparound case. The case discusses the nature and management of the company's "global teams" that design and develop new products. The case overviews specific challenges these teams face as well as the practices the company uses to manage these teams. "Self-management" is now discussed as a factor that might be considered when trying to characterize a team and understand its functioning. The discussion on virtual teams has been enhanced and now highlights how these teams are leveraged at companies such as Con Edison and Logitech. The OB at the Bookstore insert box presents students with *The Orange Revolution,* which discusses how teams can achieve breakthrough results through practices that begin with the establishment of a common mission and core set of values. The movie *Inception* is now the focus of OB on Screen. It provides a compelling example of the importance of team composition to team functioning and effectiveness. Finally, the section on diversity has been enhanced in that it now discusses ways in which potential problems with deep-level diversity can be managed effectively (and ineffectively).
- *Chapter 10: Teams: Processes and Communication*—This chapter includes a new wraparound case on Procter and Gamble (P&G). The case overviews how P&G has long used teams in innovative ways to achieve extraordinary results, and it provides a vivid illustration in the context of the teams the company employs to produce a constant stream of new and improved products. The book, *Making Ideas Happen,* is now the focus of OB at the Bookstore. The book advances the basic idea that although individual genius is important, innovations are more likely the result of teams, especially if team processes are managed effectively. The team decision-making section now includes discussion of consensus decisions and factors that influence consensus decision outcomes. The section on team communication now includes discussion of the role of "emotion" and "rumors" in the communication process. The section also discusses the role of technology, specifically user centered Web 2.0 tools and other collaboration technologies, in the communication process, and how companies such as AT&T, GE, FedEx, and Coca-Cola are leveraging these technologies to improve team effectiveness. The concept of "psychological safety" is now mentioned as an example of a team state. Finally, we feature the movie *Glory Road* for OB on Screen. The movie depicts the struggles of a highly diverse team, and how the team overcomes these struggles to become cohesive and successful.
- *Chapter 11: Leadership: Power and Negotiation*—Indra Nooyi now anchors the chapter as the new wraparound case. The discussion centers on Nooyi's bases of power within PepsiCo and how she acquired them. It also details her battle, both inside and outside the company, to push her vision of PepsiCo becoming a "healthier" snack food company. *Linchpin: Are you Indispensible?* by best-selling author Seth Godin is the new OB at the Bookstore feature. The book offers a unique (if not controversial) look at how people can put themselves in a position of power within their organizations. Updated company examples using leaders such as Larry Page (Google CEO) and Irene Rosenfeld (Kraft CEO) are used throughout. In the negotiations portion of the chapter, there is a new section which details the research surrounding negotiator biases including changing styles when negotiating from positions of power or when the negotiator becomes emotionally involved. The trials and tribulations of Google's use of "guanxi" have also been updated in the chapter's OB Internationally feature.
- *Chapter 12: Leadership: Styles and Behaviors*—The chapter's new wraparound case features the always brash and colorful stylings of the Virgin Group's Sir Richard

Branson. The discussion revolves around Branson's visionary and charismatic behaviors and what it means for Virgin. The fact that Virgin is privately owned by Branson allows him to do things that many leaders in organizations don't have the opportunity to do. Numerous new leader examples have been added, including discussions of the styles and behaviors of Sergio Marchionne (Fiat-Chrysler), Jack Griffin (Time Inc.), Jeff Immelt (GE), and Millard Drexler (J. Crew). *The King's Speech* is utilized as a new OB on Screen box to illustrate a highly unexpected transformational leader during a time of war. The chapter's new OB at the Bookstore features Adam Bryant's 2011 bestselling *The Corner Office: Indispensible and Unexpected Lessons from CEOs on How to Lead and Succeed,* which offers a unique perspective on transformational leadership behaviors and how these upper-level executives acquired them.

- *Chapter 13: Organizational Structure*—Starbucks is the focus of the chapter's new wraparound case. The case details the company's matrix structure, which allows it to deliver a standardized product while at the same time being flexible to its local markets. The case also describes Starbucks' recent restructurings (during which it laid off 12,000 employees) and how that affected employees within the well-known employee-friendly organization. OB on Screen now features *The Company Men* which features a discussion not only of layoff survivors but also of the emotional toll and ethical dilemmas that leaders in a company face during restructurings. AES is a new company highlighted in the chapter along with Yahoo, Darden Restaurants, Bristol-Myers Squibb, and Macy's.
- *Chapter 14: Organizational Culture*—The chapter features a new wraparound case on the fun-loving, crazy culture of online retailer Zappos. The case discussion revolves around how the culture was created, what CEO Tony Hseih does to keep the culture going, and why so many people want to copy it. It also details the dilemma that Zappos faces in trying to hire people to "fit"—which most people think would be easy, but in fact is quite a chore. New culture examples are taken from companies such as Davita Home Healthcare, Dyson (vacuums), Honda, Trader Joe's, and USAA among others. OB at the Bookstore features Tom Shales' recently released bestselling book: *Those Guys Have All the Fun: Inside the World of ESPN.* What looks like a great place to work from the outside is actually a pretty contemptuous place from a culture perspective. The chapter's OB Internationally has also been updated to detail the international acquisition of Swedish-based Volvo by China's Geely Holding Group and the surrounding cultural issues.

Acknowledgements
致　谢

An enormous number of persons played a role in helping us put this textbook together. Truth be told, we had no idea that we would have to rely on and put our success in the hands of so many different people! Each of them had unique and useful contributions to make toward the publication of this book, and they deserve and thus receive our sincere gratitude.

We thank Michael Ablassmeir, our executive editor, for his suggestions and guidance on this third edition, and John Weimeister for filling that same role with earlier editions. We are thankful to both for allowing us to write the book that we wanted to write. Thanks also go out to Kelly Pekelder, our Development Editor, for keeping us on track and keeping track of all the details that go into a book like this. We also owe much gratitude to our Marketing Manager, Anke Weekes. We also would like to thank Pat Frederickson, Matt Diamond, Jeremy Cheshareck, and Susan Lombardi at Irwin/McGraw Hill, as they are the masterminds of much of how the book actually looks as it sits in students' hands; their work and effort were spectacular. A special thanks also goes out to Jessica Rodell (University of Georgia) for her assistance with our CONNECT content.

We have also had the great fortune of having had over 25 faculty members from colleges and universities around the country provide feedback on various aspects of the third edition of this textbook. Whether by providing feedback on chapters or attending focus groups, their input made this book substantially better:

Tejinder K. Billing, *Rowan University*

Barbara Crandall, *Oklahoma City University*

Joseph P. Daly, *Appalachian State University*

Kristen Bell DeTienne, *Brigham Young University*

Ronald L. Dufresne, *Saint Joseph's University*

Charles R. Foley, *Columbus State Community College*

Christina Fong, *University of Washington*

Lynda Fuller, *Wilmington University*

Wayne Hochwarter, *Florida State University*

Elaine Hollensbe, *University of Cincinnati*

H. B. Karp, *Hampton University*

Pat Laidler, *Massasoit Community College*

Marcia A. Marriott, *Monroe Community College*

Steven Meisel, *La Salle University*

James Meurs, *University of Mississippi*

Paula C. Morrow, *Iowa State University*

Kanu Priya, *Arkansas State University*

Jude A. Rathburn, *University of Wisconsin–Milwaukee*

Christopher J. Roussin, *Suffolk University*

James M. Schmidtke, *California State University, Fresno*

Randall G. Sleeth, *Virginia Commonwealth University*

Edward C. Tomlinson, *John Carroll University*

Sydne West Tustison, *Columbia College*

Ethan P. Waples, *University of Central Oklahoma*

Tal Zarankin, *Radford University*

We would also like to thank our students at the undergraduate, masters, and executive levels who were taught with this book for their constructive feedback toward making it more effective in the classroom. Thanks also to our PhD students for allowing us to take time out from research projects to focus on this book.

Finally, we thank our families, who gave up substantial amounts of time with us and put up with the stress that necessarily comes at times during an endeavor such as this.

Jason Colquitt

Jeff LePine

Michael Wesson

Brief Contents
简要目录

Table of Contents
详细目录

ORGANIZATIONAL BEHAVIOR

Improving Performance and Commitment in the Workplace

PART

1

INTRODUCTION TO ORGANIZATIONAL BEHAVIOR

组织行为学导论

chapter 1

What Is Organizational Behavior?

什么是组织行为学

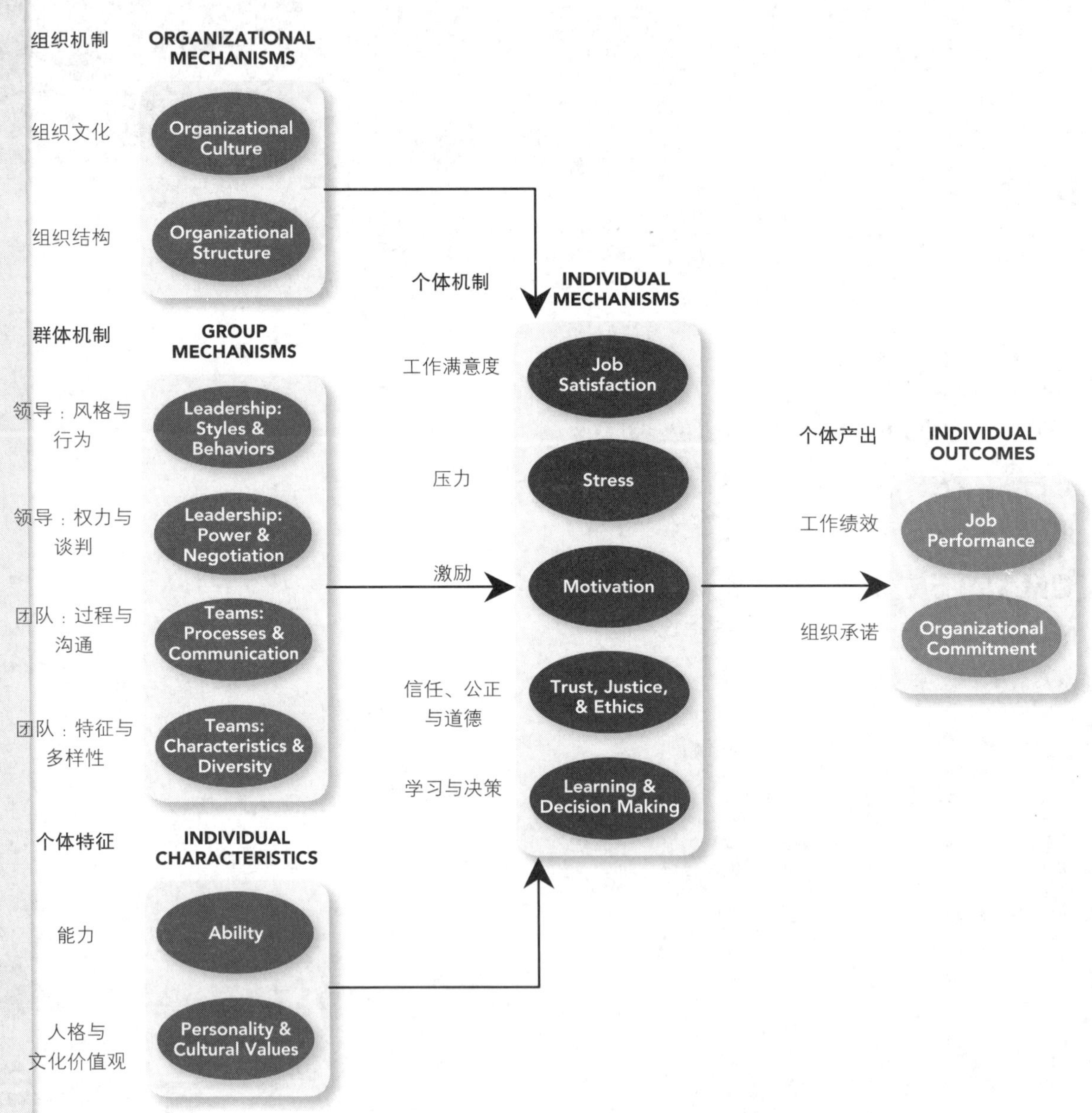

LEARNING GOALS

After reading this chapter, you should be able to answer the following questions:

1.1 What is the definition of "organizational behavior" (OB)?

1.2 What are the two primary outcomes in studies of OB?

1.3 What factors affect the two primary OB outcomes?

1.4 Why might firms that are good at OB tend to be more profitable?

1.5 What is the role of theory in the scientific method?

1.6 How are correlations interpreted?

FACEBOOK

Consider these two numbers: 310 million and 155 million. Can you guess what those numbers are summarizing? You might have pegged the first number as the approximate population of the United States (circa April of 2011). But what's the second number? It's the number of Americans who are members of Facebook at that same point in time. That means that one-half of the country is on Facebook—a 30 percent increase over one year prior. Other countries are experiencing even faster growth rates, including Indonesia, India, Mexico, Germany, and Brazil. Not bad for the Palo Alto–based company that was created in January of 2004 by Mark Zuckerberg and three of his classmates at Harvard. Borrowing elements from Friendster, MySpace, AIM, and other services, the site's initial mission was to unify all of the "facebooks" used by Harvard's dormitories while allowing students to share personal information. The site was exclusively for Harvard students in the beginning, before being extended to Columbia, then Yale, then Stanford. Of course, the expansion continued to other universities, then to high schools, before becoming open to all in September of 2006.

How did a company that started with four people accomplish so much growth, while simultaneously expanding the services offered by the site? One key was to hire the best employees they could find, and lots of them. Unlike most tech companies, Facebook continued to hire even during the economic downturn. Zuckerberg notes that the company looks for entrepreneurial "hackers" who are focused on building new things and making an impact on the world. Newly hired engineers go through a six-week "cultural indoctrination"—a sort of "boot camp" about Facebook's code and customs—that helps instill that entrepreneurial mindset. Every other month, employees take part in all-hands "hackathons" to brainstorm about new ideas, to form teams around those ideas, and to show how hard everyone else is working.

As Facebook approaches the 2,000 employee mark, a new challenge is coping with turnover in its engineering and management ranks. Zuckerberg acknowledges that entrepreneurial hires may not stick around for the long term given their impatient and ambitious nature, not to mention the hours and schedule that work at Facebook demands. One approach that Facebook uses to replace such employees is acquiring young start-up companies. For example, Facebook wound up hiring Paul Buchheit, a Google alum who had started a company called FriendFeed. Buchheit is attracted to Facebook for the same reason he wanted to start FriendFeed—the company doesn't mind breaking things in order to find a better way. It turns out that hiring ex-Googlers is becoming something of a trend at Facebook, which makes a lot of sense. After all, not only have Google employees weathered the growth phase themselves, they happen to have worked on the only website with more users than Facebook.

什么是组织行为学
WHAT IS ORGANIZATIONAL BEHAVIOR?

Before we define exactly what the field of organizational behavior represents, take a moment to ponder the following question: Who was the single *worst* coworker you've ever had? Picture fellow students who collaborated with you on class projects; colleagues from part-time or summer jobs; or peers, subordinates, or supervisors working in your current organization. What did this coworker do that earned him or her "worst coworker" status? Was it some of the behaviors shown in the right column of Table 1-1 (or perhaps all of them)? Now take a moment to consider the single *best* coworker you've ever had. Again, what did this coworker do to earn "best coworker" status—some or most of the behaviors shown in the left column of Table 1-1?

If you ever found yourself working alongside the two people profiled in the table, two questions probably would be foremost on your mind: "*Why* does the worst coworker act that way?" and "*Why* does the best coworker act that way?" Once you understand why the two coworkers act so differently, you might be able to figure out ways to interact with the worst coworker more effectively (thereby making your working life a bit more pleasant). If you happen to be a manager, you might formulate plans for how to improve attitudes and behaviors in the unit. Such plans could include how to screen applicants, train and socialize new organizational members, manage evaluations and rewards for performance, and deal with conflicts that arise between

TABLE 1-1 The Best of Coworkers, the Worst of Coworkers

THE BEST	THE WORST
Have you ever had a coworker who usually acted this way?	*Have you ever had a coworker who usually acted this way?*
Got the job done, without having to be managed or reminded	Did not got the job done, even with a great deal of hand-holding
Adapted when something needed to be changed or done differently	Was resistant to any and every form of change, even when changes were beneficial
Was always a "good sport," even when bad things happened at work	Whined and complained, no matter what was happening
Attended optional meetings or functions to support colleagues	Optional meetings? Was too lazy to make it to some required meetings and functions!
Helped new coworkers or people who seemed to need a hand	Made fun of new coworkers or people who seemed to need a hand
Felt an attachment and obligation to the employer for the long haul	Seemed to always be looking for something else, even if it wasn't better
Was first to arrive, last to leave	Was first to leave for lunch, last to return

The Million Dollar Question:
Why do these two employees act so differently?

employees. Without understanding why employees act the way they do, it's extremely hard to find a way to change their attitudes and behaviors at work.

组织行为学的定义
ORGANIZATIONAL BEHAVIOR DEFINED

Organizational behavior (OB) is a field of study devoted to understanding, explaining, and ultimately improving the attitudes and behaviors of individuals and groups in organizations. Scholars in management departments of universities and scientists in business organizations conduct research on OB. The findings from those research studies are then applied by managers or consultants to see whether they help meet "real-world" challenges. OB can be contrasted with two other courses commonly offered in management departments: human resource management and strategic management. **Human resource management** takes the theories and principles studied in OB and explores the "nuts-and-bolts" applications of those principles in organizations. An OB study might explore the relationship between learning and job performance, whereas a human resource management study might examine the best ways to structure training programs to promote employee learning. **Strategic management** focuses on the product choices and industry characteristics that affect an organization's profitability. A strategic management study might examine the relationship between firm diversification (when a firm expands into a new product segment) and firm profitability.

组织行为学是一门致力于研究理解、解释及最终改进组织中个体和群体的态度与行为的科学。

1.1
What is the definition of "organizational behavior" (OB)?

人力资源管理吸收组织行为学研究的理论与原理，并且探讨这些原理如何在组织中具体运用。

战略管理主要关注影响组织的盈利能力的产品选择及行业特性。

The theories and concepts found in OB are actually drawn from a wide variety of disciplines. For example, research on job performance and individual characteristics draws primarily from studies in industrial and organizational psychology. Research on satisfaction, emotions, and team processes draws heavily from social psychology. Sociology research is vital to research on team characteristics and organizational structure, and anthropology research helps inform the study of organizational culture. Finally, models from economics are used to understand motivation, learning, and decision making. This diversity brings a unique quality to the study of OB, as most students will be able to find a particular topic that's intrinsically interesting and thought provoking to them.

组织行为学的整合模型
AN INTEGRATIVE MODEL OF OB

Because of the diversity in its topics and disciplinary roots, it's common for students in an organizational behavior class to wonder, "How does all this stuff fit together?" How does what gets covered in Chapter 3 relate to what gets covered in Chapter 11? To clarify such issues, this textbook is structured around an integrative model of OB, shown in Figure 1-1, that's designed to provide a roadmap for the field of organizational behavior. The model shows how the topics in the next 13 chapters—represented by the 13 ovals in the model—all fit together. We should stress that there are other potential ways of combining the 13 topics, and Figure 1-1 likely oversimplifies the connections among the topics. Still, we believe the model provides a helpful guide as you move through this course. Figure 1-1 includes five different kinds of topics.

FIGURE 1-1 Integrative Model of Organizational Behavior

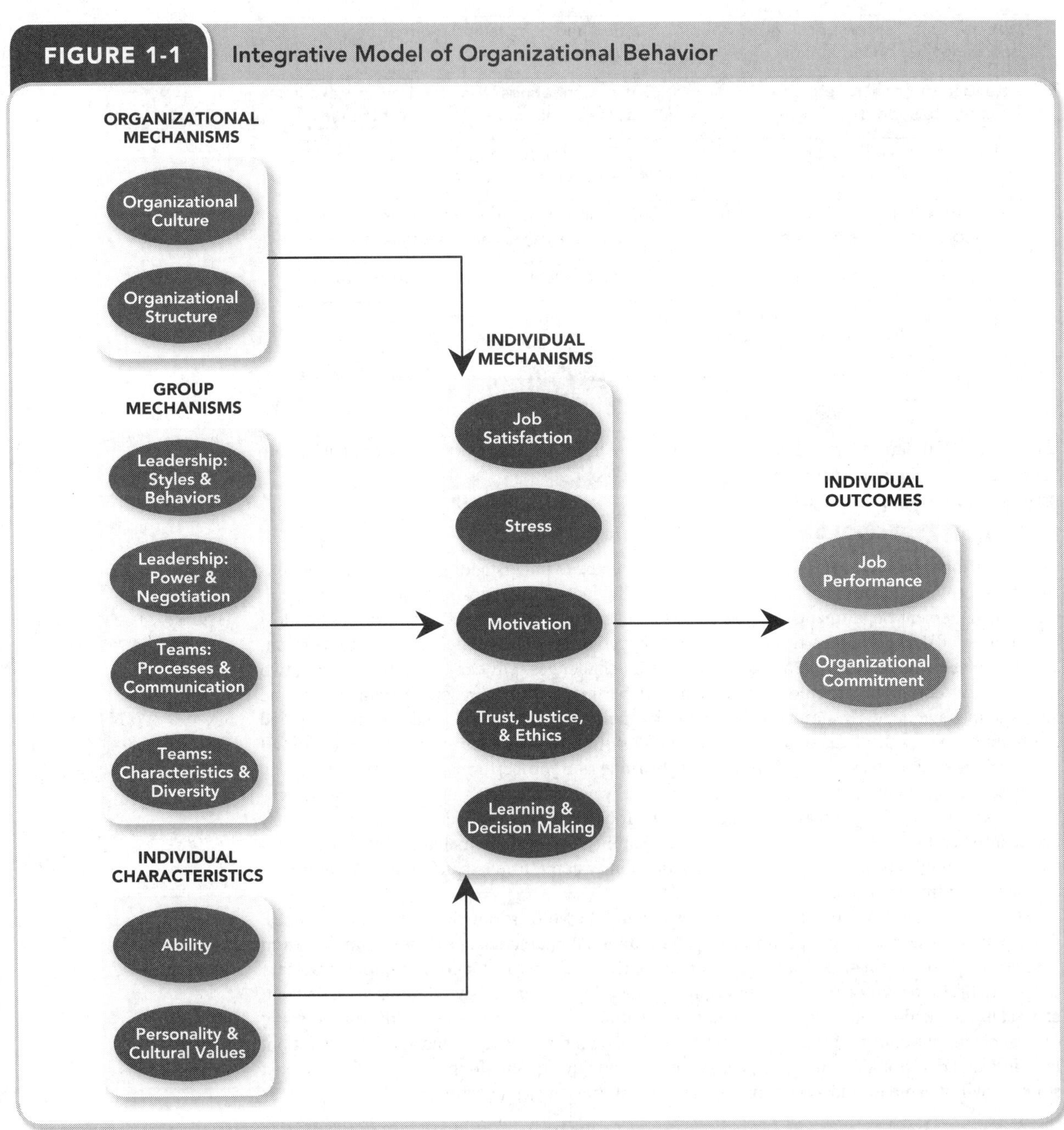

INDIVIDUAL OUTCOMES. The right-most portion of the model contains the two primary outcomes of interest to organizational behavior researchers (and employees and managers in organizations): *job performance* and *organizational commitment.* Most employees have two primary goals for their working lives: to perform their jobs well and to remain a member of an organization that they respect. Likewise, most managers have two primary goals for their employees: to maximize their job performance and to ensure that they stay with the firm for a significant length of time. As described in Chapter 2, there are several specific behaviors that, when taken together, constitute good job performance. Similarly, as described in Chapter 3, there are a number of beliefs, attitudes, and emotions that cause an employee to remain committed to an employer.

1.2
What are the two primary outcomes in studies of OB?

This book starts by covering job performance and organizational commitment so that you can better understand the two primary organizational behavior goals. Our hope is that by using performance and commitment as starting points, we can highlight the practical importance of OB topics. After all, what could be more important than having employees who perform well and want to stay with the company? This structure also enables us to conclude the other chapters in the book with sections that describe the relationships between each chapter's topic and performance and commitment. For example, the chapter on motivation concludes by describing the relationships between motivation and performance and motivation and commitment. In this way, you'll learn which of the topics in the model are most useful for understanding your own attitudes and behaviors.

INDIVIDUAL MECHANISMS. Our integrative model also illustrates a number of individual mechanisms that directly affect job performance and organizational commitment. These include *job satisfaction,* which captures what employees feel when thinking about their jobs and doing their day-to-day work (Chapter 4). Another individual mechanism is *stress,* which reflects employees' psychological responses to job demands that tax or exceed their capacities (Chapter 5). The model also includes *motivation,* which captures the energetic forces that drive employees' work effort (Chapter 6).

1.3
What factors affect the two primary OB outcomes?

INDIVIDUAL CHARACTERISTICS. Of course, if satisfaction, stress, motivation, and so forth are key drivers of job performance and organizational commitment, it becomes important to understand what factors improve those individual mechanisms. Two such factors reflect the characteristics of individual employees. *Personality and cultural values* reflect the various traits and tendencies that describe how people act, with commonly studied traits including extraversion, conscientiousness, and collectivism. As described in Chapter 7, personality and cultural values affect the way people behave at work, the kinds of tasks they're interested in, and how they react to events that happen on the job. The model also examines *ability,* which describes the cognitive abilities (verbal, quantitative, etc.), emotional skills (other awareness, emotion regulation, etc.), and physical abilities (strength, endurance, etc.) that employees bring to a job. As described in Chapter 8, ability influences the kinds of tasks an employee is good at (and not so good at).

GROUP MECHANISMS. Our integrative model also acknowledges that employees don't work alone. Instead, they typically work in one or more work teams led by some formal (or sometimes informal) leader. Like the individual characteristics, these group mechanisms shape satisfaction, stress, motivation, trust, and learning. Chapter 9 covers *team characteristics and diversity*—describing how teams are formed, staffed, and composed, and how team members come to rely on one another as they do their work. Chapter 10 then covers *team processes and communication*—how teams behave, including their coordination, conflict, and cohesion. The next two chapters focus on the leaders of those teams. We first describe how individuals become leaders in the first place, covering *leader power and negotiation* to summarize how individuals attain authority over others (Chapter 11). We then describe how leaders behave in their leadership roles, as *leader styles and behaviors* capture the specific actions that leaders take to influence others at work (Chapter 12).

ORGANIZATIONAL MECHANISMS. Finally, our integrative model acknowledges that the teams described in the prior section are grouped into larger organizations that themselves affect satisfaction, stress, motivation, and so forth. For example, every company has an *organizational structure* that dictates how the units within the firm link to (and communicate with) other units (Chapter 13). Sometimes structures are centralized around a decision-making authority, whereas other times, structures are decentralized, affording each unit some autonomy. Every company also has an *organizational culture* that captures "the way things are" in the organization—shared knowledge about the values and beliefs that shape employee attitudes and behaviors (Chapter 14).

SUMMARY. Each of the chapters in this textbook will open with a depiction of this integrative model, with the subject of each chapter highlighted. We hope that this opening will serve as a roadmap for the course—showing you where you are, where you've been, and where you're going. We also hope that the model will give you a feel for the "big picture" of OB—showing you how all the OB topics are connected. Facebook is a good example of those connections. Zuckerberg has become increasingly interested in forging a culture that sees a deeper meaning in Facebook. He himself articulates the inherent value in openness and transparency—that people could actually behave more responsibly as information becomes more widely shared. Facebook's employees, who are selected based on their intelligence, ambition, and creativity, are motivated by that vision, along with a strict performance evaluation system that ranks all employees on a 1–5 scale. High performers can earn financial rewards, with low performers quickly ushered out of the company. Finally, recent changes in the management ranks have been geared toward making the workplace less political and cliquish, in an effort to boost satisfaction and reduce stress. Says one investor with contacts throughout Silicon Valley, "I've got friends at Google who say that for the first time they feel like they're really missing something by not working at Facebook."

组织行为学至关重要吗

DOES ORGANIZATIONAL BEHAVIOR MATTER?

Having described exactly what OB is, it's time to discuss another fundamental question: Does it really matter? Is there any value in taking a class on this subject, other than fulfilling some requirement of your program? (You might guess that we're biased in our answers to these questions, given that we wrote a book on the subject!) Few would disagree that organizations need to know principles of accounting and finance to be successful; it would be impossible to conduct business without such knowledge. Similarly, few would disagree that organizations need to know principles of marketing, as consumers need to know about the firm's products and what makes those products unique or noteworthy.

However, people sometimes wonder whether a firm's ability to manage OB has any bearing on its bottom-line profitability. After all, if a firm has a good-enough product, won't people buy it regardless of how happy, motivated, or committed its workforce is? Perhaps for a time, but effective OB can help keep a product good over the long term. This same argument can be made in reverse: If a firm has a bad-enough product, isn't it true that people won't buy it, regardless of how happy, motivated, or committed its workforce is? Again, perhaps for a time, but the effective management of OB can help make a product get better, incrementally, over the long term.

Consider this pop quiz about the automotive industry: Which automaker finished behind only Lexus and Porsche in a recent study of initial quality by J.D. Power and Associates? Toyota? Nope. Honda? Uh-uh. The answer is Hyundai (yes, Hyundai). The automaker has come a long way in the decade since comedian Jay Leno likened a Hyundai to a bobsled ("It has no room, you have to push it to get going, and it only goes downhill!"). More recent models—including those built in a manufacturing plant in Montgomery, Alabama—are regarded as good looking and well made, with *Consumer Reports* tabbing the Hyundai Elantra SE as the best small sedan in a recent set of rankings. Says one investor, "Hyundai is a brand that is on the verge of being aspirational. People are saying they are proud to own it, not just to settle for it." That turnaround can be credited to the company's increased emphasis on quality. Work teams devoted to quality have been expanded eightfold, and almost all employees are enrolled in special training programs devoted to quality issues. Hyundai represents a case in which OB principles are being applied across cultures. Our **OB Internationally** feature spotlights such international and cross-cultural applications of OB topics in each chapter.

OB INTERNATIONALLY

Changes in technology, communications, and economic forces have made business more global and international than ever. To use Thomas Friedman's line, "the world is flat." The playing field has been leveled between the United States and the rest of the world. This feature spotlights the impact of globalization on the organizational behavior concepts described in this book and covers a variety of topics:

Cross-Cultural Differences. Research in cross-cultural organizational behavior has illustrated that national cultures affect many of the relationships in our integrative model. Put differently, there is little that we know about OB that is "universal" or "culture free."

International Corporations. An increasing number of organizations are international in scope, with both foreign and domestic operations. Applying organizational behavior concepts in these firms represents a special challenge—should policies and practices be consistent across locations or tailored to meet the needs of the culture?

Expatriation. Working as an expatriate—an employee who lives outside his or her native country—can be particularly challenging. What factors influence expatriates' job performance and organizational commitment levels?

Managing Diversity. More and more work groups are composed of members of different cultural backgrounds. What are the special challenges involved in leading and working in such groups?

构建概念论证
BUILDING A CONCEPTUAL ARGUMENT

Of course, we shouldn't just accept it on faith that OB matters, nor should we merely look for specific companies that appear to support the premise. What we need instead is a conceptual argument that captures why OB might affect the bottom-line profitability of an organization. One such argument is based on the **resource-based view** of organizations. This perspective describes what exactly makes resources valuable—that is, what makes them capable of creating long-term profits for the firm. A firm's resources include financial (revenue, equity, etc.) and physical (buildings, machines, technology) resources, but they also include resources related to organizational behavior, such as the knowledge, ability, and wisdom of the workforce, as well as the image, culture, and goodwill of the organization.

资源基础观描述了真正使公司资源变得有价值的原因——也就是，如何为公司创造长期利润。

The resource-based view suggests that the value of resources depends on several factors, shown in Figure 1-2. For example, a resource is more valuable when it is *rare*. Diamonds, oil, Babe Ruth baseball cards, and Action Comics #1 (the debut of Superman) are all expensive precisely because they are rare. Good people are also rare—witness the adage "good people are hard to find." Ask yourself what percentage of the people you've worked with have been talented, motivated, satisfied, and good team players. In many organizations, cities, or job markets, such employees are the exception rather than the rule. If good people really are rare, then the effective management of OB should prove to be a valuable resource.

Hyundai's emphasis on work teams and training has increased the quality of its cars, like these models built in its Montgomery, Alabama, plant.

The resource-based view also suggests that a resource is more valuable when it is **inimitable,** meaning that it cannot be imitated. Many of the firm's resources can be imitated, if competitors have enough money. For example, a new form of technology can help a firm gain an advantage for a short time, but competing firms can switch

独特意味着它不能被模仿。

FIGURE 1-2 What Makes a Resource Valuable?

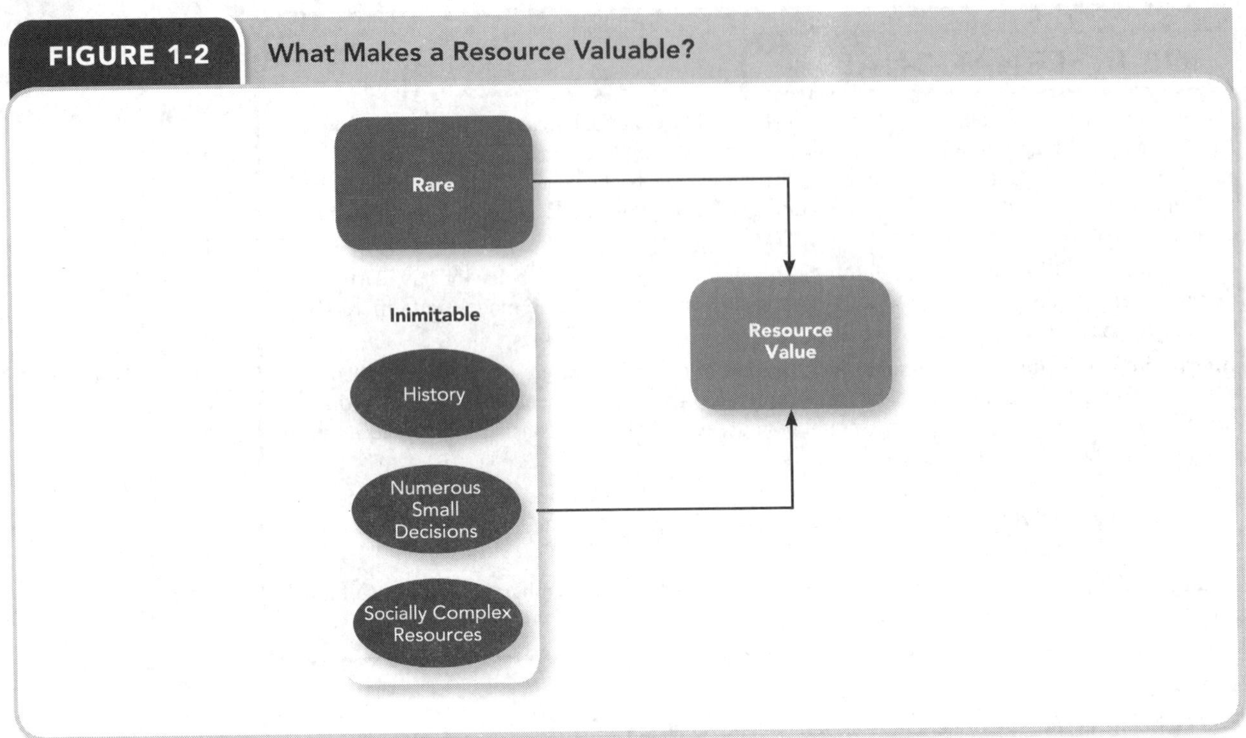

to the same technology. Manufacturing practices can be copied, equipment and tools can be approximated, and marketing strategies can be mimicked. Good people, in contrast, are much more difficult to imitate. As shown in Figure 1-2, there are three reasons people are inimitable.

人们创造了**历史**——能使组织受益的经验、智慧及知识的集合体。

HISTORY. People create a **history**—a collective pool of experience, wisdom, and knowledge that benefits the organization. History cannot be bought. Consider an example from the consumer electronics retailing industry where Microsoft, taking a cue from Apple, launched its first retail store in Scottsdale, Arizona, in 2009. The company hopes that the stores will give it a chance to showcase its computer and mobile phone operating systems, along with its hardware and gaming products. Microsoft faces an uphill climb in the retail space, however, because Apple has an eight-year head start after opening its first store in 2001, in McLean, Virginia. Microsoft's position on the "retail learning curve" is therefore quite different, suggesting that it will grapple with many of the same issues that Apple resolved years ago.

众多细小决策是指人们日复一日、周复一周地做出的许多细小决定。

NUMEROUS SMALL DECISIONS. The concept of **numerous small decisions** captures the idea that people make many small decisions day in and day out, week in and week out. "So what?" you might say, "Why worry about small decisions?" To answer that question, ask yourself what the biggest decisions are when launching a new line of retail stores. The location of them maybe, or perhaps their look and feel? It turns out that Microsoft placed their stores near Apple's, and mimicked much of their open, "Zen" sensibility. Said one patron, "It appears that the Microsoft Store in Mission Viejo is dressed up as the Apple Store

Microsoft opened its first retail stores in 2009, including this one in Mission Viejo, California. The look and feel of Microsoft's stores is very similar to Apple's retail outlets.

for Halloween." Big decisions can be copied; they are visible to competitors and observable by industry experts. In contrast, the "behind the scenes" decisions at the Apple Store are more invisible to Microsoft, especially the decisions that involve the hiring and management of employees. Apple seems to understand the inimitable advantage that such decisions can create. A recent article in *Workforce Management* included features on the top human resources executives for 20 of the most admired companies in America. Interestingly, the entry for Apple's executive was cryptic, noting only that the company "keeps its human resources executive shrouded in secrecy and refuses to respond to any questions about HR's contribution to the company's most admired status."

SOCIALLY COMPLEX RESOURCES. People also create **socially complex resources,** like culture, teamwork, trust, and reputation. These resources are termed "socially complex" because it's not always clear how they came to develop, though it is clear which organizations do (and do not) possess them. One advantage that Apple has over Microsoft in the retail wars is the unusual amount of interest and enthusiasm created by products like the iPad, iPhone, iPod, and MacBook Air. Those products have an "it factor" that brings customers into the store, and Apple itself sits atop *Fortune*'s list of 50 most admired companies in the world. Competitors like Microsoft can't just acquire "coolness" or "admiration"—they are complex resources that evolve in ways that are both murky and mysterious. For a look at how the resource-based view could explain Facebook's early success, see our **OB on Screen** feature, which appears in each chapter and uses well-known movies to demonstrate OB concepts.

人们也创造了**社会复杂资源**，如文化、团队、信任及声誉。这些资源之所以被称为"社会复杂体"是因为它们形成的过程并不清晰。

研究证据
RESEARCH EVIDENCE

1.4

Why might firms that are good at OB tend to be more profitable?

Thus, we can build a conceptual argument for why OB might affect an organization's profitability: Good people are both rare and inimitable and therefore create a resource that is valuable for creating competitive advantage. Conceptual arguments are helpful, of course, but it would be even better if there were hard data to back them up. Fortunately, it turns out that there is a great deal of research evidence supporting the importance of OB for company performance. Several research studies have been conducted on the topic, each employing a somewhat different approach.

One study began by surveying executives from 968 publicly held firms with 100 or more employees. The survey assessed so-called high performance work practices—OB policies that are widely agreed to be beneficial to firm performance. The survey included 13 questions asking about a combination of hiring, information sharing, training, performance management, and incentive practices, and each question asked what proportion of the company's workforce was involved in the practice. Table 1-2 provides some of the questions used to assess the high performance work practices (and also shows which chapter of the textbook describes each particular practice in more detail). The study also gathered the following information for each firm: average annual rate of turnover, productivity level (defined as sales per employee), market value of the firm, and corporate profitability. The results revealed that a one-unit increase in the proportion of the workforce involved in the practices was associated with an approximately 7 percent decrease in turnover, $27,000 more in sales per employee, $18,000 more in market value, and $3,800 more in profits. Put simply, better OB practices were associated with better firm performance.

Although there is no doubting the importance of turnover, productivity, market value, and profitability, another study examined an outcome that's even more fundamental: firm survival. The study focused on 136 nonfinancial companies that made initial public offerings (IPOs) in 1988. Firms that undergo an IPO typically have shorter histories and need an infusion of cash to grow or introduce some new technology. Rather than conducting a survey, the authors of this study examined the prospectus filed by each firm (the Securities and Exchange Commission requires that prospectuses contain honest information, and firms can be liable for any inaccuracies that might mislead investors). The authors coded each prospectus for information that might suggest OB issues were valued. Examples of valuing OB issues included describing employees as a source of competitive advantage in strategy and mission statements, emphasizing training and continuing education, having a human resources management executive, and emphasizing full-time rather than temporary or contract employees. By 1993, 81 of the 136 firms included in the study had survived (60 percent). The key question is whether the value placed on OB predicted which did (and did not) survive. The results revealed that firms that valued OB had a 19 percent higher survival rate than firms that did not value OB.

OB ON SCREEN

This feature is designed to illustrate OB concepts in action on the silver screen. Once you've learned about OB topics, you'll see them playing out all around you, especially in movies. This inaugural edition spotlights The Social Network (Dir.: David Fincher, Columbia Pictures, 2010).

THE SOCIAL NETWORK

Tyler: *The main difference between what we're talking about and MySpace, or Friendster, or any of those other social networking sites. . .*

Mark: *. . .is exclusivity. . .right?*

With those words, Mark Zuckerberg (Jessie Eisenberg) encapsulates the ingredient that will soon distinguish his site from its competitors in the social networking space. MySpace and Friendster were open to anyone and everyone, and you didn't need to use your real name or e-mail address when creating an account. So friend requests would often come from people that you didn't necessarily like, or really even know. To join Facebook, in the beginning, you needed what was described as the most prestigious e-mail address in the country: harvard.edu.

Of course, the exchange above occurred as Tyler and Cameron Winklevoss (both played by Armie Hammer) and Divya Narendra (Max Minghella) asked Mark to help them with their own site, the Harvard Connection. Like Mark, they realized that exclusivity would give a Harvard-focused site an inimitable advantage, because of the cache and reputation of the university. Now friend requests would come from people that you truly wanted to connect with. Of course, Facebook wound up sharing some of the same elements as Harvard Connection, and the Winklevosses (along with Divya Narendra) wound up suing Mark after his site was launched. That lawsuit was ultimately settled, with a payout of around $65 million.

Although its exclusivity advantage was critical as Facebook expanded to new universities, the decision to open the site up to everyone forever removed that source of inimitability. Fortunately for Facebook, its size and market position offers a new source of competitive advantage. Over the long term, however, its market dominance will depend on the numerous small decisions that the company makes to improve the site, and the steps the company takes to guard the "coolness" and reputation associated with using it.

A third study focused on *Fortune*'s "100 Best Companies to Work For" list, which has appeared annually since 1998. Table 1-3 provides some highlights from the 2011 version of the list. If the 100 firms on the list really do have good OB practices, and if good OB practices really do influence firm profitability, then it follows that the 100 firms should be more profitable. To explore this premise, the study went back to the original 1998 list and found a "matching firm" for those companies that were included. The matching firm consisted of the most similar company with

TABLE 1-2 Survey Questions Designed to Assess High Performance Work Practices

SURVEY QUESTION ABOUT OB PRACTICE	COVERED IN CHAPTER:
What is the proportion of the workforce whose jobs have been subjected to a formal job analysis?	2
What is the proportion of the workforce who are administered attitude surveys on a regular basis?	4
What is the proportion of the workforce who have access to company incentive plans, profit-sharing plans, and/or gain-sharing plans?	6
What is the average number of hours of training received by a typical employee over the last 12 months?	8
What proportion of the workforce are administered an employment test prior to hiring?	7, 8
What is the proportion of the workforce whose performance appraisals are used to determine compensation?	6

Source: From M.A. Huselid, "The Impact of Human Resource Management Practices on Turnover, Productivity, and Corporate Financial Performance," *Academy Of Management Journal,* Vol. 38, pp. 635–72. Copyright © 1995. Reproduced with permission of Academy of Management via Copyright Clearance Center.

respect to industry and size in that particular year, with the added requirement that the company had not appeared on the "100 Best" list. This process essentially created two groups of companies that differ only in terms of their inclusion in the "100 Best." The study then compared the profitability of those two groups of companies. The results revealed that the "100 Best" firms were more profitable than their peers. Indeed, the cumulative investment return for a portfolio based on the 1998 "100 Best" companies would have doubled the return for the broader market.

那么是什么如此之难
SO WHAT'S SO HARD?

Clearly this research evidence seems to support the conceptual argument that good people constitute a valuable resource for companies. Good OB does seem to matter in terms of company profitability. You may wonder then, "What's so hard?" Why doesn't every company prioritize the effective management of OB, devoting as much attention to it as they do accounting, finance, marketing, technology, physical assets, and so on? Some companies do a bad job when it comes to managing their people. Why is that?

One reason is that there is no "magic bullet" OB practice—one thing that, in and of itself, can increase profitability. Instead, the effective management of OB requires a belief that several different practices are important, along with a long-term commitment to improving those practices. This premise can be summarized with what might be called the **Rule of One-Eighth:**

有效的 OB 管理需要几种不同的实践，并且要长期承诺改善这些实践，这个假设可概括为**八分之一原则**。

> One must bear in mind that one-half of organizations won't believe the connection between how they manage their people and the profits they earn. One-half of those who do see the connection will do what many organizations have done—try to make a single change to solve their problems, not realizing that the effective management of people requires a more comprehensive and systematic approach. Of the firms that make comprehensive changes, probably only about one-half will persist with their practices long enough to actually derive economic benefits. Since one-half times one-half times one-half equals one-eighth, at best 12 percent of organizations will actually do what is required to build profits by putting people first.

TABLE 1-3 The "100 Best Companies to Work For" in 2011

1. SAS	23. Goldman Sachs	63. Deloitte
2. Boston Consulting	24. Whole Foods	65. Adobe Systems
3. Wegmans	34. Quicktrip	67. Publix
4. Google	35. Genentech	71. Marriott
5. NetApp	44. Intuit	72. Microsoft
6. Zappos.com	48. Build-a-Bear Workshop	73. PricewaterhouseCoopers
9. REI	49. American Express	74. Nordstrom
10. Dreamworks Anim.	51. Intel	77. Ernst & Young
12. Scottrade	53. Four Seasons Hotel	82. Teach for America
15. Mercedes-Benz USA	57. Aflac	86. KPMG
20. Cisco	58. General Mills	98. Starbucks
21. Container Store	59. Hasbro	99. Accenture

Source: From M. Moskowitz, R. Levering, and C. Tkaczyk, "100 Best Companies to Work For," *Fortune,* February 7, 2011, pp. 91–101. Copyright © 2011 Time Inc. Used under license.

The integrative model of OB used to structure this book was designed with this Rule of One-Eighth in mind. Figure 1-1 suggests that high job performance depends not just on employee motivation but also on fostering high levels of satisfaction, effectively managing stress, creating a trusting climate, and committing to employee learning. Failing to do any one of those things could hinder the effectiveness of the other concepts in the model. Of course, that systemic nature reveals another reality of organizational behavior: It's often difficult to "fix" companies that struggle with OB issues. Such companies often struggle in a number of different areas and on a number of different levels.

我们怎么"知道"我们了解了组织行为学的相关问题

HOW DO WE "KNOW" WHAT WE KNOW ABOUT ORGANIZATIONAL BEHAVIOR?

经验方法：人们之所以坚持某种信念，是因为这与他们的经验与观察有关。

直觉方法：人们之所以坚持某种信念，是因为这是理所当然的——看起来显而易见或不证自明。

权威方法：人们之所以坚持某种信念，是因为一些受人尊敬的官员、机构或来源这样说过。

科学方法：人们之所以接受某种信念，是因为科学研究运用一系列样本、情境及方法趋于重复这个结果。

Now that we've described what OB is and why it's an important topic of study, we now turn to how we "know" what we know about the topic. In other words, where does the knowledge in this textbook come from? To answer this question, we must first explore how people "know" about anything. Philosophers have argued that there are several different ways of knowing things:

- **Method of Experience:** People hold firmly to some belief because it is consistent with their own experience and observations.
- **Method of Intuition:** People hold firmly to some belief because it "just stands to reason"—it seems obvious or self-evident.
- **Method of Authority:** People hold firmly to some belief because some respected official, agency, or source has said it is so.
- **Method of Science:** People accept some belief because scientific studies have tended to replicate that result using a series of samples, settings, and methods.

Consider the following prediction: Providing social recognition, in the form of public shows of praise and appreciation for good behaviors, will increase the performance and commitment of work units. Perhaps you feel that you "know" this claim to be true because you yourself have always responded well to praise and recognition. Or perhaps you feel that you "know" it to be true because it seems like common sense—who wouldn't work harder after a few public pats on the back? Maybe you feel that you "know" it to be true because a respected boss from your past always extolled the virtue of public praise and recognition.

However, the methods of experience, intuition, and authority also might have led you to the opposite belief—that providing social recognition has no impact on the performance and commitment of work units. It may be that public praise has always made you uncomfortable or embarrassed, to the point that you've tried to hide especially effective behaviors to avoid being singled out by your boss. Or it may seem logical that social recognition will be viewed as "cheap talk," with employees longing for financial incentives rather than verbal compliments. Or perhaps the best boss you ever worked for never offered a single piece of social recognition in her life, yet her employees always worked their hardest on her behalf. From a scientist's point of view, it doesn't really matter what a person's experience, intuition, or authority suggests; the prediction must be tested with data. In other words, scientists don't simply assume that their beliefs are accurate; they acknowledge that their beliefs must be tested scientifically. To read about some interesting scientific tests of human behavior, see our **OB at the Bookstore** feature, which appears in each chapter to showcase a well-known business book that discusses OB concepts.

OB AT THE BOOKSTORE

This feature is designed to spotlight bestselling OB books that complement the content of each chapter. Drawing a bridge from our chapters to these books lets you see how the titles at the bookstore fit together and complement the content of the course.

SUPERFREAKONOMICS

by Steven Levitt and Stephen Dubner (New York: HarperCollins, 2010).

Some people may feel uneasy about reducing the vagaries of human behavior to cold numerical probabilities . . . These objections are good and true. But while there are exceptions to every rule, it's also good to know the rule.

With those words, Levitt and Dubner describe the scientific approach they use to examine human behavior in the sequel to their bestselling *Freakonomics*. What they describe as the "economic approach" is the same method of science used to study organizational behavior. As the authors note, "It usually begins by accumulating data, great gobs of it, which may have been generated on purpose or perhaps left behind by accident. A good set of data can go a long way toward describing human behavior as long as the proper questions are asked of it."

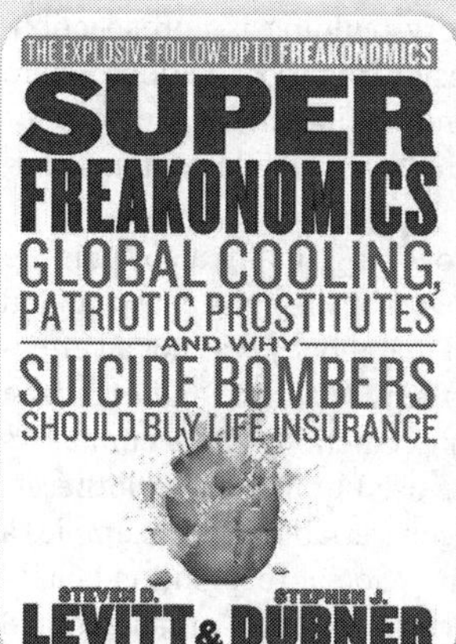

Levitt and Dubner ask a number of questions, some of which illustrate the limitations of the method of intuition. For example, which complaint is more life threatening in an emergency room: chest pains or shortness of breath? You might assume chest pains, which have a one-month mortality rate of 1.2 percent and a one-year mortality rate of 5.3 percent. But the rates for shortness of breath—2.9 percent and 12.9 percent, respectively—are twice as high! Other questions reveal the limitations of the method of authority. For example, the National Highway Traffic Safety Administration (NHTSA) notes that child safety seats reduce the risk of traffic fatalities by 54 percent. It turns out that 54 percent reduction is relative to a child riding completely unrestrained—without a car seat or a seat belt. The mortality rate in car crashes for children ages 2–6 is virtually identical for child safety seats (18.2 percent) and regular seat belts (18.1 percent).

Levitt and Dubner stress that the scientific approach "isn't meant to describe the world as any one of us might *want* it to be, or fear that it is, or pray that it becomes—but rather to explain what it actually is." Once that understanding is gained, it becomes possible to change things for the better.

FIGURE 1-3 The Scientific Method

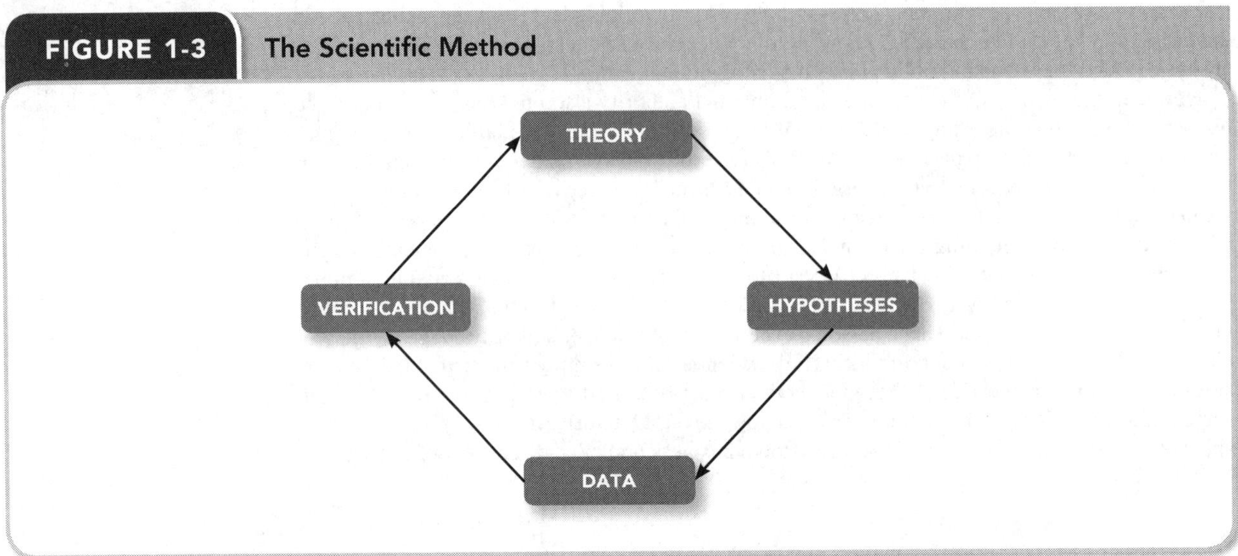

Source: Adapted from F. Bacon, M. Silverthorne, and L. Jardine, *The New Organon* (Cambridge: Cambridge University Press, 2000).

1.5
What is the role of theory in the scientific method?

科学方法从理论开始，**理论**被定义为论断的集合——包括言语和符号的——说明变量是怎样相关的，为什么相关，以及在什么条件下应该（或不应该）相关。

Scientific studies are based on the scientific method, originated by Sir Francis Bacon in the 1600s and adapted in Figure 1-3. The scientific method begins with **theory,** defined as a collection of assertions—both verbal and symbolic—that specify how and why variables are related, as well as the conditions in which they should (and should not) be related. More simply, a theory tells a story and supplies the familiar who, what, where, when, and why elements found in any newspaper or magazine article. Theories are often summarized with theory diagrams, the "boxes and arrows" that graphically depict relationships between variables. Our integrative model of OB in Figure 1-1 represents one such diagram, and there will be many more to come in the remaining chapters of this textbook.

A scientist could build a theory explaining why social recognition might influence the performance and commitment of work units. From what sources would that theory be built? Well, because social scientists "are what they study," one source of theory building is introspection. However, theories may also be built from interviews with employees or from observations where scientists take notes, keep diaries, and pore over company documents to find all the elements of a theory story. Alternatively, theories may be built from research reviews, which examine findings of previous studies to look for general patterns or themes.

Although many theories are interesting, logical, or thought provoking, many also wind up being completely wrong. After all, scientific theories once predicted that the earth was flat and the sun revolved around it. Closer to home, OB theories once argued that money was not an effective motivator and that the best way to structure jobs was to make them as simple and mundane as possible. Theories must therefore be tested to verify that their predictions are accurate. As shown in Figure 1-3, the scientific method requires that theories be used to inspire **hypotheses.** Hypotheses are written predictions that specify relationships between variables. For example, a theory of social recognition could be used to inspire this hypothesis: "Social recognition behaviors on the part of managers will be positively related to the job performance and organizational commitment of their units." This hypothesis states, in black and white, the expected relationship between social recognition and unit performance.

假设是一种表明变量之间关系的书面预测。

Assume a family member owned a chain of 21 fast-food restaurants and allowed you to test this hypothesis using the restaurants. Specifically, you decided to train the managers in a subset of the restaurants about how to use social recognition as a tool to reinforce behaviors. Meanwhile, you left another subset of restaurants unchanged to represent a control group. You then tracked the total number of social recognition behaviors exhibited by managers over the next nine months by observing the managers at specific time intervals. You measured job performance by tracking drive-through times for the next nine months and used those times to reflect the minutes it takes for a customer to approach the restaurant, order food, pay, and leave. You also measured the commitment of the work unit by tracking employee retention rates over the next nine months.

So how can you tell whether your hypothesis was supported? You could analyze the data by examining the **correlation** between social recognition behaviors and drive-through times, as well as the correlation between social recognition behaviors and employee turnover. A correlation, abbreviated *r*, describes the statistical relationship between two variables. Correlations can be positive or negative and range from 0 (no statistical relationship) to 1 (a perfect statistical relationship). Picture a spreadsheet with two columns of numbers. One column contains the total numbers of social recognition behaviors for all 21 restaurants, and the other contains the average drive-through times for those same 21 restaurants. The best way to get a feel for the correlation is to look at a scatterplot—a graph made from those two columns of numbers. Figure 1-4 presents three scatterplots, each depicting different sized correlations. The strength of the correlation can be inferred from the "compactness" of its scatterplot. Panel (a) shows a perfect 1.0 correlation; knowing the score for social recognition allows you to predict the score for drive-through times perfectly. Panel (b) shows a correlation of .50, so the trend in the data is less obvious than in Panel (a) but still easy to see with the naked eye. Finally, Panel (c) shows a correlation of .00—no statistical relationship. Understanding the correlation is important because OB questions are not "yes or no" in nature. That is, the question is not "*Does* social recognition lead to higher job performance?" but rather "*How often* does social recognition lead to higher job performance?" The correlation provides a number that expresses an answer to the "how often" question.

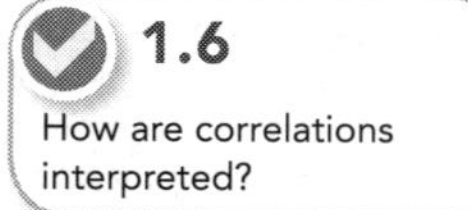

相关性，简写为 *r*，描述了两个变量间的统计关系。

So what is the correlation between social recognition and job performance (and between social recognition and organizational commitment)? It turns out that a study very similar to the

FIGURE 1-4 Three Different Correlation Sizes

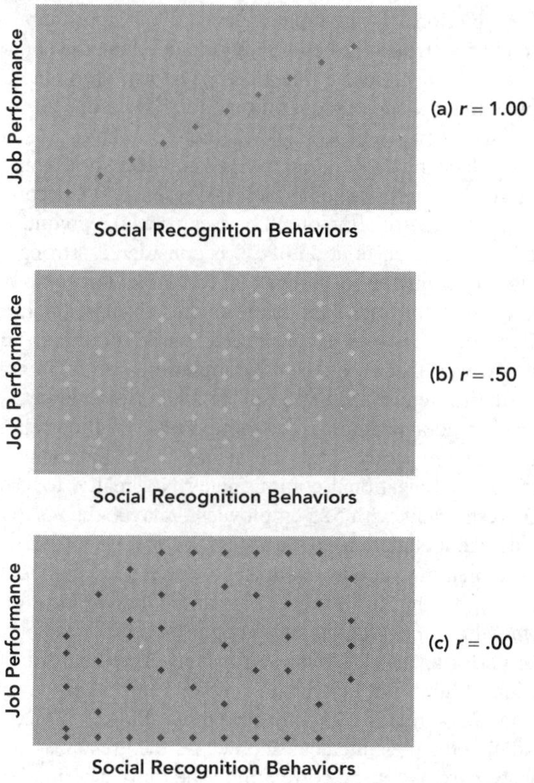

Job Performance / Social Recognition Behaviors — (a) $r = 1.00$

Job Performance / Social Recognition Behaviors — (b) $r = .50$

Job Performance / Social Recognition Behaviors — (c) $r = .00$

A study of Burger King restaurants revealed a correlation between social recognition—praise and appreciation by managers—and employees' performance and commitment. Such studies contribute to the growing body of organizational behavior knowledge.

one described was actually conducted, using a sample of 21 Burger King restaurants with 525 total employees. The correlation between social recognition and job performance was .28. The restaurants that received training in social recognition averaged 44 seconds of drive-through time nine months later versus 62 seconds for the control group locations. The correlation between social recognition and retention rates was .20. The restaurants that received training in social recognition had a 16 percent better retention rate than the control group locations nine months later. The study also instituted a financial "pay-for-performance" system in a subset of the locations and found that the social recognition effects were just as strong as the financial effects.

Of course, you might wonder whether correlations of .28 or .20 are impressive or unimpressive. To understand those numbers, let's consider some context for them. Table 1-4 provides some notable correlations from other areas of science. If the correlation between height and weight is only .44, then a correlation of .28 between social recognition and job performance doesn't sound too bad! In fact, a correlation of .50 is considered "strong" in organizational behavior research, given the sheer number of things that can affect how employees feel and act. A .30 correlation is considered "moderate," and many studies discussed in this book will have results in this range. Finally, a .10 correlation is considered "weak" in organizational behavior research. It should be noted, however, that even "weak" correlations can be important if they predict costly behaviors such as theft or ethical violations. The .08 correlation between smoking and lung cancer within 25 years is a good example of how important small correlations can be.

Does this one study settle the debate about the value of social recognition for job performance and organizational commitment? Not really, for a variety of reasons. First, it included only 21 restaurants with 525 employees—maybe the results would have turned out differently if the study had included more locations. Second, it focused only on restaurant employees—maybe there's something unique about such employees that makes them particularly responsive to social recognition. Third, it may be that the trained locations differed from the control locations on something *other than* social recognition, and it was that "something" that was responsible for the performance differences. You may have heard the phrase, "correlation does not imply causation." It turns out that making **causal inferences**—establishing that one variable really does cause another—requires establishing three things. First, that the two variables are correlated. Second, that the presumed cause precedes the presumed effect in time. Third, that no alternative explanation exists for the correlation. The third criterion is often fulfilled in experiments, where researchers have more control over the setting in which the study occurs.

做出**因果推论**——证明一个变量会导致另一个变量——需要证明三点。首先，两个变量是相关的。其次，假设原因在时间上是在假设结果之后的。第三，对于相关没有其他替代的解释。

TABLE 1-4 Some Notable Correlations

CORRELATION BETWEEN . . .	r	SAMPLE SIZE
Height and weight	.44	16,948
Ibuprofen and pain reduction	.14	8,488
Antihistamines and reduced sneezing	.11	1,023
Smoking and lung cancer within 25 years	.08	3,956
Coronary bypass surgery and 5-year survival	.08	2,649

Source: From Robert Hogan, "In Defense of Personality Measurement: New Wine for Old Whiners," *Human Performance,* Vol. 18, 2005, pp. 331–41. Reprinted by permission of the publisher, Taylor & Frances Group, www.informaworld.com.

The important point is that little can be learned from a single study. The best way to test a theory is to conduct many studies, each of which is as different as possible from the ones that preceded it. So if you really wanted to study the effects of social recognition, you would conduct several studies using different kinds of samples, different kinds of measures, and both experimental and nonexperimental methods. After completing all of those studies, you could look back on the results and create some sort of average correlation across all of the studies. This process is what a technique called **meta-analysis** does. It takes all of the correlations found in studies of a particular relationship and calculates a weighted average (such that correlations based on studies with large samples are weighted more than correlations based on studies with small samples). It turns out that a meta-analysis has been conducted on the effects of social recognition and job performance. That analysis revealed an average correlation of .21 across studies conducted in 96 different organizations in the service industry. That meta-analysis offers more compelling support for the potential benefits of social recognition than the methods of experience, intuition, or authority could have provided.

元分析是对具有特定关联的研究中的所有相关性，计算加权平均值（这种基于大规模样本基础上的相关性比小样本研究中的相关性有更大的权重）。

Indeed, meta-analyses can form the foundation for **evidence-based management**—a perspective that argues that scientific findings should form the foundation for management education, much as they do for medical education. Proponents of evidence-based management argue that human resources should be transformed into a sort of R&D department for managing people. Notes one advocate, "In R&D, you go into the laboratory, you experiment and you keep up with the research that others do. . . .Can you imagine walking into the R&D lab at a pharmaceutical company, asking the chief chemist about an important new study and having him respond that they don't keep up with the literature on chemistry?" Verizon Business, the Basking Ridge, New Jersey–based unit of Verizon Communications, is one example of a company that is moving toward evidence-based management. The company notes that the dollars spent on human resources issues demand more than an intuition-based justification for new plans. More informed decisions come from running systematic experiments in smaller units of an organization, making greater use of internal data, hiring PhD's with relevant expertise, and pursuing collaborations with academics.

循证基础的管理认为科学发现应该构成管理教育的基础，犹如医疗教育一样。

总结：本书的推进

SUMMARY: MOVING FORWARD IN THIS BOOK

The chapters that follow will begin working through the integrative model of OB in Figure 1-1, beginning with the individual outcomes and continuing with the individual, group, and organizational mechanisms that lead to those outcomes. Each chapter begins by spotlighting a company that historically has done a good job of managing a given topic or is currently struggling with a topic. Theories relevant to that topic will be highlighted and discussed. The concepts in those theories will be demonstrated in the **OB on Screen** features to show how OB phenomena have "come to life" in film. The **OB at the Bookstore** feature will then point you to bestsellers that discuss similar concepts. In addition, the **OB Internationally** feature will describe how those concepts operate differently in different cultures and nations.

Each chapter ends with three sections. The first section provides a summarizing theory diagram that explains why some employees exhibit higher levels of a given concept than others. For example, the summarizing theory diagram for Chapter 4 will explain why some employees are more satisfied with their jobs than others. As we noted in the opening of this chapter, knowledge about *why* is critical to any employee who is trying to make sense of his or her working life or any manager who is trying to make his or her unit more effective. How often have you spent time trying to explain your own attitudes and behaviors to yourself? If you consider yourself to be an introspective person, you've probably thought about such questions quite a bit. Our **OB Assessments** feature will help you find out how reflective you really are. This feature also appears in each chapter of the textbook and allows you to gain valuable knowledge about your own personality, abilities, job attitudes, and leadership styles.

The next concluding section will describe the results of meta-analyses that summarize the relationships between that chapter's topic and both job performance and organizational commitment. Over time, you'll gain a feel for which of the topics in Figure 1-1 have strong, moderate, or weak relationships with these outcomes. This knowledge will help you recognize how everything in OB fits together and what the most valuable tools are for improving performance and commitment in the workplace. As you will discover, some of the topics in OB have a greater impact on how well employees perform their jobs, whereas others have a greater impact on how long employees remain with their organizations. Finally, the third concluding section will describe how the content of that chapter can be applied, at a specific level, in an actual organization. For example, the motivation chapter concludes with a section describing how compensation practices can be used to maximize employee effort. If you're currently working, we hope that these concluding sections will help you see how the concepts you're reading about can be used to improve your own organizations. Even if you're not working, these application sections will give you a glimpse into how you will experience OB concepts once you begin your working life.

OB ASSESSMENTS

This feature is designed to illustrate how OB concepts actually get measured in practice. In many cases, these OB assessments will provide you with potentially valuable insights into your own attitudes, skills, and personality. The OB assessments that you'll see in each chapter consist of multiple survey items. Two concepts are critical when evaluating how good the OB assessments are: *reliability* and *validity.* Reliability is defined as the degree to which the survey items are free from random error. If survey items are reliable, then similar items will yield similar answers. Validity is defined as the degree to which the survey items seem to assess what they are meant to assess. If survey items are valid, then experts on the subject will agree that the items seem appropriate.

INTROSPECTION

How introspective are you? This assessment is designed to measure introspection—sometimes termed "private self-consciousness"—which is the tendency to direct attention inward to better understand your attitudes and behaviors. Answer each question using the response scale provided. Then subtract your answers to the boldfaced questions from 4, with the difference being your new answers for those questions. For example, if your original answer for question 5 was "3," your new answer is 1 (4 – 3). Then sum your answers for the ten questions. (For more assessments relevant to this chapter, please visit http://connect.mcgraw-hill.com.)

0	1	2	3	4
EXTREMELY UNCHARACTERISTIC OF ME	SOMEWHAT UNCHARACTERISTIC OF ME	NEUTRAL	SOMEWHAT CHARACTERISTIC OF ME	EXTREMELY CHARACTERISTIC OF ME

1. I'm always trying to figure myself out. ________
2. **Generally, I'm not very aware of myself.** ________
3. I reflect about myself a lot. ________
4. I'm often the subject of my own daydreams. ________
5. **I never scrutinize myself.** ________
6. I'm generally attentive to my inner feelings. ________
7. I'm constantly examining my motives. ________
8. I sometimes have the feeling that I'm off somewhere watching myself. ________
9. I'm alert to changes in my mood. ________
10. I'm aware of the way my mind works when I work through a problem. ________

SCORING AND INTERPRETATION

If your scores sum up to 26 or above, you do a lot of introspection and are highly self-aware. You may find that many of the theories discussed in this textbook will help you better understand your attitudes and feelings about working life.

Source: From A. Fenigstein, M.F. Scheier, and A.H. Buss, "Public and Private Self-Consciousness: Assessment and Theory," *Journal of Consulting and Clinical Psychology,* Vol. 43, August 1975, pp. 522–27.

chapter 2

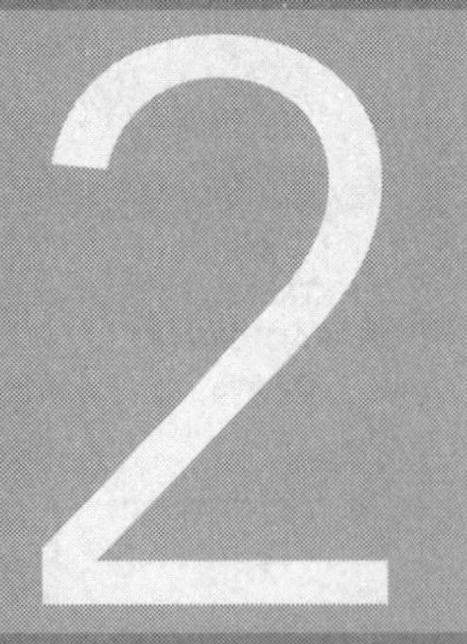

Job Performance

工作绩效

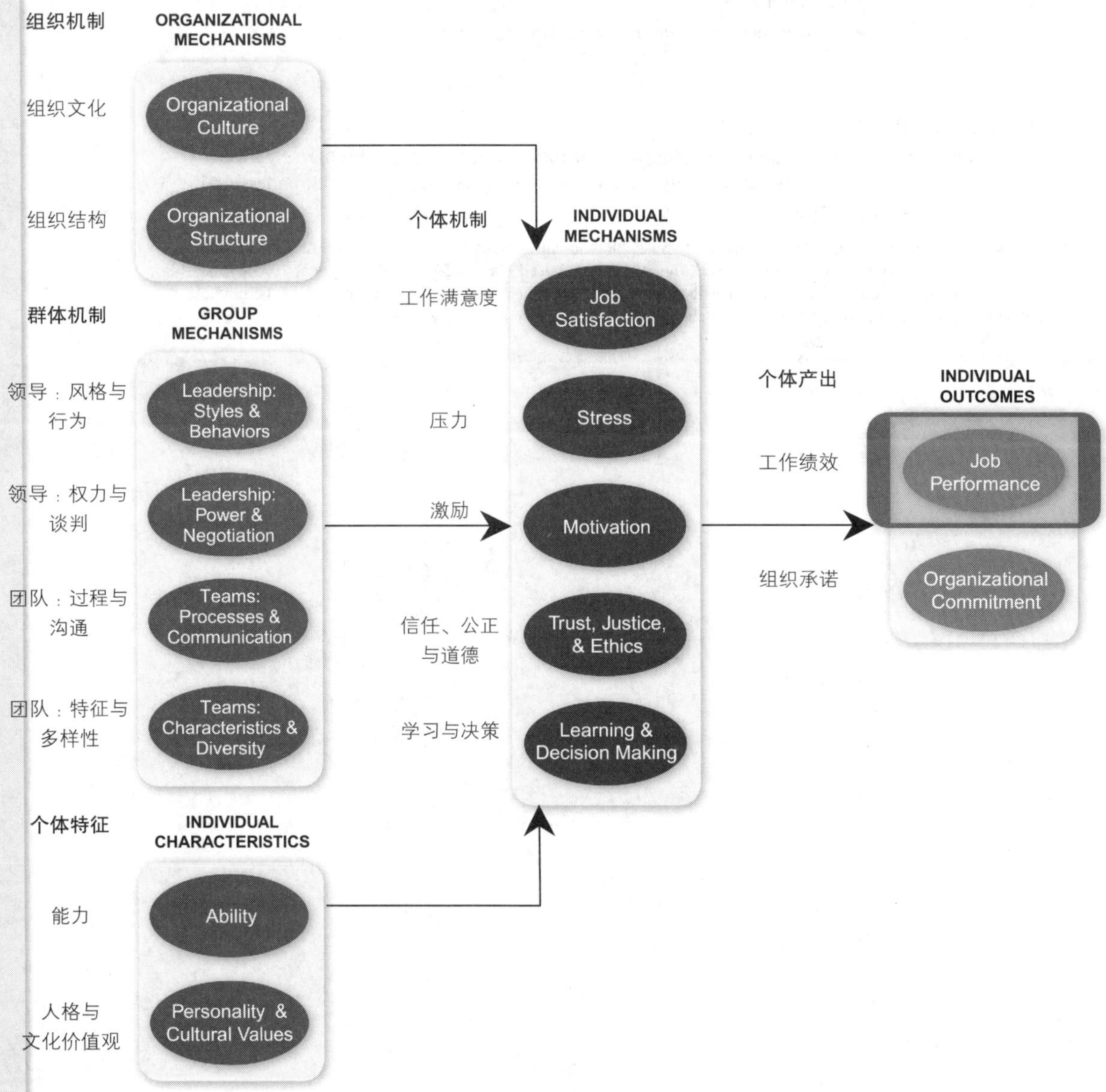

LEARNING GOALS

After reading this chapter, you should be able to answer the following questions:

2.1 What is job performance?

2.2 What is task performance?

2.3 How do organizations identify the behaviors that underlie task performance?

2.4 What is citizenship behavior?

2.5 What is counterproductive behavior?

2.6 What workplace trends are affecting job performance in today's organizations?

2.7 How can organizations use job performance information to manage employee performance?

FRITO-LAY

"What happens when 48,000 people focus on a single vision?" This question appears on the company vision page of the corporate website of Frito-Lay, the Plano, Texas–based subsidiary of PepsiCo Inc., and market leader in the salty snack food industry. But what exactly is this vision, and what does it have to do with selling $13 billion worth of Fritos, Ruffles, Lay's, Doritos, Cheetos, and Tostitos (as well as 28 other well-known brands of snack food) each year? Well, according to the Frito-Lay website, the company's vision is to provide to consumers the best snacks on earth. They begin with simple all natural ingredients—corn, potatoes, and oil—and incorporate innovations to make and sell snacks that are more tasty and fun than what competitors can offer. Frito-Lay recognizes that the job performance of its employees is a key driver of the company's success. How so? The company believes it can be successful only if each of its 48,000 employees understands the company's vision and performs in a way that helps to achieve it.

So how does Frito-Lay foster alignment of its employees' performance with the company's vision? As in most organizations, the task of managing employee performance is a fairly involved process that requires careful research and analysis. It begins with an understanding of the activities involved in each job, and how effective and ineffective performance of these various activities contributes to the company's success. This understanding, in turn, provides the basis for developing and implementing management practices that reinforce these important performance-related activities and behaviors.

As an example, consider the Frito-Lay job that's likely to be most familiar to you, the route sales representative. You've seen the folks who perform this job in the aisles of grocery, drug, and convenience stores placing the product on the shelves and displays. Although you might believe the job is important only because it determines whether your favorite snack is in stock, fresh, and not crushed, it might surprise you to learn just how crucial the job is to Frito-Lay. There are over 17,000 route sales representatives who provide service to more than 20,000 retail outlets each day. They not only load shelves and displays with the various products, but they also drive the products from warehouses to the stores, take orders for additional product, and negotiate with managers for additional display space. In an effort to manage the performance of these employees and bring it in line with their vision, Frito-Lay invests in research that identifies the factors that influence effectiveness in each of these tasks, as well as how the various job tasks should be prioritized in different situations.

工作绩效

JOB PERFORMANCE

We begin our journey through the integrative model of organizational behavior with job performance. Why begin with job performance? Because understanding one's own performance is a critical concern for any employee, and understanding the performance of employees in one's unit is a critical concern for any manager. Consider for a moment the job performance of your university's basketball coach. If you were the university's athletic director, you might gauge the coach's performance by paying attention to various behaviors. How much time does the coach spend on the road during recruiting season? How effective are the coach's practices? Are the offensive and defensive schemes well designed, and are the plays called during games appropriate? You might also consider some other behaviors that fall outside the strict domain of basketball. Does the coach run a clean program? Do players graduate on time? Does the coach represent the university well during interviews with the media and when in public?

Of course, as your university's athletic director, you might be tempted to ask a simpler question: Is the coach a winner? After all, fans and boosters may not care how good the coach is at the previously listed behaviors if the team fails to win conference championships or make it deep into the NCAA tournament. Moreover, the coach's performance in terms of wins and losses has important implications for the university because it affects ticket sales, licensing fees, and booster donations.

Still, is every unsuccessful season the coach's fault? What if the coach develops a well-conceived game plan but the players repeatedly make mistakes at key times in the game? What if the team experiences a rash of injuries or inherits a schedule that turns out to be much tougher than originally thought? What if a few games during the season are decided by fluke baskets or by bad calls by the referees?

Geno Auriemma has led the University of Connecticut women's basketball team to 34 Big East titles, seven national championships, four perfect seasons, and 100 percent graduation rate for all four-year players. If the Huskies suffered through a couple losing seasons, would Coach Auriemma be considered a low performer?

This example illustrates one dilemma when examining job performance. Is performance a set of behaviors that a person does (or does not) perform, or is performance the end result of those behaviors? You might be tempted to believe it's more appropriate to define performance in terms of results rather than behaviors. This is because results seem more "objective" and are more connected to the central concern of managers—"the bottom line." For example, the job performance of salespeople is often measured by the amount of sales revenue generated by each person over some time span (e.g., a month, a quarter, a year). For the most part, this logic makes perfect sense: Salespeople are hired by organizations to generate sales, and so those who meet or exceed sales goals are worth more to the organization and should be considered high performers. It's very easy to appreciate how the sales revenue from each salesperson might be added up and used as an indicator of a business's financial performance.

However, as sensible as this logic seems, using results to indicate job performance creates potential problems. First, employees contribute to their organization in ways that go beyond bottom-line results, and so evaluating an employee's performance based on results alone might give you an inaccurate picture of which employees are worth more to the organization. Second, results are often influenced by factors that are beyond the employee's control—product quality, competition, equipment, technology, budget constraints, coworkers, and supervision, just to name a few. Third, even if these uncontrollable factors are less relevant in a given situation, there's another problem with a results-based view of job performance: results don't tell you how to reverse a "bad year." That is, performance feedback based on results does not provide people with the information they need to improve their behavior. As our opening example illustrates, Frito-Lay believes that managing people so that they are able to improve their results requires an understanding of what the people actually do to achieve those results. Other companies, such as Walgreens, use knowledge of the performance behaviors to create comprehensive training and development programs so that employees can be effective at various jobs they may have throughout their careers with the company. In sum, given that the field of OB aims to understand, predict, and improve behavior, we refer to job performance as behavior. We use the term "results" or "job performance results" to describe the outcomes associated with those behaviors.

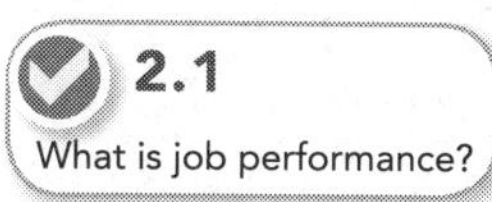

So what types of employee behaviors constitute job performance? To understand this question, consider that **job performance** is formally defined as the value of the set of employee behaviors that contribute, either positively or negatively, to organizational goal accomplishment. This definition of job performance includes behaviors that are within the control of employees, but it places a boundary on which behaviors are (and are not) relevant to job performance. For example, consider the behavior of a server in a restaurant that prides itself on world-class customer service. Texting a friend during a work break would not usually be relevant (in either a positive or negative sense) to the accomplishment of organizational goals. That behavior is therefore not relevant to the server's job performance. However, texting in the middle of taking a customer's order would be relevant (in a negative sense) to organizational goal accomplishment. That behavior, therefore, is relevant to the server's job performance.

工作绩效是指一些有意义的员工行为，这些行为对组织目标的实现产生积极或消极的影响。

成为一名“高绩效员工”意味着什么

WHAT DOES IT MEAN TO BE A "GOOD PERFORMER"?

Our definition of job performance raises a number of important questions. Specifically, you might be wondering which employee behaviors fall under the umbrella heading of "job performance." In other words, what exactly do you have to *do* to be a "good performer"? We could probably spend an entire chapter just listing various behaviors that are relevant to job performance. However, those behaviors generally fit into three broad categories. Two categories are task performance and citizenship behavior, both of which contribute positively to the organization. The third category is counterproductive behavior, which contributes negatively to the organization. The sections that follow describe these broad categories of job performance in greater detail.

任务绩效

TASK PERFORMANCE

任务绩效包括直接将组织资源转换为组织生产的产品和服务的员工行为。

Task performance includes employee behaviors that are directly involved in the transformation of organizational resources into the goods or services that the organization produces. If you read a description of a job in an employment ad online, that description will focus on task performance behaviors—the tasks, duties, and responsibilities that are a core part of the job. Put differently, task performance is the set of explicit obligations that an employee must fulfill to receive compensation and continued employment. For a flight attendant, task performance includes announcing and demonstrating safety and emergency procedures and distributing food and beverages to passengers. For a firefighter, task performance includes searching burning buildings to locate fire victims and operating equipment to put out fires. For an accountant, task performance involves preparing, examining, and analyzing accounting records for accuracy and completeness. Finally, for an advertising executive, task performance includes developing advertising campaigns and preparing and delivering presentations to clients.

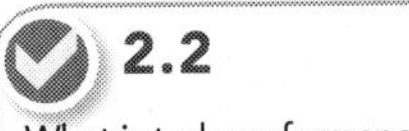
2.2
What is task performance?

常规性任务绩效是在正常的、常规的及可预测的情况下对工作需求的为人熟知的反应方式。

Although the specific activities that constitute task performance differ widely from one job to another, task performance also can be understood in terms of more general categories. One way of categorizing task performance is to consider the extent to which the context of the job is routine, changing, or requires a novel or unique solution. **Routine task performance** involves well-known responses to demands that occur in a normal, routine, or otherwise predictable way. In these cases, employees tend to behave in more or less habitual or programmed ways that vary little from one instance to another. As an example of a routine task activity, you may recall watching an expressionless flight attendant robotically demonstrate how to insert the seatbelt tongue into the seatbelt buckle before your flight takes off. Seatbelts haven't really changed since . . . oh . . . 1920, so the instructions to passengers tend to be conveyed the same way, over and over again.

适应性任务绩效，或更为一般来说的“适应性”，包括员工对新奇的、不同寻常的或不可预测的任务需求的反应。

In contrast, **adaptive task performance**, or more commonly "adaptability," involves employee responses to task demands that are novel, unusual, or, at the very least, unpredictable. For example, on August 2, 2005, Air France Flight 358, carrying 297 passengers and 12 crew members from Paris, France, to Toronto, Canada, skidded off the runway while landing and plunged into a ravine. Amid smoke and flames, the flight attendants quickly responded to the emergency and assisted three-quarters of the 297 passengers safely off the plane within 52 seconds, before the emergency response team arrived. One minute later, the remaining passengers and 12 crew members were out safely. From this example, you can see that flight attendants' task performance shifted from activities such as providing safety demonstrations and handing out beverages to performing emergency procedures to save passengers' lives. Although flight attendants receive training so they can handle emergency situations such as this one, executing these behaviors effectively in the context of an actual emergency differs fundamentally from anything experienced previously.

Adaptive behaviors are becoming increasingly important as globalization, technological advances, and knowledge-based work increase the pace of change in the workplace. In fact, adaptive task performance has become crucial in today's global economy where companies have been faced with the challenge of becoming more productive with fewer employees on staff. For example, at the German chemical and pharmaceutical company Bayer, the hiring of

TABLE 2-1 Behaviors Involved in Adaptability

BEHAVIORS	SPECIFIC EXAMPLES
Handling emergencies or crisis situations	Quickly analyzing options for dealing with danger or crises and their implications; making split-second decisions based on clear and focused thinking
Handling work stress	Remaining composed and cool when faced with difficult circumstances or a highly demanding workload or schedule; acting as a calming and settling influence to whom others can look for guidance
Solving problems creatively	Turning problems upside-down and inside-out to find fresh new approaches; integrating seemingly unrelated information and developing creative solutions
Dealing with uncertain and unpredictable work situations	Readily and easily changing gears in response to unpredictable or unexpected events and circumstances; effectively adjusting plans, goals, actions, or priorities to deal with changing situations
Learning work tasks, technologies, and work situations	Quickly and proficiently learning new methods or how to perform previously unlearned tasks; anticipating change in the work demands and searching for and participating in assignments or training to prepare for these changes
Demonstrating interpersonal adaptability	Being flexible and open-minded when dealing with others; listening to and considering others' viewpoints and opinions and altering one's own opinion when it's appropriate to do so
Demonstrating cultural adaptability	Willingly adjusting behavior or appearance as necessary to comply with or show respect for others' values and customs; understanding the implications of one's actions and adjusting one's approach to maintain positive relationships with other groups, organizations, or cultures

Source: E.E. Pulakos, S. Arad, M.A. Donovan, and K.E. Plamondon, "Adaptability in the Workplace: Development of a Taxonomy of Adaptive Performance," *Journal of Applied Psychology* 85 (2000), pp. 612–24. Copyright © 2004 by the American Psychological Association. Adapted with permission. No further reproduction or distribution is permitted without permission from the American Psychological Association.

plant directors involves the search for candidates who not only possess a wide range of skills and abilities so that they can adapt to various job demands, but in addition, competence in helping other employees adapt to changes that occur in the workplace. Table 2-1 provides a number of examples of adaptability that are relevant to many jobs in today's economy.

Finally, **creative task performance** is the degree to which individuals develop ideas or physical outcomes that are both novel and useful. The necessity of including both novelty and usefulness in the definition of creativity can be illustrated with the following example of what effective performance for a swimsuit designer involves. Consider first the case of a swimsuit designer who suggests in a meeting that next season's line of swimsuits should be made entirely out of chrome-plated steel. Although this idea might be very novel, for many reasons it's not likely to be very useful. Indeed, someone who offered an idea like this would likely be considered silly rather than creative. Another swimsuit designer suggests in the meeting that swimsuits

创造性任务绩效是指个体开发有价值的、新奇的想法或物质产出的程度。

for next season should be made out of materials that are attractive and comfortable. Although under some circumstances such an idea might be useful, the idea is not novel because attractiveness and comfort are generally accepted design elements for swimsuits. Someone who offered an idea like this might be appreciated for offering input, but no one would consider this individual's performance to be particularly creative. Finally, a third designer for this swimsuit manufacturer suggests that perhaps a two-piece design would be preferred for women, rather than a more traditional one-piece design. Although such an idea would not be considered creative today, it certainly was in 1946 when, in separate but nearly simultaneous efforts, Jacques Heim and Louis Reard introduced the bikini.

Although you might be tempted to believe that creative task performance is only relevant to jobs such as artist and inventor, its emphasis has been increasing across a wide variety of jobs. Indeed, more than half the total wages and salary in the United States are paid to employees who need to be creative as part of their jobs, and as a consequence, some have argued that we are at the "dawn of the creative age." This increase in the value of creative performance can be explained by the rapid technological change and intense competition that mark today's business landscape. In this context, employee creativity is necessary to spark the types of innovations that enable organizations to stay ahead of their competition.

2.3

How do organizations identify the behaviors that underlie task performance?

任务分析归结起来有三个步骤：第一，列举出在工作中包括的所有活动。第二，按照活动的重要性和频率，由"相关业务专家"对这份清单中的每项活动进行排序。第三，那些重要性和频率排序较高的活动被保留下来用于界定任务绩效。

Now that we've given you a general understanding of task performance behaviors, you might be wondering how organizations identify the sets of behaviors that represent "task performance" for different jobs. Many organizations identify task performance behaviors by conducting a **job analysis.** Although there are many different ways to conduct a job analysis, most boil down to three steps. First, a list of the activities involved in a job is generated. This list generally results from data from several sources, including observations, surveys, and interviews of employees. Second, each activity on this list is rated by "subject matter experts," according to things like the importance and frequency of the activity. Subject matter experts generally have experience performing the job or managing the job and therefore are in a position to judge the importance of specific activities to the organization. Third, the activities that are rated highly in terms of their importance and frequency are retained and used to define task performance. Those retained behaviors then find their way into training programs as learning objectives and into performance evaluation systems as measures to evaluate task performance.

As an example, to determine training objectives for production workers, Toyota uses a highly detailed job analysis process to identify important tasks as well as the behaviors necessary to effectively complete those tasks. The core job tasks involved in the job of a bumper-molding operator, for example, include "routine core tasks," "machine tending," and "quality," and each of these tasks further consists of several more detailed steps. For example, routine core tasks include de-molding, trimming, spray-molding, and sanding. Each of these tasks can be broken down further into more detailed steps, and in turn, the specific behaviors involved in each step become the focus of the training. For example, to de-mold the left side of the bumper, the worker must "use left thumb to push along edge of bumper," "place pressure in the crease of thumb," "push toward left side away from mold," and "grasp top edge when bumper is released." Although this level of detail might seem like an awful lot of analysis for what one might imagine to be a relatively straightforward job, Toyota competes on the basis of quality and cost, and its success in selling millions of Camrys, Corollas, and Tacomas each year has been attributed to its ability to train production workers to follow the standardized and efficient procedures.

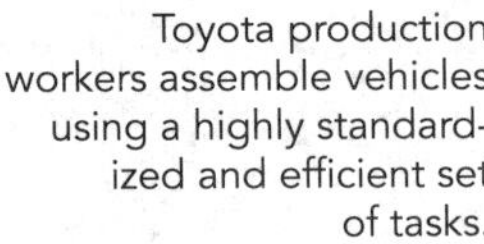

Toyota production workers assemble vehicles using a highly standardized and efficient set of tasks.

Men's Wearhouse, the Houston-based retailer, provides another good example of an organization that uses task performance information to manage its employees. The company first gathers information about the employee's on-the-job behaviors. For example, the job of wardrobe consultant involves greeting, interviewing and measuring customers properly, ensuring proper alteration revenue is collected, and treating customers in a warm and caring manner. After the information is gathered, senior managers provide feedback and coaching to the employee about which types of behaviors he or she needs to change to improve. The feedback is framed as constructive criticism meant to improve an employee's behavior. Put yourself in the place of a Men's Wearhouse wardrobe consultant for a moment. Wouldn't you rather have your performance evaluated on the basis of behaviors such as these rather than some overall index of sales? After all, those behaviors are completely within your control, and the feedback you receive from your boss will be more informative than the simple directive to "sell more suits next year than you did this year."

If organizations find it impractical to use job analysis to identify the set of behaviors needed to define task performance, they can turn to a database the government has created to help with that important activity. The **Occupational Information Network** (or O*NET) is an online database that includes, among other things, the characteristics of most jobs in terms of tasks, behaviors, and the required knowledge, skills, and abilities (http://online.onetcenter.org). Figure 2-1 shows the O*NET output for a flight attendant's position, including many of the tasks discussed previously in this chapter. Of course, O*NET represents only a first step in figuring out the important tasks for a given job. Many organizations ask their employees to perform tasks that their competitors do not, so their workforce performs in a unique and valuable way. O*NET cannot capture those sorts of unique task requirements—the "numerous small decisions" that separate the most effective organizations from their competitors.

职业信息网络是一种在线数据库，包括按照任务、行为、知识、技能和能力划分的绝大部分工作的特征。

For example, the authors of a book entitled *Nuts* identify "fun" as one of the dominant values of Southwest Airlines. Southwest believes that people are willing to work more productively and creatively in an environment that includes humor and laughter. Consistent with this belief, flight attendant task performance at Southwest includes not only generic flight attendant activities, such as those identified by O*NET, but also activities that reflect a sense of humor and playfulness. Effective flight attendants at Southwest tell jokes over the intercom such as, "We'll be dimming the lights in the cabin . . . pushing the light-bulb button will turn your reading light on. However, pushing the flight attendant button will not turn your flight attendant on." As another example, Nisshinbo Automotive, a part of the Japanese company Nisshinbo Holdings, was

FIGURE 2-1 O*NET Results for Flight Attendants

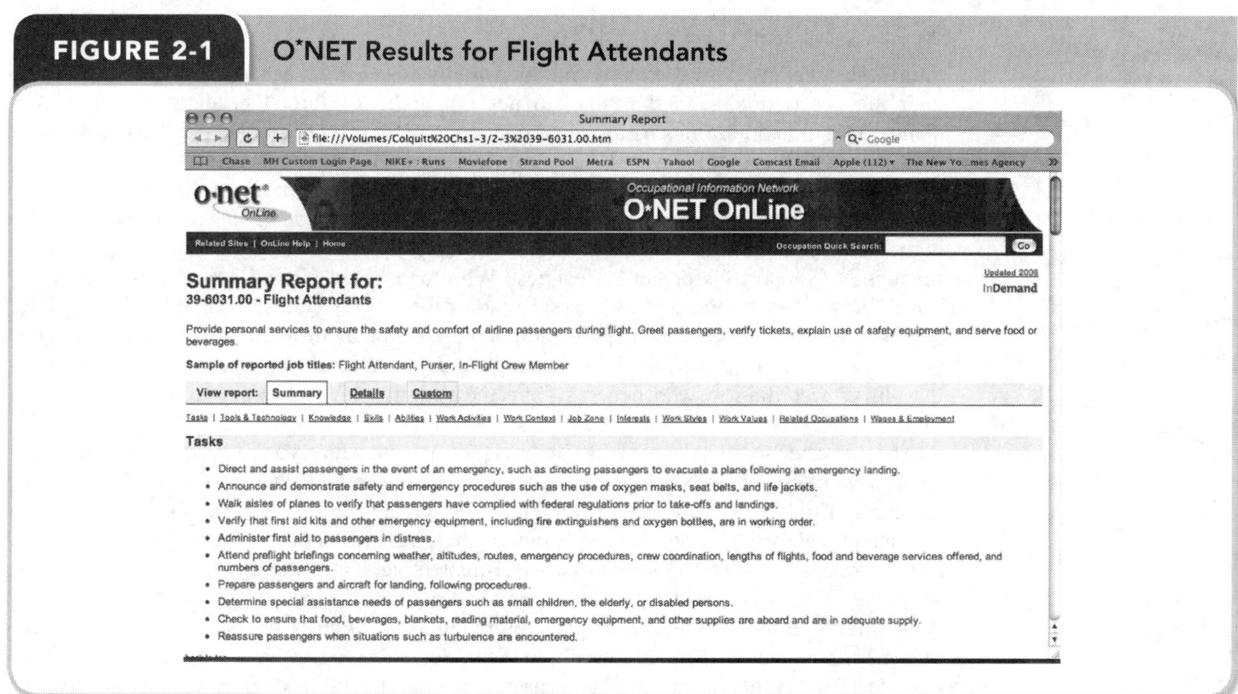

O*NET, or Occupational Information Network, is an online government database that lists the characteristics of most jobs and the knowledge required for each. This sample is for the job of flight attendant.

The pilot of Flight 1549 displayed exceptional performance and saved the lives of his passengers and crew.

faced with the challenge of increasing productivity with fewer workers. They developed a system where they not only evaluated and compensated employees for behaviors reflected in their job descriptions, but also in behaviors that supported the company's mission defined more broadly. In summary, though O*NET may be a good place to start, the task information from the database should be supplemented with information regarding behaviors that support the organization's values and strategy.

Before concluding our section on task performance, it's important to note that task performance behaviors are not simply performed or not performed. Although poor performers often fail to complete required behaviors, it's just as true that the best performers often exceed all expectations for those behaviors. In fact, you can probably think of examples of employees who have engaged in task performance that's truly extraordinary. As an example, consider the case of Chesley B. Sullenberger, the pilot of US Airways Flight 1549, which lost power after hitting a flock of birds shortly after taking off from New York's LaGuardia Airport on January 15, 2009. Sullenberger calmly discussed the problem with air traffic control and decided that the only course of action was to land in the Hudson River. Three minutes after the bird strike, he executed a textbook landing on the water, saving the lives of all 150 passengers and crew. Experts agree that Sullenberger's performance that day was remarkable. Not only did Sullenberger accurately assess the situation and make the right decision about where to ditch the aircraft, he also piloted the landing perfectly. If the plane had approached the water going too slow, it would have lost lift and crashed into the water nose first; if the plane had been going too fast when it touched, it would have flipped, cart-wheeled, and disintegrated.

公民行为是指有助于组织提高工作环境整体质量的员工自愿行为，无论其是否受到奖励。

人际公民行为主要使同伴或同事受益，并且以超过正常工作期望的方式，对组织其他成员提供帮助、支持及发展。

助人行为包括支持有繁重工作任务的同事，帮助他们处理个人事宜以及为新员工传授工作技巧。

 **2.4**
What is citizenship behavior?

公民行为
CITIZENSHIP BEHAVIOR

Sometimes employees go the extra mile by actually engaging in behaviors that are not within their job description—and thus that do not fall under the broad heading of task performance. This situation brings us to the second category of job performance, called **citizenship behavior**, which is defined as voluntary employee activities that may or may not be rewarded but that contribute to the organization by improving the overall quality of the setting in which work takes place. Have you ever had a coworker or fellow student who was especially willing to help someone who was struggling? Who typically attended optional meetings or social functions to support his or her colleagues? Who maintained a good attitude, even in trying times? We tend to call those people "good citizens" or "good soldiers." High levels of citizenship behavior earn them such titles. Although there are many different types of behaviors that might seem to fit the definition of citizenship behavior, research suggests two main categories that differ according to who benefits from the activity: coworkers or the organization (see Figure 2-2).

The first category of citizenship behavior is the one with which you're most likely to be familiar: **interpersonal citizenship behavior**. Such behaviors benefit coworkers and colleagues and involve assisting, supporting, and developing other organizational members in a way that goes beyond normal job expectations. For example, **helping** involves assisting coworkers who have heavy workloads, aiding them with personal matters, and showing new employees the ropes when they first arrive on the job. Do you consider yourself a helpful person? Check the **OB Assessments** feature to see how helpful you really are. **Courtesy** refers to keeping coworkers informed about matters that are relevant to them. Some employees have a tendency to keep relevant facts and events secret. Good citizens do the opposite; they keep others in the loop because they never know what information might be useful to someone else. **Sportsmanship** involves maintaining a good attitude with coworkers, even when they've done something annoying or

善意知会是指使同事知晓与他们相关的事件。

运动员精神是指与同事保持良好的态度。

FIGURE 2-2 Types of Citizenship Behaviors

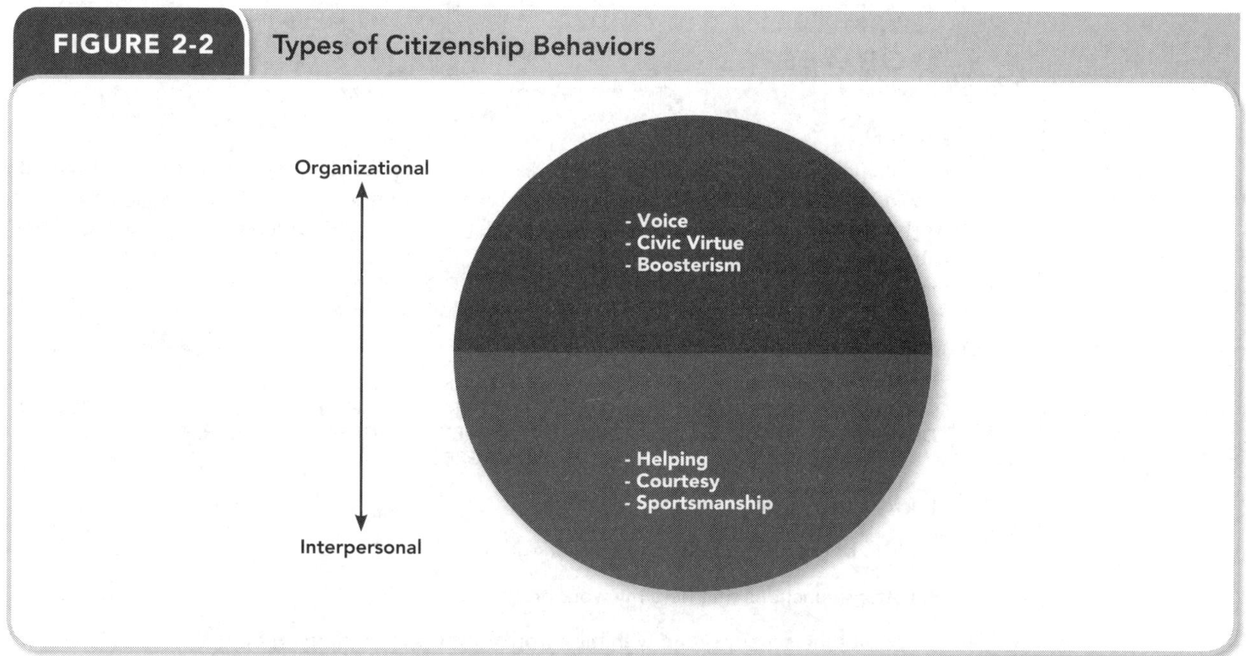

when the unit is going through tough times. Whining and complaining are contagious; good citizens avoid being the squeaky wheel who frequently makes mountains out of molehills.

Although interpersonal citizenship behavior is important in many different job contexts, it may be even more important when employees work in small groups or teams. A team with members who tend to be helpful, respectful, and courteous is also likely to have a positive team atmosphere in which members trust one another. This type of situation is essential to foster the willingness of team members to work toward a common team goal rather than goals that may be more self-serving. In fact, if you think about the behaviors that commonly fall under the "teamwork" heading, you'll probably agree that most are examples of interpersonal citizenship behavior (see Chapter 10 on Team Processes and Communication for more discussion of such issues).

The second category of citizenship behavior is **organizational citizenship behavior**. These behaviors benefit the larger organization by supporting and defending the company, working to improve its operations, and being especially loyal to it. For example, **voice** involves speaking up and offering constructive suggestions for change. Good citizens react to bad rules or policies by constructively trying to change them as opposed to passively complaining about them (see Chapter 3 on Organizational Commitment for more discussion of such issues). **Civic virtue** refers to participating in the company's operations at a deeper-than-normal level by attending voluntary meetings and functions, reading and keeping up with organizational announcements, and keeping abreast of business news that affects the company. **Boosterism** means representing the organization in a positive way when out in public, away from the office, and away from work. Think of friends you've had who worked for a restaurant. Did they always say good things about the restaurant when talking to you and keep any "kitchen horror stories" to themselves? If so, they were being good citizens by engaging in high levels of boosterism.

Three important points should be emphasized about citizenship behaviors. First, as you've probably realized, citizenship behaviors are relevant in virtually any job, regardless of the particular nature of its tasks, and research suggests that these behaviors can boost organizational effectiveness. As examples, research conducted in a paper mill found that the quantity and quality of crew output was higher in crews that included more workers who engaged in citizenship behavior. Research in 30 restaurants also showed that higher levels of citizenship behavior promoted higher revenue, better operating efficiency, higher customer satisfaction, higher performance quality, less food waste, and fewer customer complaints. Thus, it seems clear that citizenship behaviors have a significant influence on the bottom line.

组织公民行为通过支持和保护公司、努力改善公司运行以及保持对公司忠诚来使组织受益。

公民道德是指通过自愿参加会议和活动、阅读及跟踪组织公告、关注影响公司的商业报道等形式深入参与公司的运行。

热心支持指在外出参加公开活动、远离办公室及工作环境时，总能以一种积极的方式代表组织。

OB ASSESSMENTS

HELPING

How helpful are you? This assessment is designed to measure helping, an interpersonal form of citizenship behavior. Think of the people you work with most frequently, either at school or at work. The questions below refer to these people as your "work group." Answer each question using the scale below, then sum up your answers. (For more assessments relevant to this chapter, please visit http://connect.mcgraw-hill.com.)

1	2	3	4	5	6	7
STRONGLY DISAGREE	MODERATELY DISAGREE	SLIGHTLY DISAGREE	NEITHER DISAGREE NOR AGREE	SLIGHTLY AGREE	MODERATELY AGREE	STRONGLY AGREE

1. I volunteer to do things for my work group. ______
2. I help orient new members of my work group. ______
3. I attend functions that help my work group. ______
4. I assist others in my group with their work for the benefit of the group. ______
5. I get involved to benefit my work group. ______
6. I help others in this group learn about the work. ______
7. I help others in this group with their work responsibilities. ______

SCORING AND INTERPRETATION

If your scores sum up to 40 or higher, you perform a high level of helping behavior, which means you frequently engage in citizenship behaviors directed at your colleagues. This is good, as long as it doesn't distract you from fulfilling your own job duties and responsibilities. If your scores sum up to less than 40, you perform a low level of helping behaviors. You might consider paying more attention to whether your colleagues need assistance while working on their task duties.

Source: L.V. Van Dyne and J.A. LePine, "Helping and Voice Extra-Role Behaviors: Evidence of Construct and Predictive Validity," *Academy of Management Journal* 41 (1998), pp. 108–19.

Second, because citizenship behaviors are relatively discretionary and influenced by the specific situation the employee is working in, they can vary significantly over time. In other words, an employee who engages in citizenship behavior during one point in time might not engage in citizenship behavior at other points in time. As an example, it's likely that you've had a very positive experience working with another student or colleague on a project and were willing to invest a great deal of extra effort in order to be helpful. At some point, however, the person with whom you were working may have done something that made you feel much less positive about the collaboration and, as a consequence, you decided to withhold your extra help so that you could focus your energies elsewhere.

Third, from an employee's perspective, it may be tempting to discount the importance of citizenship behaviors—to just focus on your own job tasks and leave aside any "extra" stuff. After all, citizenship behaviors appear to be voluntary and optional, whereas task performance requirements are not. However, discounting citizenship behaviors is a bad idea because supervisors don't always view such actions as optional. In fact, research on computer salespeople, insurance agents, petrochemical salespeople, pharmaceutical sales managers, office furniture makers, sewing machine operators, U.S. Air Force mechanics, and first-tour U.S. Army soldiers has shown that citizenship behaviors relate strongly to supervisor evaluations of job performance, even when differences in task performance are also considered. As we discuss in our **OB Internationally** feature, the tendency of supervisors to consider citizenship behaviors in evaluating overall job performance appears to hold even across countries with vastly different cultures. Of course, this issue has a lot of relevance to you, given that in most organizations, supervisors' evaluations of employee job performance play significant roles in determining employee pay and promotions. Indeed, employee citizenship behavior has been found to influence the salary and promotion recommendations people receive, over and above their task performance. Put simply, it pays to be a good citizen.

反生产行为
COUNTERPRODUCTIVE BEHAVIOR

Now we move from the "good soldiers" to the "bad apples." Whereas task performance and citizenship behavior refer to employee activities that help the organization achieve its goals and objectives, other activities in which employees engage do just the opposite. This third broad category of job performance is **counterproductive behavior**, defined as employee behaviors that intentionally hinder organizational goal accomplishment. The word "intentionally" is a key aspect of this definition; these are things that employees mean to do, not things they accidentally do. Although there are many different kinds of counterproductive behaviors, research suggests that—like task performance and citizenship behavior—they can be grouped into more specific categories (see Figure 2-3).

反生产行为定义为员工有意识地阻止组织目标实现的行为。

OB INTERNATIONALLY

As we've already explained, citizenship behavior tends to be viewed as relatively voluntary because it's not often explicitly outlined in job descriptions or directly rewarded. However, people in organizations vary in their beliefs regarding the degree to which citizenship behavior is truly voluntary, and these differences have important implications. As an example, consider a situation in which an employee engages in citizenship behaviors because of his or her belief that the behaviors are part of the job. However, this employee works for a supervisor who believes that citizenship behaviors are unnecessary. Assuming that the supervisor would not consider the citizenship behaviors on a performance evaluation, the employee would likely react negatively because he or she has not been recognized for putting effort into activities that help other members of the organization.

So what types of factors cause differences in beliefs regarding whether or not citizenship behavior is discretionary? One factor that would appear to be important is national culture. It is widely believed that the culture in countries like the United States, Canada, and the Netherlands encourages behaviors that support competition and individual achievement, whereas the culture in countries like China, Colombia, and Portugal encourages behaviors that promote cooperation and group interests over self-interests. On the basis of these cultural differences, it seems logical to expect that people from the former set of countries would consider citizenship behavior relatively unimportant compared with people from the latter set of countries. In reality, however, the findings from one recent study comparing Canadian and Chinese managers found that this cultural stereotype was simply not true. Managers in both countries not only took citizenship behavior into account when evaluating overall job performance, but the weight they gave to citizenship behavior in their overall evaluation of employees was the same. One explanation for this result is that the realities of running effective business organizations in a global economy have a significantly stronger impact on managerial practices than do cultural norms. It is important to note that the results of this study do not mean that we can ignore culture when trying to understand employee job performance. In fact, there are reasons to believe that cultural differences are important to consider when designing and implementing systems to manage employee performance.

FIGURE 2-3 Types of Counterproductive Behaviors

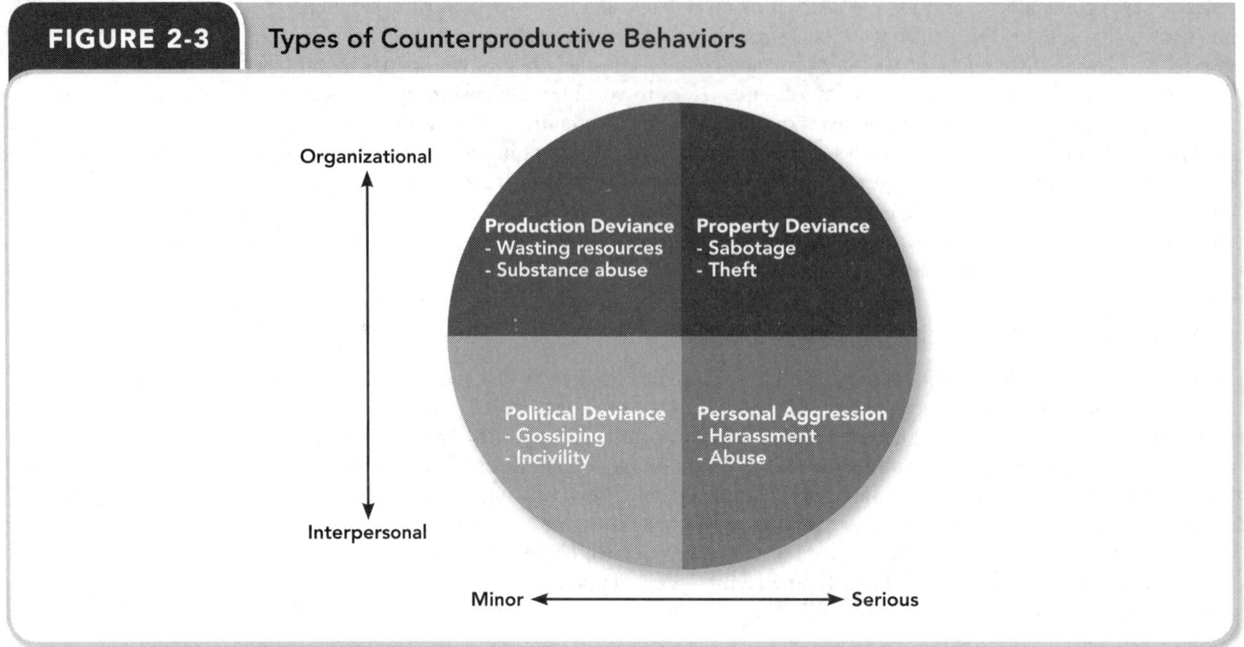

Source: Adapted from S.L. Robinson and R.J. Bennett, "A Typology of Deviant Workplace Behaviors: A Multidimensional Scaling Study," *Academy of Management Journal* 38 (1995), pp. 555–72.

2.5
What is counterproductive behavior?

财产偏差是指危害组织财产及所有权的行为。

Property deviance refers to behaviors that harm the organization's assets and possessions. For example, **sabotage** represents the purposeful destruction of physical equipment, organizational processes, or company products. Do you know what a laser disc is? Probably not—and the reason you don't is because of sabotage. A company called DiscoVision (a subsidiary of MCA) manufactured laser discs in the late 1970s, with popular movie titles like *Smokey and the Bandit* and *Jaws* retailing for $15.95. Although this level matches the price of DVDs today, it was far less than the $50–$100 needed to buy videocassettes (which were of inferior quality) at the time. Unfortunately, laser discs had to be manufactured in "clean rooms," because specs of dust or debris could cause the image on the television to freeze, repeat, skip, or drop out. When MCA merged with IBM in 1979, the morale of the employees fell, and counterproductive behaviors began to occur. Employees sabotaged the devices that measured the cleanliness of the rooms. They also began eating in the rooms—even "popping" potato chip bags to send food particles into the air. This sabotage eventually created a 90 percent disc failure rate that completely alienated customers. As a result, despite its much lower production costs and higher-quality picture, the laser disc disappeared, and the organizations that supported the technology suffered incredible losses.

Even if you've never heard of the laser disc, you've certainly eaten in a restaurant. The cost of counterproductive behaviors in the restaurant industry is estimated to be 2–3 percent of revenues per year, but what may be more disturbing is the nature of those counterproductive behaviors. Thirty-one percent of employees who responded to a survey knowingly served improperly prepared food, 13 percent intentionally sabotaged the work of other employees, and 12 percent admitted to intentionally contaminating food they prepared or served to a customer (yuck!). At a minimum, such sabotage of the restaurant's product can lead to a bad meal and a customer's promise to never return to that establishment. Of course, such behaviors can also lead to food poisoning, health code violations, and a damaging lawsuit.

偷窃表示另一种形式的财产偏差，其成本与怠工一样昂贵。

Theft represents another form of property deviance and can be just as expensive as sabotage (if not more). Research has shown that up to three-quarters of all employees have engaged in counterproductive behaviors such as theft, and the cost of these behaviors is staggering. For example, one study estimated that 47 percent of store inventory shrinkage was due to employee theft and that this type of theft costs organizations approximately $14.6 billion per year. Maybe you've had friends who worked at a restaurant or bar and been lucky enough to get discounted (or even free) food and drinks whenever you wanted. Clearly that circumstance is productive for you, but it's quite counterproductive from the perspective of the organization.

Production deviance is also directed against the organization but focuses specifically on reducing the efficiency of work output. **Wasting resources** is the most common form of production deviance, when employees use too many materials or too much time to do too little work. Manufacturing employees who use too much wood or metal are wasting resources, as are restaurant employees who use too many ingredients when preparing the food. Workers who work too slowly or take too many breaks are also wasting resources because "time is money" (see Chapter 3 on Organizational Commitment for more discussion of such issues). **Substance abuse** represents another form of production deviance. If employees abuse drugs or alcohol while on the job or shortly before coming to work, then the efficiency of their production will be compromised because their work will be done more slowly and less accurately.

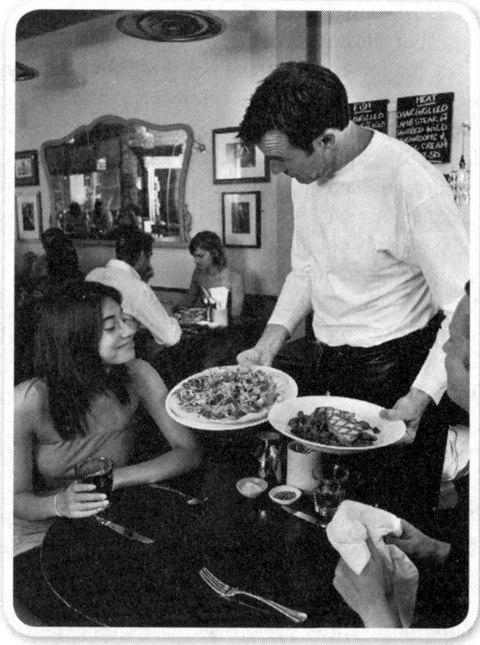

Counterproductive behavior by employees can be destructive to the organization's goals. In some settings, such as a restaurant, it can even be a problem for customers.

In contrast to property and production deviance, **political deviance** refers to behaviors that intentionally disadvantage other individuals rather than the larger organization. **Gossiping**—casual conversations about other people in which the facts are not confirmed as true—is one form of political deviance. Everyone has experienced gossip at some point in time and knows the emotions people feel when they discover that other people have been talking about them. Such behaviors undermine the morale of both friendship groups and work groups. **Incivility** represents communication that's rude, impolite, discourteous, and lacking in good manners. The erosion of manners seems like a societywide phenomenon, and the workplace is no exception. Taken one by one, these political forms of counterproductive behavior may not seem particularly serious to most organizations. However, in the aggregate, acts of political deviance can create an organizational climate characterized by distrust and unhealthy competitiveness. Beyond the productivity losses that result from a lack of cooperation among employees, organizations with this type of climate likely cannot retain good employees. Moreover, there's some evidence that gossip and incivility can "spiral"—meaning that they gradually get worse and worse until some tipping point, after which more serious forms of interpersonal actions can occur.

Those more serious interpersonal actions may involve **personal aggression**, defined as hostile verbal and physical actions directed toward other employees. **Harassment** falls under this heading and occurs when employees are subjected to unwanted physical contact or verbal remarks from a colleague. **Abuse** also falls under this heading; it occurs when an employee is assaulted or endangered in such a way that physical and psychological injuries may occur. You might be surprised to know that even the most extreme forms of personal aggression are actually quite prevalent in organizations. For example, on average in the United States about one employee each week is murdered by a current or previous coworker. As another example, about 54 million Americans are bullied at work each year. Bullying involves psychological harassment and abuse directed toward an individual or group of individuals. Examples of bullying include humiliation, social isolation, and systematic maltreatment, all of which results in the target of these behaviors feeling helpless. It might surprise you to learn that the source of the bullying is often a boss. We don't believe that bosses are inherently evil, but some undoubtedly lose sight of the line between being tough and being a bully, and that what matters isn't the intent of the behavior, but rather the perception of the person to whom the behavior is targeted. Acts of personal aggression can also be quite costly to organizations. For example, Mitsubishi Motor Manufacturing of America settled a class action sexual harassment lawsuit for $34 million after women at a plant in Normal, Illinois, complained of widespread and routine groping, fondling, lewd jokes, lewd behavior, and pornographic graffiti.

Three points should be noted about counterproductive behavior. First, there's evidence that people who engage in one form of counterproductive behavior also engage in others. In other

生产偏差也是一种背离组织的行为，但特别关注于降低工作产出的效率。

资源浪费是生产偏差行为最普遍的形式，当员工使用太多的原材料或太多的时间来做很少的工作时就是资源浪费。

药物滥用是另一种形式的生产偏差。如果员工工作时或工作前不久滥用药物或饮酒过量，他们的生产率就会大打折扣，因为他们的工作做得更慢或不够准确。

政治偏差是指有意识地做出不利于其他员工的行为。

闲言碎语是一种非正式的有关他人的沟通，其中的事实没有经过确认是否属实，属于政治偏差的一种形式。

无礼表示的是一种粗鲁的、不礼貌的、失礼的及缺乏友好方式的沟通。

个人攻击定义为直接指向其他员工的、敌对的、口头及身体上的行动。

骚扰属于一种个人攻击，是指员工受到来自于同事的非意愿的身体接触或者口头议论的影响。

虐待属于一种个人攻击，是指员工受到攻击和遭受危险时身体和心理上所受到的伤害。

words, such behaviors tend to represent a pattern of behavior rather than isolated incidents. Second, like citizenship behavior, counterproductive behavior is relevant to any job. It doesn't matter what the job entails; there are going to be things to steal, resources to waste, and people to be uncivil toward. Third, it's often surprising which employees engage in counterproductive behavior. You might be tempted to guess that poor performers would be the ones who engage in high levels of counterproductive behavior, and that highly effective task performers do not engage in counterproductive behavior. In fact, however, there's only a weak negative correlation between task performance and counterproductive behavior, and if you think about it for a moment, you can probably come up with a few examples of people who are very effective in their jobs but who also engage in high levels of counterproductive behavior. Sometimes the best task performers are the ones who can best get away with counterproductive actions, because they're less likely to be suspected or blamed. Moreover, counterproductive behaviors might even be tolerated for a while where the individual is able to effectively accomplish very challenging tasks. Our **OB on Screen** feature illustrates an amusing example of this apparent contradiction in behavior.

OB ON SCREEN

DESPICABLE ME

OK, my turn.

With those words, a criminal mastermind named Gru (Steve Carell, voice) tells a carnival barker (Jack McBrayer, voice) he wants to take a shot at winning a fluffy unicorn for his daughter Agnes (Elsie Fisher, voice) in the animated movie, *Despicable Me* (Dir.: Pierre Coffin and Chris Renaud, Universal Pictures, 2010). Agnes and her two sisters, all of whom Gru adopted as part of his evil plot to steal the moon, had been playing a carnival game to win the unicorn, only to discover the game is rigged. Agnes hit a target with a ping-pong ball she fired from her gun, but it didn't knock the target over. Gru took over the situation. He paid the barker to play the game himself, and when the target appeared, he whipped out his own weapon and fired a solar flare that disintegrated the target and carnival stand. The barker, who somehow survived, handed the unicorn to Agnes who walked away happy as a clam.

The movie centers on a dichotomy in Gru's behavior. On the one hand, Gru does things that are intentionally deviant and very illegal. Obliteration of the carnival stand fits the bill here. He also steals the Eiffel Tower and Statue of Liberty (the small ones in Vegas). On the other hand, Gru does things that are remarkably positive. At the carnival, for example, the girls want to go on a roller coaster but they need to be accompanied by an adult, so Gru goes with them even though the ride is uncomfortably small and makes him sick. As another example, Gru risks his life to save the girls by balancing on a cable connecting two spaceships in flight. Although these amusing examples occur outside the work setting as most of you think of it (we hope), they nevertheless serve as a reminder that people are complex, and that it can be a mistake to assume that if someone is good (or bad) on one dimension of performance they are also good (or bad) on the other dimensions of performance. So how does the dichotomy in Gru's behavior play out in the movie? You'll have to watch to find out!

总结：成为一名“高绩效员工”意味着什么
SUMMARY: WHAT DOES IT MEAN TO BE A "GOOD PERFORMER"?

So what does it mean to be a "good performer"? As shown in Figure 2-4, being a good performer means a lot of different things. It means employees are good at the particular job tasks that fall within their job description, whether those tasks are routine or require adaptability or creativity. But it also means that employees engage in citizenship behaviors directed at both coworkers and the larger organization. And it also means that employees refrain from engaging in the counterproductive behaviors that can badly damage the climate of an organization. The

FIGURE 2-4 What Does It Mean to be a "Good Performer"?

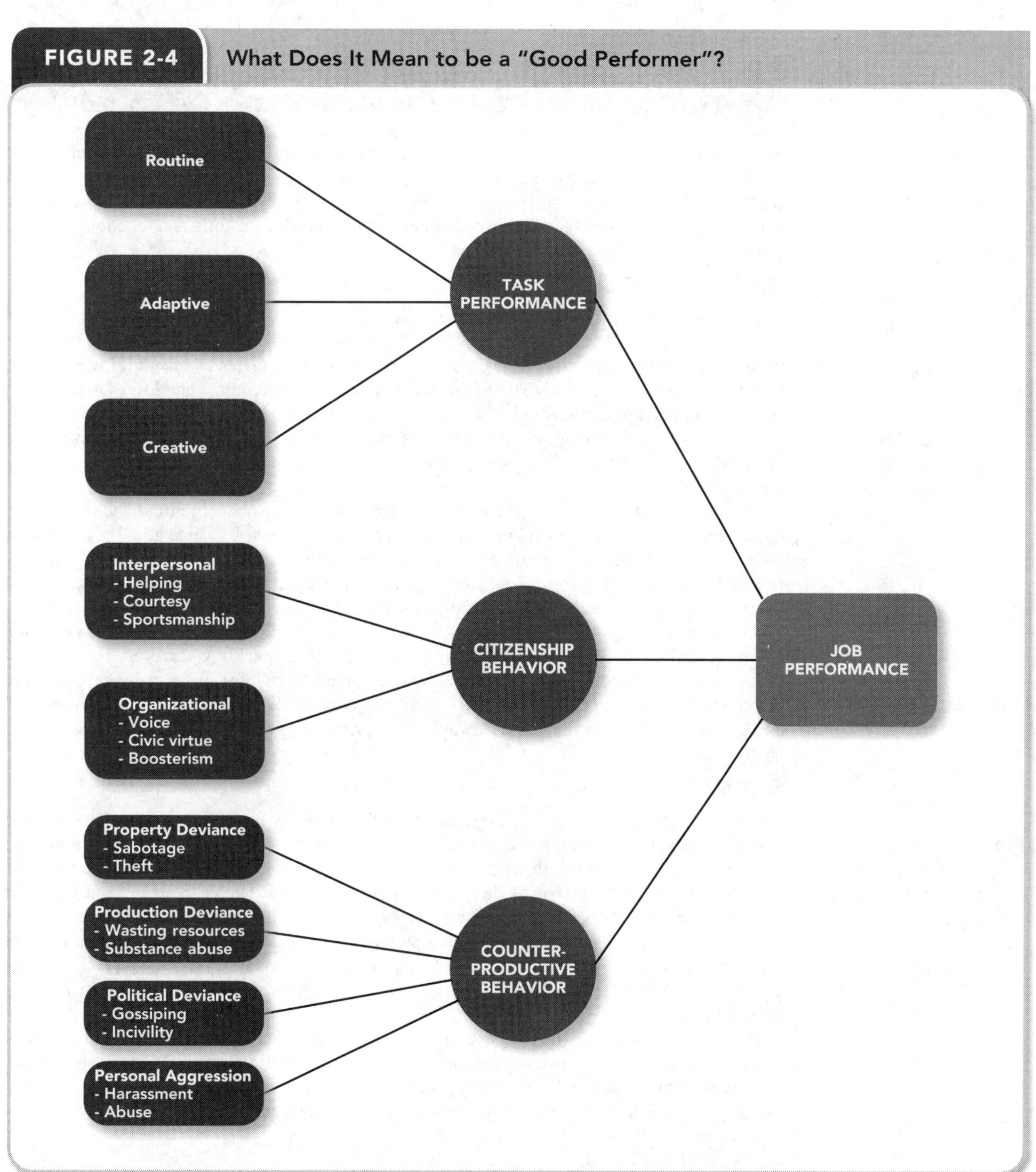

goal for any manager is therefore to have employees who fulfill all three pieces of this good performer description.

As you move forward in this book, you'll notice that almost every chapter includes a description of how that chapter's topic relates to job performance. For example, Chapter 4 on Job Satisfaction will describe how employees' feelings about their jobs affect their job performance. You'll find that some chapter topics seem more strongly correlated with task performance, whereas other topics are more strongly correlated with citizenship behavior or counterproductive behavior. Such differences will help you understand exactly how and why a given topic, be it satisfaction, stress, motivation, or something else, influences job performance. By the end of the book, you'll have developed a good sense of the most powerful drivers of job performance.

影响绩效的趋势

TRENDS AFFECTING PERFORMANCE

Now that we've described exactly what job performance is, it's time to describe some of the trends that affect job performance in the contemporary workplace. Put simply, the kinds of jobs employees do are changing, as is the way workers get organized within companies. These trends put pressure on some elements of job performance while altering the form and function of others.

知识工作

KNOWLEDGE WORK

2.6

What workplace trends are affecting job performance in today's organizations?

到了20世纪90年代初，大多数新的工作要求员工去从事认知性的工作，这些工作要求员工运用一定的理论和分析的知识来完成，而这些知识是通过正规教育和持续学习来获得的。今天，来自美国劳工部的数据证实，这类工作即**知识工作**正变得比体力工作越来越普遍。

Historically speaking, research on organizational behavior has focused on the physical aspects of job performance. This focus was understandable, given that the U.S. economy was industrial in nature and the productivity of the employees who labored in plants and factories was of great concern. However, by the early 1990s, the majority of new jobs required employees to engage in cognitive work, applying theoretical and analytical knowledge acquired through formal education and continuous learning. Today, statistics from the U.S. Department of Labor confirm that this type of work, also called **knowledge work,** is becoming more prevalent than jobs involving physical activity.

In addition to being more cognitive, knowledge work tends to be more fluid and dynamic in nature. Facts, data, and information are always changing. Moreover, as time goes by, it becomes easier to access more and more of these facts and data, using Google on an iPhone for example. In addition, the tools used to do knowledge work change quickly, with software, databases, and computer systems updated more frequently than ever. As those tools become more powerful, the expectations for completing knowledge work become more ambitious. After all, shouldn't reports and presentations be more comprehensive and finished more quickly when every book used to create them is available online 24-7 rather than at some library? In fact, as many have recently noted, expectations regarding knowledge work can become overwhelming for employees, and as a consequence, new and innovative ways of performing this type of work may be necessary.

服务工作

SERVICE WORK

服务工作是指通过直接电子的、口头的或者身体互动的形式提供给顾客无形产品的工作。

One of the largest and fastest growing sectors in the economy is not in industries that produce goods but rather in industries that provide services. **Service work**, or work that provides nontangible goods to customers through direct electronic, verbal, or physical interaction, accounts for approximately 55 percent of the economic activity in the United States, and about 20 percent of the new jobs created are service jobs, trailing only professional services in terms of growth. Retail salespersons, customer service representatives, and food service workers represent the bulk of that service job growth. By comparison, maintenance, repair, construction, and production jobs are only projected to account for 4–7 percent of new jobs over the next several years.

The increase in service jobs has a number of implications for job performance. For example, the costs of bad task performance are more immediate and more obvious. When customer service representatives do their job duties poorly, the customer is right there to notice. That failure can't be hidden behind the scenes or corrected by other employees chipping in before it's too late. In addition, service work contexts place a greater premium on high levels of citizenship behavior and low levels of counterproductive behavior. If service employees refuse to help one another or maintain good sportsmanship, or if they gossip and insult one another, those negative emotions get transmitted to the customer during the service encounter. Maintaining a positive work environment therefore becomes even more vital.

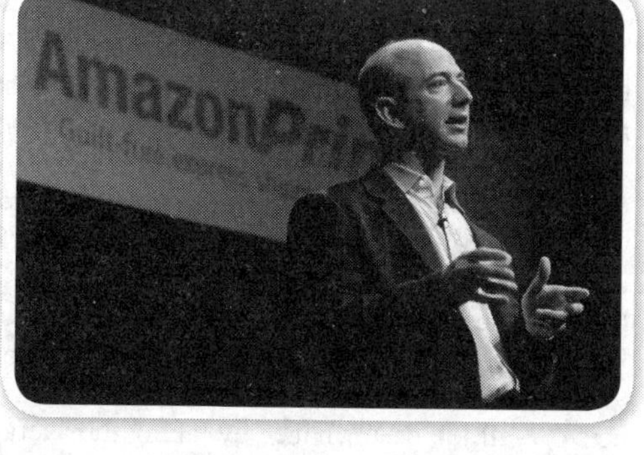

Amazon CEO Jeff Bezos stresses the importance of customer service.

In fact, some very notable organizations compete successfully by placing special emphasis on the performance of people who do service work. Amazon, for example, believes that the best way to ensure that customers keep using its website to purchase merchandise is to ensure customers are satisfied with their experience, especially when a transaction goes wrong, such as if merchandise arrives broken or an order doesn't ship because the product is back ordered. Amazon customer service employees receive a great deal of training so that they can provide timely and consistent responses to customers who have questions or problems. In fact, customer service is so important to Amazon that each and every employee, including CEO Jeff Bezos, spends two days a year answering customer service calls. Apparently all this training has paid off: Amazon now ranks number one in customer service quality, scoring above companies such as The Ritz-Carlton and Lexus, which are famous for providing world-class customer service.

应用：绩效管理

APPLICATION: PERFORMANCE MANAGEMENT

2.7

How can organizations use job performance information to manage employee performance?

Now that we've described what job performance is, along with some of the workplace trends that affect it, it's time to discuss how organizations use job performance information. As you saw in the Frito-Lay example, good companies understand the linkage between employee performance and organizational performance and, accordingly, they invest resources collecting information about employee performance so that it can be managed in a way that helps the organization achieve its mission. In this section, we describe general ways in which job performance information is used to manage employee performance. We spotlight four of the most representative practices: management by objectives, behaviorally anchored rating scales, 360-degree feedback, and forced ranking. We'll also discuss how social networking software is being used for performance management purposes in organizations.

目标管理

MANAGEMENT BY OBJECTIVES

Management by objectives (MBO) is a management philosophy that bases an employee's evaluations on whether the employee achieves specific performance goals. How does MBO work? Typically, an employee meets with his or her manager to develop a set of mutually agreed-upon objectives that are measurable and specific (see Chapter 6 on Motivation for more discussion of such issues). In addition, the employee and the manager agree on the time period for achieving those objectives and the methods used to do so. An example of a performance objective for a line manager in a factory might be something like, "Reducing production waste by 35 percent within three months by developing and implementing new production procedures." Employee performance then can be gauged by referring to the degree to which the employee achieves results that are consistent with the objectives. If the line manager cuts production waste by 37 percent within three months, the manager's performance would be deemed effective, whereas if the manager only cuts production waste by 2 percent, his or her performance would be deemed ineffective. MBO is best suited for managing the performance of employees who work in contexts in which objective measures of performance can be quantified.

目标管理是一种基于员工是否能够取得特定绩效目标评价的管理哲学。

行为锚评定量表
BEHAVIORALLY ANCHORED RATING SCALES

行为锚评定量表通过直接评价工作绩效行为来测量绩效。

You might have noticed that MBO emphasizes the results of job performance as much as it does the performance behaviors themselves. In contrast, **behaviorally anchored rating scales** (BARS) measure performance by directly assessing job performance behaviors. The BARS approach uses "critical incidents"—short descriptions of effective and ineffective behaviors—to create a measure that can be used to evaluate employee performance. As an example of a BARS approach, consider the measure of task performance shown in Table 2-2, which focuses on the "planning, organizing, and scheduling" dimension of task performance for a manager. The rater reads the behaviors on the far left column of the measure and matches actual observations of the behavior of the manager being rated to the corresponding level on the measure by placing a check in the blank.

Typically, supervisors rate several performance dimensions using BARS and score an employee's overall job performance by taking the average value across all the dimensions. Because the critical incidents convey the precise kinds of behaviors that are effective and ineffective, feedback from BARS can help an employee develop and improve over time. That is, employees can develop an appreciation of the types of behaviors that would make them effective. Such information provides a nice complement to MBO, which is less capable of providing specific feedback about why an objective might have been missed.

360 度反馈
360-DEGREE FEEDBACK

360 度反馈不仅需要从主管那里收集绩效信息，还要从其他任何人那里收集与员工绩效行为有关的第一手材料。

The **360-degree feedback** approach involves collecting performance information not just from the supervisor but from anyone else who might have firsthand knowledge about the employee's performance behaviors. These other sources of performance information typically include the

TABLE 2-2 BARS Example for "Planning Organizing, and Scheduling"

RATING	RATING	BEHAVIORAL ANCHORS
[7]	Excellent	• Develops a comprehensive project plan, documents it well, obtains required approval, and distributes the plan to all concerned.
[6]	Very Good	• Plans, communicates, and observes milestones; states week by week where the project stands relative to plans. Maintains up-to-date charts of project accomplishment and backlogs and uses these to optimize any schedule modifications required. • Experiences occasional minor operational problems but communicates effectively.
[5]	Good	• Lays out all the parts of a job and schedules each part to beat schedule; will allow for slack. • Satisfies customer's time constraints; time and cost overruns occur infrequently.
[4]	Average	• Makes a list of due dates and revises them as the project progresses, usually adding unforeseen events; investigates frequent customer complaints. • May have a sound plan but does not keep track of milestones; does not report slippages in schedule or other problems as they occur.
[3]	Below Average	• Plans are poorly defined; unrealistic time schedules are common. • Cannot plan more than a day or two ahead; has no concept of a realistic project due date.
[2]	Very Poor	• Has no plan or schedule of work segments to be performed. • Does little or no planning for project assignments.
[1]	Unacceptable	• Seldom, if ever, completes project because of lack of planning and does not seem to care. • Fails consistently due to lack of planning and does not inquire about how to improve.

Source: D.G. Shaw, C.E. Schneier, and R.W. Beatty, "Managing Performance with a Behaviorally Based Appraisal System," in *Applying Psychology in Business: The Handbook for Managers and Human Resource Professionals,* eds. J.W. Jones, B.D. Steffy, and D.W. Bray (Lexington, MA: Lexington Books, 2001), pp. 314–25. Reprinted with permission of Lexington Books.

employee's subordinates, peers, and customers. With the exception of the supervisor's ratings, the ratings are combined so that the raters can remain anonymous to the employee. Most 360-degree feedback systems also ask the employee to provide ratings of his or her own performance. The hope is that this 360-degree perspective will provide a more balanced and comprehensive examination of performance. By explicitly comparing self-provided ratings with the ratings obtained from others, employees can develop a better sense of how their performance may be deficient in the eyes of others and exactly where they need to focus their energies to improve.

Although the information from a 360-degree feedback system can be used to evaluate employees for administrative purposes such as raises or promotions, there are problems with that sort of application. First, because ratings vary across sources, there is the question of which source is most "correct." Even if multiple sources are taken into account in generating an overall performance score, it's often unclear how the information from the various sources should be weighted. Second, raters may give biased evaluations if they believe that the information will be used for compensation, as opposed to just skill development. Peers in particular may be unwilling to provide negative information if they believe it will harm the person being rated. As a result, 360-degree feedback is best suited to improving or developing employee talent, especially if the feedback is accompanied by coaching about how to improve the areas identified as points of concern.

强迫排名
FORCED RANKING

One of the most notable strategies that Jack Welch, *Fortune*'s Manager of the 20th Century, used to build a great workforce at General Electric involved evaluations that make clear distinctions among employees in terms of their job performance. Although Welch considered several systems that could differentiate employees, the most effective relied on the "vitality curve," depicted in Figure 2-5, which forces managers to rank all of their people into one of three categories: the top 20 percent (A players), the vital middle 70 percent (B players), or the bottom 10 percent (C players). The A players are thought to possess "the four Es of GE leadership: very high *energy* levels, the ability to *energize* others around common goals, the *edge* to make tough yes-and-no decisions, and finally the ability to consistently *execute* and deliver on their promises." The B players are developed. According to Welch, B players are the backbone of the company but lack the passion of As. The C players are those who cannot get the job done and are let go. The system was taken so seriously at GE that managers who couldn't differentiate their people tended to find themselves in the C category.

FIGURE 2-5 Jack Welch's Vitality Curve

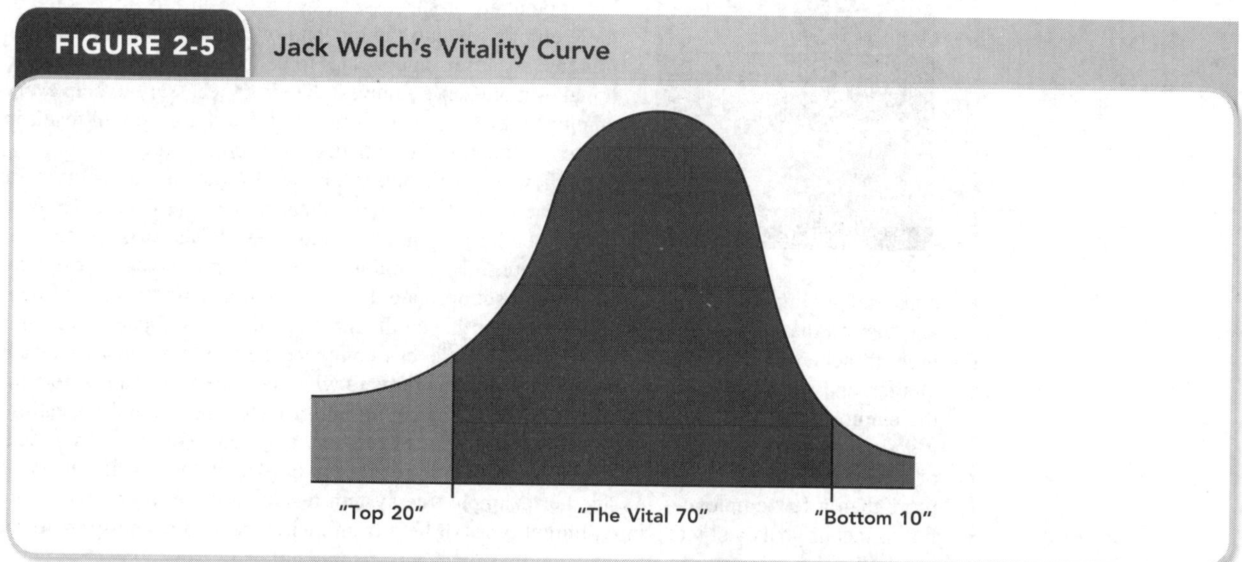

Source: From *Jack* by Jack Welch with John A. Byrne. Copyright © 2001 by the John F. Welch Jr. Foundation. By permission of Grand Central Publishing.

今天，财富 500 强公司中大约有 20% 使用韦尔奇的**强迫排名**系统的某种变式，即人们所熟知的“排名与解雇”或“死亡曲线”。

Today, approximately 20 percent of *Fortune* 500 companies use some variant of Welch's **forced ranking** system, which is popularly known as "rank and yank" or the "dead man's curve." However, there are some important controversies to consider. For example, some believe the system is inherently unfair because it forces managers to give bad evaluations to employees who may be good performers, just to reach a preestablished percentage. As another example, employees may become hypercompetitive with one another to avoid finding themselves in a lower category. This type of competitiveness is the opposite of what may be needed in today's team-based organizations. In fact, our **OB at the Bookstore** feature showcases an approach to performance management that represents somewhat of a backlash to the forced ranking approach.

社会网络系统
SOCIAL NETWORKING SYSTEMS

Most of you reading this book are familiar with social networking services such as Facebook and Twitter. Well, this technology has recently been applied in organizational contexts for the purposes of developing and evaluating employee job performance. As an example, Accenture

OB AT THE BOOKSTORE

HELPING PEOPLE WIN AT WORK
by Ken Blanchard and Garry Ridge (Upper Saddle River, New Jersey: Polvera Publishing and Garry Ridge Publishing as FT Press, 2009).

Don't mark my paper, help me get an A.

With those words, Blanchard and Ridge describe the philosophy used to review the job performance of employees at WD-40, a global consumer products company headquartered in San Diego. The authors claim that this philosophy, which was instituted by Ridge when he took over as CEO of the company in 1997, is responsible for the company's remarkable performance over the last decade. So what exactly does this philosophy involve? The authors begin by noting their approach stands in sharp contrast to forced ranking systems. They argue that companies invest a great deal in hiring employees with a proven track record of success or with high potential for success, and so it's absurd to force some of these employees into the low end of the performance distribution just because someone has to be there. Rather, they believe it makes more sense to invest the effort necessary to help every employee reach their potential, and that doing so will result in a more productive and satisfied workforce.

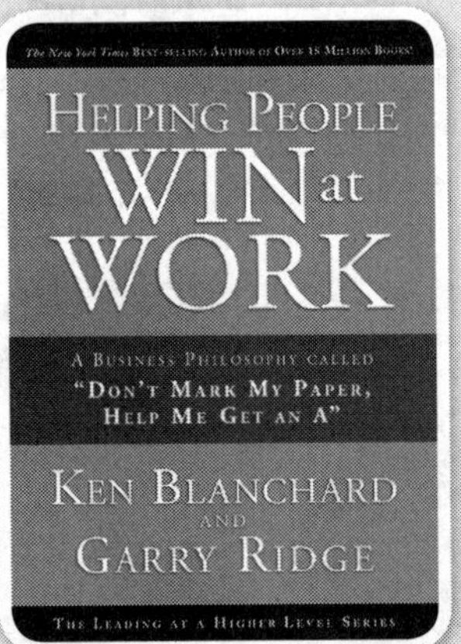

So how does this philosophy work? The starting point is for managers to work with subordinates to ensure they understand their essential job functions and to establish goals for each of the functions. These mutually agreed upon goals, in essence, constitute a "final exam." The manager and subordinate then meet and discuss the type of help and support the subordinate needs, and together they craft a plan that the subordinate will implement to achieve an "A" on this final exam. Employees complete their own report cards each quarter, and when goals haven't been met, the focus turns to what the supervisor can do to help the employee succeed. Although this system of managing performance may sound appealing, it's worthwhile to consider potential downsides. For example, the system requires a great deal of time and effort from supervisors, and so it may place a heavy burden on those who supervise more than a few employees. As another example, the system results in employees having different sets of goals and receiving different types of help from their supervisors, and so there's a possibility that some employees may feel they have been treated unfairly.

uses a Facebook-styled program called "Performance Multiplier," which requires that employees post and update weekly and quarterly goals. Managers then monitor the information and provide feedback. As another example, a Toronto–based software company called Rypple uses a Twitter-like program to enable employees to post questions about their own performance so that other employees can give them anonymous feedback. Although the effectiveness of social networking applications for performance evaluation and employee development purposes has not been studied scientifically, there are some advantages that make us believe that they will grow in popularity. For example, these types of systems provide performance information that is much more timely, relative to traditional practices that measure performance quarterly or even yearly. Although it might be unpleasant to learn from your peers that a presentation you gave was boring, it's much better than giving 50 boring presentations over the course of the year and then getting the news from your boss.

chapter 3

Organizational Commitment

组织承诺

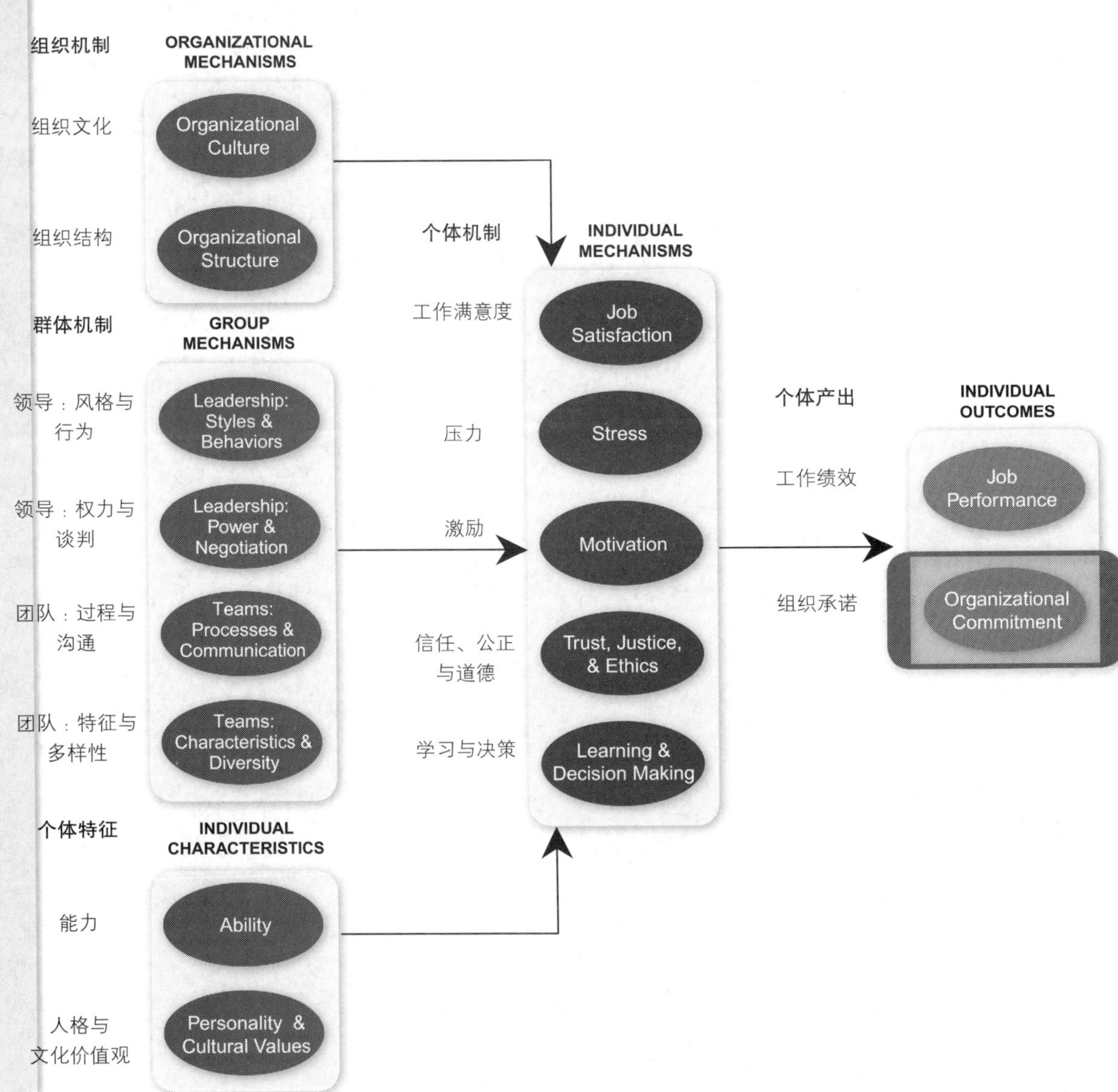

LEARNING GOALS

After reading this chapter, you should be able to answer the following questions:

3.1 What is organizational commitment? What is withdrawal behavior? How are the two connected?

3.2 What are the three types of organizational commitment, and how do they differ?

3.3 What are the four primary responses to negative events at work?

3.4 What are some examples of psychological withdrawal? Of physical withdrawal? How do the different forms of withdrawal relate to each other?

3.5 What workplace trends are affecting organizational commitment in today's organizations?

3.6 How can organizations foster a sense of commitment among employees?

NASA

Travis Thompson has an interesting job. A 31-year veteran of the Kennedy Space Center and a member of the orbiter closeout crew, Thompson is the last person astronauts see before riding a space shuttle to the heavens. "What I do," Thompson says with pride, "is put astronauts in spaceships and close the hatch." He tells each of them, "You come back and see me now." With the end of the Space Shuttle program, however, Thompson has no more hatches to close. After 30 years of shuttle flights, including building and maintaining the International Space Station, and launching the Hubble telescope, the program was terminated due to budget cuts, continuing concerns about safety, and a sense that NASA (the National Aeronautics and Space Administration) needs a new mission and direction.

The end of the shuttle program affects all 15,000 employees at the Kennedy Space Center, including 2,100 direct NASA employees and contractors with the United Space Alliance—jointly owned by Boeing and Lockheed Martin—for whom Thompson works. Although the direct NASA employees will not lose their jobs, around 8,000 employees will eventually be targeted for layoffs. Employees who remain face what one agency manager describes as "a period of sustained ambiguity." A program to go to Mars reached the initial planning stages before being shelved due to its half a trillion dollar price tag. Legislation was recently passed that would call for an asteroid landing by 2025, but government funding may prove inadequate. In the near term, any American who wants to go to space will need to hitch a ride on a Russian Soyuz capsule or a privately built spacecraft.

Imagine being an engineer, scientist, mechanic, or staff person whose days were tied to launch schedules for your entire career. Even if your own job was safe from the layoffs, would you remain committed when manned space flight was not the end result of your work? Historically, NASA has had one of the lowest attrition rates in the government, with only a quarter of eligible employees choosing to take retirement in any given year. Now observers fear that many of the most skilled employees at NASA won't wait around to learn what that next big direction is, depriving the agency of critical expertise. Not only do they fear the unknown, in terms of what their work will be, they also worry about losing valued members of their work team. For its part, NASA management is doing all that it can to ease the pain of the transition, including offering skills and resiliency-based training, résumé workshops, grief counseling, and morale events designed to highlight what the shuttle program has meant. Still, the president of a local employment agency describes the transition in stark terms: "It's gut-wrenching."

组织承诺

ORGANIZATIONAL COMMITMENT

Organizational commitment sits side by side with job performance in our integrative model of organizational behavior, reflecting one of the starting points for our journey through the concepts covered in this course. Why begin with a discussion of organizational commitment? Because as illustrated in the NASA example, it's not enough to have talented employees who perform their jobs well. You also need to be able to hang on to those employees for long periods of time so that the organization can benefit from their efforts. Put yourself in the shoes of a business owner. Let's say you spent a great deal of time recruiting a graduate from the local university, selling her on your business, and making sure that she was as qualified as you initially believed her to be. Now assume that, once hired, you took a personal interest in that employee, showing her the ropes and acting as mentor and instructor. Then, just as the company was set to improve as a result of that employee's presence, she leaves to go to work for a competitor. As an employer, can you think of many things more depressing than that scenario?

Unfortunately, that scenario is not far-fetched. The U.S. Bureau of Labor Statistics estimates that the average American will have 10.8 jobs between the ages of 18 and 42. That projection is based in part on an overall turnover (or "attrition") rate of around 16 percent across all industries. It is true that the economic downturn has reduced voluntary turnover, with just over 1 percent of employees deciding to quit their jobs at the peak of the recession. Still, one study suggested that 60 percent of employees plan to quit their jobs once the economy improves, with many already networking and circulating their résumé. Those projections should be scary to any employer because turnover can be quite expensive. Estimates suggest that turnover costs between 90 percent and 200 percent of an employee's annual salary. Why so expensive? Those estimates include various costs, including the administrative costs involved in the separation, recruitment expenses, screening costs, and training and orientation expenses for the new hire. They also include "hidden costs" due to decreased morale, lost organizational knowledge, and lost productivity.

组织承诺是指组织中的员工希望保留其组织成员身份的一种愿望。

Organizational commitment is defined as the desire on the part of an employee to remain a member of the organization. Organizational commitment influences whether an employee stays a member of the organization (is retained) or leaves to pursue another job (turns over). Our attention in this chapter is focused primarily on reducing voluntary turnover by keeping the employees that the organization wants to keep, though we will touch on involuntary turnover in a discussion of layoffs and downsizing. Employees who are not committed to their organizations engage in **withdrawal behavior**, defined as a set of actions that employees perform to avoid the work situation—behaviors that may eventually culminate in quitting the organization. The relationship between commitment and withdrawal is illustrated in Figure 3-1. Some employees may exhibit much more commitment than withdrawal, finding themselves on the green end of the continuum. Other employees exhibit much more withdrawal than commitment, finding themselves on the red end of the continuum. The sections that follow review both commitment and withdrawal in more detail.

3.1

What is organizational commitment? What is withdrawal behavior? How are the two connected?

退缩行为是指员工为了逃避工作情境而采取的一些行为，这些行为将最终使员工离开组织。

成为一名“承诺型”员工意味着什么

WHAT DOES IT MEAN TO BE "COMMITTED"?

One key to understanding organizational commitment is to understand where it comes from. In other words, what creates a desire to remain a member of an organization? To explore this question, consider the following scenario: You've been working full-time for your employer for around five years. The company gave you your start in the business, and you've enjoyed your time there. Your salary is competitive enough that you were able to purchase a home in a good school system, which is important because you have one young child and another on the way. Now assume that a competing firm contacted you while you were attending a conference and offered you a similar position in its company. What kinds of things might you think about? If you created a list to organize your thoughts, what might that list look like?

承诺的类型

TYPES OF COMMITMENT

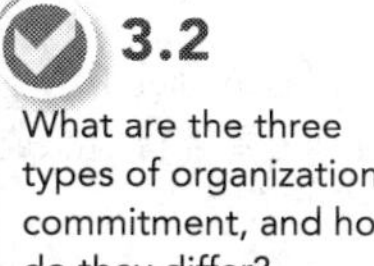

3.2

What are the three types of organizational commitment, and how do they differ?

One potential list is shown in Table 3-1. The left-hand column reflects some emotional reasons for staying with the current organization, including feelings about friendships, the atmosphere or culture of the company, and a sense of enjoyment when completing job duties. These sorts of

FIGURE 3-1 Organizational Commitment and Employee Withdrawal

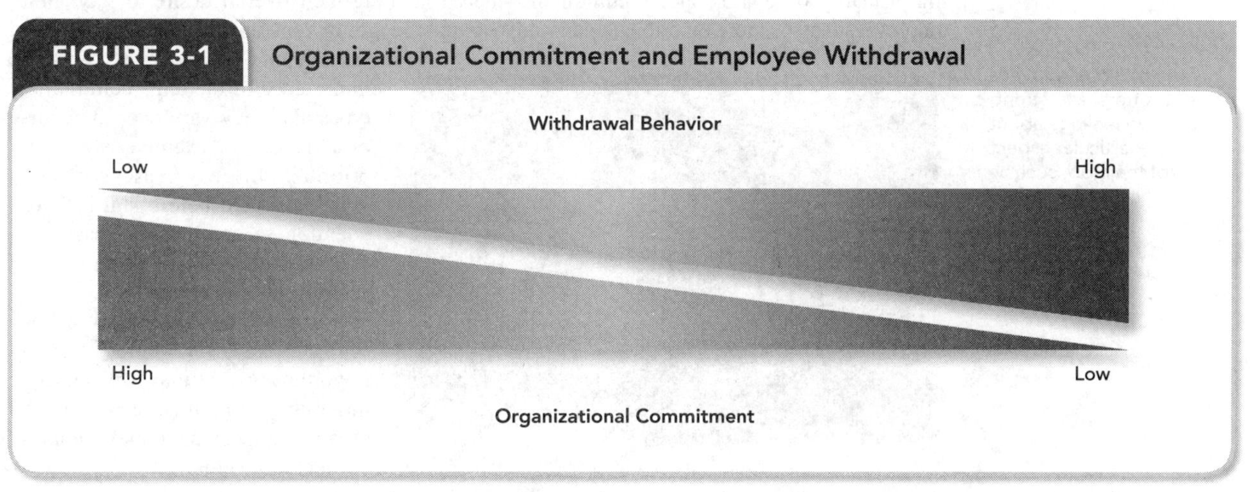

TABLE 3-1 The Three Types of Organizational Commitment

What Makes Someone Stay with their Current Organization?		
AFFECTIVE COMMITMENT (EMOTION-BASED)	**CONTINUANCE COMMITMENT (COST-BASED)**	**NORMATIVE COMMITMENT (OBLIGATION-BASED)**
Some of my best friends work in my office . . . I'd miss them if I left.	I'm due for a promotion soon . . . will I advance as quickly at the new company?	My boss has invested so much time in me, mentoring me, training me, showing me the ropes.
I really like the atmosphere at my current job . . . it's fun and relaxed.	My salary and benefits get us a nice house in our town . . . the cost of living is higher in this new area.	My organization gave me my start . . . they hired me when others thought I wasn't qualified.
My current job duties are very rewarding . . . I enjoy coming to work each morning.	The school system is good here, my spouse has a good job . . . we've really put down roots where we are.	My employer has helped me out of a jam on a number of occasions . . . how could I leave now?
Staying because you ***want*** to.	Staying because you ***need*** to.	Staying because you ***ought*** to.

情感承诺定义为员工与组织间由于情感联系而想要维持组织成员身份的愿望。

持续承诺定义为由于意识到离开组织产生的成本而想要维持组织成员身份的愿望。

规范承诺定义为员工出于义务感而想要维持组织成员身份的愿望。

emotional reasons create **affective commitment**, defined as a desire to remain a member of an organization due to an emotional attachment to, and involvement with, that organization. Put simply, you stay because you *want* to. The middle column reflects some cost-based reasons for staying, including issues of salary, benefits, and promotions, as well as concerns about uprooting a family. These sorts of reasons create **continuance commitment**, defined as a desire to remain a member of an organization because of an awareness of the costs associated with leaving it. In other words, you stay because you *need* to. The right-hand column reflects some obligation-based reasons for staying with the current organization, including a sense that a debt is owed to a boss, a colleague, or the larger company. These sorts of reasons create **normative commitment**, defined as a desire to remain a member of an organization due to a feeling of obligation. In this case, you stay because you *ought* to.

As shown in Figure 3-2, the three types of organizational commitment combine to create an overall sense of psychological attachment to the company. Of course, different people may weigh the three types differently. Some employees may be very rational and cautious by nature, focusing primarily on continuance commitment when evaluating their overall desire to stay. Other employees may be more emotional and intuitive by nature, going more on "feel" than a calculated assessment of costs and benefits. The importance of the three commitment types also may vary over the course of a career. For example, you might prioritize affective reasons early in your work life before shifting your attention to continuance reasons as you start a family or become more established in a community. Regardless of how the three types are prioritized, however, they offer an important insight into *why* someone might be committed and what an organization can do to make employees feel more committed.

Committed employees often have strong positive feelings about one particular aspect of their job, such as their colleagues, their manager, or the particular work they do.

FIGURE 3-2 Drivers of Overall Organizational Commitment

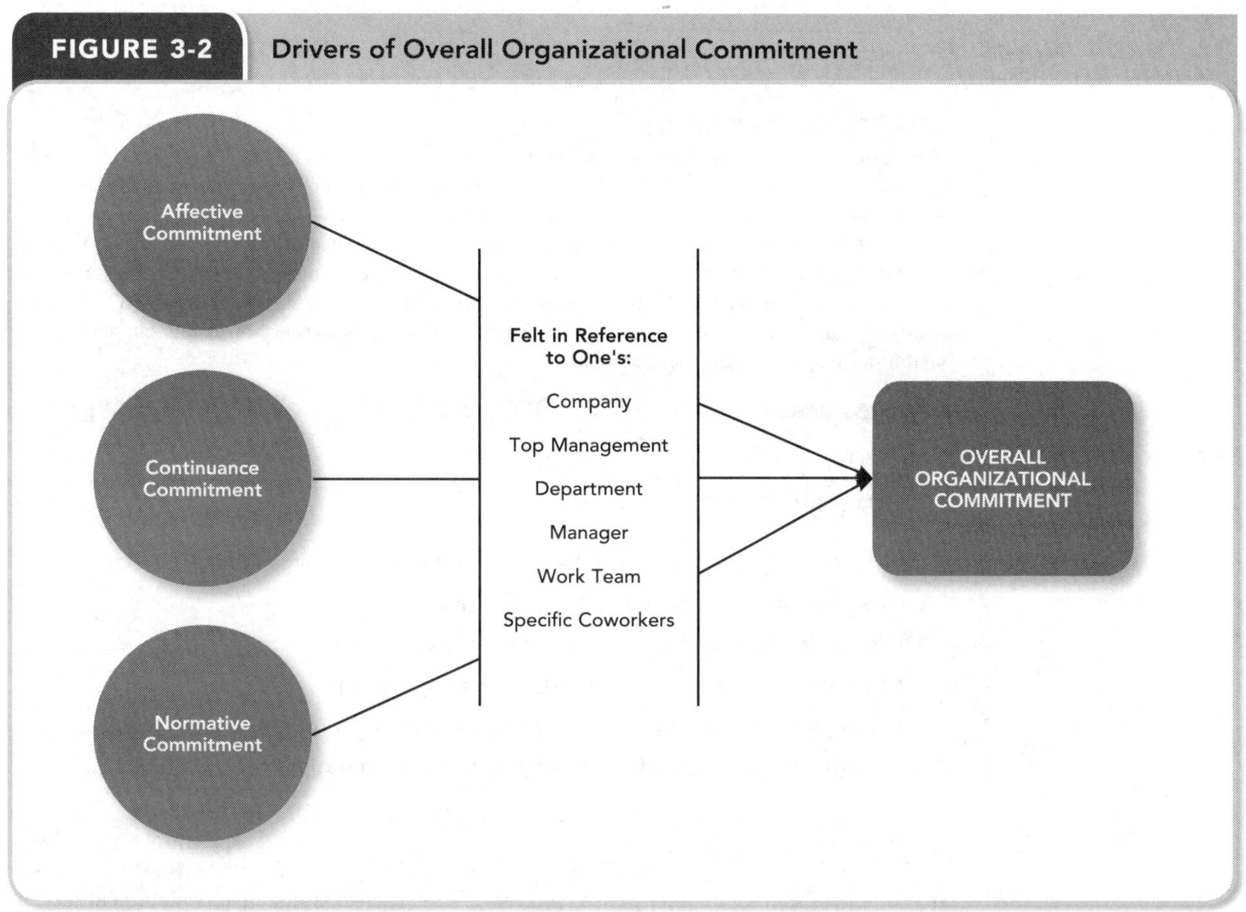

Figure 3-2 also shows that organizational commitment depends on more than just "the organization." That is, people aren't always committed to companies; they're also committed to the top management that leads the firm at a given time, the department in which they work, the manager who directly supervises them, or the specific team or coworkers with whom they work most closely. We use the term **focus of commitment** to refer to the various people, places, and things that can inspire a desire to remain a member of an organization. For example, you might choose to stay with your current employer because you're emotionally attached to your work team, worry about the costs associated with losing your company's salary and benefits package, and feel a sense of obligation to your current manager. If so, your desire to remain cuts across multiple types of commitment (affective, continuance, and normative) and multiple foci (or focuses) of commitment (work team, company, manager). Now that you're familiar with the drivers of commitment in a general sense, let's go into more depth about each type.

承诺焦点是指不同的人们、地点及事件都有激发员工维持组织成员身份的愿望。

AFFECTIVE COMMITMENT. One way to understand the differences among the three types of commitment is to ask yourself what you would feel if you left the organization. Consider the reasons listed in the left-hand column of Table 3-1. What would you feel if, even after taking all those reasons into account, you decided to leave your organization to join another one? Answer: You'd feel a sense of *sadness*. Employees who feel a sense of affective commitment identify with the organization, accept that organization's goals and values, and are more willing to exert extra effort on behalf of the organization. By identifying with the organization, they come to view organizational membership as important to their sense of self. Is affective commitment something that you feel for your current employer or have felt for a past employer? Check the **OB Assessments** feature to find out.

OB ASSESSMENTS

AFFECTIVE COMMITMENT

How emotionally attached are you to your employer? This assessment is designed to measure affective commitment—the feeling that you *want* to stay with your current organization. Think about your current job or the last job that you held (even if it was a part-time or summer job). Answer each question using the response scale provided. Then subtract your answers to the boldfaced questions from 6, with the difference being your new answers for those questions. For example, if your original answer for Question 3 was "4," your new answer is "2" (6 – 4). Then sum your answers for the six questions. (For more assessments relevant to this chapter, please visit http://connect.mcgraw-hill.com.)

1 STRONGLY DISAGREE	2 DISAGREE	3 NEUTRAL	4 AGREE	5 STRONGLY AGREE

1. I would be very happy to spend the rest of my career in this organization. ______
2. I really feel as if this organization's problems are my own. ______
3. **I do not feel like "part of the family" at my organization.** ______
4. **I do not feel "emotionally attached" to this organization.** ______
5. This organization has a great deal of personal meaning for me. ______
6. **I do not feel a strong sense of belonging to my organization.** ______

SCORING AND INTERPRETATION

If your scores sum up to 20 or above, you feel a strong sense of affective commitment to your current or past employer, which means that you feel an emotional attachment to the company, or the people within it, making it less likely that you would leave voluntarily. If your scores sum up to less than 20, you have a weaker sense of affective commitment to your current or past employer. This result is especially likely if you responded to the questions in reference to a part-time or summer job, as there might not have been enough time to develop an emotional bond.

Source: From J.P. Meyer and N.J. Allen, 1997, *Commitment in the Workplace: Theory, Research, and Application.* Reproduced with permission of Sage Publications, Inc. via Copyright Clearance Center.

It's safe to say that if managers could choose which type of commitment they'd like to instill in their employees, they'd choose affective commitment. Moreover, when a manager looks at an employee and says "She's committed" or "He's loyal," that manager usually is referring to a behavioral expression of affective commitment. For example, employees who are affectively committed to their employer tend to engage in more interpersonal and organizational citizenship behaviors, such as helping, sportsmanship, and boosterism. One meta-analysis of 22 studies with more than 6,000 participants revealed a moderately strong correlation between affective commitment and citizenship behavior. (Recall that a meta-analysis averages together results from multiple studies investigating the same relationship.) Such results suggest that emotionally committed employees express that commitment by "going the extra mile" whenever they can.

Because affective commitment reflects an emotional bond to the organization, it's only natural that the emotional bonds among coworkers influence it. We can therefore gain a better understanding of affective commitment if we take a closer look at the bonds that tie employees together. Assume you were given a sheet with the names of all the employees in your department

FIGURE 3-3 A Social Network Diagram

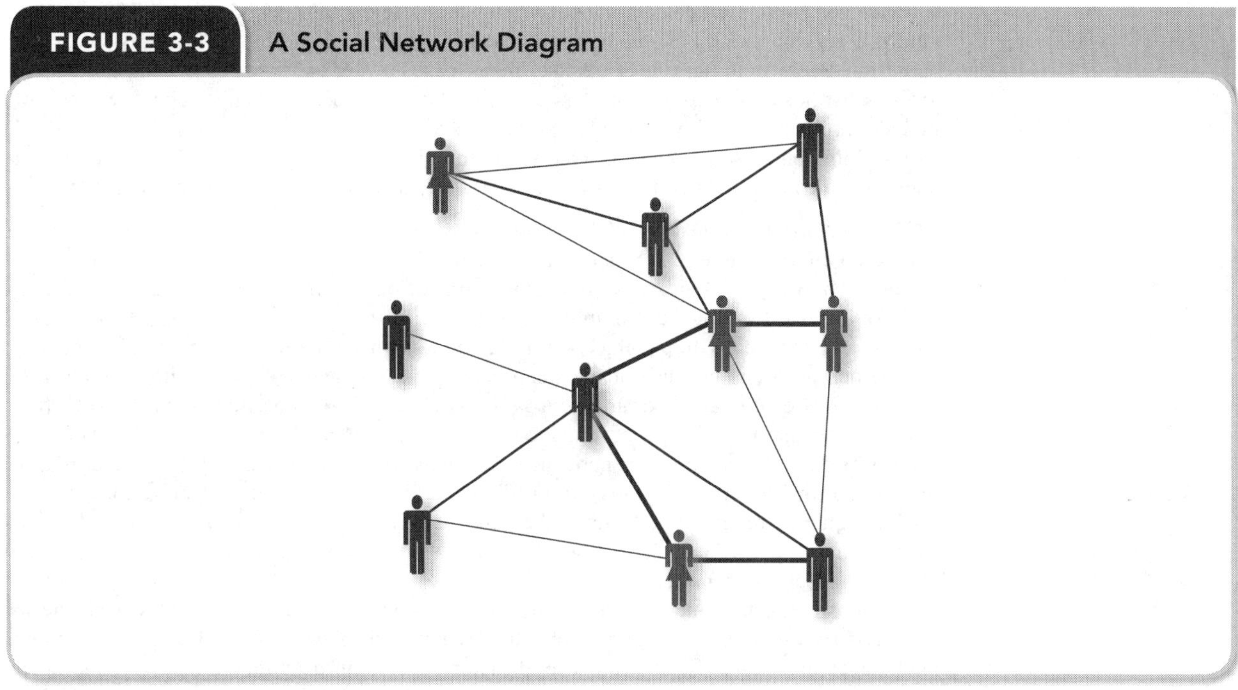

or members of your class. Then assume you were asked to rate the frequency with which you communicated with each of those people, as well as the emotional depth of those communications. Those ratings could be used to create a "social network" diagram that summarizes the bonds among employees. Figure 3-3 provides a sample of such a diagram. The lines connecting the 10 members of the work unit represent the communication bonds that tie each of them together, with thicker lines representing more frequent communication with more emotional depth. The diagram illustrates that some employees are "nodes," with several direct connections to other employees, whereas others remain at the fringe of the network.

The **erosion model** suggests that employees with fewer bonds will be most likely to quit the organization. If you look at Figure 3-3, who's most at risk for turning over? That's right—the employee who only has one bond with someone else (and a relatively weak bond at that). From an affective commitment perspective, that employee is likely to feel less emotional attachment to work colleagues, which makes it easier to decide to leave the organization. Social network diagrams can also help us understand another explanation for turnover. The **social influence model** suggests that employees who have direct linkages with "leavers" will themselves become more likely to leave. In this way, reductions in affective commitment become contagious, spreading like a disease across the work unit. Think about the damage that would be caused if the central figure in the network (the one who has linkages to five other people) became unhappy with the organization.

腐蚀模型认为与他人有较少联系的雇员更有可能辞职。

社会影响模型表明，与"离职者"有直接联系的员工更有可能选择离职。

More and more companies are beginning to understand the value in helping employees connect. SAS, the Cary, North Carolina–based

SAS, the Cary, North Carolina–based software company, offers a number of recreational perks to help employees stay connected to one another.

software company, provides a number of perks that bring employees together. Those include a billiard hall; intramural tennis, baseball, and volleyball; pool and fitness facilities; and even a hair salon. Sabre Holdings, the Southlake, Texas–based owner of Travelocity, created an internal social network system called Sabre Town. More company-focused than Facebook, Sabre Town includes profiles of employee skills, experience, and customer contacts, along with groups built around common personal interests. One such group is Mom2Mom, which allows employees to connect and converse about day care centers, pediatricians, and work-family balance issues.

CONTINUANCE COMMITMENT. Now consider the reasons for staying listed in the middle column of Table 3-1. What would you feel if, even after taking all those reasons into account, you decided to leave your organization to join another one? Answer: You'd feel a sense of *anxiety.* Continuance commitment exists when there's a profit associated with staying and a cost associated with leaving, with high continuance commitment making it difficult to change organizations because of the steep penalties associated with the switch. One factor that increases continuance commitment is the total amount of investment (in terms of time, effort, energy, etc.) employees have made in mastering their work roles or fulfilling their organizational duties. Picture a scenario in which you've worked extremely hard for a number of years to finally master the "ins and outs" of working at a particular organization, and now you're beginning to enjoy the fruits of that labor in terms of financial rewards and better work assignments. That effort might be wasted if you moved to another organization (and had to start over on the learning curve).

Another factor that increases continuance commitment is a lack of employment alternatives. If an employee has nowhere else to go, the need to stay will be higher. Employment alternatives themselves depend on several factors, including economic conditions, the unemployment rate, and the marketability of a person's skills and abilities. Of course, no one likes to feel "stuck" in a situation, so it may not be surprising that the behavioral benefits associated with affective commitment don't really occur with continuance commitment. There's no statistical relationship between continuance commitment and citizenship behavior, for example, or any other aspects of job performance. Continuance commitment therefore tends to create more of a passive form of loyalty.

It's important to note that some of the reasons in the middle column of Table 3-1 center on personal or family issues. Continuance commitment focuses on personal and family issues more than the other two commitment types, because employees often need to stay for both work and nonwork reasons. One concept that demonstrates the work and nonwork forces that can bind us to our current employer is **embeddedness**, which summarizes employees' links to their organization and community, their sense of fit with their organization and community, and what they would have to sacrifice for a job change. As demonstrated in Table 3-2, embeddedness strengthens continuance commitment by providing more reasons employees need to stay in their current positions (and more sources of anxiety if they were to leave). Research suggests that embeddedness helps employees weather negative events that occur, and that it matters across cultures.

嵌入描述了个人与组织和社区的联系，他们与组织和社区的匹配感，以及变换工作后他们的损失是什么。

Think about your current situation. If you're a college student who is working part-time, you likely don't feel very embedded. Your links to your job are probably only short-term, and you may feel that the job is more routine than you'd like from a fit perspective. You probably also wouldn't feel you were sacrificing much if you left the job. From a community perspective, you may be going to school in a different city or state than where you grew up, again resulting in few links, low perceived fit, or a lack of felt sacrifice. However, if you're a full-time employee who is relatively established in your job and community, you may feel quite embedded in your current situation. See our **OB on Screen** feature for one employee's defense of low embeddedness.

Alcon Labs seems to understand the value of continuance commitment. The Fort Worth, Texas–based leader in eye care products enjoys a voluntary turnover rate of less than 2 percent. One likely reason for that low rate is the benefits package Alcon offers its employees. For example, Alcon offers a 401(k) retirement plan in which it matches 240 percent of what employees contribute, up to a total of 5 percent of total compensation. So, for example, if an employee invests $500 toward retirement in a given month, Alcon contributes $1,200. That policy more

TABLE 3-2 Embeddedness and Continuance Commitment

"Embedded" People Feel:		
FACET	FOR THE ORGANIZATION:	FOR THE COMMUNITY:
Links	• I've worked here for such a long time. • I'm serving on so many teams and committees.	• Several close friends and family live nearby. • My family's roots are in this community.
Fit	• My job utilizes my skills and talents well. • I like the authority and responsibility I have at this company.	• The weather where I live is suitable for me. • I think of the community where I live as home.
Sacrifice	• The retirement benefits provided by the organization are excellent. • I would sacrifice a lot if I left this job.	• People respect me a lot in my community. • Leaving this community would be very hard.

Source: Adapted from T.R. Mitchell, B.C. Holtom, T.W. Lee, C.J. Sablynski, and M. Erez, "Why People Stay: Using Job Embeddedness to Predict Voluntary Turnover," *Academy of Management Journal* 44 (2001), pp. 1102–21.

than doubles the most generous rates of other companies, allowing employees to build a comfortable "nest egg" for retirement more quickly. Clearly, employees would feel a bit anxious about giving up that benefit if a competitor came calling.

NORMATIVE COMMITMENT. Now consider the reasons for staying listed in the right-hand column of Table 3-1. What would you feel if, even after taking all those reasons into account, you decided to leave your organization to join another one? Answer: You'd feel a sense of *guilt*. Normative commitment exists when there is a sense that staying is the "right" or "moral" thing to do. The sense that people *should* stay with their current employers may result from personal work philosophies or more general codes of right and wrong developed over the course of their lives. They may also be dictated by early experiences within the company, if employees are socialized to believe that long-term loyalty is the norm rather than the exception.

Aside from personal work philosophies or organizational socialization, there seem to be two ways to build a sense of obligation-based commitment among employees. One way is to create a feeling that employees are in the organization's debt—that they owe something to the organization. For example, an organization may spend a great deal of money training and developing an employee. In recognition of that investment, the employee may feel obligated to "repay" the organization with several more years of loyal service. Think about how you'd feel if your employer paid your tuition, allowing you to further your education, while also providing you with training and developmental job assignments that increased your skills. Wouldn't you feel a bit guilty if you took the first job opportunity that came your way?

Another possible way to build an obligation-based sense of commitment is by becoming a particularly charitable organization. Did you ever wonder why organizations spend time and money on charitable things—for example, building playgrounds in the local community? Don't those kinds of projects take away from research and development, product improvements, or profits for shareholders? Well, charitable efforts have several potential advantages. First, they can provide good public relations for the organization, potentially generating goodwill for its products and services and helping attract new recruits. Second, they can help existing employees feel better about the organization, creating a deeper sense of normative commitment. Those benefits may be particularly relevant with younger employees. Some evidence indicates that members of Generation Y (those born between 1977 and 1994) are somewhat more charitably minded than other generations. In support of that view, a growing number of MBA graduates

OB ON SCREEN

UP IN THE AIR

How much does your life weigh?

With those words, Ryan Bingham (George Clooney) begins his speech at a Hampton Inn in Columbus. In his spare time, Bingham hones a motivational speech extolling the virtues of being unencumbered. "Imagine for a second that you're carrying a backpack," he continues. "I want you to pack it with all the stuff that you have in your life. . . .The shelves, the drawers, the knick-knacks, then you start adding the larger stuff . . . the backpack should be getting pretty heavy now . . . Now I want you to fill it with people. . . . You get them into that backpack, feel the weight of that bag. Make no mistake, your relationships are the heaviest component in your life."

Bingham's working life represents a paradox, of sorts. On the one hand, he practices what he preaches. He travels 322 days a year, spending only 43 days in a spartan studio apartment in Omaha. He has no wife, few friends, and only the shallowest relationship with his family. On the other hand, his job revolves around understanding and appreciating how embedded people feel and react. You see, Bingham works for Career Transition Corporation (CTC). When a company wants to fire someone but doesn't want to do it themselves, they hire CTC and Bingham delivers the news. It sounds like a horrible job, but Bingham believes in it, and he's good at it.

When a "transitionee" named Bob wonders what he'll tell his children, Bingham notes that Bob once minored in French culinary arts. "How much did they first pay you to give up on your dreams," Bingham asks. "And when were you gonna stop, and come back and do what makes you happy? I see guys who work at the same company their entire lives. . . . They clock in, they clock out, and they never have a moment of happiness. You have an opportunity here, Bob . . . this is a rebirth." Ironically, when videoconferencing advancements threaten the way he does his job, it's Bingham's turn to grapple with that feeling of uncertainty. So he fights to stay on the road. Why? Because, "The slower we move the faster we die. . . . Make no mistake, moving is living."

are joining socially conscious online networks, such as Netimpact.org.

Comcast recognizes the value of normative commitment. For nine years, the Philadelphia-based media company has organized Comcast Cares Day. Originally, the day consisted of 50 employees working at a local charity event. This year, 60,500 employees, their family members, and volunteers worked with local and national nonprofits on a variety of activities, from planting gardens to cleaning up riverbanks. The head of Comcast's community involvement program contends that Comcast Cares Day was not created to help attract and maintain employees. Still, she admits that it's been a positive unintended consequence, especially for younger employees.

退缩行为
WITHDRAWAL BEHAVIOR

As noted earlier, one study suggested that 60 percent of employees plan to look for another job once the economy improves. Organizational commitment is therefore a vital concern, given that organizations will need to be fully staffed when business picks back up and industries become even more competitive. Indeed, organizational commitment is at its most important when employees are at their most needed. To paraphrase the old saying, "When the going gets tough, the organization doesn't want you to get going." In tough times, organizations need their employees to demonstrate loyalty, not "get going" right out the door. Of course, it's those same tough times that put an employee's loyalty and allegiance to the test.

Consider the following scenario: You've been working at your company for three years and served on a key product development team for the past several months. Unfortunately, the team has been struggling of late. In an effort to enhance the team's performance, the organization has added a new member to the group. This member has a solid history of product development but is, by all accounts, a horrible person to work with. You can easily see the employee's talent but find yourself hating every moment spent in the employee's presence. This situation is particularly distressing because the team won't finish its work for another nine months, at the earliest. What would you do in this situation?

Research on reactions to negative work events suggests that you might respond in one of four general ways. First, you might attempt to remove yourself from the situation, either by being absent from work more frequently or by voluntarily leaving the organization. This removal is termed **exit**, defined as an active, destructive response by which an individual either ends or restricts organizational membership. Second, you might attempt to change the circumstances by meeting with the new team member to attempt to work out the situation. This action is termed **voice**, defined as an active, constructive response in which individuals attempt to improve the situation (see Chapter 2 on Job Performance for more discussion of such issues). Third, you might just "grin and bear it," maintaining your effort level despite your unhappiness. This response is termed **loyalty**, defined as a passive, constructive response that maintains public support for the situation while the individual privately hopes for improvement. Fourth, you might just go through the motions, allowing your performance to deteriorate slowly as you mentally "check out." This reaction is termed **neglect**, defined as a passive, destructive response in which interest and effort in the job declines. Sometimes neglect can be even more costly than exit because it's not as readily noticed. Employees may neglect their duties for months (or even years) before their bosses catch on to their poor behaviors.

Taken together, the exit–voice–loyalty–neglect framework captures most of the possible responses to a negative work event. Where does organizational commitment fit in? Organizational commitment should decrease the likelihood that an individual will respond to a negative work event with exit or neglect (the two destructive responses). At the same time, organizational commitment should increase the likelihood that the negative work event will prompt voice or loyalty (the two constructive responses). Consistent with that logic, research indeed suggests that organizational commitment increases the likelihood of voice and loyalty while decreasing the likelihood of exit and neglect. For an example of loyalty, voice, and exit in the late-night talk show realm, see our **OB at the Bookstore** feature.

If we consider employees' task performance levels together with their organizational commitment levels, we can gain an even clearer picture of how people might respond to negative work events. Consider Table 3-3, which depicts combinations of high and low levels of organizational commitment and task performance. **Stars** possess high commitment and high performance and are held up as role models for other employees. Stars likely respond to negative events with voice because they have the desire to improve the status quo and the credibility needed to inspire change. It's pretty easy to spot the stars in a given unit, and you can probably think about your current or past job experiences and identify the employees who would fit that description. **Citizens** possess high commitment and low task performance but perform many of the voluntary "extra-role" activities that are needed to make the organization function smoothly. Citizens are likely to respond to negative events with loyalty because they may lack the credibility needed to inspire change but do possess the desire to remain a member of the organization. You can spot citizens by looking for the people who do the little things—showing around new employees, picking up birthday cakes, ordering new supplies when needed, and so forth.

退出是指个体通过结束或限制组织成员身份的一种主动的、破坏性的反应。

 **3.3**

What are the four primary responses to negative events at work?

建言是指个体试图改善环境而采取的一种主动的建设性反应。

忠诚是指个体表现出来的一种被动的、建设性的反应，以保持个体对环境的公开支持，同时个体私下里希望改善环境。

忽略是指一种被动的、破坏性的反应，在这种反应中工作兴趣和努力不断下降。

明星员工拥有高水平的组织承诺与高水平的任务绩效，被其他员工视为角色榜样。

公民员工拥有高水平的组织承诺与低水平的任务绩效，但却表现出许多自愿的“角色外”活动，以保证组织正常运行。

TABLE 3-3 Four Types of Employees

		Task Performance	
		HIGH	LOW
ORGANIZATIONAL COMMITMENT	HIGH	Stars	Citizens
	LOW	Lone wolves	Apathetics

Source: Adapted from R.W. Griffeth, S. Gaertner, and J.K. Sager, "Taxonomic Model of Withdrawal Behaviors: The Adaptive Response Model," *Human Resource Management Review* 9 (1999), pp. 577–90.

独狼员工拥有低水平的组织承诺与高水平的任务绩效，积极努力实现他们自己的目标，而不一定是公司目标。

冷漠员工拥有低水平的组织承诺与低水平的任务绩效，仅付出最少的努力来保住自己的工作。

心理退缩是由从精神上逃避工作环境的行为组成。有些商业文章将心理退缩比作"磨洋工"，意思是说虽然员工占据着公司中的职位，其实心已经不在这里了。

当员工看起来在工作，但实际上已经被各种想法与顾虑干扰的时候，就是在**做白日梦**。

3.4
What are some examples of psychological withdrawal? Of physical withdrawal? How do the different forms of withdrawal relate to each other?

社会化是指员工口头谈论与工作无关的主题。

装忙是员工的主观意愿，使他们看起来在工作，即使没有从事工作任务。

兼职是指员工利用工作时间和公司资源来完成与公司无关的工作，如接私活。

泡网是运用网络、E-mail及即时通话工具供个人娱乐而不是工作职责。

Lone wolves possess low levels of organizational commitment but high levels of task performance and are motivated to achieve work goals for themselves, not necessarily for their company. They are likely to respond to negative events with exit. Although their performance would give them the credibility needed to inspire change, their lack of attachment prevents them from using that credibility constructively. Instead, they rely on their performance levels to make them marketable to their next employer. To spot lone wolves, look for the talented employees who never seem to want to get involved in important decisions about the future of the company. Finally, **apathetics** possess low levels of both organizational commitment and task performance and merely exert the minimum level of effort needed to keep their jobs. Apathetics should respond to negative events with neglect, because they lack the performance needed to be marketable and the commitment needed to engage in acts of citizenship.

It's clear from this discussion that exit and neglect represent the flip side of organizational commitment: withdrawal behavior. How common is withdrawal behavior within organizations? Quite common, it turns out. One study clocked employees' on-the-job behaviors over a two-year period and found that only about 51 percent of their time was actually spent working! The other 49 percent was lost to late starts, early departures, long coffee breaks, personal matters, and other forms of withdrawal. As a manager, wouldn't you like to feel like there was more than a coin-flip's chance that your employees were actually working during the course of a given day?

As shown in Figure 3-4, withdrawal comes in two forms: psychological (or neglect) and physical (or exit). **Psychological withdrawal** consists of actions that provide a mental escape from the work environment. Some business articles refer to psychological withdrawal as "warm-chair attrition," meaning that employees have essentially been lost even though their chairs remain occupied. This withdrawal form comes in a number of shapes and sizes. The least serious is **daydreaming**, when employees appear to be working but are actually distracted by random thoughts or concerns. **Socializing** refers to the verbal chatting about nonwork topics that goes on in cubicles and offices or at the mailbox or vending machines. **Looking busy** indicates an intentional desire on the part of employees to look like they're working, even when not performing work tasks. Sometimes employees decide to reorganize their desks or go for a stroll around the building, even though they have nowhere to go. (Those who are very good at managing impressions do such things very briskly and with a focused look on their faces!) When employees engage in **moonlighting**, they use work time and resources to complete something other than their job duties, such as assignments for another job.

Perhaps the most widespread form of psychological withdrawal among white-collar employees is **cyberloafing**—using Internet, e-mail, and instant messaging access for their personal enjoyment rather than work duties. Some estimates suggest that typical cubicle dwellers stop what they're doing about once every three minutes to send e-mail, check Facebook or Twitter, surf over to YouTube, and so forth. Such distractions consume as much as 28 percent of employees' workdays and cost some $650 billion a year in lost productivity. Sports fans seem particularly vulnerable. Estimates suggest that Fantasy Football league transactions consume as much as $1.5 billion in productivity during a typical season. The spring isn't much better, as estimates suggest that employers lose $1.2 billion as employees watch NCAA tournament games online. Some employees view cyberloafing as a way of "balancing the scales" when it comes to personal versus work time. For example, one participant in a cyberloafing study noted, "It is

OB AT THE BOOKSTORE

THE WAR FOR LATE NIGHT
by Bill Carter (New York: Viking, 2010).

After only seven months, with my Tonight Show in its infancy, NBC has decided to react to their terrible difficulties in prime-time by making a change in their long-established late night schedule. Last Thursday, NBC executives told me they intended to move the Tonight Show to 12:05 to accommodate the Jay Leno Show at 11:35. For 60 years the Tonight Show has aired immediately following the late local news. I sincerely believe that delaying the Tonight Show into the next day to accommodate another comedy program will seriously damage what I consider to be the greatest franchise in the history of broadcasting. The Tonight Show at 12:05 simply isn't the Tonight Show.

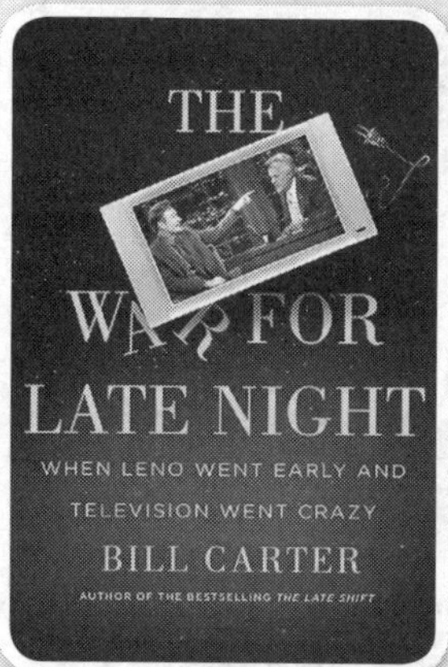

With those words, addressed in a statement to "People of Earth," Conan O'Brien voiced some significant dissatisfaction with his employer. As described in Carter's account, NBC had moved Leno to 10:00 weekdays three months after Conan inherited *The Tonight Show* from him. Leno's ratings were disappointing, but his contract required NBC to keep him on the air, in some capacity. As Conan's *Tonight Show* numbers worsened, partially due to the poor lead-in provided by Leno, the new late night status quo came up for grabs.

To fully appreciate Conan's situation, we have to journey back to 2001. After hosting *Late Night* at 12:35 on NBC for 11 years, Fox offered Conan its 11:00 slot for seven times his current salary. Conan turned it down, however, because NBC had treated him well and he had dreamed of hosting *The Tonight Show* since watching Johnny Carson as a boy. Three years later, NBC came up with an idea that would reward Conan for his affective commitment. In five years, Conan would officially take over *The Tonight Show* as Leno's contract expired.

When it all began to unravel, Conan used the events as fuel to reignite his show. He put *The Tonight Show* on Craigslist ("Guaranteed to last for up to seven months; designed for 11:35, but can easily be moved!"), along with himself ("Tall, slender redhead available for nighttime recreation, currently homeless, must meet at your place"). After several days and some of his best shows, a settlement was reached, with Leno regaining *The Tonight Show* and Conan eventually moving to TBS. Loyalty had turned to exit, with Conan summarizing, "I think they cured me of my addiction to *The Tonight Show*."

alright for me to use the Internet for personal reasons at work. After all, I do work overtime without receiving extra pay from my employer." Although such views may seem quite reasonable, other employees view cyberloafing as a means to retaliate for negative work events. One participant in the same study noted, "My boss is not the appreciative kind; I take what I can whenever I can. Surfing the net is my way of hitting back."

Physical withdrawal consists of actions that provide a physical escape, whether short-term or long-term, from the work environment. Physical withdrawal also comes in a number of shapes and sizes. **Tardiness** reflects the tendency to arrive at work late (or leave work early). Of course, tardiness can sometimes be unavoidable, as when employees have car trouble or must fight through bad weather, but it often represents a calculated desire to spend less time at work. **Long breaks** involve longer-than-normal lunches, soda breaks, coffee breaks, and so forth that provide a physical escape from work. Sometimes long breaks stretch into **missing meetings**,

身体退缩是由从身体上长期或短期逃避工作环境的行为组成。

拖拉是一种上班晚（下班早）的倾向。

长时间休息包括超出规定时间的午餐、喝咖啡等逃避工作的行为。

耽误会议意味着员工离开办公室时忽略了重要的工作活动。

FIGURE 3-4 Psychological and Physical Withdrawal

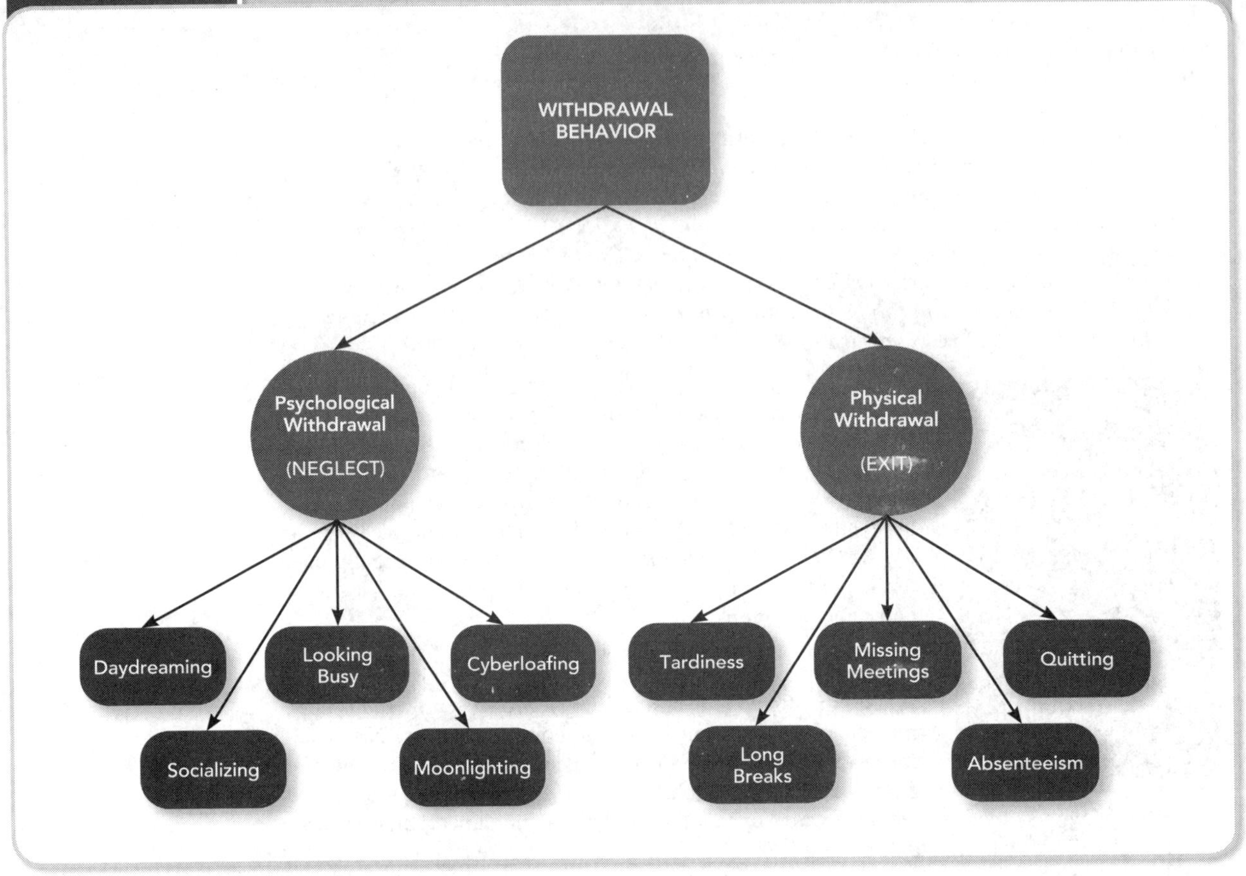

WITHDRAWAL BEHAVIOR

Psychological Withdrawal (NEGLECT)

Daydreaming

Socializing

Looking Busy

Moonlighting

Cyberloafing

Physical Withdrawal (EXIT)

Tardiness

Long Breaks

Missing Meetings

Absenteeism

Quitting

which means employees neglect important work functions while away from the office. As a manager, you'd like to be sure that employees who leave for lunch are actually going to come back, but sometimes that's not a safe bet!

当员工缺失一整天工作时就是**缺勤**。

Absenteeism occurs when employees miss an entire day of work. Of course, people stay home from work for a variety of reasons, including illness and family emergencies. There's also a rhythm to absenteeism. For example, employees are more likely to be absent on Mondays or Fridays. Moreover, streaks of good attendance create a sort of pressure to be absent, as personal responsibilities build until a day at home becomes irresistible. That type of absence can sometimes be functional, because people may return to work with their "batteries recharged." Group and departmental norms also affect absenteeism by signaling whether an employee can get away with missing a day here or there without being noticed.

One survey suggests that 57 percent of U.S. employees take sick days when they're not actually sick, a trend that has some companies going to extreme measures. Private investigation firms charge around $75 per hour to send investigators in search of employees who may be playing hooky. Rick Raymond, an investigator in Florida, once followed a supposedly sick employee to Universal Studios. The employee rode three roller coasters that take automatic pictures at the sharpest turns. Raymond bought all three, which conveniently included time and date stamps. When the employee later claimed that the photos weren't her, Raymond responded by playing back video of her volunteering

In an effort to curb absenteeism, some companies have turned to private investigators to try to catch "sick" employees who are playing hooky.

at an animal show in the park! The news isn't all bad for would-be work-skippers. Some of the same firms that track employees provide training on how to elude the boss's surveillance attempts.

Finally, the most serious form of physical withdrawal is **quitting**—voluntarily leaving the organization. As with the other forms of withdrawal, employees can choose to "turn over" for a variety of reasons. The most frequent reasons include leaving for more money or a better career opportunity; dissatisfaction with supervision, working conditions, or working schedule; family factors; and health. Note that many of those reasons reflect avoidable turnover, meaning that the organization could have done something to keep the employee, perhaps by offering more money, more frequent promotions, or a better work situation. Family factors and health, in contrast, usually reflect unavoidable turnover that doesn't necessarily signal a lack of commitment on the part of employees.

辞职指自愿离开该组织。

Regardless of their reasons, some employees choose to quit after engaging in a very thorough, careful, and reasoned analysis. Typically some sort of "shock," whether it be a critical job change, a negative work experience, or an unsolicited job offer, jars employees enough that it triggers the thought of quitting in them. Once the idea of quitting has occurred to them, employees begin searching for other places to work, compare those alternatives to their current job, and—if the comparisons seem favorable—quit. This process may take days, weeks, or even months as employees grapple with the decision. In other cases, though, a shock may result in an impulsive, knee-jerk decision to quit, with little or no thought given to alternative jobs (or how those jobs compare to the current one). Of course, sometimes a shock never occurs. Instead, an employee decides to quit as a result of a slow but steady decrease in happiness until a "straw breaks the camel's back" and voluntary turnover results.

Figure 3-4 shows 10 different behaviors that employees can perform to psychologically or physically escape from a negative work environment. A key question remains though: "How do all those behaviors relate to one another?" Consider the following testimonials from uncommitted (and admittedly fictional) employees:

- "I can't stand my job, so I do what I can to get by. Sometimes I'm absent, sometimes I socialize, sometimes I come in late. There's no real rhyme or reason to it; I just do whatever seems practical at the time."
- "I can't handle being around my boss. I hate to miss work, so I do what's needed to avoid being absent. I figure if I socialize a bit and spend some time surfing the web, I don't need to ever be absent. But if I couldn't do those things, I'd definitely have to stay home . . . a lot."
- "I just don't have any respect for my employer anymore. In the beginning, I'd daydream a bit during work or socialize with my colleagues. As time went on, I began coming in late or taking a long lunch. Lately I've been staying home altogether, and I'm starting to think I should just quit my job and go somewhere else."

Each of these statements sounds like something that an uncommitted employee might say. However, each statement makes a different prediction about the relationships among the withdrawal behaviors in Figure 3-4. The first statement summarizes the **independent forms model** of withdrawal, which argues that the various withdrawal behaviors are uncorrelated with one another, occur for different reasons, and fulfill different needs on the part of employees. From this perspective, knowing that an employee cyberloafs tells you nothing about whether that employee is likely to be absent. The second statement summarizes the **compensatory forms model** of withdrawal, which argues that the various withdrawal behaviors negatively correlate with one another—that doing one means you're less likely to do another. The idea is that any form of withdrawal can compensate for, or neutralize, a sense of dissatisfaction, which makes the other forms unnecessary. From this perspective, knowing that an employee cyberloafs tells you that the same employee probably isn't going to be absent. The third statement summarizes the **progression model** of withdrawal, which argues that the various withdrawal behaviors are positively correlated: The tendency to daydream or socialize leads to the tendency to come in late or take long breaks, which leads to the tendency to be absent or quit. From this perspective, knowing that an employee cyberloafs tells you that the same employee is probably going to be absent in the near future.

独立形式模型认为不同的退缩行为之间不相关。

补偿形式模型认为不同类型的退缩行为之间是负相关的。

演化模型认为不同的退缩行为之间是正相关的。

Which of the three models seems most logical to you? Although all three make some sense, the progression model has received the most scientific support. Studies tend to show that the withdrawal behaviors in Figure 3-4 are positively correlated with one another. Moreover, if you view the behaviors as a causal sequence moving from left (daydreaming) to right (quitting), the behaviors that are closest to each other in the sequence tend to be more highly correlated. For example, quitting is more closely related to absenteeism than to tardiness, because absenteeism is right next to it in the withdrawal progression. These results illustrate that withdrawal behaviors may begin with very minor actions but eventually can escalate to more serious actions that may harm the organization.

总结：成为一名“承诺型”员工意味着什么
SUMMARY: WHAT DOES IT MEAN TO BE "COMMITTED"?

So what does it mean to be a "committed" employee? As shown in Figure 3-5, it means a lot of different things. It means that employees have a strong desire to remain a member of the organization, maybe because they want to stay, need to stay, or feel they ought to stay. Regardless of the reasons for their attachment though, retaining these employees means stopping the progression of withdrawal that begins with psychological forms and then escalates to behavioral forms. Note that the negative sign (−) in Figure 3-5 illustrates that high levels of overall organizational commitment reduce the frequency of psychological and physical withdrawal. Note also that psychological withdrawal goes on to affect physical withdrawal, which represents the progressive nature of such behaviors.

As you move forward in this book, you'll notice that every chapter includes a description of how that chapter's topic relates to organizational commitment. For example, Chapter 4 on Job Satisfaction describes how employees' satisfaction levels influence their organizational commitment. Sometimes you'll notice that a given chapter's topic relates more strongly to organizational commitment than to job performance. Other times, however, the topic may relate similarly to commitment and performance, or even relate more strongly to performance. Regardless, such differences will help you see exactly why the various topics in this book are so important to managers.

影响承诺的趋势
TRENDS THAT AFFECT COMMITMENT

Now that we've described exactly what organizational commitment represents, it's time to describe some of the trends that affect it in the contemporary workplace. Put simply, the composition of the workforce is changing, as is the traditional relationship between employees and employers. These trends put pressure on some types of commitment and alter the kinds of withdrawal seen in the workplace.

劳动力的多样性
DIVERSITY OF THE WORKFORCE

One of the most visible trends affecting the workplace is the increased diversity of the U.S. labor force. Demographically speaking, the percentage of the workforce that is white is expected to drop to around 65 percent by 2012. Meanwhile, the percentage of minorities in the workforce is expected to rise to the following levels: African Americans (12 percent), Hispanics (15 percent), and Asians (6 percent). Thus, by 2012, minority groups will make up one-third of the workforce. Meanwhile, women have virtually matched men in terms of workforce percentages, with 53 percent of jobs filled by men and 47 percent by women. These statistics show that the "white, male-dominated" workforce is becoming a thing of the past.

3.5
What workplace trends are affecting organizational commitment in today's organizations?

The workforce is becoming diverse in other ways as well. The percentage of members of the workforce who are 60 years or older is expected to grow to 10 percent in 2012. As the 78 million Baby Boomers near retirement, they're expected to remain in the workforce significantly longer than previous generations. Research suggests that remaining a member of the workforce is actually beneficial to older people's health, keeping them more mentally and physically fit. Moreover, medical advances are helping older employees stay vital longer, just as the physical labor component of most jobs keeps shrinking. The Baby Boomers are also one of the most

FIGURE 3-5 What Does It Mean to Be "Committed"?

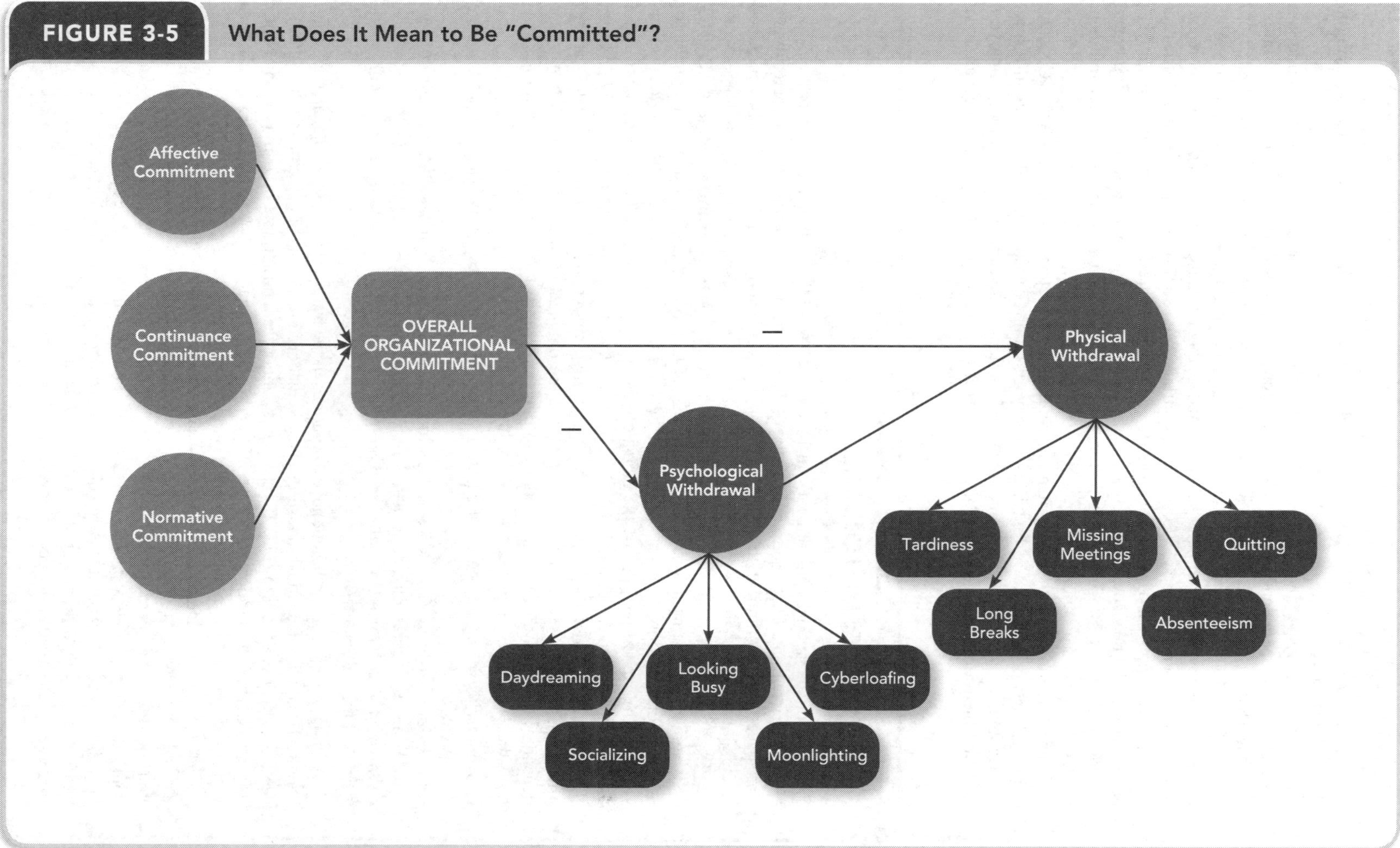

educated generations, and research suggests that their continued participation in the workforce could add $3 trillion a year to the country's economic output. That, combined with the uncertainty surrounding Social Security and stock market–based retirement plans, makes staying in the workforce a logical call.

As the economy continues to become more global, U.S. businesses face another important form of diversity: More and more employees are foreign-born. Although stereotypes view immigrants as staffing blue-collar or service jobs, many of the most educated employees come from abroad. Consider that half of the PhDs working in the United States are foreign-born, as are 45 percent of the physicists, computer scientists, and mathematicians. At the same time, more and more American employees are working as expatriates who staff offices in foreign countries for long periods of time. Serving as an expatriate can be a very stressful assignment for employees as they adjust to a new country, a new style of working, and increased distance from family and friends. See our **OB Internationally** feature for more discussion of organizational commitment in multinational corporations.

These forms of diversity make it more challenging to retain valued employees. Consider the social network diagram in Figure 3-3. As work groups become more diverse with respect to race, gender, age, and national origin, there's a danger that minorities or older employees will find themselves on the fringe of such networks, which potentially reduces their affective

OB INTERNATIONALLY

Fostering organizational commitment can be more complex in multinational corporations, for two primary reasons. First, multinational corporations provide two distinct foci of commitment: Employees can be committed to the local subsidiary in which they work, or they can be committed to the global organization. Research on commitment in multinational corporations suggests that employees draw a distinction between those two foci when judging their commitment. Specifically, employees distinguish between the prestige of their local subsidiary and the reputation of the larger organization. They also distinguish between the support provided by their local supervisor and the support provided by the global organization's top management. Such results reveal that it's possible to be committed to the local office but not the overall organization, or vice versa.

Second, multinational corporations require many employees to serve as expatriates for significant periods of time. Research suggests that the organizational commitment of expatriates depends, in part, on how well they adjust to their foreign assignments. Research further suggests that expatriates' adjustment comes in three distinct forms:

- *Work adjustment.* The degree of comfort with specific job responsibilities and performance expectations.
- *Cultural adjustment.* The degree of comfort with the general living conditions, climate, cost of living, transportation, and housing offered by the host culture.
- *Interaction adjustment.* The degree of comfort when socializing and interacting with members of the host culture.

A study of American multinational corporations in the transportation, service, manufacturing, chemical, and pharmaceutical industries showed that all three forms of adjustment relate significantly to affective commitment. If expatriates cannot feel comfortable in their assignment, it's difficult for them to develop an emotional bond to their organization. Instead, they're likely to withdraw from the assignment, both psychologically and physically.

What factors contribute to an expatriate's adjustment levels? It turns out that work adjustment depends on many of the same things that drive domestic employees' job satisfaction and motivation. Cultural and interaction adjustment, in contrast, are very dependent on spousal and family comfort. If an expatriate's spouse or children are unhappy in their new environment, it becomes very difficult for the expatriate to remain committed. Fortunately, research suggests that cultural and interaction adjustment can increase with time, as experiences in the host nation gradually increase expatriates' sense of comfort and, ultimately, their commitment to the work assignment.

commitment. At the same time, foreign-born employees are likely to feel less embedded in their current jobs and perceive fewer links to their community and less fit with their geographic area. This feeling may reduce their sense of continuance commitment. Recent trends suggest that the most educated and skilled immigrants are leaving the U.S. workforce at a rate of about 1,000 a day, particularly when their home country's economy begins to boom.

变化中的员工—雇主关系
THE CHANGING EMPLOYEE–EMPLOYER RELATIONSHIP

A few generations ago, many employees assumed that they would work for a single organization for their entire career. The assumption was that they would exchange a lifetime of loyalty and good work for a lifetime of job security. That perception changed in the 1980s and 1990s as downsizing became a more common part of working life. In 1992, downsizing statistics peaked as 3.4 million jobs were lost, and annual job losses have remained that high ever since. Downsizing represents a form of involuntary turnover, when employees are forced to leave the organization regardless of their previous levels of commitment. The increase in downsizing has gone hand-in-hand with increases in temporary workers and outsourcing, fundamentally altering the way employees view their relationships with their employers.

Companies usually downsize to cut costs, particularly during a recession or economic downturn. Does downsizing work? Does it make the company more profitable? One study suggests that the answer is "not usually." This study examined 3,628 companies between 1980 and 1994, of which 59 percent downsized 5 percent or more of their workforce at least once and 33 percent fired 15 percent or more of their workforce at least once. The most important result was that downsizing actually harmed company profitability and stock price. In fact, it typically took firms two years to return to the performance levels that prompted the downsizing in the first place. The exception to this rule was companies that downsized in the context of some larger change in assets (e.g., the sale of a line of business, a merger, an acquisition). However, such firms were relatively rare; only one-eighth of the downsizers were involved in some sort of asset change at the time the layoffs occurred.

Why doesn't downsizing tend to work? One reason revolves around the organizational commitment levels of the so-called "survivors." The employees who remain in the organization after a downsizing are often stricken with "survivor syndrome," characterized by anger, depression, fear, distrust, and guilt. One study found that downsizing survivors actually experienced more work-related stress than did the downsizing victims who went on to find new employment. Survivor syndrome tends to reduce organizational commitment levels at the worst possible time, as downsizing survivors are often asked to work extra hard to compensate for their lost colleagues. Indeed, a study of 3,500 Boeing employees revealed some particularly stark examples of survivor syndrome. Specifically, the study showed that employees who survived a 33 percent downsizing had depression scores that were nearly twice as high as those who left. They were also more likely to binge drink and experience chronic sleeping and health problems.

The change in employee–employer relationships brought about by a generation of downsizing makes it more challenging to retain valued employees. The most obvious challenge is finding a way to maintain affective commitment. The negative emotions aroused by survivor syndrome likely reduce emotional attachment to the organization. Moreover, if the downsizing has caused the loss of key figures in employees' social networks, then their desire to stay will be harmed. However, a second challenge is to find some way to maintain normative commitment. The sense that people *should* stay with their employer may have been eroded by downsizing, with personal work philosophies now focusing on maximizing marketability for the next opportunity that comes along. Even if employees felt obligated to remain at a firm in the past, seeing colleagues get dismissed in a downsizing effort could change that belief rather quickly.

One way of quantifying the change in employee–employer relationships is to assess how employees view those relationships psychologically. Research suggests that employees tend to view their employment relationships in quasi-contractual terms. Specifically, **psychological contracts** reflect employees' beliefs about what they owe the organization and what the organization owes them. These contracts are shaped by the recruitment and socialization activities that employees experience, which often convey promises and expectations that shape beliefs about reciprocal obligations. Some employees develop **transactional contracts** that are based on a narrow set of specific monetary obligations (e.g., the employee owes attendance

心理契约反映了员工关于如何对组织尽责及组织如何对他们尽责的想法。

交易契约是员工基于狭隘的金钱义务所形成的想法。

and protection of proprietary information; the organization owes pay and advancement opportunities). Other employees develop **relational contracts** that are based on a broader set of open-ended and subjective obligations (e.g., the employee owes loyalty and the willingness to go above and beyond; the organization owes job security, development, and support). Seeing one's coworkers downsized can constitute a "breach" of an employee's psychological contract, and research suggests that psychological contract breach leads to psychological and physical withdrawal. However, trends such as downsizing, use of temporary workers, and outsourcing may also cause employees to define their contracts in more transactional (as opposed to relational) terms.

关系契约是员工基于广泛的开放思维及主观义务所形成的想法。

应用：承诺措施

APPLICATION: COMMITMENT INITIATIVES

Now that you've gained a good understanding of organizational commitment, as well as some of the workforce trends that affect it, we close with a discussion of strategies and initiatives that can be used to maximize commitment. What exactly can companies do to increase loyalty? At a general level, they can be supportive. **Perceived organizational support** reflects the degree to which employees believe that the organization values their contributions and cares about their well-being. Organizations can do a number of things to be supportive, including providing adequate rewards, protecting job security, improving work conditions, and minimizing the impact of politics. In a sense, such support represents the organization's commitment to its employees. A meta-analysis of 42 research studies with almost 12,000 participants revealed that perceptions of support are strongly related to organizational commitment. That same review showed that perceptions of support are associated with lower levels of psychological and physical withdrawal.

感知到的组织支持表示员工相信组织看重他们的贡献及关心他们幸福的程度。

 3.6

How can organizations foster a sense of commitment among employees?

Beyond being supportive, organizations can engage in specific practices that target the three forms of commitment. For example, organizations could foster affective commitment by increasing the bonds that link employees together. Ben & Jerry's holds monthly "joy events" during which all production stops for a few hours, to be replaced by Cajun-themed parties, table tennis contests, and employee appreciation celebrations. Monsanto, the St. Louis, Missouri–based provider of agricultural products, groups staffers into "people teams" charged with designing employee-bonding activities like "snowshoe softball." Such tight bonding among employees may explain why Monsanto's voluntary turnover rate is only 3 percent. Companies like PepsiCo and Procter & Gamble pay particular attention to mentoring and team-building programs for female and minority employees to create a sense of solidarity among employees who might otherwise remain on the fringe of social networks.

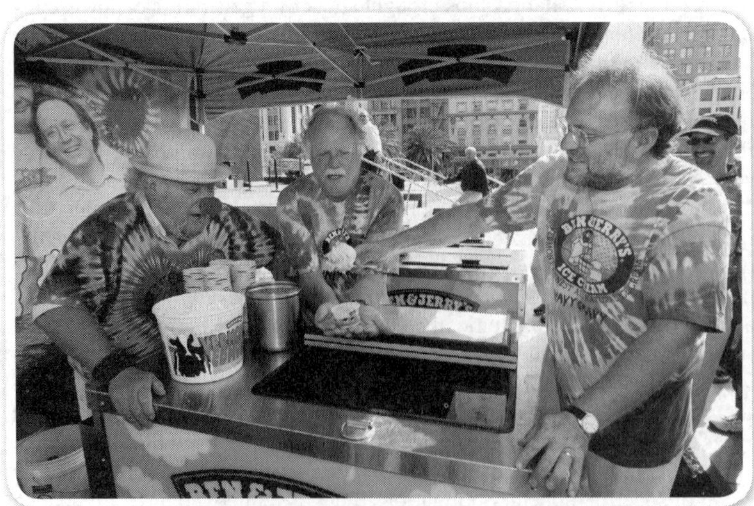

Ben & Jerry's, founded by Ben Cohen and Jerry Greenfield, goes to great lengths to encourage employees to hang out together and have fun during their workweek. Such bonding activities lower turnover and encourage valued employees to remain.

From a continuance commitment perspective, the priority should be to create a salary and benefits package that creates a financial need to stay. One study compared the impact of a variety of human resource management practices on voluntary turnover and found that two of the most significant predictors were average pay level and quality of the benefits package. Of course, one factor that goes hand-in-hand with salaries and benefits is advancement/promotion, because salaries cannot remain competitive if employees get stuck in neutral when climbing the career ladder. Perhaps that's why companies that are well-known for their commitment to promotion-from-within policies, like A.G. Edwards and the Principal Financial Group, also enjoy especially low voluntary turnover rates. Paying attention to career paths is especially important for star employees and foreign-born employees, both of whom have many options for employment elsewhere.

From a normative commitment perspective, the employer can provide various training and development opportunities for employees, which means investing in them to create the sense that they owe further service to the organization. As the nature of the employee–employer relationship has changed, opportunities for development have overtaken secure employment on the list of employee priorities. IBM is one company with a reputation for prioritizing development. Its "workforce management initiative" keeps a database of 33,000 résumés to develop a snapshot of employee skills. IBM uses that snapshot to plan its future training and development activities, with $400 million of the company's $750 million training budget devoted to giving employees the skills they may need in the future. If employees find developmental activities beneficial and rewarding, they may be tempted to repay those efforts with additional years of service.

A final practical suggestion centers on what to do if withdrawal begins to occur. Managers are usually tempted to look the other way when employees engage in minor forms of withdrawal. After all, sometimes such behaviors simply represent a break in an otherwise busy day. However, the progression model of withdrawal shows that even minor forms of psychological withdrawal often escalate, eventually to the point of absenteeism and turnover. The implication is therefore to stop the progression in its early stages by trying to root out the source of the reduced commitment. Many of the most effective companies make great efforts to investigate the causes of low commitment, whether at the psychological withdrawal stage or during exit interviews. As one senior oil executive acknowledged, the loss of a talented employee warrants the same sort of investigation as a technical malfunction that causes significant downtime on an oil rig.

PART

2

INDIVIDUAL MECHANISMS

个体机制

chapter 

Job Satisfaction

工作满意度

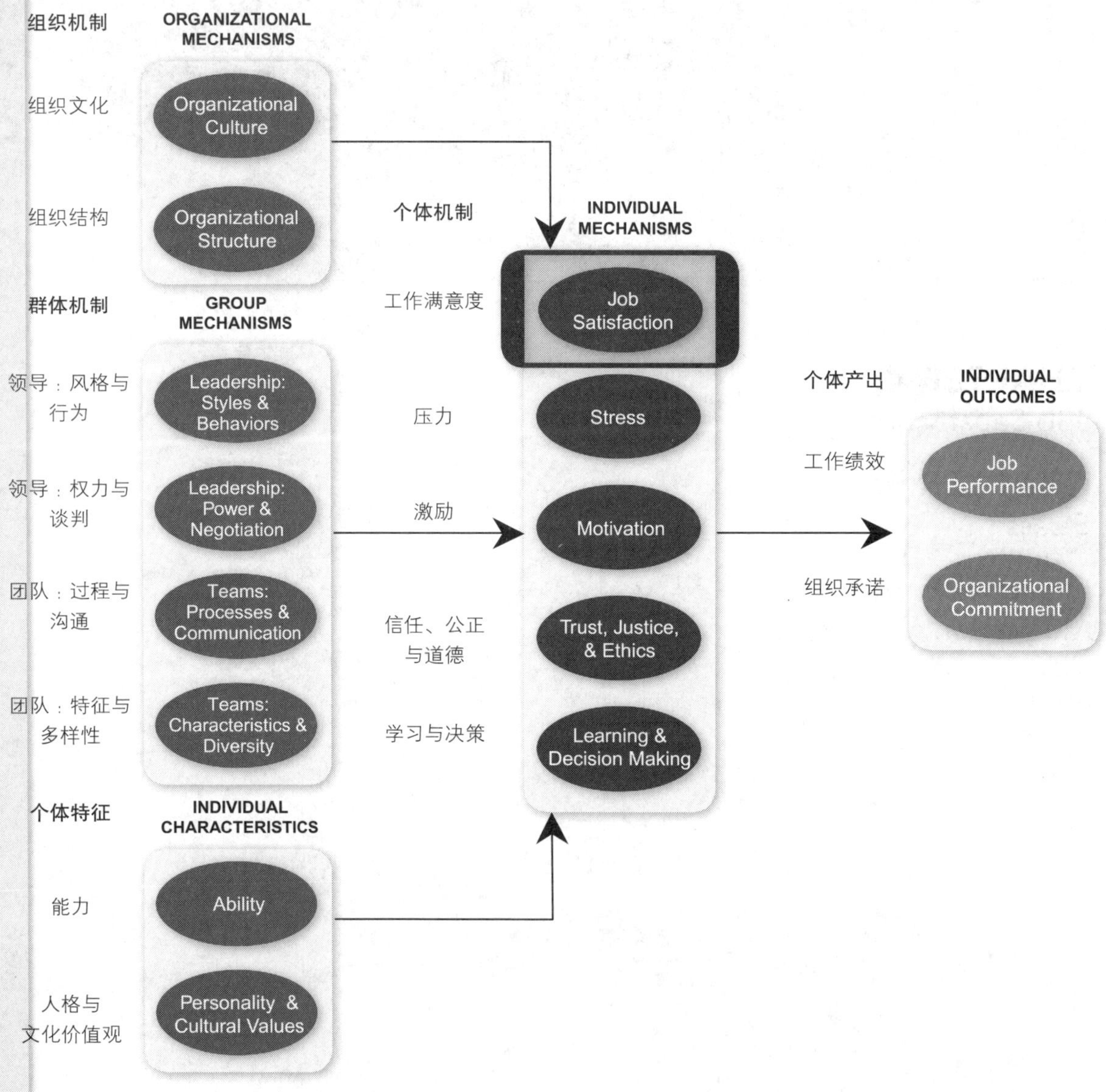

组织机制 ORGANIZATIONAL MECHANISMS

组织文化 Organizational Culture

组织结构 Organizational Structure

群体机制 GROUP MECHANISMS

领导：风格与行为 Leadership: Styles & Behaviors

领导：权力与谈判 Leadership: Power & Negotiation

团队：过程与沟通 Teams: Processes & Communication

团队：特征与多样性 Teams: Characteristics & Diversity

个体特征 INDIVIDUAL CHARACTERISTICS

能力 Ability

人格与文化价值观 Personality & Cultural Values

个体机制 INDIVIDUAL MECHANISMS

工作满意度 Job Satisfaction

压力 Stress

激励 Motivation

信任、公正与道德 Trust, Justice, & Ethics

学习与决策 Learning & Decision Making

个体产出 INDIVIDUAL OUTCOMES

工作绩效 Job Performance

组织承诺 Organizational Commitment

LEARNING GOALS

After reading this chapter, you should be able to answer the following questions:

4.1 What is job satisfaction?

4.2 What are values, and how do they affect job satisfaction?

4.3 What specific facets do employees consider when evaluating their job satisfaction?

4.4 Which job characteristics can create a sense of satisfaction with the work itself?

4.5 How is job satisfaction affected by day-to-day events?

4.6 What are mood and emotions, and what specific forms do they take?

4.7 How does job satisfaction affect job performance and organizational commitment? How does it affect life satisfaction?

4.8 What steps can organizations take to assess and manage job satisfaction?

HASBRO

"It's impossible not to have fun here . . . That's what the place is about." Those words might draw some skepticism if uttered by a typical CEO. If the CEO works for Hasbro, however, they have a definite air of believability. Indeed, the Pawtucket, Rhode Island–based toy company, led since 2008 by 47-year-old Brian Goldner, recently made *Fortune*'s "100 Best Companies to Work For" list for the first time. Who wouldn't want to work for a company whose assets include games like Monopoly, Scrabble, Cranium, Trivial Pursuit, Risk, Battleship, Candy Land, and Twister; and toys like Nerf, Play-Doh, G.I. Joe, Transformers, Mr. Potato Head, My Little Pony, and the Easy-Bake Oven? Notes Katy Fiffault, the company's vice-president of Global Consumer Insights, "Hasbro has what I believe are the deepest, most beloved and powerful brands in family entertainment. . . ."

The fun at Hasbro goes beyond those brands, however. Everyone except shift workers gets Friday afternoons off, in exchange for four extra hours of work from Monday to Thursday. Employees also get paid to do four hours of volunteer work for children each month. Compensation and benefits are also solid for the United States' number two toymaker (behind Mattel). Equity grants are increasing, as are the size and frequency of bonuses. Still, a lot of the satisfaction that comes from working at Hasbro flows out of the work that employees do. As one observer notes, employees don't return home to questions like, "Hey, Mom—just how was asphalt throughput at the plant today?" Instead, they get to spend their days directly or indirectly involved with brands that are beloved by their families, friends, and neighbors. And they get to participate in special events, like the recent establishing of a new world record for the most people playing Monopoly simultaneously (3,361).

With such venerable and well-known brands, you might think life at Hasbro would be a bit low on variety and innovation. One of Hasbro's strengths, however, is developing new and unique products, as well as novel ways to leverage its assets. Products are developed using "martini meetings," named for the shape of the glass. Researchers start at the rim by looking for new technologies, before winnowing down the options to the most promising. By the time the process reaches the stem, the form and shape of the new product is clear. This process allowed Hasbro to apply advances in animatronics to create FurReal Friends, soft animal toys with robotics inside. And Hasbro has gone beyond toys and games by transforming its brands into movie and entertainment properties. Soon the Transformers and G.I. Joe film franchises will be joined by a Battleship movie. These sorts of developments make Hasbro a place that's as interesting as it is fun.

工作满意度

JOB SATISFACTION

This chapter takes us to a new portion of our integrative model of organizational behavior. Job satisfaction is one of several individual mechanisms that directly affects job performance and organizational commitment. As shown in the Hasbro example, if employees are very satisfied with their jobs and experience positive emotions while working, they may perform their jobs better and choose to remain with the company for a longer period of time. Think about the worst job that you've held in your life, even if it was just a summer job or a short-term work assignment. What did you feel during the course of the day? How did those feelings influence the way you behaved, in terms of your time spent on task and citizenship behaviors rather than counterproductive or withdrawal behaviors?

工作满意度是一种愉快的情绪状态，源于对自身工作或工作体验的评价。

Job satisfaction is a pleasurable emotional state resulting from the appraisal of one's job or job experiences. In other words, it represents how you *feel* about your job and what you *think* about your job. Employees with high job satisfaction experience positive feelings when they think about their duties or take part in task activities. Employees with low job satisfaction experience negative feelings when they think about their duties or take part in their task activities. Unfortunately, workplace surveys suggest that satisfied employees are becoming more and more rare. For example, one recent survey showed that just 45 percent of Americans were satisfied with their jobs, down from 61 percent two decades ago. What explains the drop? The same survey revealed declines in the percentage of employees who find their work interesting (51 percent), who are satisfied with their boss (51 percent), and who like their coworkers (57 percent). Reversing such trends requires a deeper understanding of exactly what drives job satisfaction levels.

为什么某些员工比其他员工更满意

WHY ARE SOME EMPLOYEES MORE SATISFIED THAN OTHERS?

So what explains why some employees are more satisfied than others? At a general level, employees are satisfied when their job provides the things that they value. **Values** are those things that people consciously or subconsciously want to seek or attain. Think about this question for a few moments: What do you want to attain from your job, that is, what things do you want your job to give you? A good wage? A sense of achievement? Colleagues who are fun to be around? If you had to make a list of the things you value with respect to your job, most or all of them would likely be shown in Table 4-1. This table summarizes the content of popular surveys of work values, broken down into more general categories. Many of those values deal with the things that your work can give you, such as good pay or the chance for frequent promotions. Other values

价值是人们有意识或无意识寻求或希望得到的东西。

TABLE 4-1 Commonly Assessed Work Values

CATEGORIES	SPECIFIC VALUES
Pay	• High salary • Secure salary
Promotions	• Frequent promotions • Promotions based on ability
Supervision	• Good supervisory relations • Praise for good work
Coworkers	• Enjoyable coworkers • Responsible coworkers
Work Itself	• Utilization of ability • Freedom and independence • Intellectual stimulation • Creative expression • Sense of achievement
Altruism	• Helping others • Moral causes
Status	• Prestige • Power over others • Fame
Environment	• Comfort • Safety

Key Question:
Which of these things are most important to you?

Source: Adapted from R.V. Dawis, "Vocational Interests, Values, and Preferences," in *Handbook of Industrial and Organizational Psychology,* Vol. 2, Eds. M.D. Dunnette and L.M. Hough (Palo Alto, CA: Consulting Psychologists Press, 1991), pp. 834–71; and D.M. Cable and J.R. Edwards, "Complementary and Supplementary Fit: A Theoretical and Empirical Investigation," *Journal of Applied Psychology* 89 (2004), pp. 822–34.

pertain to the context that surrounds your work, including whether you have a good boss or good coworkers. Still other values deal with the work itself, like whether your job tasks provide you with freedom or a sense of achievement.

4.2
What are values, and how do they affect job satisfaction?

Consider the list of values in Table 4-1. Which would make your "top five" in terms of importance right now, at this stage of your life? Maybe you have a part-time job during college and you value enjoyable coworkers or a comfortable work environment above everything else. Or maybe you're getting established in your career and starting a family, which makes a high salary and frequent promotions especially critical. Or perhaps you're at a point in your career that you feel a need to help others or find an outlet for your creative expression. (In our case, we value fame, which is what led us to write this textbook. We're still waiting for Conan's call . . . or at least Fallon's.) Regardless of your "top five," you can see that different people value different things and that your values may change during the course of your working life.

价值实现
VALUE FULFILLMENT

价值认知理论认为工作满意度依赖于你认为工作是否提供你认为有价值的东西。

Values play a key role in explaining job satisfaction. **Value-percept theory** argues that job satisfaction depends on whether you *perceive* that your job supplies the things that you *value*. This theory can be summarized with the following equation:

$$\text{Dissatisfaction} = (V_{want} - V_{have})\,(V_{importance})$$

In this equation, V_{want} reflects how much of a value an employee wants, V_{have} indicates how much of that value the job supplies, and $V_{importance}$ reflects how important the value is to the employee. Big differences between wants and haves create a sense of dissatisfaction, especially when the value in question is important. Note that the difference between V_{want} and V_{have} gets multiplied by importance, so existing discrepancies get magnified for important values and minimized for trivial values. As an example, say that you were evaluating your pay satisfaction. You want to be earning around $70,000 a year but are currently earning $50,000 a year, so there's a $20,000 discrepancy. Does that mean you feel a great deal of pay dissatisfaction? Only if pay is one of the most important values to you from Table 4-1. If pay isn't that important, you probably don't feel much dissatisfaction.

4.3
What specific facets do employees consider when evaluating their job satisfaction?

Value-percept theory also suggests that people evaluate job satisfaction according to specific "facets" of the job. After all, a "job" isn't one thing—it's a collection of tasks, relationships, and rewards. The most common facets that employees consider in judging their job satisfaction appear in Figure 4-1. The figure includes the "want vs. have" calculations that drive satisfaction with pay, promotions, supervision, coworkers, and the work itself. The figure also shows how satisfaction with those five facets adds together to create "overall job satisfaction." Figure 4-1 shows that employees might be satisfied for all kinds of reasons. One person may be satisfied because she's in a high-paying job and working for a good boss. Another person may be satisfied because he has good coworkers and enjoyable work tasks. You may have noticed that a few of the values in Table 4-1, such as working for moral causes and gaining fame and prestige, are not represented in Figure 4-1. Those values are missing because they're not as relevant in all jobs, unlike pay, promotions, and so forth.

工资满意度是指员工对工资的感受，包括是否得到了他们应得的，是否稳定，是否足以支付正常的开销和奢侈品。

The first facet in Figure 4-1, **pay satisfaction,** refers to employees' feelings about their pay, including whether it's as much as they deserve, secure, and adequate for both normal expenses and luxury items. Similar to the other facets, pay satisfaction is based on a comparison of the pay that employees want and the pay they receive. Although more money is almost always better, most employees base their desired pay on a careful examination of their job duties and the pay given to comparable colleagues. As a result, even nonmillionaires can be quite satisfied with their pay (thankfully for most of us!). Take the employees at NuStar Energy, the San Antonio–based asphalt refiner and operator of oil pipelines storage. The company pays more than the industry average, with merit pay and equity grants for nonexecutives. And either everyone gets a bonus or no one does. Those sorts of pay policies make it more bearable to stand next to hot asphalt in a flame-retardant suit, hard hat, shatterproof glasses, and steel-toed boots!

晋升满意度是指员工对于公司晋升政策及执行方面的感受，包括晋升是否频繁、公平，是否基于能力。

The next facet in Figure 4-1, **promotion satisfaction,** refers to employees' feelings about the company's promotion policies and their execution, including whether promotions are frequent,

FIGURE 4-1 The Value-Percept Theory of Job Satisfaction

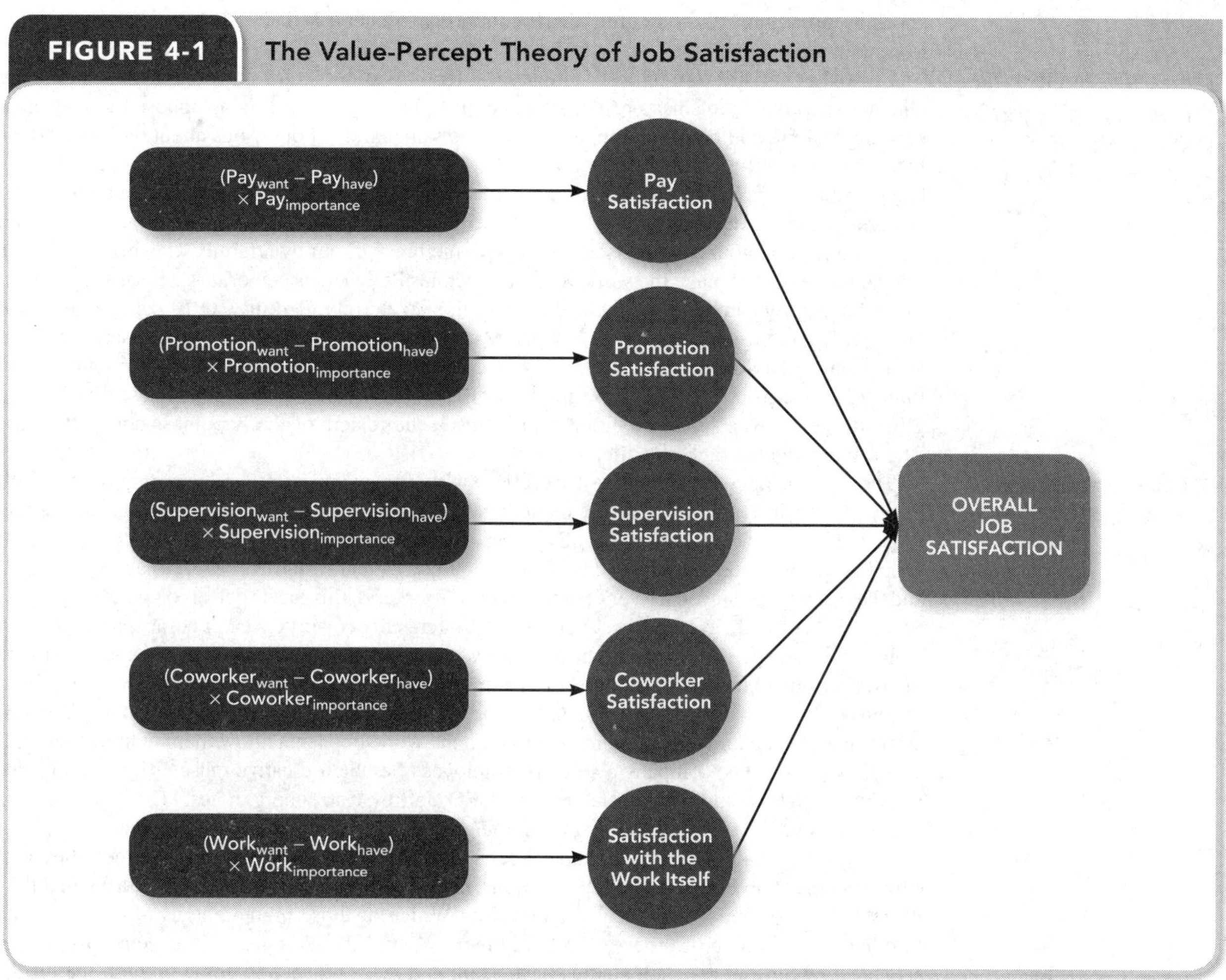

fair, and based on ability. Unlike pay, some employees may not want frequent promotions because promotions bring more responsibility and increased work hours. However, many employees value promotions because they provide opportunities for more personal growth, a better wage, and more prestige. Nordstrom, the Seattle–based high-end retailer, does a good job fostering promotion satisfaction on the part of its employees. New sales clerks are often promoted within a year, with potential leaders put on the fast track with a six-month training program. Indeed, five of the nine members of Nordstrom's executive committee started off on the sales floor. "Leadership is grounded in experience," notes one executive. "We want to make sure people get enough experiences to grow their career."

Supervision satisfaction reflects employees' feelings about their boss, including whether the boss is competent, polite, and a good communicator (rather than lazy, annoying, and too distant). Most employees ask two questions about their supervisors: (1) "Can they help me attain the things that I value?" and (2) "Are they generally likable?" The first question depends on whether supervisors provide rewards for good performance, help employees obtain necessary resources, and protect employees from unnecessary distractions. The second question depends on whether supervisors have good personalities, as well as values and beliefs similar to the employees' philosophies. General Mills, the Minneapolis–based manufacturer of food products, works hard to foster a sense of supervision satisfaction. The company stresses leadership development courses at its General Mills institute, and rotates employees across jobs to broaden the experiences they bring to leadership roles. One manager describes the company's culture this way, "I've noticed a manager three roles ago is still putting in good words for me, and still

主管满意度是指员工对老板的感受，包括老板是否能干、有礼貌，是否擅于与人沟通（而不是懒惰的、令人讨厌的和冷漠的）。

checking up on me. It's something that's common at General Mills, and something I've started to do as well."

同事满意度是指员工对同事的感受，包括同事是否聪明、负责任、乐于助人、有趣，而不是懒惰、爱讲闲话、令人讨厌和无趣。

Coworker satisfaction refers to employees' feelings about their fellow employees, including whether coworkers are smart, responsible, helpful, fun, and interesting as opposed to lazy, gossipy, unpleasant, and boring. Employees ask the same kinds of questions about their coworkers that they do about their supervisors: (1) "Can they help me do my job?" and (2) "Do I enjoy being around them?" The first question is critical because most of us rely, to some extent, on our coworkers when performing job tasks. The second question also is important because we spend just as much time with coworkers as we do with members of our own family. Coworkers who are pleasant and fun can make the workweek go much faster, whereas coworkers who are disrespectful and annoying can make even one day seem like an eternity. Perkins COIE, the Seattle–based law firm that represents Starbucks, Google, Microsoft, and Intel, fosters coworker satisfaction in an unusual—and downright sneaky—way. The firm encourages the creation of "happiness committees," small groups within each department that perform random acts of kindness, like leaving gifts at an employee's work station. The twist? The rosters of the happiness committees are kept secret from the rank-and-file.

工作本身的满意度反映了员工对于他们实际工作任务的感受，包括任务是否具有挑战性、有趣、受人重视，是否用到了核心技能，而不是枯燥的、重复性的和令人难受的。

The last facet in Figure 4-1, **satisfaction with the work itself,** reflects employees' feelings about their actual work tasks, including whether those tasks are challenging, interesting, respected, and make use of key skills rather than being dull, repetitive, and uncomfortable. Whereas the previous four facets described the outcomes that result from work (pay, promotions) and the people who surround work (supervisors, coworkers), this facet focuses on what employees actually *do.* After all, even the best boss or most interesting coworkers can't compensate for 40 or 50 hours of complete boredom each week! How can employers instill a sense of satisfaction with the work itself? One way is to emphasize the most challenging and interesting parts of the job. At DreamWorks Animation, the Glendale, California–based producer of Shrek and Kung Fu Panda, employees are encouraged to attend "Life's a Pitch" workshops that allow them to hone their presentation skills. The company also helps employees flex their creative muscles by offering free drawing, sculpting, and improv classes. The CEO, Jeffrey Katzenberg, notes, "Our philosophy is that if you love your work, and you love coming to work, then the work will be exceptional."

In summary, value-percept theory suggests that employees will be satisfied when they perceive that their job offers the pay, promotions, supervision, coworkers, and work tasks that they value. Of course, this theory begs the question: Which of those ingredients is most important? In other words, which of the five facets in Figure 4-1 has the strongest influence on overall job satisfaction? Several research studies have examined these issues and come up with the results shown in Figure 4-2. The figure depicts the correlation between each of the five satisfaction facets and an overall index of job satisfaction. (Recall that correlations of .10, .30, and .50 indicate weak, moderate, and strong relationships, respectively.)

Figure 4-2 suggests that satisfaction with the work itself is the single strongest driver of overall job satisfaction. Supervision and coworker satisfaction are also strong drivers, and promotion and pay satisfaction have moderately strong effects. Why is satisfaction with the work itself so critical? Well, consider that a typical workweek contains around 2,400 minutes. How much of that time is spent thinking about how much money you make? 10 minutes? Maybe 20? The same is true for promotions—we may want them, but we don't necessarily spend hours a day thinking about them. We do spend a significant chunk of that time with other people though. Between lunches, meetings, hallway chats, and other conversations, we might easily spend 600 minutes a week with supervisors and coworkers. That leaves almost 1,800 minutes for just us and our work. As a result, it's hard to be satisfied with your job if you don't like what you actually do.

Employees at DreamWorks Animation can express their creativity at work in a number of ways, including free drawing, sculpting, and improv classes, and courses on honing their pitching and presentation skills.

工作本身的满意度
SATISFACTION WITH THE WORK ITSELF

Given how critical enjoyable work tasks are to overall job satisfaction, it's worth spending more time describing the kinds of tasks that most people find enjoyable. Researchers began focusing on this question in the

FIGURE 4-2 Correlations between Satisfaction Facets and Overall Job Satisfaction

Correlation with Overall Job Satisfaction

.80
.70
.60
.50
.40
.30
.20
.10
.00

Pay
Promotion
Supervision
Coworker
Work Itself

Specific Facets of Job Satisfaction

Represents a strong correlation (around .50 in magnitude).
Represents a moderate correlation (around .30 in magnitude).
Represents a weak correlation (around .10 in magnitude).

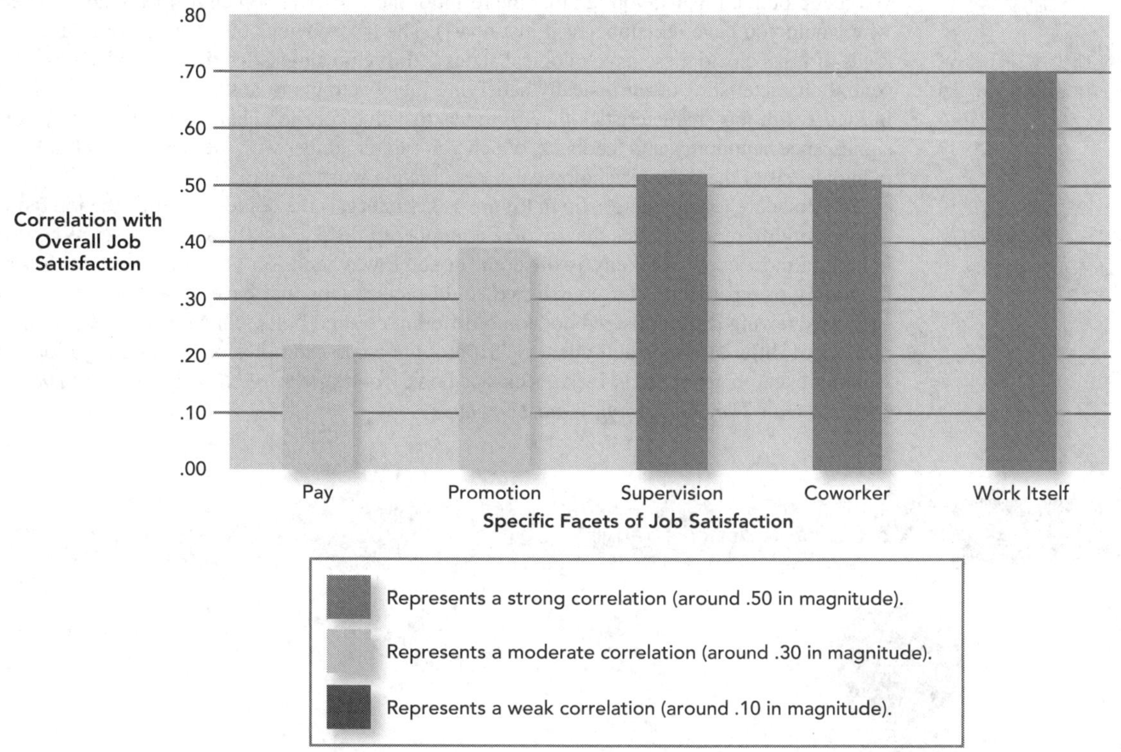

Sources: G.H. Ironson, P.C. Smith, M.T. Brannick, W.M. Gibson, and K.B. Paul, "Construction of a Job in General Scale: A Comparison of Global, Composite, and Specific Measures," *Journal of Applied Psychology* 74 (1989), pp. 193–200; and S.S. Russell, C. Spitzmuller, L.F. Lin, J.M. Stanton, P.C. Smith, and G.H. Ironson, "Shorter Can Also Be Better: The Abridged Job in General Scale," *Educational and Psychological Measurement* 64 (2004), pp. 878–93.

1950s and 1960s, partly in reaction to practices based in the "scientific management" perspective. Scientific management focuses on increasing the efficiency of job tasks by making them more simplified and specialized and using time and motion studies to plan task movements and sequences carefully. The hope was that such steps would increase worker productivity and reduce the breadth of skills required to complete a job, ultimately improving organizational profitability. Instead, the simplified and routine jobs tended to lower job satisfaction while increasing absenteeism and turnover. Put simply: Boring jobs may be easier, but they're not necessarily better.

So what kinds of work tasks are especially satisfying? Research suggests that three "critical psychological states" make work satisfying. The first psychological state is believing in the **meaningfulness of work,** which reflects the degree to which work tasks are viewed as something that "counts" in the employee's system of philosophies and beliefs (see Chapter 6 on Motivation for more discussion of such issues). Trivial tasks tend to be less satisfying than tasks that make employees feel like they're aiding the organization or society in some meaningful way. The second psychological state is perceiving **responsibility for outcomes,** which captures the degree to which employees feel that they're key drivers of the quality of the unit's work. Sometimes employees feel like their efforts don't really matter, because work outcomes are dictated by effective procedures, efficient technologies, or more influential colleagues. Finally, the third psychological state is **knowledge of results,** which reflects the extent to which employees know how well (or how poorly) they're doing. Many employees work in jobs in which they never find out about their mistakes or notice times when they did particularly well.

工作的意义是指工作任务在多大程度上被视为在员工的价值观与信仰体系中占有“一席之地”。

对产出的责任是指员工感受到他们是部门工作质量关键因素的程度。

结果知识是指员工知道他们做得有多好（或多差）的程度。

4.4
Which job characteristics can create a sense of satisfaction with the work itself?

Think about times when you felt especially proud of a job well done. At that moment, you were probably experiencing all three psychological states. You were aware of the result (after all, some job had been done well). You felt you were somehow responsible for that result (otherwise, why would you feel proud?). Finally, you felt that the result of the work was somehow meaningful (otherwise, why would you have remembered it just now?). The next obvious question then becomes, "What kinds of tasks create these psychological states?" **Job characteristics theory,** which describes the central characteristics of intrinsically satisfying jobs, attempts to answer this question. As shown in Figure 4-3, job characteristics theory argues that five core job characteristics (variety, identity, significance, autonomy, and feedback, which you can remember with the acronym "VISAF") result in high levels of the three psychological states, making work tasks more satisfying.

工作特征理论描述了令人满意的工作的内在核心特征。

The first core job characteristic in Figure 4-3, **variety,** is the degree to which the job requires a number of different activities that involve a number of different skills and talents. When variety is high, almost every workday is different in some way, and job holders rarely feel a sense of monotony or repetition. Of course, we could picture jobs that have a variety of boring tasks, such as screwing different sized nuts onto different colored bolts, but such jobs do not involve a number of different skills and talents. To provide some examples of low and high job variety, we offer excerpts from Studs Terkel's classic book *Working: People Talk About What They Do All Day and How They Feel About What They Do.*

多样性是指完成一项工作包含许多不同活动的程度，这些活动需要不同的技能与能力。

FIGURE 4-3 Job Characteristics Theory

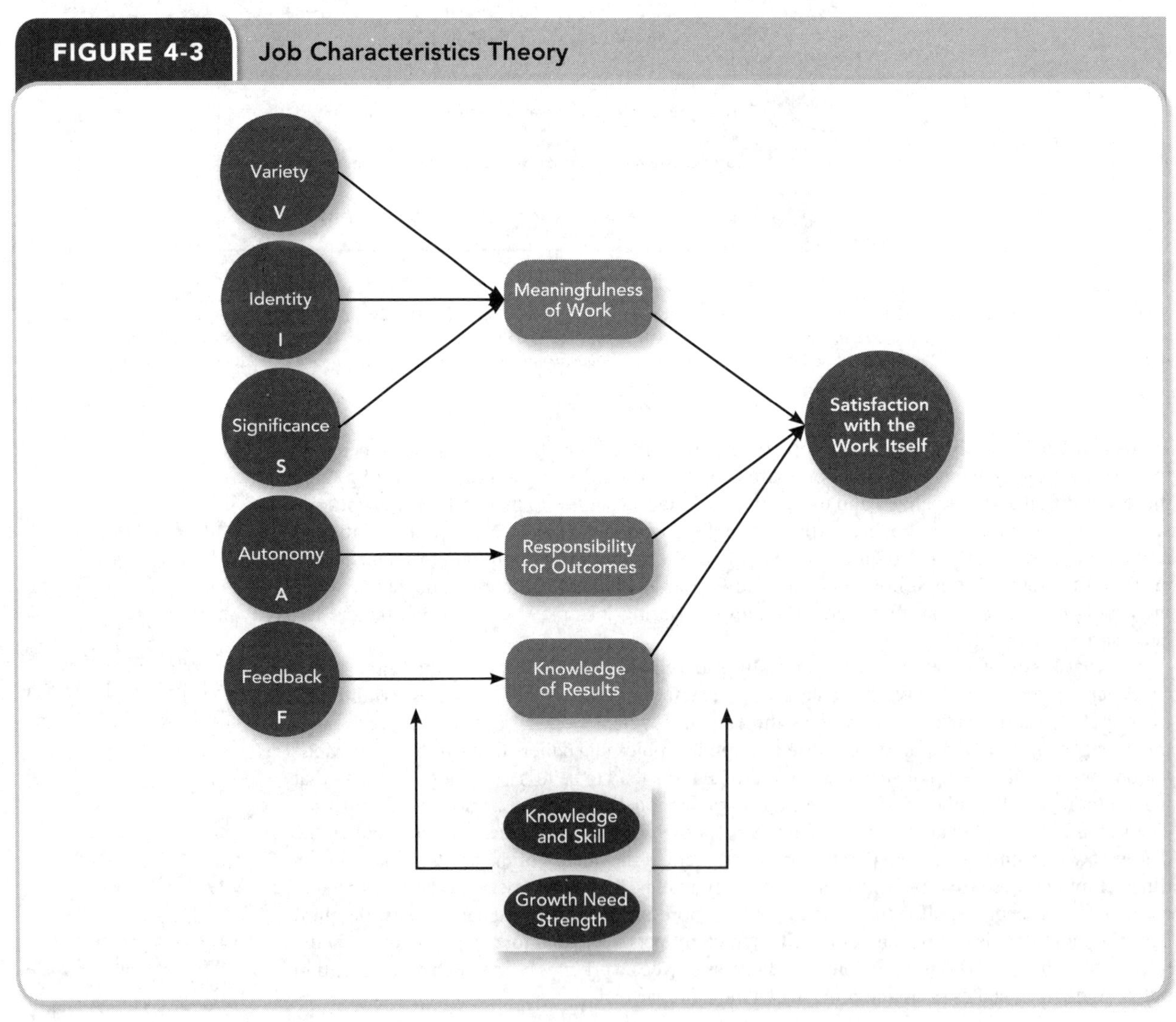

▼ Low Variety: Phil Stallings, Spot-Welder

I stand in one spot, about two- or three-feet area, all night. The only time a person stops is when the line stops. We do about thirty-two jobs per car, per unit. Forty-eight units an hour, eight hours a day. Thirty-two times forty-eight times eight. Figure it out. That's how many times I push that button. . . . It don't stop. It just goes and goes and goes. I bet there's men who have lived and died out there, never seen the end of that line. And they never will—because it's endless. It's like the serpent. It's just all body, no tail. It can do things to you . . . (Laughs).

▲ High Variety: Eugene Russell, Piano Tuner

Every day is different. I work Saturdays and Sundays sometimes. Monday I'm tuning a piano for a record company that had to be done before nine o'clock. When I finish that, I go to another company and do at least four pianos. During that day there's a couple of harpsichords mixed in.. . . I get a big kick out of it, because there are so many facets. Other people go through a routine. At a certain time they punch a clock. . . . Then they're through with it and *then* their life begins. With us the piano business is an integral part of our life. I had a discussion with another tuner, who is a great guitar man. He said "Why are we tuners?" I said, "Because we want to hear good sounds."

Evidence indicates that our preference for variety is hardwired into our brains. Research in psychiatry and neuroscience shows that the brain releases a chemical called dopamine whenever a novel stimulus (a new painting, a new meal, a new work challenge) is experienced, and we tend to find this dopamine release quite pleasurable. Unfortunately, the amount of dopamine present in our brains declines over our life spans. One neuroscientist therefore suggests that the best way to protect our dopamine system is through novel, challenging experiences, writing, "The sense of satisfaction after you've successfully handled unexpected tasks or sought out unfamiliar, physically and emotionally demanding activities is your brain's signal that you're doing what nature designed you to do." Something to think about the next time you plan to order the same old thing at your favorite restaurant!

The second core job characteristic in Figure 4-3, **identity,** is the degree to which the job requires completing a whole, identifiable, piece of work from beginning to end with a visible outcome. When a job has high identity, employees can point to something and say, "There, I did that." The transformation from inputs to finished product is very visible, and the employee feels a distinct sense of beginning and closure. Think about how you feel when you work for a while on some project but don't quite get it finished—does that lack of closure bug you? If so, identity is an important concern for you. Consider these excerpts from *Working:*

同一性是指工作需要作为一个整体来完成的程度。

▼ Low Identity: Mike Lefevre, Steelworker

It's not just the work. Somebody built the pyramids. Somebody's going to build something. Pyramids, Empire State Building—these things don't just happen. There's hard work behind it. I would like to see a building, say the Empire State, I would like to see on one side of it a foot-wide strip from top to bottom with the name of every bricklayer, the name of every electrician, with all the names. So when a guy walked by, he could take his son and say, "See, that's me over there on the forty-fifth floor. I put the steel beam in." Picasso can point to a painting. What can I point to? A writer can point to a book. Everybody should have something to point to.

▲ High Identity: Frank Decker, Interstate Truck Driver

Every load is a challenge and when you finally off-load it, you have a feeling of having completed a job—which I don't think you get in a production line. I pick up a load at the mill, going to Hotpoint in Milwaukee. I take a job and I go through all the process. . . . You feel like your day's work is well done when you're coming back. I used to have problems in the morning, a lot of heartburn, I couldn't eat. But once I off-loaded, the pressure was off. Then I could eat anything.

重要性是指工作在多大程度上影响其他人的工作或生活，特别是对广阔世界的人们产生影响。

Significance is the degree to which the job has a substantial impact on the lives of other people, particularly people in the world at large. Virtually any job can be important if it helps put food on the table for a family, send kids to college, or make employees feel like they're doing their part for the working world. That said, significance as a core job characteristic captures something beyond that—the belief that this job *really matters*. When employees feel that their jobs are significant, they can see that others value what they do and they're aware that their job has a positive impact on the people around them. There's the sense that, if their job was taken away, society would be the worse for it. Consider these excerpts from *Working:*

▼ Low Significance: Louis Hayward, Washroom Attendant

They come in. They wash their hands after using the service—you hope. (A soft chuckle.) I go through the old brush routine, stand back, expecting a tip. A quarter is what you expect when you hand the guy a towel and a couple of licks of the broom. . . . I'm not particularly proud of what I'm doing. The shine man and I discuss it quite freely. In my own habitat I don't go around saying I'm a washroom attendant at the Palmer House. Outside of my immediate family, very few people know what I do. They do know I work at the Palmer House and let that suffice. You say Palmer House, they automatically assume you're a waiter. . . . The whole thing is obsolete. It's on its way out. This work isn't necessary in the first place. It's so superfluous. It was *never* necessary. (Laughs.)

▲ High Significance: Tom Patrick, Fireman

Last month there was a second alarm. I was off duty. I ran over there. I'm a bystander. I see these firemen on the roof, with the smoke pouring out around them, and the flames, and they go in. . . . You could see the pride that they were seein'. The ***** world's so ***** up, the country's ***** up. But the firemen, you actually see them produce. You see them put out a fire. You see them come out with babies in their hands. You see them give mouth-to-mouth when a guy's dying. You can't get around that ****. That's real. To me, that's what I want to be.

自主性是指在多大程度上允许个人自由、独立、决断地完成工作。

Autonomy is the degree to which the job provides freedom, independence, and discretion to the individual performing the work. When your job provides autonomy, you view the outcomes of it as the product of your efforts rather than the result of careful instructions from your boss or a well-written manual of procedures. Autonomy comes in multiple forms, including the freedom to control the timing, scheduling, and sequencing of work activities, as well as the procedures and methods used to complete work tasks. To many of us, high levels of autonomy are the difference between "having a long leash" and being "micromanaged." Consider these excerpts from *Working:*

▼ Low Autonomy: Beryl Simpson, Airline Reservationist

They brought in a computer called Sabre. . . . It has a memory drum and you can retrieve that information forever. . . . With Sabre being so valuable, you were allowed no more than three minutes on the telephone. You had twenty seconds, busy-out time it was called, to put the information into Sabre. Then you had to be available for another phone call. It was almost like a production line. We adjusted to the machine. The casualness, the informality that had been there previously was no longer there. . . . You took thirty minutes for lunch, not thirty-one. If you got a break, you took ten minutes, not eleven. . . . With the airline I had no free will. I was just part of that stupid computer.

▲ High Autonomy: Bud Freeman, Jazz Musician

I live in absolute freedom. I do what I do because I want to do it. What's wrong with making a living doing something interesting . . .? The jazz man is expressing freedom in every note he plays. We can only please the audience doing what *we* do. We have to please ourselves first. I want to play for the rest of my life. I don't see any sense in stopping. Were I to live another thirty years—that would make me ninety-five—why not try to play? I can just hear the critics: "Did you hear that wonderful note old man Freeman played last night?" (Laughs.) As Ben Webster says, "I'm going to play this **** saxophone until they put it on top of me."

Despite the need for discipline and practice, the job of a jazz musician is one with a high degree of autonomy.

The last core job characteristic in Figure 4-3, **feedback,** is the degree to which carrying out the activities required by the job provides employees with clear information about how well they're performing. A critical distinction must be noted: This core characteristic reflects feedback obtained *directly from the job* as opposed to feedback from coworkers or supervisors. Most employees receive formal performance appraisals from their bosses, but that feedback occurs once or maybe twice a year. When the job provides its own feedback, that feedback can be experienced almost every day. Consider these excerpts from *Working:*

反馈是指在完成工作的过程中，提供给员工明确的信息使其知晓工作好坏的程度。

▼ Low Feedback: Lilith Reynolds, Government Project Coordinator

I'm very discouraged about my job right now. . . . I'm to come up with some kind of paper on economic development. It won't be very hard because there's little that can be done. At the end of sixty days I'll present the paper. But because of the reorganization that's come up I'll probably never be asked about the paper.

▲ High Feedback: Dolores Dante, Waitress

When somebody says to me, "You're great, how come you're *just* a waitress?" *Just* a waitress. I'd say, "Why, don't you think you deserve to be served by me?" . . . Tips? I feel like Carmen. It's like a gypsy holding out a tambourine and they throw the coin. (Laughs.) . . . People would ask for me. . . . I would like to say to the customer, "Go to so-and-so." But you can't do that, because you feel a sense of loyalty. So you would rush, get to your customers quickly. Some don't care to drink and still they wait for you. That's a compliment.

The passages in this section illustrate the potential importance of each of the five core characteristics. But how important are the core characteristics to satisfaction with the work itself? Meta-analyses of around 200 different research studies employing around 90,000 total participants showed that the five core job characteristics are moderately to strongly related to work satisfaction. However, those results don't mean that *every* employee wants more variety, more autonomy, and so forth. The bottom of Figure 4-3 includes two other variables: **knowledge and skill** and **growth need strength** (which captures whether employees have strong needs for personal accomplishment or developing themselves beyond where they currently are). In the jargon of theory diagrams, these variables are called "moderators." Rather than directly affecting other variables in the diagram, moderators influence the strength of the relationships between variables. If employees lack the required knowledge and skill or lack a desire for growth and development, more variety and autonomy should *not* increase their satisfaction very much. However, when employees are very talented and feel a strong need for growth, the core job characteristics become even more powerful. A graphical depiction of this moderator effect appears in Figure 4-4, where you can see that the relationship between the core job characteristics and satisfaction becomes stronger when growth need strength increases.

知识与技能是指员工拥有成功完成工作所需的天赋与能力的程度。

成长需要强度描述了员工对于个人成就或超越当前的自我是否有强烈需要。

FIGURE 4-4 Growth Need Strength as a Moderator of Job Characteristic Effects

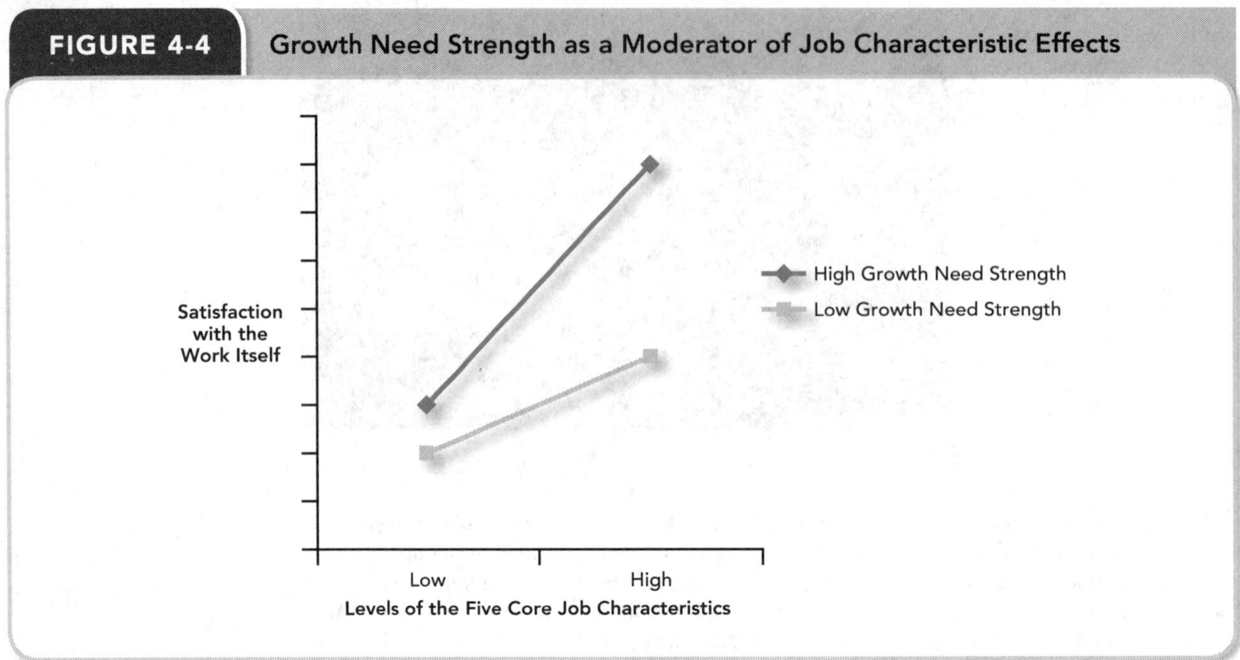

Source: Adapted from B.T. Loher, R.A. Noe, N.L. Moeller, and M.P. Fitzgerald, "A Meta-Analysis of the Relation of Job Characteristics to Job Satisfaction," *Journal of Applied Psychology* 70 (1985), pp. 280–89.

工作丰富化是指增加与工作有关的任务与责任的多样化、同一性、自主性等等。

工作重塑是指员工以一种主动的方式决定、塑造及重新界定他们的工作。

4.5 How is job satisfaction affected by day-to-day events?

Given how critical the five core job characteristics are to job satisfaction, many organizations have employed job characteristics theory to help improve satisfaction among their employees. The first step in this process is assessing the current level of the characteristics to arrive at a "satisfaction potential score." See our **OB Assessments** feature for more about that step. The organization, together with job design consultants, then attempts to redesign aspects of the job to increase the core job characteristic levels. Often this step results in **job enrichment,** such that the duties and responsibilities associated with a job are expanded to provide more variety, identity, autonomy, and so forth. Research suggests that such enrichment efforts can indeed boost job satisfaction levels. Moreover, enrichment efforts can heighten work accuracy and customer satisfaction, though training and labor costs tend to rise as a result of such changes. However, employees needn't necessarily wait for enrichment efforts to improve levels of the core job characteristics. Many employees can engage in **job crafting,** where they shape, mold, and redefine their jobs in a proactive way. For example, they might alter the boundaries of their jobs by switching certain tasks, they might change specific collaborative relationships, or they might reenvison how they view their work, relative to the broader context of the organization's mission.

心境和情绪
MOOD AND EMOTIONS

Let's say you're a satisfied employee, maybe because you get paid well and work for a good boss or because your work tasks provide you with variety and autonomy. Does this mean you'll definitely be satisfied at 11:00 a.m. next Tuesday? Or 2:30 p.m. the following Thursday? Obviously it doesn't. Each employee's satisfaction levels fluctuate over time, rising and falling like some sort of emotional stock market. This fluctuation might seem strange, given that people's pay, supervisors, coworkers, and work tasks don't change from one hour to the next. The key lies in remembering that job satisfaction reflects what you think and feel about your job. So part of it is rational, based on a careful appraisal of the job and the things it supplies. But another part of it is emotional, based on what you feel "in your gut" while you're at work or thinking about work. So satisfied employees feel good about their job *on average,* but things happen during the course of the day to make them feel better at some times (and worse at others).

OB ASSESSMENTS

CORE JOB CHARACTERISTICS

How satisfying are your work tasks? This assessment is designed to measure the five core job characteristics. Think of your current job or the last job that you held (even if it was a part-time or summer job). Answer each question using the response scale provided. Then subtract your answers to the boldfaced question from 8, with the difference being your new answer for that question. For example, if your original answer for Question 2 was "5," your new answer is "3" (8 – 5). Then use the formula to compute a satisfaction potential score (SPS).

1	2	3	4	5	6	7
VERY INACCURATE	MOSTLY INACCURATE	SLIGHTLY INACCURATE	UNCERTAIN	SLIGHTLY ACCURATE	MOSTLY ACCURATE	VERY ACCURATE

V1. The job requires me to use a number of complex or high-level skills. _____

V2. The job is quite simple and repetitive. _____

I1. The job is arranged so that I can do an entire piece of work from beginning to end. _____

I2. The job provides me the chance to completely finish the pieces of work I begin. _____

S1. This job is one where a lot of other people can be affected by how well the work gets done. _____

S2. The job itself is very significant and important in the broader scheme of things. _____

A1. The job gives me a chance to use my personal initiative and judgment in carrying out the work. _____

A2. The job gives me considerable opportunity for independence and freedom in how I do the work. _____

F1. Just doing the work required by the job provides many chances for me to figure out how well I am doing. _____

F2. After I finish a job, I know whether I performed well. _____

$$SPS = \left| \frac{V1+V2+I1+I2+S1+S2}{6} \right| \times \left| \frac{A1+A2}{2} \right| \times \left| \frac{F1+F2}{2} \right|$$

$$SPS = \left| \frac{\qquad}{6} \right| \times \left| \frac{\qquad}{2} \right| \times \left| \frac{\qquad}{2} \right|$$

$$SPS = \boxed{\qquad} \times \boxed{\qquad} \times \boxed{\qquad} = \boxed{\qquad}$$

SCORING AND INTERPRETATION

If your score is 150 or above, your work tasks tend to be satisfying and enjoyable. If your score is less than 150, you might benefit from trying to "craft" your job by taking on more challenging assignments and collaborations, or reenvisioning the way your job fits into the organization's mission.

Sources: J.R. Hackman and G.R. Oldham, *The Job Diagnostic Survey: An Instrument for the Diagnosis of Jobs and the Evaluation of Job Redesign Projects* (New Haven, CT: Yale University, 1974); J.R. Idaszak and F. Drasgow, "A Revision of the Job Diagnostic Survey: Elimination of a Measurement Artifact," *Journal of Applied Psychology* 72 (1987), pp. 69–74.

FIGURE 4-5 Hour-by-Hour Fluctuations in Job Satisfaction during the Workday

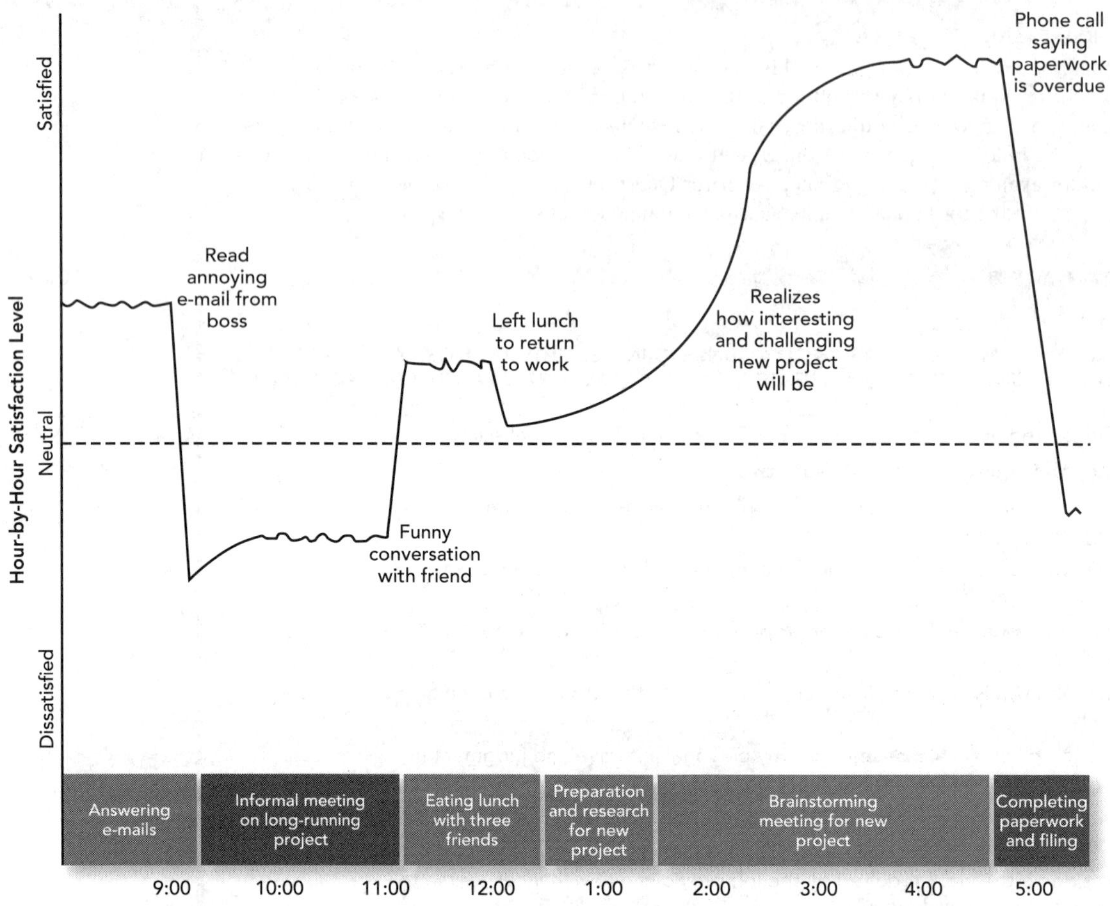

Hour-by-Hour Satisfaction Level
Satisfied
Neutral
Dissatisfied
Read annoying e-mail from boss
Funny conversation with friend
Left lunch to return to work
Realizes how interesting and challenging new project will be
Phone call saying paperwork is overdue
Answering e-mails
Informal meeting on long-running project
Eating lunch with three friends
Preparation and research for new project
Brainstorming meeting for new project
Completing paperwork and filing
9:00 10:00 11:00 12:00 1:00 2:00 3:00 4:00 5:00

Figure 4-5 illustrates the satisfaction levels for one employee during the course of a workday, from around 9:00 a.m. to 5:00 p.m. You can see that this employee did a number of different things during the day, from answering e-mails to eating lunch with friends to participating in a brainstorming meeting regarding a new project. You can also see that the employee came into the day feeling relatively satisfied, though satisfaction levels had several ebbs and flows during the next eight hours. What's responsible for those ebbs and flows in satisfaction levels? Two related concepts: mood and emotions.

4.6
What are mood and emotions, and what specific forms do they take?

What kind of mood are you in right now? Good? Bad? Somewhere in between? Why are you in that kind of mood? Do you really even know? (If it's a bad mood, we hope it has nothing to do with this book!) **Moods** are states of feeling that are often mild in intensity, last for an extended period of time, and are not explicitly directed at or caused by anything. When people are in a good or bad mood, they don't always know who (or what) deserves the credit or blame; they just happen to be feeling that way for a stretch of their day. Of course, it would be oversimplifying things to call all moods either good or bad. Sometimes we're in a serene mood; sometimes we're in an enthusiastic mood. Both are "good" but obviously feel quite different. Similarly, sometimes we're in a bored mood; sometimes we're in a hostile mood. Both are "bad" but, again, feel quite different.

心境是一种强度温和、时间持久，无明确指向或并非由某物引起的感觉状态。

It turns out that there are a number of different moods that we might experience during the workday. Figure 4-6 summarizes the different moods in which people sometimes find themselves. The figure illustrates that moods can be categorized in two ways: **pleasantness** and **activation.** First, the horizontal axis of the figure reflects whether you feel pleasant (in a "good mood") or

FIGURE 4-6 Different Kinds of Moods

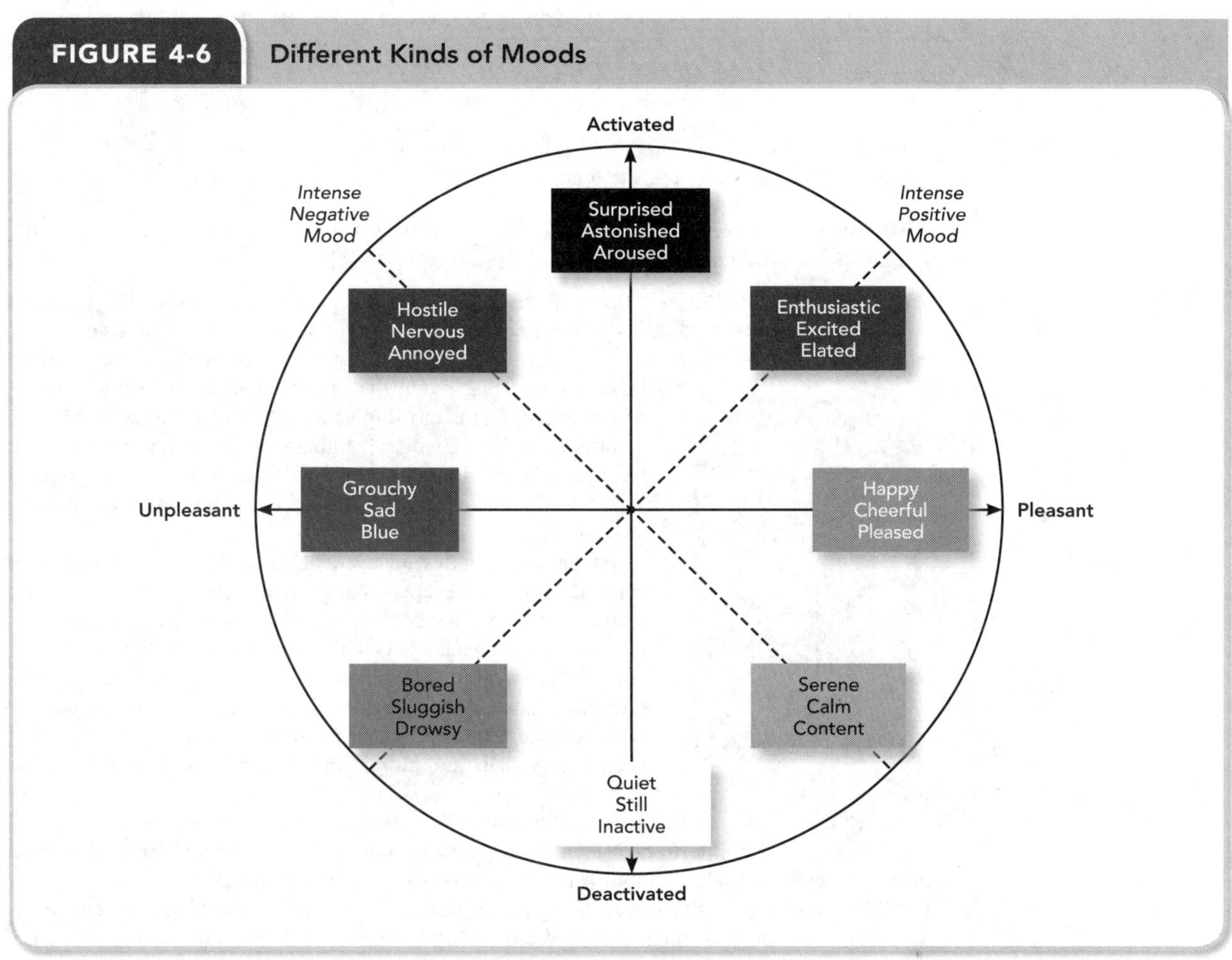

Sources: Adapted from D. Watson and A. Tellegen, "Toward a Consensual Structure of Mood," *Psychological Bulletin* 98 (1985), pp. 219–35; J.A. Russell, "A Circumplex Model of Affect," *Journal of Personality and Social Psychology* 39 (1980), pp. 1161–78; and R.J. Larsen and E. Diener, "Promises and Problems with the Circumplex Model of Emotion," in *Review of Personality and Social Psychology: Emotion,* Vol. 13, ed. M.S. Clark (Newbury Park, CA: Sage, 1992), pp. 25–59.

unpleasant (in a "bad mood"). The figure uses green colors to illustrate pleasant moods and red colors to illustrate unpleasant moods. Second, the vertical axis of the figure reflects whether you feel activated and aroused or deactivated and unaroused. The figure uses darker colors to convey higher levels of activation and lighter colors to convey lower levels. Note that some moods are neither good nor bad. For example, being surprised or astonished (high activation) and quiet or still (low activation) are neither pleasant nor unpleasant. As a result, those latter moods are left colorless in Figure 4-6.

Figure 4-6 illustrates that the most intense positive mood is characterized by feeling enthusiastic, excited, and elated. When employees feel this way, coworkers are likely to remark, "Wow, you're sure in a good mood!" In contrast, the most intense negative mood is characterized by feeling hostile, nervous, and annoyed. This kind of mood often triggers the question, "Wow, what's gotten you in such a bad mood?" If we return to our chart of hour-by-hour job satisfaction in Figure 4-5, what kind of mood do you think the employee was in while answering e-mails? Probably a happy, cheerful, and pleased mood. What kind of mood was the employee in during the informal meeting on the long-running project? Probably a grouchy, sad, and blue mood. Finally, what kind of mood do you think the employee was in during the brainstorming meeting for the new project? Clearly, an enthusiastic, excited, and elated mood. This employee would report especially high levels of job satisfaction at this point in time. For a look at some of the other feelings that can be found in the world of work, see our **OB at the Bookstore** feature.

OB AT THE BOOKSTORE

THE PLEASURES AND SORROWS OF WORK

by Alain de Botton (New York: Pantheon Books, 2009).

All societies have had work at their centre; ours is the first to suggest that it could be something much more than a punishment or a penance.

With those words, de Botton reflects on the inspiration for his book, meant to be "a hymn to the intelligence, peculiarity, beauty and horror of the modern workplace and not least, its extraordinary claim to be able to provide us, alongside love, with the principal source of life's meaning." He composed that hymn over two years by observing a variety of jobs, including cargo ship spotter, biscuit manufacturer, career counselor, rocket scientist, painter, accountant, and entrepreneur. He had a photo journalist in tow, with many images evoking some of the same emotional chords that de Botton strikes with his analysis.

As the title implies, many of those chords are unpleasant. In contrast to the shopkeepers, builders, farmers, and cooks typically featured in children's books, de Botton notes that contemporary jobs are often specialized, with anonymous and intangible outcomes. Indeed, jobs are sometimes so specific that no one quite understands what everyone else does! Moreover, when work is completed, the result is often intangible, fading into oblivion in such a way that the "glory" and "legacy" of previous eras are sacrificed.

Never quite rising to the level of "pleasures," de Botton's other observations about work revolve around its ability to help us mark time during our lives. He writes, "The start of work means the end to freedom, but also to doubt, intensity and wayward desires . . . ten thousand possibilities have been reduced to an agreeable handful." Fortunately for them, the subjects of de Botton's writings are often able to see meaning where he, as an outside observer, does not. Consider Emily Wan, an accountant in London. She likens the audit process to a piece of carpentry, while pointing out that "capitalism could not function without her." Or consider the biscuit branding expert, who notes that his decisions about width, shape, coating, and packaging can give a biscuit "a personality as subtly and appropriately nuanced as that of a protagonist in a great novel."

Some organizations take creative steps to foster positive moods among their employees. For example, Quicken Loans, the Detroit–based online lender, provides Razor scooters to help team members go from place to place inside their headquarters. Many of those places are adorned with scratch-and-sniff wallpaper and graffiti created by local artists. Or consider these offerings by Booz Allen Hamilton, the McLean, Virginia–based consulting firm. Employees can participate in ice cream socials, pet photo contests, and hula lessons. Such perks may not rival the importance of pay, promotions, supervision, coworkers, and the work itself as far as job satisfaction is concerned, but they can help boost employees' moods during a particular workday.

Although novel and unusual perks can be valuable, the most intense forms of positive mood often come directly from work activities, like the brainstorming project in Figure 4-5. Research suggests that two conditions are critical to triggering intense positive mood. First, the activity in question has to be challenging. Second, the employee must possess the unique skills needed to meet that challenge. That high challenge–high skill combination can result in **flow**—a state in which employees feel a total immersion in the task at hand, sometimes losing track of how much time has passed. People often describe flow as being "in the zone" and report heightened states of clarity, control, and concentration, along with a sense of enjoyment, interest, and loss

心流是员工感到完全沉浸于当前任务中的一种状态。

of self-consciousness. Although you may have experienced flow during leisure activities, such as playing sports or making music, research suggests that we experience flow more often in our working lives. Much of our leisure time is spent in passive recreation, such as watching TV or chatting with friends, that lacks the challenge needed to trigger flow states. Work tasks, in contrast, may supply the sorts of challenges that require concentration and immersion—particularly when those tasks contain high levels of variety, significance, autonomy, and so forth (see Chapter 6 on Motivation for more discussion of such issues).

Returning to Figure 4-5, it's clear that specific events triggered variations in satisfaction levels. According to **affective events theory,** workplace events can generate affective reactions—reactions that then can go on to influence work attitudes and behaviors. Workplace events include happenings, like an annoying e-mail from a boss or a funny conversation with a friend, that are relevant to an employee's general desires and concerns. These events can trigger **emotions,** which are states of feeling that are often intense, last for only a few minutes, and are clearly directed at (and caused by) someone or some circumstance. The difference between moods and emotions becomes clear in the way we describe them to others. We describe moods by saying, "I'm feeling grouchy," but we describe emotions by saying, "I'm feeling angry *at my boss.*" According to affective events theory, these emotions can create the ebb and flow in satisfaction levels in Figure 4-5 and can also trigger spontaneous behaviors. For example, positive emotions may trigger spontaneous instances of citizenship behavior, whereas negative emotions may trigger spontaneous instances of counterproductive behavior.

As with mood, it's possible to differentiate between specific examples of positive and negative emotions. Table 4-2 provides a summary of many of the most important. **Positive emotions** include joy, pride, relief, hope, love, and compassion. **Negative emotions** include anger,

根据**情感事件理论**，工作场所的事件能够产生情感反应——这种反应能持续影响工作态度与行为。

情绪是指强烈的、持续几分钟并有明确指向或由某人或某种环境引发的感觉状态。

积极情绪包括快乐、自豪、安心、希望、爱与同情。

消极情绪包括生气、焦虑、害怕、羞愧、悲伤、嫉妒及厌恶。

TABLE 4-2 Different Kinds of Emotions

POSITIVE EMOTIONS	DESCRIPTION
Joy	A feeling of great pleasure
Pride	Enhancement of identity by taking credit for achievement
Relief	A distressing condition has changed for the better
Hope	Fearing the worst but wanting better
Love	Desiring or participating in affection
Compassion	Being moved by another's situation
NEGATIVE EMOTIONS	
Anger	A demeaning offense against me and mine
Anxiety	Facing an uncertain or vague threat
Fear	Facing an immediate and concrete danger
Guilt	Having broken a moral code
Shame	Failing to live up to your ideal self
Sadness	Having experienced an irreversible loss
Envy	Wanting what someone else has
Disgust	Revulsion aroused by something offensive

Source: Adapted from R.S. Lazarus, *Emotion and Adaptation* (New York: Oxford University, 1991).

anxiety, fear, guilt, shame, sadness, envy, and disgust. What emotion do you think the employee experienced in Figure 4-5 when reading a disrespectful e-mail from the boss? Probably anger. What emotion do you think that same employee enjoyed during a funny conversation with a friend? Possibly joy, or maybe relief that lunch had arrived and a somewhat bad day was halfway over. Leaving lunch to return to work might have triggered either anxiety (because the bad day might resume) or sadness (because the fun time with friends had ended). Luckily, the employee's sense of joy at taking on a new project that was interesting and challenging was right around the corner. The day did end on a down note, however, as the phone call signaling overdue paperwork was likely met with some mix of anger, fear, guilt, or even disgust (no one likes paperwork!).

情绪劳动是指需要管理情绪才能成功完成工作任务。

Of course, just because employees *feel* many of the emotions in Table 4-2 during the workday doesn't mean they're supposed to *show* those emotions. Some jobs demand that employees live up to the adage "never let 'em see you sweat." In particular, service jobs in which employees make direct contact with customers often require those employees to hide any anger, anxiety, sadness, or disgust that they may feel, suppressing the urge to spontaneously engage in some negative behavior. Such jobs are high in what's called **emotional labor,** or the need to manage emotions to complete job duties successfully. Flight attendants are trained to "put on a happy face" in front of passengers, retail salespeople are trained to suppress any annoyance with customers, and restaurant servers are trained to act like they're having fun on their job even when they're not.

情绪传染是指一个人可能受另一个人的情绪影响或"传染"。

Is it a good idea to require emotional labor on the part of employees? Research on **emotional contagion** shows that one person can "catch" or "be infected by" the emotions of another person. If a customer service representative is angry or sad, those negative emotions can be transferred to a customer (like a cold or disease). If that transfer occurs, it becomes less likely that customers will view the experience favorably and spend money, which potentially harms the bottom line. From this perspective, emotional labor seems like a vital part of good customer service. Unfortunately, other evidence suggests that emotional labor places great strain on employees and that their "bottled up" emotions may end up bubbling over, sometimes resulting in angry outbursts against customers or emotional exhaustion and burnout on the part of employees (see Chapter 5 on Stress for more discussion of such issues).

总结：为什么某些员工比其他员工更满意
SUMMARY: WHY ARE SOME EMPLOYEES MORE SATISFIED THAN OTHERS?

So what explains why some employees are more satisfied than others? As we show in Figure 4-7, answering that question requires paying attention to the more rational appraisals people make about their job and the things it supplies for them, such as pay, promotions, supervision, coworkers, and the work itself. Satisfaction with the work itself, in turn, is affected by the five core job characteristics: variety, identity, significance, autonomy, and feedback. However, answering that question also requires paying attention to daily fluctuations in how people feel, in terms of their positive and negative moods and positive and negative emotions. In this way, a generally satisfied employee may act unhappy at a given moment, just as a generally dissatisfied employee may act happy at a given moment. Understanding those sorts of fluctuations can help managers separate long-term problems (boring tasks, incompetent coworkers) from more short-lived issues (a bad meeting, an annoying interaction).

工作满意度有多重要
HOW IMPORTANT IS JOB SATISFACTION?

Several factors influence an employee's job satisfaction, from pay to coworkers to job tasks to day-to-day moods and emotions. Of course, the most obvious remaining question is, "Does job satisfaction really matter?" More precisely, does job satisfaction have a significant impact on job performance and organizational commitment—the two primary outcomes in our integrative model of OB? Figure 4-8 summarizes the research evidence linking job satisfaction to job performance and organizational commitment. This same sort of figure will appear in each of the

FIGURE 4-7 Why Are Some Employees More Satisfied Than Others?

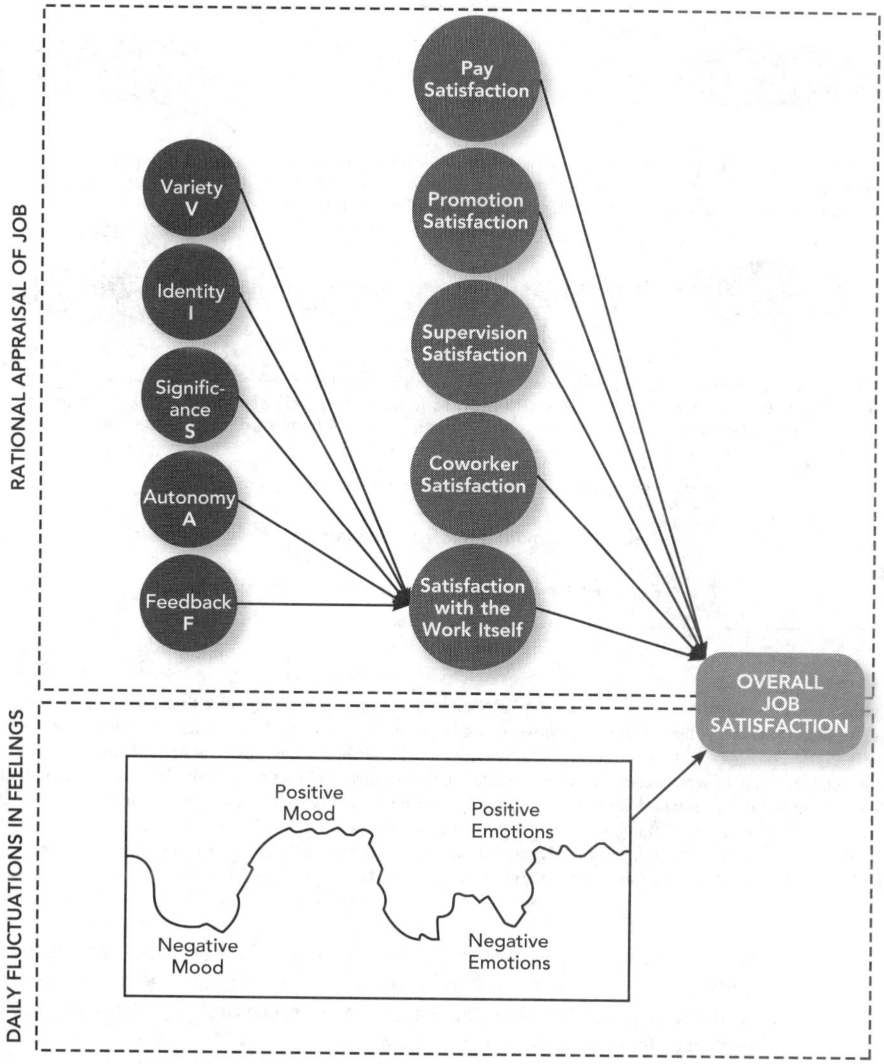

remaining chapters of this book, so that you can get a better feel for which of the concepts in our integrative model has the strongest impact on performance and commitment.

Figure 4-8 reveals that job satisfaction does predict job performance. Why? One reason is that job satisfaction is moderately correlated with task performance. Satisfied employees do a better job of fulfilling the duties described in their job descriptions, and evidence suggests that positive feelings foster creativity, improve problem solving and decision making, and enhance memory and recall of certain kinds of information. Positive feelings also improve task persistence and attract more help and support from colleagues. Apart from these sorts of findings, the benefits of job satisfaction for task performance might best be explained on an hour-by-hour basis. At any given moment, employees wage a war between paying attention to a given work task and attending to "off-task" things, such as stray thoughts, distractions, interruptions, and so forth. Positive feelings when working on job tasks can pull attention away from those distractions and channel people's attention to task accomplishment. When such concentration

4.7

How does job satisfaction affect job performance and organizational commitment? How does it affect life satisfaction?

FIGURE 4-8 Effects of Job Satisfaction on Performance and Commitment

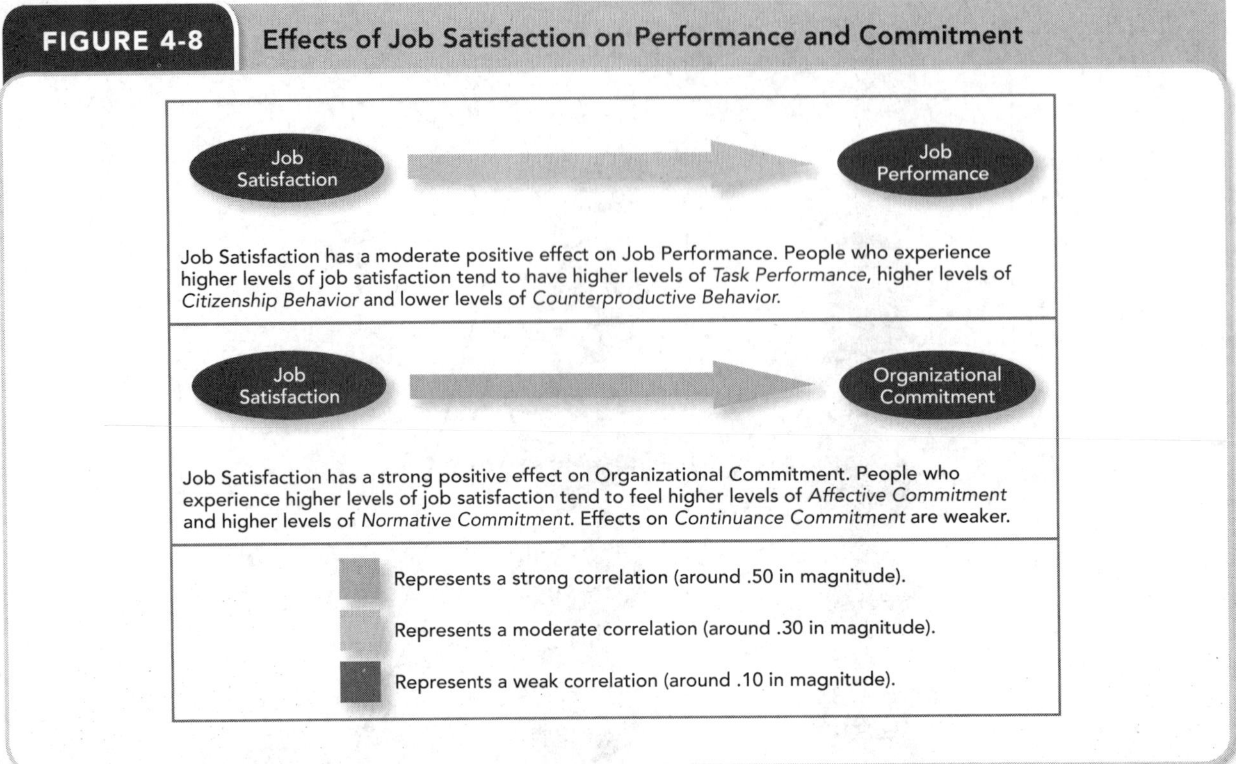

Sources: A. Cooper-Hakim and C. Viswesvaran, "The Construct of Work Commitment: Testing an Integrative Framework," *Psychological Bulletin* 131 (2005), pp. 241–59; R.S. Dalal, "A Meta-Analysis of the Relationship between Organizational Citizenship Behavior and Counterproductive Work Behavior," *Journal of Applied Psychology* 90 (2005), pp. 1241–55; D.A. Harrison, D.A. Newman, and P.L. Roth, "How Important Are Job Attitudes? Meta-Analytic Comparisons of Integrative Behavioral Outcomes and Time Sequences," *Academy of Management Journal* 49 (2006), pp. 305–25; T.A. Judge, C.J. Thoreson, J.E. Bono, and G.K. Patton, "The Job Satisfaction–Job Performance Relationship: A Qualitative and Quantitative Review," *Psychological Bulletin* 127 (2001), pp. 376–407; J.A. LePine, A. Erez, and D.E. Johnson, "The Nature and Dimensionality of Organizational Citizenship Behavior: A Critical Review and Meta-Analysis," *Journal of Applied Psychology* 87 (2002), pp. 52–65; and J.P. Meyer, D.J. Stanley, L. Herscovitch, and L. Topolnytsky, "Affective, Continuance, and Normative Commitment to the Organization: A Meta-Analysis of Antecedents, Correlates, and Consequences," *Journal of Vocational Behavior* 61 (2002), pp. 20–52.

occurs, an employee is more focused on work at a given point in time. Of course, the relationship between satisfaction and task performance can work in reverse to some extent, such that people tend to enjoy jobs that they can perform more successfully. Meta-analyses tend to be less supportive of this causal direction, however.

Job satisfaction also is correlated moderately with citizenship behavior. Satisfied employees engage in more frequent "extra mile" behaviors to help their coworkers and their organization. Positive feelings increase their desire to interact with others and often result in spontaneous acts of helping and other instances of good citizenship. In addition, job satisfaction has a moderate negative correlation with counterproductive behavior. Satisfied employees engage in fewer intentionally destructive actions that could harm their workplace. Events that trigger negative emotions can prompts employees to "lash out" against the organization by engaging in rule breaking, theft, sabotage, or other retaliatory behaviors. The more satisfied employees are, the less likely they'll feel those sorts of temptations.

Figure 4-8 also reveals that job satisfaction influences organizational commitment. Why? Job satisfaction is strongly correlated with affective commitment, so satisfied employees are more likely to want to stay with the organization. After all, why would employees want to leave a place where they're happy? Another reason is that job satisfaction is strongly correlated with normative commitment. Satisfied employees are more likely to feel an obligation to remain with their firm and a need to "repay" the organization for whatever it is that makes them so satisfied, whether good pay, interesting job tasks, or effective supervision. However, job satisfaction is uncorrelated with continuance commitment, because satisfaction does not create a cost-based need to remain with the organization. Taken together, these commitment effects become more apparent when you consider the kinds of employees who withdraw from the organization. In many cases, dissatisfied employees are the ones who sit daydreaming at their desks, come in late, are frequently absent, and eventually decide to quit their jobs.

生活满意度
LIFE SATISFACTION

Of course, job satisfaction is important for other reasons as well—reasons that have little to do with job performance or organizational commitment. For example, job satisfaction is strongly related to **life satisfaction,** or the degree to which employees feel a sense of happiness with their lives. Research shows that job satisfaction is one of the strongest predictors of life satisfaction. Put simply, people feel better about their lives when they feel better about their jobs. This link makes sense when you realize how much of our identity is wrapped up in our jobs. What's the first question that people ask one another after being introduced? That's right—"What do you do?" If you feel bad about your answer to that question, it's hard to feel good about your life. As our **OB on Screen** feature illustrates, that adage is even true for George Clooney!

"Researchers say I'm not happier for being richer, but do you know how much researchers make?"

Source: © Pat Byrnes, The New Yorker Collection, www.cartoonbank.com

The connection between job satisfaction and life satisfaction also makes sense given how much of our lives are spent at work. Table 4-3 presents the results of one study that examines time spent on daily activities, along with reported levels of positive and negative feelings during the course of those activities. The participants in the study spent most

生活满意度是指员工对生活感到幸福的程度。

TABLE 4-3 How We Spend Our Days

ACTIVITY	AVERAGE HOURS PER DAY	POSITIVE FEELINGS	NEGATIVE FEELINGS
Working	6.9	3.62	0.97
On the phone	2.5	3.92	0.85
Socializing	2.3	4.59	0.57
Eating	2.2	4.34	0.59
Relaxing	2.2	4.42	0.51
Watching TV	2.2	4.19	0.58
Computer/e-mail/Internet	1.9	3.81	0.80
Commuting	1.6	3.45	0.89
Housework	1.1	3.73	0.77
Interacting with kids	1.1	3.86	0.91
Napping	0.9	3.87	0.60
Praying/meditating	0.4	4.35	0.59
Exercising	0.2	4.31	0.50
Intimate relations	0.2	5.10	0.36

Notes: Positive and negative feelings measured using a scale of 0 (not at all) to 6 (very much).

Source: From D. Kahneman, A.B. Krueger, D.A. Schkade, N. Schwarz, and A.A. Stone, "A Survey Method for Characterizing Daily Life Experience: The Day Reconstruction Method," *Science* 306 (2004), pp. 1776–80. Reprinted with permission from AAAS.

OB ON SCREEN

MICHAEL CLAYTON

There's no play here . . . there's no angle . . . I'm not a miracle worker, I'm a janitor.

With those words, Michael Clayton (George Clooney) reveals what he thinks of his job (Dir.: Tony Gilroy, Warner Brothers, 2007). He's an attorney working for one of the largest firms in the world—Kenner, Bach, and Ledeen. His job gets him a nice car and a nice suit but unfortunately not a nice life. You see, Clayton is the firm's "fixer"—the guy who uses his contacts and street smarts to solve messy situations. One night he's flying to Milwaukee to babysit an attorney who's had a breakdown. The next night he's driving to upstate New York to help a client who has committed a hit and run.

It's difficult to find much significance in Clayton's job. Fixing the situations that demand his attention may help his firm, but they have no benefit for society in general. He also lacks autonomy, constantly waiting for his cell phone to ring to send him on his next excursion. Moreover, those excursions don't tend to provide positive affective events. Listening to a client weasel out of a hit-and-run situation triggers feelings of shame and disgust, not joy or pride. It's not even clear that Kenner, Bach appreciates his efforts, because he's still not a partner, even after 17 years. Why not? Because as one of his colleagues points out, "Michael . . . you're a bag man, not an attorney."

All of this perspective hits home for Clayton as he's driving back from the hit-and-run meeting. He sees three horses, standing still on a misty hill, next to the road at sunrise. He stops his car, gets out, and slowly walks toward them, entranced—as if the horses represent all the honor and childhood innocence that he's lost in his life. The moment is surreal and haunting—made all the more so when his car explodes in a ball of flame.

of their day at work. Unfortunately, that time resulted in the highest levels of negative feelings and the second-lowest levels of positive feelings (behind only commuting). Home and leisure activities (e.g., socializing, relaxing, exercising, intimate relations) were deemed much more satisfying but took up a much smaller portion of the day. The implication is clear: If we want to feel better about our days, we need to find a way to be more satisfied with our jobs.

Indeed, increases in job satisfaction have a stronger impact on life satisfaction than do increases in salary or income. As the old adage goes, "money can't buy happiness." This finding may seem surprising, given that pay satisfaction is one facet of overall job satisfaction (see Figure 4-1). However, you might recall that pay satisfaction is a weaker driver of overall job satisfaction than other facets, such as the work itself, supervision, or coworkers (see Figure 4-2). We should also note that pay satisfaction depends less on absolute salary levels and more on relative salary levels (i.e., how your salary compares to your circle of peers). As the writer H.L. Mencken once remarked, "A wealthy man is one who earns $100 a year more than his wife's sister's husband." For more on the relationship between money and happiness, see our **OB Internationally** feature.

OB INTERNATIONALLY

The "money can't buy happiness" adage can even be supported using nation-level data. For example, survey data in the United States, Britain, and Japan show that people are no happier today than they were 50 years ago, even though average incomes have more than doubled during that span. Another way of examining this issue explores the connection between national wealth and average happiness: Do wealthier nations have citizens with higher levels of life satisfaction? The figure below provides a representation of the relationship between average income per citizen for a nation and the percentage of respondents who describe themselves as happy, according to population surveys.

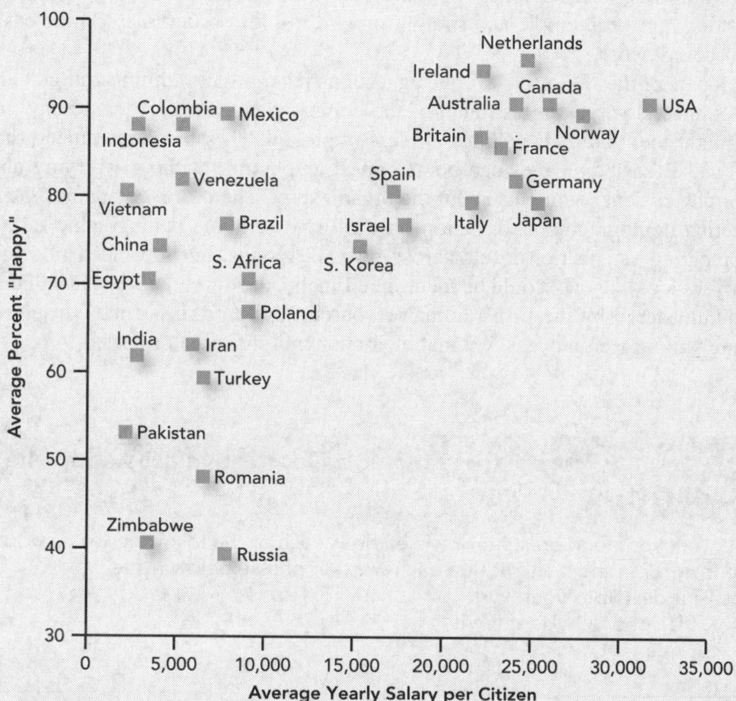

Comparing countries reveals that nations above the poverty line are indeed happier than nations below the poverty line. However, for countries with an average income of $20,000 or more, additional income is not associated with higher levels of life satisfaction. For example, the United States is the richest country on earth, but it trails nations like the Netherlands and Ireland in life satisfaction. Understanding differences in life satisfaction across nations is important to organizations for two reasons. First, such differences may influence how receptive a given nation is to the company's products. Second, such differences may affect the kinds of policies and practices an organization needs to use when employing individuals in that nation.

应用：监测满意度

APPLICATION: TRACKING SATISFACTION

Because job satisfaction seems to be a key driver of job performance, organizational commitment, and life satisfaction, it's important for managers to understand just how satisfied their employees are. Several methods assess the job satisfaction of rank-and-file employees, including focus groups, interviews, and attitude surveys. Of those three choices, attitude surveys are often

4.8

What steps can organizations take to assess and manage job satisfaction?

the most accurate and most effective. Attitude surveys can provide a "snapshot" of how satisfied the workforce is and, if repeated over time, reveal trends in satisfaction levels. They also can explore the effectiveness of major job changes by comparing attitude survey results before and after a change.

Although organizations are often tempted to design their own attitude surveys, there are benefits to using existing surveys that are already in wide use. One of the most widely administered job satisfaction surveys is the Job Descriptive Index (JDI). The JDI assesses all five satisfaction facets in Figure 4-1: pay satisfaction, promotion satisfaction, supervisor satisfaction, coworker satisfaction, and satisfaction with the work itself. The JDI also has been subjected to a great deal of research attention that, by and large, supports its accuracy. Furthermore, the JDI includes a companion survey—the Job in General (JIG) scale—that assesses overall job satisfaction. Excerpts from the JDI and JIG appear in Table 4-4. One strength of the JDI is that the questions are written in a very simple and straightforward fashion so that they can be easily understood by most employees.

The developers of the JDI offer several suggestions regarding its administration. For example, they recommend surveying as much of the company as possible because any unsurveyed employees might feel that their feelings are less important. They also recommend that surveys be anonymous so that employees can be as honest as possible without worrying about being punished for any critical comments about the organization. Therefore, companies must be careful in collecting demographic information on the surveys. Some demographic information is vital for comparing satisfaction levels across relevant groups, but too much information will make employees feel like they could be identified. Finally, the developers suggest that the survey should be administered by the firm's human resources group or an outside consulting agency. This structure will help employees feel that their anonymity is more protected.

TABLE 4-4 Excerpts from the Job Descriptive Index and the Job in General Scale

Think of the work you do at present. How well does each of the following words or phrases describe your work? In the blank beside each word or phrase below, write
Y for "Yes" if it describes your work
N for "No" if it does NOT describe it
? for "?" if you cannot decide

Pay Satisfaction[a] ____ Well-paid ____ Bad ____ Barely live on income	**Coworker Satisfaction**[a] ____ Stimulating ____ Smart ____ Unpleasant
Promotion Satisfaction[a] ____ Regular promotions ____ Promotion on ability ____ Opportunities somewhat limited	**Satisfaction with Work Itself**[a] ____ Fascinating ____ Pleasant ____ Can see my results
Supervision Satisfaction[a] ____ Knows job well ____ Around when needed ____ Doesn't supervise enough	**OVERALL JOB SATISFACTION**[b] ____ Better than most ____ Worthwhile ____ Worse than most

[a] The Job Descriptive Index, © Bowling Green State University (1975, 1985, 1997).
[b] The Job in General Scale, © Bowling Green State University (1982, 1985).
Source: W.K. Balzer, J.A. Kihn, P.C. Smith, J.L. Irwin, P.D. Bachiochi, C. Robie, E.F. Sinar, & L.F. Parra, 2000, "Users' Manual for the Job Descriptive Index (JDI; 1997 version) and the Job in General Scales." In J.N. Stanton & C.D. Crossley (eds.) *Electronic Resources for the JDI and JIG.* Bowling Green, OH, Bowling Green State University. Reprinted with permission.

Once JDI data have been collected, a number of interesting questions can be explored. First, the data can indicate whether the organization is satisfied or dissatisfied by comparing average scores for each facet with the JDI's "neutral levels" for those facets (the "neutral levels" are available in the JDI manual). Second, it becomes possible to compare the organization's scores with national norms to provide some context for the firm's satisfaction levels. The JDI manual also provides national norms for all facets and breaks down those norms according to relevant demographic groups (e.g., managers vs. nonmanagers, new vs. senior employees, gender, education). Third, the JDI allows for within-organization comparisons to determine which departments have the highest satisfaction levels and which have the lowest.

The results of attitude survey efforts should then be fed back to employees so that they feel involved in the process. Of course, attitude surveys ideally should be a catalyst for some kind of improvement effort. Surveys that never lead to any kind of on-the-job change eventually may be viewed as a waste of time. As a result, the organization should be prepared to react to the survey results with specific goals and action steps. For example, an organization with low pay satisfaction may react by conducting additional benchmarking to see whether compensation levels are trailing those of competitors. An organization with low promotion satisfaction might react by revising its system for assessing performance. Finally, an organization that struggles with satisfaction with the work itself could attempt to redesign key job tasks or, if that proves too costly, train supervisors in strategies for increasing the five core job characteristics on a more informal basis.

chapter 5

Stress

压力

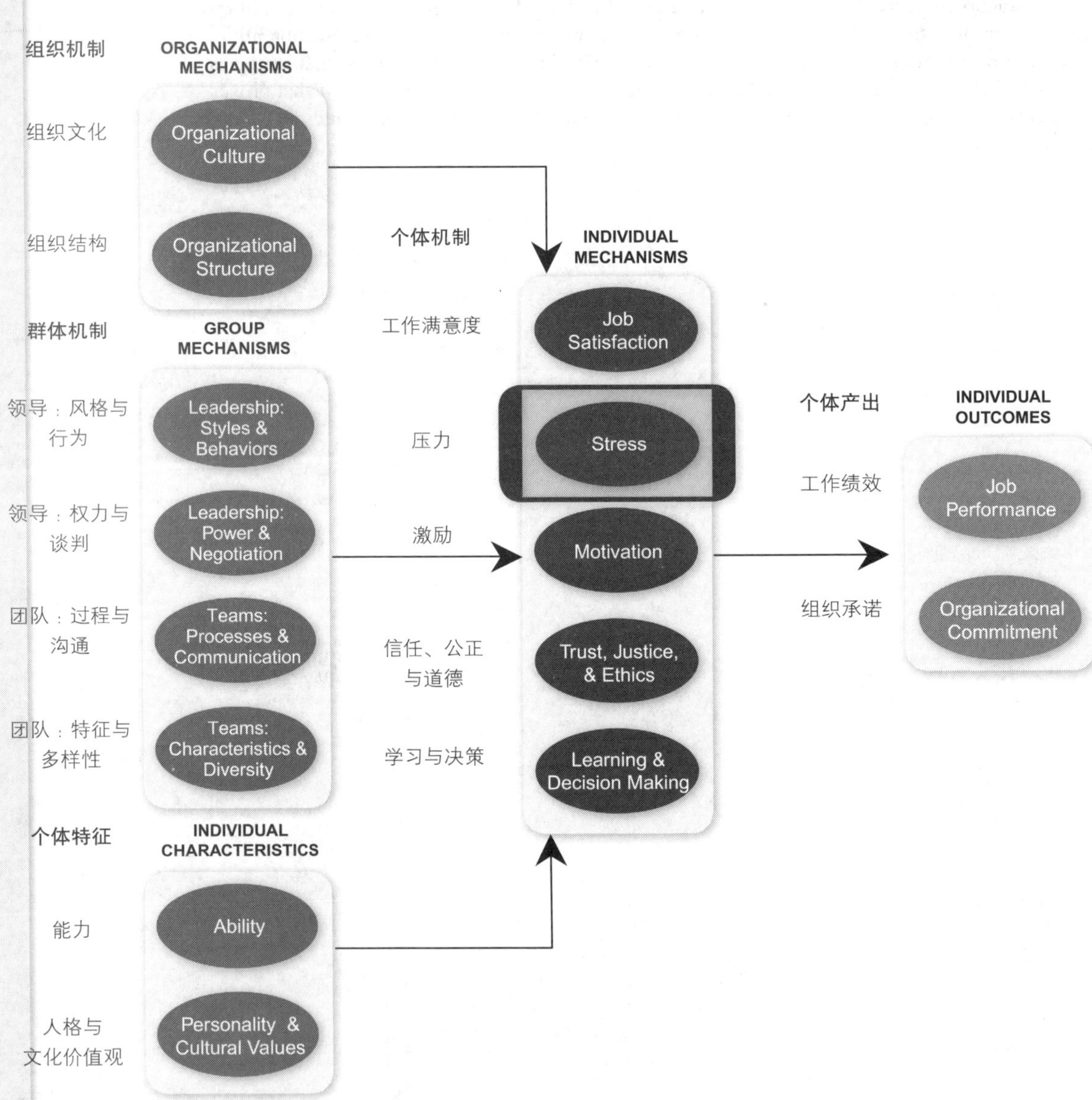

LEARNING GOALS

After reading this chapter, you should be able to answer the following questions:

5.1 What is stress, and how is it different than stressors and strains?

5.2 What are the four main types of stressors?

5.3 How do individuals cope with stress?

5.4 How does the Type A Behavior Pattern influence the stress process?

5.5 How does stress affect job performance and organizational commitment?

5.6 What steps can organizations take to manage employee stress?

GOOGLE

If you're like most people, chances are that it hasn't been more than a few hours since you've used Google to search for something on the web. In fact, in the United States each month, there are about 12 billion Google searches, a number that represents about 65 percent of all web searches conducted. Of course, you may also have used Google to e-mail (Gmail), collaborate (Google Docs), shop (Google Products), or see what something looks like from afar (Google Maps). Google has enjoyed remarkable financial success and growth since its inception in 1998, after cofounders Larry Page and Sergey Brin developed and patented the algorithm that made web searches efficient and user-friendly. Google's revenues, primarily from advertising, are nearly $30 billion, placing it among the top 100 or so companies in the United States, just ahead of household names such as McDonald's, 3M, and Time Warner.

If you picture your life as a Googler, chances are you'd have an image in mind that's quite positive. Google is highly innovative, and the nature of the work and work environment at the company create a sense of excitement for its employees. Of course, Google employees put in long hours and are under great stress to develop the innovations that lead to the new and improved products and services that we all enjoy. So how does Google help its employees cope with these stressful demands? Employees at Google headquarters and its other offices are treated to a variety of extraordinary perks that make life easier. For example, Google serves free gourmet food in cafés, allowing employees to work without having to worry about traveling off-site to eat. As another example, Google employees can take care of medical appointments, haircuts, laundry, and oil changes right at the office, so they don't have to figure out how to find the time to deal with these nonwork responsibilities. As a final example, Google offers perks that help employees cope with the demands of their work directly. For example, Google provides access to bikes so employees can travel quickly to meet team members in other buildings to collaborate on projects.

It shouldn't surprise you to learn that Google employees take great pleasure in these perks. In fact, *Fortune* magazine consistently ranks Google among the very best places in the United States to work. However, it's important to point out these perks are important to Google for reasons beyond just making life easier for their employees. By reducing the number of demands that employees have to deal with, employee stress levels are decreased, and this is important because stress is associated with a number of outcomes, such as fatigue, memory loss, and coronary heart disease, which ultimately decrease employee productivity and increase absenteeism and health care costs.

压 力

STRESS

Stress is an OB topic that's probably quite familiar to you. Even if you don't have a lot of work experience, consider how you feel toward the end of a semester when you have to cram for several final exams and finish a couple of term projects. At the same time, you might have also been looking for a job or planning a trip with friends or family. Although some people might be able to deal with all of these demands without becoming too frazzled, most people would say this type of scenario causes them to feel "stressed out." This stressed-out feeling might even be accompanied by headaches, stomach upsets, backaches, or sleeping difficulties. Although you might believe your stress will diminish once you graduate and settle down, high stress on the job is more prevalent than it's ever been before. The federal government's National Institute for Occupational Safety and Health (NIOSH) summarized findings from several sources that indicated up to 40 percent of U.S. workers feel their jobs are "very stressful" or "extremely stressful." Unfortunately, high stress is even more prevalent in the types of jobs that most of you are likely to have after you graduate. In fact, managers are approximately 21 percent more likely than the average worker to describe their jobs as stressful. Table 5-1 provides a list of jobs and their rank in terms of how stressful they are.

压力是指当个人面对特定利益的需求时所产生的心理反应，这种需求超过了个人的能力和资源。

5.1
What is stress, and how is it different than stressors and strains?

Stress is defined as a psychological response to demands that possess certain stakes for the person and that tax or exceed the person's capacity or resources. The demands that cause people to

TABLE 5-1 Jobs Rated from Least Stressful (1) to Most Stressful (250)

LEAST STRESSFUL JOBS	STRESS LEVEL	MOST STRESSFUL JOBS	STRESS LEVEL
1. Musical instrument repairer	18.77	212. Registered nurse	62.14
2. Florist	18.80	220. Attorney	64.33
4. Actuary	20.18	223. Newspaper reporter	65.26
6. Appliance repairer	21.12	226. Architect	66.92
8. Librarian	21.40	228. Lumberjack	67.60
10. File clerk	21.71	229. Fisherman	69.82
11. Piano tuner	22.29	230. Stockbroker	71.65
12. Janitor	22.44	231. U.S. Congressperson	72.05
16. Vending machine repairer	23.47	233. Real estate agent	73.06
18. Barber	23.62	234. Advertising account exec	74.55
24. Mathematician	24.67	238. Public relations exec	78.52
29. Cashier	25.11	240. Air traffic controller	83.13
30. Dishwasher	25.32	241. Airline pilot	85.35
32. Pharmacist	25.87	243. Police officer	93.89
40. Biologist	26.94	244. Astronaut	99.34
44. Computer programmer	27.00	245. Surgeon	99.46
50. Astronomer	28.06	246. Taxi driver	100.49
56. Historian	28.41	248. Senior corporate exec	108.62
67. Bank teller	30.12	249. Firefighter	110.93
78. Accountant	31.13	250. U.S. President	176.55

Source: Adapted from L. Krantz, *Jobs Rated Almanac*, 6th ed. (Fort Lee, NJ: Barricade Books, Inc., 2002). The stress level score is calculated by summing points in 21 categories, including deadlines, competitiveness, environmental conditions, speed required, precision required, initiative required, physical demands, and hazards encountered.

experience stress are called **stressors**. The negative consequences that occur when demands tax or exceed a person's capacity or resources are called **strains**. This definition of stress illustrates that it depends on both the nature of the demand and the person who confronts it. People differ in terms of how they perceive and evaluate stressors and the way they cope with them. As a result, different people may experience different levels of stress even when confronted with the exact same situation.

压力源是指那些导致人们承受压力的需求。

紧张是指个人需求超出个人的能力或资源所产生的负面结果。

为什么某些员工比其他员工压力更大

WHY ARE SOME EMPLOYEES MORE "STRESSED" THAN OTHERS?

压力的交易理论解释了压力源是如何被感知与评估以及人们如何对这些感知与评估做出反应的。

To fully understand what it means to feel "stressed," it's helpful to consider the **transactional theory of stress**. This theory explains how stressors are perceived and appraised, as well as how people respond to those perceptions and appraisals. When people first encounter stressors, the

FIGURE 5-1 Transactional Theory of Stress

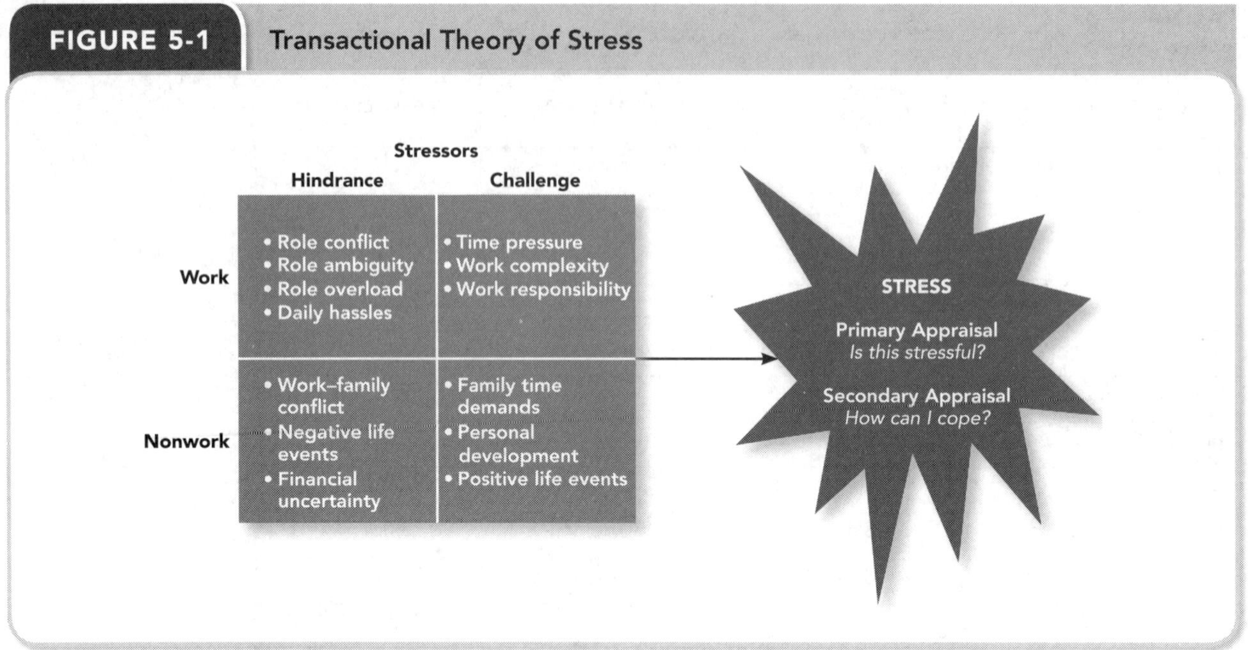

当人们首次遇到压力源时，**初级评估**过程就开始了。

process of **primary appraisal** is triggered. As shown in Figure 5-1, primary appraisal occurs as people evaluate the significance and the meaning of the stressor they're confronting. Here, people first consider whether a demand causes them to feel stressed, and if it does, they consider the implications of the stressor in terms of their personal goals and overall well-being.

As an example of a primary appraisal, consider the job of a cashier at a well-run convenience store. In this store, cashiers engage in routine sales transactions with customers. Customers walk in the store and select merchandise, and the cashiers on duty ring up the sale and collect the money. Under normal day-to-day circumstances at this store, well-trained cashiers would not likely feel that these transactions are overly taxing or exceed their capacity, so those cashiers would not likely appraise these job demands as stressful. Job demands that tend not to be appraised as stressful are called **benign job demands**.

良性工作需求是指那些没有被评估为压力的工作需求。

However, consider how convenience store cashiers would react in a different store in which the cash register and credit card machine break down often and without warning. The cashiers who work at this store would likely view their job as being more stressful. This is because they would have to diagnose and fix problems with equipment while dealing with customers who are growing more and more impatient. Furthermore, the cashiers in this store might appraise the stressful situation as one that unnecessarily prevents them from achieving their goal of being viewed as an effective employee in the eyes of the customers and the store manager.

Finally, consider a third convenience store in which the cashiers' workload is higher due to additional responsibilities that include receiving merchandise from vendors, taking physical inventory, and training new employees. In this store, the cashiers may appraise their jobs as stressful because of the higher workload and the need to balance different priorities. However, in contrast to the cashiers in the previous example, cashiers in this store might appraise these demands as providing an opportunity to learn and demonstrate the type of competence that often is rewarded with satisfying promotions and pay raises.

 5.2

What are the four main types of stressors?

压力源的类型
TYPES OF STRESSORS

In the previous two examples, the cashiers were confronted with demands that a primary appraisal would label as "stressful." However, the specific demands in the two examples have an important difference. Having to deal with equipment breakdowns or unhappy customers is not likely to be perceived by most employees as having implications that are personally beneficial;

in fact, the opposite is likely to be true. These kinds of stressors are called **hindrance stressors**, or stressful demands that people tend to perceive as hindering their progress toward personal accomplishments or goal attainment. Hindrance stressors most often trigger negative emotions such as anxiety and anger.

阻碍性压力源是指人们认为会阻碍个人成功或目标实现的压力需求。

In contrast, having to deal with additional responsibilities is likely to be perceived by most employees as having long-term benefits. These kinds of stressors are called **challenge stressors**, or stressful demands that people tend to perceive as opportunities for learning, growth, and achievement. Although challenge stressors can be exhausting, they often trigger positive emotions such as pride and enthusiasm. Figure 5-1 lists a number of hindrance and challenge stressors, some of which are experienced at work and some of which are experienced outside of work.

挑战性压力源是指人们认为会有利于个人学习、成长及成就的压力需求。

WORK HINDRANCE STRESSORS. The various roles we fill at work are the source of different types of work-related hindrance stressors. One type of work-related hindrance stressor is **role conflict**, which refers to conflicting expectations that other people may have of us. As an example of role conflict that occurs from incompatible demands within a single role that a person may hold, consider the job of a call center operator. People holding these jobs are expected to communicate with as many people as possible over a given time period. The expectation is that the call center operator will spend as little time as possible with the people on the other end of the line. At the same time, however, operators are also expected to be responsive to the questions and concerns raised by the people they talk with. Because effectiveness in this aspect of the job may require a great deal of time, call center operators are put in a position in which they simply cannot meet both types of expectations.

角色冲突是指他人对我们的冲突性期望。

Role ambiguity refers to a lack of information about what needs to be done in a role, as well as unpredictability regarding the consequences of performance in that role. Employees are sometimes asked to work on projects for which they're given very few instructions or guidelines about how things are supposed to be done. In these cases, employees may not know how much money they can spend on the project, how long it's supposed to take, or what exactly the finished product is supposed to look like. Role ambiguity is often experienced among new employees who haven't been around long enough to receive instructions from supervisors or observe and model the role behaviors of more senior colleagues. Students sometimes experience role ambiguity when professors remain vague about particular course requirements or how grading is going to be performed. In such cases, the class becomes stressful because it's not quite clear what it takes to get a good grade.

角色模糊是指员工在工作角色需求与绩效结果的不可预测性两方面缺乏信息。

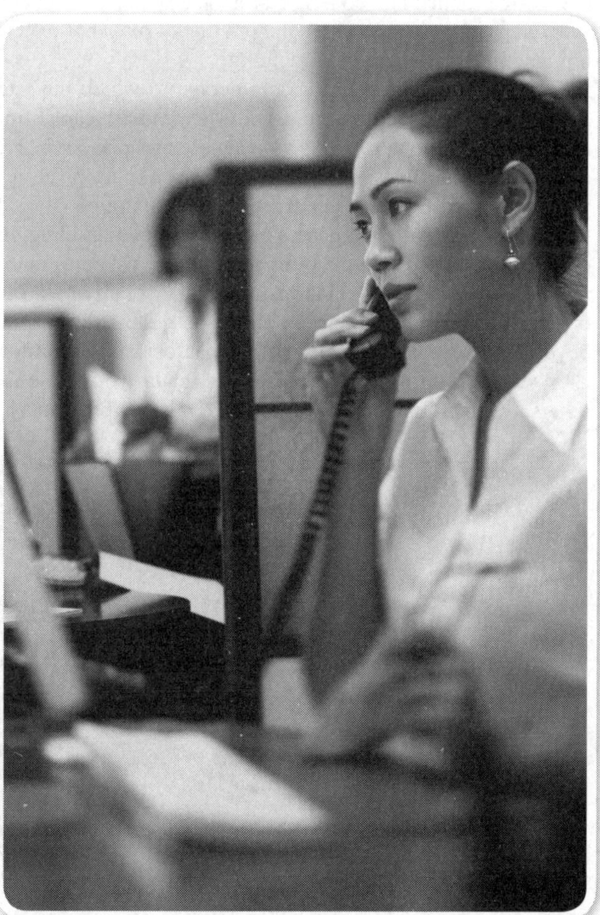

Call center operators experience role conflict. On the one hand, they need to be polite and responsive to the people with whom they're speaking. On the other hand, they need to spend as little time as possible on each call.

Role overload occurs when the number of demanding roles a person holds is so high that the person simply cannot perform some or all of the roles

当一个人承担的角色数量过多，以至于这个人根本不能有效履行某些或所有的角色时，就发生了**角色超载**。

effectively. Role overload as a source of stress is becoming very prevalent for employees in many different industries, and in fact, studies have shown that this source of stress is more prevalent than both role conflict and role ambiguity. For example, the workload for executives and managers who work in investment banking, consulting, and law is so high that 80-hour workweeks are becoming the norm. Although this trend may not be surprising to some of you, people holding these jobs also indicate that they would not be able to effectively complete most of the work that's required of them, even if they worked twice as many hours.

日常干扰是指相对微小的日常需求阻碍我们完成真正想要完成的事情。

One final type of work-related hindrance stressor, **daily hassles**, refers to the relatively minor day-to-day demands that get in the way of accomplishing the things that we really want to accomplish. Examples of hassles include having to deal with unnecessary paperwork, office equipment malfunctions, annoying interactions with abrasive coworkers, and useless communications. Although these examples of daily hassles may seem relatively minor, taken together, they can be extremely time consuming and stressful. Indeed, according to one survey, 40 percent of executives spend somewhere between a half-day and a full day each week on communications that are not useful or necessary. For a clear example of a job filled with hassles and other types of hindrance stressors, see our **OB on Screen** feature.

时间压力是指没有足够时间来完成工作的强烈感受。

WORK CHALLENGE STRESSORS. One type of work-related challenge stressor is **time pressure**—a strong sense that the amount of time you have to do a task is just not quite enough. Although most people appraise situations with high time pressure as rather stressful, they also tend to appraise these situations as more challenging than hindering. Time pressure demands tend to be viewed as something worth striving for because success in meeting such demands can be intrinsically satisfying. As an example of this positive effect of high time pressure, consider Michael Jones, an architect at a top New York firm. His job involves overseeing multiple projects with tight deadlines, and as a result, he has to work at a hectic pace. Although Jones readily acknowledges that his job is stressful, he also believes that the outcome of having all the stress is satisfying. Jones is able to see the product of his labor over the Manhattan skyline, which makes him feel like he's a part of something.

工作复杂性是指从知识、技能、能力方面来说，工作要求超出个人能力的程度。

Work complexity refers to the degree to which the requirements of the work, in terms of knowledge, skills, and abilities, tax or exceed the capabilities of the person who is responsible for performing the work. As an example of work complexity, consider the nature of employee development practices that organizations use to train future executives and organizational leaders. In many cases, these practices involve giving people jobs that require skills and knowledge that the people do not yet possess. A successful marketing manager who is being groomed for an executive-level position may, for example, be asked to manage a poorly performing production facility with poor labor relations in a country halfway around the world. Although these types of developmental experiences tend to be quite stressful, managers report that being stretched beyond their capacity is well worth the associated discomfort.

工作责任是指一个人对他人承担的责任的性质。

Work responsibility refers to the nature of the obligations that a person has toward others. Generally speaking, the level of responsibility in a job is higher when the number, scope, and importance of the obligations in that job are higher. As an example, the level of work responsibility for an air traffic controller, who may be accountable for the lives of tens of thousands of people every day, is very high. Controllers understand that if they make an error while directing an aircraft—for example, saying "turn left" instead of "turn right"—hundreds of people can die in an instant. Although controller errors that result in midair collisions and crashes

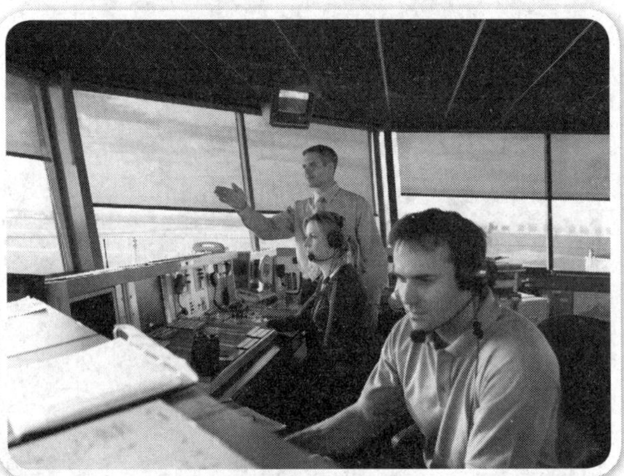

The job of an air traffic controller is stressful because of the challenging demands. In particular, air traffic controllers know that during each shift they work, they'll be responsible for ensuring that thousands of people arrive at their destinations safely and on time.

are extremely rare, the possibility weighs heavily on the minds of controllers, especially after they lose "the picture" (controller jargon for the mental representation of an assigned airspace and all the aircraft within it) due to extreme workloads, a loss of concentration, or equipment malfunctions. As with people's reactions to time pressure and work complexity, people tend to evaluate demands associated with high responsibility as both stressful and potentially positive.

OB ON SCREEN

THE DEVIL WEARS PRADA

Please bore someone else with your questions.

With those words, fashion magazine editor Miranda Priestly (Meryl Streep) foreshadows the stress she imposes on her new "second assistant," Andy Sachs (Anne Hathaway), in *The Devil Wears Prada* (Dir.: David Frankel, Fox 2000 Pictures, 2006). You see, immediately after walking into the office on her first day on the job, Andy receives an order from Miranda to get 10 or 15 skirts from Calvin Klein. When Andy asks, "What kind of skirts do you need?" Miranda responds with the line quoted above.

Unfortunately, Miranda's reply creates role ambiguity for Andy. She has no one at the magazine to turn to for help, and to make matters worse she has absolutely no clue about fashion. Later in the same conversation, Miranda gives Andy a dose of role overload. She tells Andy to do several unrelated tasks that are not only difficult to understand, but also impossible to accomplish. Of course, the fun doesn't stop there! Andy soon finds that her new job is also filled with role conflict and daily hassles. Not only does Andy have to run time-consuming personal errands for Miranda while ensuring the completion of important magazine-related tasks, but she's also subjected to constant insults from Miranda and her first assistant Emily (Emily Blunt). Andy seems to understand that the demands of working for Miranda are preventing her from reaching her goal of being a journalist, but she can't bring herself to quit because she needs money to make ends meet. Clearly, Andy's job is filled with demands that she appraises as hindrance stressors.

Later in the movie, however, things slowly begin to change for Andy. She begins to believe that if she works harder to please Miranda, she'll be able to make connections with important people in the magazine industry, which in turn will open doors for her in the competitive field of journalism. In essence, Andy begins to appraise her job demands as consisting of challenge stressors rather than hindrance stressors. So what are the consequences of Andy's reappraisal of her job demands? You'll have to watch the movie to find out.

工作－家庭冲突是一种特定形式的角色冲突，即工作角色的需求阻碍了家庭角色需求的实现（反之亦然）。

消极生活事件也是非工作阻碍性压力源的一种形式。研究表明，许多生活事件被认为非常具有压力，尤其是对人们的生活带来重大变化的事件。

NONWORK HINDRANCE STRESSORS. Although the majority of people in the United States spend more time at the office than anywhere else, there are a number of stressful demands outside of work that have implications for managing behavior in organizations. In essence, stressors experienced outside of work may have effects that "spill over" to affect the employee at work. One example of nonwork hindrance stressors is **work–family conflict**, a special form of role conflict in which the demands of a work role hinder the fulfillment of the demands of a family role (or vice versa). We most often think of cases in which work demands hinder effectiveness in the family context, termed "work to family conflict." For example, employees who have to deal with lots of hindrances at work may have trouble switching off their frustration after they get home, and as a consequence, they may become irritable and impatient with family and friends. However, work–family conflict can occur in the other direction as well. For example, "family to work conflict" would occur if a salesperson experiencing the stress of marital conflict comes to work harboring emotional pain and negative feelings, which makes it difficult to interact with customers effectively.

Nonwork hindrance stressors also come in the form of **negative life events**. Research has revealed that a number of life events are perceived as quite stressful, particularly when they result in significant changes to a person's life. Table 5-2 provides a listing of some commonly experienced life events, along with a score that estimates how stressful each event is perceived to be. As the table reveals, many of the most stressful life events do not occur at work. Rather, they include family events such as the death of a spouse or close family member, a divorce or marital separation, a jail term, or a personal illness. These events would be classified as hindrance stressors because they hinder the ability to achieve life goals and are associated with negative emotions.

TABLE 5-2 Stressful Life Events

LIFE EVENT	STRESS SCORE	LIFE EVENT	STRESS SCORE
Death of a spouse	100	Trouble with in-laws	29
Divorce	73	Outstanding achievement	28
Marital separation	65	Begin or end school	26
Jail term	63	Change in living conditions	25
Death of close family member	63	Trouble with boss	23
Personal illness	53	Change in work hours	20
Marriage	50	Change in residence	20
Fired at work	47	Change in schools	20
Marital reconciliation	45	Change in social activities	18
Retirement	45	Change in sleeping habits	16
Pregnancy	40	Change in family get-togethers	15
Gain of new family member	39	Change in eating habits	15
Death of close friend	37	Vacations	13
Change in occupation	36	The holiday season	12
Child leaving home	29	Minor violations of the law	11

Source: Adapted from T.H. Holmes and R.H. Rahe, "The Social Re-Adjustment Rating Scale," *Journal of Psychosomatic Research* 11 (1967), pp. 213–18.

A third type of nonwork hindrance stressor is **financial uncertainty**. This type of stressor refers to conditions that create uncertainties with regard to the loss of livelihood, savings, or the ability to pay expenses. This type of stressor is highly relevant during recessions or economic downturns. When people have concerns about losing their jobs, homes, and life savings because of economic factors that are beyond their control, it's understandable why nearly half of the respondents to a recent survey indicated that stress was making it hard for them to do their jobs.

财政的不确定性是非工作阻碍性压力源的第三种形式。这种压力源是指生计、储蓄或支付能力的损失带来不确定性的情况。

NONWORK CHALLENGE STRESSORS. Of course, the nonwork domain can be a source of challenge stressors as well. **Family time demands** refer to the time that a person commits to participate in an array of family activities and responsibilities. Specific examples of family time demands include time spent involved in family pursuits such as traveling, attending social events and organized activities, hosting parties, and planning and making home improvements. Examples of **personal development** activities include participation in formal education programs, music lessons, sports-related training, hobby-related self-education, participation in local government, or volunteer work. Finally, Table 5-2 includes some **positive life events** that are sources of nonwork challenge stressors. For example, marriage, the addition of a new family member, and graduating from school are stressful in their own way. However, each is associated with more positive, rather than negative, emotions.

家庭时间需求是指一个人承诺参与家庭活动和承担责任的时间。

个人发展活动的例子包括参加正式教育项目、音乐课、运动相关的培训、与爱好相关的自我教育、参加当地政府或志愿者组织的工作。

人们如何处理压力源
HOW DO PEOPLE COPE WITH STRESSORS?

5.3

How do individuals cope with stress?

According to the transactional theory of stress, after people appraise a stressful demand, they ask themselves, "What *should* I do?" and "What *can* I do?" to deal with this situation. These questions, which refer to the **secondary appraisal** shown in Figure 5-1, center on the issue of how people cope with the various stressors they face. **Coping** refers to the behaviors and thoughts that people use to manage both the stressful demands they face and the emotions associated with those stressful demands. As Table 5-3 illustrates, coping can involve many different types of activities, and these activities can be grouped into four broad categories based on two dimensions. The first dimension refers to the method of coping (behavioral versus cognitive), and the second dimension refers to the focus of coping (problem solving versus regulation of emotions).

积极生活事件也是非工作挑战性压力源的来源。例如，婚姻、增加新家庭成员及学业毕业会带来压力。

次要评价主要围绕人们如何处理不同的压力源。

处理是指人们用来管理压力需求及其相关情绪的行为与想法。

The first part of our coping definition highlights the idea that methods of coping can be categorized on the basis of whether they involve behaviors or thoughts. **Behavioral coping** involves the set of physical activities that are used to deal with a stressful situation. In one example of behavioral coping, a person who is confronted with a lot of time pressure at work might choose to cope by working faster. In another example, an employee who has several daily hassles might cope by avoiding work—coming in late, leaving early, or even staying home. As a final example, employees often cope with the stress of an international assignment by returning home from the assignment prematurely. As our **OB Internationally** feature illustrates, international assignments are becoming increasingly prevalent, and the costs of these early returns to organizations can be significant.

行为处理是指用来处理压力情境的一系列身体活动。

TABLE 5-3 Examples of Coping Strategies

	PROBLEM-FOCUSED	EMOTION-FOCUSED
Behavioral Methods	• Working harder • Seeking assistance • Acquiring additional resources	• Engaging in alternative activities • Seeking support • Venting anger
Cognitive Methods	• Strategizing • Self-motivation • Changing priorities	• Avoiding, distancing, and ignoring • Looking for the positive in the negative • Reappraising

Source: Adapted from J.C. Latack and S.J. Havlovic, "Coping with Job Stress: A Conceptual Evaluation Framework for Coping Measures," *Journal of Organizational Behavior* 13 (1992), pp. 479–508.

OB INTERNATIONALLY

The number of expatriates, or employees who are sent abroad to work for their organization, has increased recently. In one survey, for example, 47 percent of the companies reported an increase in the number of expatriate assignments over the previous year, and 54 percent projected increases in these assignments in the following year. This survey also indicated that more than half of all employees sent abroad expected their assignment to last between one and three years. Unfortunately, a significant number of expatriate assignments do not succeed because the employee returns home earlier than planned. In fact, up to 40 percent of all American expatriates return home early, and it has been estimated that each early return costs the host organization approximately $100,000. Of course, a second way that international assignments fail is when the expatriate performs at an unsatisfactory level.

One key factor that influences the commitment and effectiveness of expatriates is how they handle the stress of being abroad. Expatriates who experience more stress as a result of cultural, interpersonal, or job factors tend to be less satisfied with their assignment, more likely to think about leaving their assignment early, and more likely to perform at subpar levels. One practice that could prove useful in managing expatriate stress is cross-cultural training, which focuses on helping people appreciate cultural differences and interacting more comfortably with the host country nationals. Unfortunately, this type of training isn't offered as frequently as you might think. Surveys suggest that many U.S. companies offer no formal cross-cultural training at all. Even when training is offered, it tends to focus more on language skills than on cultural understanding and interaction skills. Given that the number of expatriate assignments is on the rise, organizations might be well served if they increased emphasis on training in these types of skills so that their expatriates are better able to cope with the stress from being abroad.

认知处理是指用来处理压力情境的想法。

In contrast to behavioral coping, **cognitive coping** refers to the thoughts that are involved in trying to deal with a stressful situation. For example, the person who is confronted with an increase in time pressure might cope by thinking about different ways of accomplishing the work more efficiently. As another example of cognitive coping, employees who are confronted with daily hassles might try to convince themselves that the hassles are not that bad after all, perhaps by dwelling on less annoying aspects of the daily events.

问题导向型处理是指人们管理压力情境时的行为与认知过程。

Whereas the first part of our coping definition refers to the method of coping, the second part refers to the focus of coping—that is, does the coping attempt to address the stressful demand or the emotions triggered by the demand? **Problem-focused coping** refers to behaviors and cognitions intended to manage the stressful situation itself. To understand problem-focused coping, consider how the people in the previous paragraphs coped with time pressure. In the first example, the person attempted to address the time pressure by working harder, whereas in the second example, the person thought about a strategy for accomplishing the work more efficiently. Although the specific coping methods differed, both of these people reacted to the time pressure similarly, in that they focused their effort on meeting the demand rather than trying to avoid it.

情绪导向型处理是指人们应对压力需求时管理自身情绪反应的不同方式。

In contrast to problem-focused coping, **emotion-focused coping** refers to the various ways in which people manage their own emotional reactions to stressful demands. The reactions to the daily hassles that we described previously illustrate two types of emotion-focused coping. In the first example, the employee used avoidance and distancing behaviors to reduce the emotional distress caused by the stressful situation. In the second example, the employee reappraised the demand to make it seem less stressful and threatening. Although people may be successful at changing the way different situations are construed to avoid feeling unpleasant emotions, the demand or problem that initially triggered the appraisal process remains.

Of course, the coping strategy that's ultimately used has important implications for how effectively people can meet or adapt to the different stressors that they face. In the work context, for example, a manager would most likely want subordinates to cope with the stress of a heavy workload by using a problem-focused strategy—working harder—rather than an emotion-focused strategy—leaving work several hours early to create distance from the stressor. Of course, there are some situations in which emotion-focused coping may be functional for the person. As an example, consider someone who repeatedly fails to make it through the auditions for *American Idol,* despite years of voice lessons and countless hours of practice. At some point, if he did not have the capability to cope emotionally—perhaps by lowering his aspirations—his self-esteem could be damaged, which could translate into reduced effectiveness in other roles that they fill.

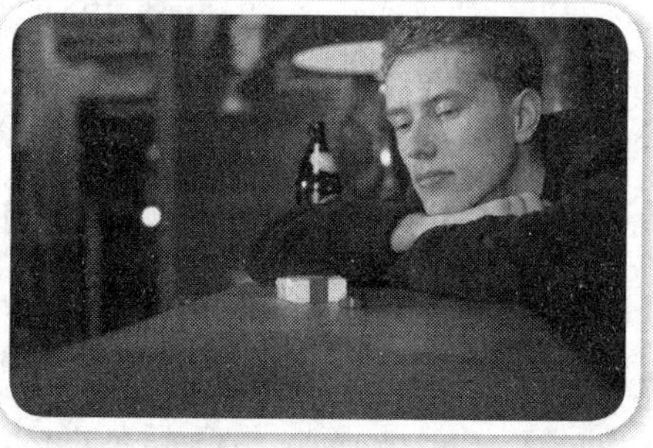

Although avoidance and distancing behaviors may reduce the emotional distress one feels, these strategies do not help manage the demand that's causing the stress.

How do people choose a particular coping strategy? One factor that influences this choice is the set of beliefs that people have about how well different coping strategies can address different demands. In essence, people are likely to choose the coping strategy they believe has the highest likelihood of meeting the demand they face. For example, successful students may come to understand that the likelihood of effectively coping with demanding final exams is higher if they study hard rather than trying to escape from the situation by going out until 3:00 a.m. The choice also depends on the degree to which people believe that they have what it takes to execute the coping strategy effectively. Returning to the previous example, if students have already failed the first two exams in the course, despite trying hard, they may come to believe that a problem-focused coping strategy won't work. In this situation, because students may feel helpless to address the demand directly, an emotion-focused coping strategy would be more likely.

Another critical factor that determines coping strategy choice is the degree to which people believe that a particular strategy gives them some degree of control over the stressor. If people believe that a demand can be addressed with a problem-focused coping strategy and have confidence that they can use that problem-focused strategy effectively, then they will feel some control over the situation and will likely use a problem-focused strategy. If people believe that a demand cannot be addressed with a problem-focused strategy or do not believe they can effectively execute that strategy, then they'll feel a lack of control over the situation and will tend to use an emotion-focused coping strategy.

So what determines how people develop a sense of control? It appears that one important factor is the nature of the stressful demand itself. In particular, people are likely to feel less control over a stressor when they appraise it as a hindrance rather than a challenge. Consider one of the life events in Table 5-2: "Trouble with boss." This event would most likely be appraised as a hindrance stressor because it serves to thwart goal achievement and triggers negative emotions. If you're like most people, you would want to change the behavior of your boss so that the trouble would stop and you could get on with your work. However, it's also likely that you would feel like you have little control over this situation because bosses are in a position of power, and complaining to your boss's boss might not be an option for you. The anxiety and hopelessness triggered by the situation would further erode any sense of control over the situation, likely leading to emotion-focused coping.

紧张体验
THE EXPERIENCE OF STRAIN

Earlier in this chapter, we defined strain as the negative consequences associated with stress. But how exactly does stress cause strain? Consider the case of Naomi Henderson, the CEO of RIVA, a Rockville, Maryland–based market research firm. The job of CEO is quite demanding, and Henderson found herself working 120 hours a week to cope with the heavy workload. One night she woke up to go to the bathroom and found that she literally could not move—she was paralyzed. After she was rushed to the emergency room, the doctor told Henderson and her husband that her diagnosis was stress. The doctor recommended rest in bed for 14 hours a day for six weeks. Although this example may seem extreme to you, the demands of many managerial and executive-level jobs are often excessive, and the negative health consequences that result are fairly predictable. In fact, if you've ever been in a situation in which you've experienced heavy stress for more than a couple of days, you can probably appreciate the toll that stress can take on you. Although people react to stress differently, you may have felt unusually exhausted, irritable, and achy. What might be surprising to you is that the mechanism within your body that gives you the ability to function effectively in the face of stressful demands is the same mechanism that ends up causing you these problems. So what is this mechanism?

Essentially, the body has a set of responses that allow it to adapt and function effectively in the face of stressful demands, but if the stressful demands do not ramp down or the demands occur too frequently, the body's adaptive responses become toxic. More specifically, when people are confronted with a stressor, their bodies secrete chemical compounds that increase their heart rate and blood pressure, as blood is redirected away from vital organs, such as the spleen, to the brain and skeletal muscles. Unfortunately, if the chemicals in the blood remain elevated because of prolonged or repeated exposure to the stressor, the body begins to break down, and several negative consequences are set into motion. As shown in Figure 5-2, those negative consequences come in three varieties: physiological strains, psychological strains, and behavioral strains.

Physiological strains that result from stressors occur in at least four systems of the human body. First, stressors can reduce the effectiveness of the body's immune system, which makes it more difficult for the body to ward off illness and infection. Have you ever noticed that you're more likely to catch a cold during or immediately after final exam week? Second, stressors can harm the body's cardiovascular system, cause the heart to race, increase blood pressure, and

FIGURE 5-2 Examples of Strain

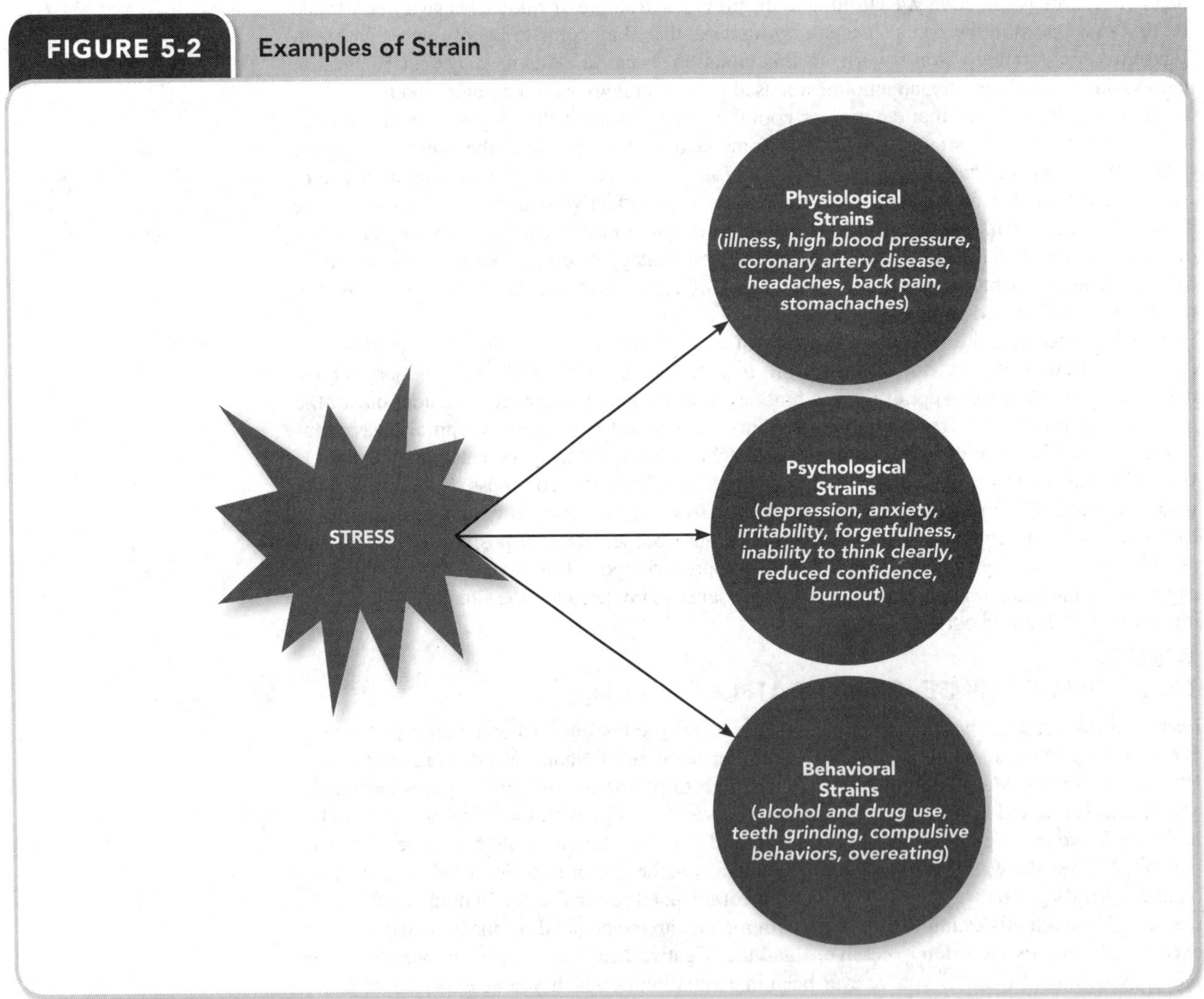

Source: From M.E. Burke, 2005 Benefits Survey Report, Society of Human Resource Management.

create coronary artery disease. Third, stressors can cause problems in the body's musculoskeletal system. Tension headaches, tight shoulders, and back pain have all been linked to a variety of stressors. Fourth, stressors cause gastrointestinal system problems. Symptoms of this type of strain include stomachaches, indigestion, diarrhea, and constipation.

Although you might be tempted to dismiss the importance of physiological strains because the likelihood of serious illness and disease is low for people in their 20s and 30s, research shows that dismissal may be a mistake. For example, high-pressure work deadlines increase the chance of heart attack within the next 24 hours by a factor of six. So even though your likelihood of suffering a heart attack may be low, who would want to increase their risk by 600 percent? Furthermore, the negative physiological effects of stress persist over time and may not show up until far into the future. One study showed that eye problems, allergic complaints, and chronic diseases could be attributed to stress measured eight years earlier.

Psychological strains that result from stressors include depression, anxiety, anger, hostility, reduced self-confidence, irritability, inability to think clearly, forgetfulness, lack of creativity, memory loss, and (not surprising, given the rest of this list) a loss of sense of humor. You might be tempted to think of these problems as isolated incidents; however, they may reflect a more general psychological condition known as **burnout**, which can be defined as the emotional, mental, and physical exhaustion that results from having to cope with stressful demands on an ongoing basis. There are many familiar examples of people who have experienced burnout, and the majority of them illustrate how burnout can lead to a decision to quit a job or even change careers. As an example, after playing for 17 seasons for the Green Bay Packers, Brett Favre decided to retire from professional football after leading his team to the NFC championship game in 2008. Favre explained to reporters that he was just tired of all the stress. The pressure of the challenge of winning compelled him to spend an ever-increasing amount of time preparing for the next game, and over time, this pressure built up and resulted in exhaustion and reduced commitment. Of course, Favre would un-retire to play for the New York Jets in 2008, only to re-retire after the season. Favre again un-retired in 2009 and joined the Minnesota Vikings. He re-retired, perhaps for the final time, after the 2010 season. Such changes of heart are not unusual after someone retires from an exciting job due to burnout. A break from stressors associated with the work not only gives the person a chance to rest and recharge, but it also provides a lot of free time to think about the excitement and challenge of performing again.

倦怠是指由于持续的压力需求而产生的情绪的、心理的及生理的耗竭。

Finally, in addition to physiological and psychological strains, the stress process can result in *behavioral strains*. Behavioral strains are unhealthy behaviors such as grinding one's teeth at night, being overly critical and bossy, excessive smoking, compulsive gum chewing, overuse of alcohol, and compulsive eating. Although it's unknown why exposure to stressors results in these specific behaviors, it's easy to see why these behaviors are undesirable both from personal and organizational standpoints.

Having started over 300 games straight, Brett Favre is well known among sports fans for his durability as an NFL quarterback. However, his durability did not mean that he was immune to the effects of stress. He retired from football three times in the span of three years, and burnout played an important role in these decisions.

解释个体的压力过程

ACCOUNTING FOR INDIVIDUALS IN THE STRESS PROCESS

So far in this chapter, we've discussed how the typical or average person reacts to different sorts of stressors. However, we've yet to discuss how people differ in terms of how they react to demands. One way that people differ in their reactions to stress depends on whether they exhibit the **Type A Behavior Pattern**. "Type A" people have a strong sense of time urgency and tend to be impatient, hard-driving, competitive, controlling, aggressive, and even hostile. If you walk, talk, and eat at a quick pace, and if you find yourself constantly annoyed with people who do things too

人们在压力反应上的区别之一在于他们是否表现出**A型行为模式**。A型人有强烈的时间紧迫感，容易不耐烦、工作努力、精力充沛、自我控制能力强、有进取心，甚至是有敌意的。

slowly, chances are that you're a Type A person. With that said, one way to tell for sure is to fill out the Type A questionnaire in our **OB Assessments** feature.

5.4 How does the Type A Behavior Pattern influence the stress process?

In the context of this chapter, the Type A Behavior Pattern is important because it can influence stressors, stress, and strains. First, the Type A Behavior Pattern may have a direct influence on the level of stressors that a person confronts. To understand why this might be true, consider that Type A persons tend to be hard-driving and have a strong desire to achieve. Because the behaviors that reflect these tendencies are valued by the organization, Type A individuals receive

OB ASSESSMENTS

TYPE A BEHAVIOR PATTERN

Do you think that you're especially sensitive to stress? This assessment is designed to measure the extent to which you're a Type A person—someone who typically engages in hard-driving, competitive, and aggressive behavior. Answer each question using the response scale provided. (For more assessments relevant to this chapter, please visit http://connect.mcgraw-hill.com.)

1	2	3	4	5	6	7
STRONGLY DISAGREE	DISAGREE	SLIGHTLY DISAGREE	NEUTRAL	SLIGHTLY AGREE	AGREE	STRONGLY AGREE

1. Having work to complete "stirs me into action" more than other people. ____
2. When a person is talking and takes too long to come to the point, I frequently feel like hurrying the person along. ____
3. **Nowadays, I consider myself to be relaxed and easygoing.** ____
4. Typically, I get irritated extremely easily. ____
5. My best friends would rate my general activity level as very high. ____
6. I definitely tend to do most things in a hurry. ____
7. I take my work much more seriously than most. ____
8. **I seldom get angry.** ____
9. I often set deadlines for myself work-wise. ____
10. I feel very impatient when I have to wait in line. ____
11. I put much more effort into my work than other people do. ____
12. **Compared with others, I approach life much less seriously.** ____

SCORING AND INTERPRETATION

Subtract your answers to the boldfaced questions from 8, with the difference being your new answers for those questions. For example, if your original answer for Question 3 was "2," your new answer is "6" (8 – 2). Then sum your answers for the twelve questions. If your scores sum up to 53 or above, you would be considered a Type A person, which means that you may perceive higher stress levels in your life and be more sensitive to that stress. If your scores sum up to 52 or below, you would be considered a Type B person. This means that you sense less stress in your life and are less sensitive to the stress that's experienced.

Source: C.D. Jenkins, S.J. Zyzanski, and R.H. Rosenman, "Progress Toward Validation of a Computer Scored Test for the Type A Coronary Prone Behavior Pattern," *Psychosomatic Medicine* Vol. 22, 193, 202 (1971). Reprinted with permission of Lippincott, Williams & Wilkins.

"rewards" in the form of increases in the amount and level of work required. In addition, because Type A people tend to be aggressive and competitive, they may be more prone to interpersonal conflict. Most of you would agree that conflict with peers and coworkers is an important stressor.

Second, in addition to the effect on stressors, the Type A Behavior Pattern is important because it influences the stress process itself. This effect of the Type A Behavior Pattern is easy to understand if you consider that hard-driving competitiveness makes people hypersensitive to demands that could potentially affect their progress toward their goal attainment. In essence, Type A individuals are simply more likely to appraise demands as being stressful rather than being benign.

Third, and perhaps most important, the Type A Behavior Pattern has been directly linked to coronary heart disease and other physiological, psychological, and behavioral strains. The size of the relationship between the Type A Behavior Pattern and these strains is not so strong as to suggest that if you're a Type A person, you should immediately call 911. However, the linkage is strong enough to suggest that the risk of these problems is significantly higher for people who typically engage in Type A behaviors.

Another individual factor that affects the way people manage stress is the degree of **social support** that they receive. Social support refers to the help that people receive when they're confronted with stressful demands, and there are at least two major types. One type of social support is called **instrumental support**, which refers to the help people receive that can be used to address the stressful demand directly. For example, if a person is overloaded with work, a coworker could provide instrumental support by taking over some of the work or offering suggestions about how to do the work more efficiently. A second type of social support is called **emotional support**. This type of support refers to the help people receive in addressing the emotional distress that accompanies stressful demands. As an example, the supervisor of the individual who is overloaded with work might provide emotional support by showing interest in the employee's situation and appearing to be understanding and sympathetic. As alluded to in these examples, social support may come from coworkers as well as from supervisors. However, social support also may be provided by family members and friends outside the context of the stressful demand.

Social support from friends, coworkers, and family can be a big help in managing stress, even though it often occurs outside the stress-causing environment

社会支持是指当人们面临压力需求时获得的帮助。

工具性支持是指能用来直接解决压力需求的帮助。

情绪性支持是指用来解决伴随压力需求产生的情绪低落时的帮助。

Similar to the Type A Behavior Pattern, social support has the potential to influence the stress process in several different ways. However, most research on social support focuses on the ways that social support buffers the relationship between stressors and strains. According to this research, high levels of social support provide a person with instrumental or emotional resources that are useful for coping with the stressor, which tends to reduce the harmful consequences of the stressor to that individual. With low levels of social support, the person does not have extra coping resources available, so the stressor tends to have effects that are more harmful. In essence, this perspective casts social support as a "moderator" of the relationship between stressors and strains (recall that moderators are variables that affect the strength of the relationship between two other variables). In this particular case, the relationship between stressors and strain tends to be weaker at higher levels of social support and stronger at lower levels of social support. Although not every research study has found support for the buffering effect of social support, the majority of research evidence has been supportive.

总结：为什么某些员工比其他员工压力更大
SUMMARY: WHY ARE SOME EMPLOYEES MORE "STRESSED" THAN OTHERS?

So what explains why some employees are more stressed than others? As shown in Figure 5-3, answering that question requires paying attention to the particular stressors the employee is experiencing, including hindrance and challenge stressors originating in both the work and

FIGURE 5-3 Why Are Some Employees More "Stressed" Than Others?

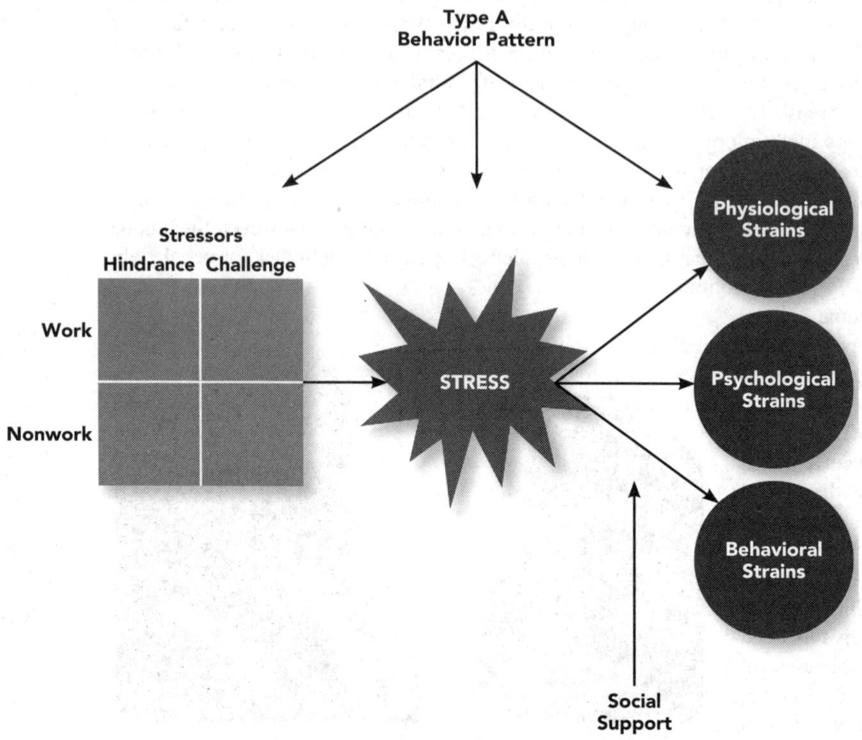

Type A Behavior Pattern
Stressors
Hindrance Challenge
Work
Nonwork
STRESS
Physiological Strains
Psychological Strains
Behavioral Strains
Social Support

nonwork domains. However, feeling stressed also depends on how those stressors are appraised and coped with, and the degree to which physiological, psychological, and behavioral strains are experienced. Finally, answering the question depends on whether the employee is "Type A" or "Type B" and whether the employee has a high or low amount of social support. Understanding all of these factors can help explain why some people can shoulder stressful circumstances for weeks at a time, whereas others seem to be "at the end of their rope" when faced with even relatively minor job demands.

压力有多重要

HOW IMPORTANT IS STRESS?

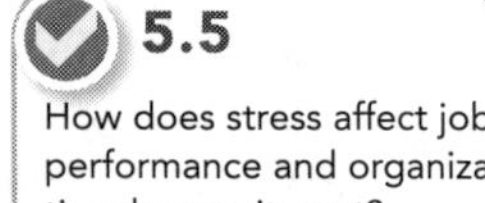

5.5

How does stress affect job performance and organizational commitment?

In the previous sections, we described how stressors and the stress process influence strains and, ultimately, people's health and well-being. Although these relationships are important to understand, you're probably more curious about the impact that stressors have on job performance and organizational commitment, the two outcomes in our integrative model of OB. Figure 5-4 summarizes the research evidence linking hindrance stressors to performance and commitment, and Figure 5-5 summarizes the research evidence linking challenge stressors to performance and commitment. We limit our discussion to relationships with work stressors rather than nonwork stressors, because this is where researchers have focused the most attention.

Figure 5-4 reveals that hindrance stressors have a weak negative relationship with job performance. A general explanation for this negative relationship is that hindrance stressors result in strains and negative emotions that reduce the overall level of physical, cognitive, and emotional

FIGURE 5-4 Effects of Hindrance Stressors on Performance and Commitment

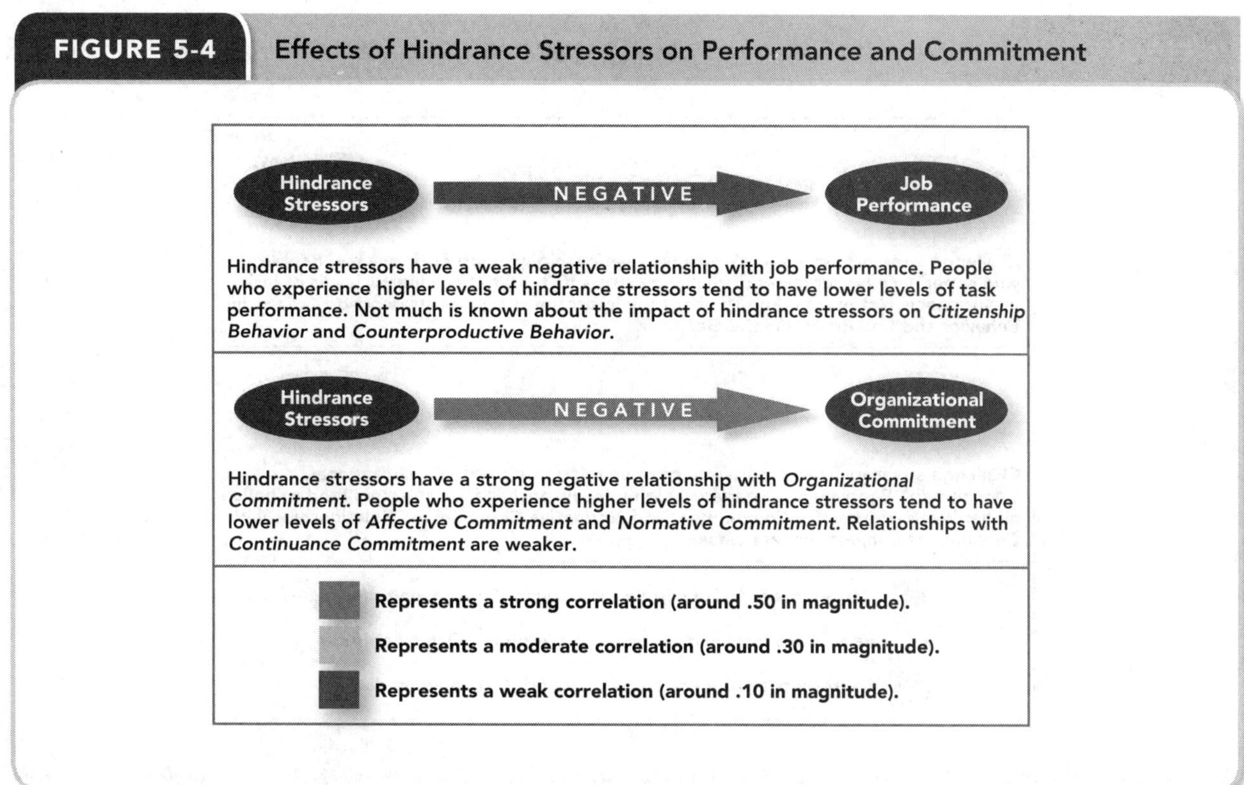

Sources: J.A. LePine, N.P. Podsakoff, and M.A. LePine, "A Meta-Analytic Test of the Challenge Stressor– Hindrance Stressor Framework: An Explanation for Inconsistent Relationships Among Stressors and Performance," *Academy of Management Journal* 48 (2005), pp. 764–75; N.P. Podsakoff, J.A. LePine, and M.A. LePine, "Differential Challenge Stressor–Hindrance Stressor Relationships with Job Attitudes, Turnover Intentions, Turnover, and Withdrawal Behavior: A Meta-Analysis," *Journal of Applied Psychology* 92 (2007), pp. 438–54.

energy that people could otherwise bring to their job duties. The detrimental effect that strains have on job performance becomes quite easy to understand when you consider the nature of the individual strains that we mentioned in the previous section. Certainly, you would agree that physiological, psychological, and behavioral strains in the form of illnesses, exhaustion, and drunkenness would detract from employee effectiveness in almost any job context.

Figure 5-4 also reveals that hindrance stressors have a strong negative relationship with organizational commitment. Why might this be? Well, hindrance stressors evoke strains, which are generally dissatisfying to people, and as we discussed in the previous chapter, satisfaction has a strong impact on the degree to which people feel committed to their organization. People who work at jobs that they know are causing them to feel constantly sick and exhausted will likely be dissatisfied with their jobs and feel less desire to stay with the organization and more desire to consider alternatives.

Turning now to challenge stressors, the story becomes somewhat different. As shown in Figure 5-5, challenge stressors have a weak relationship with job performance and a moderate relationship with organizational commitment. However, in contrast to the results for hindrance stressors, the relationships are positive rather than negative. In other words, employees who experience higher levels of challenge stressors also tend to have higher levels of job performance and organizational commitment. These relationships stand in sharp contrast with the lower levels of job performance and organizational commitment that result when employees confront higher levels of hindrance stressors. So what explains this difference? Although challenge stressors result in strains, which detract from performance and commitment, they also tend to trigger the type of positive emotions and problem-focused coping strategies that are characteristic of employees who are highly engaged in their jobs. The net benefits of these positive emotions, problem-focused

FIGURE 5-5 Effects of Challenge Stressors on Performance and Commitment

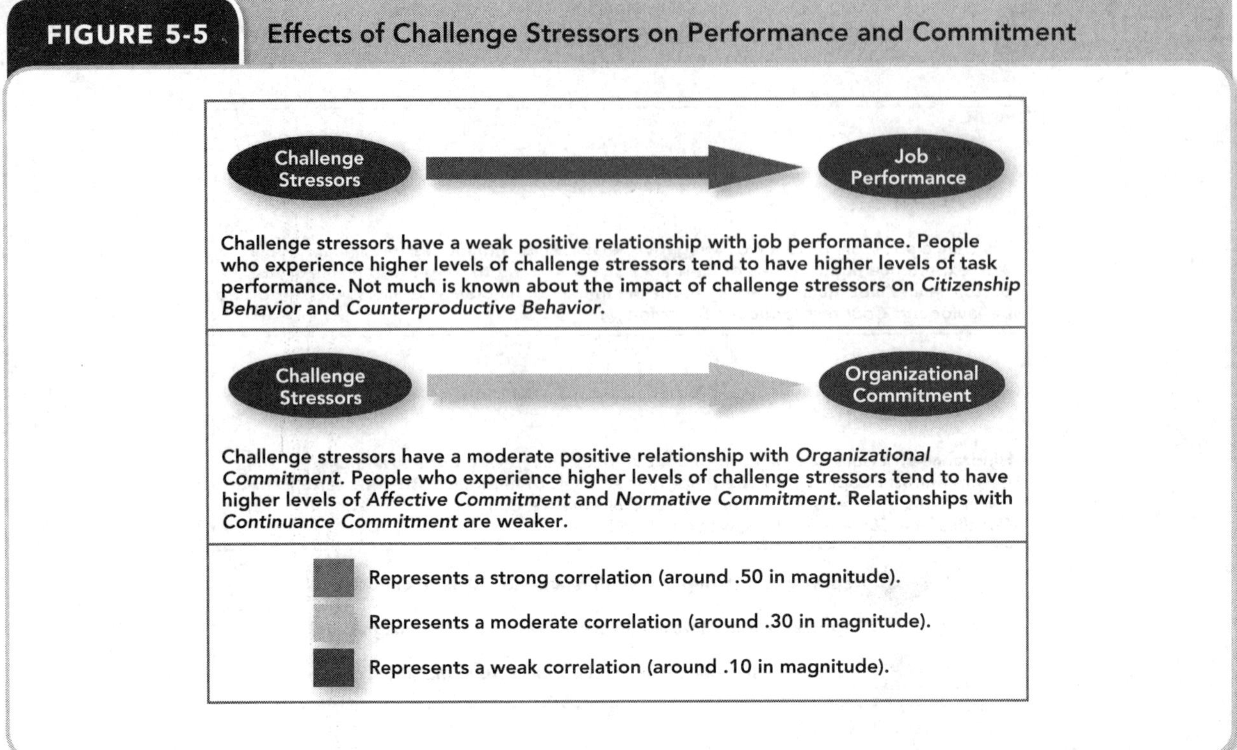

Sources: J.A. LePine, N.P. Podsakoff, and M.A. LePine, "A Meta-Analytic Test of the Challenge Stressor–Hindrance Stressor Framework: An Explanation for Inconsistent Relationships Among Stressors and Performance," *Academy of Management Journal* 48 (2005), pp. 764–75; N.P. Podsakoff, J.A. LePine, and M.A. LePine, "Differential Challenge Stressor–Hindrance Stressor Relationships with Job Attitudes, Turnover Intentions, Turnover, and Withdrawal Behavior: A Meta-Analysis," *Journal of Applied Psychology* 92 (2007), pp. 438–54.

coping strategies, and engagement outweigh the costs of the added strain, meaning that challenge stressors tend to be beneficial to employee performance and commitment when both the positives and negatives are considered. These positive effects of challenge stressors have been demonstrated for executives, employees in lower-level jobs, and even students. It's important to point out, however, that high levels of challenge stressors may have negative consequences that only become apparent over the long term. People whose jobs are filled with challenge stressors experience strains that can result in illness, but because they tend to be more satisfied, committed, and engaged with their jobs, they come to work anyway. This phenomenon, which is referred to as *presenteeism,* can result in prolonged illness, as well as the spread of illness, and ultimately a downward spiral of impaired performance and employee health. In fact, it may surprise you to learn that the reductions in productivity that result from presenteeism are even larger than reductions in productivity that result from employee absenteeism.

应用：压力管理

APPLICATION: STRESS MANAGEMENT

Previously, we described how employee stress results in strains that cost organizations in terms of reduced employee performance and commitment. However, there are other important costs to consider that relate to employee health. Most organizations provide some sort of health care benefits for their employees, and all but the smallest organizations pay worker's compensation insurance, the rates for which are determined, in part, by the nature of the job and the organization's history of work-related injuries and illnesses. So what role does stress play in these costs?

Well, it turns out that these health-related costs are driven to a great extent by employee stress. Estimates are that between 60 percent and 90 percent of all doctor visits can be attributed to stress-related causes, and the cost of providing health care to people who experience high levels of stress appears to be approximately 50 percent higher than for those who experience lower levels of stress. Statistics from jobs in different industries indicate that the frequency of worker's compensation claims is dramatically higher when the level of stress on the job is high. As one example, the frequency of claims was more than 800 percent higher for a copy machine distributor when the level of stress at the job site was high. So what do all these costs mean to you as a student of organizational behavior or as a manager?

For one thing, the relationship between stress and health care costs means that there may be huge dividends for organizations that learn how to manage their employees' stress more effectively. As the opening of this chapter suggests, companies such as Google recognize the potential for a positive return on their investments in practices aimed at reducing employee stress. In fact, surveys indicate that the vast majority of companies in the United States provide benefits, in one form or another, that are intended to help employees cope with stressful demands and reduce the associated strains. Next, we describe some approaches that organizations use to manage employee stress.

5.6
What steps can organizations take to manage employee stress?

评 估
ASSESSMENT

The first step in managing stress is to assess the level and sources of stress in the workplace. Although there are many ways to accomplish this type of evaluation, often referred to as a *stress audit,* managers can begin by asking themselves questions about the nature of the jobs in their organization to estimate whether high stress levels may be a problem. The first category of questions might involve the degree to which the organization is going through changes that would likely increase uncertainty among employees. As an example, a merger between two companies might increase employees' uncertainty about their job security and possible career paths. As another example, employees in an organization that has transitioned to team-based work might be concerned about how their individual performance contributions will be recognized and rewarded. A second category of questions might center on the work itself. These questions typically focus on the level and types of stressors experienced by the employees. The third category of questions could involve the quality of relationships between not only employees but also employees and the organization. Here, an important question to consider is whether organizational politics play a large role in administrative decisions.

减少压力源
REDUCING STRESSORS

Once a stress audit reveals that stress may be a problem, the next step is to consider alternative courses of action. One general course of action involves managing stressors, which may be accomplished in one of two ways. First, organizations could try to eliminate or significantly reduce stressful demands. As an example, companies sometimes institute policies that try to limit the demands faced by their employees. Xonex Relocation, a relocation services company located in New Castle, Delaware, prohibits employees from working during lunch and eating at their desks, and they structured workflow so that employees don't leave the office in the evening with unfinished work hanging over their heads. As another example of this approach, 19 percent of organizations in one recent survey used *job sharing* to reduce role overload and work–family conflict. Job sharing doesn't mean splitting one job into two but rather indicates that two people share the responsibilities of a single job, as if the two people were a single performing unit. The assumption underlying the practice is that "although businesses are becoming 24/7, people don't." You might be tempted to believe that job sharing would be most appropriate in lower-level jobs, where responsibilities and tasks are limited in number and relatively easy to divide. In actuality, job sharing is being used even at the highest levels in organizations. At Boston–based Fleet Bank, for example, two women shared the position of vice president for global markets and foreign exchange for six years until their department was dissolved when Fleet was acquired by Bank of America. During this time, they had one desk, one chair, one computer, one telephone, one voicemail account, one set of goals, and one performance review. They each worked 20–25 hours a week and performed the role effectively and seamlessly.

Another example of how companies reduce stressors is employee sabbaticals. A *sabbatical* gives employees the opportunity to take time off from work to engage in an alternative activity. Estimates indicate that approximately 11 percent of large companies offer paid sabbaticals, and almost one-third offer unpaid sabbaticals. American Express, for example, allows employees who have 10 years' tenure to apply for a paid sabbatical of up to six months. These employees are encouraged to work for a nonprofit organization or school, but the institution cannot have religious or political affiliations. PricewaterhouseCoopers also offers paid sabbaticals for up to six months for personal growth reasons or for work in social services; this program is available to employees with as little as two years' experience. Relative to job sharing, sabbaticals allow for a cleaner break from the stressful routine for a fairly lengthy period of time, so for the period of the sabbatical, the employee's stress may be quite low. However, because the level of stressors never changes in the job itself, the employee is likely to experience the same level of stress upon returning from the sabbatical. See our **OB at the Bookstore** feature for an additional perspective about ways to reduce the number and level of stressors in one's job.

OB AT THE BOOKSTORE

THE 4-HOUR WORKWEEK
by Timothy Ferriss (New York: Crown Publishing, 2007).

> *Most people, my past self included, have spent too much time convincing themselves that life has to be hard, a resignation to 9-to-5 drudgery in exchange for (sometimes) relaxing weekends and the occasional keep-it-short-or-get-fired vacation.*

With those words, Timothy Ferriss suggests that we can reduce the level of stress in our lives by changing the way we approach our work. According to Ferris, we should approach work by focusing on only the most important tasks and doing them well, and then not bothering much with all the rest. Although this suggestion seems like common sense, he argues that most people try to accomplish everything that's asked, and because only 20 percent of these tasks are really important, the majority of time is spent on minutiae that means very little in the grand scheme of things.

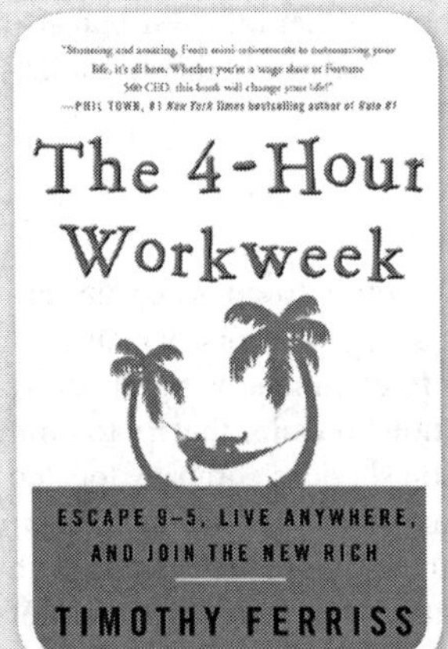

Ferriss also argues that people should schedule time for work for only as long as it takes to accomplish the most important aspects of the work. This suggestion is based on *Parkinson's Law,* which asserts that the perceived importance and complexity of tasks will grow in relation to the time we have to do them. In other words, if we give ourselves longer to do something than is absolutely necessary, we'll find ways to fill that time. If we instead give ourselves tight deadlines, we're forced to focus on the most important priorities, and we think of the creative ways to accomplish them.

Although the book presents some interesting ideas about ways of reducing stress, there are important questions about their practicality, especially in jobs that involve collaboration. For example, a certain task might seem like a "time waster" to you, and so according to Ferris, it should be given very low priority. But to your colleague, your work on this task may mean the difference between success and failure on an important project. What do you think will happen if you blow-off this task and should need help from this colleague in the future? In summary, though it may be possible to implement many of the lessons of *The 4-Hour Workweek* to reduce your stress, there may be some unintended consequences as well.

提供资源
PROVIDING RESOURCES

Although reducing stressors may reduce the overall level of stress that a person experiences, this approach is likely to be most beneficial when the focus of the effort is on hindrance stressors rather than challenge stressors. Hindrance stressors such as role ambiguity, conflict, and overload not only cause strain but also decrease commitment and job performance. In contrast, though challenge stressors such as time pressure and responsibility cause strain, they also tend to be motivating and satisfying, and as a consequence, they generally are positively related to commitment and performance.

So as a supplement to reducing stressors, organizations can provide resources that help employees cope with stressful demands. One way that organizations provide resources to employees is through *training interventions* aimed at increasing job-related competencies and skills. Employees who possess more competencies and skills can handle more demands before they begin to appraise these demands as overly taxing or exceeding their capacity. Training that increases employee competencies and skills is also beneficial to the extent that it promotes a sense that the demands are more controllable, and as we discussed in a previous section, a sense of control promotes problem-focused coping strategies.

A second way that organizations provide resources to employees so that they can cope more effectively is through *supportive practices* that help employees manage and balance the demands that exist in the different roles they have. Although we only have room in this chapter to describe a few of these practices, Table 5-4 lists many examples, as well as the percentage of organizations that were found to use them in a survey of almost 400 organizations.

The first supportive practice example is flextime, which was used by 56 percent of the organizations in the survey. Organizations that use flextime give employees some degree of latitude in terms of which hours they need to be present at the workplace. Flexible working hours give employees the ability to cope with demands away from work, so they don't have to worry about these demands while they're at work. As another example, 37 percent of the organizations in the survey allowed telecommuting on a part-time basis. By providing the opportunity to work at

TABLE 5-4 Supportive Practices Used by Organizations

PRACTICE	% OF SMALL ORGANIZATIONS	% OF MEDIUM ORGANIZATIONS	% OF LARGE ORGANIZATIONS
Flextime	57%	56%	56%
Part-time telecommuting	36%	33%	43%
Compressed workweek	27%	30%	41%
Bring child to work if needed	43%	25%	18%
Full-time telecommuting	14%	18%	24%
Lactation program	8%	20%	28%
On-site child care	1%	3%	13%
Company-supported child care center	0%	1%	11%

Source: From M.E. Burke, 2005 Benefits Survey Report, Society of Human Resource Management.

home or some other location with computer access, employees are put in a better position to cope with demands that might be impossible to cope with otherwise. Compressed workweeks, which is used by approximately one-third of all companies in the survey, allows full-time employees to work additional hours on some days and have shorter days or time off on others. As with flextime and telecommuting, compressed workweeks give employees the ability to manage both work and nonwork role demands. As an example of a company that takes these types of supportive practices to the extreme, Best Buy has implemented a program called the Results Only Work Environment for the 4,000 employees who work at their corporate headquarters in Richfield, Minnesota. The employees in this program get to work wherever and whenever they please as long as they achieve the results required by the work assigned to them. We should also note that practices such as flextime, telecommuting, and compressed workweeks not only facilitate stress management but also appear to have other benefits. At companies such as Xerox, Corning, and United Parcel Service, implementing these types of practices resulted in improvements in productivity, innovation, absenteeism, and turnover.

降低紧张
REDUCING STRAINS

As an alternative to managing stressors, many organizations use practices that reduce strains. One type of strain-reducing practice involves training in *relaxation techniques,* such as progressive muscle relaxation, meditation, and miscellaneous calming activities like taking walks, writing in a journal, and deep breathing. Although these relaxation techniques differ, the basic idea is the same—they teach people how to counteract the effects of stressors by engaging in activities that slow the heart rate, breathing rate, and blood pressure. As an example of a relatively simple relaxation technique, consider the recommendation of Herbert Benson, a physician and president of the Mind/Body Medical Institute in Boston. He suggests that people under stress should repeat a word, sound, prayer, phrase, or motion for 10–20 minutes once or twice a day and, during that time, try to completely ignore other thoughts that may come to mind. As another example, recall the case of Naomi Henderson, the market research firm CEO who literally became paralyzed by all the stress in her job. Well, we're happy to say that Henderson got better, but she was able to do so only after being treated by a physician who helped her learn how to reduce her own strains by doing "mental aerobics." Those exercises involved taking breaks every hour to stretch and do deep breathing, taking short naps to replenish energy, and learning how to say no politely to unreasonable demands. As a final example, BlueCross BlueShield of Tennessee has trained approximately one-fifth of its 4,500 employees in the use of biofeedback technology to reduce the stress associated with financial uncertainties stemming from the economic downturn. The training uses a heart monitor and software to help people learn how to change their heart rhythms from an irregular pattern to a regular pattern by shifting from an anxious emotional state to a more positive one. Apparently, the training worked: A preliminary evaluation of the program revealed that those employees who received biofeedback training reported being less exhausted and anxious than they were before the training.

A second general category of strain-reducing practices involves *cognitive–behavioral techniques.* In general, these techniques attempt to help people appraise and cope with stressors in a more rational manner. To understand what these techniques involve, think of someone you know who not only exaggerates the level and importance of stressful demands but also predicts doom and disaster after quickly concluding that the demands simply cannot be met. If you know someone like this, you might recommend cognitive–behavioral training that involves "self-talk," a technique in which people learn to say things about stressful demands that reflect rationality and optimism. So, when confronted with a stressful demand, this person might be trained to say, "This demand isn't so tough; if I work hard I can accomplish it." Cognitive–behavioral training also typically involves

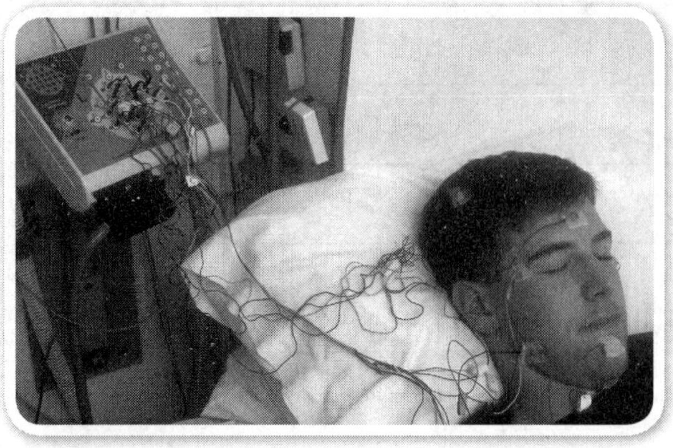

People can learn how to reduce strain using biofeedback technology.

instruction about tools that foster effective coping. So, in addition to the self-talk, the person might be trained on how to prioritize demands, manage time, communicate needs, and seek support. As an example of this type of training, Austin, Texas–based Freescale Semiconductor Inc. trains its 6,000 employees how to be "resilient" to stressful situations, such as those that occur when employees have to interact with team members from other departments in the organization that do not share the same goals. The training teaches employees strategies, such as planning for the stressful encounter and using social support, which give them the ability to use a problem-focused approach to coping with their stress.

A third category of strain-reducing practices involves *health and wellness programs.* For example, almost three-quarters of the organizations in one survey reported having *employee assistance programs* intended to help people with personal problems such as alcoholism and other addictions. More than 60 percent of organizations in this survey provided employees with wellness programs and resources. The nature of these programs and resources varies a great deal from organization to organization, but in general, they're comprehensive efforts that include health screening (blood pressure, cholesterol levels, pulmonary functioning) and health-related courses and information. Other examples of health and wellness programs intended to reduce strain include smoking cessation programs, on-site fitness centers or fitness center memberships, and weight loss and nutrition programs. Today, health and wellness programs that encourage and support exercise are a growing trend. As an example, Humana, a Fortune 100 health care administration company, implemented a program that allows the 8,500 employees who work at their corporate headquarters in Louisville, Kentucky, to borrow bikes for free from kiosks located throughout the city. As another example, consider how Grant Thornton, the Chicago–based tax, audit, and advisory firm, encourages exercise: It spent more than $200,000 helping 230 of its employees train and compete in a marathon. It also reimburses employees for participation in up to three races or walks per year, and it even set up running clubs in each of its 50 offices. How well do efforts such as this pay off? L.L. Bean initiated a comprehensive wellness program for roughly 5,000 of its employees that included health assessments, health-coaching, and on-site fitness and nutrition programs, and found that the program had a positive return on investment after the first year and reduced health care costs by almost $400 per employee.

chapter

Motivation

激　励

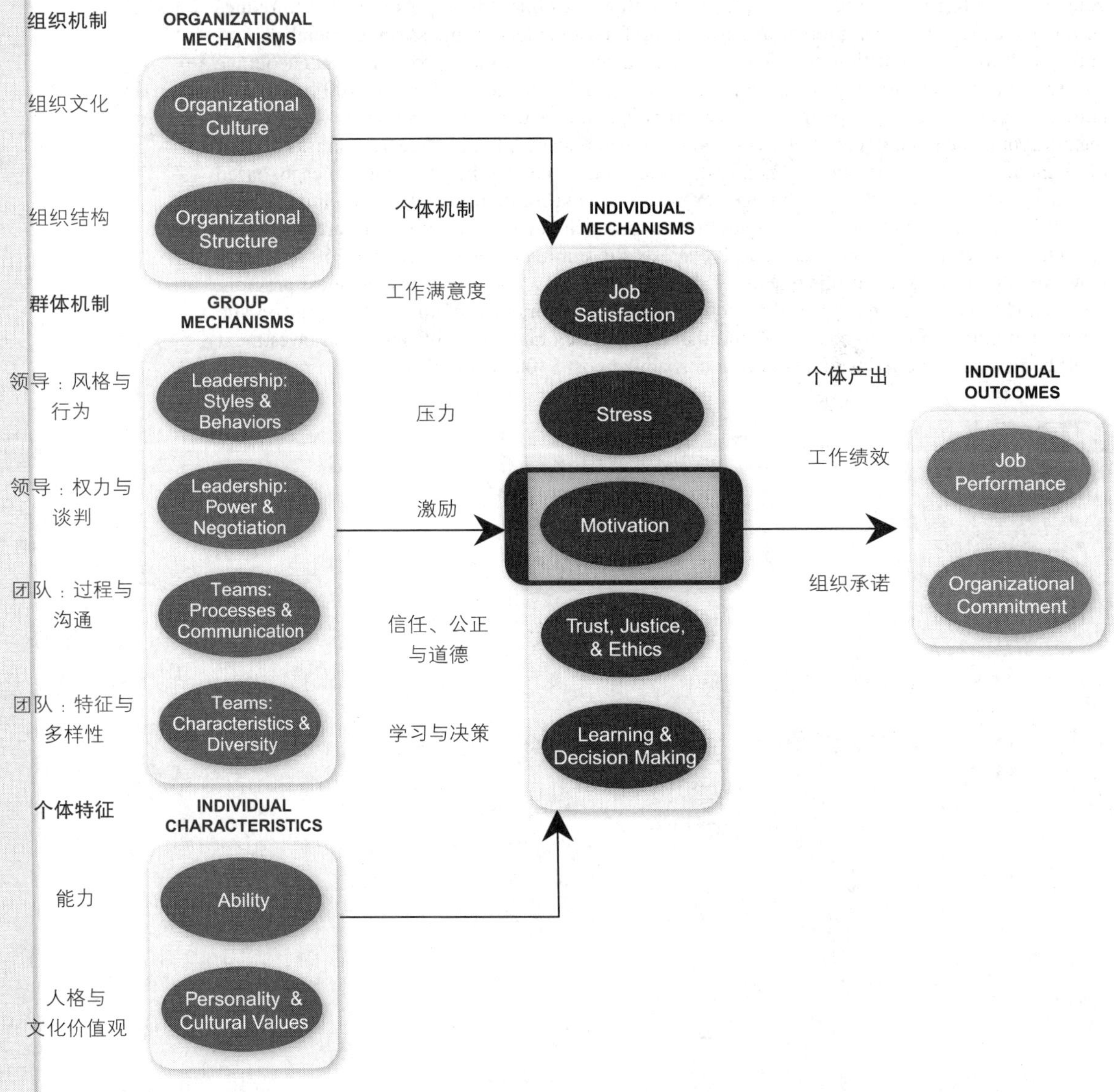

LEARNING GOALS

After reading this chapter, you should be able to answer the following questions:

6.1 What is motivation?

6.2 What three beliefs help determine work effort, according to expectancy theory?

6.3 What two qualities make goals strong predictors of task performance, according to goal setting theory?

6.4 What does it mean to be equitably treated according to equity theory, and how do employees respond to inequity?

6.5 What is psychological empowerment, and what four beliefs determine empowerment levels?

6.6 How does motivation affect job performance and organizational commitment?

6.7 What steps can organizations take to increase employee motivation?

AMERICAN EXPRESS

Picture this scenario: You're on the second leg of a three-leg trip, and you realize you've lost your American Express card. You've got a second credit card, but you still call customer service right away, to report the card stolen and to order a new one. When the agent puts you on hold for a moment during the call, your mind wanders to his job and his surroundings. It must be boring, you think to yourself—being chained to a desk, going through the same motions over and over. Who could stay motivated? Indeed, call centers have been called the factories of the 21st century, with assembly lines being replaced by the rigid scripts that govern the actions of service agents.

If you had placed your call 10 years ago, the picture you painted wouldn't have been far off. American Express service agents were tasked with maximizing the number of transactions per day as they monitored a checklist with standard rules and procedures. Say a customer's name three times, avoid 10 seconds of "dead time," and so forth. Eventually the company learned a valuable lesson in customer service, which one consultant sums up this way: "Unengaged employees can't create engaged customers." In 2005, Jim Bush, executive vice president for world service, launched the Relationship Care strategy to make customer service jobs more motivational. With the help of suggestions from employees, the strategy makes customer service jobs more empowering while also supplying more intrinsic and extrinsic incentives. Bush noted that American Express is a company that was founded on service, way back in the 1850s when it specialized in freight and delivery. "We brought it back to its heritage," he notes.

For example, the focus on cost cutting has been replaced with a focus on outstanding customer service. Rather than getting a client off the phone as quickly as possible, agents are now encouraged to have longer open-ended conversations to build rapport. Agents are encouraged to think on their feet, and given much more latitude and authority on service decisions for their clients. Such conversations often lead to customers signing up for services that they didn't know about previously. Notes Teresa Tate, an agent in American Express's Phoenix center who's gotten to know one small business client especially well, "I genuinely feel like I'm in this company's finance department." Indeed, the company's overarching goal for its agents is a challenging one: "To become the world's most respected service brand." From that perspective, the operative competitor is Ritz Carlton, not just MasterCard and Visa. The efforts seem to be paying off, as American Express has earned J.D. Power and Associates' top ranking for service among credit card issuers three years in a row.

激 励

MOTIVATION

Few OB topics matter more to employees and managers than motivation. How many times have you wondered to yourself, "Why can't I get myself going today?" Or how many times have you looked at a friend or coworker and wondered, "Why are they working so slowly right now?" Both of these questions are asking about "motivation," which is a derivation of the Latin word for movement, *movere.* Those Latin roots nicely capture the meaning of motivation, as motivated employees simply move faster and longer than unmotivated employees. More formally, **motivation** is defined as a set of energetic forces that originates both within and outside an employee, initiates work-related effort, and determines its direction, intensity, and persistence. Motivation is a critical consideration because effective job performance often requires high levels of both ability and motivation (see Chapter 8 on Ability for more discussion of such issues).

激励定义为发自于员工内外积极力量的组合，它能够激发与工作有关的活动，并决定其方向、强度和持续性。

The first part of our motivation definition illustrates that motivation is not one thing but rather a set of distinct forces. Some of those forces are internal to the employee, such as a sense of purpose or confidence, whereas others are external to the employee, such as the goals or incentives an employee is given. The next part of that definition illustrates that motivation determines a number of facets of an employee's work effort. These facets are summarized in Figure 6-1, which depicts a scenario in which your boss has given you an assignment to work on. Motivation determines *what* employees do at a given moment—the direction in which their effort is channeled. Every moment of the workday offers choices between task and citizenship sorts of actions or withdrawal and counterproductive sorts of actions. When it's 3:00 p.m. on a Thursday, do you

FIGURE 6-1 Motivation and Effort

MOTIVATION DETERMINES THE . . .

DIRECTION of Effort:	INTENSITY of Effort:	PERSISTENCE of Effort:
What are you going to do right now?	*How hard are you going to work on it?*	*How long are you going to work on it?*
☑ The assignment your boss gave you yesterday	As hard as you can, or only at half-speed?	For five hours or five minutes?
☐ Send e-mails to your friends		
☐ Surf the web for a while		

keep working on the assignment your boss gave you, or do you send e-mails or surf the web for a while? Once the direction of effort has been decided, motivation goes on to determine *how hard* an employee works—the intensity of effort—and *for how long*—the persistence of effort. We all have friends or coworkers who work extremely hard for . . . say . . . 5 minutes. We also have friends or coworkers who work extremely long hours but always seem to be functioning at half-speed. Neither of those groups of people would be described as extremely motivated.

As the American Express example illustrates, organizations are always on the lookout for new and better ways to motivate their employees. These days, however, those discussions are more likely to focus on a concept called **engagement.** You can think of engagement as a contemporary synonym, more or less, for high levels of intensity and persistence in work effort. Employees who are "engaged" completely invest themselves and their energies into their jobs. Outwardly, engaged employees devote a lot of energy to their jobs, striving as hard as they can to take initiative and get the job done. Inwardly, engaged employees focus a great deal of attention and concentration on their work, sometimes becoming so absorbed, involved, and interested in their tasks that they lose track of time (see Chapter 4 on Job Satisfaction for more discussion of such issues). Many companies attempt to measure engagement on their annual employee surveys, often by assessing factors that are believed to foster intense and persistent work effort. Most of those surveys reveal a decline in engagement during the economic downturn, with one estimate pointing to a 9 percent drop overall, and a 23 percent drop among top performers. Given those numbers, it's not surprising that a recent survey of human resources executives indicated an increased emphasis on improving engagement levels. That emphasis is critical, as research suggests that low levels of engagement can be contagious, crossing over from one employee to another.

投入是与工作活动中的高强度和高持续性含义相同的一个现代同义词。

为什么某些员工比其他员工受到更多激励

WHY ARE SOME EMPLOYEES MORE MOTIVATED THAN OTHERS?

There are a number of theories and concepts that attempt to explain why some employees are more motivated (or engaged) than others. The sections that follow review those theories and concepts in some detail. Most of them are relevant to each of the effort facets described in

Figure 6-1. However, some of them are uniquely suited to explaining the direction of effort, whereas others do a better job of explaining the intensity and persistence of effort.

期望理论
EXPECTANCY THEORY

期望理论描述了员工在不同的自发反应中做出选择所经历的认知过程。

6.2
What three beliefs help determine work effort, according to expectancy theory?

What makes you decide to direct your effort to work assignments rather than taking a break or wasting time? Or what makes you decide to be a "good citizen" by helping out a colleague or attending some optional company function? **Expectancy theory** describes the cognitive process that employees go through to make choices among different voluntary responses. Drawing on earlier models from psychology, expectancy theory argues that employee behavior is directed toward pleasure and away from pain or, more generally, toward certain outcomes and away from others. How do employees make the choices that take them in the "right direction"? The theory suggests that our choices depend on three specific beliefs that are based in our past learning and experience: expectancy, instrumentality, and valence. These three beliefs are summarized in Figure 6-2, and we review each of them in turn.

期望是指付出大量努力就会获得成功的任务绩效的信念。

EXPECTANCY. **Expectancy** represents the belief that exerting a high level of effort will result in the successful performance of some task. More technically, expectancy is a subjective probability, ranging from 0 (no chance!) to 1 (a mortal lock!) that a specific amount of effort will result in a specific level of performance (abbreviated E $\longrightarrow$ P). Think of a task at which you're not particularly good, such as writing romantic poetry. You may not be very motivated to write romantic poetry because you don't believe that your effort, no matter how hard you try, will result in a poem that "moves" your significant other. As another example, you'll be more motivated to work on the assignment described in Figure 6-1 if you're confident that trying hard will allow you to complete it successfully.

FIGURE 6-2 Expectancy Theory

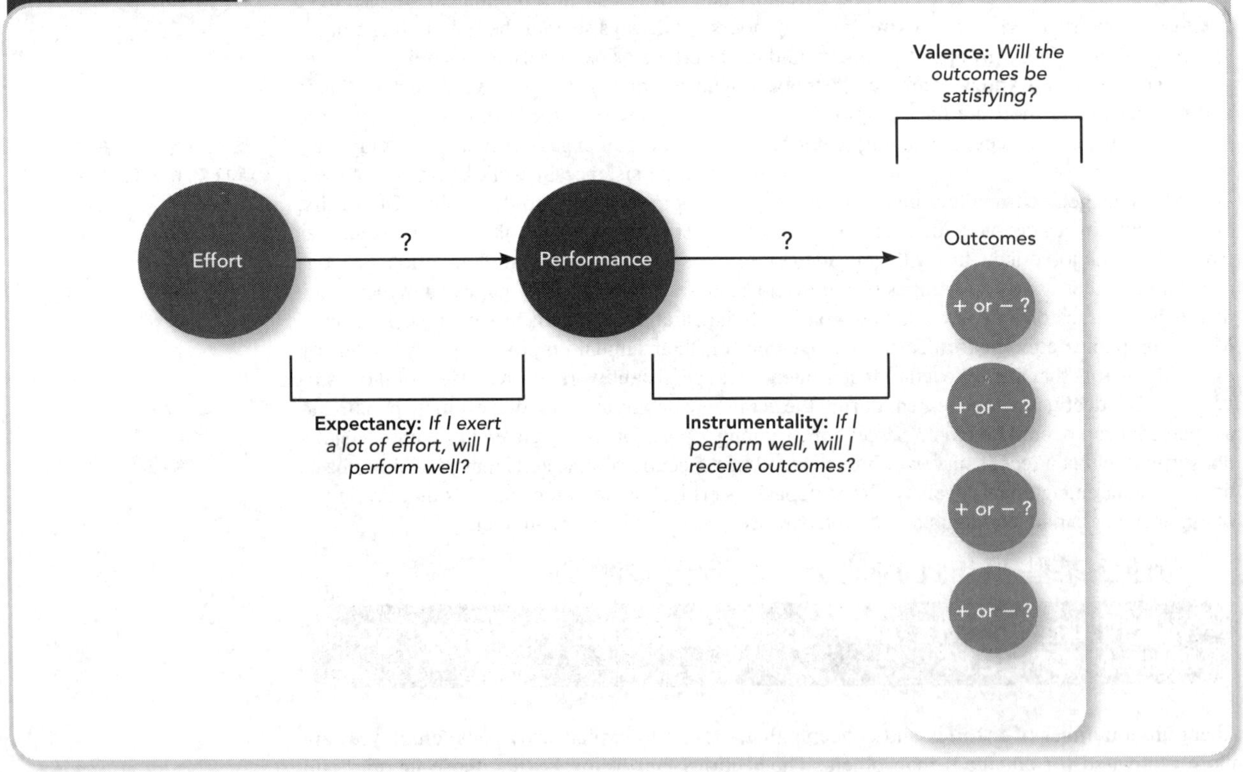

Source: Adapted from V.H. Vroom, *Work and Motivation* (New York: Wiley, 1964).

What factors shape our expectancy for a particular task? One of the most critical factors is **self-efficacy,** defined as the belief that a person has the capabilities needed to execute the behaviors required for task success. Think of self-efficacy as a kind of self-confidence or a task-specific version of self-esteem. Employees who feel more "efficacious" (that is, self-confident) for a particular task will tend to perceive higher levels of expectancy—and therefore be more likely to choose to exert high levels of effort. Why do some employees have higher self-efficacy for a given task than other employees? Figure 6-3 can help explain such differences.

自我效能定义为个人对具备成功完成任务所需能力的信念。

When employees consider efficacy levels for a given task, they first consider their **past accomplishments**—the degree to which they have succeeded or failed in similar sorts of tasks in the past. They also consider **vicarious experiences** by taking into account their observations and discussions with others who have performed such tasks. Self-efficacy is also dictated by **verbal persuasion,** because friends, coworkers, and leaders can persuade employees that they can "get the job done." Finally, efficacy is dictated by **emotional cues,** in that feelings of fear or anxiety can create doubts about task accomplishment, whereas pride and enthusiasm can bolster confidence levels. Taken together, these efficacy sources shape analyses of how difficult the task requirements are and how adequate an employee's personal and situational resources will prove to be. They also explain the content of most pregame speeches offered by coaches before the big game; such speeches commonly include references to past victories (past accomplishments), pep talks about how good the team can be (verbal persuasion), and cheers to rally the troops (emotional cues).

过去的成就是指在过去一些相似的任务中成功或失败的程度。

替代性经验是指员工与完成了相同任务的其他人进行的对话和讨论。

口头说服是指朋友、同事及领导者会说服员工"他们能够完成这项工作"。

情绪提示是指害怕或焦虑的情绪会形成对任务完成的疑问，而自豪和热情将提升自信水平。

INSTRUMENTALITY. **Instrumentality** represents the belief that successful performance will result in some outcome(s). More technically, instrumentality is a set of subjective probabilities, each ranging from 0 (no chance!) to 1 (a mortal lock!) that successful performance will bring a set of outcomes (abbreviated P $\longrightarrow$ O). The term "instrumentality" makes sense when you consider the meaning of the adjective "instrumental." We say something is "instrumental" when it helps attain something else—for example, reading this chapter is instrumental for getting a good grade in an OB class (at least, we hope so!). Unfortunately, evidence indicates that many employees don't perceive high levels of instrumentality in their workplace. One survey of more

工具性表示成功地履行职责就会带来成果的信念。

FIGURE 6-3 Sources of Self-Efficacy

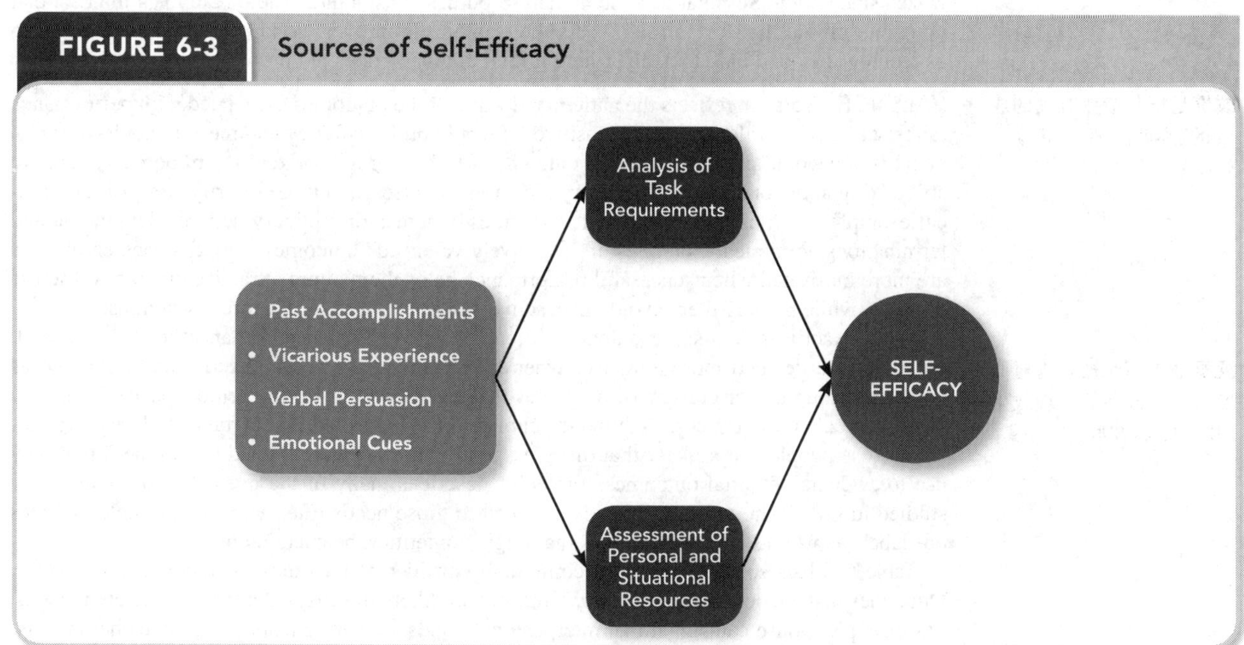

Source: Adapted from A. Bandura, "Self-Efficacy: Toward a Unifying Theory of Behavioral Change," *Psychological Review* 84 (1977), pp. 191–215; and M.E. Gist and T.R. Mitchell, "Self-Efficacy: A Theoretical Analysis of its Determinants and Malleability," *Academy of Management Review* 17 (1992), pp. 183–211.

Pregame speeches, like this dramatization of Herb Brooks's in *Miracle*, are often geared around bolstering a team's self-efficacy. Said Brooks before the USA took on the Soviet Union in the 1980 Olympics, "Tonight, we skate with 'em. Tonight, we stay with 'em. . . . Tonight, we are the greatest hockey team in the world!"

than 10,000 employees revealed that only 35 percent viewed performance as the key driver of their pay. By comparison, 60 percent viewed seniority as the key driver.

Although organizations often struggle to foster instrumentality in the best of times, linking performance to outcomes is even more difficult during an economic downturn. One human resources consulting firm estimated that 31 percent of organizations froze pay in 2009, with that estimate falling to 13 percent in 2010, and an expected 2 percent in 2011. 3M, the St. Paul, Minnesota–based maker of Post-it notes and Scotch tape, is one example of a firm that is only now unfreezing its pay. Executives at 3M indicated that pay increases would return after being frozen since 2009. Summarizes one human resources consultant, "There really is a mindset that you can only do that for so long." As the economy improves, good performers will begin to expect rewards, and may look elsewhere if their company does not provide them.

效价是指与绩效有关的成果的预期价值（简写为V）。

VALENCE. **Valence** reflects the anticipated value of the outcomes associated with performance (abbreviated V). Valences can be positive ("I would prefer *having* outcome X to not having it"), negative ("I would prefer *not having* outcome X to having it"), or zero ("I'm bored . . . are we still talking about outcome X?"). Salary increases, bonuses, and more informal rewards are typical examples of "positively valenced" outcomes, whereas disciplinary actions, demotions, and terminations are typical examples of "negatively valenced" outcomes. In this way, employees are more motivated when successful performance helps them attain attractive outcomes, such as bonuses, while helping them avoid unattractive outcomes, such as disciplinary actions.

需要是指那些被认为对成果具有关键性的心理或生理影响的认知群或认知集。

What exactly makes some outcomes more "positively valenced" than others? In general, outcomes are deemed more attractive when they help satisfy needs. **Needs** can be defined as cognitive groupings or clusters of outcomes that are viewed as having critical psychological or physiological consequences. Although scholars once suggested that certain needs are "universal" across people, it's likely that different people have different "need hierarchies" that they use to evaluate potential outcomes. Table 6-1 describes many of the needs that are commonly studied in OB. The terms and labels assigned to those needs often vary, so the table includes our labels as well as alternative labels that might sometimes be encountered.

外在激励是指取决于任务绩效的某些偶然性因素所控制的激励。

Table 6-2 lists some of the most commonly considered outcomes in studies of motivation. Outcomes that are deemed particularly attractive are likely to satisfy a number of different needs. For example, praise can signal that interpersonal bonds are strong (satisfying relatedness needs) while also signaling competence (satisfying esteem needs). Note also that some of the outcomes in Table 6-2, such as bonuses, promotions, and praise, result from other people acknowledging successful performance. These outcomes foster **extrinsic motivation**—motivation that is controlled by some contingency that depends on task performance. Other outcomes in the table,

TABLE 6-1 Commonly Studied Needs in OB

NEED LABEL	ALTERNATIVE LABELS	DESCRIPTION
Existence	Physiological, Safety	The need for the food, shelter, safety, and protection required for human existence.
Relatedness	Love, Belongingness	The need to create and maintain lasting, positive, interpersonal relationships.
Control	Autonomy, Responsibility	The need to be able to predict and control one's future.
Esteem	Self-regard, Growth	The need to hold a high evaluation of oneself and to feel effective and respected by others.
Meaning	Self-actualization	The need to perform tasks that one cares about and that appeal to one's ideals and sense of purpose.

Sources: Adapted from E.L. Deci and R.M Ryan, "The 'What' and 'Why' of Goal Pursuits: Human Needs and the Self-Determination of Behavior," *Psychological Inquiry* 11 (2000), pp. 227–68; R. Cropanzano, Z.S. Byrne, D.R. Bobocel, and D.R. Rupp, "Moral Virtues, Fairness Heuristics, Social Entities, and Other Denizens of Organizational Justice," *Journal of Vocational Behavior* 58 (2001), pp. 164–209; A.H. Maslow, "A Theory of Human Motivation," *Psychological Review* 50 (1943), pp. 370–96; and C.P. Alderfer, "An Empirical Test of a New Theory of Human Needs," *Organizational Behavior and Human Performance* 4 (1969), pp. 142–75.

such as enjoyment, interestingness, and personal expression, are self-generated, originating in the mere act of performing the task. These outcomes foster **intrinsic motivation**—motivation that is felt when task performance serves as its own reward. Taken together, extrinsic and intrinsic motivation represent an employee's "total motivation" level.

内在激励是指当任务绩效本身作为奖励时员工所感到的激励。

You might wonder which of the outcomes in the table are most attractive to employees. That's a difficult question to answer, given that different employees emphasize different needs. However, two things are clear. First, the attractiveness of many rewards varies across cultures. One expert on cross-cultural recognition programs notes, "Different cultures have different motivators. In fact, giving a gift card could be extremely insulting because it could be saying that you are bribing them to do what they already do." Good performance on a project in an American company might earn a trip to Las Vegas. However, trips to alcohol- and gambling-intensive areas are taboo in parts of Asia or the Middle East. A better award in India would be tickets to a newly released movie or a moped for navigating in congested areas.

Second, research suggests that employees underestimate how powerful a motivator pay is to them. When employees rank the importance of extrinsic and intrinsic outcomes, they often put pay in fifth or sixth place. However, research studies show that financial incentives often have a stronger impact on motivation than other sorts of outcomes. One reason is that money is relevant to many of the needs in Table 6-1. For example, money can help satisfy existence needs by helping employees buy food, afford a house, and save for retirement. However, money also conveys a sense of esteem, as it signals that employees are competent and well-regarded. In fact, research suggests that people differ in how they view the **meaning of money**—the degree to which they view money as having symbolic, not just economic, value. The symbolic value of money can be summarized in at least three dimensions: achievement (i.e., money symbolizes success), respect (i.e., money brings respect in one's community), and freedom (i.e., money provides opportunity).

金钱的意义是指将金钱视为具有象征意义而不仅仅是经济价值的程度。

Who's more likely to view money from these more symbolic perspectives? Some research suggests that men are more likely to view money as representing achievement, respect, and freedom than are women. Research also suggests that employees with higher salaries are more likely to view money in achievement-related terms. Younger employees are less likely to view money in a positive light, relative to older employees. Differences in education do not appear to impact the meaning of money, however. How do you view the meaning of money? See our **OB Assessments** feature to find out.

TABLE 6-2 Extrinsic and Intrinsic Outcomes

EXTRINSIC OUTCOMES	INTRINSIC OUTCOMES
Pay	Enjoyment
Bonuses	Interestingness
Promotions	Accomplishment
Benefits and perks	Knowledge gain
Spot awards	Skill development
Praise	Personal expression
Job security	(Lack of) Boredom
Support	(Lack of) Anxiety
Free time	(Lack of) Frustration
(Lack of) Disciplinary actions	
(Lack of) Demotions	
(Lack of) Terminations	

Sources: Adapted from E.E. Lawler III and J.L. Suttle, "Expectancy Theory and Job Behavior," *Organizational Behavior and Human Performance* 9 (1973), pp. 482–503; J. Galbraith and L.L. Cummings, "An Empirical Investigation of the Motivational Determinants of Task Performance: Interactive Effects between Instrumentality–Valence and Motivation–Ability," *Organizational Behavior and Human Performance* 2 (1967), pp. 237–57; E. McAuley, S. Wraith, and T.E. Duncan, "Self-Efficacy, Perceptions of Success, and Intrinsic Motivation for Exercise," *Journal of Applied Social Psychology* 21 (1991), pp. 139–55; and A.S. Waterman, S.J. Schwartz, E. Goldbacher, H. Green, C. Miller, and S. Philip, "Predicting the Subjective Experience of Intrinsic Motivation: The Roles of Self-Determination, the Balance of Challenges and Skills, and Self-Realization Values," *Personality and Social Psychology Bulletin* 29 (2003), pp. 1447–58.

MOTIVATIONAL FORCE. According to expectancy theory, the direction of effort is dictated by three beliefs: expectancy (E ⟶ P), instrumentality (P ⟶ O), and valence (V). More specifically, the theory suggests that the total "motivational force" to perform a given action can be described using the following formula:

$$\text{Motivational Force} = \boxed{E \longrightarrow P} \times \boxed{\Sigma[(P \longrightarrow O) \times V]}$$

The Σ symbol in the equation signifies that instrumentalities and valences are judged with various outcomes in mind, and motivation increases as successful performance is linked to more and more attractive outcomes. Note the significance of the multiplication signs in the formula: Motivational force equals zero if any one of the three beliefs is zero. In other words, it doesn't matter how confident you are if performance doesn't result in any outcomes. Similarly, it doesn't matter how well performance is evaluated and rewarded if you don't believe you can perform well.

目标设置理论
GOAL SETTING THEORY

So, returning to the choice shown in Figure 6-1, let's say that you feel confident you can perform well on the assignment your boss gave you and that you also believe successful performance will bring valued outcomes. Now that you've chosen to direct your effort to that assignment, two critical questions remain: How hard will you work, and for how long? To shed some more light on these questions, you stop by your boss's office and ask her, "So, when exactly do you need this done?" After thinking about it for a while, she concludes, "Just do your best." After returning

OB ASSESSMENTS

THE MEANING OF MONEY

How do you view money—what meaning do you attach to it? This assessment will tell you where you stand on the three facets of the meaning of money—money as achievement, money as respect, and money as freedom. Answer each question using the response scale provided. Then follow the instructions below to score yourself. (For more assessments relevant to this chapter, please visit http://connect.mcgraw-hill.com.)

1 STRONGLY DISAGREE	2 DISAGREE	3 SLIGHTLY DISAGREE	4 NEUTRAL	5 SLIGHTLY AGREE	6 AGREE	7 STRONGLY AGREE

1. Money represents one's achievement. _____
2. Money is a symbol of success. _____
3. Money is the most important goal in my life. _____
4. Money can buy everything. _____
5. Money makes people respect you in the community. _____
6. Money will help you express your competence and abilities. _____
7. Money can bring you many friends. _____
8. Money is honorable. _____
9. Money gives you autonomy and freedom. _____
10. Money can give you the opportunity to be what you want to be. _____
11. Money in the bank is a sign of security. _____
12. Money means power. _____

SCORING AND INTERPRETATION

Money as Achievement: Sum up items 1–4. ________
Money as Respect: Sum up items 5–8. ________
Money as Freedom: Sum up items 9–12. ________

Money as Achievement: High = 13 or above. Low = 12 or below.
Money as Respect: High = 15 or above. Low = 14 or below.
Money as Freedom: High = 20 or above. Low = 19 or below.

If you scored high on all three dimensions, then you view money as having multiple, non-economic meanings. This result means that money is likely to be a powerful motivator for you.

Source: Adapted from T.L. Tang, "The Meaning of Money Revisited," *Journal of Organizational Behavior* 13 (1992), pp. 197–202.

目标设置理论将目标看做是努力强度和持续性的主要驱动力。

6.3

What two qualities make goals strong predictors of task performance, according to goal setting theory?

to your desk, you realize that you're still not sure how much to focus on the assignment, or how long you should work on it before turning to something else.

Goal setting theory views goals as the primary drivers of the intensity and persistence of effort. Goals are defined as the objective or aim of an action and typically refer to attaining a specific standard of proficiency, often within a specified time limit. More specifically, the

该理论认为，与不指定目标、指定简单的目标或“尽力而为”的目标相比，为员工制定**具体且有难度的目标**会导致更高水平的绩效。

theory argues that assigning employees **specific and difficult goals** will result in higher levels of performance than assigning no goals, easy goals, or “do-your-best” goals. Why are specific and difficult goals more effective than do-your-best ones? After all, doesn’t “your best” imply the highest possible levels of effort? The reason is that few people know what their “best” is (and even fewer managers can tell whether employees are truly doing their “best”). Assigning specific and difficult goals gives people a number to shoot for—a “measuring stick” that can be used to tell them how hard they need to work and for how long. So if your boss had said, “Have the assignment on my desk by 10:30 a.m. on Tuesday, with no more than two mistakes,” you would have known exactly how hard to work and for how long.

Of course, a key question then becomes, “What’s a difficult goal?” Figure 6-4 illustrates the predicted relationship between goal difficulty and task performance. When goals are easy, there’s no reason to work your hardest or your longest, so task effort is lower. As goals move from moderate to difficult, the intensity and persistence of effort become maximized. At some point, however, the limits of a person’s ability get reached, and self-efficacy begins to diminish. Also at that point, goals move from difficult to impossible, and employees feel somewhat helpless when attempting to achieve them. In turn, effort and performance inevitably decline. So a difficult goal is one that stretches employees to perform at their maximum level while still staying within the boundaries of their ability.

The effects of specific and difficult goals on task performance have been tested in several hundred studies using many kinds of settings and tasks. A sampling of those settings and tasks is shown in Table 6-3. Overall, around 90 percent of the goal setting studies support the beneficial effects of specific and difficult goals on task performance. Although some of the settings and tasks shown in the table are unlikely to be major parts of your career (archery, handball, LEGO construction), others should be very relevant to the readers (and authors!) of this book (managing and supervision, studying, faculty research). Then again, who wouldn’t want a career in LEGO construction?

自我设定目标是指人们用来监督自己任务进程的内化目标。

Why exactly do specific and difficult goals have such positive effects? Figure 6-5 presents goal setting theory in more detail to understand that question better. First, the assignment of a specific and difficult goal shapes people’s own **self-set goals**—the internalized goals that people use to monitor their own task progress. In the absence of an assigned goal, employees may not even consider what their own goals are, or they may self-set relatively easy goals that

FIGURE 6-4 Goal Difficulty and Task Performance

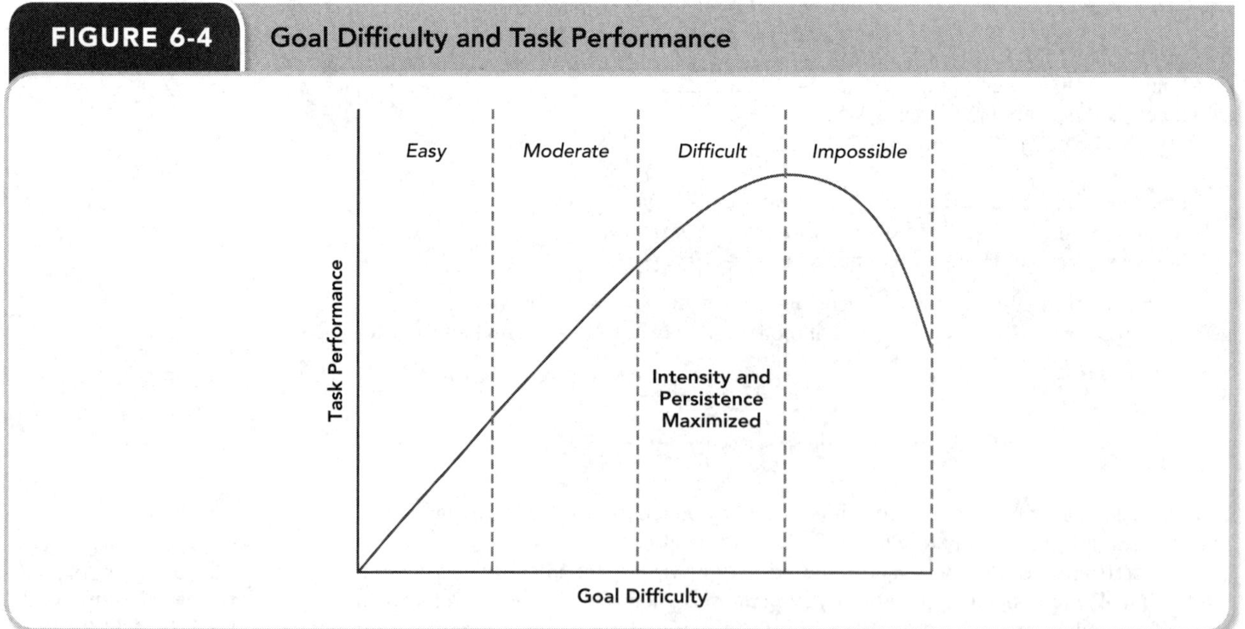

Source: Adapted from E.A. Locke and G.P. Latham, *A Theory of Goal Setting and Task Performance* (Englewood Cliffs, NJ: Prentice Hall, 1990).

TABLE 6-3 Settings and Tasks Used in Goal Setting Research

SETTINGS AND TASKS	
Air traffic control	Management training
Archery	Marine recruit performance
Arithmetic	Maze learning
Beverage consumption	Mining
Chess	Proofreading
Computer games	Production and manufacturing
Course work	Puzzles
Energy conservation	Safety behaviors
Exercise	Sales
Faculty research	Scientific and R&D work
Juggling	Sit-ups
LEGO construction	Studying
Logging	Weight lifting
Managing and supervision	Weight loss

Source: Adapted from E.A. Locke and G.P. Latham, *A Theory of Goal Setting and Task Performance* (Englewood Cliffs, NJ: Prentice Hall, 1990).

FIGURE 6-5 Goal Setting Theory

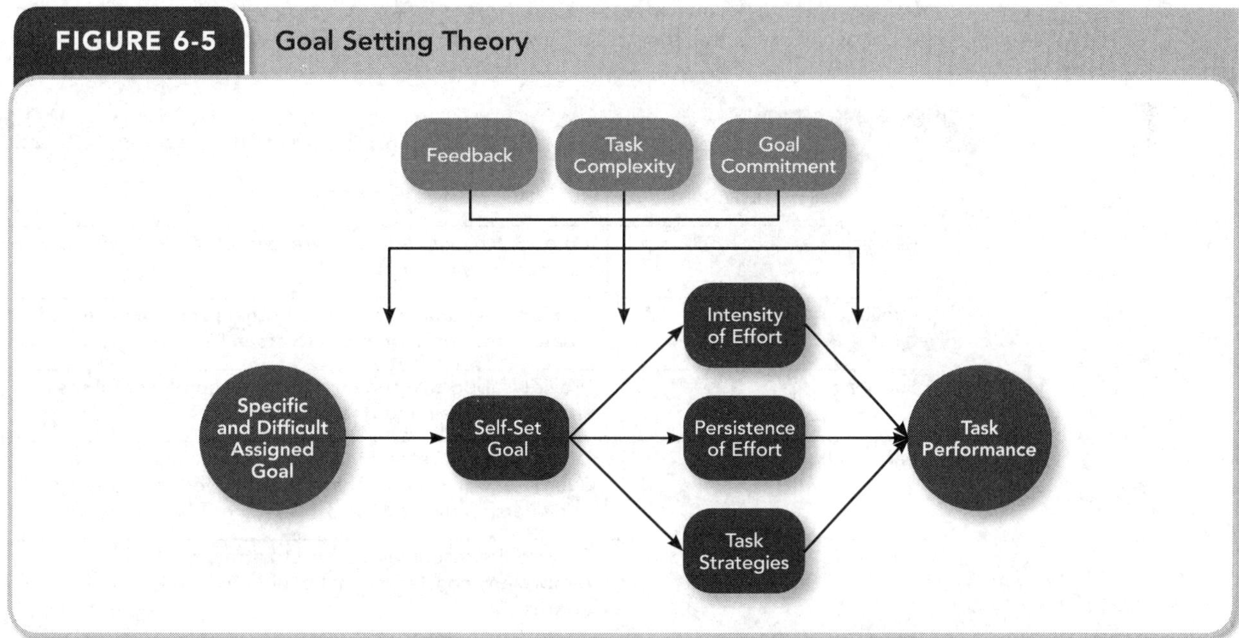

Sources: Adapted from E.A. Locke and G.P. Latham, *A Theory of Goal Setting and Task Performance* (Englewood Cliffs, NJ: Prentice Hall, 1990); E.A. Locke and G.P. Latham, "Building a Practically Useful Theory of Goal Setting and Task Motivation: A 35-Year Odyssey," *American Psychologist* 57 (2002), pp. 705–17; and G.P. Latham, "Motivate Employee Performance through Goal-Setting," in *Blackwell Handbook of Principles of Organizational Behavior,* ed. E.A. Locke (Malden, MA: Blackwell, 2000), pp. 107–19.

任务策略是指为了实现成功的绩效而制订学习计划和解决问题的方法。

反馈是指员工实现目标的过程中不断更新的进展。

任务复杂性反映了任务中信息和行动的复杂程度以及任务的多变程度。

目标承诺是指一个人接受目标并且决心实现目标的程度。

they're certain to meet. As a self-set goal becomes more difficult, the intensity of effort increases, and the persistence of effort gets extended. However, goals have another effect; they trigger the creation of **task strategies,** defined as learning plans and problem-solving approaches used to achieve successful performance. In the absence of a goal, it's easy to rely on trial and error to figure out how best to do a task. Under the pressure of a measuring stick, however, it becomes more effective to plan out the next move. Put differently, goals can motivate employees to work both harder and smarter.

Figure 6-5 also includes three variables that specify when assigned goals will have stronger or weaker effects on task performance. In the jargon of theory diagrams, these variables are called "moderators." Rather than directly affecting other variables in the diagram, moderators affect the strength of the relationships between variables. One moderator is **feedback,** which consists of updates on employee progress toward goal attainment. Imagine being challenged to beat a friend's score on a video game but having your own score hidden as you played. How would you know how hard to try? Another moderator is **task complexity,** which reflects how complicated the information and actions involved in a task are, as well as how much the task changes. In general, the effects of specific and difficult goals are almost twice as strong on simple tasks as on complex tasks, though the effects of goals remain beneficial even in complex cases. Goal setting at Wyeth, the Madison, New Jersey–based pharmaceuticals company, illustrates the value of goals for complex tasks (after all, what's more complicated than chemistry?). When Robert Ruffolo was appointed the new chief of R&D several years ago, he was concerned about the low number of new drug compounds being generated by Wyeth's labs. His solution? He gave scientists a goal of discovering 12 new drug compounds every year, up from the 4 compounds they were previously averaging, with bonuses contingent on reaching the goals. Wyeth's scientists have reached the goal every year since, and the goal was eventually upped to 15 compounds per year.

The final moderator shown in Figure 6-5 is **goal commitment,** defined as the degree to which a person accepts a goal and is determined to try to reach it. When goal commitment is high, assigning specific and difficult goals will have significant benefits for task performance. However, when goal commitment is low, those effects become much weaker. The importance of goal commitment raises the question of how best to foster commitment when assigning goals to employees. Table 6-4 summarizes some of the most powerful strategies for fostering goal commitment, which range from rewards to supervisory support to employee participation.

TABLE 6-4 Strategies for Fostering Goal Commitment

STRATEGY	DESCRIPTION
Rewards	Tie goal achievement to the receipt of monetary or nonmonetary rewards.
Publicity	Publicize the goal to significant others and coworkers to create some social pressure to attain it.
Support	Provide supportive supervision to aid employees if they struggle to attain the goal.
Participation	Collaborate on setting the specific proficiency level and due date for a goal, so that the employee feels a sense of ownership over the goal.
Resources	Provide the resources needed to attain the goal and remove any constraints that could hold back task efforts.

Sources: Adapted from J.R. Hollenbeck and H.J. Klein, "Goal Commitment and the Goal-Setting Process: Problems, Prospects, and Proposals for Future Research," *Journal of Applied Psychology* 72 (1987), pp. 212–20; H.J. Klein, M.J. Wesson, J.R. Hollenbeck, and B.J. Alge, "Goal Commitment and the Goal-Setting Process: Conceptual Clarification and Empirical Synthesis," *Journal of Applied Psychology* 84 (1999), pp. 885–96; E.A. Locke, G.P. Latham, and M. Erez, "The Determinants of Goal Commitment," *Academy of Management Review* 13 (1988), pp. 23–29; and G.P. Latham, "The Motivational Benefits of Goal-Setting," *Academy of Management Executive* 18 (2004), pp. 126–29.

Microsoft recently revised its use of goal setting principles in an effort to boost goal commitment and task performance. The company had become concerned that employees viewed their goals as objectives they *hoped* to meet rather than objectives they were *committed* to meeting. Moreover, approximately 25–40 percent of employees were working under goals that were either not specific enough or not measurable enough to offer feedback. To combat these trends, managers are now trained to identify five to seven **S.M.A.R.T. goals** for each employee and to link rewards directly to goal achievement. The S.M.A.R.T. acronym summarizes many beneficial goal characteristics, standing for **S**pecific, **M**easurable, **A**chievable, **R**esults-Based, and **T**ime-Sensitive. (Although that acronym is a useful reminder, note that it omits the all-important "Difficult" characteristic). Managers and employees at Microsoft participate jointly in the goal setting process, and managers offer support by suggesting task strategies that employees can use to achieve the goals. In this way, managers and employees come to understand the "how" of achievement, not just the "what." For insights into how goal setting operates across cultures, see our **OB Internationally** feature.

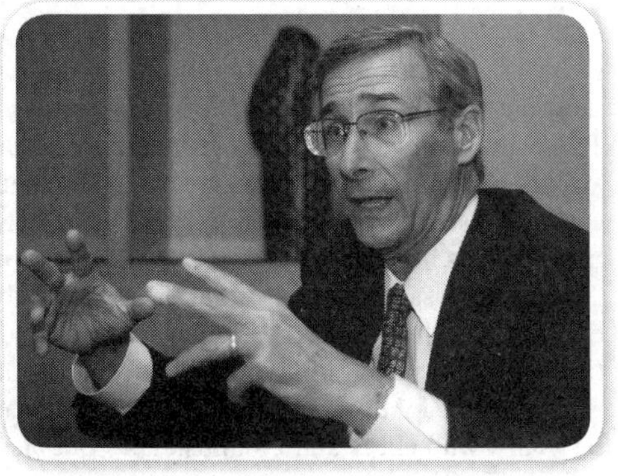

As the chief of research and development at Wyeth, Inc., a pharmaceutical company, Robert Ruffolo offered company scientists a bonus for discovering 12 new drug compounds every year. They've done it every year and are now reaching for a new goal of 15.

S.M.A.R.T. 是具体、可衡量、可达到、结果导向及时间敏感的首字母缩写，概括了许多有利的目标特征。

OB INTERNATIONALLY

Research in cross-cultural OB suggests that there are some "universals" when it comes to motivation. For example, interesting work, pay, achievement, and growth are billed as motivating forces whose importance does not vary across cultures. Of course, some motivation principles do vary in their effectiveness across cultures, including some of the strategies for fostering goal commitment.

Types of Goals. Should goals be given on an individual or a groupwide basis? Employees in the United States usually prefer to be given individual goals. In contrast, employees in other countries, including China and Japan, prefer to receive team goals. This difference likely reflects the stronger emphasis on collective responsibility and cooperation in those cultures.

Rewards. Rewards tend to increase goal commitment across cultures, but cultures vary in the types of rewards that they value. Employees in the United States prefer to have rewards allocated according to merit. In contrast, employees in other countries, including China, Japan, and Sweden, prefer that rewards be allocated equally across members of the work unit. Employees in India prefer a third allocation strategy—doling out rewards according to need. These cultural differences show that nations differ in how they prioritize individual achievement, collective solidarity, and the welfare of others.

Participation. National culture also affects the importance of participation in setting goals. Research suggests that employees in the United States are likely to accept assigned goals because the culture emphasizes hierarchical authority. In contrast, employees in Israel, which lacks a cultural emphasis on hierarchy, do not respond as well to assigned goals. Instead, employees in Israel place a premium on participation in goal setting.

Feedback. Culture also influences how individuals respond when they receive feedback regarding goal progress. As with participation, research suggests that employees in the United States are more likely to accept feedback because they are comfortable with hierarchical authority relationships and have a strong desire to reduce uncertainty. Other cultures, like England, place less value on reducing uncertainty, making feedback less critical to them.

公平理论
EQUITY THEORY

Returning to our running example in Figure 6-1, imagine that at this point, you've decided to work on the assignment your boss gave you, and you've been told that it's due by Tuesday at 10:30 a.m. and can't have more than two mistakes in it. That's a specific and difficult goal, so your browser hasn't been launched in a while, and you haven't even thought about checking your e-mail. In short, you've been working very hard for a few hours, until the guy from across the hall pops his head in. You tell him what you're working on, and he nods sympathetically, saying, "Yeah, the boss gave me a similar assignment that sounds just as tough. I think she realized how tough it was though, because she said I could use the company's playoff tickets if I finish it on time." Playoff tickets? Playoff tickets?? Looks like it's time to check that e-mail after all. . . .

公平理论认为激励不仅依赖于个人的信念和环境，还取决于发生在他人身上的情况。

Unlike the first two theories, **equity theory** acknowledges that motivation doesn't just depend on your own beliefs and circumstances but also on what happens to *other people.* More specifically, equity theory suggests that employees create a "mental ledger" of the outcomes (or rewards) they get from their job duties. What outcomes might be part of your mental ledger? That's completely up to you and depends on what you find valuable, though Table 6-5 provides a listing of some commonly considered outcomes. Equity theory further suggests that employees create a mental ledger of the inputs (or contributions and investments) they put into their job duties. Again, the composition of your mental ledger is completely specific to you, but Table 6-5 provides a listing of some inputs that seem to matter to most employees.

6.4
What does it mean to be equitably treated according to equity theory, and how do employees respond to inequity?

比较对象是指能为公平的评判提供直觉参照系的一些人。

公平伤害是指只能通过重新平衡投入产出比才能减轻的内部紧张感。

So what exactly do you do with these mental tallies of outcomes and inputs? Equity theory argues that you compare your ratio of outcomes and inputs to the ratio of some **comparison other**—some person who seems to provide an intuitive frame of reference for judging equity. There are three general possibilities that can result from this "cognitive calculus," as shown in Figure 6-6. The first possibility is that the ratio of outcomes to inputs is balanced between you and your comparison other. In this case, you feel a sense of equity, and you're likely to maintain the intensity and persistence of your effort. This situation would have occurred if you had been offered playoff tickets, just like your colleague.

The second possibility is that your ratio of outcomes to inputs is less than your comparison other's ratio. According to equity theory, any imbalance in ratios triggers **equity distress**—an internal tension that can only be alleviated by restoring balance to the ratios. In an underreward case, the equity distress likely takes the form of negative emotions such as anger or envy. One way to stop feeling those emotions is to try to restore the balance in some way, and Figure 6-6 reveals two methods for doing so. You could be constructive and proactive by talking to your boss and explaining why you deserve better outcomes. Such actions would result in the growth of your outcomes, restoring balance to the ratio. Of course, anger often results in actions that are destructive rather than constructive, and research shows that feelings of underreward inequity are among the strongest predictors of counterproductive behaviors, such as employee theft.

TABLE 6-5 Some Outcomes and Inputs Considered by Equity Theory

OUTCOMES	INPUTS
Pay	Effort
Seniority benefits	Performance
Fringe benefits	Skills and abilities
Status symbols	Education
Satisfying supervision	Experience
Workplace perks	Training
Intrinsic rewards	Seniority

Sources: Adapted from J.S. Adams, "Inequity in Social Exchange," in *Advances in Experimental Social Psychology,* Vol. 2, ed. L. Berkowitz (New York: Academic Press, 1965), pp. 267–99.

FIGURE 6-6 Three Possible Outcomes of Equity Theory Comparisons

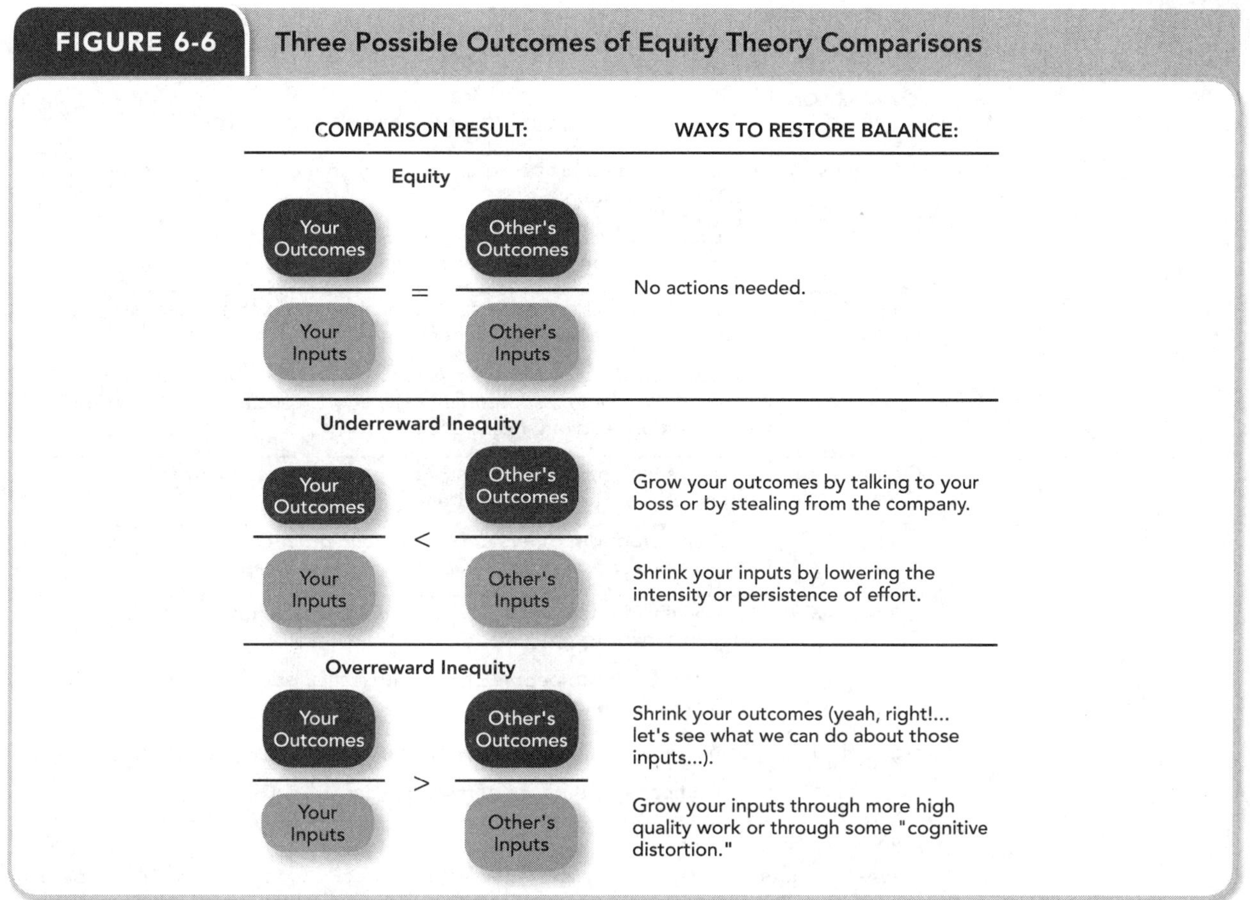

Sources: Adapted from J.S. Adams, "Inequity in Social Exchange," in *Advances in Experimental Social Psychology*, Vol. 2, ed. L. Berkowitz (New York: Academic Press, 1965), pp. 267–99.

More relevant to this chapter, another means of restoring balance is to shrink your inputs by lowering the intensity and persis tence of effort. Remember, it's not the total outcomes or inputs that matter in equity theory—it's only the ratio.

The third possibility is that your ratio of outcomes to inputs is greater than your comparison other's ratio. Equity distress again gets experienced, and the tension likely creates negative emotions such as guilt or anxiety. Balance could be restored by shrinking your outcomes (taking less money, giving something back to the comparison other), but the theory acknowledges that such actions are unlikely in most cases. Instead, the more likely solution is to increase your inputs in some way. You could increase the intensity and persistence of your task effort or decide to engage in more "extra mile" citizenship behaviors. At some point though, there may not be enough hours in the day to increase your inputs any further. An alternative (and less labor-intensive) means of increasing your inputs is to simply rethink them—to reexamine your mental ledger to see if you may have "undersold" your true contributions. On second thought, maybe your education or seniority is more critical than you realized, or maybe your skills and abilities are more vital to the organization. This **cognitive distortion** allows you to restore balance mentally, without altering your behavior in any way.

认知歪曲可以让你在心理上重新恢复平衡，而不需以任何方式改变行为。

There is one other way of restoring balance, regardless of underreward or overreward circumstances, that's not depicted in Figure 6-6: Change your comparison other. After all, we compare our "lots in life" to a variety of other individuals. Table 6-6 summarizes the different kinds of comparison others that can be used. Some of those comparisons are **internal comparisons,** meaning that they refer to someone in the same company. Others are **external comparisons,**

内部比较是指与同一公司的某人进行比较。

外部比较是指与另一公司的某人进行比较。

TABLE 6-6 Judging Equity with Different Comparison Others

COMPARISON TYPE	DESCRIPTION AND SAMPLE SURVEY ITEM
Job Equity	Compare with others doing the same job in the same organization. Sample survey item: *Compared with others doing the same job as me in my company with similar education, seniority, and effort, I earn about:*
Company Equity	Compare with others in the same organization doing substantially different jobs. Sample survey item: *Compared with others in my company on other jobs doing work that is similar in responsibility, skill, effort, education, and working condition required, I earn about:*
Occupational Equity	Compare with others doing essentially the same job in other organizations. Sample survey item: *Compared with others doing my job in other companies in the area with similar education, seniority, and effort, I earn about:*
Educational Equity	Compare with others who have attained the same education level. Sample survey item: *Compared with people I know with similar education and responsibility as me, I earn about:*
Age Equity	Compare with others of the same age. Sample survey item: *Compared with those of my age, I earn about:*

40% less	30% less	20% less	10% less	About the same	10% more	20% more	30% more	40% more

Source: R.W. Scholl, E.A. Cooper, and J.F. McKenna, "Referent Selection in Determining Equity Perceptions: Differential Effects on Behavioral and Attitudinal Outcomes," *Personnel Psychology* 40 (1987), pp. 113–24. Copyright © 1987, John Wiley & Sons. Reprinted with permission.

meaning that they refer to someone in a different company. If a given comparison results in high levels of anger and envy or high levels of guilt and anxiety, the frame of reference may be shifted. In fact, research suggests that employees don't just compare themselves to one other person; instead, they make multiple comparisons to a variety of different others. Although it may be possible to create a sort of "overall equity" judgment, research shows that people draw distinctions between the various equity comparisons shown in the table. For example, one study showed that job equity was the most powerful driver of citizenship behaviors, whereas occupational equity was the most powerful driver of employee withdrawal. For an example of someone who's never quite satisfied, no matter what the comparison, see our **OB on Screen** feature.

These mechanisms make it clear that judging equity is a very subjective process. Recent data from a Salary.com report highlight that very subjectivity. A survey of 1,500 employees revealed that 65 percent of the respondents planned to look for a new job in the next three months, with 57 percent doing so because they felt underpaid. However, Salary.com estimated that only 19 percent of those workers really were underpaid, taking into account their relevant inputs and the current market conditions. In fact, it was estimated that 17 percent were actually being overpaid by their companies! On the one hand, that subjectivity is likely to be frustrating to most managers in charge of compensation. On the other hand, it's important to realize that the intensity and persistence of employees' effort is driven by their own equity perceptions, not anyone else's.

Perhaps many employees feel they're underpaid because they compare their earnings with their CEOs'. Just consider the 10 highest-paid CEOs in a 2010 *Bloomberg Businessweek* list:

OB ON SCREEN

WALL STREET: MONEY NEVER SLEEPS

Jake Moore: *What's your number . . . the amount of money you would need to just walk away from it and live?*

Bretton James: *More.*

With that simple answer, Bretton James (Josh Brolin) provides some insight into his motivation, in *Wall Street: Money Never Sleeps* (Dir.: Oliver Stone, 20th Century Fox, 2010). James is the head of Churchill Schwartz, one of the largest investment banks on Wall Street. Jake Moore (Shia LaBeouf) believes that James helped bring about the fall of his firm, Keller Zabel, which resulted in the suicide of his mentor, Lewis Zabel (Frank Langella). With the help of Gordon Gecko (Michael Douglas), the central figure of the original *Wall Street,* Moore gets back at James by starting a rumor that hurts Churchill Schwartz's stock price. That act puts Moore on James's radar, resulting in the meeting with the exchange above.

To James, money means many things. It's a symbol of achievement, success, respect, and power. But mostly it's a way to win—a way to have more than everyone else. James doesn't have "a number"—a figure at which he'd be content to retire and live out his days in a more relaxing fashion—because as soon as his wealth stops growing, envy will kick in. James's response exemplifies *greed,* an intense and selfish desire for more of something than is needed (in this case, money). It was Gecko who once famously proclaimed that "Greed is good." In James's case, his greed does cause him to work hard, but it also causes him to do unethical and illegal things to fulfill his competitive zeal. For his part, Gecko seems to have gained perspective after a stint in jail for insider trading. "The one thing I learned in jail," he notes, "is that money is not the prime asset in life. Time is." It turns out that Gecko has a bit of a score to settle with James, one reason he's only too happy to serve as a mentor to Moore. As he mounts his climb back to the top, Gecko summarizes his own motivation: "It's not about the money—it's about the game."

Leslie Moonves of CBS ($43 million), Philippe Dauman of Viacom ($34 million), Ray Irani of Occidental Petroleum ($31 million), William Weldon of Johnson and Johnson ($30 million), Thomas Ryan of CVS Caremark ($30 million), Glen Senk of Urban Outfitters ($30 million), Randall Stephenson of AT&T ($29 million), James Hackett of Anadarko Petroleum ($27 million), Brian Roberts of Comcast ($27 million), and Rex Tillerson of ExxonMobil ($27 million). Those figures include salary, bonuses, stock and option awards, nonequity incentive awards, pension plan contributions, and other forms of compensation.

Estimates suggest that CEO pay fell by 5–10 percent last year, which commonly occurs during economic downturns. Even those diminished values, however, reflect a disconnect between what CEOs make and what the typical employee makes. In 1980, the median compensation for CEOs was 33 times that of the average worker. Three decades later, that ratio is more than 100 times the average worker's compensation. Why do boards of directors grant such large compensation packages to CEOs? Although there are many reasons, some have speculated that the pay packages represent status symbols, with many CEOs viewing themselves in celebrity terms, along the lines of professional athletes. Alternatively, CEO pay packages may represent rewards for years of climbing the corporate ladder or insurance policies against the low job security for most CEOs.

Can such high pay totals ever be viewed as equitable in an equity theory sense? Well, CEOs likely have unusually high levels of many inputs, including effort, skills and abilities, education, experience, training, and seniority. CEOs may also use other CEOs as their comparison others—as opposed to rank-and-file employees—making them less likely to feel a sense of overreward inequity. Ultimately, however, the equity of their pay depends on how the company performs under them. An analysis of the CEOs listed above compared their pay to what might have been deserved using models of stock performance and company revenues. That comparison suggested that Brian Roberts was paid about 256 percent too much, given Comcast's shareholder return of 2 percent, with Rex Tillerson being overpaid by 278 percent given ExxonMobil's –13 percent return. Who are some of the best bargains as CEO? One is Jeff Bezos of Amazon. His salary of just under $2 million represents a 90 percent underpayment, given Amazon's shareholder return of 162 percent. Overall, the analysis revealed a near-zero correlation between CEO pay and shareholder returns.

Some organizations grapple with concerns about equity by emphasizing pay secrecy (though that doesn't help with CEO comparisons, given that the Securities and Exchange Commission demands the disclosure of CEO pay for all publicly traded companies). One survey indicated that 36 percent of companies explicitly discourage employees from discussing pay with their colleagues, and surveys also indicate that most employees approve of pay secrecy. Is pay secrecy a good idea? Although it has not been the subject of much research, there appear to be pluses and minuses associated with pay secrecy. On the plus side, such policies may reduce conflict between employees while appealing to concerns about personal privacy. On the minus side, employees may respond to a lack of accurate information by guessing at equity levels, possibly perceiving more underpayment inequity than truly exists. In addition, the insistence on secrecy might cause employees to view the company with a sense of distrust.

"This is sloth—greed is on the top floor."

Source: © Tom Cheney, The New Yorker Collection, www.cartoonbank.com

心理授权
PSYCHOLOGICAL EMPOWERMENT

Now we return, for one last time, to our running example in Figure 6-1. When last we checked in, your motivation levels had suffered because you learned your coworker was offered the company's playoff tickets for successfully completing a similar assignment. As you browse the web in total "time-wasting mode," you begin thinking about all the reasons you hate working on this assignment. Even aside from the issue of goals and rewards, you keep coming back to this issue: You would never have taken on this project *by choice*. More specifically, the project itself doesn't seem very meaningful, and you doubt that it will have any real impact on the functioning of the organization.

Those sentiments signal a low level of **psychological empowerment,** which reflects an energy rooted in the belief that work tasks contribute to some larger purpose. Psychological empowerment represents a form of intrinsic motivation, in that merely performing the work tasks serves as its own reward and supplies many of the intrinsic outcomes shown in Table 6-2. The concept of psychological empowerment has much in common with our discussion of "satisfaction with the work itself" in Chapter 4 on Job Satisfaction. That discussion illustrated that jobs with high levels of variety, significance, and autonomy can be intrinsically satisfying. Models of psychological empowerment argue that a similar set of concepts can make work tasks intrinsically motivating. Four concepts are particularly important: meaningfulness, self-determination, competence, and impact.

心理授权是指来源于工作任务有助于实现更大目标这一信念的能量。

Meaningfulness captures the value of a work goal or purpose, relative to a person's own ideals and passions. When a task is relevant to a meaningful purpose, it becomes easier to concentrate on the task and get excited about it. You might even find yourself cutting other tasks short so you can devote more time to the meaningful one or thinking about the task outside of work hours. In contrast, working on tasks that are not meaningful brings a sense of emptiness and detachment. As a result, you might need to mentally force yourself to keep working on the task. Managers can instill a sense of meaningfulness by articulating an exciting vision or purpose and fostering a noncynical climate in which employees are free to express idealism and passion without criticism. For their part, employees can build their own sense of meaningfulness by identifying and clarifying their own passions. Employees who are fortunate enough to be extremely passionate about their work sometimes describe it as "a calling"—something they were born to do.

意义是指相对于一个人自己的理想和激情来说，工作目标或目的的价值。

6.5
What is psychological empowerment, and what four beliefs determine empowerment levels?

Self-determination reflects a sense of choice in the initiation and continuation of work tasks. Employees with high levels of self-determination can choose what tasks to work on, how to structure those tasks, and how long to pursue those tasks. That sense of self- determination is a strong driver of intrinsic motivation, because it allows employees to pursue activities that they themselves find meaningful and interesting. Managers can instill a sense of self-determination in their employees by delegating work tasks, rather than micromanaging them, and by trusting employees to come up with their own approach to certain tasks. For their part, employees can gain more self-determination by earning the trust of their bosses and negotiating for the latitude that comes with that increased trust.

自我决定反映了在工作任务的启动和持续中的一种选择感。

Competence captures a person's belief in his or her capability to perform work tasks successfully. Competence is identical to the self-efficacy concept reviewed previously in this chapter; employees with a strong sense of competence (or self-efficacy) believe they can execute the particular behaviors needed to achieve success at work. Competence brings with it a sense of pride and mastery that is itself intrinsically motivating. Managers can instill a sense of competence in their employees by providing opportunities for training and knowledge gain, expressing positive feedback, and providing challenges that are an appropriate match for employees' skill levels. Employees can build their own competence by engaging in self-directed learning, seeking out feedback from their managers, and managing their own workloads.

能力是指一个人相信他的能力足以成功完成工作任务的信念。

Impact reflects the sense that a person's actions "make a difference"—that progress is being made toward fulfilling some important purpose. Phrases such as "moving forward," "being on track," and "getting there" convey a sense of impact. The polar opposite of impact is "learned helplessness"—the sense that it doesn't matter what a person does, nothing will make a difference. Here, phrases such as "stuck in a rut," "at a standstill," or "going nowhere" become more relevant. Managers can instill a sense of impact by celebrating milestones along the journey

影响反映了对一个人的行为起到"重要作用"的认识，即正在朝达成某些重要目标迈进。

OB AT THE BOOKSTORE

DRIVE

by Daniel Pink (New York: Penguin Group, 2009).

. . . the upgrade that's needed to meet the new realities of how we organize, think about, and do what we do—depends on what I call Type I behavior. Type I behavior is fueled more by intrinsic desires than extrinsic ones.

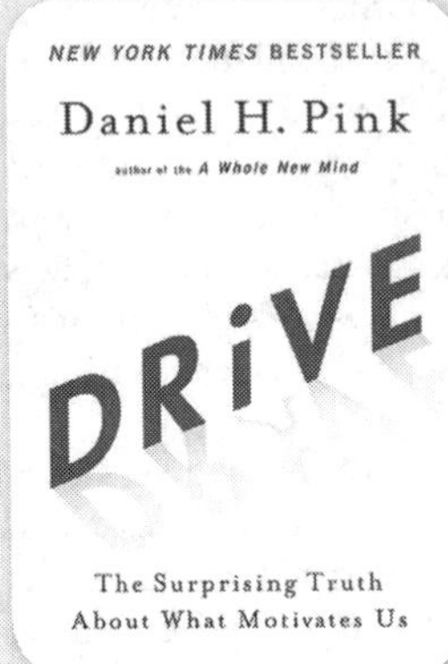

With those words, Pink makes the case for a new motivational "operating system." He refers to humankind's earliest drive to survive as "Motivation 1.0." As collaboration replaced individualism, that operating system gave way to "Motivation 2.0," exemplified by "carrot and stick" or "if-then" approaches. Motivation 2.0 encourages what Pink calls "Type X behavior," which revolves around extrinsic rewards. Pink argues that Type X behavior has served organizations well in a number of jobs for a number of years, but that it's less effective in jobs that demand creativity and nonprogrammed actions.

To illustrate his point, Pink discusses a psychology study that used the candle problem, pictured below. Participants are asked to take a candle, some tacks, and a book of matches and attach the candle to the wall so that the wax doesn't drip onto the table. How would you do it? We won't give away the answer (though you can Google "candle problem" to find out). The study compared the time it took participants to solve the problem with and without a monetary incentive. The results showed that participants who were offered the incentive took longer to solve it, presumably because the reward narrowed their focus—making them less likely to focus on "outside the box" solutions.

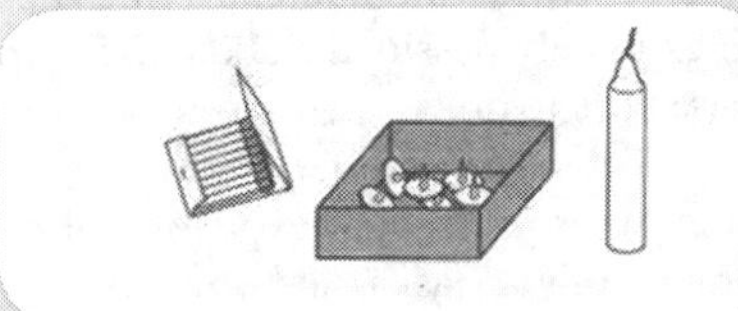

Pink argues that a "Motivation 3.0" operating system is needed for such tasks—one that revolves around intrinsic motivation (or "Type I behavior"). Much of his discussion echoes our review of control, esteem, and meaning needs, along with intrinsic outcomes. But it is his discussion of the "three elements of Type I behavior" that evokes psychological empowerment. Those elements are autonomy (acting with choice), mastery (getting better at something that matters), and purpose (hitching oneself to a larger cause). As Pink summarizes, "We know that human beings are not merely smaller, slower, better-smelling horses galloping after that day's carrot. . . . We're designed to be active and engaged."

to task accomplishment, particularly for tasks that span a long time frame. Employees can attain a deeper sense of impact by building the collaborative relationships needed to speed task progress and initiating their own celebrations of "small wins" along the way. See our **OB at the Bookstore** feature for a similar set of empowering concepts.

Studies of generational trends point to the increasing interest of psychological empowerment as a motivating force. For example, one survey of 3,332 teens worldwide revealed that 78 percent viewed personal fulfillment as a key motivator. There is also a sense that younger employees enter the workplace with higher expectations for the importance of their roles, the autonomy they'll be given, and the progress they'll make in their organizational careers. That trend is especially apparent in India, where the younger generation is coming of age in a time of unprecedented job opportunities due to the tech-services boom. MindTree, an IT consulting firm headquartered in New Jersey and Bangalore, India, takes steps to prevent young employees from feeling "lost in a sea of people." The company places new hires into "houses" with their own assembly space and work areas, providing opportunities for more personal attention and mentoring. Infosys, another IT consulting firm based in Bangalore, established a "Voice of Youth Council" that places a dozen under-30 employees on its executive management committee. The committee gives younger employees the chance to impact the company's operations. Bela Gupta, the council's youngest member at 24 years of age, describes the experience as "very empowering."

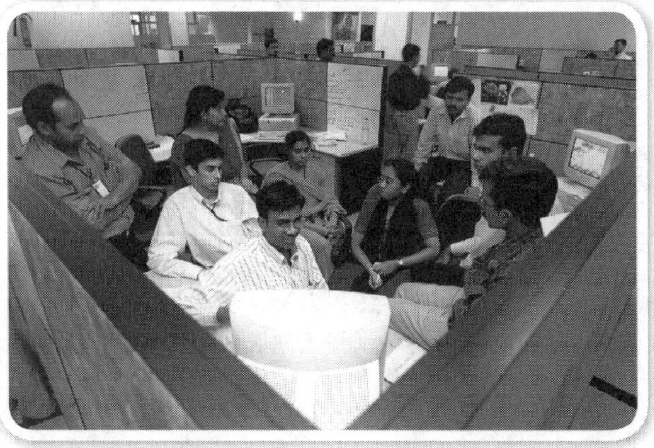

Young employees at MindTree, an information technology consulting firm, are given mentoring and personal attention to build a sense of empowerment.

总结：为什么某些员工比其他员工受到更多激励

SUMMARY: WHY ARE SOME EMPLOYEES MORE MOTIVATED THAN OTHERS?

So what explains why some employees are more motivated than others? As shown in Figure 6-7, answering that question requires considering all the energetic forces that initiate work-related effort, including expectancy theory concepts (expectancy, instrumentality, valence), the existence (or absence) of specific and difficult goals, perceptions of equity, and feelings of psychological empowerment. Unmotivated employees may simply lack confidence due to a lack of expectancy or competence or the assignment of an unachievable goal. Alternatively, such employees may feel their performance is not properly rewarded due to a lack of instrumentality, a lack of valence, or feelings of inequity. Finally, it may be that their work simply isn't challenging or intrinsically rewarding due to the assignment of easy or abstract goals or the absence of meaningfulness, self-determination, and impact.

激励有多重要

HOW IMPORTANT IS MOTIVATION?

Does motivation have a significant impact on the two primary outcomes in our integrative model of OB—does it correlate with job performance and organizational commitment? Answering that question is somewhat complicated, because motivation is not just one thing but rather a set of energetic forces. Figure 6-8 summarizes the research evidence linking motivation to job performance and organizational commitment. The figure expresses the likely combined impact of those energetic forces on the two outcomes in our OB model.

6.6

How does motivation affect job performance and organizational commitment?

Turning first to job performance, literally thousands of studies support the relationships between the various motivating forces and task performance. The motivating force with the strongest performance effect is self-efficacy/competence, because people who feel a sense of internal self-confidence tend to outperform those who doubt their capabilities. Difficult goals are the second most powerful motivating force; people who receive such goals outperform the recipients of easy goals. The motivational force created by high levels of valence, instrumentality, and expectancy is the next most powerful motivational variable for task performance. Finally, perceptions of equity have a somewhat weaker effect on task performance.

Less attention has been devoted to the linkages between motivation variables and citizenship and counterproductive behavior. With respect to the former, employees who engage in more work-related effort would seem more likely to perform "extra mile" sorts of actions, because

FIGURE 6-7 Why Are Some Employees More Motivated Than Others?

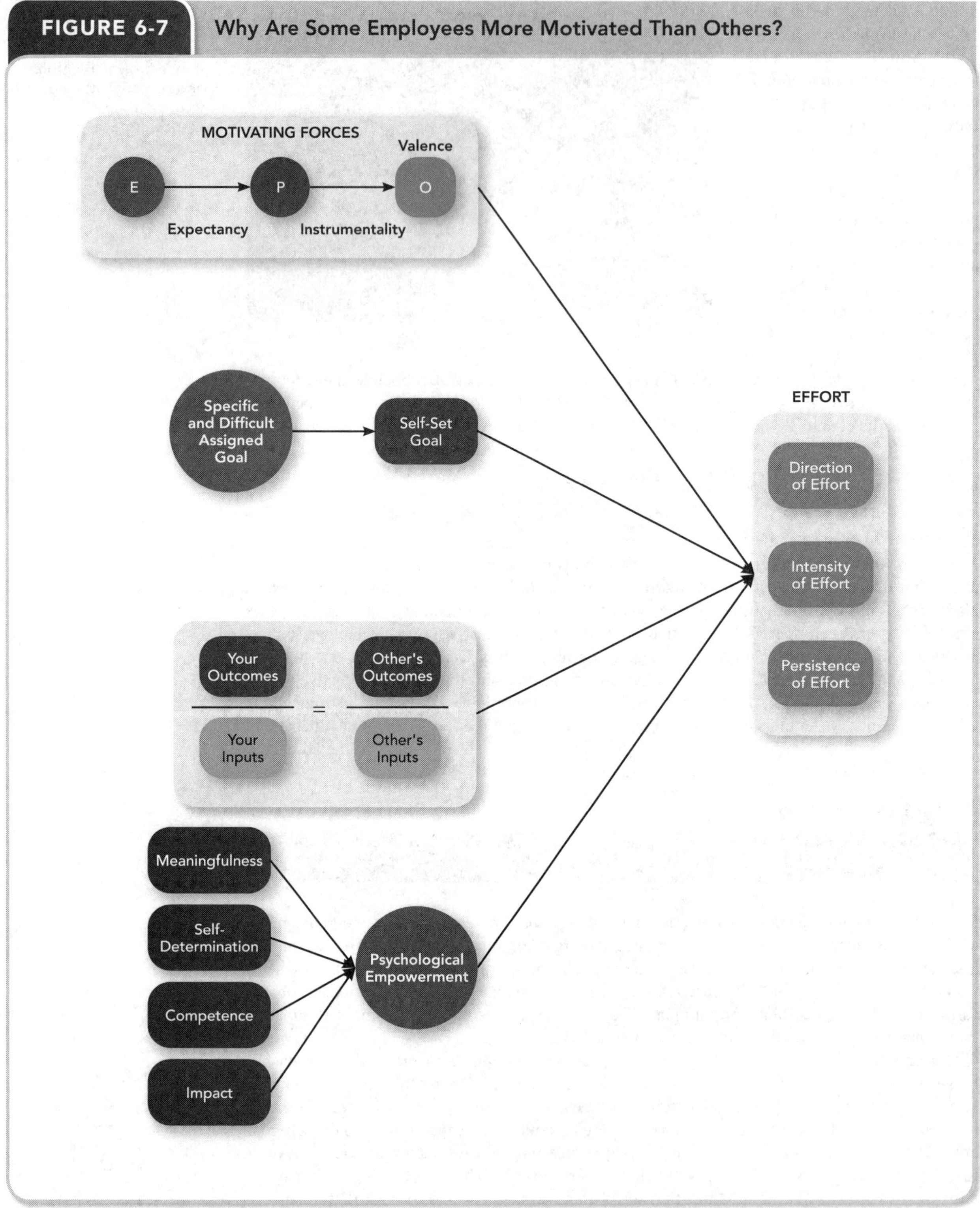

FIGURE 6-8 Effects of Motivation on Performance and Commitment

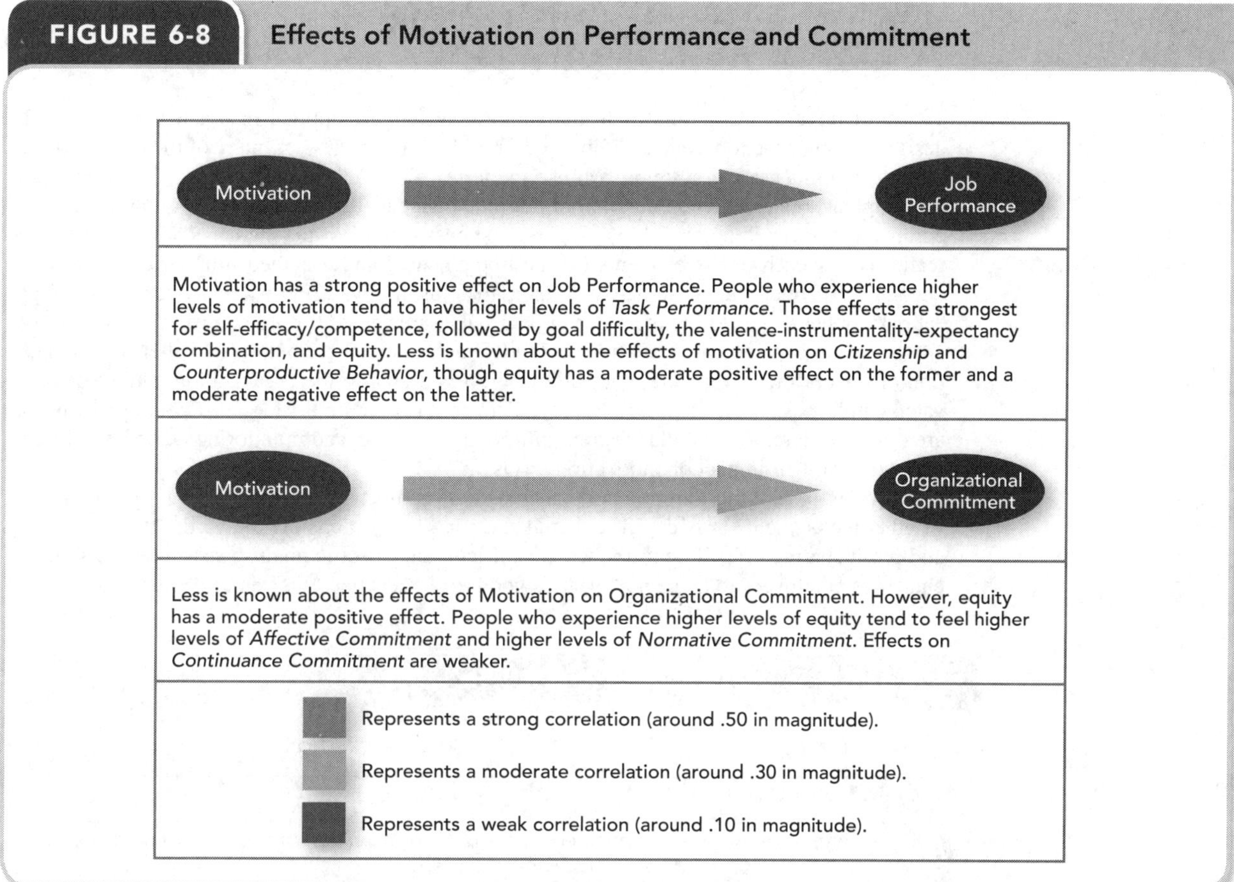

Sources: Y. Cohen-Charash and P.E. Spector, "The Role of Justice in Organizations: A Meta-Analysis," *Organizational Behavior and Human Decision Processes* 86 (2001), pp. 287–321; J.A. Colquitt, D.E. Conlon, M.J. Wesson, C.O.L.H. Porter, and K.Y. Ng, "Justice at the Millennium: A Meta-Analytic Review of 25 Years of Organizational Justice Research," *Journal of Applied Psychology* 86 (2001), pp. 425–45; J.P. Meyer, D.J. Stanley, L. Herscovitch, and L. Topolnytsky, "Affective, Continuance, and Normative Commitment to the Organization: A Meta-Analysis of Antecedents, Correlates, and Consequences," *Journal of Vocational Behavior* 61 (2002), pp. 20–52; A.D. Stajkovic and F. Luthans, "Self-Efficacy and Work-Related Performance: A Meta-Analysis," *Psychological Bulletin* 124 (1998), pp. 240–61; W. Van Eerde and H. Thierry, "Vroom's Expectancy Models and Work-Related Criteria: A Meta-Analysis," *Journal of Applied Psychology* 81 (1996), pp. 575–86; and R.E. Wood, A.J. Mento, and E.A. Locke, "Task Complexity as a Moderator of Goal Effects: A Meta-Analysis," *Journal of Applied Psychology* 72 (1987), pp. 416–25.

those actions themselves require extra effort. The best evidence in support of that claim comes from research on equity. Specifically, employees who feel a sense of equity on the job are more likely to engage in citizenship behaviors, particularly when those behaviors aid the organization. The same employees are less likely to engage in counterproductive behaviors, because such behaviors often serve as a retaliation against perceived inequities.

As with citizenship behaviors, the relationship between motivation and organizational commitment seems straightforward. After all, the psychological and physical forms of withdrawal that characterize less committed employees are themselves evidence of low levels of motivation. Clearly employees who are daydreaming, coming in late, and taking longer breaks are struggling to put forth consistently high levels of work effort. Research on equity and organizational commitment offers the clearest insights into the motivation–commitment relationship. Specifically, employees who feel a sense of equity are more emotionally attached to their firms and feel a stronger sense of obligation to remain.

应用：薪酬体系

APPLICATION: COMPENSATION SYSTEMS

The most important area in which motivation concepts are applied in organizations is in the design of compensation systems. Table 6-7 provides an overview of many of the elements used in typical compensation systems. We use the term "element" in the table to acknowledge that most organizations use a combination of multiple elements to compensate their employees. Two points must be noted about Table 6-7. First, the descriptions of the elements are simplistic; the reality is that each of the elements can be implemented and executed in a variety of ways. Second, the elements are designed to do more than just motivate. For example, plans that put pay "at risk" rather than creating increases in base salary are geared toward control of labor costs. As another example, elements that stress individual achievement are believed to alter the composition of a workforce over time, with high achievers drawn to the organization while less motivated employees are selected out. Finally, plans that reward unit or organizational performance are designed to reinforce collaboration, information sharing, and monitoring among employees, regardless of their impact on motivation levels.

6.7
What steps can organizations take to increase employee motivation?

One way of judging the motivational impact of compensation plan elements is to consider whether the elements provide difficult and specific goals for channeling work effort. Merit pay and profit sharing offer little in the way of difficult and specific goals, because both essentially challenge employees to make next year as good (or better) than this year. In contrast, lump-sum

TABLE 6-7 Compensation Plan Elements

ELEMENT	DESCRIPTION
Individual-Focused	
Piece-Rate	A specified rate is paid for each unit produced, each unit sold, or each service provided.
Merit Pay	An increase to base salary is made in accordance with performance evaluation ratings.
Lump-Sum Bonuses	A bonus is received for meeting individual goals but no change is made to base salary. The potential bonus represents "at risk" pay that must be re-earned each year. Base salary may be lower in cases in which potential bonuses may be large.
Recognition Awards	Tangible awards (gift cards, merchandise, trips, special events, time off, plaques) or intangible awards (praise) are given on an impromptu basis to recognize achievement.
Unit-Focused	
Gainsharing	A bonus is received for meeting unit goals (department goals, plant goals, business unit goals) for criteria controllable by employees (labor costs, use of materials, quality). No change is made to base salary. The potential bonus represents "at risk" pay that must be re-earned each year. Base salary may be lower in cases in which potential bonuses may be large.
Organization-Focused	
Profit Sharing	A bonus is received when the publicly reported earnings of a company exceed some minimum level, with the magnitude of the bonus contingent on the magnitude of the profits. No change is made to base salary. The potential bonus represents "at risk" pay that must be re-earned each year. Base salary may be lower in cases in which potential bonuses may be large.

bonuses and gain sharing provide a forum for assigning difficult and specific goals; the former does so at the individual level and the latter at the unit level. Partly for this reason, both types of plans have been credited with improvements in employee productivity.

Another way of judging the motivational impact of the compensation plan elements is to consider the correspondence between individual performance levels and individual monetary outcomes. After all, that correspondence influences perceptions of both instrumentality and equity. Profit sharing, for example, is unlikely to have strong motivational consequences because an individual employee can do little to improve the profitability of the company, regardless of his or her job performance. Instrumentality and equity are more achievable with gain sharing, because the relevant unit is smaller and the relevant outcomes are more controllable. Still, the highest instrumentality and equity levels will typically be achieved through individual-focused compensation elements, such as piece-rate plans or merit pay plans.

Of the two individual-focused elements, merit pay is by far the more common, given that it is difficult to apply piece-rate plans outside of manufacturing, sales, and service contexts. Indeed, one review estimated that merit pay is used by around 90 percent of U.S. organizations. Criticisms of merit pay typically focus on a smaller than expected differentiation in pay across employees. One survey reported that pay increases for top performers (5.6 percent on average) are only modestly greater than the pay increases for average performers (3.3 percent on average). Such differences seem incapable of creating a perceived linkage between performance and outcomes (though merit reviews can also have indirect effects on pay by triggering promotions).

A number of factors constrain instrumentality and equity in most applications of merit pay. As noted earlier, one such factor is budgetary constraints, as many organizations freeze or limit pay increases during an economic downturn. Another factor is the accuracy of the actual performance evaluation. Think of all the times you've been evaluated by someone else, whether in school or in the workplace. How many times have you reacted by thinking, "Where did that rating come from?" or "I think I'm being evaluated on the wrong things!" Performance evaluation experts suggest that employees should be evaluated on behaviors that are controllable by the employees (see Chapter 2 on Job Performance for more discussion of such issues), observable by managers, and critical to the implementation of the firm's strategy. The managers who conduct evaluations also need to be trained in how to conduct them, which typically involves gaining knowledge of the relevant behaviors ahead of time and being taught to keep records of employee behavior between evaluation sessions.

Even if employees are evaluated on the right things by a boss who has a good handle on their performance, other factors can still undermine accuracy. Some managers might knowingly give inaccurate evaluations due to workplace politics or a desire to not "make waves." One survey showed that 70 percent of managers have trouble giving poor ratings to underachieving employees. Unfortunately, such practices only serve to damage instrumentality and equity, because they fail to separate star employees from struggling employees. To ensure that such separation occurs, Yahoo instituted a "stacked ranking" system to determine compensation, in which managers rank all the employees within their unit from top to bottom. Employees at the top end of those rankings then receive higher bonuses than employees at the bottom end. Although such practices raise concerns about employee morale and excessive competitiveness, research suggests that such forced distribution systems can boost the performance of a company's workforce, especially for the first few years after their implementation.

Finally, another factor that can hinder the effectiveness of merit pay is its typical once-a-year schedule. How long a shelf life can the motivational benefits of a salary increase really have? One month? Two months? Six? Such concerns have led a number of organizations to supplement other compensation elements with more widespread use of recognition awards. For example, Symantec, the Mountain View, California–based software firm, launched its Applause Program in 2008. It honors employees in real time with a combination of gift cards (worth up to $1,000) and electronic thank you cards. Estimates suggest that around 65 percent of employees have been recognized with some form of "applause" since the program launched. The Everett Clinic, based in Everett, Washington, uses a number of different recognition awards, colorfully named Hero-Grams, Caught in the Act cards, and Pat on the Back cards. Explains Daniel Debow, the founder of Rypple, a performance management system that resembles Facebook in its look and feel, "We live in a real-time world . . . so it's crazy to think people wouldn't want real-time feedback."

PART

3

INDIVIDUAL CHARACTERISTICS

个体特征

chapter 7

Personality and Cultural Values

人格与文化价值观

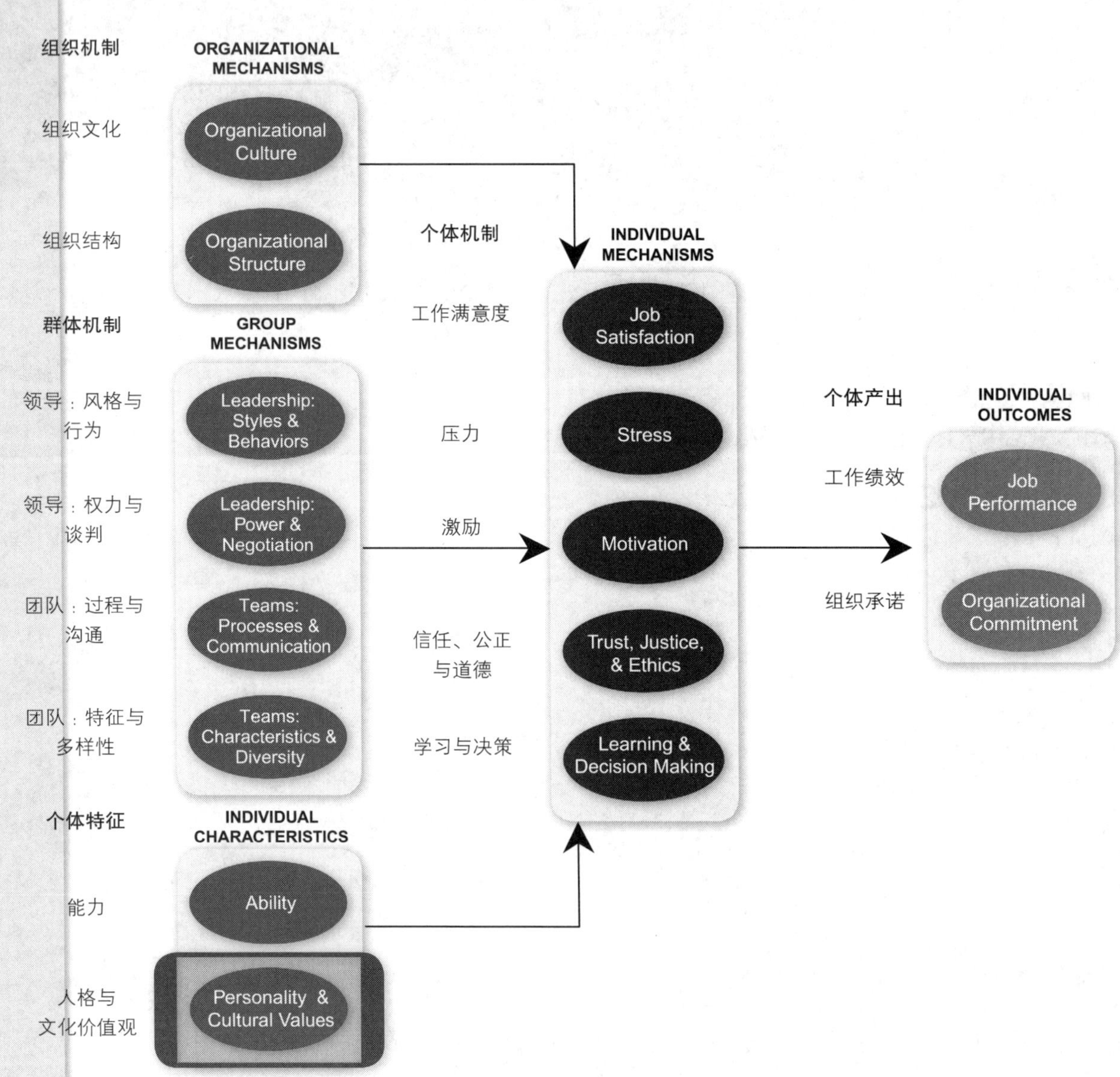

LEARNING GOALS

After reading this chapter, you should be able to answer the following questions:

7.1 What is personality? What are cultural values?

7.2 What are the "Big Five?"

7.3 Is personality driven by nature or by nurture?

7.4 What taxonomies can be used to describe personality, other than the Big Five?

7.5 What taxonomies can be used to describe cultural values?

7.6 How does personality affect job performance and organizational commitment?

7.7 Are personality tests useful tools for organizational hiring?

PANDA EXPRESS

"Hi, I'm Francis Yee and I'm making a commitment to being more open." Sound like a greeting that might be offered at a psychology seminar, or maybe a self-help workshop? Actually, it's a greeting offered at a corporate meeting of Panda Express. You see, the CEO of Panda Express, 62-year-old Andrew Cherng, has long been an avid consumer of business, management, and self-improvement materials. Even when he opened his first restaurant, the Panda Inn in Pasadena, California, in 1973, his waiters recall him bringing in cassette recordings of whatever seminar he'd recently attended. "Business is a playground," notes Cherng. "Business is where you practice your human skills. It's where you grow! You grow as a person, and then you will grow in business. That's how you go forward."

Panda Express has certainly done its share of growing since 1973. The still privately held company has 1,350 locations, with $1.4 billion in sales in the "fast casual" segment of the restaurant market. Despite the economic downturn, the chain enjoyed 7 percent same-store sales growth over the past year. And the optimistic-by-nature Cherng sees more where that came from. He wants to be at 2,300 stores by 2015, and wants to increase sales from $1.4 million per store to $2 million per store (one of Panda's benchmarks, California's In-N-Out Burger, averages $8–10 million in sales per store). Cherng provides a call to arms at one corporate meeting, telling the "Pandas"—the term used for employees at the company—"We need to be at $2 million per store. . . . I'm challenging all of you to be impeccable, to aim higher, to grow!"

Like most service-sector jobs, being an employee at Panda Express requires the warmth and patience needed for dealing with customers, along with the care and diligence to do the job well. Employees also need to be able to work with (and for) individuals from different cultures. Although Panda's employees are predominantly Asian and Latino, many customers are Caucasian. Cherng himself embodies a number of those traits, being described as the quintessential "front of the house" maître d': welcoming, eager, and even joyous. But Cherng's emphasis on self-improvement also demands more of what Francis Yee was working on: openness. Employees need to be willing to take an honest look at their strengths and weaknesses, and be open to new and different avenues for growth. As Cherng summarizes, "Before 2003 we used to be more task-based. But now, if you want to be a manager at Panda, you have to be committed to being positive, to continuous learning."

人格与文化价值观

PERSONALITY AND CULTURAL VALUES

人格（也译作“个性”）是指解释个体的思维、情绪及行为特性的内在结构与倾向。

特质是指个体应对环境时重复发生的规律或倾向。

7.1
What is personality? What are cultural values?

文化价值观是指在既定的文化中，人们对理想的终极状态或行为模式的共同信念。

It seems clear that Panda Express pays close attention to the personality of its employees when making decisions about hiring and development. **Personality** refers to the structures and propensities inside people that explain their characteristic patterns of thought, emotion, and behavior. Personality creates people's social reputations—the way they are perceived by friends, family, coworkers, and supervisors. In this way, personality captures *what people are like.* That's in contrast to ability, the subject of Chapter 8, which captures *what people can do.* Although we sometimes describe people as having "a good personality," personality is actually a collection of multiple traits. **Traits** are defined as recurring regularities or trends in people's responses to their environment. Adjectives such as responsible, easygoing, polite, and reserved are examples of traits that can be used to summarize someone's personality.

As we'll describe later, personality traits are a function of both your genes and your environment. One important piece of the environmental part of that equation is the culture in which you were raised. **Cultural values** are defined as shared beliefs about desirable end states or modes of conduct in a given culture. You can think of cultural values as capturing *what cultures are like.* Adjectives such as traditional, informal, risk averse, or assertive are all examples of values that can be used to summarize a nation's culture. Cultural values can influence the development of people's personality traits, as well as how those traits are expressed in daily life. In this way, a responsible person in the United States may act somewhat differently than a responsible person in China, just as an easygoing person in France may act somewhat differently than an easygoing person in Indonesia.

我们如何描述员工是什么样的

HOW CAN WE DESCRIBE WHAT EMPLOYEES ARE LIKE?

We can use personality traits and cultural values to describe what employees are like. For example, how would you describe your first college roommate to one of your classmates? You'd start off using certain adjectives—maybe the roommate was funny and outgoing, or maybe frugal and organized. Of course, it would take more than a few adjectives to describe your roommate fully. You could probably go on listing traits for several minutes, maybe even coming up with 100 traits or more. Although 100 traits may sound like a lot, personality researchers note that the third edition of *Webster's Unabridged Dictionary* contained 1,710 adjectives that can be used to describe someone's traits! Was your roommate abrasive, adulterous, agitable, alarmable, antisocial, arbitrative, arrogant, asocial, audacious, aweless, and awkward? We hope not!

“大五” 分类系统

THE BIG FIVE TAXONOMY

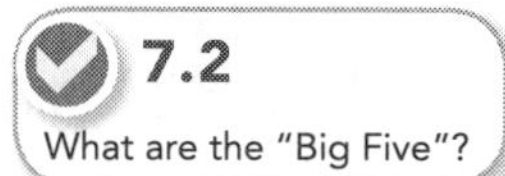

“大五” 模型是指个体人格特征的五个维度：尽责性、宜人性、神经质、对经验的开放性以及外倾性。

With 1,710 adjectives, you might be worrying about the length of this chapter (or the difficulty of your next exam!). Fortunately, it turns out that most adjectives are variations of five broad dimensions or "factors" that can be used to summarize our personalities. Those five personality dimensions include **conscientiousness, agreeableness, neuroticism, openness to experience,** and **extraversion.** Collectively, these dimensions have been dubbed the **Big Five.** Figure 7-1 lists the traits that can be found within each of the Big Five dimensions. We acknowledge that it can be hard to remember the particular labels for the Big Five dimensions, and we only wish there was some acronym that could make the process easier. . . .

FIGURE 7-1 Trait Adjectives Associated with the Big Five

C	A	N	O	E
Conscientiousness	Agreeableness	Neuroticism	Openness	Extraversion
• Dependable • Organized • Reliable • Ambitious • Hardworking • Persevering	• Kind • Cooperative • Sympathetic • Helpful • Courteous • Warm	• Nervous • Moody • Emotional • Insecure • Jealous • Unstable	• Curious • Imaginative • Creative • Complex • Refined • Sophisticated	• Talkative • Sociable • Passionate • Assertive • Bold • Dominant
NOT	NOT	NOT	NOT	NOT
• Careless • Sloppy • Inefficient • Negligent • Lazy • Irresponsible	• Critical • Antagonistic • Callous • Selfish • Rude • Cold	• Calm • Steady • Relaxed • At ease • Secure • Contented	• Uninquisitive • Conventional • Conforming • Simple • Unartistic • Traditional	• Quiet • Shy • Inhibited • Bashful • Reserved • Submissive

Sources: G. Saucier, "Mini-Markers: A Brief Version of Goldberg's Unipolar Big-Five Markers," *Journal of Personality Assessment* 63 (1994), pp. 506–516; L.R. Goldberg, "The Development of Markers for the Big-Five Factor Structure," *Psychological Assessment* 4 (1992), pp. 26–42; R.R. McCrae and P.T. Costa Jr., "Validation of the Five-Factor Model of Personality across Instruments and Observers," *Journal of Personality and Social Psychology* 52 (1987), pp. 81–90; and C.M. Gill and G.P. Hodgkinson, "Development and Validation of the Five-Factor Model Questionnaire (FFMQ): An Adjectival-Based Personality Inventory for Use in Occupational Settings," *Personnel Psychology* 60 (2007), pp. 731–766.

Would you like to see what your Big Five profile looks like? Our **OB Assessments** feature will show you where you stand on each of the five dimensions. After you've gotten a feel for your personality profile, you might be wondering about some of the following questions: How does personality develop? Why do people have the traits that they possess? Will those traits change

OB ASSESSMENTS

THE BIG FIVE

What does your personality profile look like? This assessment is designed to measure the five major dimensions of personality: conscientiousness (C), agreeableness (A), neuroticism (N), openness to experience (O), and extraversion (E). Listed below are phrases describing people's behaviors. Please write a number next to each statement that indicates the extent to which it accurately describes you. Answer each question using the response scale provided. Then subtract your answers to the boldfaced questions from 6, with the difference being your new answer for those questions. For example, if your original answer for question 6 was "2," your new answer is "4" (6 –2). (For more assessments relevant to this chapter, please visit http://connect.mcgraw-hill.com.)

1	2	3	4	5
VERY INACCURATE	MODERATELY INACCURATE	NEITHER INACCURATE NOR ACCURATE	MODERATELY ACCURATE	VERY ACCURATE

1. I am the life of the party.
2. I sympathize with others' feelings.
3. I get chores done right away.
4. I have frequent mood swings.
5. I have a vivid imagination.
6. **I don't talk a lot.**
7. **I am not interested in other people's problems.**
8. **I often forget to put things back in their proper place.**
9. **I am relaxed most of the time.**
10. **I am not interested in abstract ideas.**
11. I talk to a lot of different people at parties.
12. I feel others' emotions.
13. I like order.
14. I get upset easily.
15. **I have difficulty understanding abstract ideas.**
16. **I keep in the background.**
17. **I am not really interested in others.**
18. **I make a mess of things.**
19. **I seldom feel blue.**
20. **I do not have a good imagination.**

SCORING AND INTERPRETATION

Conscientiousness: Sum up items 3, 8, 13, and 18. ________
Agreeableness: Sum up items 2, 7, 12, and 17. ________
Neuroticism: Sum up items 4, 9, 14, and 19. ________
Openness to Experience: Sum up items 5, 10, 15, and 20. ________
Extraversion: Sum up items 1, 6, 11, and 16. ________

Now chart your scores in the figure below to see whether you are above or below the norm for each dimension.

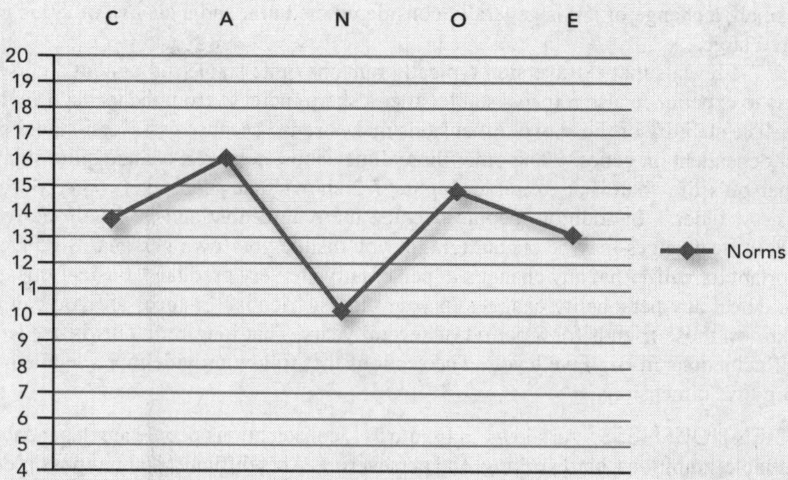

Source: Copyright © 2006 by the American Psychological Association. Reproduced with permission from M.B. Donnellan, F.L. Oswald, B.M. Baird, and R.E. Lucas, "The Mini-IPIP Scales: Tiny-Yet-Effective Measures of the Big Five Factors of Personality," *Psychological Assessment* 18 (2006), pp. 192–203. No further reproduction or distribution is permitted without written permission from the American Psychological Association.

over time? All of these questions are variations on the "nature vs. nurture" debate: Is personality a function of our genes, or is it something that we develop as a function of our experiences and environment? As you might guess, it's sometimes difficult to tease apart the impact of nature and nurture on personality. Let's assume for a moment that you're especially extraverted and so are your parents. Does this mean you've inherited their "extraversion gene"? Or does it mean that you observed and copied their extraverted behavior during your childhood (and were rewarded with praise for doing so)? It's impossible to know, because the effects of nature and nurture are acting in combination in this example.

One method of separating nature and nurture effects is to study identical twins who've been adopted by different sets of parents at birth. For example, the University of Minnesota has been conducting studies of pairs of identical twins reared apart for several decades. Such studies find, for example, that extraversion scores tend to be significantly correlated across pairs of identical twins. Such findings can clearly be attributed to "nature," because identical twins share 100 percent of their genetic material, but cannot be explained by "nurture," because the twins were raised in different environments. A review of several different twin studies concludes that genes have a significant impact on people's Big Five profile. More specifically, 49 percent of the variation in extraversion is accounted for by genetic differences. The genetic impact is somewhat smaller for the rest of the Big Five: 45 percent for openness, 41 percent for neuroticism, 38 percent for conscientiousness, and 35 percent for agreeableness.

7.3
Is personality driven by nature or by nurture?

Another method of examining the genetic basis of personality is to examine changes in personality traits over time. Longitudinal studies require participants to complete personality assessments at multiple time periods, often separated by several years. If personality has a strong genetic component, then people's Big Five profiles at, say, age 21 should be very similar to their profiles at age 50. Figure 7-2 summarizes the results of 92 studies that assessed personality changes in more than 50,000 people. The figure notes personality changes across seven time periods, including teenage years (age 10–18), college years (18–22), and people's 20s, 30s, 40s, 50s, and 60s. The *y*-axis expresses changes in personality in standard deviation terms, ranging from +1 (one standard deviation increase on a given dimension) to −1 (one standard deviation decrease on a given dimension). In standard deviation terms, a change of .20 is generally considered small, a change of .50 is generally considered medium, and a change of .80 is generally considered large.

Figure 7-2 reveals that extraversion typically remains quite stable throughout a person's life. Openness to experience also remains stable, after a sharp increase from the teenage years to college age. The stability of those two dimensions makes sense because extraversion and openness are most dependent on genes. The other three dimensions, however, change quite significantly over a person's life span. For example, Figure 7-2 shows that people get more conscientious as they grow older. In addition, people become more agreeable and less neurotic over time. Although those changes may be encouraging if you dislike your own personal Big Five profile, it's important to realize that any changes in personality are very gradual. Consider this question: Can you detect any personality changes in your closest friends? Chances are you can't, unless you've known those friends for a period of several years. That long-term lens is needed to spot gradual fluctuations in Big Five levels. The sections that follow provide more detail about each of the Big Five dimensions.

CONSCIENTIOUSNESS. As shown in Figure 7-1, conscientious people are dependable, organized, reliable, ambitious, hardworking, and persevering. It's difficult, if not impossible, to envision a job in which those traits will not be beneficial. That's not a claim we make about all of the Big Five, because some jobs require high levels of agreeableness, extraversion, or openness, while others demand low levels of those same traits. We don't want to spoil the "how important

FIGURE 7-2 Changes in Big Five Dimensions over the Life Span

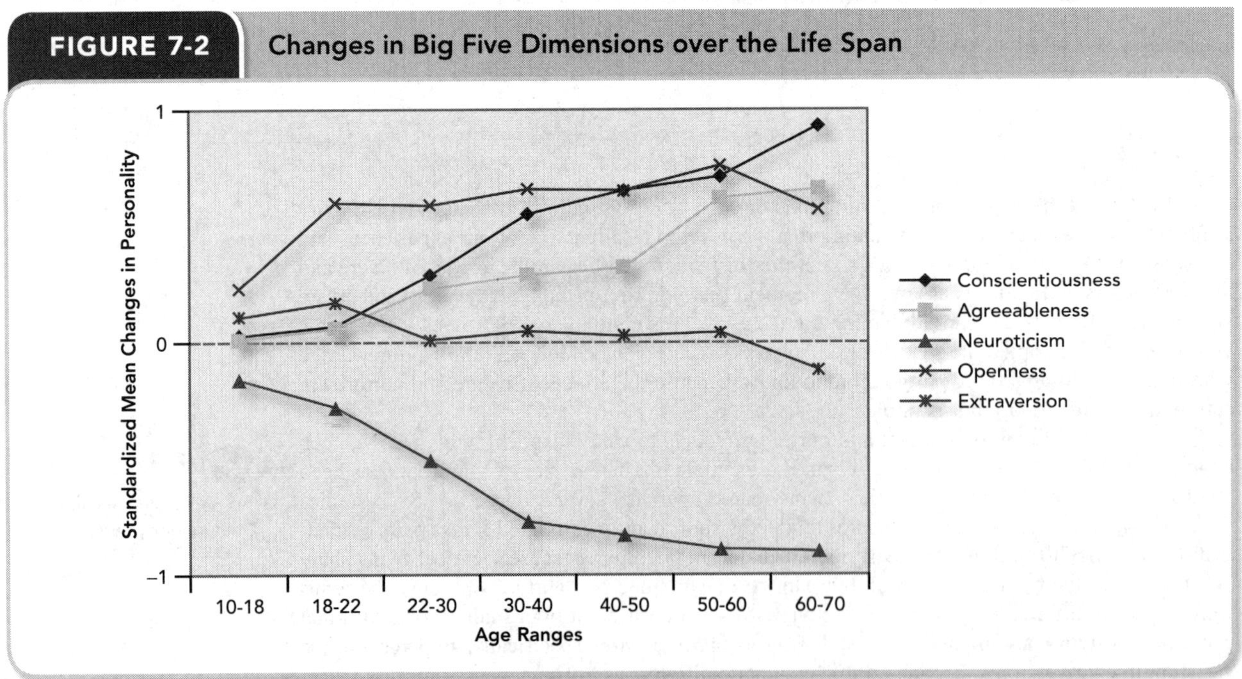

Source: Adapted from B.W. Roberts, K.E. Walton, and W. Viechtbauer, "Patterns of Mean-Level Change in Personality Traits across the Life Course: A Meta-Analysis of Longitudinal Studies," *Psychological Bulletin* 132 (2006), pp. 1–25.

is personality?" discussion that concludes this chapter, but suffice it to say that conscientiousness has the biggest influence on job performance of any of the Big Five. Of course, the key question therefore becomes: Why is conscientiousness so valuable?

One reason can be found in the general goals that people prioritize in their working life. Conscientious employees prioritize **accomplishment striving,** which reflects a strong desire to accomplish task-related goals as a means of expressing personality. People who are "accomplishment strivers" have a built-in desire to finish work tasks, channel a high proportion of their efforts toward those tasks, and work harder and longer on task assignments. As evidence of their accomplishment-striving nature, one research study showed that conscientious salespeople set higher sales goals for themselves than unconscientious salespeople and were more committed to meeting those goals. Another study of salespeople showed that conscientious salespeople's organizational skills were particularly valuable during their first year of employment, and their ambitious nature became more critical as they gained tenure and experience.

成就动机是指个体完成与任务有关的目标的强烈愿望。

A third research study provides particularly compelling evidence regarding the benefits of conscientiousness. The study used data from the University of California, Berkeley's, Intergenerational Studies Center, which collected data about a set of children in the late 1920s and early 1930s. Those researchers gathered personality data using interviews and assessments of the children by trained psychologists. Follow-up studies collected data on the same sample as they reached early adulthood, middle age, and late adulthood. This last time period included assessments of career success, which included ratings of annual income and occupational prestige. The results of the study showed that childhood conscientiousness was strongly correlated with ratings of career success five decades later! In fact, those conscientiousness effects were roughly twice as strong as the effects of the other Big Five dimensions.

Such findings show that it pays to be conscientious; other research even suggests that conscientiousness is good for your health. For example, one study gathered data about the conscientiousness of 1,528 children in the early 1920s. Data on health-relevant behaviors were then gathered in 1950 for 1,215 of the original participants. By 1986, 419 of the participants had died and 796 were still living. The results of the study revealed that childhood conscientiousness was negatively related to mortality, including death from injuries, death from cardiovascular disease, and death from cancer. Why did conscientious participants live longer? The study also showed that conscientiousness was negatively related to alcohol consumption and smoking during adulthood. Other research has shown that conscientious people are less likely to abuse drugs, more likely to take preventative steps to remain healthy, and less likely to perform risky behaviors as a driver or pedestrian.

AGREEABLENESS. Agreeable people are warm, kind, cooperative, sympathetic, helpful, and courteous. Agreeable people prioritize **communion striving,** which reflects a strong desire to obtain acceptance in personal relationships as a means of expressing personality. Put differently, agreeable people focus on "getting along," not necessarily "getting ahead." Unlike conscientiousness, agreeableness is not related to performance across all jobs or occupations. Why not? The biggest reason is that communion striving is beneficial in some positions but detrimental in others. For example, managers often need to prioritize the effectiveness of the unit over a desire to gain acceptance. In such cases, effective job performance may demand being disagreeable in the face of unreasonable requests or demands.

共享动机是指在人际关系中获得接纳的强烈愿望。

Of course, there are some jobs in which agreeableness can be beneficial. The most obvious example is service jobs—jobs in which the employee has direct, face-to-face, or verbal contact with a customer. How many times have you encountered a customer service person who is cold, rude, or antagonistic? Did you tend to buy the company's product after such experiences? Research suggests that agreeable employees have stronger customer service skills. One reason for their effectiveness in customer service environments is that they're reluctant to react to conflict with criticism, threats, or manipulation. Instead, they tend to react to conflict by walking away, adopting a "wait-and-see" attitude, or giving in to the other person.

Research suggests that conscientious individuals actually live longer. One potential reason is that conscientiousness is associated with less risky driving behavior.

One study provides unique insights into the effects of agreeableness. The study used a variation of "lived day analysis," where a portion of a participant's daily routine is recorded and analyzed. Ninety-six undergraduates completed assessments of the Big Five personality dimensions before being fitted with a digital recorder and an electronic microphone that could be clipped to their shirt collar. The microphone recorded 30 seconds of footage at 12-minute intervals over the course of two weekdays, with participants unable to track when footage was actually being recorded. Trained coders then rated the sounds and conversations recorded on the microphone. The results of the study revealed a number of interesting expressions of agreeableness. Agreeable participants were significantly less likely to be at home in their apartment during recordings; instead, they spent more time in public places. They were also less likely to use swear words and more likely to use words that conveyed personal rapport during conversations.

零相识是指两人第一次见面的情境。

EXTRAVERSION. Extraverted people are talkative, sociable, passionate, assertive, bold, and dominant (in contrast to introverts, who are quiet, shy, and reserved). Of the Big Five, extraversion is the easiest to judge in **zero acquaintance** situations—situations in which two people have only just met. Consider times when you've been around a stranger in a doctor's office, in line at a grocery store, or in an airport terminal. It only takes about 5 minutes to figure out whether that stranger is extraverted or introverted. Extraversion is also the Big Five dimension that you knew your standing on, even before taking our self-assessment. People rarely consider how open they are to new experiences or how agreeable they are, but almost everyone already self-identifies as an "extravert" or "introvert."

地位动机是指在社会结构中获得权力与影响力的强烈愿望。

Like agreeableness, extraversion is not necessarily related to performance across all jobs or occupations. However, extraverted people prioritize **status striving,** which reflects a strong desire to obtain power and influence within a social structure as a means of expressing personality. Extraverts care a lot about being successful and influential and direct their work efforts toward "moving up" and developing a strong reputation. Indeed, research suggests that extraverts are more likely to emerge as leaders in social and task-related groups. They also tend to be rated as more effective in a leadership role by the people who are following them. One potential reason for these findings is that people tend to view extraverts, who are more energetic and outgoing, as more "leaderlike" than introverts.

积极情感是指个体体验愉快心境的个性倾向，如热情、兴奋和快乐。

In addition to being related to leadership emergence and effectiveness, research suggests that extraverts tend to be happier with their jobs. You may recall from Chapter 4 on Job Satisfaction that people's day-to-day moods can be categorized along two dimensions: pleasantness and activation. As illustrated in Figure 7-3, extraverted employees tend to be high in what's called **positive affectivity**—a dispositional tendency to experience pleasant, engaging moods such as enthusiasm, excitement, and elation. That tendency to experience positive moods across situations explains why extraverts tend to be more satisfied with their jobs. Research now acknowledges that employees' genes have a significant impact on their job satisfaction and that much of that genetic influence is due to extraversion (and neuroticism, as discussed next). For example, one study of identical twins reared apart showed that twins' job satisfaction levels were significantly correlated, even when the twins held jobs that were quite different in terms of their duties, their complexity, and their working conditions. In fact, this study suggested that around 30 percent of the variation in job satisfaction is due to genetic factors such as personality.

"I could cry when I think of the years I wasted accumulating money, only to learn that my cheerful disposition is genetic."

Source: © J.B. Handelsman, The New Yorker Collection, www.cartoonbank.com

Other research suggests that extraverts have more to be happy about than just their jobs. Specifically, research suggests that extraversion is positively related to more general life satisfaction. To shed light on that finding, one study asked students to complete a "life event checklist" by indicating whether various events had happened to them in the preceding four years. The results showed that extraversion was associated with more positive events, such as joining a club or athletic team, going on vacation with friends, getting a raise at work, receiving an award for nonacademic reasons, and getting married or engaged. Other studies have linked extraversion to the number of same-sex peers, number of dating partners, frequency of alcohol consumption, and frequency of attending parties. However, extraverts spend so much time doing those things that

FIGURE 7-3 Extraversion, Neuroticism, and Typical Moods

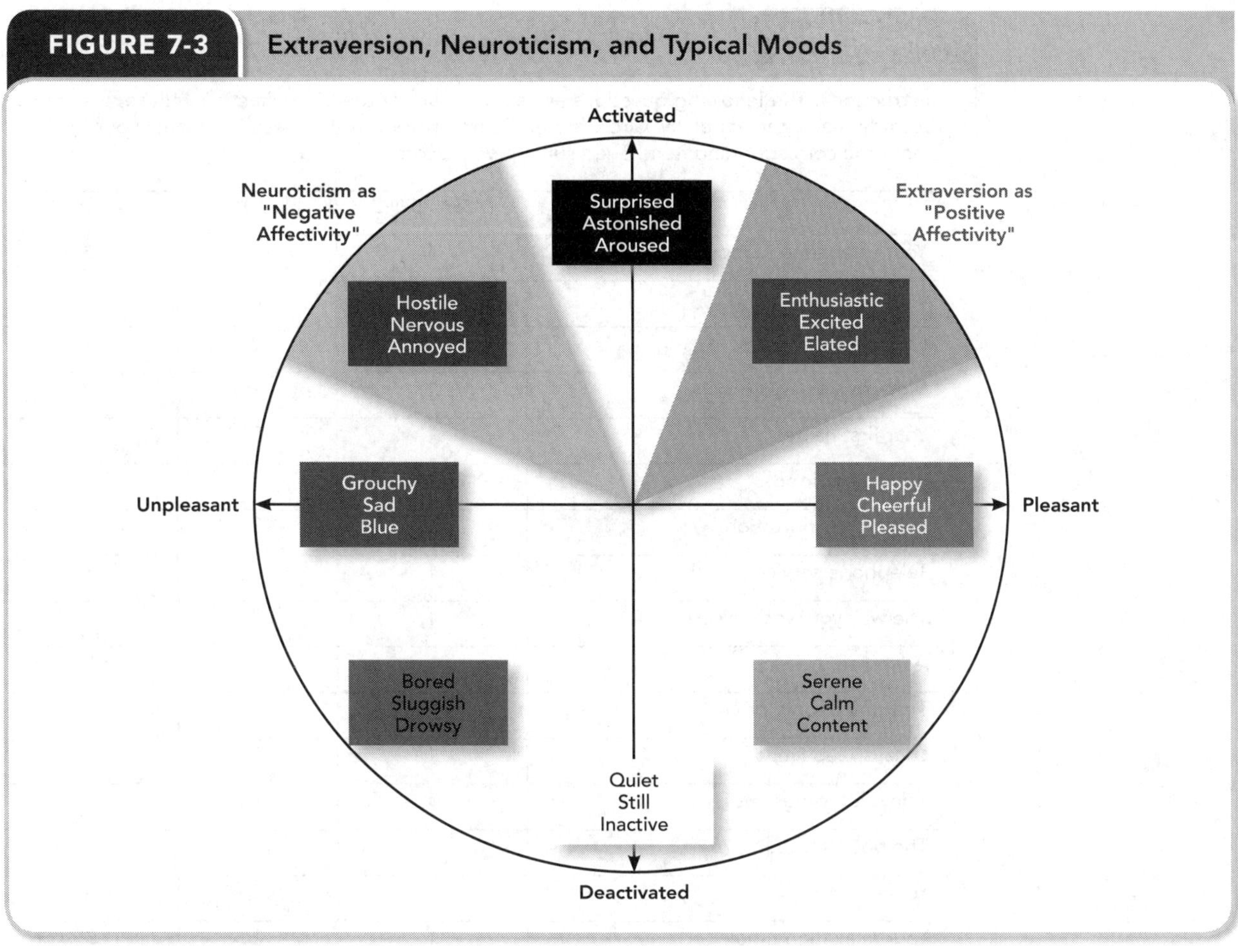

they wind up having less frequent interactions with their family. Even parents of extraverts enjoy a phone call home now and again!

NEUROTICISM. Neurotic people are nervous, moody, emotional, insecure, and jealous. Occasionally you may see this Big Five dimension called by its flip side: "Emotional Stability" or "Emotional Adjustment." If conscientiousness is the most important of the Big Five from the perspective of job performance, neuroticism is the second most important. There are few jobs for which the traits associated with neuroticism are beneficial to on-the-job behaviors. Instead, most jobs benefit from employees who are calm, steady, and secure.

Whereas extraversion is synonymous with positive affectivity, neuroticism is synonymous with **negative affectivity**—a dispositional tendency to experience unpleasant moods such as hostility, nervousness, and annoyance (see Figure 7-3). That tendency to experience negative moods explains why neurotic employees often experience lower levels of job satisfaction than their less neurotic counterparts. Along with extraversion, neuroticism explains much of the impact of genetic factors on job satisfaction. Research suggests that the negative affectivity associated with neuroticism also influences life satisfaction, with neurotic people tending to be less happy with their lives in general. In fact, one method of assessing neuroticism (or negative affectivity) is to determine how unhappy people are with everyday objects and things. This "gripe index" is shown in Table 7-1. If you find yourself dissatisfied with several of the objects in that table, then you probably experience negative moods quite frequently.

消极情感是指个体体验不愉快心境的个性倾向，如敌对、紧张和恼怒。

Neuroticism also influences the way that people deal with stressful situations. Specifically, neuroticism is associated with a **differential exposure** to stressors, meaning that neurotic people are more likely to appraise day-to-day situations as stressful (and therefore feel like they are exposed

差别暴露是指神经质个体更有可能将每天的情境看做是压力情境（因而感觉他们更频繁地暴露在压力源之下）。

TABLE 7-1 The Neutral Objects Questionnaire (a.k.a. The "Gripe Index")

Instructions: The following questions ask about your degree of satisfaction with several items. Consider each item carefully. Circle the numbered response that best represents your feelings about the corresponding item. Then sum up your score.

	DISSATISFIED	NEUTRAL	SATISFIED
Your telephone number	1	2	3
$8^{1/2} \times 11$ paper	1	2	3
Popular music	1	2	3
Modern art	1	2	3
Your first name	1	2	3
Restaurant food	1	2	3
Public transportation	1	2	3
Telephone service	1	2	3
The way you were raised	1	2	3
Advertising	1	2	3
The way people drive	1	2	3
Local speed limits	1	2	3
Television programs	1	2	3
The people you know	1	2	3
Yourself	1	2	3
Your relaxation time	1	2	3
Local newspapers	1	2	3
Today's cars	1	2	3
The quality of food you buy	1	2	3
The movies being produced today	1	2	3
The climate where you live	1	2	3
The high school you attended	1	2	3
The neighbors you have	1	2	3
The residence where you live	1	2	3
The city in which you live	1	2	3

Interpretation: If you scored below a 50, you tend to be less satisfied with everyday objects than the typical respondent. Such a score may indicate negative affectivity, a tendency to feel negative emotional states frequently. (Or perhaps you should change your phone number!)

Sources: Adapted from T.A. Judge, "Does Affective Disposition Moderate the Relationship Between Job Satisfaction and Voluntary Turnover?" *Journal of Applied Psychology* 78 (1993), pp. 395–401; and J. Weitz, "A Neglected Concept in the Study of Job Satisfaction," *Personnel Psychology* 5 (1952), pp. 201–205.

to stressors more frequently). Neuroticism is also associated with a **differential reactivity** to stressors, meaning that neurotic people are less likely to believe they can cope with the stressors that they experience. Neuroticism is largely responsible for the Type A Behavior Pattern that has been shown to affect employees' health and ability to manage stressful environments. That is, neurotic people are much more likely to be "Type As," whereas less neurotic individuals are much more likely to be "Type Bs" (see Chapter 5 on Stress for more discussion of such issues).

差别反应是指神经质个体更不可能相信自己能够处理压力源。

Neuroticism is also strongly related to **locus of control,** which reflects whether people attribute the causes of events to themselves or to the external environment. Neurotic people tend to hold an *external* locus of control, meaning that they often believe that the events that occur around them are driven by luck, chance, or fate. Less neurotic people tend to hold an *internal* locus of control, meaning that they believe that their own behavior dictates events. Table 7-2 provides more detail about the external versus internal distinction. The table includes a number of beliefs that are representative of an external or internal viewpoint, including beliefs about life in general, work, school, politics, and relationships. If you tend to agree more strongly with the beliefs in the left column, then you have a more external locus of control. If you tend to agree more with the right column, your locus is more internal.

控制点是指个体将事件的原因归于自身还是外部环境。

How important is locus of control? One meta-analysis of 135 different research studies showed that an internal locus of control was associated with higher levels of job satisfaction and job performance. A second meta-analysis of 222 different research studies showed that people with an internal locus of control enjoyed better health, including higher self-reported mental well-being, fewer self-reported physical symptoms, lower blood pressure, and lower stress hormone secretion. Internals also enjoyed more social support at work than externals and sensed that they had a stronger relationship with their supervisors. They viewed their jobs as having more beneficial characteristics, such as autonomy and significance, and fewer negative characteristics, such as conflict and ambiguity. In addition, those with an internal locus of control earned a higher salary than those with an external locus. See our **OB on Screen** feature for a character with an exceptionally internal locus of control.

OPENNESS TO EXPERIENCE. The final dimension of the Big Five is openness to experience. Open people are curious, imaginative, creative, complex, refined, and sophisticated. Of all the Big Five, openness to experience has the most alternative labels. Sometimes it's called "Inquisitiveness" or "Intellectualness" or even "Culture" (not in the national culture sense—rather, in the "high culture" sense of knowing fine wine, art, and classical music). Much like agreeableness and extraversion, the traits associated with openness are beneficial in some jobs but not others. As a result, openness is not related to job performance across all occupations.

TABLE 7-2 External and Internal Locus of Control

PEOPLE WITH AN EXTERNAL LOCUS OF CONTROL TEND TO BELIEVE:	PEOPLE WITH AN INTERNAL LOCUS OF CONTROL TEND TO BELIEVE:
Many of the unhappy things in people's lives are partly due to bad luck.	People's misfortunes result from the mistakes they make.
Getting a good job depends mainly on being in the right place at the right time.	Becoming a success is a matter of hard work; luck has little or nothing to do with it.
Many times exam questions tend to be so unrelated to course work that studying is really useless.	In the case of the well-prepared student, there is rarely if ever such a thing as an unfair test.
This world is run by the few people in power, and there is not much the little guy can do about it.	The average citizen can have an influence in government decisions.
There's not much use in trying too hard to please people; if they like you, they like you.	People are lonely because they don't try to be friendly.

Source: Adapted from J.B. Rotter, "Generalized Expectancies for Internal versus External Control of Reinforcement," *Psychological Monographs* 80 (1966), pp. 1–28.

OB ON SCREEN

THE ADJUSTMENT BUREAU

You've just seen behind a curtain that you weren't even supposed to know existed. . . . Your path through the world this morning was supposed to be adjusted.

With those words, an agent known only as Richardson (John Slattery) tries to explain a great many things to David Norris (Matt Damon) in *The Adjustment Bureau* (Dir.: George Nolfi, Universal Pictures, 2011). David's concession speech in a New York senate race—inspired by a chance meeting with a mysterious woman (Emily Blunt)—has put him on the fast track to front-runner status in the next election. After several months of wondering about her, David just bumped into the woman on the bus on his way to work. And this time, he got her name—Elise. The problem is that David was never supposed to see Elise again. An agent named Harry was supposed to make David spill coffee on his shirt at 7:05, causing him to miss that bus and arrive late to work (late enough for other "adjustments" to be made at the office).

His on-time arrival allows David to stumble across several Adjustment Bureau agents as they are "recalibrating" some of his colleague's decision making. Explains Richardson, "See, sometimes when people spill their coffee, or their Internet goes out, or they misplace their keys, they think it's chance. And sometimes it is. But sometimes it's us, nudging people back on plan." Then Richardson drops another bomb, telling David that he was never supposed to see Elise again, that their encounter on the bus wasn't "part of the plan." As Richardson lights the card containing Elise's phone number on fire, he assumes the Adjustment Bureau has contained this particular problem. But Richardson doesn't know David quite well enough. Not content to leave his fate up to the bureau, David proceeds to ride the exact same bus every day, for three years. That internal locus of control—with a high level of conscientiousness mixed in—fuels David as he tries to become master of his own fate. As he tells Richardson, "I don't care what you put in my way, I'm not giving up."

What jobs benefit from high levels of openness? Generally speaking, jobs that are very fluid and dynamic, with rapid changes in job demands. Research shows that open employees excel in learning and training environments, because their curiosity gives them a built-in desire to learn new things. They also tend to be more adaptable and quick to identify when the "old way of doing things" is no longer effective, excelling at the search for a new and better approach. In fact, conscientious employees are sometimes less effective than open employees in such environments, because their persevering nature sometimes prevents them from abandoning "tried-and-true" task strategies.

FIGURE 7-4 Openness to Experience and Creativity

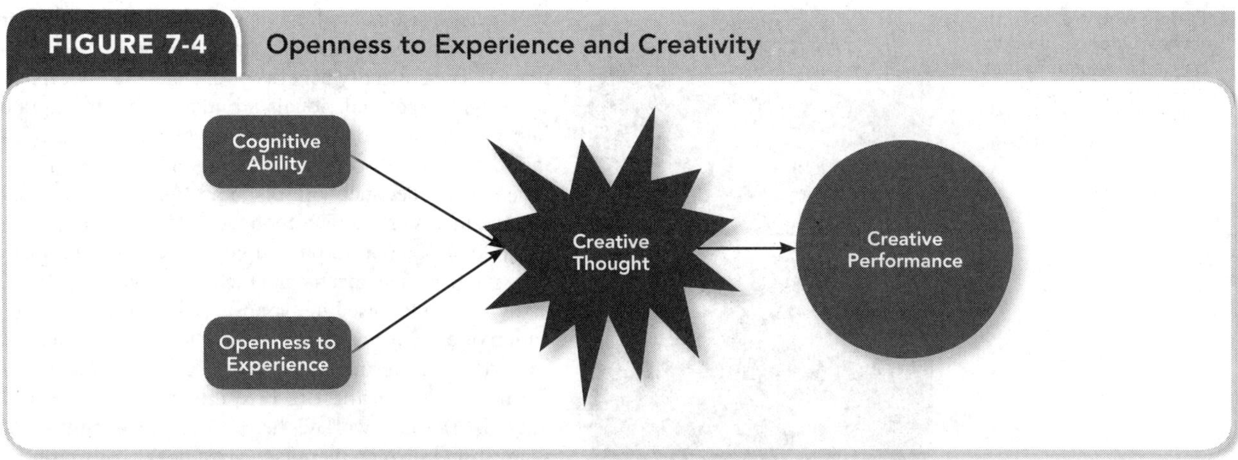

Openness to experience is also more likely to be valuable in jobs that require high levels of creative performance, where job holders need to be able to generate novel and useful ideas and solutions. The relationship between openness and creative performance can be seen in Figure 7-4. Together with cognitive ability, openness to experience is a key driver of creative thought, as smart and open people excel at the style of thinking demanded by creativity (see Chapter 8 on Ability for more discussion of such issues). How good are you at creative thinking? See Figure 7-5 to find out. Creative thought results in creative performance when people come up

FIGURE 7-5 Tests of Creative Thinking

Instructions: Do you consider yourself to be a creative thinker? See if you can solve the problems below. If you need help, the answers can be found in the Takeaways section of this chapter.

1. What gets wetter as it dries?
2. A woman had two sons who were born on the same hour of the same day of the same year. But they were not twins. How could this be so?
3. What occurs once in June, once in July, and twice in August?
4. Make this mathematical expression true by drawing only a single noncurving line:

$$5+5+5 = 550$$

5. Join all nine of the dots below using only four (or fewer) noncurving lines, without lifting your pen from the paper and without retracing the lines.

Source: http://home.swipnet.se/~w-19502/puzzles.htm; http://www.mycoted.com/Category:Puzzles

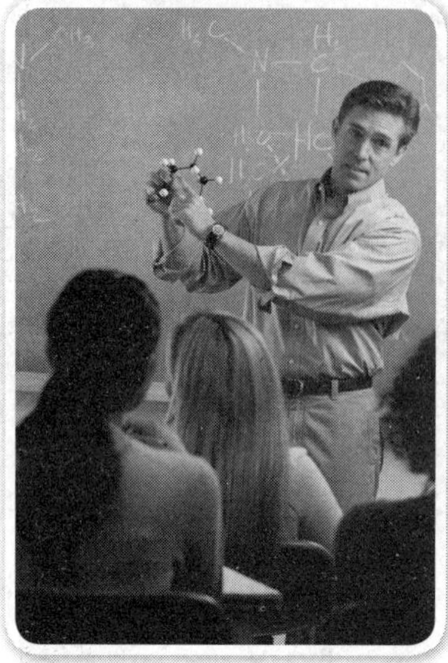
People who are open to new experiences tend to do well in situations that offer frequent opportunities to learn new things, such as teaching.

with new ideas, create fresh approaches to problems, or suggest new innovations that can help improve the workplace. The creativity benefits of openness likely explain why highly open individuals are more likely to migrate into artistic and scientific fields, in which novel and original products are so critical. Dragonfly, a New York–based Web video–networking company, goes to unusual lengths to foster creative thought. The company pays $10,000 to $20,000 to put employees through six hours of hypnotism. The idea is that the relaxation, meditation, and visualization used in hypnosis can unlock the imagination of employees, even if they're lower in openness.

BMW, the German automaker, seems to understand the importance of the Big Five dimensions of personality. BMW has worked hard to create a culture of innovation in which there is never a penalty for proposing new and outlandish ways of improving its cars. Those proposed improvements include a "smart card" that can be taken out of your own BMW and plugged into a rented one, passing along your music, podcast, and comfort settings to the new vehicle. Openness is needed to foster such creative thought, but agreeableness is also key to BMW's culture. Stefan Krause, BMW's chief financial officer, summarizes how to push a creative idea successfully: "You can go into fighting mode or you can ask permission and get everyone to support you. If you do it without building ties, you will be blocked."

BMW employees also draw on their conscientiousness in those critical times when a new technology is introduced or production volume is expanded. During those time periods, employees from other factories may move into temporary housing far from home to put in extra hours on another plant's line. Why are employees so devoted? For one thing, no one at BMW can remember a layoff—something that is incredibly unique in the auto industry. That's part of the reason BMW's human resources group receives more than 200,000 applications annually. Those fortunate enough to make it to the interview stage participate in elaborate, day-long drills in teams to make sure that their personalities provide a good match for the company.

BMW's Leipzig facility, where the assembly line moves above work spaces to give employees a feel for the rhythm of the plant.

人格的其他分类系统
OTHER TAXONOMIES OF PERSONALITY

Although the Big Five is the dominant lens for examining personality, it's not the only framework with which you might be familiar. One of the most widely administered personality measures in organizations is the **Myers-Briggs Type Indicator** (or MBTI). This instrument was originally created to test a theory of psychological types advanced by the noted psychologist Carl Jung. The MBTI evaluates individuals on the basis of four types of preferences:

迈尔斯－布里基斯人格类型指标是在组织中实施人格测量使用最广泛的量表之一。它最初是用来检验著名心理学家荣格提出的心理类型理论。

7.4
What taxonomies can be used to describe personality, other than the Big Five?

- *Extraversion* (being energized by people and social interactions) versus *Introversion* (being energized by private time and reflection).

- *Sensing* (preferring clear and concrete facts and data) versus *Intuition* (preferring hunches and speculations based on theory and imagination).
- *Thinking* (approaching decisions with logic and critical analysis) versus *Feeling* (approaching decisions with an emphasis on others' needs and feelings).
- *Judging* (approaching tasks by planning and setting goals) versus *Perceiving* (preferring to have flexibility and spontaneity when performing tasks).

The MBTI categorizes people into one of 16 different types on the basis of their preferences. For example, an "ISTJ" has a preference for Introversion, Sensing, Thinking, and Judging. Research on the MBTI suggests that managers are more likely to be "TJs" than the general population. Moreover, the different personality types seem to approach decision-making tasks with differing emphases on facts, logic, and plans. That said, there is little evidence that the MBTI is a useful tool for predicting the job satisfaction, motivation, performance, or commitment of employees across jobs. Indeed, one of the reasons the MBTI is so widely used is that there really isn't a "bad type"—no one who gets their profile is receiving negative news. As a result, the most appropriate use of the MBTI is in a team-building context, to help different members understand their varying approaches to accomplishing tasks. Using the MBTI as any kind of hiring or selection tool does not appear to be warranted, based on existing research.

A second alternative to the Big Five is offered by research on vocational interests. **Interests** are expressions of personality that influence behavior through preferences for certain environments and activities. Interests reflect stable and enduring likes and dislikes that can explain why people are drawn toward some careers and away from others. Holland's **RIASEC model** suggests that interests can be summarized by six different personality types:

兴趣是由于对特定情境及活动的偏好而对行为产生影响的个性表现。

RIASEC 模型认为兴趣可以概括成六种不同的个性类型。

- *Realistic:* Enjoys practical, hands-on, real-world tasks. Tends to be frank, practical, determined, and rugged.
- *Investigative:* Enjoys abstract, analytical, theory-oriented tasks. Tends to be analytical, intellectual, reserved, and scholarly.
- *Artistic:* Enjoys entertaining and fascinating others using imagination. Tends to be original, independent, impulsive, and creative.
- *Social:* Enjoys helping, serving, or assisting others. Tends to be helpful, inspiring, informative, and empathic.
- *Enterprising:* Enjoys persuading, leading, or outperforming others. Tends to be energetic, sociable, ambitious, and risk-taking.
- *Conventional:* Enjoys organizing, counting, or regulating people or things. Tends to be careful, conservative, self-controlled, and structured.

As shown in Figure 7-6, the RIASEC model further suggests that the personality types can be classified along two dimensions: the degree to which employees prefer to work with data versus ideas and the degree to which they prefer to work with people versus things. For example, those with a Realistic personality prefer to work with things and data more than people and ideas. The model arranges the personality types in a hexagonal fashion, with types adjacent to one another being more similar than types that are more distant. The central premise of the RIASEC model is that employees will have more career satisfaction, job knowledge, and longevity in occupations that match their personality type. For example, Realistic people should be happier and more effective as craftspeople than as counselors because a craftsperson's duties provide a good match to their personality. One of the most common applications of the RIASEC model is interest inventories, which provide people their scores on relevant personality dimensions, along with a list of occupations that could provide a good match for that profile.

文化价值观
CULTURAL VALUES

As noted previously, our personalities are influenced by both our genes and our environment. One significant aspect of that environment is the society in which we were raised. Societies can be described in a number of ways, including their climate and habitat, their sovereignty and political system, their language and religion, their education and technology levels, and their economic development. However, one of the most important aspects of societies is culture.

FIGURE 7-6 Holland's RIASEC Model

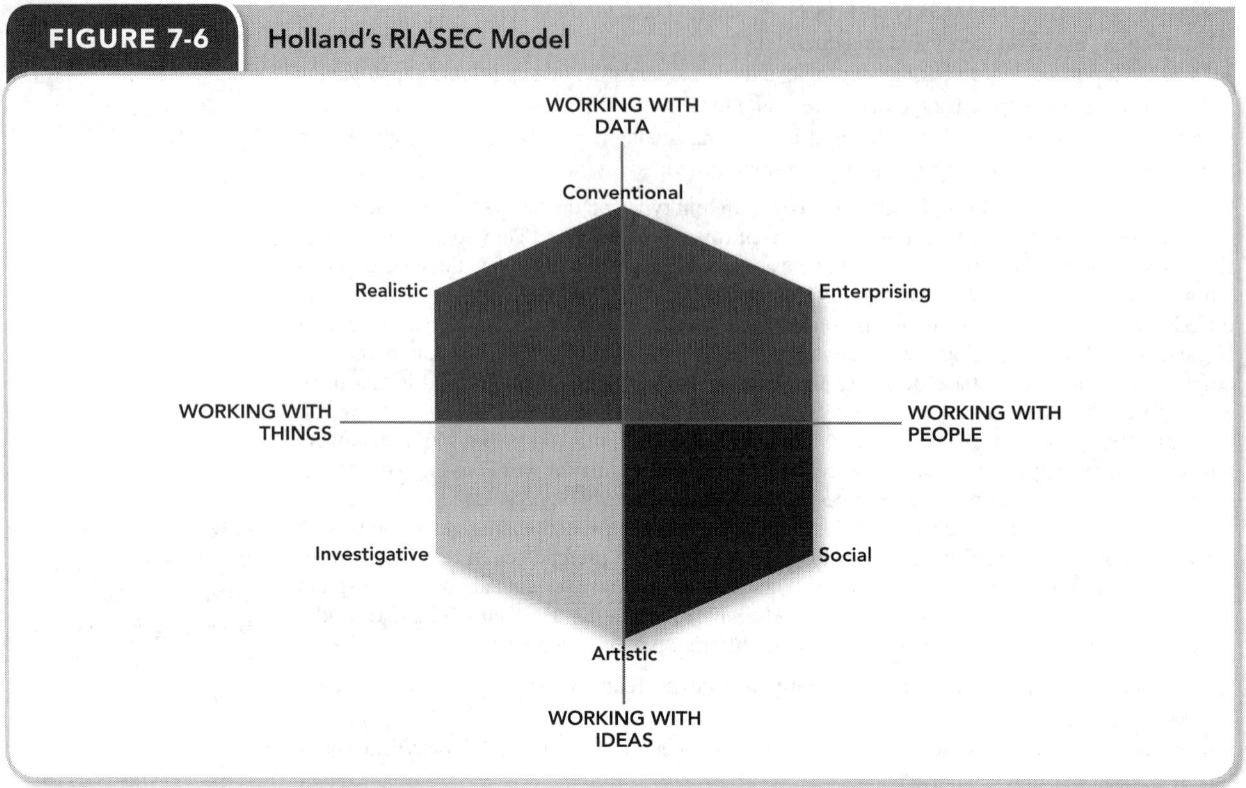

Source: Adapted from J.L. Holland, *Making Vocational Choices: A Theory of Careers* (Englewood Cliffs, NJ: Prentice-Hall, 1973).

Culture is defined as the shared values, beliefs, motives, identities, and interpretations that result from common experiences of members of a society and are transmitted across generations. Culture has been described as patterns resulting from societal traditions and as the collective programming of the mind that separates one society from another. The shared values, societal traditions, and collective programming that underlies culture influences the development of our personalities while also shaping the way our traits are expressed. In this way, explaining "what we're like" requires an awareness of "where we're from."

To some extent, cultures provide societies with their own distinct personalities. One study on the Big Five profiles of 51 different cultures showed that some societies tend to value certain personality traits more than other societies. For example, people from India tend to be more conscientious than people from Belgium. People from the Czech Republic tend to be more agreeable than people from Hong Kong of China. People from Brazil tend to be more neurotic than people from China. People from Australia tend to be more extraverted than people from Russia. People from Denmark tend to be more open than people from Argentina. For their part, people in the United States trend toward the high end of the 51-culture sample on extraversion and openness, staying near the middle for the other Big Five dimensions. Of course, that doesn't mean that all of the members of these societies have exactly the same personality. Instead, those results merely convey that certain cultures tend to place a higher value on certain traits.

7.5
What taxonomies can be used to describe cultural values?

Although it's possible to contrast nations using the Big Five, as we just did, cross-cultural research focuses more attention on the shared values aspect of culture. The values that are salient in a given culture influence how people select and justify courses of action and how they evaluate themselves and other people. To some extent, cultural values come to reflect the way things *should be done* in a given society. Acting in a manner that's consistent with those values helps people to fit in, and going against those values causes people to stand out. Just as there are a number of traits that can be used to describe personality, there are a number of values that can be used to describe cultures. Given the sheer complexity of culture, it's not surprising that different studies have arrived at different taxonomies that can be used to summarize cultural values.

The most well-known taxonomy of cultural values was derived from a landmark study in the late 1960s and early 1970s by Geert Hofstede, who analyzed data from 88,000 IBM employees from 72 countries in 20 languages. His research showed that employees working in different countries tended to prioritize different values, and those values clustered into several distinct dimensions. Those dimensions are summarized in Table 7-3 and include **individualism–collectivism, power distance, uncertainty avoidance,** and **masculinity–femininity.** A subsequent study added a fifth dimension to the taxonomy: **short-term vs. long-term orientation.** Hofstede's research introduced scores on each of the dimensions for various cultures, providing researchers with a quantitative tool to summarize and compare and contrast the cultures of different societies. Table 9-3 includes some of the countries that have high or low scores on Hofstede's dimensions.

文化价值观的维度包括个**人主义－集体主义**、**权力距离**、**不确定性规避**、**男性－女性**。后来的研究增加了第五个维度：**短期与长期取向**。

TABLE 7-3 Hofstede's Dimensions of Cultural Values

Individualism-Collectivism	
INDIVIDUALISTIC	**COLLECTIVISTIC**
The culture is a loosely knit social framework in which people take care of themselves and their immediate family.	The culture is a tight social framework in which people take care of the members of a broader ingroup and act loyal to it.
United States, the Netherlands, France	*Indonesia, China, West Africa*
Power Distance	
LOW	**HIGH**
The culture prefers that power be distributed uniformly where possible, in a more egalitarian fashion.	The culture accepts the fact that power is usually distributed unequally within organizations.
United States, Germany, the Netherlands	*Russia, China, Indonesia*
Uncertainty Avoidance	
LOW	**HIGH**
The culture tolerates uncertain and ambiguous situations and values unusual ideas and behaviors.	The culture feels threatened by uncertain and ambiguous situations and relies on formal rules to create stability.
United States, Indonesia, the Netherlands	*Japan, Russia, France*
Masculinity–Femininity	
MASCULINE	**FEMININE**
The culture values stereotypically male traits such as assertiveness and the acquisition of money and things.	The culture values stereotypically female traits such as caring for others and caring about quality of life.
United States, Japan, Germany	*The Netherlands, Russia, France*
Short-Term vs. Long-Term Orientation	
SHORT-TERM ORIENTED	**LONG-TERM ORIENTED**
The culture stresses values that are more past- and present-oriented, such as respect for tradition and fulfilling obligations.	The culture stresses values that are more future-oriented, such as persistence, prudence, and thrift.
United States, Russia, West Africa	*China, Japan, the Netherlands*

Sources: G. Hofstede, *Culture's Consequences: Comparing Values, Behaviors, Institutions, and Organizations across Nations* (Thousand Oaks, CA: Sage, 2001); G. Hofstede, "Cultural Constraints in Management Theories," *Academy of Management Executive* 7 (1993), pp. 81–94; and G. Hofstede and M.H. Bond, "The Confucius Connection: From Cultural Roots to Economic Growth," *Organizational Dynamics* 16 (1988), pp. 5–21.

Research on cultural values categorizes China as a highly collective culture, meaning that its citizens tend to prioritize taking care of ingroup members, and staying loyal to them.

Although Hofstede's dimensions have formed the foundation for much of the research on cross-cultural management, more recent studies have painted a more nuanced picture of cultural values. **Project GLOBE** (Global Leadership and Organizational Behavior Effectiveness) is a collection of 170 researchers from 62 cultures who have studied 17,300 managers in 951 organizations since 1991. The main purpose of Project GLOBE is to examine the impact of culture on the effectiveness of various leader attributes, behaviors, and practices (see Chapter 12 on Leadership: Styles and Behaviors for more discussion of such issues). In pursing that goal, project researchers asked managers to rate the values held within their organizations and within their societies. That research identified nine different dimensions that are used to summarize cultures within Project GLOBE. Some of those dimensions can be viewed as replications of Hofstede's work. For example, Project GLOBE identified both *power distance* and *uncertainty avoidance* as key dimensions of cultural values. The project also identified collectivism, though it was differentiated into *institutional collectivism* (where formalized practices encourage collective action and collective distribution of resources) and *ingroup collectivism* (where individuals express pride and loyalty to specific ingroups).

Other dimensions bear some similarity to Hofstede's work but are conceptually distinct. Those dimensions are listed below, along with some information on the cultures that score at the higher and lower ends on a given value. Note that Project GLOBE groups cultures into "country clusters." Those clusters include Anglo (United States, Canada, Australia, England), Latin America (Mexico, Brazil, Colombia, Venezuela), Latin Europe (France, Spain, Italy, Israel), Germanic Europe (Germany, Austria, the Netherlands, Switzerland), Nordic Europe (Denmark, Finland, Sweden), Eastern Europe (Poland, Hungary, Russia, Greece), Middle East (Turkey, Egypt, Kuwait, Morocco), Southern Asia (India, Thailand, Indonesia, Malaysia), Confucian Asia (China, South Korea, Japan, Singapore), and Sub-Sahara Africa (Zimbabwe, Namibia, Nigeria). The following descriptions note some of the country clusters that earn high and low scores on a given cultural value. Note that the Anglo group, which includes the United States, scores in the middle on most of the cultural values.

- *Gender Egalitarianism.* The culture promotes gender equality and minimizes role differences between men and women. High: Nordic Europe, Eastern Europe. Low: Middle East.
- *Assertiveness.* The culture values assertiveness, confrontation, and aggressiveness in social relationships. High: Germanic Europe, Eastern Europe. Low: Nordic Europe.
- *Future Orientation.* The culture engages in planning and investment in the future while delaying individual or collective gratification. High: Germanic Europe, Nordic Europe. Low: Middle East, Latin America, Eastern Europe.
- *Performance Orientation.* The culture encourages and rewards members for excellence and performance improvements. High: Anglo, Confucian Asia, Germanic Europe. Low: Latin America, Eastern Europe.
- *Humane Orientation.* The culture encourages and rewards members for being generous, caring, kind, fair, and altruistic. High: Southern Asia, Sub-Saharan Africa. Low: Latin Europe, Germanic Europe.

Taken together, Hofstede's work and the Project GLOBE studies have identified between five and nine cultural value dimensions. However, the lion's share of cross-cultural research focuses on individualism–collectivism, perhaps the most fundamental means of differentiating cultures. The individualism–collectivism distinction is relevant to various topics within organizational behavior. For example, collectivists exhibit higher levels of task performance and citizenship behaviors in work team settings, and also exhibit lower levels of counterproductive and withdrawal behaviors. They are also more likely to feel affectively and normatively committed to their employers than are individualists. Research also suggests that collectivists tend to prefer rewards that are allocated equally on a group-wide basis as opposed to rewards tied solely to individual achievement.

Regardless of the particular value of focus, research on cultural values illustrates the potential differences between the attitudes and beliefs of U.S. employees and the attitudes and beliefs of employees in other societies. Awareness of such cultural variations is critical, given that those differences can influence reactions to change, conflict management styles, negotiation approaches, and reward preferences, just to name a few. Failing to understand those differences can compromise the effectiveness of multinational groups and organizations. Such problems are particularly likely if employees are high in **ethnocentrism,** defined as a propensity to view one's own cultural values as "right" and those of other cultures as "wrong." For more discussion of this issue, see our **OB Internationally** feature.

种族中心主义是一种将自己的文化价值观视为“正确”而将其他的文化价值观视为“错误”的倾向。

OB INTERNATIONALLY

Research suggests that ethnocentrism hinders the effectiveness of expatriates, who are employees working full-time in other countries. Ethnocentrism makes expatriates less likely to adjust to a new culture, less likely to fulfill the duties required of their international assignment, and more likely to withdraw from that assignment. How can organizations identify employees with the right personalities to serve as expatriates? One useful tool is the *multicultural personality questionnaire,* which assesses five personality dimensions that can maximize the performance and commitment of expatriates. Those dimensions are listed below, along with some sample items.

Cultural Empathy. A tendency to empathize with the feelings, thoughts, and behaviors of individuals with different cultural values.

- I understand other people's feelings.
- I take other people's habits into consideration.

Open-mindedness. A tendency to have an open and unprejudiced attitude toward other cultural values and norms.

- I get involved in other cultures.
- I find other religions interesting.

Emotional Stability. A tendency to remain calm in the kinds of stressful situations that can be encountered in foreign environments.

- I can put setbacks in perspective.
- I take it for granted that things will turn out right.

Social Initiative. A tendency to be proactive when approaching social situations, which aids in building connections.

- I easily approach other people.
- I am often the driving force behind things.

Flexibility. A tendency to regard new situations as a challenge and to adjust behaviors to meet that challenge.

- I could start a new life easily.
- I feel comfortable in different cultures.

Research has linked these five personality traits to a number of expatriate success factors. For example, individuals with a "multicultural personality" are more likely to aspire to international positions, more likely to gain international experience, more likely to adjust to new assignments, and more likely to be happy with their lives during those assignments.

FIGURE 7-7 How Can We Describe What Employees Are Like?

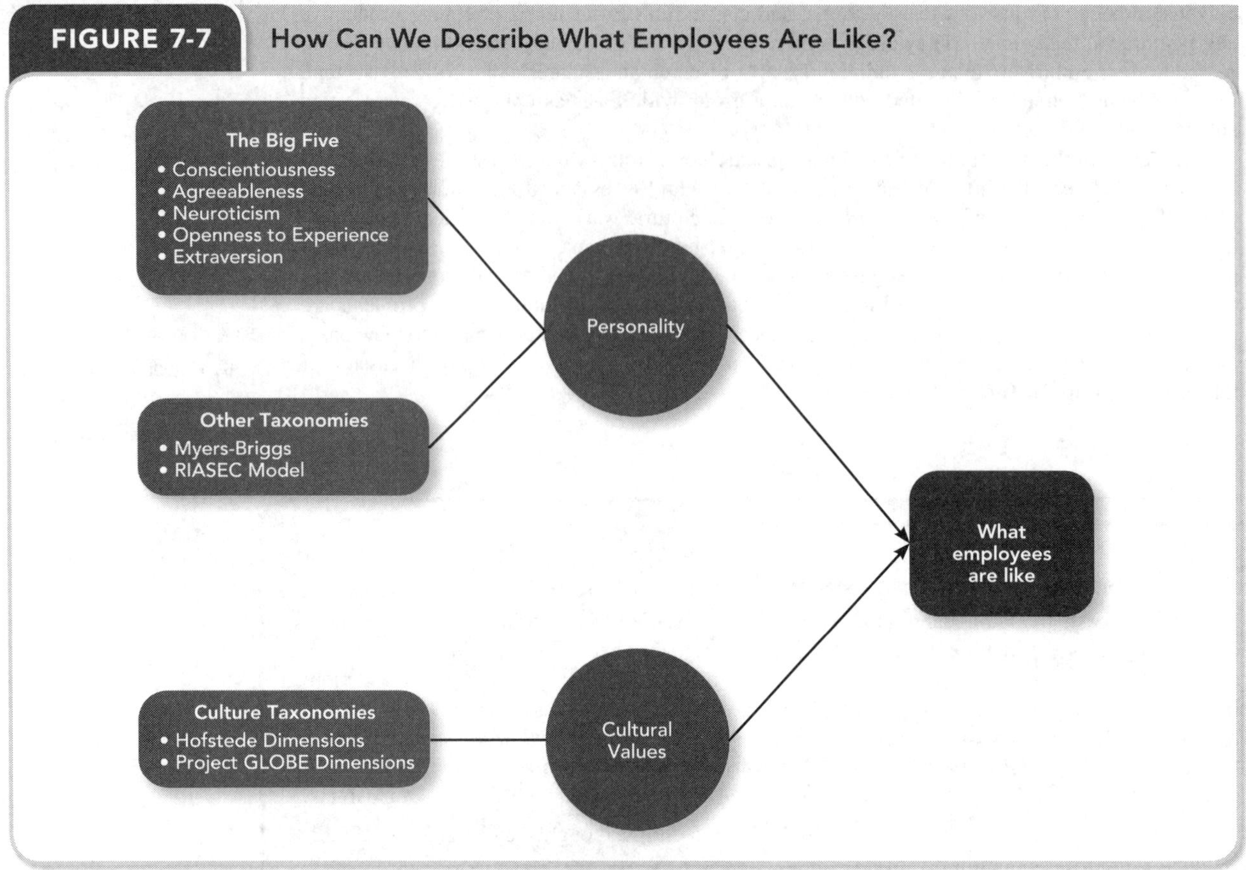

总结：我们如何描述员工是什么样的
SUMMARY: HOW CAN WE DESCRIBE WHAT EMPLOYEES ARE LIKE?

So how can we explain what employees are like? As shown in Figure 7-7, many of the thousands of adjectives we use to describe people can be boiled down into the Big Five dimensions of personality. Conscientiousness reflects the reliability, perseverance, and ambition of employees. Agreeableness captures their tendency to cooperate with others in a warm and sympathetic fashion. Neuroticism reflects the tendency to experience negative moods and emotions frequently on a day-to-day basis. Individuals who are high on openness to experience are creative, imaginative, and curious. Finally, extraverts are talkative, sociable, and assertive and typically experience positive moods and emotions. Other personality taxonomies, like the MBTI or the RIASEC model, can also capture many employee traits. Beyond personality, however, what employees are like also depends on the culture in which they were raised. Cultural values like individualism–collectivism, power distance, and so forth also influence employees' thoughts, emotions, and behaviors.

人格和文化价值观有多重要
HOW IMPORTANT ARE PERSONALITY AND CULTURAL VALUES?

We've already described a number of reasons why the Big Five should be important considerations, particularly in the case of conscientiousness. What if we focus specifically on the two outcomes in our integrative model of OB, performance and commitment? Figure 7-8 summarizes the research evidence linking conscientiousness to those two outcomes. The figure reveals that

FIGURE 7-8 Effects of Personality on Performance and Commitment

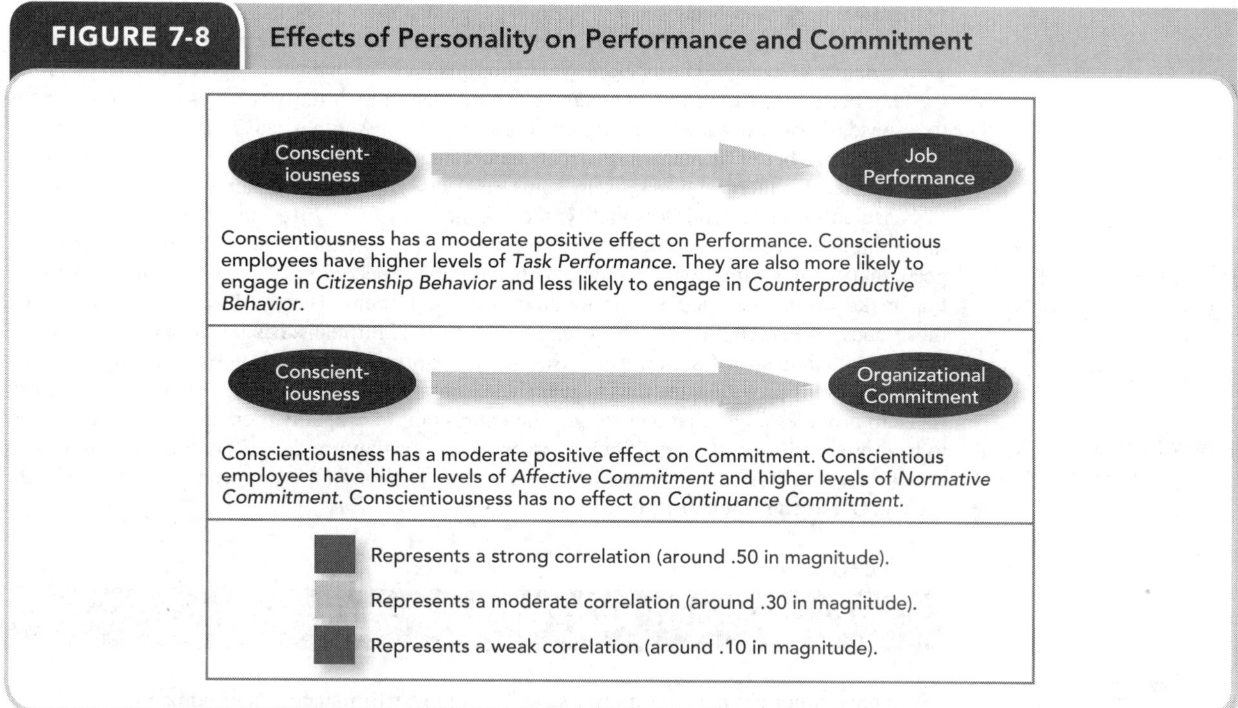

Sources: M.R. Barrick, M.K. Mount, and T.A. Judge, "Personality and Performance at the Beginning of the New Millennium: What Do We Know and Where Do We Go Next?" *International Journal of Selection and Assessment* 9 (2001), pp. 9–30; C.M. Berry, D.S. Ones, and P.R. Sackett, "Interpersonal Deviance, Organizational Deviance, and Their Common Correlates: A Review and Meta-Analysis," *Journal of Applied Psychology* 92 (2007), pp. 410–24; A. Cooper-Hakim and C. Viswesvaran, "The Construct of Work Commitment: Testing an Integrative Framework," *Psychological Bulletin* 131 (2005), pp. 241–59; L.M. Hough and A. Furnham, "Use of Personality Variables in Work Settings," in *Handbook of Psychology,* Vol. 12, eds. W.C. Borman, D.R. Ilgen, and R.J. Klimoski (Hoboken, NJ: Wiley, 2003), pp. 131–69; J.E. Mathieu and D.M. Zajac, "A Review and Meta-Analysis of the Antecedents, Correlates, and Consequences of Organizational Commitment," *Psychological Bulletin* 108 (1990), pp. 171–94; and J.F. Salgado, "The Big Five Personality Dimensions and Counterproductive Behaviors," *International Journal of Selection and Assessment* 10 (2002), pp. 117–25.

conscientiousness affects job performance. Of the Big Five, conscientiousness has the strongest effect on task performance, partly because conscientious employees have higher levels of *motivation* than other employees. They are more self-confident, perceive a clearer linkage between their effort and their performance, and are more likely to set goals and commit to them. For these reasons, conscientiousness is a key driver of what's referred to as **typical performance,** which reflects performance in the routine conditions that surround daily job tasks. An employee's ability, in contrast, is a key driver of **maximum performance,** which reflects performance in brief, special circumstances that demand a person's best effort.

典型绩效是在以日常工作任务为中心的常规情境下取得的绩效。

最大化绩效是在需要个体付出最大努力的特定情境下取得的绩效。

 **7.6**

How does personality affect job performance and organizational commitment?

Conscientious employees are also more likely to engage in citizenship behaviors. Why? One reason is that conscientious employees are so punctual and have such good work attendance that they are simply more available to offer "extra mile" sorts of contributions. Another reason is that they engage in so much more work-related effort that they have more energy to devote to citizenship behaviors. A third reason is that they tend to have higher levels of *job satisfaction,* and positive feelings tend to foster spontaneous instances of citizenship. Finally, conscientious employees are less likely to engage in counterproductive behaviors, for two major reasons. First, their higher job satisfaction levels make it less likely that they'll feel a need to retaliate against their organization. Second, even if they do perceive some slight or injustice, their dependable and reliable nature should prevent them from violating organizational norms by engaging in negative actions.

Figure 7-8 also reveals that conscientious employees tend to be more committed to their organization. They're less likely to engage in day-to-day psychological and physical withdrawal behaviors because such actions go against their work habits. They're also significantly less likely to voluntarily leave the organization. Why? One reason is that the persevering nature of conscientious employees prompts them to persist in a given course of action for long periods of time. That persistence can be seen in their daily work effort, but it extends to a sense of commitment to the organization as well. Another reason is that conscientious employees are better at managing *stress,* perceiving lower levels of key stressors, and being less affected by them at work. In some respects, Figure 7-8 understates the importance of conscientiousness (and personality, more generally). Why? Because personality becomes more important in some contexts than in others. The principle of **situational strength** suggests that "strong situations" have clear behavioral expectations, incentives, or instructions that make differences between individuals less important, whereas "weak situations" lack those cues. Personality variables tend to be more significant drivers of behavior in weak situations than in strong situations. Similarly, the principle of **trait activation** suggests that some situations provide cues that trigger the expression of a given trait. For example, a cry for help provides a cue that can trigger the expression of empathy. Personality variables tend to be more significant drivers of behaviors in situations that provide relevant cues than in situations in which those cues are lacking. For more discussion of the importance of the situation, see our **OB at the Bookstore** feature.

情境强度原则提出，"强情境"有明确的行为期望、激励或指令，从而使个体间的差异变得不那么重要，而"弱情境"则缺乏这些线索。

特质激活原则提出，有些情境提供了引发特定特质表达的线索。

应用：人格测验

APPLICATION: PERSONALITY TESTS

Given how important personality traits can be to job performance and organizational commitment, it's not surprising that many organizations try to gauge the personality of job applicants. What's the best way to do that? Well, many organizations try to gauge personality through interviews by looking for cues that an applicant is conscientious or agreeable or has high levels of some other relevant personality dimension. Can you see a potential problem with this approach? Here's a hint: When was the last time you went into an interview and acted careless, sloppy, moody, or insecure? It's probably been a while. People engage in a number of impression management and self-presentation tactics when interviewing, sometimes to appear to possess traits that they don't really have. In fact, most interview preparation courses and books train applicants to exhibit the very personality traits that most employers are looking for!

To examine whether interviewers can gauge the Big Five, one study asked 26 interviewers, all of whom were human resources practitioners with more than 12 years of hiring experience, to assess the personalities of undergraduate business students who were on the job market. The interviewers met with an average of three students for 30 minutes and were instructed to follow the interview protocols used in their own organizations. Once the interviews had concluded, the study gathered multiple ratings of the Big Five, including ratings from the interviewer, the student, and a close friend of the student. The results of the study showed that the interviewers' ratings of extraversion, agreeableness, and openness were fairly consistent with the students' own ratings, as well as their friends' ratings. In contrast, interviewers' ratings of conscientiousness and neuroticism were only weakly related to the students' and friends' ratings. This study therefore shows that interviewers are unable to gauge the two Big Five dimensions that are most highly related to job performance.

7.7

Are personality tests useful tools for organizational hiring?

Rather than using interviews to assess personality, more and more companies are relying on paper-and-pencil "personality tests" like the kind shown in our OB Assessments. A recent survey of Fortune 1000 firms suggests that around a third of those organizations rely on, or plan to implement, some form of personality testing. If you've ever applied for an hourly position at Best Buy, Target, Toys "R" Us, Marriott, Universal Studios, Sports Authority, CVS Pharmacy, Albertsons, or the Fresh Market, you may have been asked to take a personality test at a computer kiosk as part of your application. That test was designed by Kronos, a workforce management software and services provider headquartered in Chelmsford, Massachusetts. Kronos's test includes 50 questions, many of which are clearly tapping the Big Five:

OB AT THE BOOKSTORE

STRENGTHSFINDER 2.0

by Tom Rath (Gallup Press: New York, 2007).

> *Far too many people spend a lifetime headed in the wrong direction. They go not only from the cradle to the cubicle, but then to the casket, without uncovering their greatest talents and potential.*

With those words, Tom Rath emphasizes the importance of discovering your talents in a sequel to the best-selling *Now, Discover Your Strengths.* Talents are defined as naturally recurring and relatively enduring patterns of thought, feeling, or behavior. The book provides an overview of 34 different "talent themes" and includes a link to an online assessment for discovering your top five themes. As shown below, the Big Five dimensions of personality seem to underlie many of the 34 talent themes:

- *Conscientiousness:* May underlie talents such as Achiever, Arranger, Deliberative, Focus, and Responsibility.
- *Agreeableness:* May underlie talents such as Empathy, Harmony, Includer, and Relator.
- *Neuroticism:* Low neuroticism may underlie talents such as Connectedness, Maximizer, and Self-Assurance.
- *Openness to Experience:* May underlie talents such as Adaptability, Ideation, Input, Intellection, and Learner.
- *Extraversion:* May underlie talents such as Command, Communication, Positivity, and Woo.

The central thesis of the book is that people will be more successful if they "play to their strengths" as opposed to focusing on improving their weaknesses. Rath notes that the Gallup Organization has asked over 10 million people whether they agree with this statement: "At work, I have the opportunity to do what I do best every day." Research suggests that respondents who agree with that statement are six times more likely to be satisfied with their job and three times more likely to be happy with their lives. Unfortunately, only one-third of respondents strongly agreed that they could focus on their talents every day. The bottom line is this: Don't let yourself be "miscast" into jobs and assignments that don't suit your personality. Instead, figure out what makes you stand out, and place yourself into situations where those talents are valued.

- You do things carefully so you don't make mistakes. (high conscientiousness)
- You can easily cheer up and forget a problem. (low neuroticism)
- You don't act polite when you don't want to. (low agreeableness)
- You'd rather blend into the crowd than stand out. (low extraversion)

Ten minutes after an applicant completes the personality test at the kiosk, the hiring manager receives an emailed or faxed report that identifies the applicant with a "green light," "yellow light," or "red light." Green lights earn an automatic follow-up interview, yellow lights require some managerial discretion, and red lights are excused from the hiring process. The report also includes some recommended interview questions to follow-up on any concerns that might have arisen based on personality responses. Kronos has built a database of 370,000 employee personality profiles, together with the actual job results for those employees, allowing them to look for profiles of effective and committed employees. Kronos also encourages employers to save the data from the personality tests for several years, to verify that responses correlate with performance evaluations and turnover over time.

Of course, personality testing is not without controversy. Privacy advocates worry about the security of the personality profiles that are stored in large databases. There's also no guarantee that the personality tests used by a company are actually valid assessments, because few of them have been subject to scientific investigation. For example, we're not aware of any scientific studies in peer-reviewed journals that have comprehensively validated Kronos's personality test. Because the personality testing industry is not regulated, the best bet for companies that are thinking about using personality tests is to start with tests that have been validated in scientific journals. Table 7-4 provides a list of some of the most well-validated measures of the Big Five personality dimensions. The vendors that own these measures typically offer software and services for scoring the instruments, interpreting the data against relevant population norms, and creating feedback sheets.

正直测验有时也称为“诚实测验”，主要是针对偷窃及其他反生产行为倾向的人格测验。

清晰目标测验询问申请者对于不诚实行为的态度、关于不诚实行为频率的看法、对常见不诚实行为合理化的支持、惩罚不诚实行为的愿望以及对过去发生不诚实行为的坦白。

隐藏目标测验并不明确涉及不诚实行为，而是评估与不诚实行为有关的一般人格特质。

One particular subset of personality tests is particularly controversial. **Integrity tests,** sometimes also called "honesty tests," are personality tests that focus specifically on a predisposition to engage in theft and other counterproductive behaviors. Integrity tests were created, in part, as a reaction to Congress's decision to make polygraph (or "lie detector") tests illegal as a tool for organizational hiring. Integrity tests typically come in two general varieties. **Clear purpose tests** ask applicants about their attitudes toward dishonesty, beliefs about the frequency of dishonesty, endorsements of common rationalizations for dishonesty, desire to punish dishonesty, and confessions of past dishonesty. **Veiled purpose tests** do not reference dishonesty explicitly but instead assess more general personality traits that are associated with dishonest acts. Table 7-5 provides sample items for both types of integrity tests. You might notice that the veiled purpose items resemble some of the items in our OB Assessment for the Big Five. Most integrity tests actually assess, in large part, a combination of high conscientiousness, high agreeableness, and low neuroticism, along with an honesty or humility factor that may lay beyond the Big Five.

Do integrity tests actually work? One study examined the effectiveness of integrity tests in a sample of convenience store clerks. The chain had been struggling with inventory "shrinkage" due to theft and began using a clear purpose integrity test to combat that trend. The study compared the integrity test scores for employees who were fired for theft-related reasons (e.g., taking merchandise, mishandling cash, having frequent cash register shortages) with a sample of demographically similar employees who remained in good standing. The results of the study revealed that employees who were terminated for theft had scored significantly lower on the integrity test when they were hired than employees who were not terminated. These sorts of results are not unusual; a meta-analysis of 443 studies including more than 500,000 employees has shown that integrity test scores have a moderately strong, negative correlation with counterproductive behaviors such as theft. In fact, integrity test scores are actually more strongly related to job performance than conscientiousness scores, largely because integrity tests sample a blend of multiple Big Five dimensions.

TABLE 7-4 A Sampling of Well-Validated Measures of the Big Five

NAME OF INSTRUMENT	VENDOR	TIME REQUIRED
NEO Five-Factor Inventory (NEO-FFI)	Sigma Assessment Systems	15 minutes
Personal Characteristics Inventory (PCI)	Wonderlic	20 minutes
Personality Research Form (PRF)	Sigma Assessment Systems	45 minutes
Hogan Personality Inventory (HPI)	Hogan Assessment Systems	15 minutes
Big Five Inventory (BFI)	TestMaster	10 minutes

TABLE 7-5 Sample Integrity Test Items

TYPE OF TEST	SAMPLE ITEMS
Clear Purpose	• Did you ever think about taking money from where you worked, but didn't go through with it? • Have you ever borrowed something from work without telling anyone? • Is it OK to get around the law if you don't break it? • If you were sent an extra item with an order, would you send it back? • Do most employees take small items from work? • What dollar value would a worker have to steal before you would fire them?
Veiled Purpose	• I like to plan things carefully ahead of time. • I often act quickly without stopping to think things through. • I've never hurt anyone's feelings. • I have a feeling someone is out to get me. • I don't feel I've had control over my life.

Source: From J.E. Wanek, P.R. Sackett, and D.S. Ones, "Towards an Understanding of Integrity Test Similarities and Differences: An Item-Level Analysis of Seven Tests," *Personnel Psychology* 56 (2003), pp. 873–94. Reprinted with permission of John Wiley & Sons, Inc.

You might find it surprising that integrity tests (or personality tests in general) can be effective. After all, don't applicants just lie on the test? Before we answer that question, consider what you would do if you applied for a job and had to answer a set of questions on a 1 ("Strongly Disagree") to 5 ("Strongly Agree") scale that were obviously measuring integrity. If a response of 5 indicated high integrity, how would you answer? You probably wouldn't answer all 5s because it would be clear that you were **faking**—exaggerating your responses to a personality test in a socially desirable fashion. You might worry that the computers that score the test have some ability to "flag" faked responses (indeed, the scoring procedures for many personality tests do flag applicants with an unusual pattern of responses).

伪装是以社会期望的方式对人格测验做出夸大的反应。

So how would you answer? Chances are, you'd allow your answers to have "a grain of truth"—you'd just exaggerate that true response a bit to make yourself look better. Figure 7-9 summarizes what this sort of faking might look like, with red circles representing below-average scores on an integrity test and green circles representing above-average scores. Research on personality testing suggests that virtually everyone fakes their responses to some degree, as evidenced in the difference between the faded circles (which represent the "true" responses) and the unfaded circles (which represent the exaggerated responses). Do dishonest people fake more? To some degree. Figure 7-9 reveals that applicants who scored below average on the test faked a bit more than applicants who scored above average on the test. But the disparity in the amount of faking is not large, likely because dishonest people tend to view their behavior as perfectly normal—they believe everyone feels and acts just like they do.

The figure reveals that it could be dangerous to set some artificial cutoff score for making hiring decisions, because it's possible for someone to "fake their way" across that cutoff (note that two of the individuals in the figure went from a below-average score to an above-average score by faking). With that caution in mind, here's the critical point illustrated by Figure 7-9: *Because everyone fakes to some degree, correlations with outcomes like theft or other counterproductive behaviors are relatively unaffected.* Picture the scatterplot in the figure with just the faded circles—what does the correlation between integrity test scores and supervisor ratings of counterproductive behavior look like? Now picture the scatterplot with just the

FIGURE 7-9 The Effects of Faking on Correlations with Integrity Tests

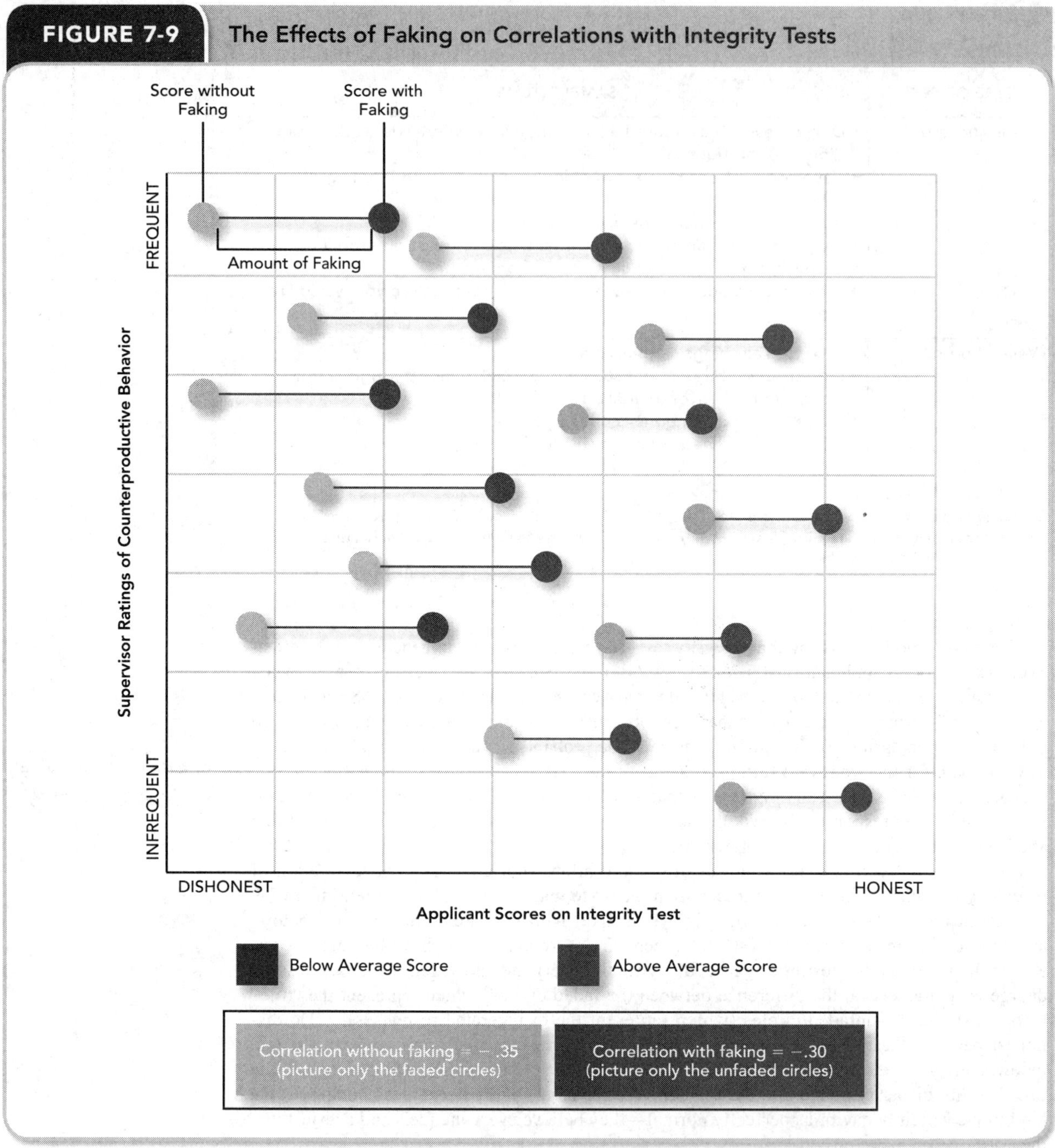

unfaded circles—what does that correlation look like? About the same, right? The tendency to fake doesn't really alter the rank order in scores from most dishonest to most honest, so the test is still useful as a tool for predicting counterproductive behavior. In fact, experts on personnel selection agree that personality and integrity tests are among the most useful tools for hiring—more useful even than the typical version of the employment interview. One of the only tools that's more useful than a personality test is an ability test—as noted in our next chapter.

chapter 8

Ability

能 力

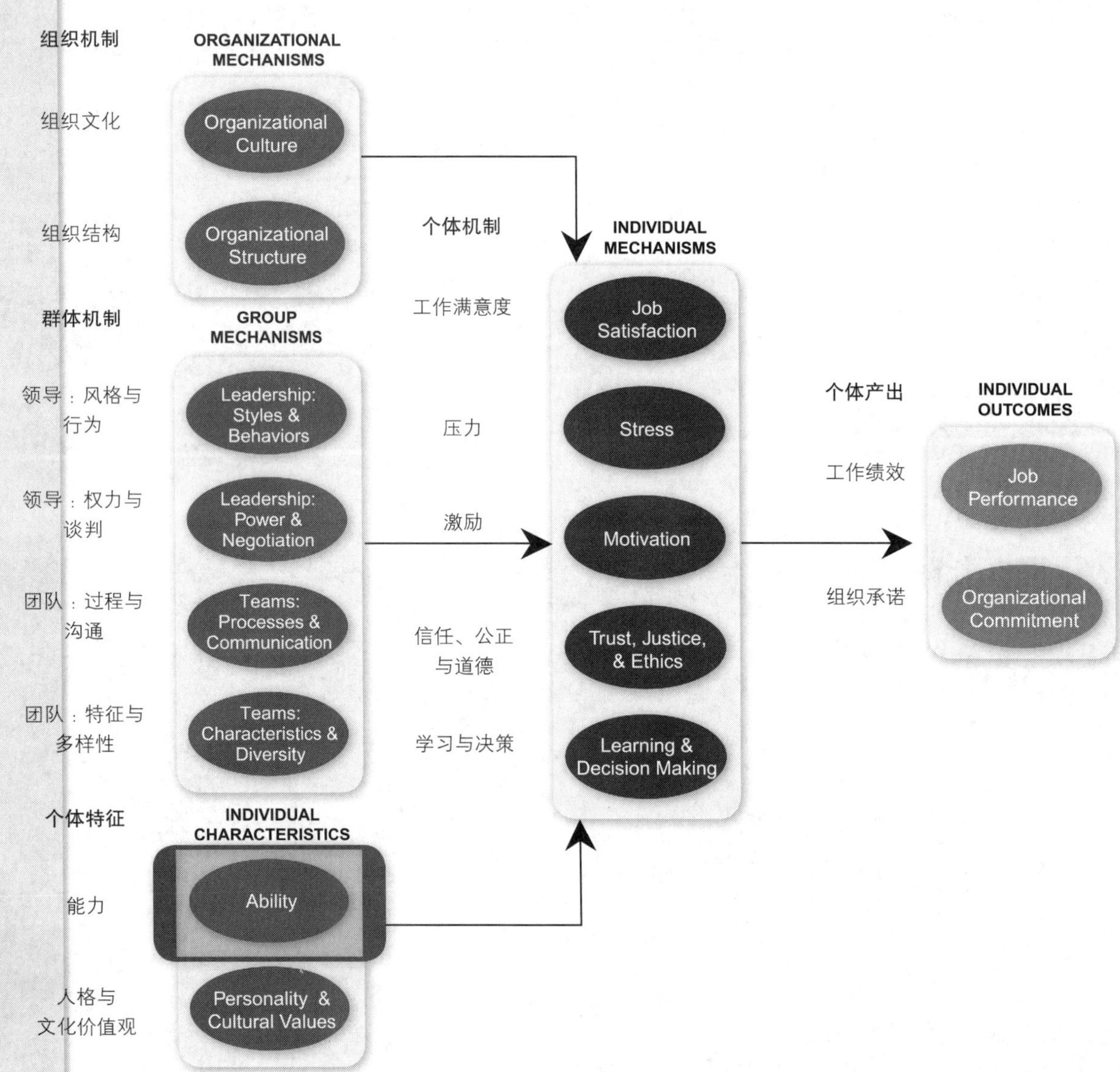

LEARNING GOALS

After reading this chapter, you should be able to answer the following questions:

8.1 What is ability?

8.2 What are the various types of cognitive ability?

8.3 What are the various types of emotional ability?

8.4 What are the various types of physical ability?

8.5 How does cognitive ability affect job performance and organizational commitment?

8.6 What steps can organizations take to hire people with high levels of cognitive ability?

JOHNSON & JOHNSON

Think for a second about the shampoo you used when you were a child, and the pink bandages you applied to cover scraped knees and minor cuts and scratches. Take another second and consider your preferred remedy for the occasional headache or aching muscles, and how you care for the heartburn and bloodshot eyes that result from overwork or being overtired. Chances are that in thinking about these things, images of Johnson & Johnson products appear in your mind. Do Johnson & Johnson's Baby Shampoo, Band-Aid, Tylenol, Motrin, Bengay, Rolaids, and Visine brands ring a bell? If so, you're not alone. Many people use Johnson & Johnson consumer products on a fairly routine basis throughout their lives, many from the day they were born. These Johnson & Johnson brands, as well as many others such as Acuvue, Listerine, Neutrogena, Stayfree, and Zyrtec are household names, and have helped the 125-year-old Brunswick, New Jersey–based company achieve revenues of over $62 billion in 2011, enough to make it number 40 on *Fortune*'s list of the 500 largest companies in the United States.

Barron's has consistently ranked Johnson & Johnson at or near the top of its annual list of the world's most admired large companies, primarily because it achieves consistent financial performance regardless of societal and economic trends. Johnson & Johnson's success is rooted, at least in part, in its managers who possess some remarkable abilities. The company has about 250 operating units that function like small businesses. To be successful in this setting, managers of these units need the ability to resolve business problems that require quantitative skills, reasoning and originality, as well as interpersonal problems that require the ability to empathize and to read what others are feeling. Given the demands and responsibilities of a job like this, it's likely that stamina is needed as well.

Unfortunately, however, a number of recent setbacks have prompted Johnson & Johnson to think about new ways to manage the company and its nearly 120,000 employees. The global economic downturn that began in the late 2000s has put a great deal of pressure on the company to perform at a higher level in order to maintain its stellar reputation. In response to this pressure, and also to ensure the company is positioned for future growth in an increasingly dynamic global marketplace, Johnson & Johnson has made it a top priority to develop the abilities of its entire workforce. The first step required to do this involves the identification of the specific abilities needed to perform each job effectively. With this knowledge, the company can then develop and implement practices to ensure that its employees possess these abilities.

能 力

ABILITY

The topic of ability is probably already familiar to you. One reason is because "ability" is an everyday word in our language, and we've all developed a pretty good understanding of our own abilities. All of us have experience doing things that require different abilities, and we received feedback, in one form or another, as to how well we did. So knowing that you're already familiar with the topic of ability, why would we write an entire chapter on it for this textbook? Well for one thing, there are many different abilities, some of which are important but might not be as familiar to you. Another reason we've included a chapter on ability is, although it might seem obvious that abilities are highly related to effectiveness in jobs, this relationship is truer in some circumstances than in others. Finally, it may be useful to understand how organizations use information about abilities to make good managerial decisions. Our chapter is organized around these three issues.

能力是指人们拥有的相对稳定的才能，用以完成某些不同但相关的活动。

8.1
What is ability?

Ability refers to the relatively stable capabilities people have to perform a particular range of different but related activities. In contrast to skills, which can be improved over time with training and experience, ability is relatively stable. Although abilities can change slowly over time with instruction, repeated practice, and repetition, the level of a given ability generally limits how much a person can improve, even with the best training in the world. One reason for this stability relates to the "nature vs. nurture" question, an issue that has been much debated in OB (see Chapter 7 on Personality and Cultural Values for more discussion of such issues). Are abilities a function of our genes, or are they something we develop as a function of our experiences and surroundings?

Few people have the physical abilities necessary to compete with professional golfers such as Annika Sorenstam.

As it turns out, abilities are a function of both genes and the environment, and the amount attributable to each source depends somewhat on the nature of the ability. Consider for a moment abilities that are physical in nature. Although training that involves weightlifting, dancing, and swimming can improve a person's strength, equilibrium, and endurance, there are limits to how much improvement is possible with such training. As an example, there are millions of people who take golf lessons and practice their swing for countless hours on a driving range, yet the vast majority of these people could never compete in a professional golf tournament because they just can't manage to consistently hit that little white ball straight or far enough. As an example of abilities that are cognitive in nature, you likely know people who, even if they went to the best schools on earth, would have great difficulty doing well in jobs such as theoretical astrophysics that require a lot of brainpower.

For cognitive abilities, it appears that genes and the environment play roughly equal roles. However, differences in cognitive abilities due to the environment become less apparent as people get older, and this may be especially true for the effect of the family environment. As an example, though neglect, abuse, and deprivation may have a negative impact on how children fare on standardized intelligence tests, that negative impact does not tend to carry over into adulthood. Beyond the family situation, what are some other factors in the environment that affect cognitive abilities? First, the quantity of schooling may be important because it provides opportunities for people to develop knowledge and critical thinking skills. Second, there's evidence that our choice of occupations may influence our cognitive abilities. It appears that complex work develops and exercises our minds, which promotes higher performance on intelligence tests. Third, certain biological factors are known to affect cognitive abilities negatively during childhood. Examples include malnutrition, exposure to toxins such as lead, and prenatal exposure to alcohol.

员工“拥有能力”意味着什么

WHAT DOES IT MEAN FOR AN EMPLOYEE TO BE "ABLE"?

As the examples in the previous paragraph imply, there are different types of ability. Whereas the golf example refers to physical ability, the theoretical astrophysics example refers to cognitive ability. In fact, there are many different facets of ability, and they can be grouped into subsets by considering similarities in the nature of the activities involved. As we'll talk about in the sections to follow, abilities can be grouped into three general categories: cognitive, emotional, and physical. Taken together, these abilities refer to *what people can do.* That's in contrast to personality (the subject of Chapter 7), which refers to *what people are like* or *what people will likely do.* As with personality, organizational personnel and hiring systems focus on finding an applicant whose abilities match the requirements of a given job.

8.2

What are the various types of cognitive ability?

认知能力是指在问题解决中与获得和运用知识有关的能力。

认知能力
COGNITIVE ABILITY

Cognitive ability refers to capabilities related to the acquisition and application of knowledge in problem solving. Cognitive abilities are very relevant in the jobs most of you will be involved with—that is, work involving the use of information to make decisions and solve problems. Chances are good that your cognitive abilities have been tested several times throughout your life. For example, almost all children in the United States take standardized tests of intelligence at some point during elementary school. Although you might not remember taking one of these, you probably remember taking the Scholastic Assessment Test (SAT). And though you probably only thought about the SAT as a test that would have a major impact on where you could and could not go to college, the SAT is actually a test of cognitive ability.

You might also remember that the SAT included a variety of different questions; some tested your ability to do math problems, whereas other questions assessed your ability to complete sentences and make analogies. The different types of questions reflect that there are several specific types of cognitive ability that contribute to effectiveness on intellectual tasks. Table 8-1 lists many of these cognitive ability types, along with their specific facets and some jobs in which they're thought to be important. The information in this table, as well as that discussed in

TABLE 8-1 Types and Facets of Cognitive Ability

TYPE	MORE SPECIFIC FACET	JOBS WHERE RELEVANT
Verbal	*Oral* and *Written Comprehension:* Understanding written and spoken words and sentences *Oral* and *Written Expression:* Communicating ideas by speaking or writing so that others can understand	Business executives; police, fire, and ambulance dispatchers; clinical psychologists
Quantitative	*Number Facility:* Performing basic math operations quickly and correctly *Mathematical Reasoning:* Selecting the right method or formula to solve a problem	Treasurers; financial managers; mathematical technicians; statisticians
Reasoning	*Problem Sensitivity:* Understanding when there is a problem or when something may go wrong *Deductive Reasoning:* Applying general rules to specific problems *Inductive Reasoning:* Combining specific information to form general conclusions *Originality:* Developing new ideas	Anesthesiologists; surgeons; business executives; fire inspectors; judges; police detectives; forensic scientists; cartoonists; designers
Spatial	*Spatial Orientation:* Knowing where one is relative to objects in the environment *Visualization:* Imagining how something will look after it has been rearranged	Pilots; drivers; boat captains; photographers; set designers; sketch artists
Perceptual	*Speed and Flexibility of Closure:* Making sense of information and finding patterns *Perceptual Speed:* Comparing information or objects with remembered information or objects	Musicians; firefighters; police officers; pilots; mail clerks; inspectors

Sources: Adapted from E.A. Fleishman, D.P. Costanza, and J. Marshall-Mies, "Abilities," in *An Occupational Information System for the 21st Century: The Development of O*NET,* eds. N.G. Peterson, M.D. Mumford, W.C. Borman, P.R. Jeanneret, and E.A. Fleishman (Washington, DC: American Psychological Association, 1999), pp. 175–95; and *O*NET Web site, The O*NET Content Model: Detailed Outline With Descriptions, http://www.onetcenter.org/content.html/1.a?d=1#cm_1.a (May 20, 2009).*

the following sections, comes from research that produced a public database called O*NET, which outlines requirements of employees in different types of jobs and occupations.

Tom Cruise has dyslexia, and so he struggles with written comprehension. He learns the lines for his movies by listening to them on tape.

VERBAL ABILITY. **Verbal ability** refers to various capabilities associated with understanding and expressing oral and written communication. *Oral comprehension* is the ability to understand spoken words and sentences, and *written comprehension* is the ability to understand written words and sentences. Although these two aspects of verbal ability would seem highly related—that is, people who have high oral comprehension would tend to have high written comprehensive, and vice versa—it's not difficult to think of people who might be high on one ability but low on the other. As an example, it's been reported that as a result of his dyslexia, Tom Cruise has poor written comprehension and can only learn his lines after listening to them on tape.

语言能力是指与理解和表达口头及书面交流有关的能力。

Two other verbal abilities are *oral expression,* which refers to the ability to communicate ideas by speaking, and *written expression,* which refers to the ability to communicate ideas in writing. Again, though it might seem that these abilities should be highly related, this is not necessarily so. You may have taken a class with a professor who has published several well-regarded books and articles but had a very difficult time expressing concepts and theories to students effectively. Although there could be many reasons why this might happen, one explanation is that the professor had high ability in terms of written expression but low ability in terms of oral expression.

Generally speaking, verbal abilities are most important in jobs in which effectiveness depends on understanding and communicating ideas and information to others. The effectiveness of business executives depends on their ability to consider information from reports and other executives and staff, as well as their ability to articulate a vision and strategy that promotes employee understanding. As another example, consider how important the verbal abilities of a 9-1-1 dispatcher might be if a loved one suddenly became ill and stopped breathing one evening.

QUANTITATIVE ABILITY. **Quantitative ability** refers to two types of mathematical capabilities. The first is *number facility,* which is the capability to do simple math operations (adding, subtracting, multiplying, and dividing). The second is *mathematical reasoning,* which refers to the ability to choose and apply formulas to solve problems that involve numbers. If you think back to the SAT, you can probably remember problems such as the following: "There were two trains 800 miles apart, and they were traveling toward each other on the same track. The first train began traveling at noon and averaged 45 miles per hour. The second train started off two hours later. At what speed did the second train average if the two trains smashed into each other at 10:00 p.m. of the same day"?

定量能力是指两种类型的数学能力。

Although number facility may be necessary to solve this problem, mathematical reasoning is crucial because the test taker needs to know which formulas to apply. Although most of us wish that problems like this would be limited to test-taking contexts (especially this particular problem), there are countless situations in which quantitative abilities are important. For example, consider the importance of quantitative ability in jobs involving statistics, accounting, and engineering. Quantitative abilities may be important in less complex, lower-level jobs as well. Have you ever been at a fast-food restaurant or convenience store when the cash register wasn't working and the clerk couldn't manage to count out change correctly or quickly? If you have, you witnessed a very good example of low quantitative ability, and perhaps some very annoyed customers.

推理能力是指与运用洞察力、规则与逻辑来感知和解决问题相关的各种能力。

REASONING ABILITY. **Reasoning ability** is actually a diverse set of abilities associated with sensing and solving problems using insight, rules, and logic. The first reasoning ability, *problem sensitivity,* is the ability to sense that there's a problem right now or likely to be one in the near future. Anesthesiology is a great example of a job for which problem sensitivity is crucial. Before surgeries, anesthesiologists give drugs to patients so that surgical procedures can take place without the patients experiencing pain. However, during the surgery, patients can have negative reactions to the drugs that might result in the loss of life. So the ability of the anesthesiologist to sense when something is wrong even before the problem is fully apparent can be a life-or-death matter.

The second type of reasoning ability is called *deductive reasoning.* This ability, which refers to the use of general rules to solve problems, is important in any job in which people are presented with a set of facts that need to be applied to make effective decisions. The job of a judge requires deductive reasoning because it centers on making decisions by applying the rules of law to make verdicts. In contrast, *inductive reasoning* refers to the ability to consider several specific pieces of information and then reach a more general conclusion regarding how those pieces are related. Inductive reasoning is required of police detectives and crime scene investigators who must consider things like tire tracks, blood spatter, fibers, and fingerprints to reach conclusions about perpetrators of crimes and causes of death.

Finally, *originality* refers to the ability to develop clever and novel ways to solve problems. Larry Page and Sergey Brin, the two founders of Google, provide good examples of originality. They not only developed the Internet search software that gave Google a competitive advantage, and created the first completely new advertising medium in nearly half a century, but they also refuse to follow conventional wisdom when it comes to managerial practices and business decisions. Clearly, originality is important in a wide variety of occupations, but in some jobs, originality is the most critical ability. For example, a cartoonist, designer, writer, or advertising executive without originality would find it difficult to be successful.

空间能力是与视觉和心理表征以及空间物体的操作有关的能力。

SPATIAL ABILITY. There are two main types of **spatial ability,** or capabilities associated with visual and mental representation and manipulation of objects in space. The first is called *spatial orientation,* which refers to a good understanding of where one is relative to other things in the environment. A tourist with high spatial organization would have no trouble finding her way back to her hotel on foot after a long day of sightseeing, even without a map or help from anyone on the street. The second spatial ability is called *visualization,* which is the ability to imagine how separate things will look if they were put together in a particular way. If you're good at imagining how a room would look if it were rearranged, or if your friends are impressed that you can buy things that go together well, chances are that you would score high on visualization.

知觉能力是指能对信息模式进行感知、理解及回忆的能力。

PERCEPTUAL ABILITY. **Perceptual ability** refers to being able to perceive, understand, and recall patterns of information. More specifically, *speed and flexibility of closure* refers to being able to pick out a pattern of information quickly in the presence of distracting information, even without all the information present. People who work for the Central Intelligence Agency likely need speed and flexibility of closure to break secret codes. Related to this ability is *perceptual speed,* which refers to being able to examine and compare numbers, letters, and objects quickly. If you can go into the produce section of a supermarket and choose the best tomatoes faster than the people around you, chances are you have high perceptual speed. Effectiveness in jobs in which people need to proofread documents, sort things, or categorize objects depends a lot on perceptual speed.

Pilots flying in conditions where there's poor visibility have to rely on various instruments and their spatial ability to visualize their absolute position, and just as important, their position relative to other objects, some of which are also moving.

GENERAL COGNITIVE ABILITY. If you've read the preceding sections carefully, you probably thought about where you stand on the different types of cognitive abilities. In doing so, you may have also reached the conclusion that you're higher on some of these abilities and lower on others. Maybe you think of yourself as being smart in verbal abilities but not as smart in quantitative abilities. In fact, most people score more similarly across their cognitive abilities than they realize. People who are high on verbal abilities also tend to be high on reasoning, quantitative, spatial, and perceptual abilities, and people who are low on verbal abilities tend to be low on the other abilities. Although this consistency might not apply to everyone, it applies often enough that researchers have been trying to understand why this occurs for well over 100 years.

The most popular explanation for the similarity in the levels of different cognitive abilities within people is that there's a **general cognitive ability**—sometimes called *g* or the *g-factor*—that underlies or causes all of the more specific cognitive abilities we've discussed so far. To understand what this means more clearly, consider the diagram in Figure 8-1 that depicts general cognitive ability as the area in common across the more specific cognitive abilities that we've discussed. This overlap exists because each of the specific abilities depends somewhat on the brain's ability to process information effectively. So, because some brains are capable of processing information more effectively than others, some people tend to score higher across the specific abilities, whereas others tend to score lower.

一般认知能力有时称为*g*或*g*因素，是所有我们目前讨论过的很多具体能力的基础或依据。

You're probably familiar with the intelligence quotient, which is known as IQ. Well, IQ was something originally used in educational contexts to diagnose learning disabilities, and accordingly, tests to measure IQ were developed using questions with which disabled students might struggle. IQ tests were then scaled as a percentage that indicated a person's mental age relative to his or her chronological age. IQ scores lower than 100 were interpreted as indicating a potential learning or educational deficiency, whereas scores higher than 100 were interpreted as indicating that someone was particularly bright for their age. However, it turns out that IQ tests and tests of general cognitive ability are often quite similar in terms of the types of questions included, and more importantly, scores on the two types of tests say pretty much the same thing about the people who take them. Does a high IQ boost effectiveness of people in work contexts? We'll discuss this matter in some detail later, but it's worth pointing out here that IQ is associated with outcomes that are very relevant to you, your employer, and perhaps society in general. For example, researchers have shown that individuals with higher IQ tend to be healthier and economically better off, and as a consequence of these two factors, they tend to feel more happy and satisfied with their lives. They also tend to have fewer accidents that cause injury, less cardiovascular disease, and not surprisingly given the first two associations, they also tend to live longer. Although the explanation for these relationships is not altogether clear, it's likely that people with higher IQ become more knowledgeable about the prevention and management of injury and disease, and in addition, may have advantages with respect to the availability of health care and knowledge that helps them to adapt to challenging circumstances. However, as our **OB at the Bookstore** feature discusses, the effects of IQ on important outcomes may be more complex than meets the eye.

FIGURE 8-1 The "g-factor"

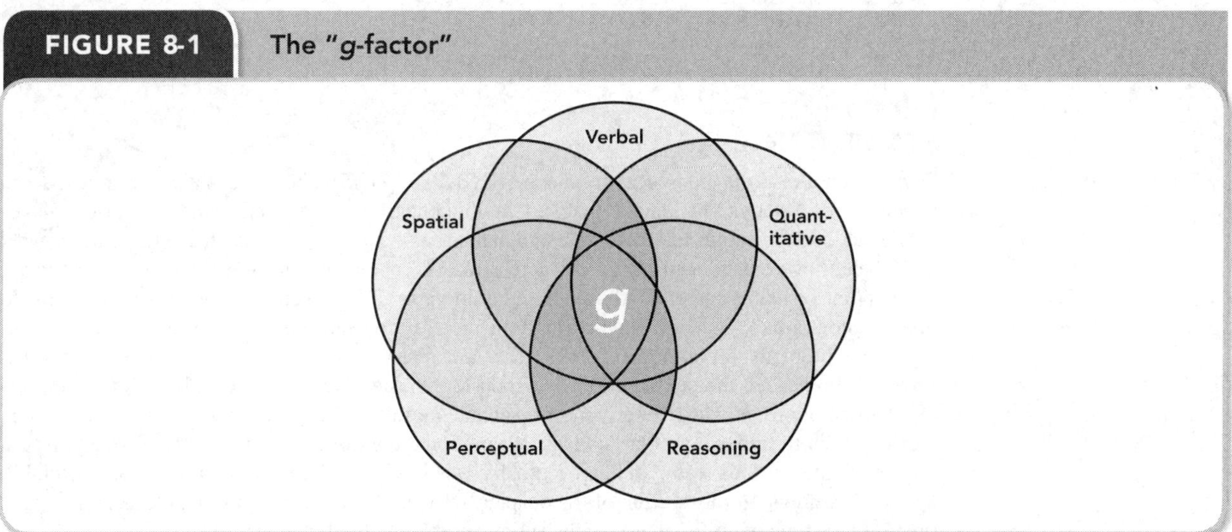

Source: Adapted from J.J. Johnson and J.B. Cullen, "Trust in Cross-Cultural Relationships," in Blackwell Handbook of Cross-Cultural Management, eds. M.J. Gannon and K.L. Newman (Malden, MA: Blackwell, 2002), pp. 335–60.

OB AT THE BOOKSTORE

OUTLIERS

by Malcolm Gladwell (New York: Little, Brown and Company, 2008).

Geniuses are the ultimate outliers. Surely there is nothing that can hold someone like that back? But is that true?

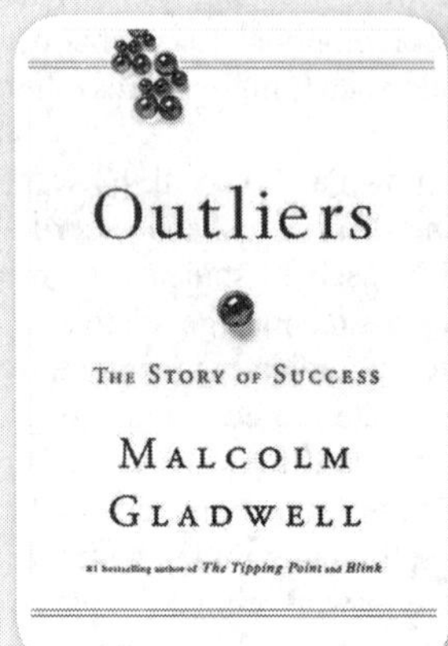

With those words, Malcolm Gladwell presents a very interesting question that he sets out to answer in his bestselling book. The central premise of the book is that you don't have to have genius-level IQ to be an outlier, which Gladwell defines as someone who achieves extraordinary success. Rather, as long as *enough* IQ is present, other factors become much more important in determining whether someone becomes an outlier in most situations. So what are these "other" factors that determine whether someone becomes an outlier? As one example, Gladwell explains how people can become outliers because luck provides opportunities that others in a given field may lack. As another example, Gladwell believes that becoming an outlier takes experience and hard work. How much experience and hard work? Gladwell believes it's about 10,000 hours' worth.

Although the book is framed as an unbiased explanation of how outliers come to be, it also conveys a message that should be very appealing to most readers. Becoming an outlier isn't just for the very few people who are lucky enough to be born with genius-level IQ. Instead, people of reasonable intelligence can become outliers as long as they take advantage of the opportunities bestowed upon them, make opportunities for themselves, and work long and hard enough. However, the book also illustrates how the potential of intelligent people to become outliers can be thwarted by factors that are beyond their control. For example, Gladwell recounts the life of Chris Langdon, who bounced around from menial job to menial job and ended up becoming a doorman at a bar, despite having an extraordinarily high IQ (somewhere in the range of 200). Langdon was born into a very poor and unstable family situation, and though he eventually made it to a very prestigious college, his mother forgot to fill out a financial statement, which resulted in the loss of his scholarship and his deep disenchantment with higher education.

情绪能力
EMOTIONAL ABILITY

Dwight Schrute, as played by Rainn Wilson on NBC's *The Office,* believes that he's a great asset to his employer, Dunder Mifflin, and that he's multitalented, intelligent, and funny. He also believes that he really understands his coworkers and that he can control them to get his way. Unbeknownst to Dwight, however, he actually comes across to everyone as being insensitive and incompetent to the point of being pathetic. Although entertaining to TV viewers, it shouldn't be too hard to imagine how a lack of self-awareness and an inability to read others' emotions could result in significant problems for bosses and employees. As a real-world example, consider the case of Dick Snyder, who headed the publishing firm Simon & Schuster. He seemed unable to control or perceive his emotions, and he regularly blew up at and humiliated his subordinates. To make matters worse, he didn't understand that his lack of emotional control and understanding were having a negative impact on his team, and he eventually was fired, despite leading his company to higher levels of earnings. In this section of the chapter, we describe the concept of emotional abilities—precisely the type of ability that Dwight Schrute and Dick Snyder appear to lack.

So how are emotional abilities different than cognitive abilities? Most of us know someone who is very smart from a "cognitive ability" or IQ standpoint, but at the same time, the person just can't manage to be effective in real-world situations that involve other people. As an example, you may have played *Trivial Pursuit* with a group of friends and found someone at the table who could not only answer the majority of the questions correctly but also managed to say odd or inappropriate things throughout the game. You may also know someone who doesn't seem very "book smart" but always seems able to get things done and says the right things at the right time. In the context of the same *Trivial Pursuit* game, such a person might have answered most of the game questions incorrectly but, sensing how uncomfortable and angry people were becoming with the annoying player, made jokes to lighten things up.

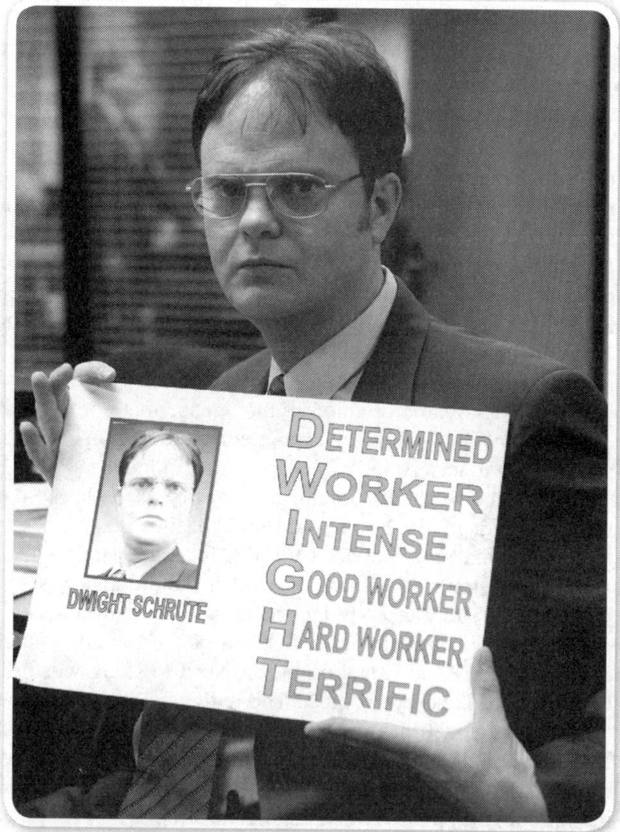

Dwight Schrute has an inflated view of himself, and absolutely no understanding or regard for how his antics affect the emotions of his coworkers.

In fact, for several decades now, researchers have been investigating whether there's a type of ability that influences the degree to which people tend to be effective in social situations, regardless of their level of cognitive abilities. Although there has been some debate among these researchers, many believe that there's a human ability that affects social functioning, called **emotional intelligence.** Emotional intelligence is defined in terms of a set of distinct but related abilities, which we describe next. As our **OB Internationally** insert box discusses, emotional intelligence may provide the foundation for capabilities that enables people to be effective in a wide variety of social contexts, even those that are quite foreign to the individual.

情绪智力是指一些不同但相关的能力，包括自我感知、他人感知、情绪调节及运用四个方面。

SELF-AWARENESS. The first type of emotional intelligence is **self-awareness,** or the appraisal and expression of emotions in oneself. This facet refers to the ability of an individual to understand the types of emotions he or she is experiencing, the willingness to acknowledge them, and the capability to express them naturally. As an example, someone who is low in this aspect of emotional intelligence might not admit to himself or show anyone else that he's feeling somewhat anxious during the first few days of a new job. These types of emotions are perfectly natural in this job context, and ignoring them might increase the stress of the situation. Ignoring those emotions might also send the wrong signal to new colleagues, who might wonder, "Why isn't the new hire more excited about his new job?"

自我感知，或者说是对自己内在情绪的评价与表达，是指个体理解他正在体验的情绪、愿意承认并自然表达情绪的能力。

OTHER AWARENESS. The second facet of emotional intelligence is called **other awareness,** or the appraisal and recognition of emotion in others. As the name of this facet implies, it refers to a person's ability to recognize and understand the emotions that other people are feeling. People who are high in this aspect of emotional intelligence are not only sensitive to the feelings of others but also can anticipate the emotions that people will experience in different situations. In contrast, people who are low in this aspect of emotional intelligence do not effectively sense the emotions that others are experiencing, and if the emotions are negative, this inability could result in the person doing something that worsens the situation. As an example, have you ever had a professor who couldn't sense that students in class didn't understand the material being presented in a lecture? When that professor continued to press on with the slides, oblivious to the fact that the students were becoming even more confused, it was poor other awareness in action. As another example,

 **8.3**
What are the various types of emotional ability?

他人感知，或者说是对他人情绪的评价与认知，是指对他人情绪体验的认知与理解的能力。

OB INTERNATIONALLY

What makes some people more or less effective in culturally diverse organizational contexts? According to some, the answer to this question is *cultural intelligence*, or the ability to discern differences among people that are due to culture, and to understand what these differences mean in terms of the way people tend to think and behave in different situations. There are three sources of cultural intelligence that correspond to the "head," "body," and "heart." The source of cultural intelligence that corresponds to the head is called *cognitive cultural intelligence*. This concept refers to the ability to sense differences among people due to culture and to use this knowledge in planning how to interact with others in anticipation of a cross-cultural encounter. The source of cultural intelligence that corresponds to the body is called *physical cultural intelligence*, which refers to the ability to adapt one's behavior when a cultural encounter requires it. Finally, the source of cultural intelligence that corresponds to the heart is called *emotional cultural intelligence*. This concept refers to the level of effort and persistence an individual exerts when trying to understand and adapt to new cultures.

Understanding cultural intelligence may be useful because it's an ability that can be improved through training. Such a program could begin with an assessment to identify sources of cultural intelligence that may be weak. Consider, for example, an individual who was very knowledgeable about the customs and norms of another culture and was very willing to learn more but who just couldn't alter her body language and eye contact so that it was appropriate for the other culture. In this particular case, the aim of the training would be to improve physical cultural intelligence. The individual might be asked to study video that contrasts correct and incorrect body language and eye contact. The individual might also be asked to engage in role-playing exercises to model the appropriate behavior and receive feedback from an expert. Finally, the individual might be asked to take acting classes. Although such training may seem to be quite involved and expensive, the costs of poor performance in cross-cultural contexts can be devastating for both the employee and the organization.

an accountant at Chemical Bank in New York recalls that his boss asked him to refine his skills in this aspect of emotional intelligence. Although he was a good accountant, he needed help showing interest in other people's emotions so that discussions with clients were less contentious. As a final example, the CEO of Forte Hotels, a chain of luxury hotels in Europe, prizes employees who have the ability to understand the customer's emotions so they can react accordingly. "I know the most amazing waitress," he says. "She can look at a counterful of people eating breakfast and tell immediately who wants chatting up, who wants to be left alone. Uncanny. Just uncanny."

情绪调节是指从情绪体验中迅速恢复的能力。

EMOTION REGULATION. The third facet of emotional intelligence, **emotion regulation,** refers to being able to recover quickly from emotional experiences. As an example of this aspect of emotional intelligence, consider the possible responses of someone on his way to work, who is driving just below the speed limit in his brand new Chevy Volt, who gets cut off by an aggressive driver who, as she passes by, throws a soda bottle out the window and shouts an obscenity. If the Volt driver can regulate his emotions effectively, he recovers quickly from the initial anger and shock of the encounter. He would be able to get back to whatever he was listening to on the radio, and by the

"Other awareness" is one aspect of emotional intelligence that allows us to empathize with others and understand their feelings.

time he got to work, the incident would likely be all but forgotten. However, if this person were not able to regulate his emotions effectively, he might lose his temper, tailgate the aggressive driver, and then ram the new Volt into her vehicle at the next stoplight. We hope it's obvious to you that the former response is much more appropriate than the latter, which could prove quite costly to the individual. Although this example highlights the importance of regulating negative emotions, we should also point out that this aspect of emotional intelligence also applies to positive emotions. Consider, for example, the response of someone who is told that she's about to receive a significant pay raise. If this person is unable to regulate her own emotions effectively, she might feel joyous and giddy the rest of the day and, as a consequence, not be able to accomplish any more work.

USE OF EMOTIONS. The fourth aspect of emotional intelligence is the **use of emotions.** This capability reflects the degree to which people can harness emotions and employ them to improve their chances of being successful in whatever they're seeking to do. To understand this facet of emotional intelligence, consider a writer who's struggling to finish a book but is under a serious time crunch because of the contract with the publisher. If the writer were high in this aspect of emotional intelligence, she would likely psych herself up for the challenge and encourage herself to work hard through any bouts of writer's block. In contrast, if the writer were low in this aspect of emotional intelligence, she might begin to doubt her competence as a writer and think about different things she could do with her life. Because these behaviors will slow progress on the book even further, the number and intensity of self-defeating thoughts might increase, and ultimately, the writer might withdraw from the task entirely.

情绪运用是指人们能够驾驭情绪并运用情绪提高成功机会的程度。

APPLYING EMOTIONAL INTELLIGENCE. Although you may appreciate how emotional intelligence can be relevant to effectiveness in a variety of interpersonal situations, such as those that are illustrated in our **OB on Screen** feature, you might be wondering whether knowledge of emotional intelligence can be useful to managers in their quest to make their organizations more effective. It turns out there's growing evidence that the answer to this question is "yes," albeit with a few caveats.

As one example of the usefulness of emotional intelligence, the U.S. Air Force found that recruiters who were high in some aspects of emotional intelligence were three times more likely to meet recruiting quotas than recruiters who scored lower in the same aspects of emotional intelligence. Recruiters with high emotional intelligence were more effective because they projected positive emotions and could quickly sense and appropriately respond to recruits' concerns. Because these capabilities made recruiting easier, there was less pressure to meet performance quotas, which translated into fewer hours at the office, higher satisfaction, and ultimately higher retention. In fact, after the Air Force began requiring new recruiters to pass an emotional intelligence test, turnover among new recruiters dropped from 25 percent to 2 percent. Given that, on average, it costs about $30,000 to train a new recruiter, this lower turnover translated into about $2.75 million in savings a year.

As a second example of the usefulness of emotional intelligence, Paris based L'Orèal, the world's largest manufacturer of cosmetics and beauty products, was interested in the use of emotional intelligence in the hiring of sales agents who could perform their jobs more effectively. How well did this idea work out for the company? The sales agents who were hired, in part, based on the their emotional intelligence scores had sales that were $91,370 greater than agents who were hired on the basis of other information. The company also found that the agents who were selected on the basis of their emotional intelligence scores were 63 percent less likely to quit during their first year as compared to the other agents. Sales agents with high emotional intelligence were able to better understand client needs, and because this results in higher performance and less frustration, these agents tend to stay with the company longer.

Although the two previous examples illustrate the usefulness of staffing and training practices based on emotional intelligence, there's some evidence that emotional intelligence may have a significantly stronger impact on the job performance of some people more than others. One recent study, for example, found that emotional intelligence is a more important determinant of job performance for people with lower levels of cognitive intelligence. The explanation for this relationship is easy to understand if you consider that, in many circumstances, high emotional intelligence can compensate somewhat for low cognitive intelligence. In other words, exceptional "people smarts" can, to some extent, make up for deficiencies in "book smarts."

Although the picture of emotional intelligence we've painted so far is very upbeat, it's important to mention that there may be a "dark side" to this ability. Specifically, there's some

OB ON SCREEN

SHERLOCK HOLMES

"Well done, old boy."

With those words, Dr. John Watson (Jude Law) sarcastically lets his friend and partner Detective Sherlock Holmes (Robert Downey, Jr.) know that he's not happy with his latest display of paradoxical abilities in the film *Sherlock Holmes* (Dir.: Guy Ritchie, Warner Bros., 2009). You see, Watson's date for the evening, Mary Morstan (Kelly Reilly), asks Holmes, whom she is meeting for the first time, to use his extraordinary reasoning abilities to tell her something about herself. Holmes starts off well enough, deducing that she tutors a boy who earlier in the day flicked ink onto her, and because she didn't react irrationally, was rewarded by the mother of the boy with a loan of the jeweled necklace she was wearing. Although Mary is impressed, Holmes can't stop himself. He begins to reveal things about Mary of a more personal nature, and despite the discomfort that's clear in Mary and Watson's expressions, Holmes continues until Mary tosses a drink in his face and leaves the restaurant.

As this scene illustrates, cognitive abilities are not strongly correlated with emotional abilities. Sherlock Holmes is highly intelligent from a cognitive ability standpoint, and in particular, reasoning ability, but at the same time, he demonstrates questionable emotional ability. Interestingly, however, the film raises a question about how the dimensions of emotional ability are interrelated. Later in the movie, for example, Holmes is engaged in a bare-knuckles fight, and as he begins to walk away after admitting defeat, the opponent spits on his back. Holmes then tells himself, "this mustn't register on an emotional level," and he devises a complex sequence of moves to disable his opponent. Here, in contrast to showing poor emotional ability in terms of other awareness during his interaction with Mary, he shows incredible emotional ability in terms of emotion regulation. He quickly recovers from the anger he feels after being spat upon, and as a consequence, he is able to rationally deal with the problem at hand. Of course, if you want to know if Holmes is successful in defeating this opponent, you'll have to watch the movie to find out.

evidence that emotional intelligence is correlated positively with behaviors at work that are more counterproductive in nature. That is, certain individuals with higher levels of emotional intelligence may tend to engage in more counterproductive behaviors such as gossiping, harassment, and even theft. This might come as some surprise to you given all the positives of emotional intelligence we mentioned in the previous paragraphs. However, consider that the ability to understand and influence others' emotions can be used to achieve personal goals that are not necessarily compatible with the goals and values of the organization or society. In essence, emotional intelligence may provide individuals with a gift of being able to influence how other people feel, and unfortunately, that gift can be abused if the individual is inclined toward questionable ends.

ASSESSING EMOTIONAL INTELLIGENCE. As we discussed previously, cognitive abilities are typically assessed using measures with questions such as those included in SAT or IQ tests. So how is emotional intelligence assessed? One type of emotional intelligence assessment is similar to a SAT-style test, because questions are scored as correct or incorrect. As the example items in Figure 8-2 illustrate, test takers are asked to describe the emotions of people depicted in pictures, predict emotional responses to different situations, and identify appropriate and inappropriate emotional responses. After a person takes the test, it gets sent back to the test publisher to be scored.

FIGURE 8-2 Sample Items from an Emotional Intelligence Test

1. **Indicate how much of each emotion is expressed by this face:**

	None				Very Much
a) Happiness	1	2	3	4	5
b) Anger	1	2	3	4	5
c) Fear	1	2	3	4	5
d) Excitement	1	2	3	4	5
e) Surprise	1	2	3	4	5

2. **What mood(s) might be helpful to feel when meeting in-laws for the very first time?**

	Not Useful				Useful
a) Slight Tension	1	2	3	4	5
b) Surprise	1	2	3	4	5
c) Joy	1	2	3	4	5

3. **Tom felt anxious, and became a bit stressed when he thought about all the work he needed to do. When his supervisor brought him an additional project, he felt _____. (Select the best choice.)**

   a) Overwhelmed
   b) Depressed
   c) Ashamed
   d) Self-conscious
   e) Jittery

4. **Debbie just came back from vacation. She was feeling peaceful and content. How well would each action preserve her mood?**

   Action 1: She started to make a list of things at home that she needed to do.

   Very Ineffective 1 2 3 4 5 Very Effective

   Action 2: She began thinking about where and when she would go on her next vacation.

   Very Ineffective 1 2 3 4 5 Very Effective

   Action 3: She decided it was best to ignore the feeling since it wouldn't last anyway.

   Very Ineffective 1 2 3 4 5 Very Effective

Source: Copyright © 2006 J. Mayer, P. Salovey, and D. Caruso. Reprinted with permission.
Note that the photo in item 1 does not appear in the test published by Multi-Health Systems.

Another type of assessment asks people about behaviors and preferences that are thought to reflect emotional intelligence. One of the first tests of this type, the "Emotional Quotient Inventory (EQ-i)," includes 133 such questions. Although the EQ-i has been used by many organizations in an attempt to improve managerial practices and organizational effectiveness, it has been criticized for measuring personality traits more than actual abilities. More recently, a group of researchers published a very short and easy-to-score measure specifically designed to assess each of the four facets of emotional intelligence described in this section. Although this assessment is similar in format to the EQ-i, the items don't appear to overlap as much with items that measure different aspects of personality. You can take the test yourself in our **OB Assessments** feature to see where you stand in terms of emotional intelligence.

身体能力
PHYSICAL ABILITIES

Physical abilities are likely very familiar to you because many of you took physical education classes early in your school career. Maybe you were evaluated on whether you could climb a rope to the ceiling of a gymnasium, run around a track several times, or kick a ball to a teammate who was running full stride. Or maybe you've applied for a job and had to take a test that assessed your ability to manipulate and assemble small mechanical parts. As a final example, and the one likely to be most familiar, you've probably been subject to tests that measure the quality of your vision and hearing. Although these examples may not seem to be related, each refers to a different type of physical ability. In this section, we review a few important types of physical abilities, which are illustrated in Table 8-2.

力量通常是指身体能够施力的程度。

STRENGTH. Although **strength** generally refers to the degree to which the body is capable of exerting force, there are actually several different types of strength that are important, depending on the job. *Static strength* refers to the ability to lift, push, or pull very heavy objects using the hands, arms, legs, shoulders, or back. Static strength is involved in jobs in which people need to lift objects like boxes, equipment, machine parts, and heavy tools. With *explosive strength,* people exert short bursts of energy to move the body or an object. Employees who are required to run, jump, or throw things at work depend on their explosive strength to be effective. The final type of strength, *dynamic strength,* refers to the ability to exert force for a prolonged period of time without becoming overly fatigued and giving out. Dynamic strength is involved in jobs in which employees have to climb ropes or ladders or pull themselves up onto platforms. Although jobs requiring physical strength may vary as to which category is important, there are also many jobs that require all three categories. Firefighters, for example, must typically pass grueling tests of strength before being hired. In Dublin, California, one part of the firefighter strength test involves climbing a long flight of stairs under time constraints without touching the rails while wearing a 50-pound vest and carrying another 25 pounds of equipment. Another part of the test involves safely moving a 165-pound dummy out of harm's way.

耐力是指一个人持续进行体力活动时，肺部及循环系统有效工作的能力。

8.4
What are the various types of physical ability?

STAMINA. **Stamina** refers to the ability of a person's lungs and circulatory system to work efficiently while he or she is engaging in prolonged physical activity. Stamina may be important in jobs that require running, swimming, and climbing. In fact, stamina is involved whenever the nature of the physical activity causes the heart rate to climb and the depth and rate of breathing to increase for prolonged periods of time. As you can imagine, the firefighter test described in the previous paragraph assesses stamina as well as strength.

灵活性是指进行弯曲、伸展、扭转和触及的能力。

FLEXIBILITY AND COORDINATION. Generally speaking, **flexibility** refers to the ability to bend, stretch, twist, or reach. When a job requires extreme ranges of motion—for example, when people need to work in a cramped compartment or an awkward position—the type of flexibility involved is called *extent flexibility.* If you've ever watched a person working inside the trunk of a car installing speakers, you've seen extent flexibility. When a job requires repeated and somewhat quick bends, stretches, twists, or reaches, the type of flexibility involved is called *dynamic flexibility.* To understand what dynamic flexibility involves, picture a house painter on a ladder trying to paint some trim just barely within reach.

协调性是指身体运动的质量，对某些工作很重要。

In addition to flexibility, **coordination,** or the quality of physical movement, may be important in some jobs. *Gross body coordination* refers to the ability to synchronize the movements of the body, arms, and legs to do something while the whole body is in motion. In contrast, *gross body equilibrium* involves the ability to maintain the balance of the body in unstable contexts or when the person has to change directions. Jumping rope effectively requires gross body

OB ASSESSMENTS

EMOTIONAL INTELLIGENCE

How high is your emotional intelligence? This assessment will tell you where you stand on the four facets of emotional intelligence discussed in this chapter—self-awareness, other awareness, emotion regulation, and emotion use. Answer each question using the response scale provided. Then follow the instructions below to score yourself. (For more assessments relevant to this chapter, please visit http://connect.mcgraw-hill.com.)

1 TOTALLY DISAGREE	2 DISAGREE	3 SOMEWHAT DISAGREE	4 NEUTRAL	5 SOMEWHAT AGREE	6 AGREE	7 TOTALLY AGREE

1. I have a good sense of why I have certain feelings most of the time. _______
2. I have a good understanding of my own emotions. _______
3. I really understand what I feel. _______
4. I always know whether or not I am happy. _______
5. I am a good observer of others' emotions. _______
6. I always know my friends' emotions from their behavior. _______
7. I am sensitive to the feelings and emotions of others. _______
8. I have a good understanding of the emotions of people around me. _______
9. I always set goals for myself and then try my best to achieve them. _______
10. I always tell myself I am a competent person. _______
11. I am a self-motivating person. _______
12. I would always encourage myself to try my best. _______
13. I am able to control my temper so that I can handle difficulties rationally. _______
14. I am quite capable of controlling my own emotions. _______
15. I can always calm down quickly when I am very angry. _______
16. I have good control over my own emotions. _______

SCORING AND INTERPRETATION:

Self-Awareness: Sum up items 1–4. _____
Other Awareness: Sum up items 5–8. _____
Emotion Use: Sum up items 9–12. _____
Emotion Regulation: Sum up items 13–16. _____

If you scored 19 or above, then you are above average on a particular dimension. If you scored 18 or below, then you are below average on a particular dimension.

Sources: K.S. Law, C.S. Wong, and L.J. Song, "The Construct and Criterion Validity of Emotional Intelligence and its Potential Utility for Management Studies," *Journal of Applied Psychology* 89 (2004), pp. 483–96; and C.S. Wong and K.S. Law, "The Effects of Leader and Follower Emotional Intelligence on Performance and Attitude," *The Leadership Quarterly* 13 (2002), pp. 243–74.

TABLE 8-2 Physical Abilities

TYPE	MORE SPECIFIC FACET	JOBS WHERE RELEVANT
Strength	*Static:* Lifting, pushing, pulling heavy objects *Explosive:* Exerting a short burst of muscular force to move oneself or objects *Dynamic:* Exerting muscular force repeatedly or continuously	Structural iron and steel workers; tractor trailer and heavy truck drivers; farm workers; firefighters
Stamina	Exerting oneself over a period of time without circulatory system giving out	Athletes; dancers; commercial divers; firefighters
Flexibility & Coordination	*Extent Flexibility:* Degree of bending, stretching, twisting of body, arms, legs *Dynamic Flexibility:* Speed of bending, stretching, twisting of body, arms, legs *Gross Body Coordination:* Coordinating movement of body, arms, and legs in activities that involve all three together *Gross Body Equilibrium:* Ability to regain balance in contexts where balance is upset	Athletes; dancers; riggers; industrial machinery mechanics; choreographers; commercial divers; structural iron and steel workers
Psychomotor	*Fine Manipulative Abilities:* Keeping hand and arm steady while grasping, manipulating, and assembling small objects *Control Movement Abilities:* Making quick, precise adjustments to a machine while operating it *Response Orientation:* Quickly choosing among appropriate alternative movements *Response Time:* Quickly responding to signals with body movements	Fabric menders; potters; timing device assemblers; jewelers; construction drillers; agricultural equipment operators; photographers; highway patrol pilots; athletes
Sensory	*Near and Far Vision:* Seeing details of an object up close or at a distance *Night Vision:* Seeing well in low light *Visual Color Discrimination:* Detecting differences in colors and shades *Depth Perception:* Judging relative distances *Hearing Sensitivity:* Hearing differences in sounds that vary in terms of pitch and loudness *Auditory Attention:* Focusing on a source of sound in the presence of other sources *Speech Recognition:* Identifying and understanding the speech of others	Electronic testers and inspectors; highway patrol pilots; tractor trailer, truck, and bus drivers; airline pilots; photographers; musicians and composers; industrial machine mechanics; speech pathologists

Source: Adapted from E.A. Fleishman, D.P. Costanza, and J. Marshall-Mies, "Abilities," in *An Occupational Information System for the 21st Century: The Development of O*NET,* eds. N.G. Peterson, M.D. Mumford, W.C. Borman, P.R. Jeanneret, and E.A. Fleishman (Washington, DC: American Psychological Association, 1999), pp. 175–95; and *O*NET Web site, The O*NET Content Model: Detailed Outline With Descriptions, http://www.onet center.org/content.html/1.A?D=1#Cm_1.A (May 20, 2009).*

coordination; walking on a balance beam requires gross body equilibrium. Both types of coordination are important in contexts that involve quick movements. However, gross body equilibrium is more important when the work environment is artificially elevated and inherently unstable.

心理运动能力一般是指操纵与控制物体的能力。

PSYCHOMOTOR ABILITIES. There are several different examples of **psychomotor abilities,** which generally refer to the capacity to manipulate and control objects. *Fine manipulative abilities* refer to the ability to keep the arms and hands steady while using the hands to do precise work, generally on small or delicate objects such as arteries, nerves, gems, and watches. *Control movement abilities* are important in tasks for which people have to make different precise adjustments, using machinery to complete the work effectively. Anyone who drills things for a living, whether it be wood, concrete, or teeth, needs this type of ability. The ability to choose the right action quickly in response to several different signals is called *response orientation.* It shouldn't be too difficult to imagine the importance of response orientation for an airline pilot who responds to the flashing lights, buzzers, and verbal information triggered during an in-flight emergency. The final psychomotor ability we describe is called *response time.* This ability reflects how quickly an individual responds to signaling information after it occurs. Returning to the previous example, most of us would feel more secure if our airline pilot had both a fast response orientation and a quick response time. After all, making the right decision may not be useful in this context if the decision is made too late!

SENSORY ABILITIES. **Sensory ability** refers to capabilities associated with vision and hearing. Examples of important visual abilities include the ability to see things up close and at a distance (*near and far vision*) or in low light contexts (*night vision*), as well as the ability to perceive colors and judge relative distances between things accurately (*visual color discrimination* and *depth perception*). There are many different jobs that emphasize only one or two of these visual abilities. For example, whereas effectiveness as a watch repairer depends on good near vision, effectiveness as an interior designer depends on visual color discrimination. However, there are other jobs in which effectiveness might depend on almost all categories of visual abilities. A fighter pilot needs near vision to read instruments and checklists, far vision and depth perception to see enemy targets and landmarks, night vision to conduct operations in low light, and visual color discrimination to interpret information from warning lights and computer readouts correctly.

感觉能力是与视觉和听觉有关的能力。

Abilities related to hearing, also referred to as auditory abilities, include the capability to hear and discriminate sounds that vary in terms of loudness and pitch (*hearing sensitivity*), being able to focus on a single sound in the presence of many other sounds (*auditory attention*), and the ability to identify and understand the speech of another person (*speech recognition*). Perhaps the most obvious jobs for which auditory abilities would be important are musicians and composers (yes, we are going to ignore exceptions like Beethoven, who was deaf at the time he wrote his Ninth Symphony). However, with these jobs, the emphasis would likely be on hearing sensitivity and auditory attention rather than speech recognition (who listens to lyrics these days?). Another job for which auditory abilities might be crucially important is a restaurant server, especially if the restaurant is crowded and noisy. In this context, a server needs auditory attention and speech recognition to be able to isolate and understand the words of a single patron against the backdrop of the loud chatter. As an example of a company that exists because of auditory ability, consider the case of Monster Cable, the Brisbane, California–based manufacturer of audiovisual cables and accessories. Noel Lee, the company's founder, started out by comparing the sound of Tchaikovsky's 1812 Overture and Michael Jackson's "Liberian Girl"

Noel Lee founded Monster Cable after using his extraordinary auditory ability to identify which type of speaker wire sounds best.

using different types of speaker wire. He listened to the music over and over again and carefully considered the dynamics, loudness, bass response, and high frequencies of the music to determine which combination of wire thickness, composition, and braiding pattern sounded best.

总结：员工“拥有能力”意味着什么
SUMMARY: WHAT DOES IT MEAN FOR AN EMPLOYEE TO BE "ABLE"?

Thus far in the chapter, we've presented you with a fairly detailed description of the domain of human abilities, which are summarized in Figure 8-3. Although the list of abilities included in the figure may seem somewhat daunting, we hope that you can appreciate that this set of abilities describes each and every one of us. Moreover, as we have alluded to throughout the chapter, these abilities play an important role in determining how effective we can be at different tasks and jobs.

能力有多重要
HOW IMPORTANT IS ABILITY?

8.5
How does cognitive ability affect job performance and organizational commitment?

So, now that you know what ability is and where it comes from, let's turn to the next important question: Does ability really matter? That is, does ability have a significant impact on job performance and organizational commitment—the two primary outcomes in our integrative model of OB? The answer to this question depends on what type of ability you are referring to—cognitive, emotional, or physical. We focus our discussion on general cognitive ability because it's the most relevant form of ability across all jobs and is likely to be important in the kinds of positions that students in an OB course will be pursuing. As it turns out, there's a huge body of research linking general cognitive ability to job performance, as summarized in Figure 8-4.

The figure reveals that general cognitive ability is a strong predictor of job performance—in particular, the task performance aspect. Across all jobs, smarter employees fulfill the requirements

FIGURE 8-3 What Does It Mean for an Employee to Be "Able"?

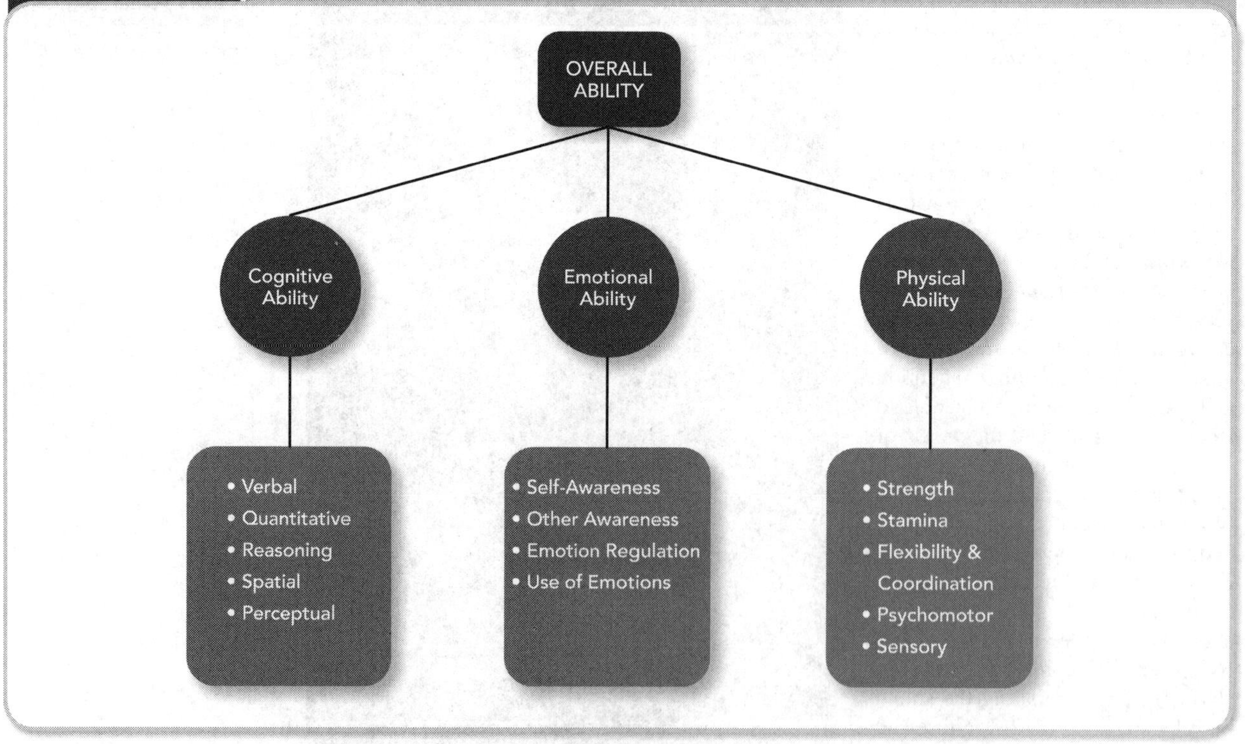

Source: Adapted from J.J. Johnson and J.B. Cullen, "Trust in Cross-Cultural Relationships," in Blackwell Handbook of Cross-Cultural Management, eds. M.J. Gannon and K.L. Newman (Malden, MA: Blackwell, 2002), pp. 335–60.

FIGURE 8-4 Effects of General Cognitive Ability on Performance and Commitment

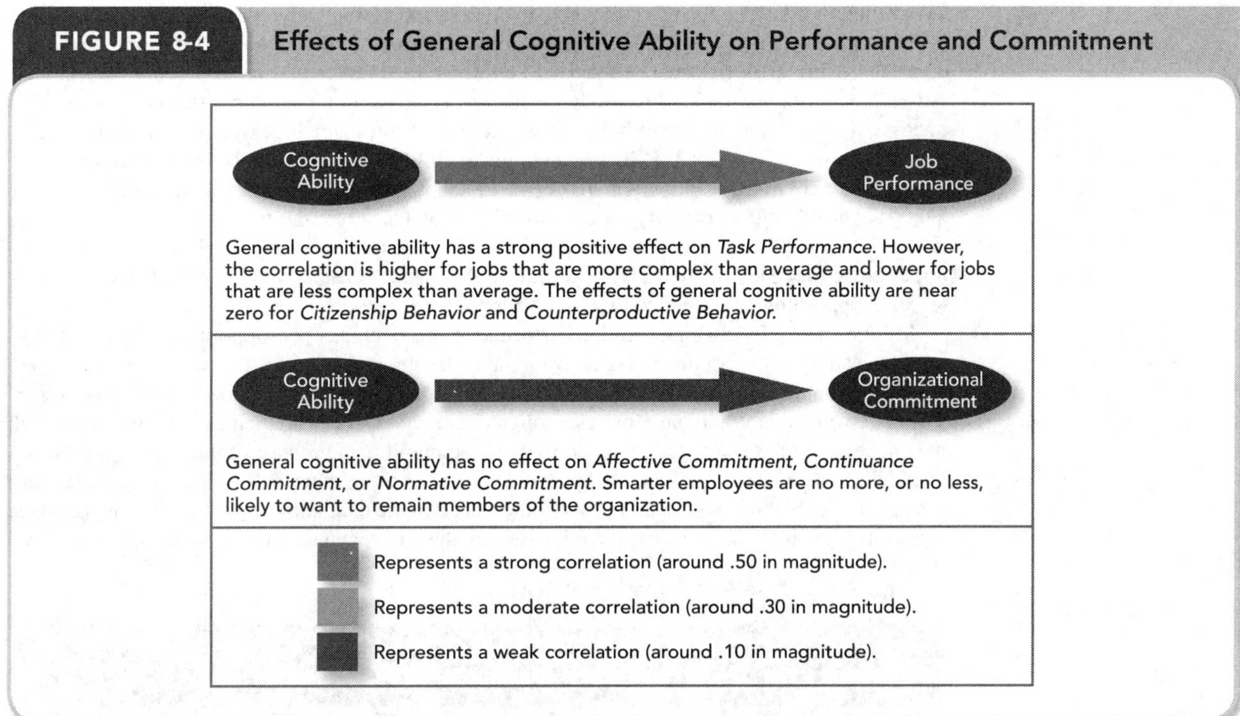

Sources: J.W. Boudreau, W.R. Boswell, T.A. Judge, and R.D Bretz, "Personality and Cognitive Ability as Predictors of Job Search Among Employed Managers," *Personnel Psychology* 54 (2001), pp. 25–50; S.M. Colarelli, R.A. Dean, and C. Konstans, "Comparative Effects of Personal and Situational Influences on Job Outcomes of New Professionals," *Journal of Applied Psychology* 72 (1987), pp. 558–66; D.N. Dickter, M. Roznowski, and D.A. Harrison, "Temporal Tempering: An Event History Analysis of the Process of Voluntary Turnover," *Journal of Applied Psychology* 81 (1996), pp. 705–16; and F.L. Schmidt and J. Hunter, "General Mental Ability in the World of Work: Occupational Attainment and Job Performance," *Journal of Personality and Social Psychology* 86 (2004), pp. 162–73.

of their job descriptions more effectively than do less smart employees. In fact, of all the variables discussed in this book, none has a stronger correlation with task performance than general cognitive ability. Thousands of organizations, many of which are quite well-known, assess cognitive ability in efforts to select the best candidates available for specific jobs. The use of cognitive ability tests for this purpose appears to be quite reasonable, given that scores on such tests have a strong positive correlation with measures of performance across different types of jobs.

In fact, this relationship holds even for performance in academic contexts. We mentioned the Scholastic Assessment Test, or the SAT, several times in this chapter because it's likely to be quite familiar to you and because it largely reflects general cognitive ability. Most colleges and universities in the United States take these scores into account when deciding which students to admit because they believe that higher scores increase the chances that students will be successful in college. But does the SAT really relate to how well someone does in college? Many of you are likely to be skeptical because you probably know someone who did extremely well on the SAT but performed poorly as a college student. Similarly, you probably know someone who didn't do that well on the SAT but who performed well as a college student. As it turns out, the SAT is actually good at predicting college performance. Students with higher SAT scores tend to perform much better in their first year of college, end up with a higher cumulative grade point average, and have a higher likelihood of graduating. The same finding applies to predicting success in graduate-level school as well. The Graduate Management Admission Test, or GMAT, is similar to the SAT in structure and content, and students who score higher on this test prior to admission to graduate school tend to achieve better grade point averages over the course of their graduate program.

So what explains why general cognitive ability relates to task performance? People who have higher general cognitive ability tend to be better at *learning and decision making*. They're able to gain more knowledge from their experiences at a faster rate, and a result, they develop a bigger pool of knowledge regarding how to do their jobs effectively. There are, however, three important caveats that we should mention. First, cognitive ability tends to be more strongly correlated with task performance than with citizenship behavior or counterproductive behavior. An increased amount of job knowledge helps an employee complete job tasks, but it doesn't necessarily affect the choice to help a coworker or refrain from breaking an important rule. Second, the positive correlation between cognitive ability and performance is even stronger in jobs that are complex or situations that demand adaptability. Third, people may do poorly on a test of general cognitive ability for reasons other than a lack of cognitive ability. As an example, people who come from economically disadvantaged backgrounds may do poorly on such tests, not because they lack the underlying cognitive ability but because they may not have had the learning opportunities needed to provide the appropriate responses.

In contrast to relationships with job performance, research has not supported a significant linkage between cognitive ability and organizational commitment. On the one hand, we might expect a positive relationship with commitment because people with higher cognitive ability tend to perform more effectively, and therefore, they might feel they fit well with their job. On the other hand, we might expect to see a negative relationship with commitment because people with higher cognitive ability possess more job knowledge, which increases their value on the job market, and in turn the likelihood that they would leave for another job. In the end, knowing how smart an employee is tells us very little about the likelihood that he or she will remain a member of the organization.

应用：选择认知能力强的员工

APPLICATION: SELECTING HIGH COGNITIVE ABILITY EMPLOYEES

Given the strong relationship between general cognitive ability and job performance, it isn't surprising that many organizations apply the content of this chapter to hire new employees. As an example, consider how Google goes about hiring employees whom they believe are the best and the brightest. To attract intelligent people to apply for a job, the company placed billboards in Silicon Valley and Harvard Square with the brainteaser, "first 10-digit prime found in consecutive digits of *e*.com." (The "*e*" in the question refers to the transcendental number used as the basis for natural logarithms, and the first 10-digit prime number in this string turns out to be 7427466391). People who solved the brainteaser went to the website where there was a more difficult brainteaser. Solving that one resulted in Google asking for the person's résumé. The company also developed something called the *Google Labs Aptitude Test* (GLAT for short) and published it in magazines that smart techies might read. The GLAT is similar to the SAT and includes questions such as, "How many different ways can you color an icosahedron with one of three colors on each face?" Google used the GLAT to attract people who are smart and who are interested in the types of problems in the test. The people who are ultimately brought in for a job interview typically face 10-person interview panels, and are confronted with very difficult questions. Someone who applies for a technical job might be asked to solve math algorithms and answer technical questions about software and computer networking. It's also likely that they'll be asked brainteaser questions that rely upon both general intelligence and the originality facet of reasoning ability. For example, "How many golf balls fit in a school bus," and "You are shrunk to the height of a nickel and your mass is proportionally reduced so as to maintain your original density. You are then thrown into an empty glass blender. The blades will start moving in 60 seconds. What do you do?" Although you might not look forward to the prospect of having to answer these types of questions in an already stressful job interview, other companies such as Microsoft use a similar approach to hire highly intelligent employees, and so it's something for which you might want to be prepared.

Of course, companies outside the high-technology sector are also interested in hiring employees who have high cognitive ability, and applicants for jobs in many of these companies are given a cognitive ability test as part of the selection process. One of the most widely used tests is the **Wonderlic Personnel Test,** a 12-minute test of general cognitive ability that consists of 50 questions. It's been in use for several decades now and has been given to more than 120 million people by thousands of organizations. From the example items that appear in Figure 8-5, you

旺德利人事测验是对一般认知能力的 12 分钟测验，由 50 道题目构成。

FIGURE 8-5 Sample Wonderlic Questions

1. Which of the following is the earliest date?

   A) Jan. 16, 1898 B) Feb. 21, 1889 C) Feb. 2, 1898 D) Jan. 7, 1898 E) Jan. 30, 1889

2. LOW is to HIGH as EASY is to ___?___.

   J) SUCCESSFUL K) PURE L) TALL M) INTERESTING N) DIFFICULT

3. A featured product from an Internet retailer generated 27, 99, 80, 115 and 213 orders over a 5-hour period. Which graph below best represents this trend?

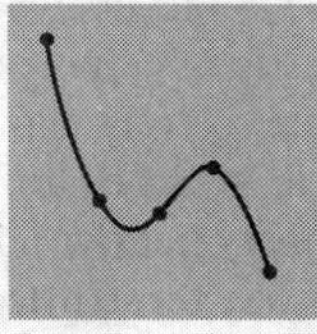
A

B

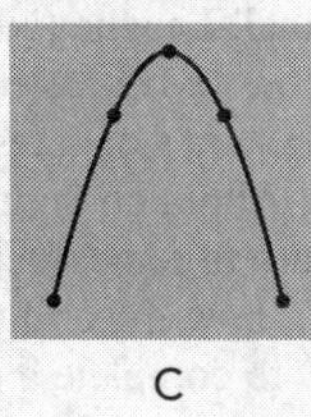
C

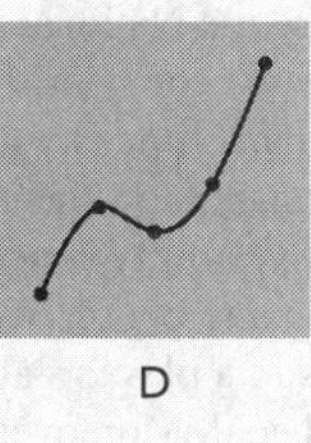
D

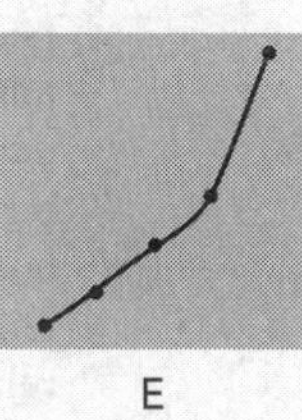
E

4. What is the next number in the series? 29 41 53 65 77 ___?___

   J) 75 K) 88 L) 89 M) 98 N) 99

5. *One word below appears in color. What is the OPPOSITE of that word?* She gave a complex answer to the question and we all agreed with her.

   A) long B) better C) simple D) wrong E) kind

6. Jose's monthly parking fee for April was $150; for May it was $10 more than April; and for June $40 more than May. His average monthly parking fee was? for these 3 months.

   J) $66 K) $160 L) $166 M) $170 N) $200

7. *If the first two statements are true, is the final statement true?*

   Sandra is responsible for ordering all office supplies.

   Notebooks are office supplies.

   Sandra is responsible for ordering notebooks.

   A) yes B) no C) uncertain

8. Which THREE choices are needed to create the figure on the left? Only pieces of the same color may overlap.

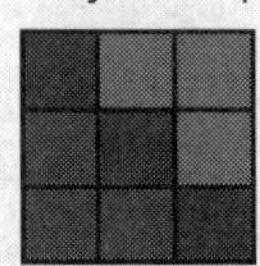

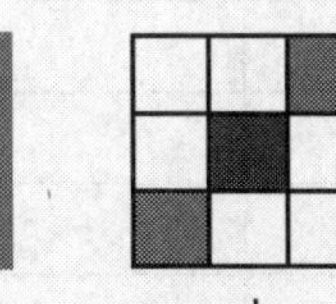
J

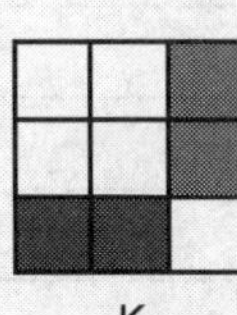
K

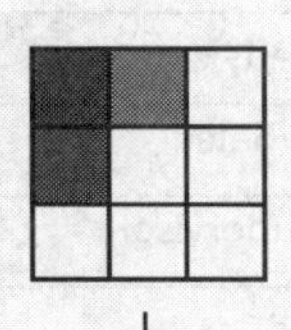
L

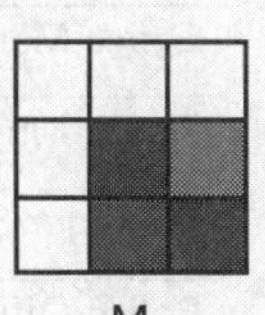
M

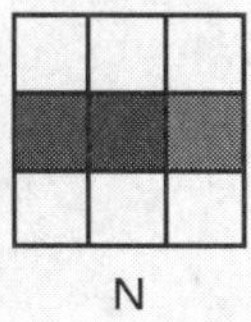
N

9. Which THREE of the following words have similar meanings?

   A) observable B) manifest C) hypothetical D) indefinite E) theoretical

10. Last year, 12 out of 600 employees at a service organization were rewarded for their excellence in customer service, which was ? of the employees.

    J) 1% K) 2% L) 3% M) 4% N) 6%

Answers:

1. E, 2. N, 3. D, 4. L, 5. C, 6. M, 7. A, 8. KLM, 9. CDE, 10. K

should be able to see how the items correspond with many of the cognitive abilities that we've described previously.

8.6
What steps can organizations take to hire people with high levels of cognitive ability?

People who take the test receive one point for each correct response, and those points are summed to give a total score that can be used as a basis for selecting people for different jobs. The Wonderlic User's Manual offers recommendations for minimum passing scores for different job families, some of which are included in Table 8-3. For example, a score of 17 is the minimum suggested score for an unskilled laborer, a score of 21—which is the average for high school graduates and corresponds to an IQ of approximately 100—is the minimum suggested score for a firefighter. A score of 28 is the minimum suggested score for upper-level managerial and executive work and around the average for all college graduates.

Chances are you'll hear about the Wonderlic Personnel Test every March and April. This is because the National Football League (NFL) administers the test to players who enter the draft, and teams consider the scores when selecting players. One question that people always debate during this time is whether scores on a test of cognitive ability are relevant to a football player's performance on the field. Although supporters of the Wonderlic's use in the NFL argue that cognitive ability is necessary to remember plays and learn complex offensive and defensive systems, many people wonder how the ability to answer questions like those listed in Figure 8-5 relates to a player's ability to complete a pass, run for a touchdown, tackle an opponent, or kick a field goal. Moreover, detractors of the Wonderlic wonder why a poor score should overshadow a record of superior accomplishments on the playing field. So who's right? Well, the results of at least one study indicate that a player's Wonderlic score does not predict subsequent performance in the NFL, and that this effect is not influenced much by the position of the player being considered.

TABLE 8-3 Suggested Minimum Wonderlic Scores for Various Jobs

JOB	MINIMUM SCORES
Mechanical Engineer	30
Attorney	29
Executive	28
Teacher	27
Nurse	26
Office Manager	25
Advertising Sales	24
Manager/Supervisor	23
Police Officer	22
Firefighter	21
Cashier	20
Hospital Orderly	19
Machine Operator	18
Unskilled Laborer	17
Maid-Matron	16

Source: *Wonderlic Personnel Test and Scholastic Level Exam: User's Manual* (Vernon Hills, IL: Wonderlic Personnel Test, Inc., 1992), pp. 28–29. Reprinted with permission.

Nevertheless, it appears that teams do take these scores seriously. As an example, after directing his Texas Longhorns to the national championship over the University of Southern California, quarterback Vince Young was one of the hottest players coming into the 2006 NFL draft. Before the draft, however, reports began circulating that he scored a 6 on the Wonderlic, a score thought to be too low for an NFL quarterback. Sportswriters then began to project that Young would end up being drafted after players with clearly inferior records of accomplishments on the field. Later, Young retook the test and scored a 16. Although the score was considered low for quarterback prospects (who averaged 25.5 in 2005), it was enough of an improvement for the Tennessee Titans, who drafted him third overall that year. Someone on the Tennessee staff may have recalled that Dan Marino also scored a 16 on the way to his Hall-of-Fame–worthy career.

PART

4

GROUP MECHANISMS

群体机制

chapter

Teams: Characteristics and Diversity

团队：特征与多样性

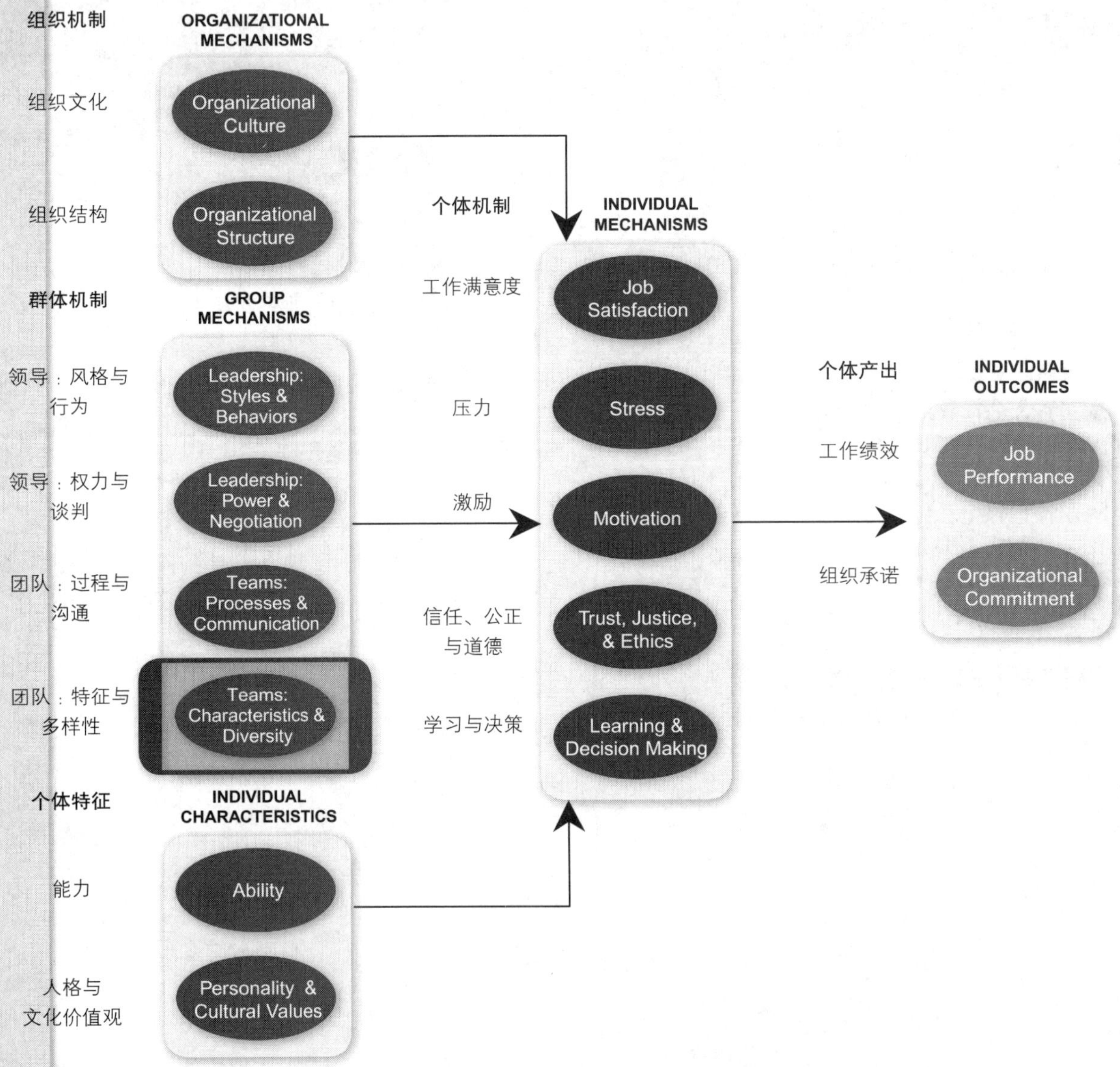

组织机制 ORGANIZATIONAL MECHANISMS

组织文化 Organizational Culture

组织结构 Organizational Structure

群体机制 GROUP MECHANISMS

领导：风格与行为 Leadership: Styles & Behaviors

领导：权力与谈判 Leadership: Power & Negotiation

团队：过程与沟通 Teams: Processes & Communication

团队：特征与多样性 Teams: Characteristics & Diversity

个体特征 INDIVIDUAL CHARACTERISTICS

能力 Ability

人格与文化价值观 Personality & Cultural Values

个体机制 INDIVIDUAL MECHANISMS

工作满意度 Job Satisfaction

压力 Stress

激励 Motivation

信任、公正与道德 Trust, Justice, & Ethics

学习与决策 Learning & Decision Making

个体产出 INDIVIDUAL OUTCOMES

工作绩效 Job Performance

组织承诺 Organizational Commitment

LEARNING GOALS

After reading this chapter, you should be able to answer the following questions:

9.1 What are the five general team types and their defining characteristics?

9.2 What are the three general types of team interdependence?

9.3 What factors are involved in team composition?

9.4 What are the types of team diversity and how do they influence team functioning?

9.5 How do team characteristics influence team effectiveness?

9.6 How can team compensation be used to manage team effectiveness?

TRW

How would you react if your boss told you that your new assignment is to lead a team responsible for designing an important new product for your company? Although it's likely you'd have many questions about the details of your new assignment, chances are you'd be pretty excited about the opportunity. But what if the next words out of your boss's mouth were, "your team will consist of members located on three continents in six different time zones, and most likely you'll never get the chance to meet together face to face." At this point, your feelings about this new assignment would likely turn from enthusiasm to trepidation. After all, how can a project team that consists of members who are so diverse and who are scattered all over the world, work collaboratively on a complex task to deliver an effective outcome? As far-fetched as this scenario sounds, you could be faced with something similar if you were one of the 60,000 or so people employed by TRW Automotive Holdings, the world's largest and most diversified supplier of automotive systems, modules, and components.

You're probably not very familiar with Livonia, Michigan–based TRW. With 2011 revenues of over $14 billion, the company is quite large, however, it designs and manufactures automobile parts such as airbags, braking systems, and safety electronics that most people never see (thankfully so). The company believes that continued research, development, and engineering activities are critical to maintaining the company's leadership position in the automotive parts and components industry, and they employ teams of employees from a global network of technical centers to accomplish projects related to this work. There are certainly challenges to accomplishing work in TRW's global teams. Most obviously, because members are not colocated, technology must be used to facilitate interaction and collaboration. Moreover, given differences in time zones, it may be difficult to schedule meetings where members can interact virtually. There may also be differences in language and culture that make virtual collaborations difficult and prone to misunderstanding.

In spite of these challenges, TRW believes there are advantages to their global teams that far outweigh the disadvantages. For example, global teams are not limited to including members who happen to live in close proximity. Rather, teams can be composed of the most qualified individuals regardless of where they are in the world. As another example, because members work in different time zones, the team's work can be accomplished almost continuously as members hand off their work to teammates in different locations at the end of their workday. Finally, because members are culturally diverse and have different perspectives that can be drawn upon, TRW teams can produce innovative solutions that can be applied anywhere around the globe.

团队特征与多样性

TEAM CHARACTERISTICS AND DIVERSITY

The topic of teams is likely familiar to almost anyone who might be reading this book. In fact, you've probably had firsthand experience with several different types of teams at different points in your life. As an example, most of you have played a team sport or two (yes, playing soccer in gym class counts). Most of you have also worked in student teams to complete projects or assignments for courses you've taken. Or perhaps you've worked closely with a small group of people to accomplish a task that was important to you—planning an event, raising money for a charity, or starting and running a small cash business. Finally, some of you have been members of organizational teams responsible for making a product, providing a service, or generating recommendations for solving company problems.

团队是指在一段时间内，两个或两个以上的个体为了完成与任务导向目的有关的目标而在工作上相互依赖的群体。

But what exactly is a team, and what is it that makes a team more than a "group"? A **team** consists of two or more people who work *interdependently* over some time period to accomplish *common goals* related to some *task-oriented purpose.* You can think of teams as a special type of group, where a group is just a collection of two or more people. Teams are special for two reasons. First, the interactions among members within teams revolve around a deeper dependence on one another than the interactions within groups. Second, the interactions within teams occur with a specific task-related purpose in mind. Although the members of a friendship group may engage in small talk or in-depth conversations on a frequent basis, the members of a team depend

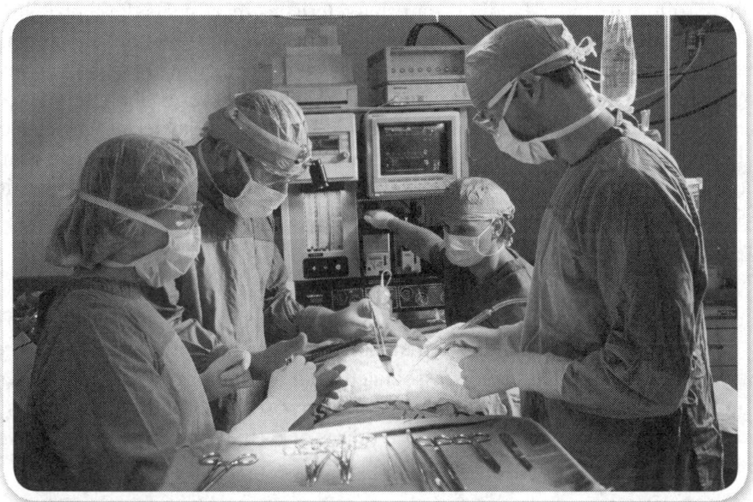

A surgical team consists of specialized members who depend on one another to accomplish tasks that are both complex and important. Why might you not want to have surgery conducted by a surgical team that functions like a group?

on one another for critical information, materials, and actions that are needed to accomplish goals related to their purpose for being together.

The use of teams in today's organizations is widespread. National surveys indicate that teams are used in the majority of organizations in the United States, regardless of whether the organization is large or small. In fact, some researchers suggest that almost all major U.S. companies are currently using teams or planning to implement them and that up to 50 percent of all employees in the United States work in a team as part of their job. Thus, whereas the use of teams was limited to pioneers such as Procter & Gamble in the 1960s, teams are currently used in all types of industries to accomplish all the types of work necessary to make organizations run effectively.

Why have teams become so widespread? The most obvious reason is that the nature of today's work requires them. As work has become more complex, interactions among multiple team members have become more vital. This is because interactions allow the team to pool complementary knowledge and skills. As an example, surgical teams consist of individuals who receive specialized training in the activities needed to conduct surgical procedures. The team consists of a surgeon who received training for the procedure in question, an anesthesiologist who received training necessary to manage patient pain, and an operating room nurse who was trained to provide overall care for the patient.

Teams may also be useful to organizations in ways beyond just accomplishing the work itself. For example, one study revealed that problem-solving teams composed primarily of rank-and-file workers could boost productivity in steel mills by devising ways to increase the efficiency of production lines and quality control processes. Although implementing teams often makes sense in settings such as these, for which the nature of the work and work-related problems are complex, teams vary a great deal from one another in terms of their effectiveness. The goal of this chapter, as well as the next, is to help you understand factors that influence team effectiveness.

什么特征可以用来描述团队

WHAT CHARACTERISTICS CAN BE USED TO DESCRIBE TEAMS?

This is the first of two chapters on teams. This chapter focuses on team characteristics—the task, unit, and member qualities that can be used to describe teams and that combine to make some teams more effective than others. Team characteristics provide a means of categorizing and examining teams, which is important because teams come in so many shapes and sizes. Team characteristics play an important role in determining what a team is capable of achieving and may influence the strategies and processes the team uses to reach its goals. As you will see, however, there's more to understanding team characteristics than meets the eye. Team characteristics such as diversity, for example, have many meanings, and its effect on team functioning and effectiveness depends on what type of diversity you're concerned with as well as several additional complicating factors. Chapter 10 will focus on team processes and communication—the specific actions and behaviors that teams can engage in to achieve synergy. The concepts in that chapter will help explain why some teams are more or less effective than their characteristics would suggest they should be. For now, however, we turn our attention to this question: "What characteristics can be used to describe teams?"

团队类型
TEAM TYPES

9.1
What are the five general team types and their defining characteristics?

One way to describe teams is to take advantage of existing taxonomies that place teams into various types. One such taxonomy is illustrated in Table 9-1. The table illustrates that there are five general types of teams and that each is associated with a number of defining characteristics. The most notable characteristics include the team's purpose, the length of the team's existence, and the amount of time involvement the team requires of its individual members. The sections to follow review these types of teams in turn.

工作团队指的是为生产产品或提供服务，通常要求成员全职投入的相对持久的团队。

WORK TEAMS. **Work teams** are designed to be relatively permanent. Their purpose is to produce goods or provide services, and they generally require a full-time commitment from their members. As an example of a work team, consider how cars and trucks are manufactured at Toyota. Teams are composed of four to eight members who do the physical work, and a leader who supports the team and coordinates with other teams. Although the teams are responsible for the work involved in the assembly of the vehicles, they are also responsible for quality control and developing ideas for improvements in the production process. Team members inspect each other's work, and when they see a problem, they stop the line until they are able to resolve the problem.

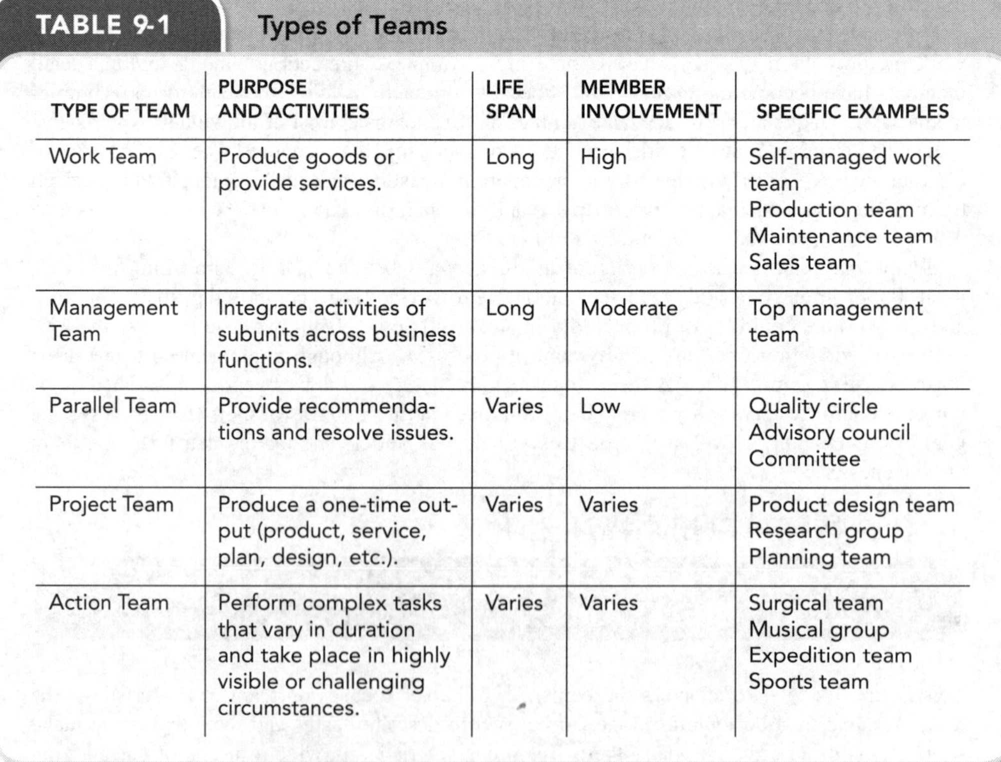

TABLE 9-1 Types of Teams

TYPE OF TEAM	PURPOSE AND ACTIVITIES	LIFE SPAN	MEMBER INVOLVEMENT	SPECIFIC EXAMPLES
Work Team	Produce goods or provide services.	Long	High	Self-managed work team Production team Maintenance team Sales team
Management Team	Integrate activities of subunits across business functions.	Long	Moderate	Top management team
Parallel Team	Provide recommendations and resolve issues.	Varies	Low	Quality circle Advisory council Committee
Project Team	Produce a one-time output (product, service, plan, design, etc.).	Varies	Varies	Product design team Research group Planning team
Action Team	Perform complex tasks that vary in duration and take place in highly visible or challenging circumstances.	Varies	Varies	Surgical team Musical group Expedition team Sports team

Sources: S.G. Cohen and D.E. Bailey, "What Makes Teams Work: Group Effectiveness Research from the Shop Floor to the Executive Suite," *Journal of Management* 27 (1997), pp. 239–90; and E. Sundstrom, K.P. De Meuse, and D. Futrell, "Work Teams: Applications and Effectiveness." *American Psychologist* 45 (1990), pp. 120–33.

MANAGEMENT TEAMS. **Management teams** are similar to work teams in that they are designed to be relatively permanent; however, they are also distinct in a number of important ways. Whereas work teams focus on the accomplishment of core operational-level production and service tasks, management teams participate in managerial-level tasks that affect the entire organization. Specifically, management teams are responsible for coordinating the activities of organizational subunits—typically departments or functional areas—to help the organization achieve its long-term goals. Top management teams, for example, consist of senior-level executives who meet to make decisions about the strategic direction of the organization. It may also be worth mentioning that because members of management teams are typically heads of departments, their commitment to the management team is offset somewhat by the responsibilities they have in leading their unit.

A Toyota work team is responsible for vehicle assembly and quality control.

管理团队在设计的相对持久上与工作团队相似；但是，在很多重要方面上还是有所区别。工作团队是针对核心操作层面的生产和服务任务，而管理团队则参与影响整个组织的管理层面的任务。

PARALLEL TEAMS. **Parallel teams** are composed of members from various jobs who provide recommendations to managers about important issues that run "parallel" to the organization's production process. Parallel teams require only part-time commitment from members, and they can be permanent or temporary, depending on their aim. Quality circles, for example, consist of individuals who normally perform core production tasks, but who also meet regularly with individuals from other work groups to identify production-related problems and opportunities for improvement. As an example of a more temporary parallel team, committees often form to deal with unique issues or issues that arise only periodically. Examples of issues that can spur the creation of committees include changes to work procedures, purchases of new equipment or services, and nonroutine hiring.

平行团队是由来自不同工作岗位的成员组成的团队，他们就与组织的生产过程"平行"的重要问题向管理者提出建议。

PROJECT TEAMS. **Project teams** are formed to take on "one-time" tasks that are generally complex and require a lot of input from members with different types of training and expertise. Although project teams only exist as long as it takes to finish a project, some projects are quite complex and can take years to complete. Members of some project teams work full-time, whereas other teams only demand a part-time commitment. A planning team comprised of engineers, architects, designers, and builders, charged with designing a suburban town center, might work together full-time for a year or more. In contrast, the engineers and artists who constitute a design team responsible for creating an electric toothbrush might work together for a month on the project while also serving on other project teams.

项目团队的组成是为了完成"一次性"任务，这些任务通常很复杂，要求具有不同类型的培训和经验的成员投入大量的时间与精力。

ACTION TEAMS. **Action teams** perform tasks that are normally limited in duration. However, those tasks are quite complex and take place in contexts that are either highly visible to an audience or of a highly challenging nature. Some types of action teams work together for an extended period of time. For example, sports teams remain intact for at least one season, and musical groups like AC/DC may stick together for decades. Other types of action teams stay together only as long as the task

The Australian Band AC/DC, which was formed in 1973, is an example of an action team that has stayed together for an extended period of time.

行动团队执行的任务通常在时间上是有限制的。这些任务十分复杂，并且是在观众高度可视或高度挑战的情境下完成的。

The Pixar team, shown here at the Academy Awards, has characteristics of both work teams and project teams. Trying to characterize this team is even more complicated when you consider that key members are involved in the management of the company, and their involvement in the films runs parallel to these other responsibilities.

takes to complete. Surgical teams and aircraft flight crews may only work together as a unit for a single two-hour surgery or flight.

SUMMARY. So how easy is it to classify teams into one of the types summarized in Figure 9-1? Well, it turns out that teams often fit into more than one category. As an example, consider the teams at Pixar, the company that has produced many computer-animated hit films, such as *Toy Story, Monsters Inc., Finding Nemo, Cars, Wall-E,* and *Up.* On the one hand, because the key members of Pixar teams have stuck together for each film the company has produced, it might seem like Pixar uses work teams. On the other hand, because the creation of each film can be viewed as a project, and because members are likely involved in multiple ongoing projects, it might seem reasonable to say that Pixar uses project teams. It's probably most appropriate to say that at Pixar, teams have characteristics of both work teams and project teams.

团队类型的变化
VARIATIONS WITHIN TEAM TYPES

Even knowing whether a team is a project team, an action team, or some other type of team doesn't tell you the whole story. Often there are important variations within those categories that are needed to understand a team's functioning. As one example, teams can vary with respect to the degree to which they have autonomy and are self-managed. If you've ever been on a team where members have a great deal of freedom to work together to establish their own goals, procedures, roles, and membership, you've worked on a team where the level of autonomy and self-management is high. You may also have worked on a team where the level of autonomy and self-management is low. In these teams, there are strict rules regarding goals, procedures, and roles, and team leaders or managers make most of the decisions regarding management of the team with respect to membership. Research has shown that although people generally prefer working in teams where the level of autonomy and self-management is high, the appropriate level of self-management with regard to overall team effectiveness may depend on a variety of factors. For example, research has shown that high levels of self-management may be most advantageous for teams where team members' have high levels of team-relevant knowledge obtained from outside experts and others in their social networks.

虚拟团队指主要通过电子邮件、即时信息和网络会议等电子通讯工具将地理上分隔的成员联系起来实现互动活动的团队。

Another way that teams can vary relates to how the members typically communicate with each other. **Virtual teams** are teams in which the members are geographically dispersed, and interdependent activity occurs through electronic communications—primarily e-mail, instant messaging, and web conferencing. Although communications and group networking software is far from

FIGURE 9-1 Types of Teams

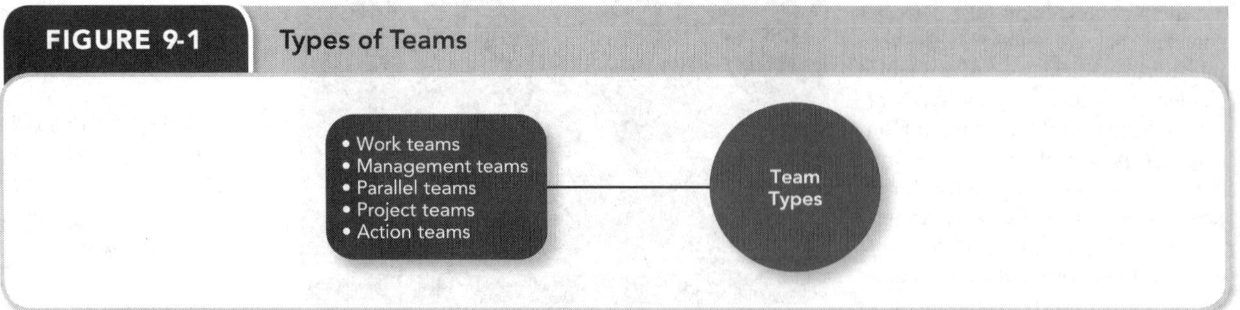

perfect, it has advanced to the point that it's possible for teams doing all sorts of work to function virtually. In fact, there has been an 800 percent increase in the number of virtual employees over the last decade or so, and it's likely that there are tens of millions of virtual teams operating today. Companies such as Con Edison, New York's giant electric and gas utility, has invested significant resources in technology and training to help these teams function and perform more effectively. The same is true at IBM, where at least 40 percent of the employees work virtually. As we described in the chapter opening on TRW, virtual teams are not just an efficient way to accomplish work when members are geographically separated. In fact, many companies in high-tech industries are leveraging virtual teams to make continuous progress on work tasks without members having to work 24/7. For example, Logitech, the Swiss company that makes things such as computer mice and keyboards, universal remotes for home entertainment systems, and gaming controllers, attributes its success to teams of designers and engineers who are located in different places around the world. Although you might be inclined to believe that time-zone differences would be a hindrance to this sort of team, Logitech turned it into a competitive advantage by letting the work *follow the sun*. Specifically, work at Logitech is accomplished continuously because members of a team who have finished their workday in one country electronically hand off the work to team members in another country who have just arrived at the office. Because these electronic hand-offs occur continuously, product development and other work needed to bring innovative products to the market can be completed much more quickly.

In addition to varying in their "virtuality," teams of any type can differ in the amount of experience they have working together. One way to understand this point is to consider what occurs in teams at different stages of their development as they progress from a newly formed team to one that's well-established. According to the most well-known theory, teams go through a progression of five stages shown in the top panel of Figure 9-2. In the first stage, called **forming,** members orient themselves by trying to understand their boundaries in the team. Members try to get a feel for what is expected of them, what types of behaviors are out of bounds, and who's in charge. In the next stage, called **storming,** members remain committed to ideas they bring with them to the team. This initial unwillingness to accommodate others' ideas triggers conflict

形成期指团队成员通过了解自己在团队中的边界以使自己适应团队的阶段。

震荡期指团队成员继续保持他们进入团队前的思想的阶段。

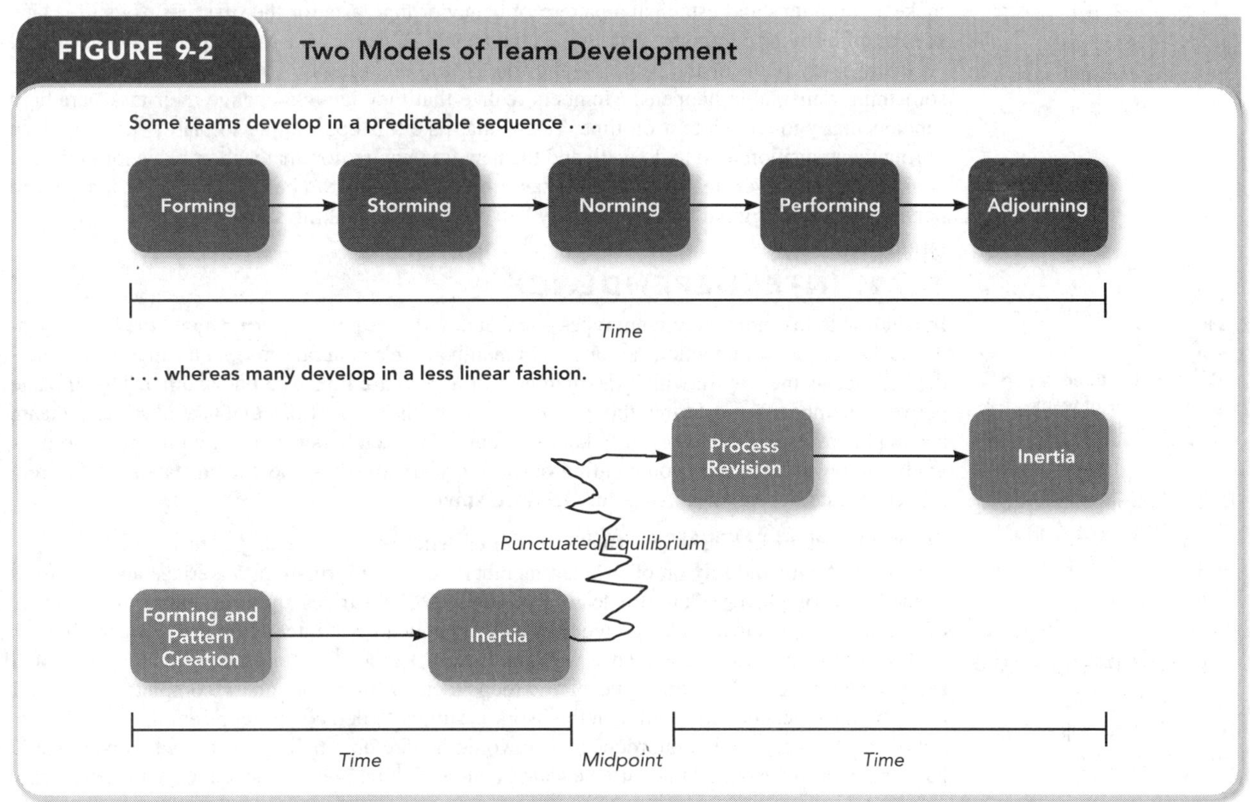

FIGURE 9-2 Two Models of Team Development

规范期指团队成员认识到他们需要共同协作以实现团队目标并开始合作的阶段。

执行期指团队成员已经适应自己的工作角色，团队朝着工作目标努力的阶段。

解散期指团队成员经历焦虑和其他情绪，离开并最终脱离团队的阶段。

that negatively affects some interpersonal relationships and harms the team's progress. During the next stage, **norming,** members realize that they need to work together to accomplish team goals, and consequently, they begin to cooperate with one another. Feelings of solidarity develop as members work toward team goals. Over time, norms and expectations develop regarding what different members are responsible for doing. In the fourth stage of team development, which is called **performing,** members are comfortable working within their roles, and the team makes progress toward goals. Finally, because the life span of many teams is limited, there's a stage called **adjourning.** In this stage, members experience anxiety and other emotions as they disengage and ultimately separate from the team.

But does this sequence of forming, storming, norming, performing, and adjourning apply to the development of all types of teams? Chances are that you've had some experience with teams that would lead you to answer this question with a "no." In fact, although this theory of group development is intuitively appealing and identifies things that may occur as teams gain experience working together, there are factors in work organizations that can significantly alter what occurs during a team's life. One situation in which this developmental sequence is less applicable is when teams are formed with clear expectations regarding what's expected from the team and its members. With many action teams, for example, there are established rules and standard operating procedures that guide team members' behaviors and their interactions with one another. As a specific example, an aircraft flight crew doesn't have to go through the forming, storming, norming, and performing stages to figure out that the pilot flies the plane and the flight attendant serves the beverages. As another example, though the adjourning stage only happens once for each type of team, the implications are likely to be more significant for team types with longer life spans that require high member involvement. Dissolving a work team that's been together for four years is likely to trigger greater anxiety and stronger emotions among members than a situation in which a committee that meets briefly once a month for a year is disbanded.

间断式平衡指的是在最初团队会议上，团队成员确定了团队生命周期前半段的行为模式，这种行为模式持续主导着团队的行为直到成为某种惯性。

Another situation in which the development sequence is less applicable may be in certain types of project teams that follow a pattern of development called **punctuated equilibrium.** This sequence appears in the bottom panel of Figure 9-2. At the initial team meeting, members make assumptions and establish a pattern of behavior that lasts for the first half of its life. That pattern of behavior continues to dominate the team's behavior as it settles into a sort of inertia. At the midway point of the project—and this is true regardless of the length of the project—something remarkable happens: Members realize that they have to change their task paradigm fundamentally to complete it on time. Teams that take this opportunity to plan a new approach during this transition tend to do well, and the new framework dominates their behavior until task completion. However, teams that don't take the opportunity to change their approach tend to persist with their original pattern and may "go down with a sinking ship."

团队依赖
TEAM INTERDEPENDENCE

9.2
What are the three general types of team interdependence?

In addition to taxonomies of team types, we can describe teams by talking about the interdependence that governs connections among team members. In a general sense, you can think of interdependence as the way in which the members of a team are linked to one another. That linkage between members is most often thought of in terms of the interactions that take place as the team accomplishes its work. However, linkages among team members also exist with respect to their goals and rewards. In fact, you can find out where your student project team stands on different aspects of interdependence using our **OB Assessments** feature.

任务依赖是指为完成团队工作，团队成员在信息、原材料和资源方面与其他成员相互作用、相互依赖的程度。

集中式依赖是指团队成员独立完成各自的工作任务，然后这些工作“累积”就构成团队的总产出。

TASK INTERDEPENDENCE. **Task interdependence** refers to the degree to which team members interact with and rely on other team members for the information, materials, and resources needed to accomplish work for the team. As Figure 9-3 illustrates, there are four primary types of task interdependence, and each requires a different degree of interaction and coordination.

The type of task interdependence with the lowest degree of required coordination is **pooled interdependence.** With this type of interdependence, group members complete their work assignments independently, and then this work is simply "piled up" to represent the group's output. Consider what pooled interdependence would be like on a fishing boat. Each person would bait a pole, drop the baited line into the water, reel the fish in, remove the fish from the hook, and,

OB ASSESSMENTS

INTERDEPENDENCE

How interdependent is your student project team? This assessment is designed to measure three types of interdependence: task interdependence, goal interdependence, and outcome interdependence. Read each of the following questions with a relevant student team in mind. Answer each question using the response scale provided. Then follow the instructions below to score yourself. (For more assessments relevant to this chapter, please visit http://connect.mcgraw-hill.com.)

1	2	3	4	5	6	7
TOTALLY DISAGREE	DISAGREE	SOMEWHAT DISAGREE	NEUTRAL	SOMEWHAT AGREE	AGREE	TOTALLY AGREE

1. I cannot accomplish my tasks without information or materials from other members of my team. ______
2. Other members of my team depend on me for information or materials needed to perform their tasks. ______
3. Within my team, jobs performed by team members are related to one another. ______
4. My work goals come directly from the goals of my team. ______
5. My work activities on any given day are determined by my team's goals for that day. ______
6. I do very few activities on my job that are not related to the goals of my team. ______
7. Feedback about how well I am doing my job comes primarily from information about how well the entire team is doing. ______
8. Evaluations of my performance are strongly influenced by how well my team performs. ______
9. Many rewards from my work (e.g., pay, grades) are determined in large part by my contributions as a team member. ______

SCORING AND INTERPRETATION

Task Interdependence: Sum up items 1–3. _____
Goal Interdependence: Sum up items 4–6. _____
Outcome Interdependence: Sum up items 7–9. _____

If you scored 14 or above, then you are above average on a particular dimension. If you scored 13 or below, then your team is below average on a particular dimension.

Source: From M.A. Campion, E.M. Papper, and G.J. Medsker, "Relations Between Work Team Characteristics and Effectiveness: A Replication and Extension," *Personnel Psychology* 49 (1996), pp. 429–52. Reprinted with permission of John Wiley & Sons, Inc.

finally, throw the fish into a tank filled with ice and other fish. At the end of the day, the boat's production would be the total weight of the fish that were caught.

The next type of task interdependence is called **sequential interdependence.** With this type of interdependence, different tasks are done in a prescribed order, and the group is structured such that the members specialize in these tasks. Although members in groups with sequential interdependence interact to carry out their work, the interaction only occurs between members

顺序式依赖指不同的任务按照指定的顺序完成，团队的结构化使成员能够分工完成这些任务。

FIGURE 9-3 Task Interdependence and Coordination Requirements

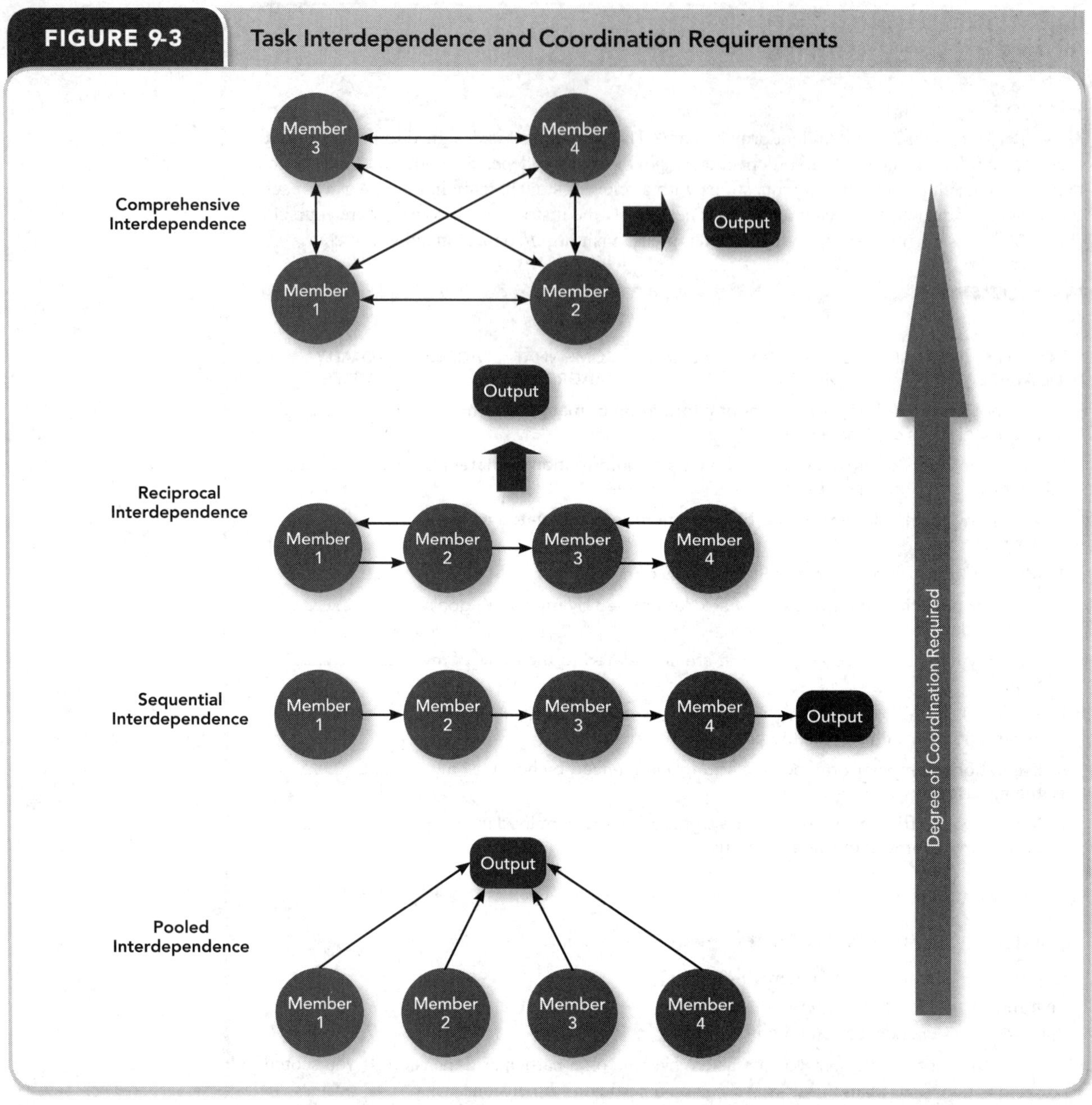

who perform tasks that are next to each other in the sequence. Moreover, the member performing the task in the latter part of the sequence depends on the member performing the task in the earlier part of the sequence, but not the other way around. The classic assembly line in manufacturing contexts provides an excellent example of this type of interdependence. In this context, an employee attaches a part to the unit being built, and once this is accomplished, the unit moves on to another employee who adds another part. The process typically ends with the unit being inspected and then packaged for shipping.

与顺序式依赖相似，**互惠式依赖**团队中的成员也是分工完成具体的任务。但是，与严格的活动顺序不同的是，互惠式依赖团队中的成员为完成团队工作还要与其他成员互动。

Reciprocal interdependence is the next type of task interdependence. Similar to sequential interdependence, members are specialized to perform specific tasks. However, instead of a strict sequence of activities, members interact with a subset of other members to complete the team's work. To understand reciprocal interdependence, consider a team of people who are involved in a business that designs custom homes for wealthy clients. After meeting with a client, the salesperson would provide general criteria, structural and aesthetic details, and some rough sketches to an architect who would work up some initial plans and elevations. The architect then would submit the initial plans to the salesperson, who would review the plans with the customer. Typically, the plans need to be revised by the architect several times, and during this process, customers have questions and requests that require the architect to consult with other members of the team. For example, the architect and structural engineer may have to meet to decide where to locate support beams and load-bearing walls. The architect and construction supervisor might also have to meet to discuss revisions to a design feature that turns out to be too costly. As a final example, the salesperson might have to meet with the designers to assist the customer in the selection of additional features, materials, and colors, which would then need to be included in a revision of the plan by the architect.

Face-to-face team meetings that involve comprehensive interdependence can consume a lot of time, yet these meetings are an important part of accomplishing work that requires collaboration.

Finally, **comprehensive interdependence** requires the highest level of interaction and coordination among members as they try to accomplish work. In groups with comprehensive interdependence, each member has a great deal of discretion in terms of what they do and with whom they interact in the course of the collaboration involved in accomplishing the team's work. Teams at IDEO, arguably the world's most successful product design firm, function with comprehensive interdependence. These teams are composed of individuals from very diverse backgrounds, and they meet as a team quite often to share knowledge and ideas to solve problems related to their design projects.

当完成工作时，**广泛依赖**要求团队成员间有最高水平的互动和合作。

It's important to note that there's no one right way to design teams with respect to task interdependence. However, it's also important to recognize the trade-offs associated with the different types. On the one hand, as the level of task interdependence increases, members must spend increasing amounts of time communicating and coordinating with other members to complete tasks. This type of coordination can result in decreases in productivity, which is the ratio of work completed per the amount of time worked. On the other hand, increases in task interdependence increase the ability of the team to adapt to new situations. The more members interact and communicate with other members, the more likely it is that the team will be able to devise solutions to novel problems it may face.

GOAL INTERDEPENDENCE. In addition to being linked to one another by task activities, members may be linked by their goals. A high degree of **goal interdependence** exists when team members have a shared vision of the team's goal and align their individual goals with that vision as a result. To understand the power of goal interdependence, visualize a small boat with several people on board, each with a paddle. If each person on the boat wants to go to the exact same place on the other side of a lake, they will all row in the same direction, and the boat will arrive at the desired location. If, however, each person believes the boat should go someplace different, each person will row in a different direction, and the boat will have major problems getting anywhere.

当团队成员共同享有团队目标的愿景，并将个人目标与愿景联系起来时，团队就形成较高的**目标依赖**。

So how do you create high levels of goal interdependence? One thing to do would be to ensure that the team has a formalized mission statement that members buy in to. Mission statements can take a variety of forms, but good ones clearly describe what the team is trying to accomplish in a way that creates a sense of commitment and urgency among team members. Mission statements can come directly from the organization or team leaders, but in many circumstances, it makes more sense for teams to go through the process of developing their own mission statements. This process not only helps members identify important team goals and the actions the team needs to take to achieve these goals, but it also increases feelings of ownership toward the mission statement itself. Table 9-2 describes a set of recommended steps that teams can take to develop their own mission statements.

Although you might believe that the mission for some team tasks is very obvious, all too often this isn't the case. In student teams, for example, you might expect that the obvious goal in the minds of the team members would be to learn the course material. However, it's typically

TABLE 9-2 The Mission Statement Development Process

Steps in Mission Statement Development
1. The team should meet in a room where there can be uninterrupted discussion for 1–3 hours.
2. A facilitator should describe the purpose of a mission statement, along with important details that members of the team should consider. Those details may include the products, outcomes, or services that the team is responsible for providing, as well as relevant time constraints.
3. The team should brainstorm to identify potential phrases or elements to include in the mission statement.
4. If the team is large enough, subgroups should be formed to create "first draft" mission statements. Those mission statements should include action verbs and be no more than four sentences.
5. The subgroups should share the first drafts with one another.
6. The team should then try to integrate the best ideas into a single mission statement.
7. The resulting mission statement should be evaluated using the following criteria: *Clarity*—It should focus clearly on a single key purpose. *Relevance*—It should focus on something that is desired by the team members. *Significance*—If achieved, there are benefits that excite the members. *Believability*—It reflects something that members believe they can achieve. *Urgency*—It creates a sense of challenge and commitment.
8. The team should then revise any weak areas of the mission statement. The team should continue to work on the mission statement until there is consensus that it inspires dedication and commitment among members toward a common purpose.

Source: From P.S. MacMillan, *The Performance Factor: Unlocking the Secrets of Teamwork,* Nashville, Broadman & Holman Publishers, 2001, pp. 51–53. Copyright © 2001 B&H Publishing Group. Used by permission.

the case that students come to a team like this with individual goals that are surprisingly different. Some students might be more interested in "just getting by" with a passing grade because they already have a job and just need their degree. Others students might want to do well in the course, but are more concerned with maintaining balance with the demands of their lives outside of school. Finally, other students might be focused solely on their grades, perhaps because they want to get into a prestigious graduate school in an unrelated discipline. Of course, the problem here is that each of these goals is associated with a different approach to working in the team. Students who want to learn the course material will work hard on the team assignments and will want to spend extra time discussing assignment-related issues with teammates, students who just want to get by will do the minimum amount of work, students who want to maintain their work–life balance will look for the most efficient way to do things, and students who are focused on their grades would be willing to take shortcuts that might inhibit learning. Although trying to reach a consensus on a team mission may not be easy in a situation in which the members have goals that vary along these lines, research has shown that teams of students experience significantly greater effectiveness if they invest time and effort doing so soon after the team first forms. For more discussion regarding the importance of goal interdependence, see our **OB at the Bookstore** feature.

结果依赖指的是团队成员共享团队获得的报酬，包括工资、奖金、正式反馈及认可、鼓励、额外休息时间及团队的持续存在。

OUTCOME INTERDEPENDENCE. The final type of interdependence relates to how members are linked to one another in terms of the feedback and outcomes they receive as a consequence of working in the team. A high degree of **outcome interdependence** exists when team members share in the rewards that the team earns, with reward examples including pay, bonuses, formal feedback and recognition, pats on the back, extra time off, and continued team survival. Of course, because team achievement depends on the performance of each team member, high

OB AT THE BOOKSTORE

THE ORANGE REVOLUTION

by Adrian Gostick and Chester Elton (New York: Free Press, 2010).

Here's what geniuses do: they build great teams.

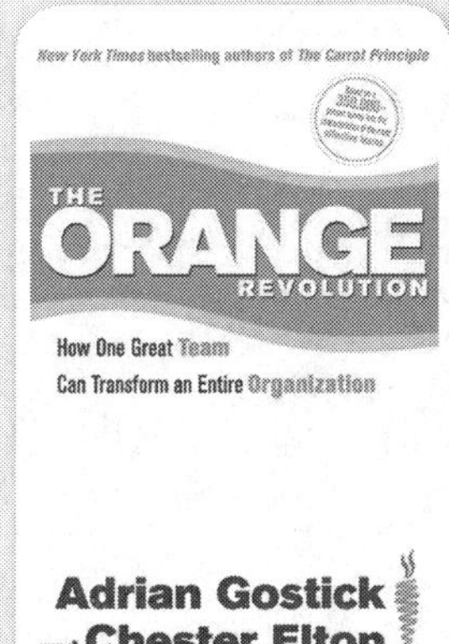

With those words, Gostick and Elton assert that important "breakthroughs" that give companies a competitive advantage are not the product of a lone genius, but rather a special form of high-performing team that works together in the passionate pursuit of a shared vision. The authors provide many examples where this has been the case. For example, the book opens with a colorful description of how the lightbulb was invented. Although most often attributed to Edison himself, the lightbulb was actually invented by a small team that worked tirelessly until Edison's vision of it was realized. The book argues that Edison's genius rested in the way he designed teams to make his visions a reality. He would compose small teams with people who possessed high levels of knowledge and character, a desire to learn, and a commitment to excellence. He then gave the teams a goal and didn't interfere with their progress much afterwards. He didn't have to. The team members became engrossed with their work, and eventually, breakthroughs occurred.

Drawing from examples like this, and also from survey data collected from 350,000 people employed in 28 different industries, Gostick and Elton offer a model that teams can follow to achieve breakthrough results and sustained success. The three elements of the model include members' commitment to a standard of world-class performance; members knowing what to expect from one another; and members who support, recognize, and cheer each other to victory. The authors claim that for these three things to happen, members first need to clearly visualize and become passionate about the same common cause. How does a team establish these types of "transformational common causes"? The authors suggest that every member of the team should be involved in establishing the cause as well as the values that guide the team as they work together to achieve the cause. The authors also suggest that the team should write a mission statement that reflects this cause, and then refer to it often, like a rallying flag. Finally, the authors suggest that team practices—things like goals, deadlines, and celebrations—should be aligned with the team's cause.

outcome interdependence also implies that team members depend on the performance of other team members for the rewards that they receive. In contrast, low outcome interdependence exists in teams in which individual members receive rewards and punishments on the basis of their own performance, without regard to the performance of the team. Research into project teams involved in consulting, financial planning, and research and development shows that in teams in which members reflect on their performance, higher levels of outcome interdependence increase the amount of information shared among members, which promotes learning, and, ultimately, team performance. As we discuss in the Application section at the end of this chapter, the way a team is designed with respect to outcome interdependence also has important implications for the level of cooperation and motivation in the team.

团队构成指的是组成团队的人们的混合体。

团队构成
TEAM COMPOSITION

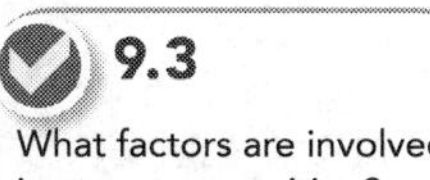
9.3
What factors are involved in team composition?

You probably already have a sense that team effectiveness hinges on **team composition**—or the mix of people who make up the team. If you've been a member of a particularly effective team, you may have noticed that the team seemed to have the right mix of knowledge,

FIGURE 9-4 Five Aspects of Team Composition

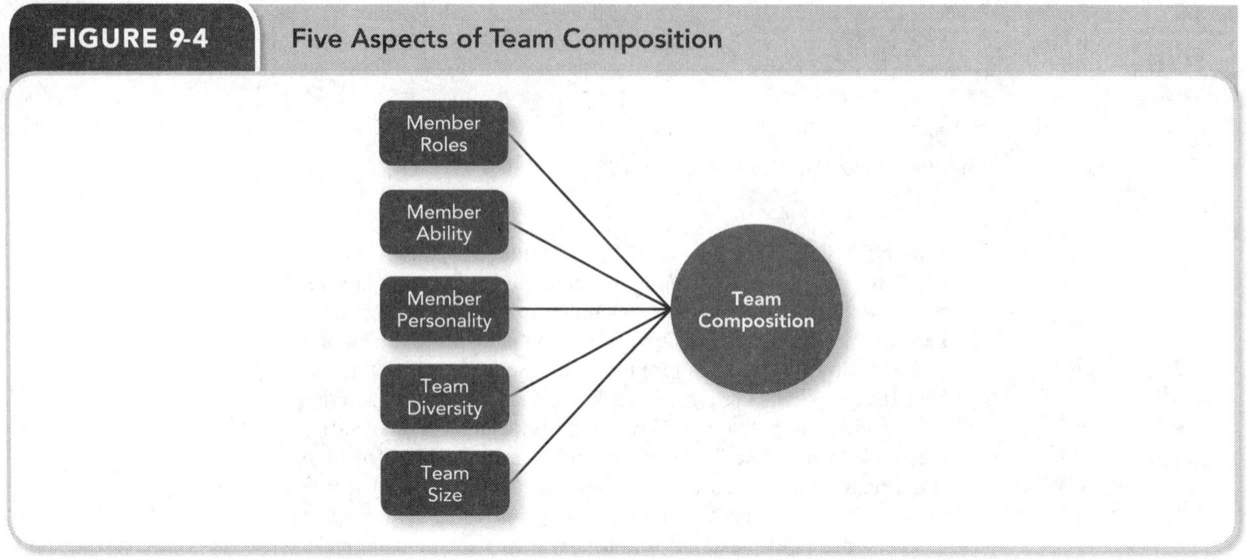

skills, abilities, and personalities. Team members were not only capable of performing their role responsibilities effectively, but they also cooperated and got along fairly well together. In this section, we identify the most important characteristics to consider in team composition, and we describe how these elements combine to influence team functioning and effectiveness. As shown in Figure 9-4, five aspects of team composition are crucial: roles, ability, personality, diversity, and team size.

角色是指在一个特定的情境中，个体被期望表现出来的行为模式。

MEMBER ROLES. A **role** is defined as a pattern of behavior that a person is expected to display in a given context. In a team setting, there are a variety of roles that members can take or develop in the course of interacting with one another, and depending on the specific situation, the presence or absence of members who possess these roles may have a strong impact on team effectiveness. One obvious way that roles can be distinguished is by considering the specific sets of task-focused activities that define what the individual members are expected to do for their team. As our **OB on Screen** feature illustrates, one of the main considerations when creating a team is to ensure that it has members who are skilled in performing the duties and responsibilities involved in their specific roles.

在**领导者–员工团队**中，由领导者为团队做决策，指导和控制其他所有团队成员，成员需要完成指定的工作。

Another way to distinguish roles is to consider what leaders and members do. In **leader–staff teams,** the leader makes decisions for the team and provides direction and control over members who perform assigned tasks, so this distinction makes sense in that the responsibilities of the leader and the rest of the team are distinct. Typically, however, team members have some latitude with respect to the behaviors they exhibit. In these situations, team roles can be described in terms of categories that are more general than the task-focused roles described above. By general we mean that these roles can apply to many different types of teams. As shown in Table 9-3, these general roles include team task roles, team building roles, and individualistic roles.

团队任务角色指的是直接有利于团队任务完成的行为。

Team task roles refer to behaviors that directly facilitate the accomplishment of team tasks. Examples include the *orienter* who establishes the direction for the team, the *devil's advocate* who offers constructive challenges to the team's status quo, and the *energizer* who motivates team members to work harder toward team goals. As you may have realized, the importance of specific task-oriented roles depends on the nature of the work in which the team is involved. The orienter role may be particularly important in teams that have autonomy over how to accomplish their work. The devil's advocate role may be particularly important in team contexts in which decisions are "high stakes" in nature. Finally, the energizer role may be most important in team contexts in which the work is important but not intrinsically motivating.

团队构建角色指的是影响团队社会氛围质量的行为。

In contrast to task-oriented roles, **team building roles** refer to behaviors that influence the quality of the team's social climate. Examples of team building roles include the *harmonizer*

OB ON SCREEN

INCEPTION

"Assemble your team Mr. Cobb, and choose your people more wisely."

With those words, Saito (Ken Watanabe) lets Dom Cobb (Leonardo DiCaprio) know that he must carefully choose members for a team needed for a high-stakes job (Dir.: Christopher Nolan, Warner Brothers, 2010). You see, Cobb is on the run from authorities, and to clear his name he must perform an inception for Saito, a powerful and politically connected businessman. What does an inception involve? Only infiltrating someone's dreams to plant an idea, and in this specific case, the idea will cause the subject to make an important decision that will help Saito's business interests. We should mention that performing an inception is dangerous. The dreamer's subconscious can detect infiltrators, and as a defense, it creates projections (many of whom carry guns and knives) to fight them off. A member of Cobb's previous team made an error that resulted in the subject detecting the infiltration, and Saito reminds Cobb that a similar failure won't be tolerated.

First, Cobb recruits an architect named Ariadne (Ellen Page). The role of the architect is to create the raw environment of the dreams—buildings and streetscape—that will be filled in with the other dreamers' projections. Cobb then recruits an imitator named Eames (Tom Hardy). This role involves taking on the identity of people who are familiar to the subject of the inception, with the object being to subtly influence the dreaming subject. Finally, Cobb recruits a chemist named Yusef (Dileep Rao) who will need to make a sedative capable of putting the team and subject into a deep sleep. The team's success depends on the execution of each role. An element in the environment that's too foreign, a misstatement by the imitator, or the sedative wearing off, could alert the subject to the infiltration and cause disaster. Members killed by projections prior to being awakened could find themselves trapped in limbo, a constant dream state where people lose their grip on reality. Although you've likely been on a team where some members didn't perform their roles effectively, we hope you didn't experience an outcome like this!

who steps in to resolve differences among teammates, the *encourager* who praises the work of teammates, and the *compromiser* who helps the team see alternative solutions that teammates can accept. As you might have gathered as you read these examples, the presence of members who take on social roles helps teams manage conflicts that could hinder team effectiveness.

TABLE 9-3 Team and Individualistic Roles

TEAM TASK ROLES	DESCRIPTION
Initiator-contributor	Proposes new ideas
Coordinator	Tries to coordinate activities among team members
Orienter	Determines the direction of the team's discussion
Devil's advocate	Offers challenges to the team's status quo
Energizer	Motivates the team to strive to do better
Procedural-technician	Performs routine tasks needed to keep progress moving
TEAM BUILDING ROLES	**DESCRIPTION**
Encourager	Praises the contributions of other team members
Harmonizer	Mediates differences between group members
Compromiser	Attempts to find the halfway point to end conflict
Gatekeeper/expediter	Encourages participation from teammates
Standard setter	Expresses goals for the team to achieve
Follower	Accepts the ideas of teammates
INDIVIDUALISTIC ROLES	**DESCRIPTION**
Aggressor	Deflates teammates, expresses disapproval with hostility
Blocker	Acts stubbornly resistant and disagrees beyond reason
Recognition seeker	Brags and calls attention to him- or herself
Self-confessor	Discloses personal opinions inappropriately
Slacker	Acts cynically, nonchalantly, or goofs off
Dominator	Manipulates team members for personal control

Source: Adapted from K. Benne and P. Sheats, "Functional Roles of Group Members." *Journal of Social Issues* 4 (1948), pp. 41–49.

个人角色指的是以团队为代价的对个人有利的行为。

Finally, whereas task roles and team building roles focus on activities that benefit the team, **individualistic roles** reflect behaviors that benefit the individual at the expense of the team. For example, the *aggressor* "puts down" or deflates fellow teammates. The *recognition seeker* takes credit for team successes. The *dominator* manipulates teammates to acquire control and power. If you've ever had an experience in a team in which members took on individualistic roles, you probably realize just how damaging they can be to the team. Individualistic role behaviors foster negative feelings among team members, which serve to hinder a team's ability to function and perform effectively.

MEMBER ABILITY. Team members possess a wide variety of abilities (see Chapter 8 on Ability for more discussion of such issues). Depending on the nature of the tasks involved in the team's work, some of these may be important to consider in team design. For example, for teams involved in physical work, relevant physical abilities will be important to take into account. Consider the types of abilities that are required of pit crew members in stock car racing, where margins of victory can be one-tenth of a second. When a car pulls into pit row, pit crew members need to leap over the pit wall and lift heavy tires, jacks, and other equipment to get the race car back on the track—ideally in about 14 seconds. In this setting, flexibility, cardiovascular endurance, and explosive strength are required, and in fact, racing teams have hired professional trainers and even built gyms to improve these abilities of their pit crew members.

It's also important to take cognitive abilities into account when designing teams. General cognitive ability is important to many different types of teams. In general, smarter teams perform better because teamwork tends to be quite complex. Team members not only have to be involved in several different aspects of the team's task, but they also have to learn how best to combine their individual efforts to accomplish team goals. In fact, the more that this type of learning is required, the more important member cognitive ability becomes. For example, research has shown that cognitive ability is more important to teams when team members have to learn from one another to adapt to unexpected changes, compared with contexts in which team members perform their assigned tasks in a routine fashion.

Of course, not every member needs high levels of these physical or cognitive abilities. If you've ever played Trivial Pursuit using teams, you might recall playing against another team in which only one of the team members was smart enough to answer any of the questions correctly. In fact, in tasks with an objectively verifiable best solution, the member who possesses the highest level of the ability relevant to the task will have the most influence on the effectiveness of the team. These types of tasks are called **disjunctive tasks.** You may also recall situations in which it was crucial that everyone on the team possessed the relevant abilities. Returning to the pit crew example, stock cars cannot leave the pit area until all the tires are mounted, and so the length of the pit stop is determined by the physical abilities of the slowest crew member. Tasks like this, for which the team's performance depends on the abilities of the "weakest link," are called **conjunctive tasks.** Finally, there are **additive tasks,** for which the contributions resulting from the abilities of every member "add up" to determine team performance. The amount of money that a Girl Scout troop earns from selling Thin Mints and Samoas is the sum of what each Girl Scout is able to sell on her own.

在具有客观证实为最佳方案的任务中，掌握与任务相关的最有能力的成员对团队的高效性产生的影响最大。这类任务被称为“**分离性任务**”。

在**连续性任务**中，团队的绩效取决于“最薄弱环节”的能力。

在**递增性任务**中，每个成员的能力带来的贡献“累加”决定团队的绩效。

MEMBER PERSONALITY. Team members also possess a wide variety of personality traits (see Chapter 7 on Personality and Cultural Values for more discussion of such issues). These personality traits affect the roles that team members take on, as well as how teams function and perform as units. For example, the agreeableness of team members has an important influence on team effectiveness. Why? Because agreeable people tend to be more cooperative and trusting, and these tendencies promote positive attitudes about the team and smooth interpersonal interactions. Moreover, because agreeable people may be more concerned about their team's interests than their own, they should work hard on behalf of the team. There's a caveat regarding agreeableness in teams, however. Because agreeable people tend to prefer harmony and cooperation rather than conflict and competition, they may be less apt to speak up and offer constructive criticisms that might help the team improve. Thus, if a team is composed of too many highly agreeable members, there's a chance that the members will behave in a way that enhances harmony of the team at the expense of task accomplishment.

As another example, team composition in terms of members' conscientiousness is important to teams. After all, almost any team would benefit from having members who tend to be dependable and work hard to achieve team goals. What might be less obvious to you is the strong negative effect on the team of having even one member who is particularly low on conscientiousness. To understand why this is true, consider how you would react to a team member who was not dependable and did not appear to be motivated to work hard toward team goals. If you're like most people, you would find the situation dissatisfying, and you would consider different ways of dealing with it. Some people might try to motivate the person to be more responsible and work harder; others might try to get the person ejected from the team. The problem is that these natural reactions to a low conscientiousness team member not only divert attention away from accomplishing work responsibilities, but they also can result in some very uncomfortable and time-consuming interpersonal conflicts. Moreover, even if you and the other members of the team work harder to compensate for this person, it would be difficult for your team to perform as effectively as other teams in which all members are more interpersonally responsible and engaged in the team's work.

A task that can go only as quickly as the slowest team member, like a pit stop in a car race, is a conjunctive task.

Finally, the personality characteristic of extraversion is relevant to team composition. People who are extraverted tend to perform more effectively in interpersonal contexts and are more positive and optimistic in general. Therefore, it shouldn't surprise you to hear that having extraverted team members is generally beneficial to the social climate of the group, as well as to team effectiveness in the eyes of supervisors. At the same time, however, research has shown that having too many members who are very high on extraversion can hurt the team. The reason for this can be attributed to extraverts' tendency to be assertive and dominant. As you would expect when there are too many members with these types of tendencies, power struggles and unproductive conflict occur with greater frequency.

团队多元化是指按照某种特征来划分的成员之间差异的程度。

 9.4

What are the types of team diversity and how do they influence team functioning?

DIVERSITY. Another aspect of team composition refers to the degree to which members are different from one another in terms of any attribute that might be used by someone as a basis of categorizing people. We refer to those differences as **team diversity.** Trying to understand the effects of team diversity is somewhat difficult because there are so many different characteristics that may be used to categorize people. Beyond obvious differences among people in their physical appearance, there can be separation among members in terms of their values and beliefs, variety among members in their knowledge and expertise, and disparity among members in their social status and power. Moreover, diversity of team member characteristics may matter more or less depending on the nature of the team and organizational context. For example, you might imagine how the dynamics in a team consisting of both men and women could vary depending on whether the team is in an organization dominated by men (or women) or whether it's balanced in terms of the employees' sex. There are also several reasons diversity might influence team functioning and effectiveness, and some of these reasons seem contradictory.

用于解释多元化为何具有积极作用的一个主导理论被称为**多元化问题解决价值观点**。按照这种观点，多元化可令团队受益，主要在于它为团队提供了开展工作时可以从中汲取知识与观点的蓄水池。

One predominant theory that has been used to explain why diversity has positive effects is called the **value in diversity problem-solving approach.** According to this perspective, diversity in teams is beneficial because it provides for a larger pool of knowledge and perspectives from which a team can draw as it carries out its work. Having greater diversity in knowledge perspectives stimulates the exchange of information, which in turn fosters learning among team members. The knowledge that results from this learning is then shared and integrated with the knowledge of other members, ultimately helping the team perform more effectively. Research has shown that these benefits of diversity are more likely to occur when the team includes members who are able and willing to put in the effort necessary to understand and integrate different perspectives. Teams that engage in work that's relatively complex and requires creativity tend to benefit most from diversity, and research on teams that are diverse in terms of many different characteristics related to knowledge and perspectives—ethnicity, expertise, personality, attitudes—supports this idea.

相似吸引观点是一种被广泛用来解释为什么多元化可能对团队具有破坏性作用的理论。按照这种观点，人们倾向于被感知与自己相似的人的吸引。

A theory that's been used widely to explain why diversity may have detrimental effects on teams is called the **similarity-attraction approach.** According to this perspective, people tend to be more attracted to others who are perceived as more similar. People also tend to avoid interacting with those who are perceived to be dissimilar, to reduce the likelihood of having uncomfortable disagreements. Consistent with this perspective, research has shown that diversity on attributes such as cultural background, race, and attitudes are associated with communication problems and ultimately poor team effectiveness.

Surface-level diversity can sometimes create issues for teams as they begin their tasks, but such problems usually disappear over time.

So it appears that there are two different theories about diversity effects that are relevant to teams, and each has been supported in research. Which perspective is correct? As it turns out, a key to understanding the impact of team diversity requires that you consider both the general type of diversity and the length of time the team has been in existence. **Surface-level diversity** refers to diversity regarding observable attributes such as race, ethnicity, sex, and age. Although this type of diversity may have a negative impact on teams early in their existence because of similarity-attraction issues, those negative effects tend to disappear as members become more knowledgeable about one another. In essence, the stereotypes that members have about one another based on surface differences are replaced with knowledge regarding underlying characteristics that are more relevant to social and task interactions.

表面多元化是指基于可观察的特性如种族、族裔、性别和年龄等方面的多元化。

One complication here is that *fault lines* often occur in diverse groups, whereby informal subgroups develop based on similarity in surface-level attributes such as gender or other characteristics. The problem with fault lines is that knowledge and information possessed by one subgroup may not be communicated to other subgroups in a manner that might help the entire team perform more effectively. In a study of boards of directors, for example, the presence of strong fault lines decreased the amount of discussion that board members had with each other in regards to entrepreneurial issues that could affect their companies. Research has shown, however, that the detrimental effects of having subgroups can be offset with training that reinforces the idea that teams may benefit from their diversity. Leadership or reward practices that reinforce the value of sharing information and promote a strong sense of team identity also help diverse teams perform more effectively.

Deep-level diversity, in contrast, refers to diversity with respect to attributes that are less easy to observe initially but that can be inferred after more direct experience. Differences in attitudes, values, and personality are good examples of deep-level diversity. In contrast to the effects of surface-level diversity, time appears to increase the negative effects of deep-level diversity on team functioning and effectiveness. Over time, as team members learn more about one another, differences that relate to underlying values and goals become increasingly apparent. Those differences can therefore create problems among team members that ultimately result in reduced effectiveness.

深层多元化是指在那些最初不容易观察到，但通过直接体验后可能推断出的特性方面的多元化。

Fortunately, it appears that the negative effects of deep-level diversity can be managed. As an example, diversity in members' approach to pursing goals has been shown to hinder team functioning and effectiveness, but this effect can be reduced if teams are instructed to take the time to reflect on their progress toward goals and their strategies. As another example, negative effects of deep-level diversity with respect to members' values have been found to be reduced when team leaders emphasize the teams' task and provide explicit direction regarding team procedures, standards, roles, and expectations. We should also point out, however, that team leaders can also exacerbate problems associated with deep-level diversity. Conflict that results from diversity in members' values appears to increase in teams with leaders who emphasize things like freedom of expression and participation. See our **OB Internationally** feature for a discussion of the challenges of managing deep-level diversity in teams that include members from different cultures.

We also should mention an important caveat here. Although personality is normally considered a deep-level diversity variable, some specific personality types do not function this way. In the previous section on personality, for example, we pointed out that though having team members who are extraverted and agreeable is generally a good thing, problems arise if a team has too many members with these attributes. So whereas diversity on most deep-level characteristics is problematic for teams, this claim does not apply to extraversion and agreeableness, because for these two personality characteristics, teams are likely to benefit from having a mix of members.

TEAM SIZE. Two adages are relevant to team size: "the more the merrier" and "too many cooks spoil the pot." Which statement do you believe is true in terms of how many members to include

OB INTERNATIONALLY

Businesses are increasingly using teams composed of members from different cultures, and so teams today often possess members who differ from one another in terms of their attitudes, values, ideas, goals, and behaviors. These types of teams, called *multicultural teams,* can approach problems from several different perspectives, which opens the door to highly innovative solutions. Cultural diversity also allows teams to serve a diverse customer base that may differ in terms of culture and nationality.

Unfortunately, the attributes that give multicultural teams these advantages also give them disadvantages. As an example, people from different cultures communicate differently, which can lead to misunderstandings. For example, to people in the United States, the phrase "to table something" means to put it off until later, whereas to people in some European countries, it means discuss it right now. Imagine your reaction if you didn't know this difference, and you told a team you were leading that you wanted to table something, and then one of your team members started to discuss options and recommendations about the issue. There are differences in the directness of communications as well. Westerners tend to be very direct and to the point, but to people in other countries, such as Japan, this directness may cause embarrassment and a sense of disrespect. There are also cultural differences in decision-making processes. In some cultures, decisions can be made only after careful consideration and reconsideration of all relevant issues, which is much different from the style in other cultures, such as the United States, where decisions are made rather quickly and with less analysis. Although these differences might seem trivial, they often lead to misunderstandings that reduce the willingness of team members to cooperate. So how can multicultural teams be managed to ensure the advantages outweigh the disadvantages? Although there's no one best way to manage multicultural teams, one proven approach is to encourage team members to take the time to communicate openly with each other about cultural differences and to proactively develop strategies the team can use to accommodate them.

on a team? The answer, according to the results of one meta-analysis, is that having a greater number of members is beneficial for management and project teams but not for teams engaged in production tasks. Management and project teams engage in work that's complex and knowledge intensive, and these teams therefore benefit from the additional resources and expertise contributed by additional members. In contrast, production teams tend to engage in routine tasks that are less complex. Having additional members beyond what's necessary to accomplish the work tends to result in unnecessary coordination and communication problems. Additional members therefore may be less productive because there's more socializing, and they feel less accountable for team outcomes. Although making a claim about the absolute best team size is impossible, research with undergraduate students concluded that team members tend to be most satisfied with their team when the number of members is between four and five. Of course, there are other rules of thumb you can use to keep team size optimal. Jeff Bezos, the CEO of Amazon.com, uses the two-pizza rule: "If a team can't be fed by two pizzas, it's too large."

总结：什么特征可以用来描述团队
SUMMARY: WHAT CHARACTERISTICS CAN BE USED TO DESCRIBE TEAMS?

The preceding sections illustrate that there are a variety of characteristics that can be used to describe teams. As Figure 9-5 illustrates, teams can be described using taxonomies of team types. For example, teams can be described by categorizing them as a work team, a management team, a parallel team, a project team, or an action team. Teams can also be described using the nature of the team's interdependence with regard to its task, goals, and outcomes. Finally, teams can be described in terms of their composition. Relevant member characteristics include member roles, member ability, member personality, member diversity, and team size.

FIGURE 9-5 What Characteristics Can Be Used to Describe Teams?

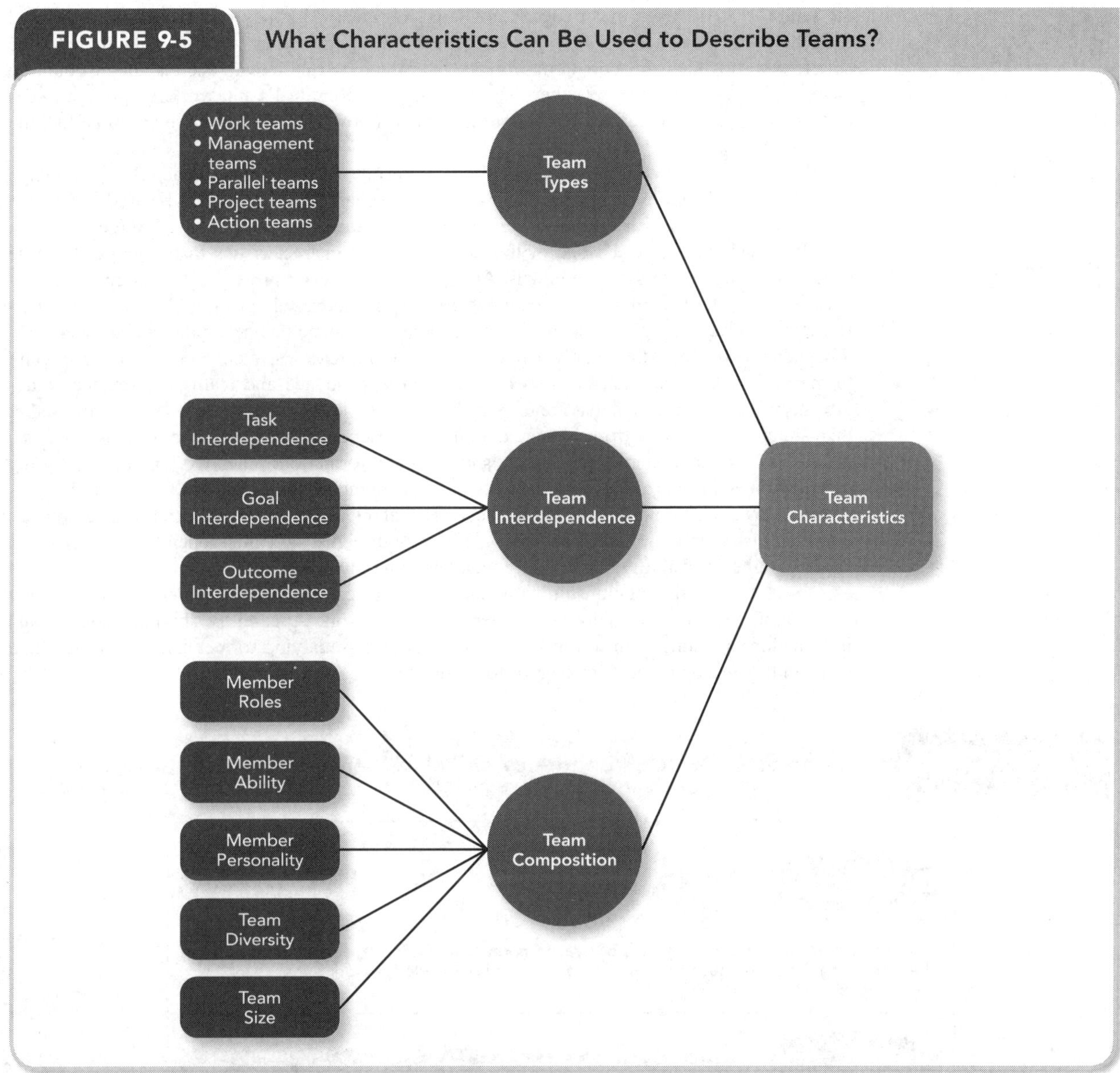

团队特征有多重要

HOW IMPORTANT ARE TEAM CHARACTERISTICS?

In previous chapters, we have described individual characteristics and mechanisms and discussed how these variables affect individual performance and commitment. In this chapter, we're concerned with team characteristics, and so naturally, we're interested in how they influence team effectiveness. One aspect of team effectiveness is *team performance,* which may include metrics such as the quantity and quality of goods or services produced, customer satisfaction, the effectiveness or accuracy of decisions, victories, completed reports, and successful investigations. Team performance in the context of student project teams most often means the quality with which the team completes assignments and projects, as well as the grades they earn.

A second aspect of team effectiveness is team commitment, which is sometimes called *team viability.* **Team viability** refers to the likelihood that the team can work together effectively into

团队生命力是指团队可以在一起有效工作直到未来的可能性。

the future. If the team experience is not satisfying, members may become disillusioned and focus their energy on activities away from the team. Although a team with low viability might be able to work together on short-term projects, over the long run, a team such as this is bound to have significant problems. Rather than planning for future tasks and working through issues that might improve the team, members of a team with low viability are more apt to be looking ahead to the team's ultimate demise.

9.5 How do team characteristics influence team effectiveness?

Of course, it's difficult to summarize the relationship between team characteristics and team performance and commitment when there are so many characteristics that can be used to describe teams. Here we focus our discussion on the impact of task interdependence. We focus on task interdependence because it's one of the most important characteristics that distinguishes true teams from mere groups of individuals. As Figure 9-6 shows, it turns out that the relationship between task interdependence and team performance is moderately positive. That is, task performance tends to be higher in teams in which members depend on one another and have to coordinate their activities rather than when members work more or less independently. It's important to mention that the relationship between task interdependence and team performance is significantly stronger in teams that are responsible for completing complex knowledge work rather than simple tasks. When work is more complex, interdependence is necessary because there's a need for members to interact and share resources and information. When work is simple, sharing information and resources is less necessary because members can do the work by themselves.

In the lower portion of Figure 9-6, you can see that the relationship between task interdependence and team commitment is weaker. Teams with higher task interdependence have only a slightly higher probability of including members who are committed to their team's continued existence. As with the relationship with team performance, task interdependence has a stronger effect on viability for teams doing complex knowledge work. Apparently, sharing resources and information in a context in which it's unnecessary is dissatisfying to members and results in a team with reduced prospects of continued existence.

FIGURE 9-6 Effects of Task Interdependence on Performance and Commitment

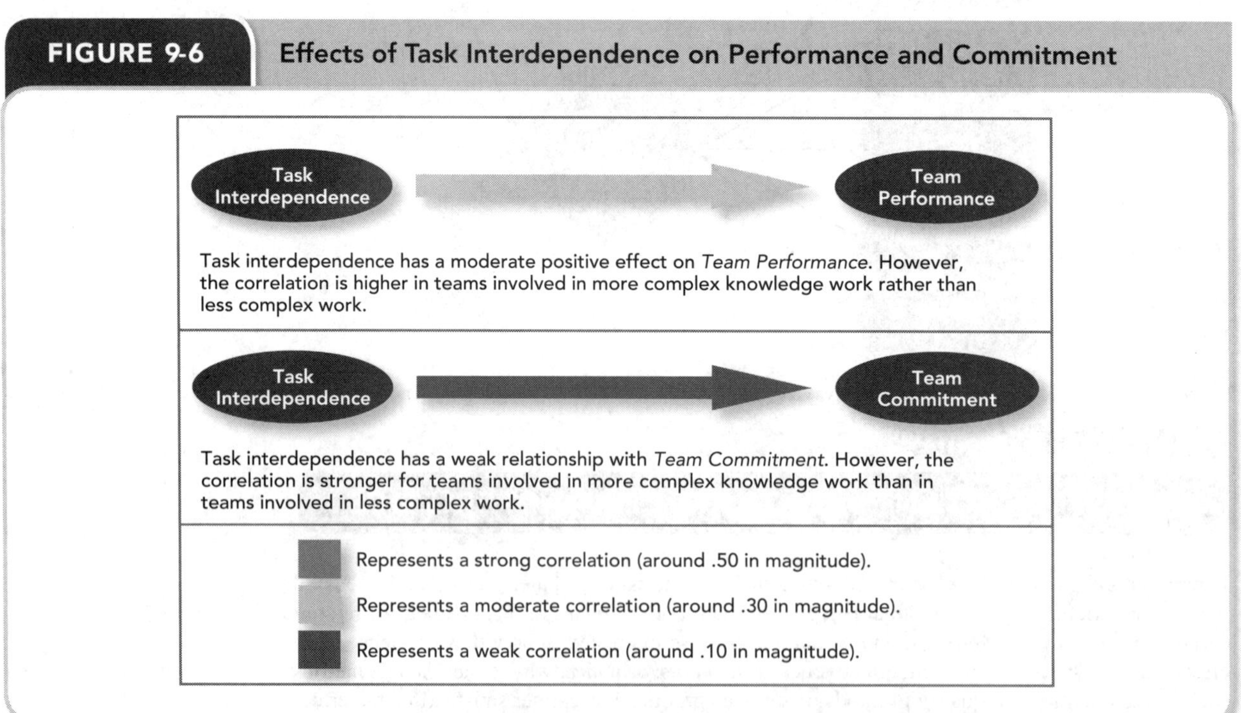

Sources: M.A. Campion, G.J. Medsker, and A.C. Higgs, "Relations Between Work Group Characteristics and Effectiveness: Implications for Designing Effective Work Groups," *Personnel Psychology* 46 (1993), pp. 823–49; M.A. Campion, E.M. Papper, and G.J. Medsker, "Relations Between Work Team Characteristics and Effectiveness: A Replication and Extension," *Personnel Psychology* 49 (1996), pp. 429–52; and G.L. Stewart, "A Meta-Analytic Review of Relationships Between Team Design Features and Team Performance," *Journal of Management* 32 (2006), pp. 29–54.

应用：团队薪酬

APPLICATION: TEAM COMPENSATION

Although all team characteristics have implications for managerial practices, outcome interdependence is particularly relevant for two reasons. First, outcome interdependence has obvious connections to compensation practices in organizations, and most of us are interested in factors that determine how we get paid. If you work for an organization with compensation that has high outcome interdependence, a higher percentage of your pay will depend on how well your team does. If you work for an organization with compensation that has low outcome interdependence, a lower percentage of your pay will depend on how well your team does.

A second reason outcome interdependence is important to consider is that it presents managers with a tough dilemma. High outcome interdependence promotes higher levels of cooperation because members understand that they share the same fate—if the team wins, everyone wins, and if the team fails, everyone fails. At the same time, high outcome interdependence may result in reduced motivation, especially among higher performing members. High performers may perceive that they're not paid in proportion to what they contributed to the team and that their teammates are taking advantage of this inequity for their own benefit.

9.6
How can team compensation be used to manage team effectiveness?

One solution to this dilemma has been to design team reward structures with **hybrid outcome interdependence,** which means that members receive rewards that are dependent on both their team's performance and how well they perform as individuals. In fact, the majority of organizations that use teams use some sort of hybrid outcome interdependence. But what percentage of team members' pay is typically based on team performance in business organizations? This is a difficult question to answer, because as we discussed earlier in the chapter, there are so many different types of teams doing so many different types of tasks, and also because organizations vary dramatically in their approaches to rewarding their employees. For example, the size of team-based pay in the goods and service sectors averages around 10–12 percent of an employee's base pay. In contrast, production workers at Nucor, the Crawfordsville, Indiana–based steel company, earn team-based bonuses of 170 percent of their base pay, on average. It's important to note that hybrid outcome interdependence, in and of itself, may not always be that effective in promoting team functioning and effectiveness. Research conducted at Xerox, for example, shows that service teams with hybrid outcome interdependence are less effective than service teams with very high or very low levels of outcome interdependence. Part of the problem with hybrid outcome interdependence is that it can lead to uncertainty about which types of behaviors are being rewarded and how pay ultimately is determined. To make hybrid interdependence work, organizations need to ensure that the system makes sense to employees. At Nucor, most production workers know within one-tenth of 1 percent what the team's bonus is for the week, as well as which products will be produced next and how these future operations will likely affect their bonuses.

混合式结果依赖指团队成员得到的报酬取决于所在团队的绩效以及他们个人的表现。

One way to resolve the dilemma of outcome interdependence is to implement a level of team-based pay that matches the level of task interdependence. Members tend to be more productive in high task interdependence situations when there's also high outcome interdependence. Similarly, members prefer low task interdependent situations when there's low outcome interdependence. To understand the power of aligning task and outcome interdependence, consider scenarios in which there's not a good match. For example, how would you react to a situation in which you worked very closely with your teammates on a team project in one of your classes, and though your professor said the team's project was outstanding, she awarded an A to one of your team members, a B to another, and a C to you? Similarly, consider how you would react to a situation in which you scored enough points for an A on your final exam, but your professor averaged everyone's grades together and gave all students a C. Chances are you wouldn't be happy with either scenario.

chapter 10

Teams: Processes and Communication

团队：过程与沟通

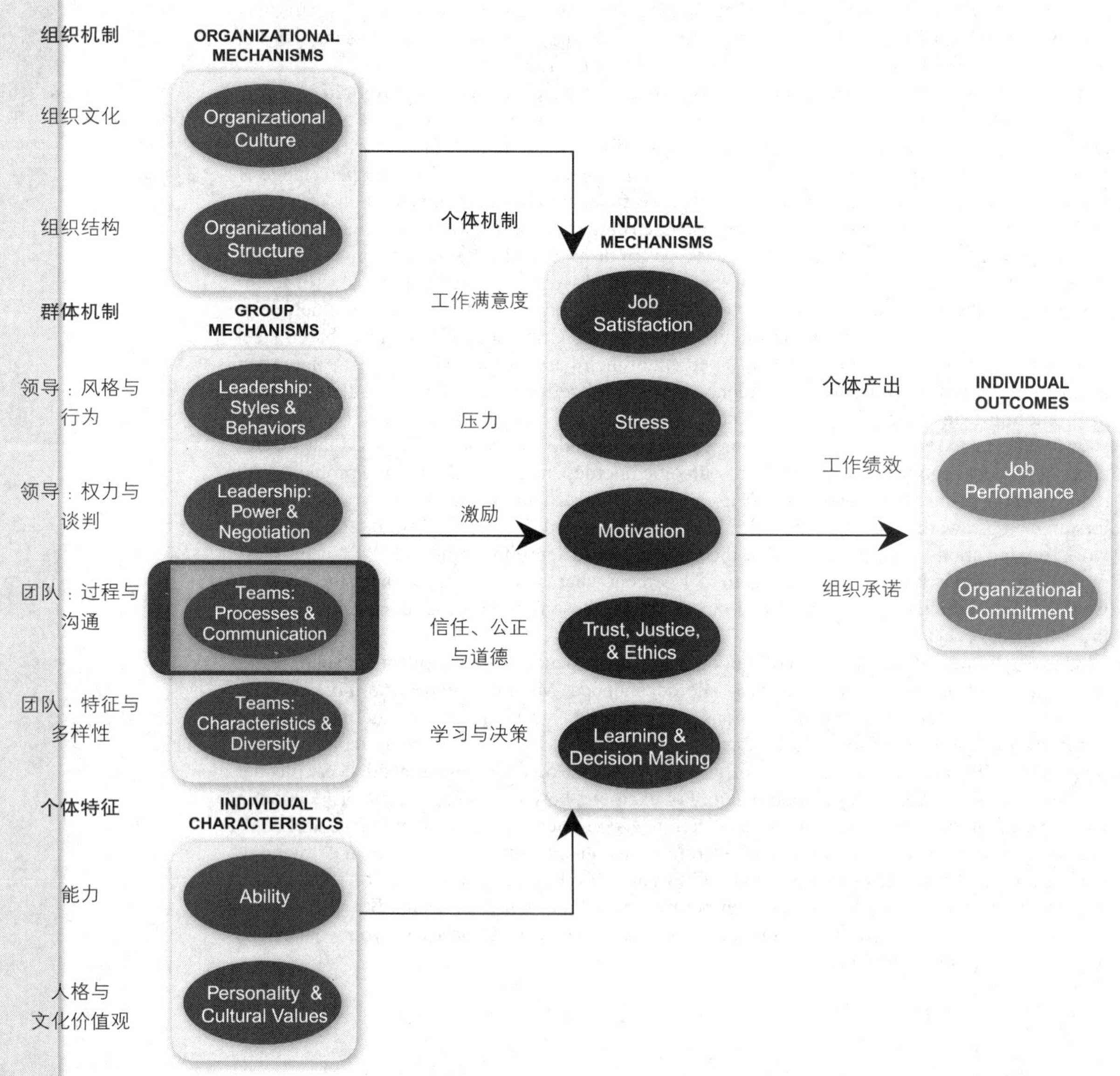

LEARNING GOALS

After reading this chapter, you should be able to answer the following questions:

10.1 What are taskwork processes, and what are some examples of team activities that fall into this process category?

10.2 What are teamwork processes, and what are some examples of team activities that fall into this process category?

10.3 What factors influence the communication process in teams?

10.4 What are team states, and what are some examples of the states that fall into this process category?

10.5 How do team processes affect team performance and team commitment?

10.6 What steps can organizations take to improve team processes?

PROCTER & GAMBLE

"Three billion times a day, Procter and Gamble (P&G) brands touch the lives of people around the world." The number "three billion" might seem like hyperbole, but consider that P&G brands such as Tide, Downy, Crest, Ivory, Charmin, Pantene, Duracell, Pampers, and Vicks are household names across the globe. So how did P&G become so successful? For one thing, the company has been on the forefront of using teams to achieve extraordinary results. For example, in the 1960s P&G experimented with self-managed work teams in the production of Downy Fabric Softener in its Lima, Ohio, plant. These teams, which had a great deal of autonomy with respect to the way they managed their work processes, could make, pack, and ship the product less expensively than a factory in California that did not use teams, while at the same time setting safety and quality records. In fact, these self-managed teams were so successful that P&G treated them as a trade secret and took security precautions so that competitors would not learn of their existence.

Today P&G uses teams throughout the organization, and has instituted numerous practices to facilitate their processes and performance. For example, the company has designed open workspaces and offices to promote communication among team members involved in product development and management so that decision making and problem solving become team efforts. The basic idea is simple, take down walls that separate people, fill the open spaces with comfortable furniture and things like coffee machines, and team members will sit down and share ideas. As another example, P&G fosters team creativity in product development by allowing teams to experiment with new ideas in a 10,000-square-foot "Innovation Gym." The gym is a dedicated space where teams meet, usually for three days or less, with a P&G employee who facilitates various activities that inspire creativity. Teams are led through brainstorming sessions, after which, ideas are formed into prototypes. Consumers are then brought into the gym to evaluate the prototypes and to provide feedback to the team.

P&G also recognizes that for teams to function effectively, they need to be coached in a way that encourages cooperation and teamwork. As an example, team leaders ensure their teams monitor progress toward goals and are open to feedback regarding their effectiveness. As another example, team leaders encourage their teams to expand their boundaries to connect with other teams so that they can learn how to cope with challenges. Finally, team leaders ensure there is open and frank communication with regard to challenges the teams may be facing, but the conversations focus on what the teams can do to move forward rather than pointing fingers and placing blame for things that happened in the past.

团队过程与沟通

TEAM PROCESSES AND COMMUNICATION

团队过程是指在团队中为达成终极目标而产生的各种不同类型的沟通、活动以及互动。

As we described in Chapter 9 on Team Characteristics and Diversity, a team consists of two or more people who work interdependently over some time period to accomplish common goals related to some task-oriented purpose. The effectiveness of organizations depends to a large extent on the activities and interactions that occur within teams as they move toward their task-related objectives. **Team process** is a term that reflects the different types of communication, activities, and interactions that occur within teams that contribute to their ultimate end goals. Team characteristics, like member diversity, task interdependence, team size, and so forth, affect team processes and communication. Those processes, in turn, have a strong impact on team effectiveness. In fact, some have argued that extraordinary teams are defined in terms of their processes.

Some of the team processes and forms of communication that we describe in this chapter are observable by the naked eye. An outside observer would be able to see members of a product team at Procter & Gamble communicating with one another in regards to the type of advertising that will be used to launch a new product. Other processes, in contrast, are less visible. An outside observer wouldn't be able to see the sense of "cohesion" felt by the members of this team or the shared "mental models" that cause them to work together so efficiently. Thus, team processes include interactions among members that occur behaviorally, as well as the hard-to-see feelings and thoughts that coalesce as a consequence of member interactions.

为什么某些团队大于其部分之和

WHY ARE SOME TEAMS MORE THAN THE SUM OF THEIR PARTS?

Take a second and try to think of a few teams that have been successful. It's likely that the success of some of these teams was expected because the team had members who are very talented and skilled. The success of other teams may be more difficult to understand just by looking at the rosters of their members. These teams might have members who appear to be less talented and skilled, but as they work together, they somehow became "more than the sum of their parts." Getting more from the team than you would expect according to the capabilities of its individual members is called **process gain**. This capability, which is synonymous with "synergy," is most critical in situations in which the complexity of the work is high or when tasks require members to combine their knowledge, skills, and efforts to solve problems. In essence, process gain is important because it results in useful resources and capabilities that did not exist before the team created them.

过程收益是指在团队中获得的收益超过依据成员个人能力而形成的收益。

Having described process gain, we now consider its polar opposite. Consider the following names: LeBron James, Dwyane Wade, and Chris Bosh. You don't have to be much more than a casual sports fan to recognize those names as some of the best in professional basketball, and it just so happens they ended up on the same NBA team, the Miami Heat. With these three superstars, it seemed certain that the Heat would've routinely crushed their opponents. To the surprise of most basketball fans, however, the team only won about half the games they played the first two months of their first season together. The Heat managed to get better as the season progressed, and although the team made it to the NBA Finals, they wound up being "less than the sum of their parts" and as a result, they were handily defeated by the Dallas Mavericks. In organizational behavior terms, the Heat were harmed by **process loss,** or getting less from the team than you would expect based on the capabilities of its individual members.

过程损失是指在团队中获得的收益少于依据成员个人能力而形成的收益。

What factors conspire to create process loss? One factor is that in teams, members have to work to not only accomplish their own tasks but also coordinate their activities with the activities of their teammates. Although this extra effort focused on integrating work is a necessary aspect

In their first season together, NBA superstars Chris Bosh, LeBron James, and Dwyane Wade were unable to consistently make use of their individual talents while playing together at the same time.

协调损失是指在团队的协调活动中，消耗了原本能够用于任务活动的时间和精力。

生产阻碍是指在团队工作中，某一成员必须等待另一成员完成后才能开展自己的工作。

激励损失，或称为团队生产率损失，是指当团队成员不能尽力工作时所带来的团队绩效损失。

of the team experience, it's called **coordination loss** because it consumes time and energy that could otherwise be devoted to task activity. Such coordination losses are often driven by **production blocking,** which occurs when members have to wait on one another before they can do their part of the team task. If you've ever worked in a team in which you felt like you couldn't get any of your own work done because of all the time spent in meetings, following up requests for information from other team members, and waiting on team members to do their part of the team task, you already understand how frustrating production blocking (and coordination loss) can be. In the context of our basketball example, production blocking occurs when a player has to wait too long for a teammate to get in position before passing the ball.

The second force that fosters process loss in team contexts is **motivational loss,** or the loss in team productivity that occurs when team members don't work as hard as they could. Why does motivational loss occur in team contexts? One explanation is that it's often quite difficult to gauge exactly how much each team member contributes to the team. Members of teams can work together on projects over an extended period of time, and as a consequence, it's difficult to keep an accurate accounting of who does what. Similarly, members contribute to their team in many different ways, and contributions of some members may be less obvious than others. Finally, members of teams don't always work together at the same time as a unit. Regardless of the reasons for it, uncertainty regarding "who contributes what" results in team members feeling less accountable for team outcomes. Those feelings of reduced accountability, in turn, cause members to exert less effort when working on team tasks than they would if they worked alone on those same tasks. This phenomenon is called **social loafing,** and it can significantly hinder a team's effectiveness. Returning to our basketball example, motivational loss and social loafing may result if players come to depend on a star player to win games for the team.

社会惰化是指个体在完成团队任务时，由于责任感减弱而导致其付出的努力比单独完成相同任务时的要少。

任务工作过程
TASKWORK PROCESSES

任务工作过程是指那些与完成团队任务直接相关的团队成员的活动。

Having described process gains and process losses, it's time to describe the particular team processes that can help teams increase their synergy while reducing their inefficiency. One relevant category of team processes is **taskwork processes,** which are the activities of team members that relate directly to the accomplishment of team tasks. In a general sense, taskwork occurs any time that team members interact with the tools or technologies that are used to complete their work. In this regard, taskwork is similar to the concept of task performance described in Chapter 2 on Job Performance. However, in the context of teams, especially those that engage in knowledge work, three types of taskwork processes are crucially important: creative behavior, decision making, and boundary spanning. These three taskwork processes are shown in Figure 10-1.

CREATIVE BEHAVIOR. When teams engage in creative behavior, their activities are focused on generating novel and useful ideas and solutions. In Chapter 7 on Personality and Cultural Values, we noted that creative behavior is driven in part by the creativity of individual employees, because some employees are simply more original and imaginative than others. However,

FIGURE 10-1 Taskwork Processes

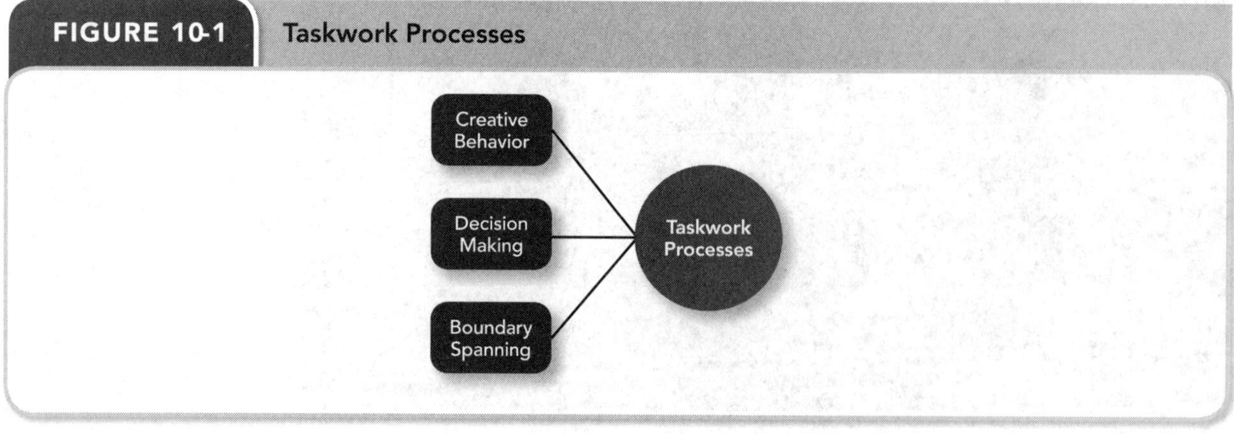

the team environment is also uniquely suited to fostering creative behavior. As a consequence, organizations like Palo Alto–based IDEO, arguably the world's most successful product design firm, rely on teams to come together and combine their members' unique sets of knowledge and skill in a manner that results in novel and useful ideas. However, achieving such outcomes depends on much more than just putting a diverse mix of people together and letting them go at it. In fact, creative behavior in teams can be fostered when members participate in a specific set of activities. See one author's take on this issue in our **OB at the Bookstore** feature.

10.1

What are taskwork processes, and what are some examples of team activities that fall into this process category?

Perhaps the best-known activity that teams use to foster creative behavior is **brainstorming.** Generally speaking, brainstorming involves a face-to-face meeting of team members in which each offers as many ideas as possible about some focal problem or issue. Most brainstorming sessions center around the following rules:

一般来说，**头脑风暴法**是指团队成员召开的面对面会议，要求每个人都提出尽可能多的有关焦点问题或议题的想法。

1. Express all ideas that come to mind (no matter how strange).
2. Go for quantity of ideas rather than quality.
3. Don't criticize or evaluate the ideas of others.
4. Build on the ideas of others.

OB AT THE BOOKSTORE

MAKING IDEAS HAPPEN

by Scott Belsky (New York: Portfolio, 2010).

For the creative mind, inspiration comes easily. But what makes up the other 99 percent of making ideas happen?

With those words, Scott Belsky asks a very practical follow-up question to Thomas Edison's famous quote, "Genius is 1 percent inspiration and 99 percent perspiration." Belsky's book tries to answer this question, and it turns out that many of the book's lessons center on the use of teams. Belsky readily acknowledges that creative ideas come from creative individuals, however, he emphasizes that using teams can improve the chances of generating creative ideas. Maybe more important, Belsky argues that a well-functioning team is necessary to keep good ideas alive and to set them into motion. He suggests that most good ideas from individuals die a premature death because of human limitations. When we think of good ideas, we experience excitement, but in a short amount of time, other demands in our lives start to crowd them out until the excitement fades and eventually they're forgotten. Sharing ideas in a team keeps ideas alive and allows them to grow and flourish. Although this recommendation might seem fairly obvious, it runs against human nature. That is, creative geniuses are admired and rewarded for the results of their efforts, and so most of us have a tendency to keep our ideas to ourselves.

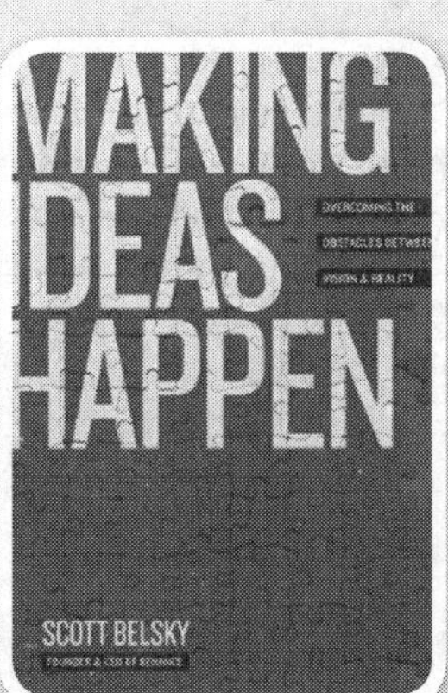

So what recommendations does Belsky have for making ideas happen in teams? For one thing, it may be important to change the reward structure in an organization so that there's less focus on short-term recognition of individual accomplishments and more focus on long-term creative outcomes that are accomplished by teams. As another example, because good ideas happen in so many different ways, there needs to be a lot of flexibility regarding where and when teams work. As a final example, teams need to foster a healthy degree of skepticism and task focused conflict so that bad ideas can be killed before too much time is wasted on them. Although suggestions like this have a great deal of merit, they may require some fundamental and expensive changes in the practices that organizations use to manage individuals and teams.

The theory is that if a team follows these rules, it will develop a large pool of ideas that it can use to address the issue at hand. This concept sounds good in theory, and almost all of us have been in some sort of brainstorming meeting at some point. It may surprise you to learn then that such brainstorming sessions rarely work as well as intended. In fact, research suggests that team members would be better off coming up with ideas on their own, as individuals, before pooling those ideas and evaluating them to arrive at a solution.

Why doesn't brainstorming work as well as individual idea generation? There appear to be at least three reasons. First, there may be a tendency for people to social loaf in brainstorming sessions. That is, members may not work as hard thinking up ideas as they would if they had to turn in an individually generated list with their name on it. Second, though the brainstorming rules explicitly forbid criticizing others' ideas, members may be hesitant to express ideas that seem silly or not well thought-out. Third, brainstorming results in production blocking because members have to wait their turn to express their ideas. This waiting around consumes time that could otherwise be used by individuals to generate new ideas.

Given the problems associated with brainstorming, why do organizations continue to use it? One reason is that the general idea of brainstorming is well known, and common sense leads people to believe that it works as advertised. Another reason is that there are benefits of brainstorming beyond just generating ideas. For example, brainstorming builds morale and results in the sharing of knowledge that might otherwise be locked inside the minds of the individual team members. Although this knowledge may not be useful for the particular problem that's being debated, it might be useful for issues that arise in the future. To achieve the benefits of brainstorming, some companies take extra steps to ensure team members are fully engaged in the process of generating ideas. At IDEO, for example, brainstorming meetings often open with a warm-up session, typically a fast-paced word game to clear the minds of the participants. Table 10-1 lists secrets of better brainstorming, as practiced at IDEO.

名义小组技术与传统的头脑风暴会谈相似，进程开始时，成员们聚在一起，概述会议的目的。下一步发生在个体水平上，团队成员在限定时间内将自己的想法写在一张纸上。接下来的一步回到团队情境中，成员们以循环的方式分享各自的观点。

One offshoot of brainstorming that addresses some of its limitations is the **nominal group technique.** Similar to a traditional brainstorming session, this process starts off by bringing the team together and outlining the purpose of the meeting. The next step takes place on an individual level however, as members have a set period of time to write down their own ideas on a piece of paper. The subsequent step goes back into the team setting, as members share their ideas with the team in a round-robin fashion. After the ideas are recorded, members have a discussion intended to clarify the ideas and build on the ideas of others. After this, it's back to an individual environment; members rank order ideas on a card that they submit to a facilitator. A facilitator then tabulates the scores to determine the winning idea. From this description, you probably can guess how the nominal group technique addresses the problems with brainstorming. By making people write down ideas on their own, it decreases social loafing and production blocking. Although team members might still be hesitant about expressing wild ideas to the group, doing so might be less threatening than having nothing to contribute to the group. In addition, ranking items as individuals makes people less apprehensive about going "against the grain" of the group by voicing support for an unpopular idea.

DECISION MAKING. In team contexts, decisions result from the interaction among team members. In some team contexts, for example, members share information regarding a problem or task, and they work together to reach a *consensus,* or general agreement among members in regards to the final solution. Juries provide a good example of how this type of decision making works. Members of a jury listen to information provided by attorneys and witnesses, and after they're given instructions by a judge, they meet privately to discuss the information with the goal being to reach a consensus regarding the verdict.

There has been a great deal of research on consensus decision making in the context of juries; however, the most important lesson from this research is that the strongest predictor of the final verdict is the distribution of the positions the individual members have in mind going into deliberations. In fact, the position held by the majority of the members prior to deliberation turns out to be the final verdict 90 percent of the time. It's not that members with the minority position

TABLE 10-1 IDEO's Secrets for Brainstorming

WHAT TO DO	DESCRIPTION
Have a sharp focus	Begin the brainstorming with a clearly stated problem.
Playful rules	Encourage playfulness, but don't debate or critique ideas.
Number the ideas	Make it easier to jump back and forth between ideas.
Build and jump	Build on and explore variants of ideas.
The space remembers	Use space to keep track of the flow of ideas in a visible way.
Stretch your brain	Warm up for the session by doing word games.
Get physical	Use drawings and props to make the ideas three-dimensional.
WHAT NOT TO DO	**DESCRIPTION**
The boss speaks first	Boss's ideas limit what people will say afterwards.
Give everybody a turn	Forcing equal participation reduces spontaneity.
Only include experts	Creative ideas come from unexpected places.
Do it off-site	You want creativity at the office too.
Limit the silly stuff	Silly stuff might trigger useful ideas.
Write down everything	The writing process can reduce spontaneity.

Source: T. Kelley and J. Littman, *The Art of Innovation* (New York: Doubleday, 2001).

simply acquiesce to the majority because of pressure, but rather, having more members in the majority increases the information and arguments available that supports the majority. Interestingly, however, despite all the research on consensus decision making, there is not a lot of evidence that this research has been very useful to attorneys and trial consultants in composing juries in a way that would lead to favorable decisions for their side.

In many other team contexts, decision making involves multiple members gathering and considering information that's relevant to their area of specialization, and then making recommendations to a team leader who is ultimately responsible for the final decision. Although the degree of member specialization and hierarchical structure of teams vary a great deal, you can understand this type of decision-making process if you consider what happens on the TV show, *Celebrity Apprentice.* The show typically begins with Donald Trump assigning two teams a fairly complex task. A celebrity member from each team then volunteers to be project leader, and this person assigns roles like marketing, logistics, and sales to the other team members. Throughout the project, members make suggestions and recommendations to the leader, who's ultimately responsible for making the decisions that determine the success of the project. Of course, project success is important because someone from the losing team—most often the project leader—gets to hear Trump say those famous words: "You're fired."

What factors account for a team's ability to make effective decisions? At least three factors appear to be involved. The first factor is **decision informity,** which reflects whether members possess adequate information about their own task responsibilities. Project teams on *Celebrity Apprentice* often fail, for example, because the team member in charge of marketing doesn't gather information necessary to help the team understand the desires and needs of the client. The second factor is **staff validity,** which refers to the degree to which members make good

决策告知指团队成员对自己的任务责任是否拥有足够的信息。

员工有效性指团队成员向领导者提出好建议的程度。

Like many teams in the real world, the teams on the television show *Celebrity Apprentice* often struggle to make good decisions.

层级敏感性反映了领导者有效衡量团队成员所提建议的程度。

recommendations to the leader. Team members can possess all the information needed to make a good recommendation but then fail to do so because of a lack of ability, insight, or good judgment. The third factor is **hierarchical sensitivity,** which reflects the degree to which the leader effectively weighs the recommendations of the members. Whom does the leader listen to, and whom does the leader ignore? Teams that make good decisions tend to have leaders that do a good job giving recommendations the weight they deserve. Together, these three variables play a large role in how effective teams are in terms of their decision making.

The decision informity, staff validity, and hierarchical sensitivity concepts can be used to make specific recommendations for improving team decision making. For example, research shows that more experienced teams tend to make better decisions because they develop an understanding of the information that's needed and how to use it, and have leaders that develop an understanding of which members provide the best recommendations. As another example, team decision making may be improved by giving members feedback about the three variables involved in the decision-making process. For instance, a team can improve its decision making if the members are told that they have to share and consider additional pieces of information before making recommendations to the leader. Although this recommendation may seem obvious, all too often teams only receive feedback about their final decision. In addition, there may be a benefit to separating the process of sharing information from the process of making recommendations and final decisions, at least in terms of how information is communicated among members. Whereas teams tend to share more information when they meet face-to-face, leaders do a better job considering recommendations and making final decisions when they're away from the members. Leaders who are separated don't have to deal with pressure from members who may be more assertive or better at articulating and defending their positions. Our **OB Internationally** feature describes additional considerations that need to be taken into account to improve decision making in culturally diverse teams.

边界跨越是指与个体和群体开展的三种不同类型的活动，这些个体和群体被认为并不属于团队。

使节活动是指通过沟通保护团队，说服他人支持团队，或者为团队获取重要的资源。

任务协调活动是指与其他职能部门的人或群体进行沟通，以协调解决任务相关的问题。

侦查活动是指团队成员为获取有关技术、竞争者或更大市场的信息而做的事情。

BOUNDARY SPANNING. The third type of taskwork process is **boundary spanning,** which involves three types of activities with individuals and groups other than those who are considered part of the team. **Ambassador activities** refer to communications that are intended to protect the team, persuade others to support the team, or obtain important resources for the team. As you might have guessed from this description, members who engage in ambassador activities typically communicate with people who are higher up in the organization. For example, a member of a marketing team might meet with senior management to request an increase in the budget for an expanded television ad campaign. **Task coordinator activities** involve communications that are intended to coordinate task-related issues with people or groups in other functional areas. Continuing with the marketing team example, a member of the team might meet with someone from manufacturing to work out how a coupon might be integrated into the product packaging materials.

Finally, **scout activities** refer to things team members do to obtain information about technology, competitors, or the broader marketplace. The marketing team member who meets with an engineer to seek information about new materials is engaging in scout activities. Taken together, research suggests that these boundary-spanning activities may be as important to determining team success as the processes that occur entirely within the team.

团队工作过程是指为促进团队工作的完成而开展的人际交往活动，但并不直接涉及任务完成活动本身。

团队工作过程
TEAMWORK PROCESSES

Another category of team process that helps teams increase their process gain while minimizing their process loss is teamwork processes. **Teamwork processes** refer to the interpersonal activities that facilitate the accomplishment of the team's work but do not directly involve task accomplishment itself. You can think of teamwork processes as the behaviors that create the

OB INTERNATIONALLY

In today's global economy, organizations have become increasingly reliant on multinational teams, or teams composed of individuals who do not share the same national identification. One benefit of multinational teams is economic. Rather than having separate businesses or products in several different countries, organizations leverage economies of scale by establishing multinational teams to develop and manage global products. A second benefit is that diversity in terms of national origin may result in business decisions that are more innovative. Such innovation stems from the team having a diverse set of experiences and perspectives from which to draw when trying to accomplish work. However, along with these benefits are potential team process problems. The most obvious problem is language barriers that prevent team members from communicating effectively with one another. Beyond simple misunderstandings, communication barriers can result in difficulties in coordinating tasks and may hinder members from receiving or understanding the information they need to make good recommendations and decisions. So what can multinational teams do to address some of these problems?

One solution is *group decision support systems,* which involve the use of computer technology to help the team structure its decision-making process. As an example, team members might meet in a room where each member sits at a networked laptop. At different points during the meeting, members are directed to enter their ideas and recommendations into the computer. These inputs are then summarized and shared visually with the entire team on their computer screens. Advantages of this approach are that the system keeps the meeting focused squarely on the task, and information can be presented in a logical sequence at a pace that makes it easier to digest. Moreover, no single member can dominate the meeting. As a consequence of these advantages, team members may participate more uniformly in the meeting and develop a more consistent understanding of the information that was exchanged. Another advantage is that the technique can be modified and used when members are geographically dispersed.

setting or context in which taskwork can be carried out. So what types of behaviors do teamwork processes involve? Figure 10-2 summarizes the set of teamwork processes discussed in this chapter.

10.2

What are teamwork processes, and what are some examples of team activities that fall into this process category?

TRANSITION PROCESSES. Teamwork processes become important as soon as teams first begin their work. **Transition processes** are teamwork activities that focus on preparation for future work. For example, *mission analysis* involves an analysis of the team's task, the challenges that face the team, and the resources available for completing the team's work. *Strategy formulation* refers to the development of courses of action and contingency plans, and then adapting those plans in light of changes that occur in the team's environment. Finally, *goal specification* involves the development and prioritization of goals related to the team's mission and strategy. Each of these transition processes is relevant before the team actually begins to conduct the core aspects of its work. However, these transition processes also may be important between periods of work activity. For example, think about the halftime adjustments made by a basketball team that's losing a game badly. The team could consider the strengths of its opponent and develop a new strategy intended to neutralize them. In this way, teams may switch from transition processes to taskwork, then back to transition processes.

转变过程是指主要关注为未来工作做准备的团队活动。

ACTION PROCESSES. Whereas transition processes are important before and between periods of taskwork, **action processes** are important as the taskwork is being accomplished. One type of action process involves *monitoring progress toward goals.* Teams that pay attention to goal-related information—perhaps by charting the team's performance relative to team goals—are typically in a good position to realize when they are "off-track" and need to make changes. *Systems monitoring* involves keeping track of things that the team needs to accomplish its work. A team that does not engage in systems monitoring may fail because it runs out of inventory,

行动过程在任务完成的过程中很重要，包括监督、助人和协调。

FIGURE 10-2 Teamwork Processes

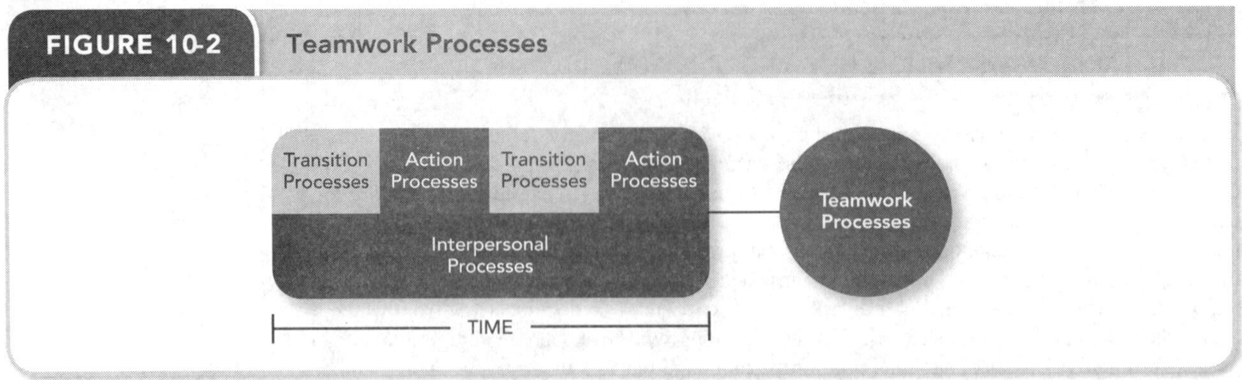

time, or other necessary resources. *Helping behavior* involves members going out of their way to help or back up other team members. Team members can provide indirect help to their teammates in the form of feedback or coaching, as well as direct help in the form of assistance with members' tasks and responsibilities. Helping behavior may be most beneficial when workload is distributed unequally among team members. *Coordination* refers to synchronizing team members' activities in a way that makes them mesh effectively and seamlessly. Poor coordination results in team members constantly having to wait on others for information or other resources necessary to do their part of the team's work.

人际过程主要与团队成员处理人际关系的方式有关。

INTERPERSONAL PROCESSES. The third category of teamwork processes is called **interpersonal processes.** The processes in this category are important before, during, or between periods of taskwork, and each relates to the manner in which team members manage their relationships. The first type of interpersonal process is *motivating and confidence building,* which refers to things team members do or say that affect the degree to which members are motivated to work hard on the team's task. Expressions that create a sense of urgency and optimism are examples of communications that would fit in this category. Similarly, *affect management* involves activities that foster a sense of emotional balance and unity. If you've ever worked in a team in which members got short-tempered when facing pressure or blamed one another when there were problems, you have firsthand experience with poor affect management.

关系冲突是指团队成员间人际关系的不一致，或者因个人价值观或偏好的不同而产生的不相容。

任务冲突是指成员在团队任务上产生的不一致。

Another important interpersonal process is *conflict management,* which involves the activities that the team uses to manage conflicts that arise in the course of its work. Conflict tends to have a negative impact on a team, but the nature of this effect depends on the focus of the conflict as well as the manner in which the conflict is managed. **Relationship conflict** refers to disagreements among team members in terms of interpersonal relationships or incompatibilities with respect to personal values or preferences. This type of conflict centers on issues that are not directly connected to the team's task. Relationship conflict is not only dissatisfying to most people, it also tends to result in reduced team performance. **Task conflict,** in contrast, refers to disagreements among members about the team's task. Logically speaking, this type of conflict can be beneficial to teams if it stimulates conversations that result in the development and expression of new ideas. Research findings, however, indicate that task conflict tends to result in reduced team effectiveness unless two conditions are present. First, members need to trust one another and be confident that they can express their opinions openly without fear of reprisals. Second, team members need to engage in effective conflict management processes. (For more discussion of conflict management issues, see Chapter 11 on Leadership: Power and Negotiation.)

What does effective conflict management involve? First, when trying to manage conflict, it's important for members to stay focused on the team's mission. If members do this, they can rationally evaluate the relative merits of each position. Second, any benefits of task conflict disappear if the level of the conflict gets too heated, if parties appear to be acting in self-interest rather than in the best interest of the team, or if there's high relationship conflict. Third, to effectively manage task conflict, members need to discuss their positions openly and be willing to exchange information in a way that fosters collaborative problem solving. If you've ever had an experience in an ongoing relationship in which you tried to avoid uncomfortable conflict by ignoring it, you probably already understand that this strategy only tends to make things worse in the end.

For task conflict to be productive, team members must feel free to express their opinions and know how to manage conflict effectively.

 10.3

What factors influence the communication process in teams?

沟 通 COMMUNICATION

So far in this chapter, we've described the focus of the activities and interactions among team members as they work to accomplish the team's purpose. For example, taskwork processes involve members sharing ideas, making recommendations, and acquiring resources from parties outside the team. As another example, teamwork processes involve members planning how to do the team's work, helping other team members with their work, and saying things to lift team members' spirits. Now we shift gears a bit and focus our attention on **communication,** the process by which information and meaning gets transferred from a sender to a receiver. Much of the work that's done in a team is accomplished interdependently and involves communication among members, and therefore, the effectiveness of communication plays an important role in determining whether there is process gain or process loss.

沟通是指信息和意图由发送者向接收者传递的过程。

One way to understand communication is to consider the model depicted in Figure 10-3. On the left side of the model is the source or *sender* of information. In a team that manufactures steel engine parts, for example, the sender might be a team member who wants to share information with another team member. More specifically, the sender might want to let another member know that the team has to work more quickly to reach a difficult performance goal. Generally speaking, senders may use verbal and written language, as well as nonverbal language and cues, to *encode* the information into a *message.* Continuing with our example, the sender may choose to quickly wave an arm up and down to convey the idea that the team needs to work faster. This encoded message is transmitted to a *receiver,* who needs to interpret or *decode* the message to form an understanding of the information it contains. In our example, the message is transmitted visually because the members are working face-to-face, but messages can be transmitted in written form, electronically, or even indirectly through other individuals. With this basic model of communication in mind, we can consider factors that may influence the effectiveness of this process.

COMMUNICATOR ISSUES. One important factor that influences the communication process is the communicators themselves. Communicators need to encode and interpret messages, and it turns out that these activities can be major sources of communication problems. In our example, the receiver may interpret the arm waving as a message that something is going wrong and that the team needs to slow down to cope with the problem. Of course, this interpretation is the exact opposite of what the sender intended to convey. The communication process may also suffer if the participants lack *communication competence,* which refers to the skills involved in encoding, transmitting, and receiving messages. In fact, it may have already occurred to you that perhaps the sender in our example should have chosen an alternative way to communicate the idea that the team needs to work more quickly. Along the same lines, a receiver who isn't skilled in listening carefully to a sender's message may misinterpret a message or miss it altogether.

An additional communicator issue relevant to the communication process in teams relates to the *emotions* and *emotional intelligence* of team members, issues we discussed in Chapter 4 on Job Satisfaction and Chapter 8 on Ability. Emotions can impact how people express themselves and can also cloud their interpretation of information they receive from others. Therefore, team members' ability to regulate their emotions and understand the emotions of others can result in clearer communications that are less prone to misunderstanding. Although you might think that emotions are mostly relevant to communications involving face-to-face interactions among team members, emotions can interfere with electronically mediated communications and, therefore, they are relevant to virtual teams as well.

FIGURE 10-3 The Communication Process

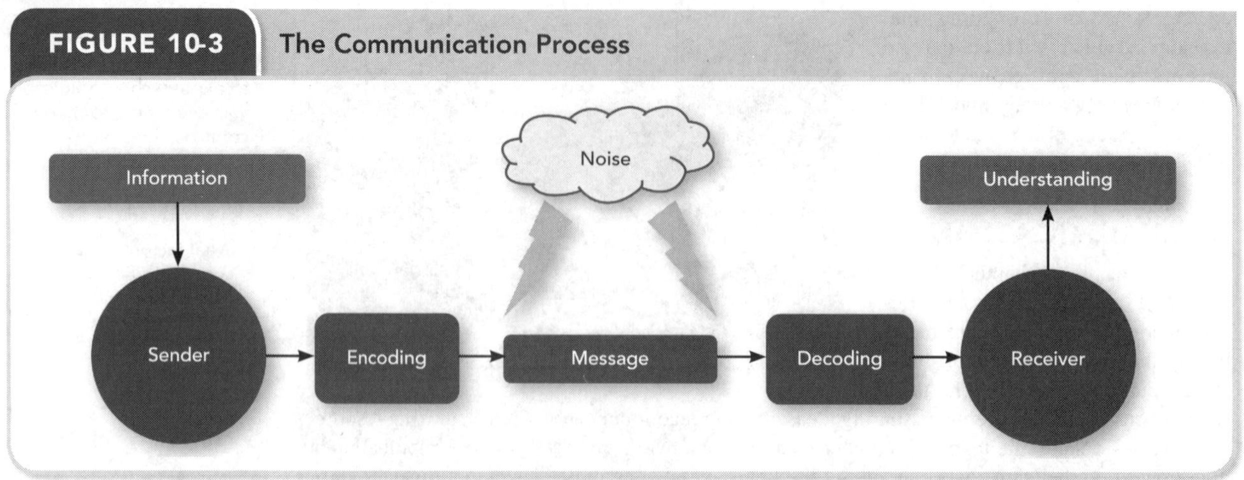

Communicator emotions can play a big role in the communication process.

NOISE. A second factor that influences the communication process is the presence of *noise* that interferes with the message being transmitted. Depending on how the message is being transmitted, noise can take on several different forms. In the context of our example, the sender and receiver may be working several feet from one another, and steam from the manufacturing process may make it difficult to see and appreciate the meaning of the gestures members make. As another example, you've probably had difficulty trying to hold a conversation with someone in a restaurant or at a party because of blaring music or crowd noise. If so, you can understand that noise increases the effort that the communicators need to exert to make the communication process work. The sender has to talk louder and more clearly, and perhaps increase the use of alternative means of communicating, such as using hand gestures to help clarify messages. In addition, the receiver has to listen more carefully and think harder to fill in the spaces left by spoken words that are impossible to hear. If one of the two parties to the communication isn't willing to put in the extra effort to send and receive messages when there is noise, the conversation likely will not last very long.

信息丰富性是指消息中传递信息的数量和深度。

INFORMATION RICHNESS. A third factor that influences the communication process is **information richness,** which is the amount and depth of information that gets transmitted in a message. Messages that are transmitted through face-to-face channels have the highest level of information richness, because senders can convey meaning through not only words but also their body language, facial expressions, and tone of voice. Face-to-face communication also achieves high information richness because it provides the opportunity for senders and receivers to receive feedback, which allows them to verify and ensure their messages are received and interpreted correctly. At the opposite end of the information richness spectrum are computer-generated reports that consist largely of numbers. Although these types of reports may include a lot of information, they're limited to information that's quantifiable, and there's an absence of additional cues that could provide context and meaning to the numbers. A personal written note is a good example of a message with a moderate level of information richness. Although the information in a note is limited to the words written down on the page, the choice of words and punctuation can add meaning beyond the words themselves. For example, research shows that recipients of e-mails try to interpret the emotions of the sender from the content of the message, and unfortunately, they often mistakenly perceive the emotion as negative even when it's not.

From our description, it may sound as though higher levels of information richness are preferable to lower levels. This assertion is true when the situation or task at hand is complex and difficult to understand. In this case, the more cues that are available to the receiver, the more likely it is that the message will be understood the way the sender intended it to be. However, the benefits of information richness may overcomplicate the communication process when the task at hand is relatively simple and straightforward. The additional information that needs to be interpreted by the receiver increases the chance that some of the cues will seem contradictory, and when this happens, receivers may feel like they're being sent "mixed messages." In summary, the appropriate level of information richness depends on the nature of the team's situation: The greater the level of complexity in the work being accomplished by the team, the more likely it is that the benefits of information richness outweigh its costs.

NETWORK STRUCTURE. So far in our discussion of communication, we've kept things simple by focusing on the flow of information between two people—a sender and a receiver. Of course, teams typically have more than just two people, so it's important at this point to consider the implications of this additional complexity. One way to understand communication in teams composed of more than two people is to consider the concept of **network structure,** which is defined as the pattern of communication that occurs regularly among each member of the team.

网络结构指在团队中每个成员之间经常使用的沟通模式。

As depicted in Figure 10-4, communication network patterns can be described in terms of *centralization,* or the degree to which the communication in a network flows through some members rather than others. The more communication flows through fewer members of the team, the higher the degree of centralization. You can think of the circles in the figure as team members, and the lines between the circles represent the flow of communication back and forth between the two members. On the left side of the figure is the *all channel* network structure, which is highly decentralized. Every member can communicate with every other member. Student teams typically communicate using this type of structure. On the right side of the figure, at the other extreme, is the *wheel* network structure. This network structure is highly centralized because all the communication flows through a single member. Teams that use a wheel structure often consist of an "official" leader who makes final decisions based on recommendations from members who have expertise in different fields. Although there are many other configurations you can easily think of, we also included the *circle* and *Y* structures to illustrate examples that fall between the extremes in terms of the level of centralization.

So why are network structures important to learn about? Quite a bit of research on this topic suggests that network structure has important implications for team effectiveness, though those implications depend on the nature of the team's work. On the one hand, when the work is simple and straightforward, a centralized structure tends to result in faster solutions with fewer mistakes. On the other hand, when the work is complex and difficult to understand, a decentralized structure tends to be more efficient. Apparently, when work is complex and difficult to understand, the team can benefit if members have the ability to communicate with anyone on the

FIGURE 10-4 Communication Network Structures

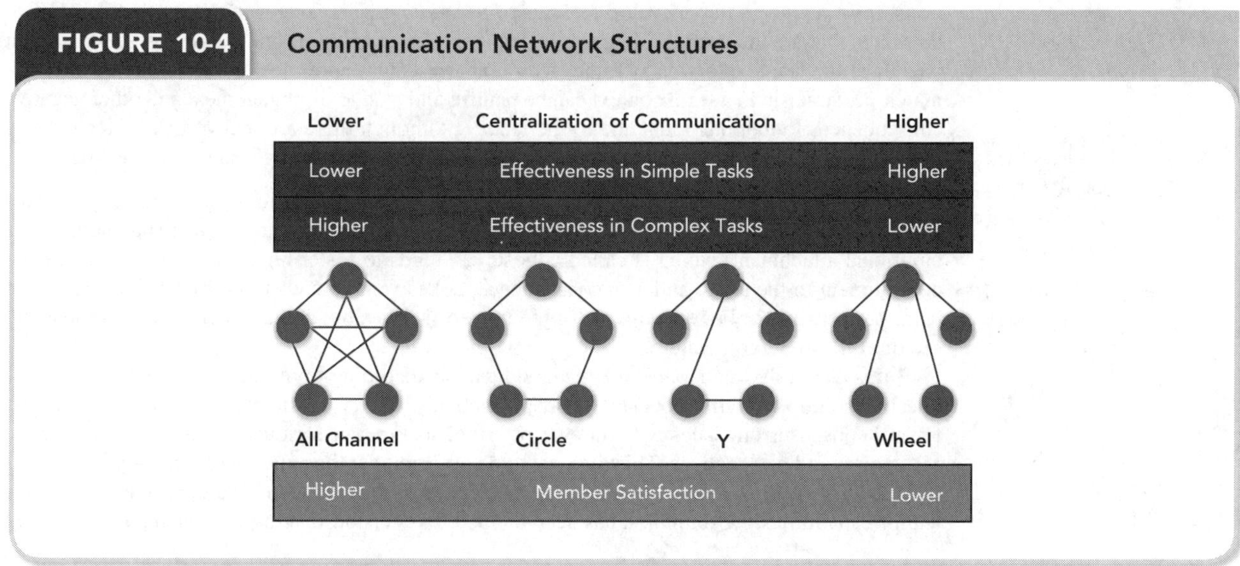

team to get assistance or resolve problems. When the work is simple and easy to understand, the additional communication channels afforded by a decentralized structure become unnecessary and divert members' attention from the task. It's important to mention, however, that members tend to prefer decentralized network structures. That is, they tend to be more satisfied with the team when they are "in the loop," even though their position in the loop might not help the team perform more effectively.

Communication among team members in organizations has become more decentralized over the past decade or so. One reason for this trend is that social network media has become inexpensive and easy to use. User-centered Web 2.0 tools and collaboration software such as Microsoft SharePoint and Jive allow individuals to share information and collaborate in real time, and many companies, such as AT&T, General Electric, FedEx, and Atlanta–based Manheim Auctions, Inc., have developed their own versions of Facebook and LinkedIn for their employees to use internally. Individuals working together can use these tools, along with mobile devices to communicate with each other at a moment's notice. While such technologies provide obvious advantages to virtual teams, teams that work together at the same office also benefit from these tools. A team member who has an inspiration or discovers an important breakthrough over the weekend no longer has to wait until Monday to share it and get feedback from teammates. It also might surprise you to learn that the use of mobile devices for communication among teammates is especially popular in underdeveloped regions such as Africa, where the number of these devices far exceeds the number of computers. In fact, companies such as Coca-Cola train in the use of mobile devices so that teams that operate in these regions can communicate and interact more effectively.

Before moving on to the next topic, we should note that the use of technology does not necessarily improve the communication process. Some individuals may lack the competence or confidence to use these newer means of communication, resulting in their reluctance or inability to participate fully in collaborative efforts that take place using these technologies. As another example, social media reduces an individual's perceived cost of expressing their ideas and opinions. This could result in an overabundance of information, and the spread of misinformation and rumors that add noise to communication. The use of Twitter during the Haiti earthquake, for example, led to rumors that contributed to anxiety and uncertainty of those directly and indirectly involved in the disaster.

团队状态是指由团队成员共同工作的经历所带来的，形成于团队成员头脑中的具体感受和想法。

团队状态
TEAM STATES

10.4
What are team states, and what are some examples of the states that fall into this process category?

A fourth category of team processes that helps teams increase their process gain while minimizing their process loss is less visible to the naked eye. **Team states** refer to specific types of feelings and thoughts that coalesce in the minds of team members as a consequence of their experience working together. For example, as a consequence of supportive leadership and member interactions, team members may develop feelings of *psychological safety,* or the sense that it is OK to do things that are interpersonally risky, or that expressing opinions and making suggestions that challenge the status quo won't be met with embarrassment and rejection at the hands of teammates. Ostracism in a team context can be painful and lead to disengagement and other negative consequences to the individual and to the team. Although there are many types of team states that we could review in this chapter, Figure 10-5 summarizes the set of team states we discuss.

凝聚力是因某些原因如信任关系而使团队成员与团队中的其他成员及团队本身形成强有力的情感纽带。

在高凝聚力的团队中，团队成员在某些议题上保持一致，从不提出、寻求或认真考虑其他可行的观点及方案，以此来维持和谐。这种以其他团队重要事项为代价的一致性动机，称为**群体思维**。

COHESION. For a number of reasons, such as having trusting relationships, members of teams can develop strong emotional bonds to other members of their team and to the team itself. This emotional attachment, which is called **cohesion,** tends to foster high levels of motivation and commitment to the team, and as a consequence, cohesiveness tends to promote higher levels of team performance. For an example of the power of cohesion, and the factors that influence it, see our **OB on Screen** feature.

But is a cohesive team *necessarily* a good team? According to researchers, the answer to this question is no. In highly cohesive teams, members may try to maintain harmony by striving toward consensus on issues without ever offering, seeking, or seriously considering alternative viewpoints and perspectives. This drive toward conformity at the expense of other team priorities is called **groupthink** and is thought to be associated with feelings of overconfidence about the team's capabilities. Groupthink has been blamed for decision-making fiascos in politics as well

FIGURE 10-5 Team States

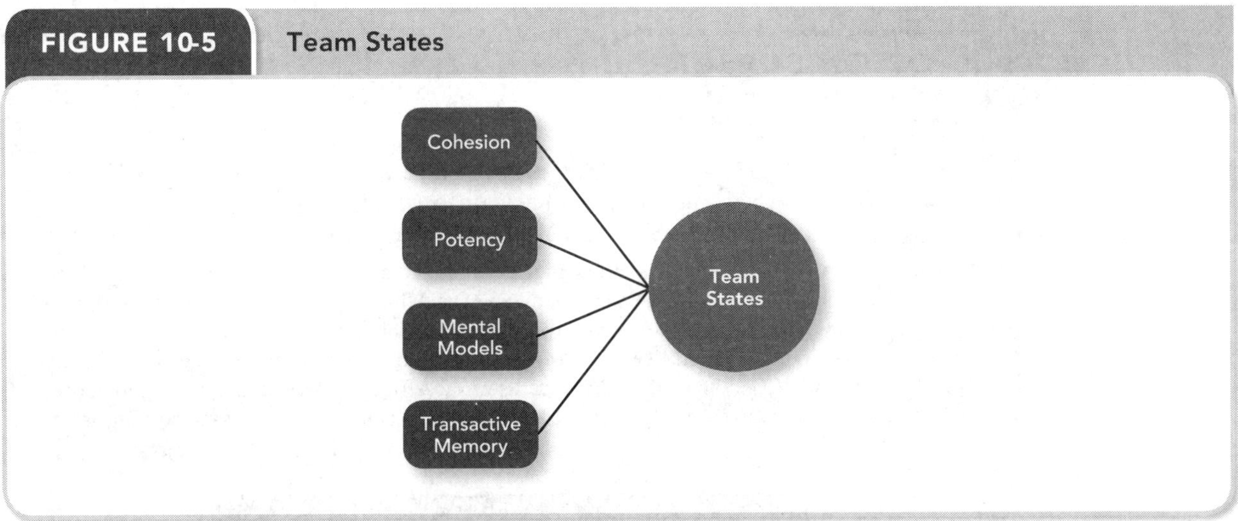

as in business. Some famous examples include John F. Kennedy's decision to go forward with the Bay of Pigs invasion of Cuba, NASA's decision to launch the space shuttle Challenger in unusually cold weather, and Enron's board of directors' decisions to ignore illegal accounting practices.

So how do you leverage the benefits of cohesion without taking on the potential costs? One way is to acknowledge that cohesion can potentially have detrimental consequences. A good first step in this regard would be to assess the team's cohesion using a scale such as the one in our **OB Assessments** feature. A high score on this sort of assessment indicates the team may be vulnerable to groupthink. A second step in preventing problems associated with cohesion would be to formally institute the role of devil's advocate. The person filling this role would be responsible for evaluating and challenging prevailing points of view in a constructive manner and also bringing in fresh perspectives and ideas to the team. Although the devil's advocate role could be filled by an existing team member, it's also possible that the team could bring in an outsider to fill that role.

POTENCY. The second team state, **potency,** refers to the degree to which members believe that the team can be effective across a variety of situations and tasks. When a team has high potency, members are confident that their team can perform well, and as a consequence, they focus more of their energy on team tasks and teamwork in hopes of achieving team goals. When a team has low potency, members are not as confident about their team, and so they begin to question the team's goals and one another. Ultimately, this reaction can result in members focusing their energies on activities that don't benefit the team. In the end, research has shown that potency has a strong positive impact on team performance. The one caveat here is that a strong sense of confidence too early in a team's existence can decrease the amount of beneficial discussions centered on different positions that are relevant to a team. So how does high potency develop in teams? Team members' confidence in their own capabilities, their trust in other members' capabilities, and feedback about past performance are all likely to play a role. Specifically, team potency is promoted in teams in which members are confident in themselves and their teammates and when the team has experienced success in the past.

效能是指成员相信团队能够有效应对各种情境及任务的程度。

MENTAL MODELS. **Mental models** refer to the level of common understanding among team members with regard to important aspects of the team and its task. A team may have shared mental models with respect to the capabilities that members bring to the team as well as the processes the team needs to use to be effective. How can these two types of mental models foster team effectiveness? When team members share in their understanding of one another's capabilities, they're more likely to know where to go for the help they might need to complete their work. In addition, they should be able to anticipate when another member needs help to do his or her work. When members have a shared understanding of which processes are necessary

心智模式是指团队成员在团队及其任务的重要方面的共识水平。

OB ON SCREEN

GLORY ROAD

Right now the Miners are just plain flat . . . there's no chemistry, no energy, it's every man for themselves out there, they're not playing like a team.

With those words, a courtside announcer (David Born) describes the play of the Texas Western Miners against the University of Seattle Chieftains, in the "based on a true story" movie, *Glory Road* (Dir.: James Gartner, Walt Disney Pictures). The Miners are undefeated with a record of 23–0 going into the game, and with a win over the 15–10 Chieftains, will likely secure a number one ranking. This might sound like a run-of-the-mill sports movie. However, the story has historical significance. The 1966 Miners included several African American players whom Coach Don Haskins (Josh Lucas) started and played regularly, and at the time, doing so was unheard of.

The movie depicts struggles the Miners went through to become a cohesive team. Although the players seemed to handle the team's diversity and their differences quite well throughout most of the season, racism outside the team created tension among team members, and this manifested in the Miners' poor play against the Chieftains. Unspoken distrust and resentment developed, and this weakened the emotional bonds among the team members, and to the team itself. The result was the players didn't work together to achieve the level of synergy necessary to defeat the opponent, and they ended up losing the game 74–63. As the announcer stated in the game's closing minutes, "Well, they've got only themselves to blame. They didn't play together, they didn't find the open man, and the Miners' perfect season is slipping away."

In the locker room after the game, the players get into an argument in which they reveal their feelings for the first time. Although heated, the conflict helps the team members appreciate the perspective of others in the team. The conflict also provides an opportunity to rally the team around a common cause and reestablish cohesion. Haskin's confidant and team trainer Ross Moore (Red West) first tells the team, "You've all forgotten what you're doing here," and Haskins follows this up with, "Shut them up, win."

to help the team be effective, they can carry out these processes efficiently and smoothly. To help you understand why this is true, consider what would happen in a team of students who had different understandings about how the team should manage conflict. Few disagreements would

OB ASSESSMENTS

COHESION

How cohesive is your team? This assessment is designed to measure cohesion—the strength of the emotional bonds that develop among members of a team. Think of your current student project team or an important team that you belong to in your job. Answer each question using the response scale provided. Then subtract your answers to the boldfaced questions from 8, with the difference being your new answers for those questions. For example, if your original answer for question 6 was "5", your new answer is "3" (8 – 5). Then sum up your answers for the eight questions. (For more assessments relevant to this chapter, please visit http://connect.mcgraw-hill.com.)

1	2	3	4	5	6	7
STRONGLY DISAGREE	DISAGREE	SLIGHTLY DISAGREE	NEUTRAL	SLIGHTLY AGREE	AGREE	STRONGLY AGREE

1. **If given a chance, I would choose to leave my team to join another.** _______
2. The members of my team get along well together. _______
3. The members of my team will readily defend each other from criticism. _______
4. I feel that I am really a part of my team. _______
5. I look forward to being with the members of my team every day. _______
6. **I find that I generally do not get along with other members of my team.** _______
7. I enjoy belonging to this team because I am friends with many members. _______
8. The team to which I belong is a close one. _______

SCORING AND INTERPRETATION

If your scores sum up to 48 or above, you feel a strong bond to your team, suggesting that your team is cohesive. If your scores sum up to less than 48, you feel a weaker bond to your team, suggesting that your team is not as cohesive.

Source: G.H. Dobbins and S.J. Zacarro, "The Effects of Group Cohesion and Leader Behavior on Subordinate Satisfaction," *Group and Organization Management,* Vol. 11, 1986, pp. 203–19. Group & Organization Management by Sage Publications, Inc., Reproduced with permission of Sage Publications, Inc., via Copyright Clearance Center.

get resolved if some of the members believed that direct confrontation was best, whereas others believed that avoidance was best.

TRANSACTIVE MEMORY. Whereas mental models refer to the degree to which the knowledge is shared among members, **transactive memory** refers to how specialized knowledge is distributed among members in a manner that results in an effective system of memory for the team. This concept takes into account the idea that not everyone on a team has to possess the same knowledge. Instead, team effectiveness requires that members understand when their own specialized knowledge is relevant to the team and how their knowledge should be combined with the specialized knowledge of other members to accomplish team goals. If you've ever worked on a team that had effective transactive memory, you may have noticed that work got done very efficiently. Everyone focused on his or her specialty and what he or she did best, members knew exactly where to go to get information when there were gaps in their knowledge, and the team produced synergistic results. Of course, transactive memory can also be fragile because the memory system depends on each and every member. If someone is slow to

交互记忆是指使团队形成有效记忆系统的专业知识如何在成员间进行分配。

respond to another member's request for information or forgets something important, the team's system of memory fails. Alternatively, if a member of the team leaves, you lose an important node in the memory system.

总结：为什么某些团队大于其部分之和
SUMMARY: WHY ARE SOME TEAMS MORE THAN THE SUM OF THEIR PARTS?

So what explains why some teams become more than the sum of their parts (whereas other teams become less)? As shown in Figure 10-6, teams become more than the sum of their parts if their team process achieves process gain rather than process loss. Teams can accomplish that goal by engaging in activities involved in effective taskwork processes, teamwork processes, communication, and team states. Important taskwork processes include creative behavior, decision making, and boundary spanning. Important teamwork processes include transition processes, action processes, and interpersonal processes. Communication can be enhanced by ensuring that members are competent communicators, noise is minimized, and appropriate levels of information richness and network complexity are chosen. Team states refer to variables such as cohesion, potency, mental models, and transactive memory. In contrast to the taskwork processes, teamwork processes, and communication, team states offer less visible and observable reasons for why some teams possess an effective synergy whereas others seem quite inefficient.

团队过程有多重要
HOW IMPORTANT ARE TEAM PROCESSES?

10.5
How do team processes affect team performance and team commitment?

Do team processes affect performance and commitment? Answering this question is somewhat complicated for two reasons. First, as in Chapter 9 on Team Characteristics and Diversity, when we say "performance and commitment," we are not referring to the performance of individuals or their attachment to the organization. Instead, we are referring to the performance of teams and the degree to which teams are capable of remaining together as ongoing entities. In the jargon of research on teams, this form of commitment is termed "team viability." Second, as we have described throughout this chapter, there are several different types of team processes that we could consider in our summary. In Figure 10-7, we characterize the relationship among team processes, performance, and commitment by focusing specifically on research involving teamwork processes. The figure therefore represents a summary of existing research on transition processes, action processes, and interpersonal processes.

Research conducted in a wide variety of team settings has shown that teamwork processes have a moderate positive relationship with team performance. This same moderate positive relationship appears to hold true, regardless of whether the research examines transition processes, action processes, or interpersonal processes. Why might the relationships between these different types of processes and team performance be so similarly positive? Apparently, effectiveness with respect to a wide variety of interactions is needed to help teams achieve process gain and, in turn, perform effectively. The interpersonal activities that prepare teams for future work appear to be just as important as those that help members integrate their taskwork and those that build team confidence and a positive team climate. Researchers have also found that the importance of team processes to team performance may be more strongly positive in teams in which there are higher levels of interdependence. This relationship can be explained quite easily: Activities that are meant to improve the integration of team members' work are simply more important in team contexts in which the work of team members needs to be integrated.

Research also indicates that teamwork processes have a strong positive relationship with team commitment. In other words, teams that engage in effective teamwork processes tend to continue to exist together into the future. Why should teamwork and team commitment be so strongly related? One reason is that people tend to be satisfied in teams in which there are effective interpersonal interactions, and as a consequence, they go out of their way to do things that they believe will help the team stick together. Think about a team situation that you've been in when everyone shared the same goals for the team, work was coordinated smoothly, and everyone was positive, pleasant to be around, and willing to do their fair share of the work. If you've

FIGURE 10-6 Why Are Some Teams More Than the Sum of Their Parts?

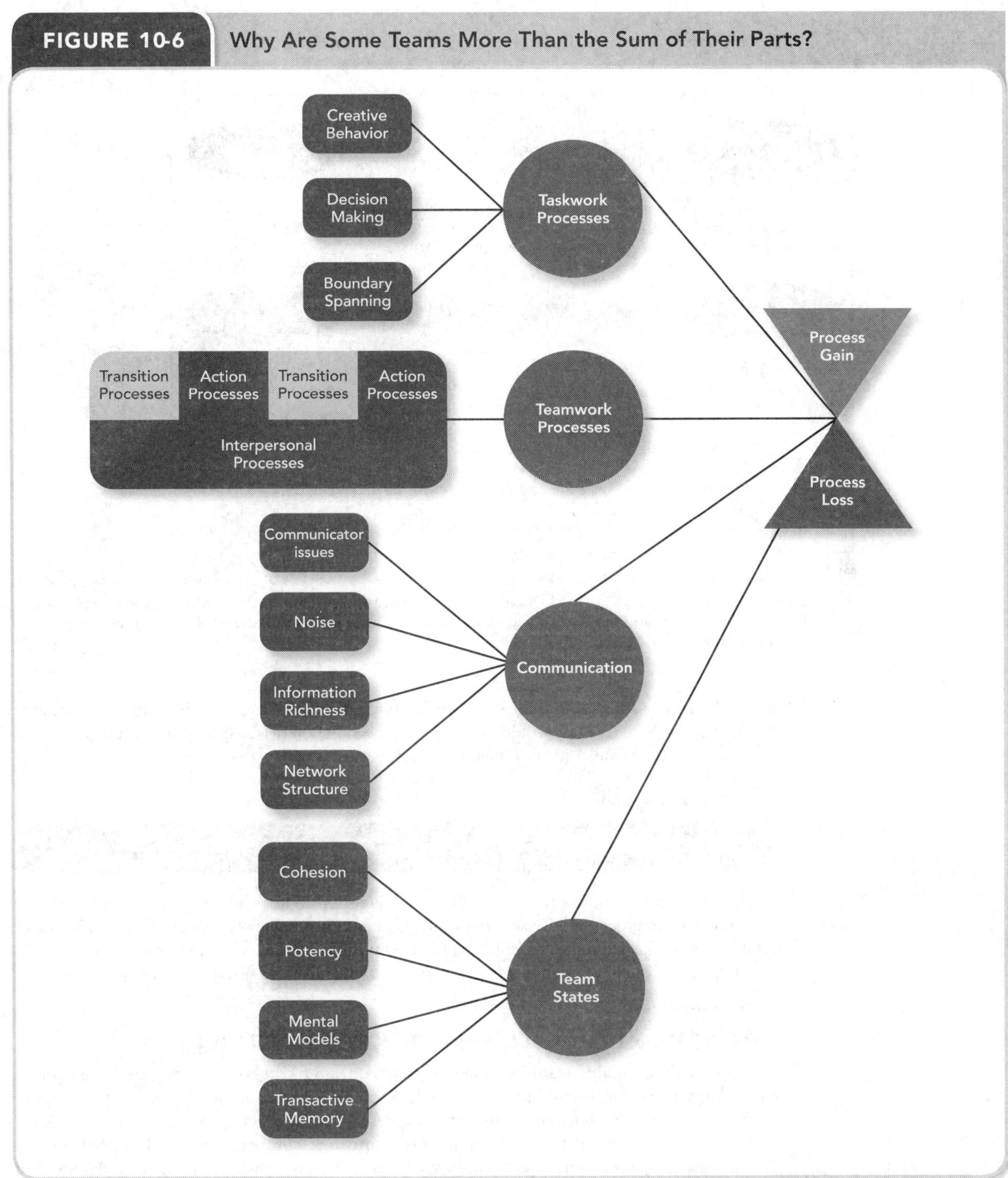

ever actually been in a situation like this—and we hope that you have—chances are that you did your best to make sure the team could continue on together. It's likely that you worked extra hard to make sure that the team achieved its goals. It's also likely that you expressed positive sentiments about the team and your desire for the team to remain together. Of course, just the opposite would be true in a team context in which members had different goals for the team, coordination

FIGURE 10-7 Effects of Teamwork Processes on Performance and Commitment

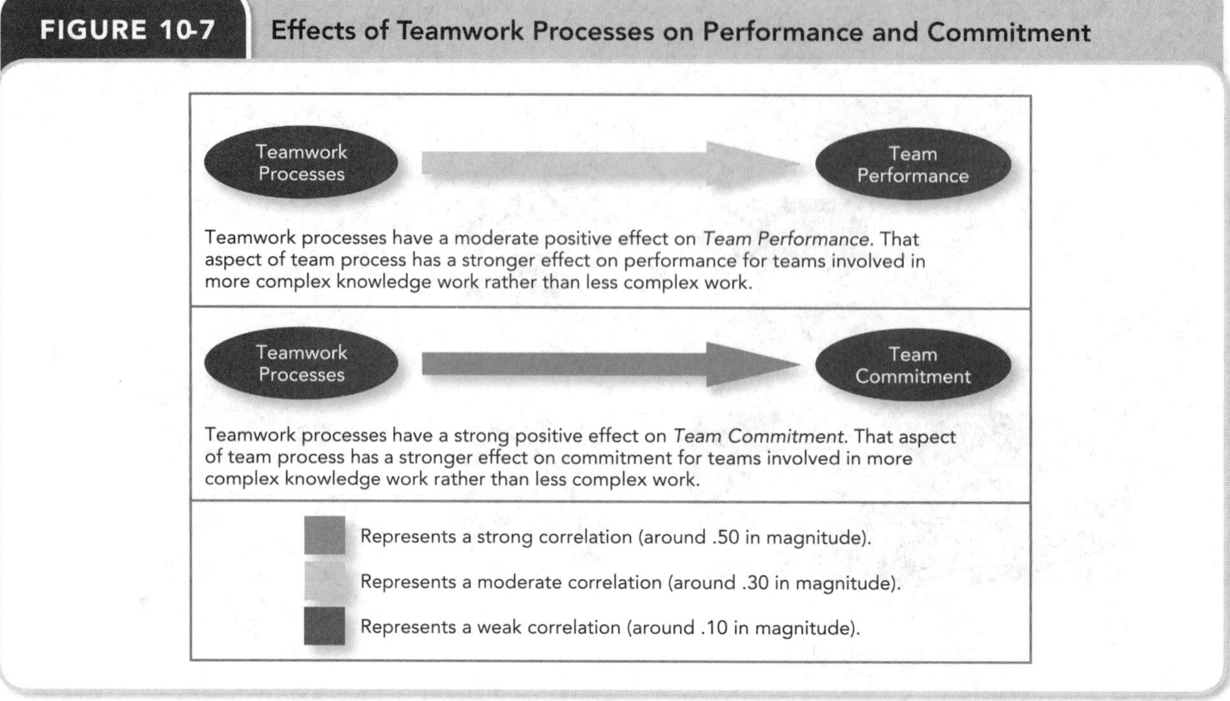

Source: J.A. LePine, R.F. Piccolo, C.L. Jackson, J.E. Mathieu, and J.R. Saul, "A Meta-Analysis of Team Process: Towards a Better Understanding of the Dimensional Structure and Relationships with Team Effectiveness Criteria," *Personnel Psychology* 61 (2008), pp. 356–76.

was difficult and filled with emotional conflict, and everyone was pessimistic and disagreeable. Members of a team like this would not only find the situation dissatisfying, but would also make it known that they would be very open to a change of scenery.

应用：培训团队

APPLICATION: TRAINING TEAMS

10.6
What steps can organizations take to improve team processes?

Team-based organizations invest a significant amount of resources into training that's intended to improve team processes. These types of investments seem to be a smart thing to do, given that team processes have a positive impact on both team performance and team commitment. In this section, we review several different approaches that organizations use to train team processes.

可转移式团队能力
TRANSPORTABLE TEAMWORK COMPETENCIES

可转移式团队能力是指受训人员可以将其在某一团队学到的知识转移到另一个团队并进行应用。

One approach to training teams is to help individual team members develop general competencies related to teamwork activities. Table 10-2 shows that this type of training could involve many different forms of knowledge, skills, and abilities. Taken together, such knowledge, skills, and abilities are referred to as **transportable teamwork competences.** This label reflects the fact that trainees can transport what they learn about teamwork from one team context and apply it in another. As a specific example of how this type of training might work, consider a recent study of teamwork training for naval aviators in an advanced pilot training program. In this study, one group of pilots went through two days of training, during which they received instruction on preferred communication practices, communicating suggestions and asking questions, and communicating about potential problems. The pilots who went through the training believed that in addition to building teamwork knowledge and skills, the training would increase their mission effectiveness and flight safety. Most important, teams that were composed of pilots who went through the training were significantly more effective than teams composed of pilots who did not go through the training. Effectiveness was judged by performance in dangerous scenarios, such as ice buildup on the aircraft wings and instructions from the air traffic control tower that were conflicting or ambiguous.

The Orpheus Chamber Orchestra has been able to perform effectively over the past 35 years because of extraordinary levels of teamwork and commitment. While all members of the orchestra help refine the interpretation and execution of each work in its repertoire, they also select a concertmaster and principal players to lead each piece.

交叉培训
CROSS-TRAINING

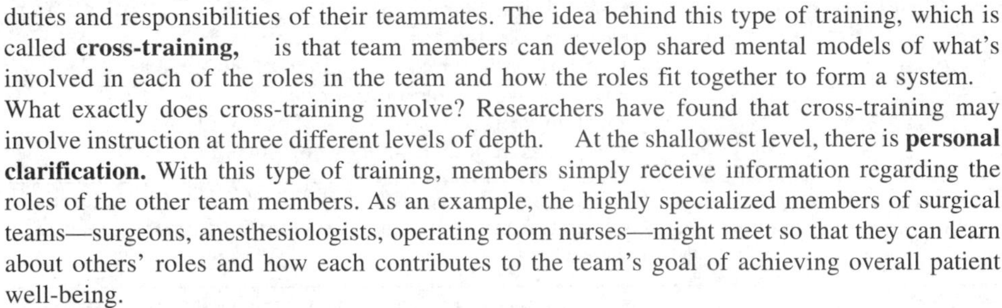

A second type of team training involves training members in the duties and responsibilities of their teammates. The idea behind this type of training, which is called **cross-training,** is that team members can develop shared mental models of what's involved in each of the roles in the team and how the roles fit together to form a system. What exactly does cross-training involve? Researchers have found that cross-training may involve instruction at three different levels of depth. At the shallowest level, there is **personal clarification.** With this type of training, members simply receive information regarding the roles of the other team members. As an example, the highly specialized members of surgical teams—surgeons, anesthesiologists, operating room nurses—might meet so that they can learn about others' roles and how each contributes to the team's goal of achieving overall patient well-being.

交叉培训是指团队成员对于团队中扮演的角色以及角色之间如何匹配形成系统方面形成共享的心智模式。

在**个人澄清**这类培训中，成员仅接收有关团队其他成员角色的信息。

At the next level of cross-training, there is **positional modeling,** which involves team members observing how other members perform their roles. In the case of the surgical teams, the surgeons might spend a day shadowing operating room nurses as they perform their duties. The shadowing not only helps the surgeons gain a better understanding of what the job of a nurse entails but also may provide insight into how the activities involved in their respective jobs could be integrated more effectively.

职位模仿是指团队成员观察其他成员如何扮演他们的角色。

Finally, the deepest level of cross-training involves **positional rotation.** This type of training gives members actual experience carrying out the responsibilities of their teammates. Although this type of hands-on experience could expand skills of members so that they might actually perform the duties of their teammates if they had to, the level of training required to achieve proficiency or certification in many situations may be prohibitive. For example, because it takes years of specialized training to become a surgeon, it would be impractical to train an operating room nurse to perform this job for the purposes of positional rotation.

职位轮换是指给予成员履行其队友职责的真实体验。

团队过程培训
TEAM PROCESS TRAINING

Cross-training and training in transportable teamwork competencies focus on individual experiences that promote individual learning. **Team process training,** in contrast, occurs in the context of a team experience that facilitates the team being able to function and perform more effectively as an intact unit. One type of team process training is called **action learning.** With this type of training, which has been used successfully at companies such as Motorola and General Electric, a team is given a real problem that's relevant to the organization and then held accountable for analyzing the problem, developing an action plan, and finally carrying out the action plan. How does this type of experience develop effective team processes? First, the team receives coaching to help facilitate more effective processes during different phases of the project. Second, there are meetings during which team members are encouraged to reflect on the team processes they've used as they worked on the project. In these meetings, the members not only discuss what they observed and learned from their experiences, but also what they would do differently in the future.

团队过程培训是指促进团队作为一个完整的单元更有效地运转和执行任务的培训。

在**行动学习**这类培训中，先给团队一个与组织相关的真实问题，要求认真分析该问题，制订行动计划，并最终实施行动计划。

A second type of team process training involves experience in a team context when there are task demands that highlight the importance of effective teamwork processes. As an example, United Airlines uses pit crew training for its ramp crews. Although teams of ramp workers at

TABLE 10–2 Teamwork Knowledge, Skills, and Abilities

COMPETENCY	DESCRIPTION
Conflict resolution	• Can distinguish between desirable and undesirable conflict. • Encourages desirable conflict and discourages undesirable conflict. • Uses win–win strategies to manage conflict.
Collaborative problem solving	• Can identify situations requiring participative problem solving. • Uses the appropriate degree of participation. • Recognizes and manages obstacles to collaborative problem solving.
Communications	• Understands communication networks. • Communicates openly and supportively. • Listens without making premature evaluations. • Uses active listening techniques. • Can interpret nonverbal messages of others. • Engages in ritual greetings and small talk.
Goal setting and performance management	• Helps establish specific and difficult goals for the team. • Monitors, evaluates, and provides performance-related feedback.
Planning and task coordination	• Coordinates and synchronizes activities among team members. • Establishes expectations to ensure proper balance of workload within the team.

Source: Adapted from M.J. Stevens and M.A. Campion, "The Knowledge, Skill, and Ability Requirements for Teamwork: Implications for Human Resource Management," *Journal of Management* 20 (1994), pp. 503–30.

an airline like United must work with luggage, belt loaders, and baggage carts, there are parallels with the work of NASCAR pit crews that work with tires, jacks, and air guns. Primarily, effective performance in both contexts means performing work safely within tight time constraints. Moreover, in both of these contexts, achieving goals requires teamwork, communication, and strict adherence to standardized team procedures. The real value of the pit crew training to the ramp crews is that it conveys the lessons of teamwork in a very vivid way. If a team fails to follow procedures and work together when trying to change tires, tools will be misplaced, parts will be dropped, and members will get in one another's way. As a consequence, a pit stop may last for minutes rather than seconds.

团队建设
TEAM BUILDING

团队建设这类培训通常是由顾问负责实施的，目的在于促进与目标设置、人际关系、问题解决与角色澄清有关的团队过程的发展。

The fourth general type of team process training is called **team building.** This type of training normally is conducted by a consultant and intended to facilitate the development of team processes related to goal setting, interpersonal relations, problem solving, and role clarification. The ropes course is a very popular task used in team building. It requires team members to work together to traverse wooden beams, ropes, and zip lines while dangling in a harness 20–50 feet in the air. Other examples include laser tag and paintball, WhirlyBall (think lacrosse played in bumper cars with a whiffle ball and plastic scoops), whitewater rafting, scavenger hunts, and beating drums in a drum circle. Team-building activities such as these are hugely popular with organizations of all sizes, and they do seem like an awful lot of fun.

But can you really build effective teams by having them participate in enjoyable activities that seem so unrelated to their jobs? In fact, this was the basis for Senators Byron Dorgan and Ron Wyden's request that the inspector general of the U.S. Postal Service be fired. In their letter to the chairman of the Post Office Board of Governors, they wrote that the inspector general "has spent millions of agency dollars on expensive and silly 'team building' exercises, diverting massive resources from the task of finding waste and improving efficiency. . . . On tapes, you see images of public servants dressed up as the Village People, wearing cat costumes, doing a striptease, and participating in mock trials—all on official time, all at the public's expense." Although it's somewhat difficult to gauge the effectiveness of team-building interventions because so many different types of exercises have been used, research has been conducted that provides mixed support for the senators' claim. The findings of one meta-analysis found that team building did not have a significant effect on team performance when performance was defined in terms of productivity. However, the research found that team building is most likely to have positive effects for smaller teams and when the exercise emphasizes the importance of clarifying role responsibilities. The facilitator of the team building session also needs to be competent in helping members see the connections between the exercise and their work, and also to ensure inclusion and participation of all members.

Ropes courses are enjoyable to participants and provide a unique opportunity for team members to get to know each other. But can they really build effective teams?

chapter 11

Leadership: Power and Negotiation

领导：权力与谈判

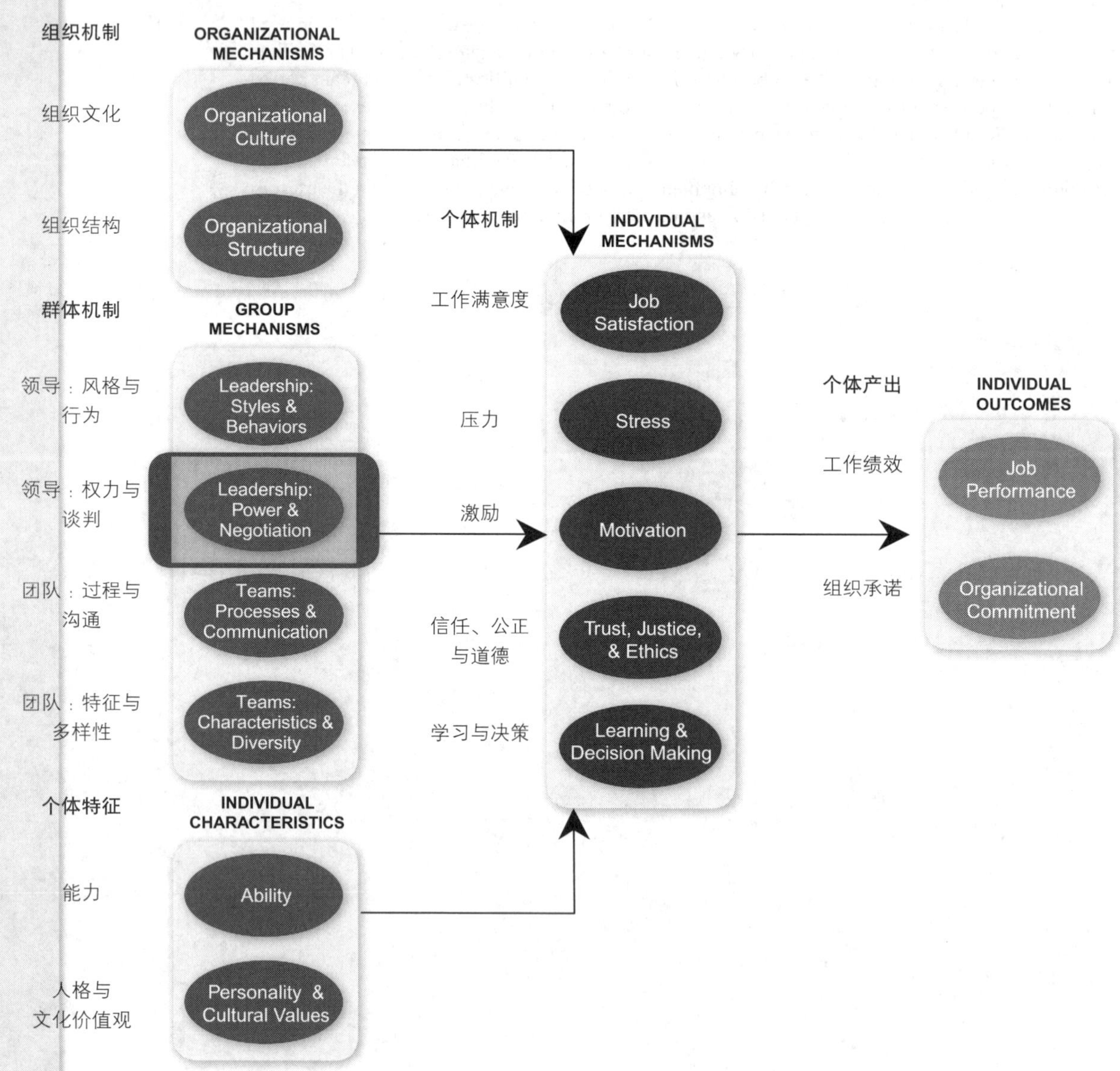

LEARNING GOALS

After reading this chapter, you should be able to answer the following questions:

11.1 What is leadership, and what role does power play in leadership?

11.2 What are the different types of power that leaders possess, and when can they use those types most effectively?

11.3 What behaviors do leaders exhibit when trying to influence others, and which of these is most effective?

11.4 What is organizational politics, and when is political behavior most likely to occur?

11.5 How do leaders use their power and influence to resolve conflicts in the workplace?

11.6 What are the ways in which leaders negotiate in the workplace?

11.7 How do power and influence affect job performance and organizational commitment?

PEPSICO

Indra Nooyi, chairman and CEO of PepsiCo, has been at the top of *Fortune's* Most Powerful Women in Business list for five straight years. She has earned this recognition not only because as CEO she runs close to a $60 billion company, but also because she has proven that she has the ability to be highly influential both inside and outside of business. *Time* magazine has twice named her as one of the 100 most influential people in the world, and Howard Schultz, CEO of Starbucks, has called her a "world-class leader" and says that she is "single-minded about following the path she believes is best for her company." Nooyi is the major driver behind PepsiCo's overall company strategy, "Performance with a Purpose," which pushes all company divisions to become more green and healthy while still pulling in profits. Nooyi's vision has pushed the company's product portfolio into three subbrands: fun for you (Pepsi, Doritos), better for you (Diet Pepsi, Baked Lay's Potato Crisps), and good for you (Tropicana, Naked Juice, Quaker Oats), and her goal is to push the United States as a whole toward a healthier eating environment. Quite a feat for a soft drink and snack-food giant!

Nooyi rose through the ranks of the company by being known as an individual with the ability to influence others. Famed ex-Pepsi CEO Roger Enrico, who made Nooyi his CFO, says to this day that Indra is "the best negotiator I've ever seen in my entire life." She has demonstrated those skills by overseeing PepsiCo's acquisition of Tropicana and Quaker Oats ($13 billion) as well as influencing the divestiture of Taco Bell, Pizza Hut, and KFC because she felt they didn't add enough value to PepsiCo (at the time, the sale reduced the company's size by a third). Nooyi is the first to recognize that her skills and influence tactics were learned over time and are partly due to mentors who provided feedback when they felt she was being too harsh.

While some of Nooyi's power now certainly comes from sitting atop the company's organizational chart, her ability as a leader to influence others comes just as much from more personal forms of power. Coworkers say she "brings her whole self" to work with her every day. Her charisma is contagious. She is known for insisting that everyone's birthday is celebrated with a cake, walking barefoot around the office, and her constant singing—in the hallways, with coworkers, and karaoke at dinner parties (her sister was nominated for a Grammy in 2011). She never refuses a phone call from her kids—board meeting or not. Enrico says, "Indra can drive as deep and hard as anyone I've ever met, but she can do it with a sense of heart and fun."

领导：权力与谈判

LEADERSHIP: POWER AND NEGOTIATION

As evidenced by PepsiCo, leaders within organizations can make a huge difference to the success of an organization or group. It would be easy after reading the opening example to anoint Indra Nooyi as a great leader and try to simply adopt her behavioral examples to follow in her footsteps. However, things aren't quite that simple. Many other leaders have exhibited similar behaviors and not been nearly as successful. As we'll discover in this and the next chapter, there are many different types of leaders, many of whom can excel, given the right circumstances.

11.1

What is leadership, and what role does power play in leadership?

领导是指运用权力与影响力指挥下属的活动，从而实现目标。

There is perhaps no subject that's written about more in business circles than the topic of leadership. A quick search on Amazon.com for "leadership" will generate a list of more than 200,000 books! That number doesn't even count the myriad videos, calendars, audio recordings, and other items, all designed to help people become better leaders. Given all the interest in this topic, a natural question becomes, "What exactly is a leader?" We define **leadership** as the use of power and influence to direct the activities of followers toward goal achievement. That direction can affect followers' interpretation of events, the organization of their work activities, their commitment to key goals, their relationships with other followers, and their access to cooperation and support from other work units. This chapter focuses on how leaders *get* the power and influence they use to direct others and the ways in which power and influence are utilized in organizations, including through negotiation. Chapter 12 will focus on how leaders actually *use* their power and influence to help followers achieve their goals.

为什么某些领导者比其他领导者更有权力
WHY ARE SOME LEADERS MORE POWERFUL THAN OTHERS?

What exactly comes to mind when you think of the term "power"? Does it raise a positive or negative image for you? Certainly it's easy to think of leaders who have used power for what we would consider good purposes, but it's just as easy to think of leaders who have used power for unethical or immoral purposes. For now, try not to focus on how leaders use power but instead on how they acquire it. **Power** can be defined as the ability to influence the behavior of others and resist unwanted influence in return. Note that this definition gives us a couple of key points to think about. First, just because a person has the ability to influence others does not mean they will actually choose to do so. In many organizations, the most powerful employees don't even realize how influential they could be! Second, in addition to influencing others, power can be seen as the ability to resist the influence attempts of others. This resistance could come in the form of the simple voicing of a dissenting opinion, the refusal to perform a specific behavior, or the organization of an opposing group of coworkers. Sometimes leaders need to resist the influence of other leaders or higher-ups to do what's best for their own unit. Other times leaders need to resist the influence of their own employees to avoid being a "pushover" when employees try to go their own way.

权力是指影响他人行为，并相应抵制不利影响的能力。

获得权力
ACQUIRING POWER

Think about the people you currently work with or have worked with in the past, or think of students that are involved in many of the same activities you are. Do any of those people seem to have especially high levels of power, meaning that they have the ability to influence your behavior? What is it that gives them that power? In some cases, their power may come from some formal position (e.g., supervisor, team leader, teaching assistant, resident advisor). However, sometimes the most powerful people we know lack any sort of formal authority. It turns out that power in organizations can come from a number of different sources. Specifically, there are five major types of power that can be grouped along two dimensions: organizational power and personal power. These types of power are illustrated in Figure 11-1.

FIGURE 11-1 Types of Power

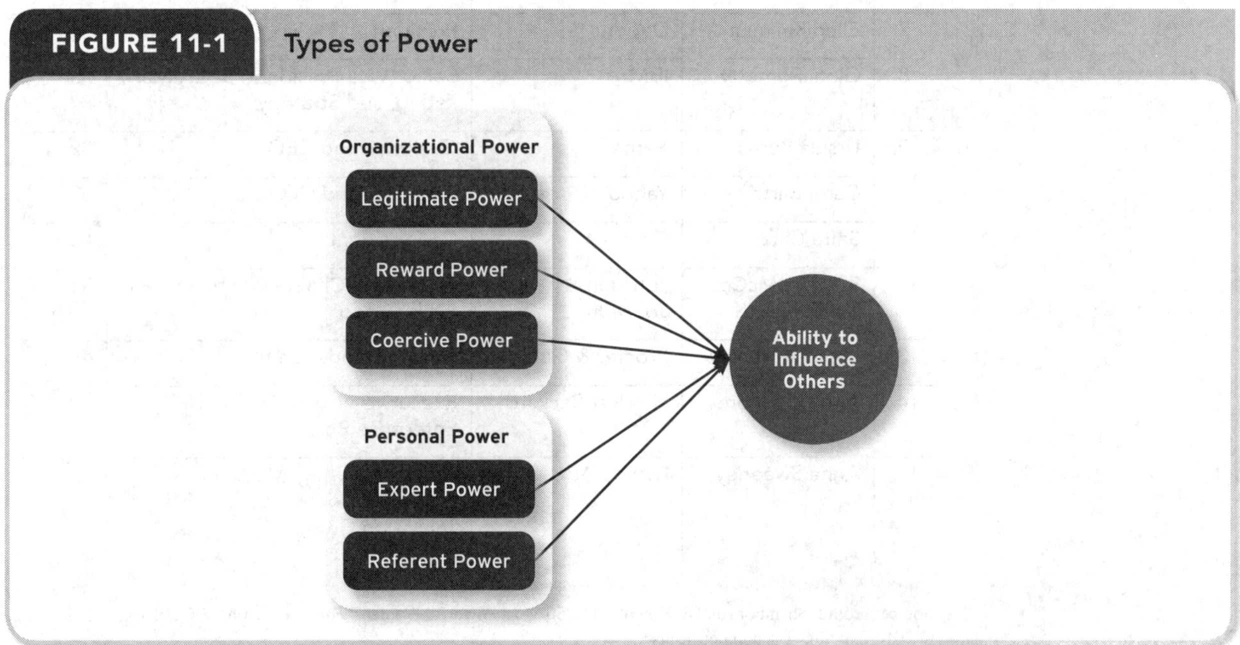

11.2
What are the different types of power that leaders possess, and when can they use those types most effectively?

合法权是来自于组织内部的职权所获得的权力，有时称为“正式职权”。

ORGANIZATIONAL POWER. The three types of organizational power derive primarily from a person's position within the organization. These types of power are considered more formal in nature. **Legitimate power** derives from a position of authority inside the organization and is sometimes referred to as "formal authority." People with legitimate power have some title—some term on an organizational chart or on their door that says, "Look, I'm supposed to have influence over you." Those with legitimate power have the understood right to ask others to do things that are considered within the scope of their authority. When managers ask an employee to stay late to work on a project, work on one task instead of another, or work faster, they are exercising legitimate power. The higher up in an organization a person is, the more legitimate power they generally possess. *Fortune* magazine provides rankings of the most powerful women in business. As shown in Table 11-1, all of those women possess legitimate power, in that they hold a title that affords them the ability to influence others.

Legitimate power does have its limits, however. It doesn't generally give a person the right to ask employees to do something outside the scope of their jobs or roles within the organization. For example, if a manager asked an employee to wash their car or mow their lawn, it would likely be seen as an inappropriate request. As we'll see later in this chapter, there's a big difference between having legitimate power and using it effectively. When used ineffectively, legitimate power can be a very weak form of power. In our opening example, Nooyi doesn't simply

TABLE 11-1 ***Fortune's* 15 Most Powerful Women in Business in 2010**

	NAME	COMPANY	POSITION	AGE
1	Indra Nooyi	PepsiCo	Chairman and CEO	54
2	Irene Rosenfeld	Kraft Foods	Chairman and CEO	59
3	Pat Woertz	Archer Daniels Midland	Chairman, President, and CEO	57
4	Andrea Jung	Avon Products	Chairperson and CEO	52
5	Angela Braly	WellPoint	Chairman, President and CEO	50
6	Oprah Winfrey	Harpo, Inc.	Chairperson	56
7	Ellen Kullman	Dupont	President	54
8	Ginni Rometty	IBM	Senior Vice-President, Sales, Marketing, and Strategy	53
9	Ursula Burns	Xerox	Chairman and CEO	52
10	Carol Bartz	Yahoo	President and CEO	62
11	Safra Catz	Oracle	Co-President	48
12	Sherilyn McCoy	Johnson & Johnson	Worldwide Chairman, Pharmaceuticals Group	51
13	Melanie Healey	Procter & Gamble	Group President, NA	49
14	Ann Livermore	Hewlett-Packard	Executive Vice President, HP Enterprise Business	52
15	Anne Sweeney	Disney-ABC	Co-Chair, Disney Media Networks; President, Disney-ABC Television Group	52

Source: From J. Shambora and B. Kowitt, "The 50 Most Powerful Women," *Fortune,* October 18, 2010, p. 131.

go bossing everyone in the organization around; she manages her legitimate power effectively to earn respect and get people to commit to their endeavors.

The next two forms of organizational power are somewhat intertwined with legitimate power. **Reward power** exists when someone has control over the resources or rewards another person wants. For example, managers generally have control over raises, performance evaluations, awards, more desirable job assignments, and the resources an employee might require to perform a job effectively. Those with reward power have the ability to influence others if those being influenced believe they will get the rewards by behaving in a certain way. **Coercive power** exists when a person has control over punishments in an organization. Coercive power operates primarily on the principle of fear. It exists when one person believes that another has the ability to punish him or her and is willing to use that power. For example, a manager might have the right to fire, demote, suspend, or lower the pay of an employee. Sometimes the limitations of a manager to impose punishments are formally spelled out in an organization. However, in many instances, managers have a considerable amount of leeway in this regard. Coercive power is generally regarded as a poor form of power to use regularly, because it tends to result in negative feelings toward those that wield it.

当某人控制另外一个人想要的资源或报酬的控制权时，**报酬权**就产生了。

当一个人控制着组织中的处罚时，**强制权**就产生了。

PERSONAL POWER. Of course, the women in Table 11-1 don't appear on that list just because they have some formal title that affords them the ability to reward and punish others. There's something else about them, as people, that provides them additional capabilities to influence others. Personal forms of power capture that "something else." **Expert power** derives from a person's expertise, skill, or knowledge on which others depend. When people have a track record of high performance, the ability to solve problems, or specific knowledge that's necessary to accomplish tasks, they're more likely to be able to influence other people who need that expertise. Consider a lone programmer who knows how to operate a piece of antiquated software, a machinist who was recently trained to operate a new piece of equipment, or the only engineer who has experience working on a specific type of project. All of these individuals will have a degree of expert power because of what they individually bring to the organization. Pat Woertz, the CEO of Archer Daniels Midland (ADM), the Decatur, Illinois–based agricultural firm, appears third in Table 11-1 largely because of her expert power. ADM hired Woertz as CEO because it felt that her time at Chevron provided her with energy expertise that could help the firm in its push for renewable fuels. There is perhaps no place where expert power comes into play more than in Silicon Valley, where it's widely perceived that the best leaders are those with significant technological experience and expertise. At Intel, Senior Advisor and former CEO Andy Grove "fostered a culture in which 'knowledge power' would trump 'position power.' Anyone could challenge anyone else's idea, so long as it was about the idea and not the person—and so long as you were ready for the demand 'Prove it.'"

专家权源自他人所依赖的专长、技能和知识。

Referent power exists when others have a desire to identify and be associated with a person. This desire is generally derived from affection, admiration, or loyalty toward a specific individual. Although our focus is on individuals within organizations, there are many examples of political leaders, celebrities, and sports figures who seem to possess high levels of referent power. Barack Obama, Angelina Jolie, and Peyton Manning all possess referent power to some degree, because others want to emulate them. The same could be said of leaders in organizations who possess a good reputation, attractive personal qualities, or a certain level of charisma. The people who have watched Oprah Winfrey (number 6 in Table 11-1) on TV, listen to her on satellite radio, or worked for her at Harpo, Inc., admire her views and seek to emulate her actions. Indra Nooyi, as detailed in our opening chapter case, clearly wields referent power. The people who surround her constantly refer to the "presence" she has whenever she walks into the room—something she had well before she became CEO. For another take on these issues, check out this chapter's **OB at the Bookstore** feature.

当其他人有强烈的愿意来认同某人或与其发生关联时，**参照权**就产生了。这种愿望一般源于对特定个体的感情、钦佩与忠诚。

Of course, it's possible for a person to possess all of the forms of power at the same time. In fact, the most powerful leaders—like those in Table 11-1—have bases of power that include all five dimensions. From an employee's perspective, it's sometimes difficult to gauge what form of power is most important. Why, exactly, do you do what your boss asks you to do? Is it because the boss has the formal right to provide direction, because the boss controls your evaluations, or because you admire and like the boss? Many times, we don't know exactly what type of power leaders possess until they attempt to use it. Generally speaking, the personal forms of power are more strongly related to organizational commitment and job performance than are the organizational forms. If you think about the authorities for whom you worked the hardest, they probably possessed some form of expertise and charisma, rather than just an ability to reward and punish. That's not to say

OB AT THE BOOKSTORE

LINCHPIN: ARE YOU INDISPENSIBLE?
by Seth Godin (New York: Penguin, 2010).

The linchpin is an individual who can walk into chaos and create order, someone who can invent, connect, create, and make things happen. Every worthwhile institution has indispensable people who make differences like these.

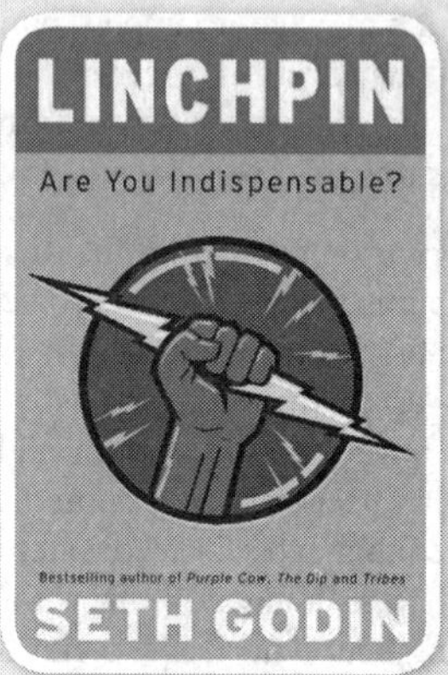

With these words, author and entrepreneur Seth Godin describes what he terms a "linchpin." The book essentially starts with the premise that the world of work as we know it is changing and so are the types of jobs that most of us will occupy. Although we have been trained since childhood to follow instructions and simply fit in, employees will no longer be able to move ahead in organizations by being compliant. The book begins with a question: Are you going to spend the rest of your career following orders and waiting for the weekend or are you going to rise above and learn to solve problems and become a person that your organization can't live without? In order to do this you must (1) stand out, (2) exert emotional labor (passion) in your job, and (3) produce interactions that those around you care about. Godin believes that you become a linchpin by giving your art (gifts, talents, effort) to others with no reciprocity in mind. By putting forth effort and giving our all in the jobs we do, rewards and recognition will follow—but not if we do it for that reason. You cannot wait to find a job that you are passionate about, you must find a way to bring passion to the job you have.

While Godin's book doesn't provide a roadmap for acquiring power (in fairness, he would argue strongly that there is no such roadmap and the word "power" is never explicitly used in the book), the book consistently skirts the ideas that in order to become a linchpin one must develop the two personal forms of power and that organizational forms of power will not set you apart. The book's descriptions of "emotional labor" and connecting with people resonate with referent power, and its descriptions of needing to develop unique talents and having a depth of knowledge combined with good judgment resonate with expert power.

though that organizational forms of power cannot successfully achieve objectives at times. Some useful guidelines for wielding each of the forms of power can be found in Table 11-2.

CONTINGENCY FACTORS. There are certain situations in organizations that are likely to increase or decrease the degree to which leaders can use their power to influence others. Most of these situations revolve around the idea that the more other employees depend on a person, the more powerful that person becomes. A person can have high levels of expert and referent power, but if he or she works alone and performs tasks that nobody sees, the ability to influence others is greatly reduced. That being said, there are four factors that have an effect on the strength of a person's ability to use power to influence others. These factors are summarized in Table 11-3. **Substitutability** is the degree to which people have alternatives in accessing resources. Leaders that control resources to which no one else has access can use their power to gain greater influence. **Discretion** is the degree to which managers have the right to make decisions on their own. If managers are forced to follow organizational policies and rules, their ability to influence others is reduced. **Centrality** represents how important a person's job is and how many people depend on that person to accomplish their tasks. Leaders who perform critical tasks and interact with others regularly have a greater ability to use their power to influence

替代性指人们在获取资源方面可选择的程度。

自由性指管理者有权单独做出决策的程度。

中心性表示一个人工作的重要程度，以及有多少人依赖于这个人完成任务。

TABLE 11-2 Guidelines for Using Power

TYPE OF POWER	GUIDELINES FOR USE
Legitimate	• Make polite, clear requests. • Explain the reason for the request. • Don't exceed your scope of authority. • Follow up to verify compliance. • Insist on compliance if appropriate.
Reward	• Offer the types of rewards people desire. • Offer rewards that are fair and ethical. • Don't promise more than you can deliver. • Explain the criteria for giving rewards and keep it simple. • Provide rewards as promised if requirements are met. • Don't use rewards in a manipulative fashion.
Coercive	• Explain rules and requirements and ensure people understand the serious consequences of violations. • Respond to infractions promptly and without favoritism. • Investigate to get facts before following through. • Provide ample warnings. • Use punishments that are legitimate, fair, and commensurate with the seriousness of noncompliance.
Expert	• Explain the reasons for a request and why it's important. • Provide evidence that a proposal will be successful. • Don't make rash, careless, or inconsistent statements. • Don't exaggerate or misrepresent the facts. • Listen seriously to the person's concerns and suggestions. • Act confidently and decisively in a crisis.
Referent	• Show acceptance and positive regard. • Act supportive and helpful. • Use sincere forms of ingratiation. • Defend and back up people when appropriate. • Do unsolicited favors. • Make self-sacrifices to show concern. • Keep promises.

Source: From Gary A. Yukl, *Leadership in Organizations,* 7th edition © 2010. Reproduced by permission of Pearson Education, Inc., Upper Saddle River, New Jersey.

others. **Visibility** is how aware others are of a leader's power and position. If everyone knows that a leader has a certain level of power, the ability to use that power to influence others is likely to be high.

可见性指其他人意识到领导者的权力与职位的程度。

MWH, a $1 billion revenue Broomfield, Colorado, engineering firm specializing in water projects, recently asked 500 employees in all of its departments where they went to when they came up with a new idea. This would allow MWH to determine who possessed certain types of expertise and who offered the most help to employees. In a sense, MWH is identifying the individuals in the organization who are likely to have the most power. Companies such as Microsoft, Pfizer, and Google are increasingly using such networking maps to understand the power structures in their organizations and who holds the most influence.

运用影响力
USING INFLUENCE

Up until now, we've discussed the types of power leaders possess and when their opportunities to use that power will grow or diminish. Now we turn to the specific strategies that leaders use to translate that power into actual influence.

TABLE 11-3 The Contingencies of Power

CONTINGENCY	LEADER'S ABILITY TO INFLUENCE OTHERS INCREASES WHEN ...
Substitutability	There are no substitutes for the rewards or resources the leader controls.
Centrality	The leader's role is important and interdependent with others in the organization.
Discretion	The leader has the freedom to make his or her own decisions without being restrained by organizational rules.
Visibility	Others know about the leader and the resources he or she can provide.

影响力指通过实际的行为来引起他人行为或态度的改变。

Recall that having power increases our *ability* to influence behavior. It doesn't mean that we will use or exert that power. **Influence** is the use of an actual behavior that causes behavioral or attitudinal changes in others. There are two important aspects of influence to keep in mind. First, influence can be seen as directional. It most frequently occurs downward (managers influencing employees) but can also be lateral (peers influencing peers) or upward (employees influencing managers). Second, influence is all relative. The absolute power of the "influencer" and "influencee" isn't as important as the disparity between them.

11.3
What behaviors do leaders exhibit when trying to influence others, and which of these is most effective?

理性说服指利用逻辑分析和客观事实来表明要求是合理的。

诉诸鼓励指通过诉诸目标对象的价值观和理想，从而引起其情感和态度的反应。

当目标对象被允许参与实施或执行一个要求的决策时，**协商**就产生了。

合作包括领导者帮助完成任务、提供必要的资源或者消除任务完成的阻碍。

讨好指通过采用奉承、称赞或其他友好的行为，使目标对影响者产生好感。

当要求者基于个人友情或忠诚要求某件事情时，**诉诸个人**就发生了。

INFLUENCE TACTICS. Leaders depend on a number of tactics to cause behavioral or attitudinal changes in others. In fact, there are at least 10 types of tactics that leaders can use to try to influence others. These tactics and their general levels of effectiveness are illustrated in Figure 11-2. The four most effective tactics have been shown to be rational persuasion, inspirational appeals, consultation, and collaboration. **Rational persuasion** is the use of logical arguments and hard facts to show the target that the request is a worthwhile one. Research shows that rational persuasion is most effective when it helps show that the proposal is important and feasible. Rational persuasion is particularly important because it's the only tactic that is consistently successful in the case of upward influence. At Google, for example, data is all-important. CEO Larry Page has been willing to change his mind in the face of conflicting information. Douglas Merrill, former Google CIO, said, "Larry would wander around the engineers and he would see a product being developed, and sometimes he would say, 'Oh I don't like that,' but the engineers would get some data to back up their idea, and the amazing thing was that Larry was fine to be wrong. As long as the data supported them, he was okay with it. And that was such an incredibly morale-boosting interaction for engineers." An **inspirational appeal** is a tactic designed to appeal to the target's values and ideals, thereby creating an emotional or attitudinal reaction. To use this tactic effectively, leaders must have insight into what kinds of things are important to the target. **Consultation** occurs when the target is allowed to participate in deciding how to carry out or implement a request. This tactic increases commitment from the target, who now has a stake in seeing that his or her opinions are valued. A leader uses **collaboration** by attempting to make it easier for the target to complete the request. Collaboration could involve the leader helping complete the task, providing required resources, or removing obstacles that make task completion difficult.

Four other influence tactics are sometimes effective and sometimes not. **Ingratiation** is the use of favors, compliments, or friendly behavior to make the target feel better about the influencer. You might more commonly hear this referred to as "sucking up," especially when used in an upward influence sense. Ingratiation has been shown to be more effective when used as a long-term strategy and not nearly as effective when used immediately prior to making an influence attempt. **Personal appeals** occur when the requestor asks for something based on personal friendship or loyalty. The stronger the friendship, the more successful the attempt is likely to be. As described in our **OB Internationally** feature, there are cultural differences when it comes to

FIGURE 11-2 Influence Tactics and Their Effectiveness

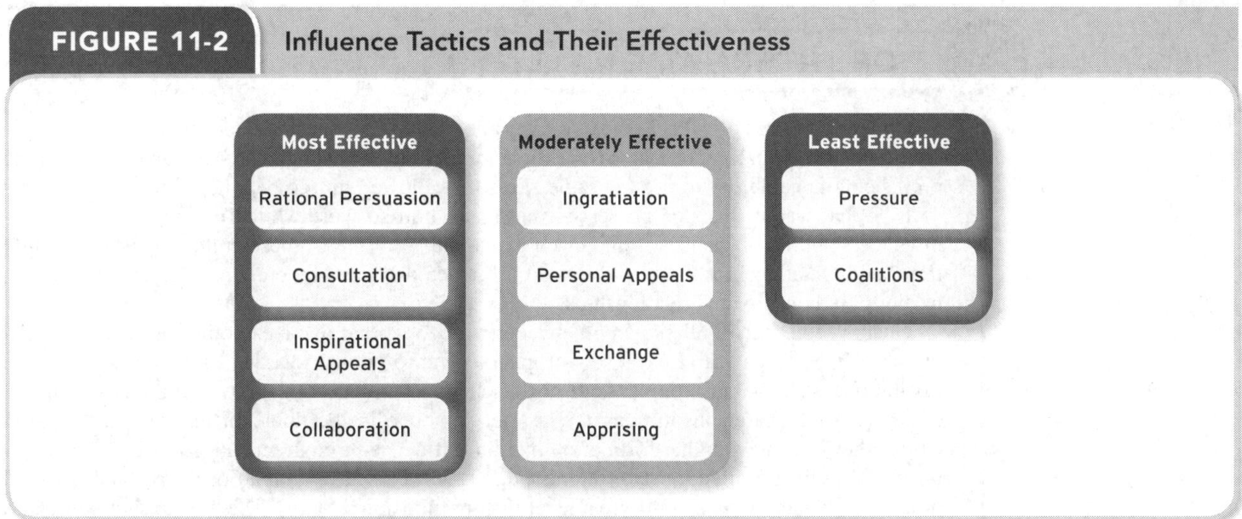

Source: Adapted from J.J. Johnson and J.B. Cullen, "Trust in Cross-Cultural Relationships," in Blackwell Handbook of Cross-Cultural Management, eds. M.J. Gannon and K.L. Newman (Malden, MA: Blackwell, 2002), pp. 335–60.

this kind of an appeal, as there are with other influence attempts. An **exchange tactic** is used when the requestor offers a reward or resource to the target in return for performing a request. This type of request requires that the requestor have something of value to offer. Finally, **apprising** occurs when the requestor clearly explains why performing the request will benefit the target personally. It differs from rational persuasion in that it focuses solely on the benefit to the target as opposed to simple logic or benefits to the group or organization. It differs from exchange, in that the benefit is not necessarily something that the requestor gives to the target but rather something that results from the action.

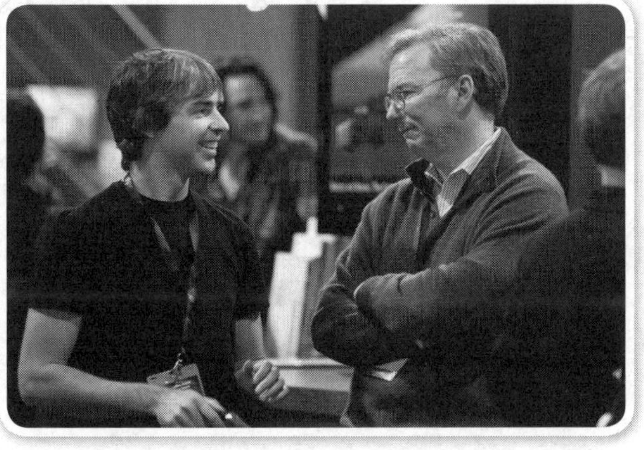

Larry Page (left), CEO of Google, is known for his willingness to allow employees to use rational persuasion (data) to change his mind on an issue.

交换策略是指要求者提供报酬或资源以换取目标执行要求的策略。

告知是指要求者明确阐明为什么执行这项要求会使目标对象个人收益的策略。

The two tactics that have been shown to be least effective and could result in resistance from the target are pressure and coalitions. Of course, this statement doesn't mean that they aren't used or can't be effective at times. **Pressure** is the use of coercive power through threats and demands. As we've discussed previously, such coercion is a poor way to influence others and may only bring benefits over the short term. The last tactic is the formation of coalitions. **Coalitions** occur when the influencer enlists other people to help influence the target. These people could be peers, subordinates, or one of the target's superiors. Coalitions are generally used in combination with one of the other tactics. For instance, if rational persuasion is not strong enough, the influencer might bring in another person to show that that person agrees with the logic of the argument.

施压是指对目标对象采用威胁、要求等强制权手段的策略。

联盟是指影响者通过获取其他人的帮助来影响目标对象的策略。

Two points should be noted about leaders' use of influence tactics. First, influence tactics tend to be most successful when used in combination. Many tactics have some limitations or weaknesses that can be overcome using other tactics. Second, the influence tactics that tend to be most successful are those that are "softer" in nature. Rational persuasion, consultation, inspirational appeals, and collaboration take advantage of personal rather than organizational forms of power. Leaders that are the most effective at influencing others will generally rely on the softer

OB INTERNATIONALLY

When Google hired Kai-Fu Lee to be vice president of engineering and president of Google Greater China, with a more than $10 million compensation package, the company was counting on his continued ability to use the same skills that allowed him to be a huge success at Microsoft. What was it that Lee possessed that made him so worthwhile? Lee argues that it was his understanding of guanxi (pronounced gwan-she). In the Chinese culture, guanxi (literally translated "relationships") is the ability to influence decisions by creating obligations between parties based on personal relationships.

Guanxi represents a relationship between two people that involves both sentiment and obligation. Individuals with high levels of guanxi tend to be tied together on the basis of shared institutions, such as kinship, places of birth, schools attended, and past working relationships. Although such shared institutions might "get someone in the door" in the United States, in China, they become a higher form of obligation. Influence through guanxi just happens—it's an unspoken obligation that must be addressed. It is, in a sense, a blend of formal and personal relationships that exists at a different level than in the United States. There is no such thing as a "business-only" relationship, and the expectation is simply that if you take, you must also give back. Lee (who recently left Google) and his guanxi were so great that Google's Chinese product managers insisted that their business cards read "Special Assistant to Kai-Fu Lee" and that their desks be placed within 100 feet of his so that they could effectively do business outside the company.

Google has been beset on all sides by cultural problems in China when it comes to influence. The company was forced to fire its first government relations head (a Chinese national) when she bought iPods as gifts for Chinese officials—something seen as normal within China—but an explicit violation of Google policy. Shortly after that, different expectations about censorship with the Chinese government caused Google to pull out of its search business in China altogether. American managers who go to work overseas must be conscious of these different types of relationships and expectations. In addition to understanding the power of guanxi, evidence suggests that Chinese managers from different areas (e.g., Hong Kong, Taiwan, Mainland China) have different beliefs when it comes to which influence tactics are the most effective. If anything, it goes to show that managers need to be acutely aware of both general and more specific cultural differences when trying to influence others in China.

tactics, make appropriate requests, and ensure the tactics they use match the types of power they have. Kraft CEO Irene Rosenfeld (number 2 in table 11-1) is known for her ability to persuade. A former executive with Kraft said, "When she is trying to persuade you of something, she will be relentless in coming back with facts and showing you she has the support of other people, she will be totally emotionally and intellectually committed to her idea."

内部化是指受影响的目标对象同意并承诺影响者的要求。

服从是指受影响的目标对象愿意完成领导者所要求的事情，但还怀有某种矛盾心理。

抵制是指目标对象拒绝执行影响者的要求，并尽力避免去做。

RESPONSES TO INFLUENCE TACTICS. As illustrated in Figure 11-3, there are three possible responses people have to influence tactics. **Internalization** occurs when the target of influence agrees with and becomes committed to the influence request. For a leader, this is the best outcome, because it results in employees putting forth the greatest level of effort in accomplishing what they are asked to do. Internalization reflects a shift in both the behaviors and the attitudes of employees. **Compliance** occurs when targets of influence are willing to do what the leader asks, but they do it with a degree of ambivalence. Compliance reflects a shift in the behaviors of employees but not their attitudes. This behavior is the most common response to influence attempts in organizations, because anyone with some degree of power who makes a reasonable request is likely to achieve compliance. That response allows leaders to accomplish their purpose, but it doesn't bring about the highest levels of employee effort and dedication. Still, it's clearly preferable to **resistance,** which occurs when the target refuses to perform the influence request and puts forth an effort to avoid having to do it. Employee resistance could come in the

FIGURE 11-3 Responses to Influence Attempts

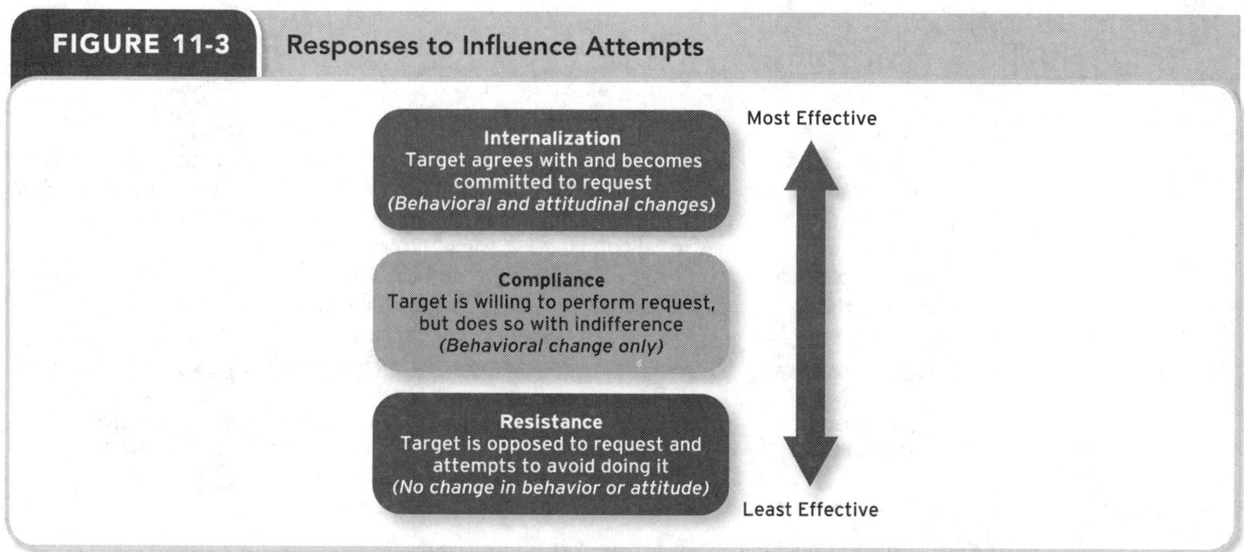

form of making excuses, trying to influence the requestor in return, or simply refusing to carry out the request. Resistance is most likely when the influencer's power is low relative to the target or when the request itself is inappropriate or unreasonable.

行动中的权力与影响力
POWER AND INFLUENCE IN ACTION

In this section, we look at two major areas in which leaders have the ability to use power to influence others. The first is through navigating the environment of organizational politics within the organization. The second is through using power and influence to help solve conflicts within the organization. As it turns out, it's easy for these two areas to coincide.

 **11.4**
What is organizational politics, and when is political behavior most likely to occur?

ORGANIZATIONAL POLITICS. If there was perhaps one term that had a more negative connotation than power, it might be politics. You've probably had people give you career advice such as, "Stay away from office politics" or "Avoid being seen as political." The truth is that you can't escape it; politics are a fact of life in organizations! Although you might hear company executives, such as former Vodafone CEO Sir Christopher Gent, make statements such as, "[When I was CEO], we were mercifully free of company politics and blame culture," you can be pretty sure that wasn't actually the case—especially given that England's Vodaphone is one of the world's largest mobile phone operators. Most leaders, such as Allison Young, vice president of Blue Cross and Blue Shield of Louisiana, will tell you that "You have to assess the political situation early on and make decisions on forward-looking strategy not only on the facts, but also the political landscape." Whether we like it or not, organizations are filled with independent, goal-driven individuals who must take into account the possible actions and desires of others to get what they want.

Organizational politics can be seen as actions by individuals that are directed toward the goal of furthering their own self-interests. Although there's generally a negative perception of politics, it's important to note that this definition doesn't imply that furthering one's self-interests is necessarily in opposition to the company's interests. A leader needs to be able to push his or her own ideas and influence others through the use of organizational politics. Research has recently supported the notion that, to be effective, leaders must have a certain degree of political skill. In fact, universities and some organizations such as Becton, Dickinson, and Company—a leading global medical technology company based in Franklin Lakes, New Jersey—are training their future leaders to be attuned to their political environment and develop their political skill.

组织政治是指与促进自我利益目标实现有关的个人行动。

Political skill is the ability to effectively understand others at work and use that knowledge to influence others in ways that enhance personal and/or organizational objectives. Two aspects of political skill are *networking ability,* or an adeptness at identifying and developing diverse contacts, and *social astuteness,* or the tendency to observe others and accurately interpret

政治技能是指在工作中能有效地理解他人，并利用知识影响他人，从而实现个人和（或）组织目标的一种能力。

OB ASSESSMENTS

POLITICAL SKILL

How much political skill do you have? This assessment is designed to measure two dimensions of political skill. Please write a number next to each statement that indicates the extent to which it accurately describes your attitude toward work while you were on the job. Alternatively, consider the statements in reference to school rather than work. Answer each question using the response scale provided. Then sum up your answers for each of the dimensions. (For more assessments relevant to this chapter, please visit http://connect.mcgraw-hill.com.)

1 STRONGLY DISAGREE	2 DISAGREE	3 NEUTRAL	4 AGREE	5 STRONGLY AGREE

1. I spend a lot of time and effort networking with others. _______
2. I know a lot of important people and am well connected. _______
3. I am good at using my connections and networks to make things happen. _______
4. I have developed a large network of colleagues and associates whom I can call on for support when I really need to get things done. _______
5. I spend a lot of time making connections. _______
6. I always seem to instinctively know the right thing to say or do to influence others. _______
7. I have a good intuition or savvy about how to present myself to others. _______
8. I am particularly good at sensing the motivations and hidden agendas of others. _______
9. I pay close attention to people's facial expressions. _______
10. I understand people very well. _______

SCORING AND INTERPRETATION:

Networking Ability: Sum up items 1–5. _______

Social Astuteness: Sum up items 6–10. _______

For networking ability, scores of 18 or more are above average and scores of 17 or less are below average. For social astuteness, scores of 19 or more are above average and scores of 18 or less are below average.

Source: Adapted from G.R. Ferris, D.C. Treadway, R.W. Kolodinsky, W.A. Hochwarter, C.J. Kacmar, C. Douglas, and D.D. Frink, "Development and Validation of the Political Skill Inventory," *Journal of Management*, 31 (2005), pp. 126–52. Reproduced with permission of Sage Publications, Inc. via Copyright Clearance Center.

their behavior. To see where you stand on these two dimensions, see our **OB Assessments** feature. Political skill also involves two other capabilities. *Interpersonal influence* involves having an unassuming and convincing personal style that's flexible enough to adapt to different situations. *Apparent sincerity* involves appearing to others to have high levels of honesty and genuineness. Taken together, these four skills provide a distinct advantage when navigating the political environments in organizations.

Although organizational politics can lead to positive outcomes, people's perceptions of politics are generally negative. This perception is certainly understandable, as anytime someone acts in a self-serving manner, it's potentially to the detriment of others. In a highly charged political environment in which people are trying to capture resources and influence one another toward potentially opposing goals, it's only natural that some employees will feel stress about the uncertainty they face at work. Environments that are perceived as extremely political have been shown to cause lower job satisfaction, increased strain, lower job performance (both task and extra-role related), higher turnover intentions, and lower organizational commitment among employees. In fact, high levels of organizational politics have even been shown to be detrimental to company performance as a whole.

"You have no idea how political this place is."

Source: © Alex Gregory, The New Yorker Collection, www.cartoonbank.com

As a result, organizations (and leaders) do their best to minimize the perceptions of self-serving behaviors that are associated with organizational politics. This goal requires identifying the particular organizational circumstances that cause politics to thrive. As illustrated in Figure 11-4, organizational politics are driven by both personal characteristics and organizational characteristics. Some employees have a strong need for power that provides them with an incentive to engage in political behaviors. Still others have "Machiavellian" tendencies, meaning that they're willing to manipulate and deceive others to acquire power.

Organizational factors that are the most likely to increase politics are those that raise the level of uncertainty in the environment. When people are uncertain about an outcome or event, they'll generally act in ways that help reduce that uncertainty. A number of events can trigger uncertainty,

FIGURE 11-4 The Causes and Consequences of Organizational Politics

Personal Characteristics
- Need for power
- Machiavellianism

Organizational Characteristics
- Lack of participation in decision making
- Limited or changing resources
- Ambiguity in roles
- High performance pressure
- Unclear performance evaluations

↓

Organizational Politics

↓

Negative Employee Reactions
- Decreased job satisfaction
- Decreased organizational commitment
- Decreased task performance
- Increased strain

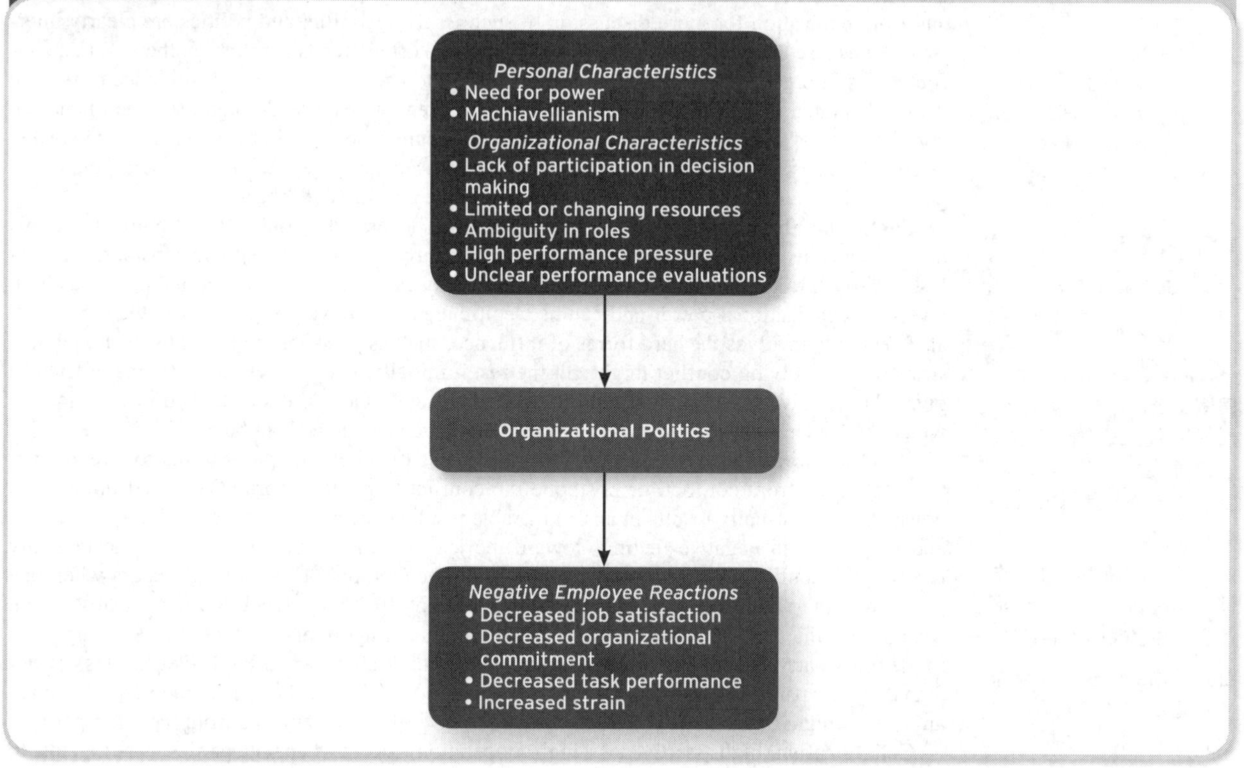

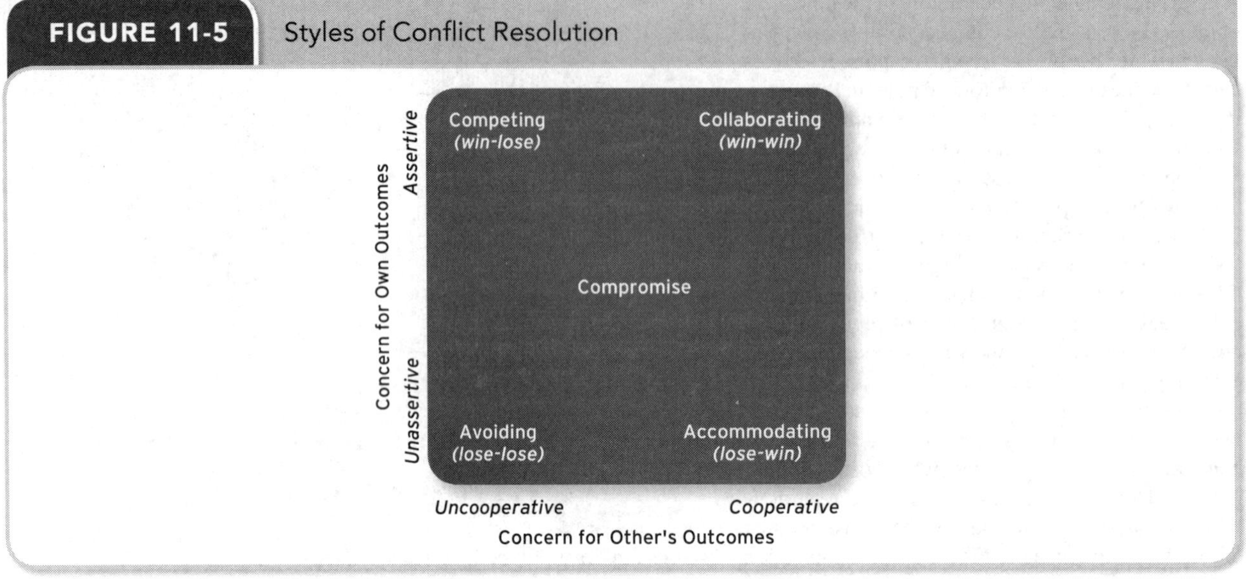

FIGURE 11-5 Styles of Conflict Resolution

including limited or changing resources, ambiguity in role requirements, high performance pressures, or unclear performance evaluation measures. A lack of employee participation in decision making has also been found to increase perceptions of organizational politics. These sorts of organizational factors generally have a much stronger effect on political behavior than do personal factors. That's actually a good thing for organizations, because it may be easier to clarify performance measures and roles than it is to change the personal characteristics of a workforce.

CONFLICT RESOLUTION. In addition to using their power to shape office politics, leaders can use their influence in the context of conflict resolution. Conflict arises when two or more individuals perceive that their goals are in opposition (see Chapter 10 on Team Processes and Communication for more discussion of such issues). Conflict and politics are clearly intertwined, because the pursuit of one's own self-interests often breeds conflict in others. When conflict arises in organizations, leaders have the ability to use their power and influence to resolve it. As illustrated in Figure 11-5, there are five different styles a leader can use when handling conflict, each of which is appropriate in different circumstances. The five styles can be viewed as combinations of two separate factors: how *assertive* leaders want to be in pursuing their own goals and how *cooperative* they are with regard to the concerns of others.

竞争（高决断性，低合作性）指一方寻求自我利益的满足，而不关注另一方的结果。

 **11.5**

How do leaders use their power and influence to resolve conflicts in the workplace?

Competing (high assertiveness, low cooperation) occurs when one party attempts to get his or her own goals met without concern for the other party's results. It could be considered a win–lose approach to conflict management. Competing occurs most often when one party has high levels of organizational power and can use legitimate or coercive power to settle the conflict. It also generally involves the hard forms of influence, such as pressure or coalitions. Although this strategy for resolving conflict might get the result initially, it won't win a leader many friends, given the negative reactions that tend to accompany such tactics. It's best used in situations in which the leader knows he or she is right and a quick decision needs to be made.

回避（低决断性，低合作性）指一方试图保持中立，远离冲突或者推迟冲突，目的在于收集信息或者让事态冷却。

迁就（低决断性，高合作性）指一方对另一方做出让步，并表现得非常慷慨。

合作（高决断性，高合作性）指双方共同努力以实现利益最大化。

Avoiding (low assertiveness, low cooperation) occurs when one party wants to remain neutral, stay away from conflict, or postpone the conflict to gather information or let things cool down. Avoiding usually results in an unfavorable result for everyone, including the organization, and may result in negative feelings toward the leader. Most important, avoiding never really resolves the conflict. **Accommodating** (low assertiveness, high cooperation) occurs when one party gives in to the other and acts in a completely unselfish way. Leaders will typically use an accommodating strategy when the issue is really not that important to them but is very important to the other party. It's also an important strategy to think about when the leader has less power than the other party. If leaders know they are going to lose the conflict due to their lack of power anyway, it might be a better long-term strategy to give in to the demands from the other party.

Collaboration (high assertiveness, high cooperation) occurs when both parties work together to maximize outcomes. Collaboration is seen as a win–win form of conflict resolution. Collaboration is generally regarded as the most effective form of conflict resolution, especially in reference to task-oriented rather than personal conflicts. However, it's also the most difficult to come by because it requires full sharing of information by both parties, a full discussion of concerns, relatively equal power between parties, and a lot of time investment to arrive at a resolution. However, this style also results in the best outcomes and reactions from both parties. **Compromise** (moderate assertiveness, moderate cooperation) occurs when conflict is resolved through give-and-take concessions. Compromise is perhaps the most common form of conflict resolution, whereby each party's losses are offset by gains and vice versa. It is seen as an easy form of resolution, maintains relations between parties, and generally results in favorable evaluations for the leader. Women are also more likely to use compromise as a tactic in comparison to men, whereas men are more likely than women to use competing as a tactic. Like most things when it comes to power and influence, it's not as much a function of which style you use, but rather when you use it that determines success. It is a mistake to think that one specific style is superior to another—research has shown that whether a certain style is effective is dependent on lots of situational issues. For more discussion of when to use the various conflict resolution strategies, see Table 11-4

妥协（中等决断性，中等合作性）指通过相互妥协的方式解决冲突。

TABLE 11-4 When to Use the Various Conflict Resolution Styles

RESOLUTION STYLE	USE DURING THE FOLLOWING SITUATIONS:
Competing	• When quick decisive action is vital (i.e., emergencies). • On important issues for which unpopular actions need implementation. • On issues vital to company welfare when you know you're right. • Against people who take advantage of noncompetitive people.
Avoiding	• When an issue is trivial or more important issues are pressing. • When you perceive no chance of satisfying your concerns. • When potential disruption outweighs the benefits of resolution. • To let people cool down and regain perspective. • When gathering information supersedes an immediate decision. • When others can resolve the conflict more effectively. • When issues seem tangential or symptomatic of other issues.
Collaborating	• To find an integrative solution when both sets of concerns are too important to be compromised. • When your objective is to learn. • To merge insights from people with different perspectives. • To gain commitment by incorporating concerns into a consensus. • To work through feelings that have interfered with a relationship.
Accommodating	• When you find you are wrong, to allow a better position to be heard, to learn, and to show your reasonableness. • When issues are more important to others than yourself, to satisfy others and maintain cooperation. • To build social credits for later issues. • To minimize loss when you are outmatched and losing. • When harmony and stability are especially important. • To allow subordinates to develop by learning from mistakes.
Compromising	• When goals are important but not worth the effort of potential disruption of more assertive modes. • When opponents with equal power are committed to mutually exclusive goals. • To achieve temporary settlements to complex issues. • To arrive at expedient solutions under time pressure. • As a backup when collaboration or competition is unsuccessful.

Source: From K.W. Thomas, "Toward Multi-Dimensional Values in Teaching: The Example of Conflict Behaviors," *Academy of Management Review*, 1, pp. 484–90. Copyright © 1997. Reproduced with permission of Academy of Management via Copyright Clearance Center.

The One Laptop Per Child project intends to provide millions of laptops for the world's poorest children. Founder and Chairman Nicholas Negroponte put together a large team of volunteers, "borrowed" workers from many different organizations, and worked to establish an effective collaboration among them by adopting a wide variety of conflict resolution strategies, even competing.

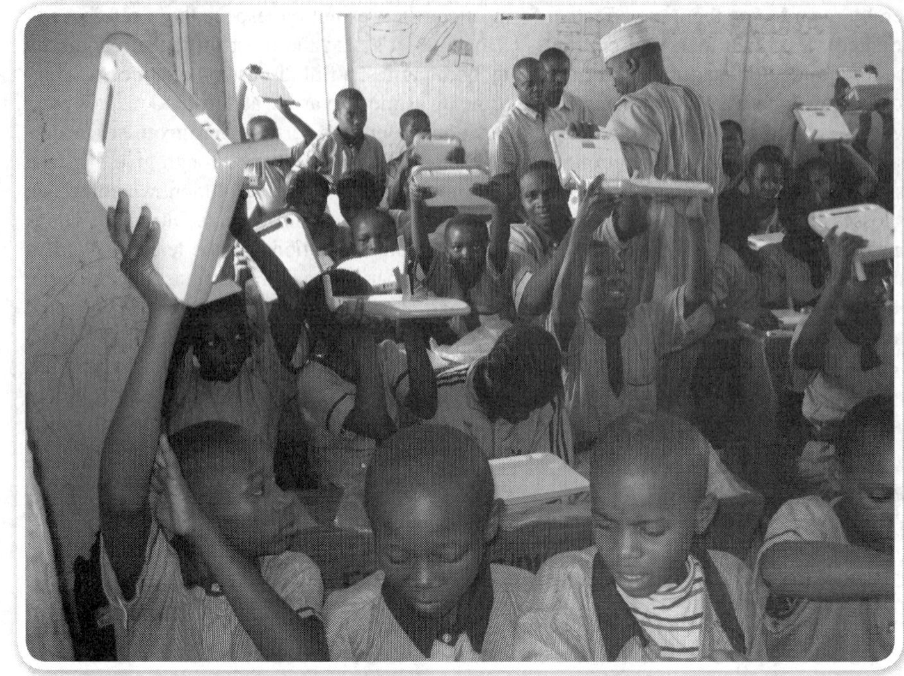

One example of conflict resolution is the One Laptop Per Child project. Nicolas Negroponte is the founder and chairperson of this nonprofit organization, whose mission is to give millions of laptops to undereducated children in the world's poorest nations. Five hundred thousand laptops—one for each primary schoolchild—have already been distributed in Uruguay; 1 million have gone out in Peru; and 25,000 are being handed out in Nicaragua. Needless to say, manufacturing a cheap laptop (named the XO and generally costing around $200 to produce) is no small feat. During the founding, Negroponte had to lead a network of vastly different individuals, all working on their own time or on loan from other organizations, through a painstaking collaboration process of design and manufacturing. The process wasn't always easy. Negroponte had to adopt a competing style of conflict resolution to make a custom wireless system for the laptop function. This competitive response upset a faction of volunteers who subsequently quit the project. However, Negroponte also has facilitated collaboration among very disparate groups. As a leader with varying degrees of power, Negroponte constantly has to balance the needs of the project with the needs of individuals and attempt to resolve conflict effectively. Surprisingly, conflict arises most frequently with regard to the countries to which the project wants to give the laptops!

谈 判
NEGOTIATIONS

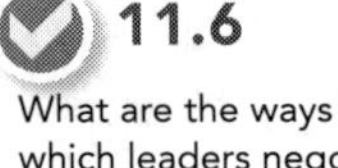

11.6

What are the ways in which leaders negotiate in the workplace?

谈判是两个或两个以上相互依赖的个体就其不同的偏向进行讨论并试图达成一致的过程。

There is perhaps no better place for leaders to use their power, influence, political, and conflict resolution skills than when conducting negotiations. **Negotiation** is a process in which two or more interdependent individuals discuss and attempt to come to an agreement about their different preferences. Negotiations can take place inside the organization or when dealing with organizational outsiders. Negotiations can involve settling a contract dispute between labor and management, determining a purchasing price for products, haggling over a performance review rating, or determining the starting salary for a new employee. Clearly, negotiations are a critical part of organizational life, for both leaders and employees. Successful leaders are good at negotiating outcomes of all types, and doing it well requires knowledge of power structures, how best to influence the other party, and awareness of their own biases in decision making.

NEGOTIATION STRATEGIES. There are two general strategies leaders must choose between when it comes to negotiations: distributive bargaining and integrative bargaining.

Distributive bargaining involves win–lose negotiating over a "fixed-pie" of resources. That is, when one person gains, the other person loses (also known as a "zero-sum" condition). The classic example of a negotiation with distributive bargaining is the purchase of a car. When you walk into a car dealership, there's a stated price on the side of the car that's known to be negotiable. In these circumstances though, every dollar you save is a dollar the dealership loses. Similarly, every dollar the salesperson negotiates for, you lose. Distributive bargaining is similar in nature to a competing approach to conflict resolution. Some of the most visible negotiations that have traditionally been approached with a distributive bargaining tactic are union–management labor negotiations. Whether it be automobile manufacturers, airlines, or nurses at hospitals, the negotiations for these sessions are typically viewed through a win–lose lens. For an example of a man who always takes a distributive bargaining position, see this chapter's **OB on Screen** feature.

分配式谈判是指对固定的资源进行的输赢谈判。也就是说，当一个人赢时，另一个就会损失（也称为"零和"条件）。

OB ON SCREEN

THERE WILL BE BLOOD

I have a competition in me. I want no one else to succeed.

With those words, Daniel Plainview (Daniel Day-Lewis) summarizes his view toward business, relationships, and life in *There Will Be Blood* (Dir.: Paul Thomas Anderson, Paramount, 2007). Daniel is an oil man through and through. He cares about nothing other than making money, will remove anyone who stands in his way, and eschews contact with other people unless it stands to benefit him somehow. As Daniel states at one point in the movie, "I look at people and I see nothing worth liking." He is the epitome of greed, and his approach to all conflict and negotiation adopts a win–lose philosophy.

Toward the beginning of the movie, Daniel appears in front of a group of townspeople with his "son and partner," H.W. Plainview (Dillon Freasier), trying to convince them why they should sell him a lease to drill for oil on their land. When the townspeople cannot come to an agreement quickly, Daniel finds someone willing to split from the group to lease him the rights to drill just on their property. He has little patience or need for compromise or collaboration. When executives from Standard Oil Company offer to make him rich beyond his wildest dreams, by buying the oil leases he has accumulated in California, Daniel simply cannot stand the thought of negotiating with a large conglomerate that might benefit from his hard work. Remember, he can't win if someone else does too. His goal is to make extraordinary amounts of money, all by himself, and at the expense of others. Daniel subsequently loses contact and significant relationships with anyone he has ever known. His nemesis is Eli Sunday (Paul Dano), an evangelical minister whose family and church lie on the land and in the town where Daniel wants to build a large series of oil derricks. The movie climaxes in a final negotiation between Daniel and Eli, featuring the now classic line, "I drink your milkshake!"

综合式谈判旨在达成一个双赢的解决方案。它包括通过问题解决与相互尊重的方式，取得一个双方满意的结果。

Many negotiations within organizations, including labor–management sessions, are beginning to occur with a more integrative bargaining strategy. **Integrative bargaining** is aimed at accomplishing a win–win scenario. It involves the use of problem solving and mutual respect to achieve an outcome that's satisfying for both parties. Leaders who thoroughly understand the conflict resolution style of collaboration are likely to thrive in these types of negotiations. In general, integrative bargaining is a preferable strategy whenever possible, because it allows a long-term relationship to form between the parties (because neither side feels like the loser). In addition, integrative bargaining has a tendency to produce a higher level of outcome favorability when both parties' views are considered, compared with distributive bargaining. As an example, picture a married couple negotiating where to go on vacation. The husband wants to go to stay in a log cabin in the mountains while the wife wants to stay at a luxury resort on the beach. This would seem to be a case of distributive bargaining—one party will win and the other will lose! After much discussion though, the couple finds that location (in the mountains) is more important to the husband and style of accommodations (luxury hotel) is more important to the wife. The two can come to a solution that provides mutually beneficial outcomes to both parties—a luxury hotel in the mountains. However, not all situations are appropriate for integrative bargaining. Integrative bargaining is most appropriate in situations in which multiple outcomes are possible, there is an adequate level of trust, and parties are willing to be flexible. Please don't approach your next used car purchase with an integrative bargaining strategy!

NEGOTIATION STAGES. Regardless of the strategy used, the actual negotiating process typically goes through a series of stages:

准备阶段可以说是谈判过程中最重要的阶段。在准备阶段，每一方都要决定谈判目标是什么，另一方是否会提出什么。

- **Preparation.** Arguably the single most important stage of the negotiating process, during preparation each party determines what its goals are for the negotiation and whether or not the other party has anything to offer. Each party also should determine its best alternative to a negotiated agreement, or **BATNA.** A BATNA describes each negotiator's bottom line. In other words, at what point are you willing to walk away? At the BATNA point, a negotiator is actually better off not negotiating at all. In their seminal book, *Getting to Yes: Negotiating Without Giving In,* Roger Fisher and William Ury state that people's BATNA is the standard by which all proposed agreements should be measured.

交流信息阶段。在这个非对抗阶段，各方会阐明自己的立场，并公布所有有利的信息。

- **Exchanging information.** In this nonconfrontational process, each party makes a case for its position and attempts to put all favorable information on the table. Each party also informs the other party how it has arrived at the conclusions it has and which issues it believes are important. When the other party is unfamiliar, this stage likely contains active listening and lots of questions. Studies show that successful negotiators ask many questions and gather much information during this stage.

讨价还价阶段。这是当人们听到"谈判"这个词时，大多数人都会想到的阶段。在这个阶段，双方可能必须妥协并做出让步以换得某个东西。

- **Bargaining.** This stage is the one most people imagine when they hear the term "negotiation." Success at this stage depends mightily on how well the previous two stages have proceeded. The goal is for each party to walk away feeling like it has gained something of value (regardless of the actual bargaining strategy). During this stage, both parties likely must make concessions and give up something to get something in return. To the degree that each party keeps the other party's concerns and motives in mind, this stage will go much more smoothly.

结束与承诺。这个阶段是将以前阶段已经达成的协议规范化。

- **Closing and commitment.** This stage entails the process of formalizing an agreement reached during the previous stage. For large, complex negotiations such as labor contracts established between an organization and a union, it can be a very long stage. For others, such as a negotiation between two coworkers about how they might handle their future relationship, no formal documents or contracts are required, and a simple handshake might suffice. Ideally, there will be no issues or misconceptions about the agreement arrived at during the bargaining stage. If they do exist, the negotiation process can regress back into the bargaining stage, and the process starts all over again. The stage also might be simply a recognition that the parties ended at an impasse with no agreement! In this case, several options are still available, as we discuss in the Application section at the end of this chapter.

NEGOTIATOR BIASES. It is important for negotiators to be aware of their biases when approaching a negotiation. While there are numerous biases to be aware of, the perceived power relationship between the parties and negotiator emotions are two of the most important. Research has shown that when negotiators perceive themselves as being in a position of power in comparison to the other party, they are more likely to demand more, concede less, and behave more aggressively during negotiations—in other words, they are likely to take a more distributive approach to negotiations. Similarly, when two parties perceive themselves as relatively equal in power, they take a more integrative approach to negotiations. As we all know, negotiations are generally a very emotion-laden affair, and negotiator emotions can also play a large role in the ability of two parties to reach successful conclusions during bargaining. (See Chapter 8 for a discussion of the ability of individuals to control their emotions during stressful times such as negotiations.) As it turns out, both positive and negative emotions can influence negotiation success in a negative way. Positive emotions, while they generally lead to a more integrative bargaining approach, can also cause negotiators to be overconfident and make decisions too quickly. Negative emotions tend to lead toward a more distributive bargaining approach and lower judgment accuracy.

总结：为什么某些领导者比其他领导者更有权力

SUMMARY: WHY ARE SOME LEADERS MORE POWERFUL THAN OTHERS?

So what explains why some leaders are more powerful and influential than others? As shown in Figure 11-6, answering that question requires an understanding of the types of power leaders acquire, what kinds of influence tactics they have available to them, and how they can use that influence to alter the attitudes and behaviors of their employees. Leaders acquire both organizational (legitimate, reward, coercive) and personal (expert, referent) forms of power, which gives them the ability to influence others. They can then use that power to influence others through influence tactics. Those tactics can help achieve organizational goals or may be applied more specifically to dealing with organizational politics, conflict resolution, or negotiation situations. In the end, there are three possible responses to influence attempts: internalization, compliance, and resistance. The effectiveness of those attempts will depend on leaders' skill at performing them and how well they match the forms of power they have with the appropriate types of influence.

权力与影响力有多重要

HOW IMPORTANT ARE POWER AND INFLUENCE?

11.7

How do power and influence affect job performance and organizational commitment?

How important is a leader's ability to use power and influence? In other words, does a leader's power and influence correlate with job performance and organizational commitment? Figure 11-7 summarizes the research evidence linking power and influence to job performance and organizational commitment. The figure reveals that power and influence are moderately correlated with job performance. When used correctly and focused on task-related outcomes, power and influence can create internalization in workers, such that they are both behaviorally and attitudinally focused on high levels of task performance. That internalization also helps increase citizenship behavior, whereas the compliance associated with power and influence can decrease counterproductive behavior. These job performance benefits make sense given that the effective use of power and influence can increase the *motivation* levels of employees, whereas the ineffective use of power and influence can increase the *stress* levels of employees.

Figure 11-7 also reveals that power and influence are moderately related to organizational commitment. When a leader draws on personal sources of power, such as expert power and referent power, a stronger emotional bond can be created with the employee, boosting affective commitment. The effective use of such power should increase *job satisfaction* and a sense of *trust* in the leader, all of which are associated with increased commitment levels. As with job performance, however, it's important to note that an ineffective use of power can also decrease commitment levels. In particular, repeated uses of coercive power or repeated reliance on hard influence tactics such as pressure or coalitions could actually decrease organizational commitment levels.

FIGURE 11-6 Why Are Some Leaders More Powerful Than Others?

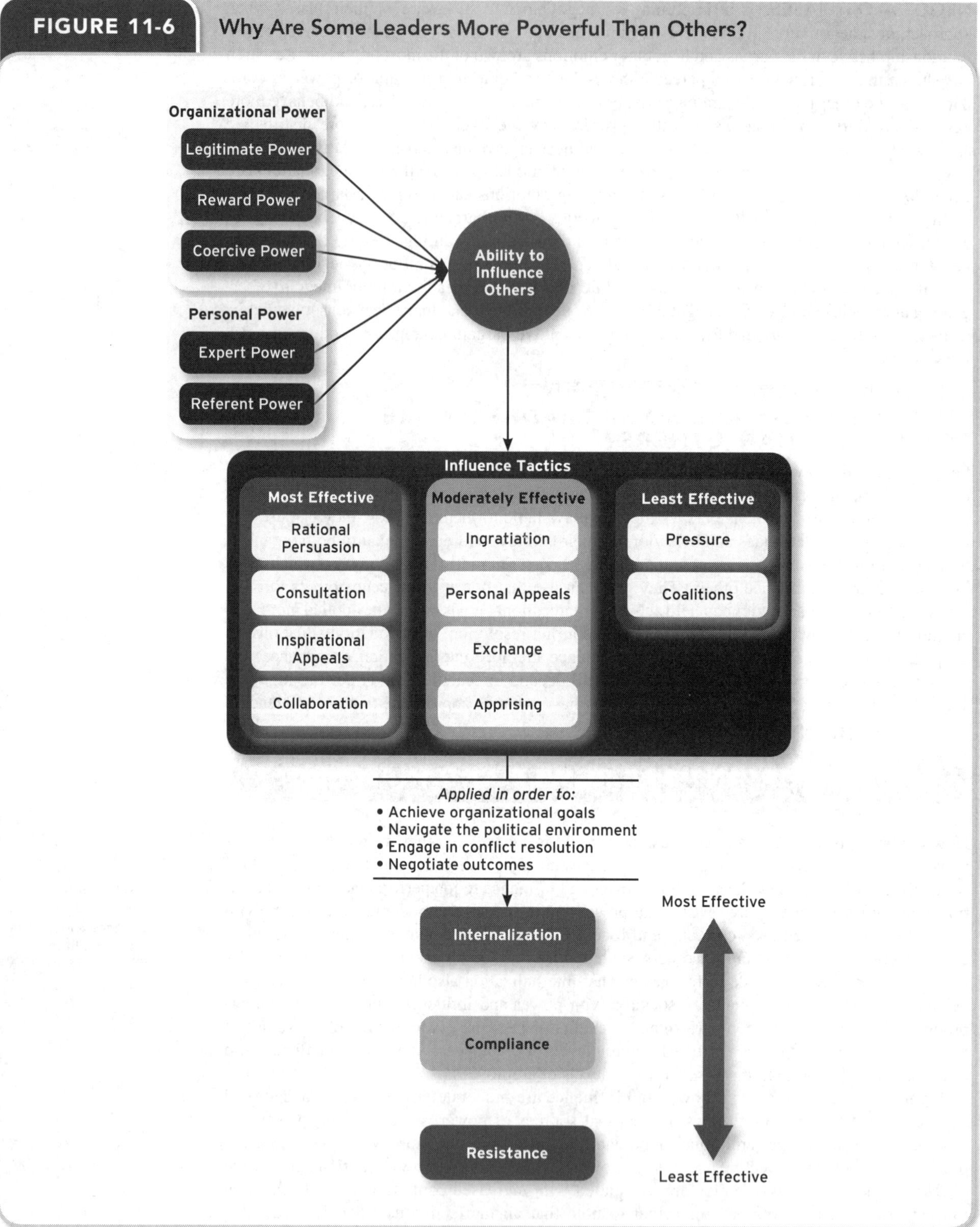

FIGURE 11-7 Effects of Power and Influence on Performance & Commitment

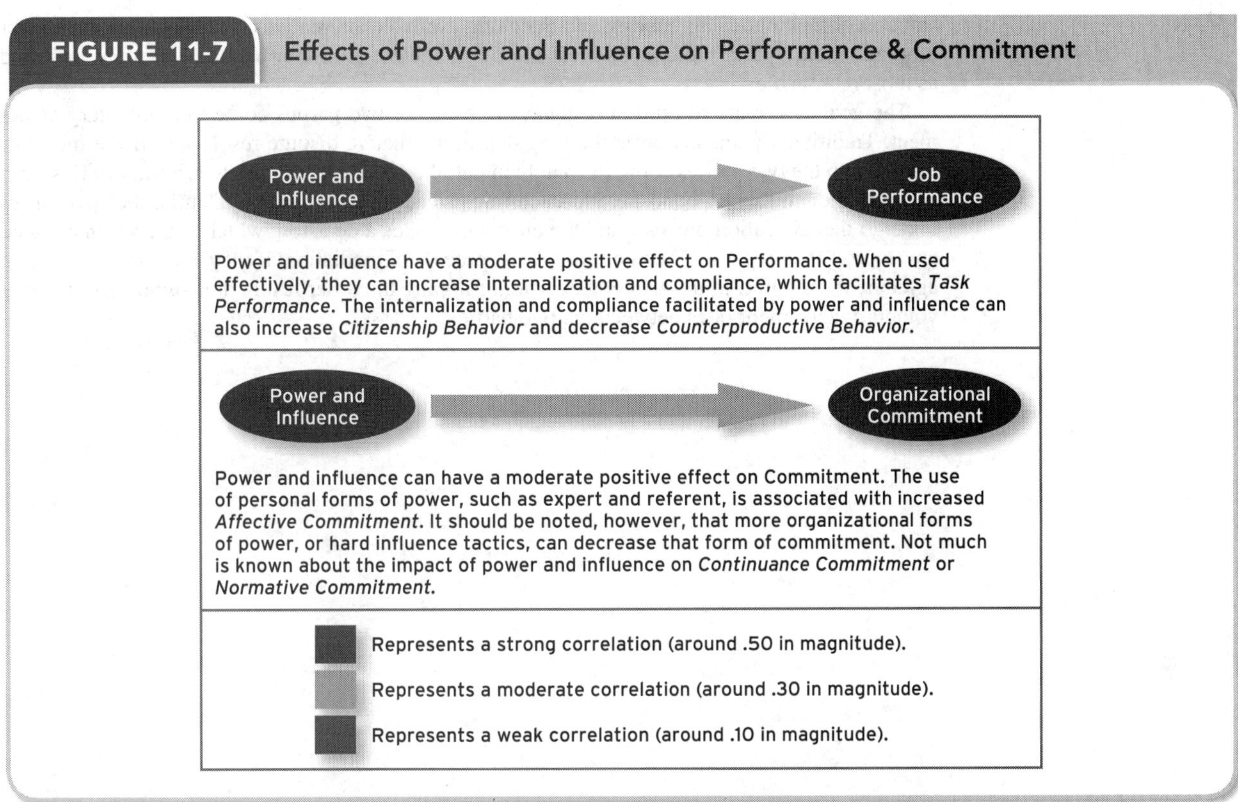

Sources: R.T. Sparrowe, B.W. Soetjipto, and M.L. Kraimer, "Do Leaders' Influence Tactics Relate to Members' Helping Behavior? It Depends on the Quality of the Relationship," *Academy of Management Journal* 49 (2006), pp. 1194–1208; G. Yukl, H. Kim, and C.M. Falbe, "Antecedents of Influence Outcomes," *Journal of Applied Psychology* 81 (1996), pp. 309–17; and P.P. Carson, K.D. Carson, and C.W. Rowe, "Social Power Bases: A Meta-Analytic Examination of Interrelationships and Outcomes," *Journal of Applied Social Psychology* 23 (1993), pp. 1150–69.

应用：其他冲突解决机制

APPLICATION: ALTERNATIVE DISPUTE RESOLUTION

There is always the possibility that, despite a leader's best effort, negotiations and/or conflict management will result in an impasse between two parties. In many organizations, disputes that might escalate into actual legal battles are settled through alternative dispute resolution. **Alternative dispute resolution** is a process by which two parties resolve conflicts through the use of a specially trained, neutral third party. There are various types of alternative dispute resolution that offer each party more or less control over the outcomes in question. Which types of resolution are chosen are generally a function of time pressures, dispute intensity, and the type of conflict involved. Two of the most common forms are mediation and arbitration.

非诉讼解决机制指双方通过经专门训练的、中立的第三方来调解冲突的过程。

Mediation requires a third party to facilitate the dispute resolution process, though this third party has no formal authority to dictate a solution. In essence, a mediator plays the role of a neutral, objective party who listens to the arguments of each side and attempts to help two parties come to an agreement. In serious, potentially litigious situations, trained mediators offer a relatively easy and quick way out of difficult disputes. A more definite form of alternative resolution is the process of arbitration. **Arbitration** occurs when a third party determines a binding settlement to a dispute. The arbitrator can be an individual or a group (board) whose job is to listen to the various arguments and then make a decision about the solution to the conflict. In some ways, arbitration is much riskier for both parties, because the outcome of the dispute rests solely in the arbitrator's hands. The arbitrator's role isn't to make everyone happy but rather to arrive at the most equitable solution in his or her opinion. In conventional arbitrations, arbitrators can create a

调解指双方需要第三方来推动争端解决的过程，但第三方并没有正式的权威进行强制解决。

仲裁指第三方确定一个约束性的解决争端的方案。仲裁者可以是个人或群体（委员会），其工作职责是听取双方不同的争论，并提出冲突解决方案。

solution of their choosing, mixing and matching available alternatives. In contrast, in final-offer arbitration, each party presents its most fair offer, and the arbitrator chooses the offer identified as most reasonable.

The goal of dispute resolution is always to have the two parties come to a voluntary agreement. Traditionally, mediation is the first step in alternative dispute resolution; if the mediator cannot help the two parties come to an agreement, the process continues to arbitration. Research suggests though that an opposite approach might lead to better results. That is, the two parties undergo the arbitration process, and the arbitrator makes a decision, which is placed in a sealed envelope. The two parties then go through the process of mediation; if they still can't come to an agreement, they turn to the arbiter's decision. Flipping the order resulted in significantly higher voluntary agreement rates between the two parties.

chapter 12

Leadership: Styles and Behaviors

领导：风格与行为

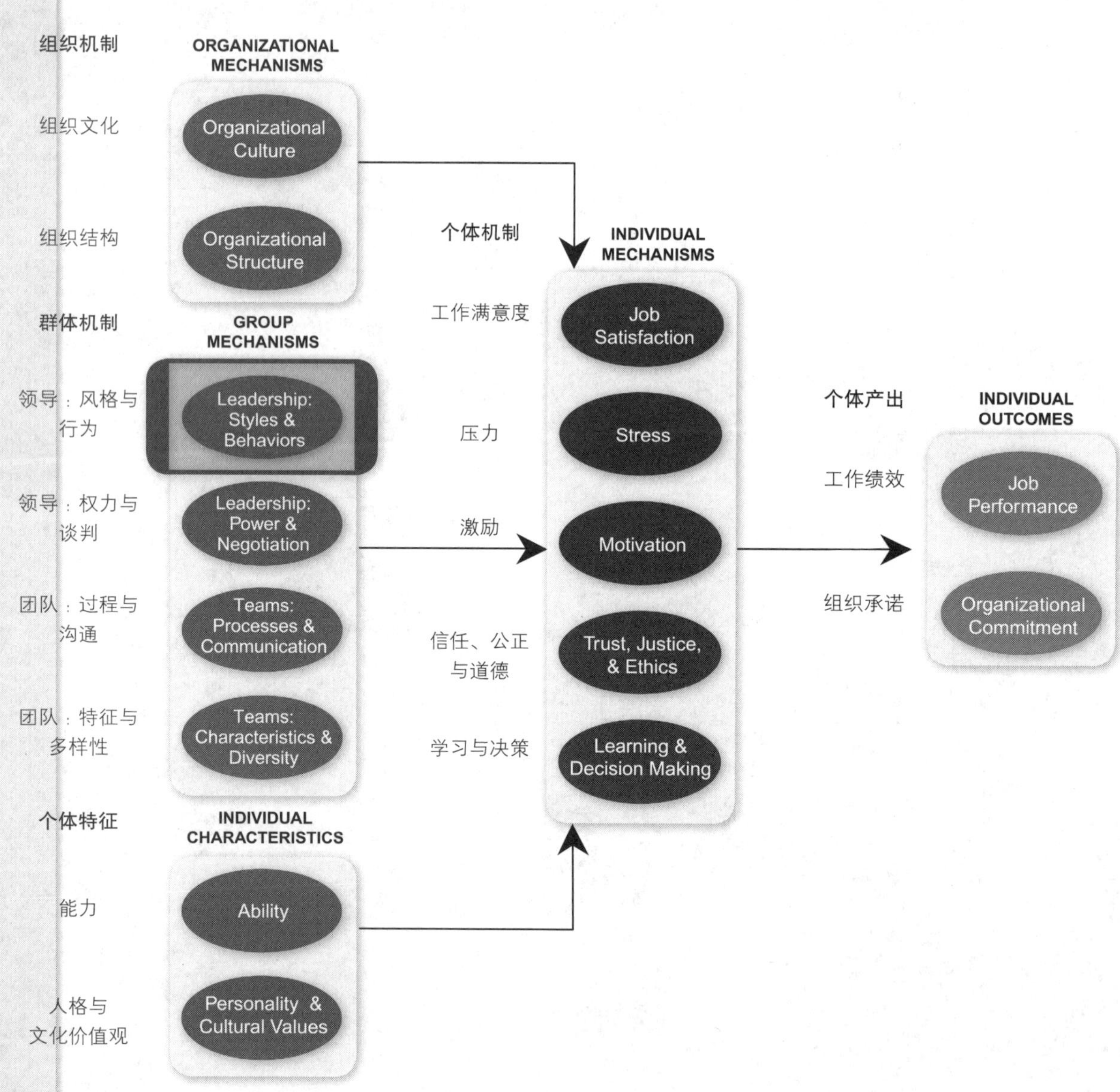

LEARNING GOALS

After reading this chapter, you should be able to answer the following questions:

12.1 What is leadership and what does it mean for a leader to be "effective"?

12.2 What traits and characteristics are related to leader emergence and leader effectiveness?

12.3 What four styles can leaders use to make decisions, and what factors combine to make these styles more effective in a given situation?

12.4 What two dimensions capture most of the day-to-day leadership behaviors in which leaders engage?

12.5 How does transformational leadership differ from transactional leadership, and which behaviors set it apart?

12.6 How does leadership affect job performance and organizational commitment?

12.7 Can leaders be trained to be more effective?

VIRGIN GROUP

It's somewhat difficult to describe exactly what the Virgin Group is. Officially, it would best be classified as a venture capital organization. It is a conglomerate of well over 300 companies all bearing the Virgin brand and dealing with businesses such as mobile telephones, transportation, travel, financial services, media, music, fitness, and even space travel. Virgin companies employ 50,000 workers in 30 countries and bring in an estimated $18 billion in revenue a year. The remarkable thing is that each of those 50,000 employees are just as likely to tell you that they "work for Richard" as they are to tell you they work at Virgin. Richard, of course, is Sir Richard Branson (yes, he has been knighted) who just spent his 60th birthday trying to break a speed record by "kiteboarding" across the English Channel. Depending on how old you are, you might also remember Branson attempting to break records by speed-sailing across the Atlantic ocean and trying to fly around the world (literally) in a hot air balloon. While these stunts gather much publicity for the Virgin brand, you are just as likely to see Branson aboard a Virgin Atlantic flight serving drinks to passengers and leading games over the public address system.

Branson (worth an estimated $4.2 billion) founded Virgin as a mail-order phonograph record retailer and has helped build the company into one of the most recognizable global brands. Known as one of the most charismatic corporate executives in the world—he has also been described as a "coaching leader" and a "nurturing leader." Branson realizes that his role as a leader at Virgin has changed over time. He states, "For as much as you need a strong personality to build a business from scratch, you must also understand the art of delegation. I have to be willing to step back now. I have to be good at helping people run the individual businesses—it can't be just me that sets the culture when we recruit people. The company must be set up so it can run without me."

Branson is known for creating far-reaching visions for the Virgin Group and inspiring employees to do what they can to help the company meet those visions. He is a leader who has proven to have the ability to change his style to match the situation he finds himself in. Branson surrounds himself with complementary employees and gives them lots of leeway in terms of doing their job or running their company. Still, that doesn't keep him from going his own way every now and then. Branson states, "Before I do anything, I first get tons of feedback. But sometimes I still say 'screw it' even if everybody thinks I'm mad."

领导：风格与行为

LEADERSHIP: STYLES AND BEHAVIORS

12.1 What is leadership and what does it mean for a leader to be "effective"?

领导是指运用权力与影响力指挥下属的活动，从而实现目标。

This is the second of two chapters on **leadership,** defined as the use of power and influence to direct the activities of followers toward goal achievement. That direction can affect followers' interpretation of events, the organization of their work activities, their commitment to key goals, their relationships with other followers, or their access to cooperation and support from other work units. The last chapter described how leaders *get* the power and influence needed to direct others. In the case of Sir Richard Branson, his power derives from his formal role as Virgin's chairman, his expertise and success in starting multiple businesses, and his charisma. This chapter describes how leaders actually *use* their power and influence in an effective way. From the very beginning of Virgin when he opened his first store, Branson has been adept at recognizing business opportunities and making money by serving customers in unique ways.

Of course, most leaders can't judge their performance by pointing to the number of companies they have created. Fortunately, leader effectiveness can be gauged in a number of ways. Leaders might be judged by objective evaluations of unit performance, such as profit margins, market share, sales, returns on investment, productivity, quality, costs in relation to budgeted expenditures, and so forth. If those sorts of indices are unavailable, the leader's superiors may judge the performance of the unit on a more subjective basis. Other approaches to judging leader effectiveness center more on followers, including indices such as absenteeism, retention of talented employees, grievances filed, requests for transfer, and so forth. Those sorts of indices can be complemented by employee surveys that assess the perceived performance of the leader, the perceived respect and legitimacy of the leader, and employee commitment, satisfaction, and psychological well-being. The top panel of Table 12-1 provides one example of these sorts of measures.

TABLE 12-1 Employee-Centered Measures of Leader Effectiveness

Unit-Focused Approach
Ask all members of the unit to fill out the following survey items, then average the responses across the group to get a measure of leader effectiveness.
1. My supervisor is effective in meeting our job-related needs.
2. My supervisor uses methods of leadership that are satisfying.
3. My supervisor gets us to do more than we expected to do.
4. My supervisor is effective in representing us to higher authority.
5. My supervisor works with us in a satisfactory way.
6. My supervisor heightens our desire to succeed.
7. My supervisor is effective in meeting organizational requirements.
8. My supervisor increases our willingness to try harder.
9. My supervisor leads a group that is effective.
Dyad-Focused Approach
Ask members of the unit to fill out the following survey items in reference to their particular relationship with the leader. The responses are not averaged across the group; rather, differences across people indicate differentiation into "ingroups" and "outgroups" within the unit.
1. I always know how satisfied my supervisor is with what I do.
2. My supervisor understands my problems and needs well enough.
3. My supervisor recognizes my potential.
4. My supervisor would use his/her power to help me solve work problems.
5. I can count on my supervisor to 'bail me out' at his/her expense if I need it.
6. My working relationship with my supervisor is extremely effective.
7. I have enough confidence in my supervisor to defend and justify his/her decisions when he/she is not present to do so.

Sources: Adapted from B. Bass and B. Avolio, *MLQ Manual* (Menlo Park, CA: Mind Garden, Inc., 2004); and G.B. Graen and M. Uhl-Bien, "Relationship-Based Approach to Leadership: Development of Leader–Member Exchange (LMX) Theory of Leadership over 25 Years: Applying a Multi-Level Multi-Domain Perspective," *Leadership Quarterly* 6 (1995), pp. 219–47.

One source of complexity when judging leader effectiveness, particularly with more subjective, employee-centered approaches, is "Whom do you ask?" The members of a given unit often disagree about how effective their leader is. **Leader–member exchange theory,** which describes how leader–member relationships develop over time on a dyadic basis, can explain why those differences exist. The theory argues that new leader–member relationships are typically marked by a **role taking** phase, during which a manager describes role expectations to an employee and the employee attempts to fulfill those expectations with his or her job behaviors. In this period of sampling and experimentation, the leader tries to get a feel for the talent and motivation levels of the employee. For some employees, that initial role taking phase may eventually be supplemented by **role making,** during which the employee's own expectations for the dyad get mixed in with those of the leader. The role making process is marked by a free-flowing exchange in which the leader offers more opportunities and resources and the employee contributes more activities and effort.

领导－成员交换理论描述了领导者与下属双方经过一段时间形成的关系。

在**角色承担**阶段，管理者向员工描述角色期望，员工以其工作行为实现期望。

在**角色形成**阶段，员工自身对双方关系的预期与领导者对双方关系的预期混合在一起。

FIGURE 12-1 Leader–Member Exchange Theory

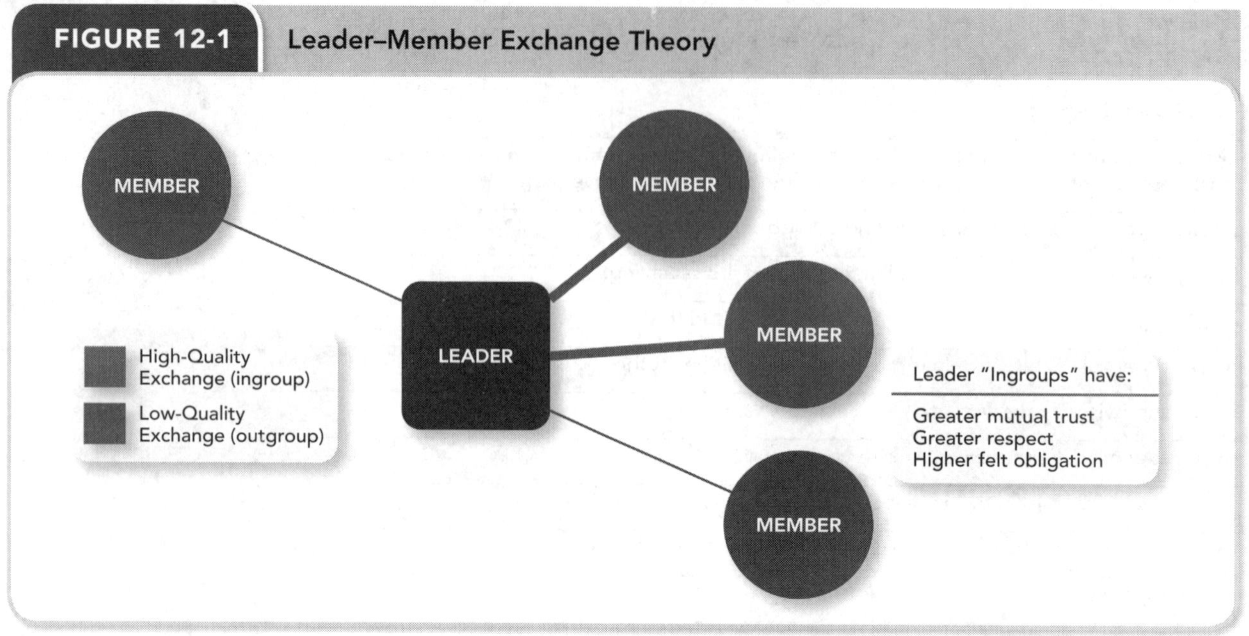

Over time, the role taking and role making processes result in two general types of leader–member dyads, as shown in Figure 12-1. One type is the "high-quality exchange" dyad, marked by the frequent exchange of information, influence, latitude, support, and attention. Those dyads form the leader's "ingroup" and are characterized by higher levels of mutual trust, respect, and obligation. The other type is the "low-quality exchange" dyad, marked by a more limited exchange of information, influence, latitude, support, and attention. Those dyads form the leader's "outgroup" and are characterized by lower levels of trust, respect, and obligation. Tests of the theory suggest that employees who are competent, likable, and similar to the leader in personality will be more likely to end up in the leader's ingroup; those factors have even greater impact than age, gender, or racial similarity. These ingroup relationships can be very powerful attachments for some workers. Research suggests that employees are less likely to leave an organization when they have a high LMX relationship with a specific leader, but they are more likely to leave following a leadership succession. Leader–member exchange theory also suggests that judgments of leader effectiveness should gauge how effective the most critical leader–member dyads appear to be. The bottom panel of Table 12-1 provides one example of this sort of measure, with more agreement indicating a higher-quality exchange relationship and thus higher levels of leader effectiveness on a dyadic basis. A recent meta-analysis found that employees who have higher-quality exchange relationships are more likely to exhibit organizational citizenship behaviors.

为什么某些领导者比其他领导者更有效

WHY ARE SOME LEADERS MORE EFFECTIVE THAN OTHERS?

领导者的有效性是指领导者的行为影响单位实现目标、员工持续性承诺以及领导—成员双方的相互信任、尊重和义务建立的程度。

For our purposes, **leader effectiveness** will be defined as the degree to which the leader's actions result in the achievement of the unit's goals, the continued commitment of the unit's employees, and the development of mutual trust, respect, and obligation in leader–member dyads. Now that we've described what it means for a leader to be effective, we turn to the critical question in this chapter: "Why are some leaders more effective than others?" That is, why exactly are some leaders viewed as more effective on a unitwide basis, and why exactly are some leaders better at fostering high-quality exchange relationships? Beginning as far back as 1904, research on leadership has attempted to answer such questions by looking for particular traits or characteristics

TABLE 12-2 Traits/Characteristics Related to Leader Emergence and Effectiveness

DESCRIPTION OF TRAIT/ CHARACTERISTIC	LINKED TO EMERGENCE?	LINKED TO EFFECTIVENESS?
High conscientiousness	√	
Low agreeableness	√	
Low neuroticism		
High openness to experience	√	√
High extraversion	√	√
High general cognitive ability	√	√
High energy level	√	√
High stress tolerance	√	√
High self-confidence	√	√

Sources: Adapted from T.A. Judge, J.E. Bono, R. Ilies, and M.W. Gerhardt, "Personality and Leadership: A Qualitative and Quantitative Review," *Journal of Applied Psychology* 87 (2002), pp. 765–80; T.A. Judge, A.E. Colbert, and R. Ilies, "Intelligence and Leadership: A Quantitative Review and Test of Theoretical Propositions," *Journal of Applied Psychology* 89 (2004), pp. 542–52; and G. Yukl, *Leadership in Organizations,* 4th ed. (Englewood Cliffs, NJ: Prentice-Hall, 1998).

of effective leaders. The search for traits and characteristics is consistent with "great person" theories of leadership that suggest that "leaders are born, not made." Early research in this area frequently focused on physical features (e.g., gender, height, physical attractiveness, energy level), whereas subsequent research focused more squarely on personality and ability (see Chapter 7 on Personality and Cultural Values and Chapter 8 on Ability for more discussion of such issues).

After a century of research, leadership scholars now acknowledge that there is no generalizable profile of effective leaders from a trait perspective. In fact, most studies have concluded that traits are more predictive of **leader emergence** (i.e., who becomes a leader in the first place) than they are of leader effectiveness (i.e., how well people actually do in a leadership role). Table 12-2 reviews some of the traits and characteristics that have been found to be correlated with leader emergence and leader effectiveness. Although a number of traits and characteristics are relevant to leadership, two limitations of this work have caused leadership research to move in a different direction. First, many of the trait–leadership correlations are weak in magnitude, particularly when leader effectiveness serves as the outcome. Second, the focus on leader traits holds less practical relevance than a focus on leader actions. Although research shows that traits can seemingly have an effect on leader effectiveness, these effects are generally explained much more strongly by leader behavior. What exactly can leaders *do* that can make them more effective? This chapter reviews three types of leader actions: decision-making styles, day-to-day behaviors, and behaviors that fall outside of a leader's typical duties.

12.2
What traits and characteristics are related to leader emergence and leader effectiveness?

领导者诞生是指谁首先成为领导者的过程。

领导者的决策风格
LEADER DECISION-MAKING STYLES

Of course, one of the most important things leaders do is make decisions. Think about the job you currently hold or the last job you had. Now picture your boss. How many decisions did he or she have to make in a given week? How did he or she go about making those decisions? A leader's decision-making style reflects the process the leader uses to generate and choose from a set of alternatives to solve a problem. Decision-making styles capture *how* a leader decides as opposed to *what* a leader decides.

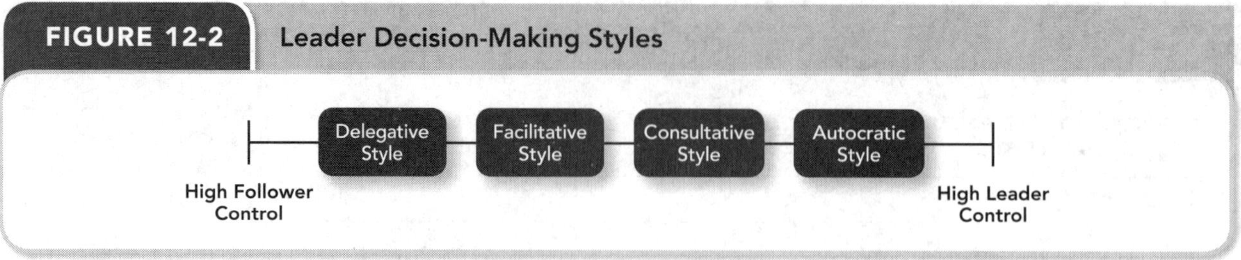

12.3

What four styles can leaders use to make decisions, and what factors combine to make these styles more effective in a given situation?

The most important element of a leader's decision-making style is this: Does the leader decide most things for him- or herself, or does the leader involve others in the process? We've probably all had bosses (or professors, or even parents) who made virtually all decisions by themselves, stopping by to announce what had happened once the call had been made. We've probably also had other bosses (or professors, or parents) who tended to do the opposite—involving us, asking our opinions, or seeking our vote even when we didn't care about what was being discussed. It turns out that this issue of leader versus follower control can be used to define some specific decision-making styles. Figure 12-2 shows those styles, arranged on a continuum from high follower control to high leader control.

独裁式风格是指领导者不征询工作单位中员工的看法和意见而独自做出决策。

DEFINING THE STYLES. With an **autocratic style,** the leader makes the decision alone without asking for the opinions or suggestions of the employees in the work unit. The employees may provide information that the leader needs but are not asked to generate or evaluate potential solutions. In fact, they may not even be told about the decision that needs to be made, knowing only that the leader wants information for some reason. This decision-making style seems to be a favorite of Fiat-Chrysler CEO Sergio Marchionne, who is doing his best to make sure decisions are made extraordinarily quickly at Chrysler—and he's doing that by making them himself. Marchionne has flattened Chrysler's organizational chart with him at the top and has 25 direct reports (not counting 21 at Fiat). One might think this would cause a major bottleneck with regard to decisions, but Marchionne swears that speed is the only thing that will save Chrysler at this point and he is always within reach through the use of one of his six BlackBerrys. Marchionne says, "BlackBerrys are divine instruments. They [his direct reports] have access to me 24/7." The CEO is known for making decisions within minutes, or seconds.

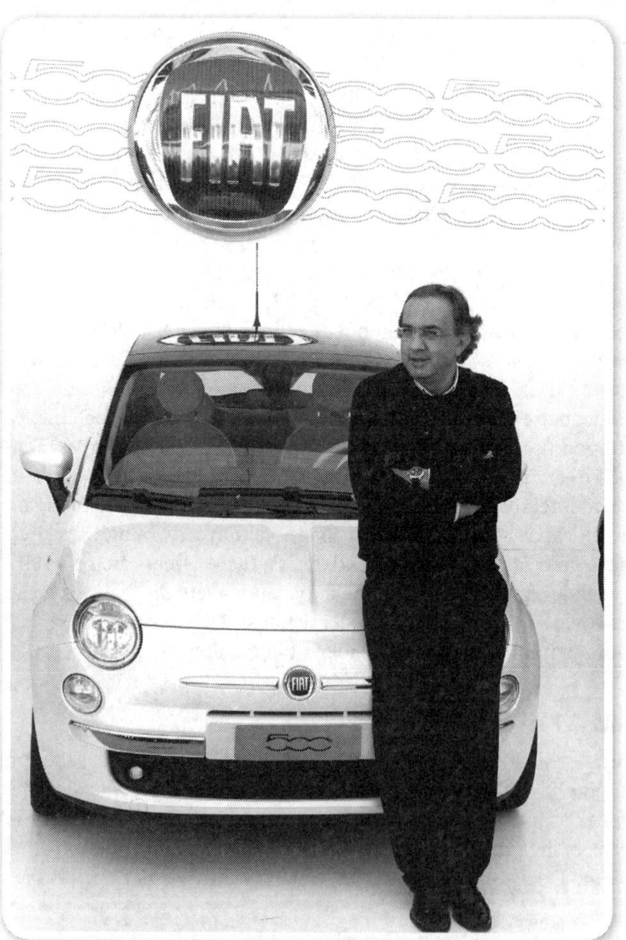

Sergio Marchionne, CEO of Fiat-Chrysler, is known for his autocratic and speedy decision-making style.

The next two styles in Figure 12-2 offer more employee involvement. With a **consultative style,** the leader presents the problem to individual employees or a group of employees, asking for their opinions and suggestions before ultimately making the decision him- or herself. With this style, employees do "have a say" in the process, but the ultimate authority still rests with the leader. That ultimate authority changes with a **facilitative style,** in which the leader presents the problem to a group of employees and seeks consensus on a solution, making sure that his or her own opinion receives no more weight than anyone else's. With this style, the leader is more facilitator than decision maker. Robert W. Selander, executive vice-chairman of MasterCard, said he had learned over time to encourage discussion in a group. "From sort of a style standpoint, I prefer to do what I call more of a consensus style of decision-making," he said. "So when I'm around the table with our executive committee, the senior leadership of the company, I could easily make a bilateral decision. You're knowledgeable about your area. I may have the best knowledge about your area or second best around the table. You and I agree. Let's get on with it. What we haven't done is we haven't benefited from the wisdom, the insight, and the experience of the others around the table. And while they may not have as much insight or knowledge about your area as you do, there's a chance that we missed something. So I try to get more engagement and discussion around topics and avoid what I would call bilateralism. I think what happens is sometimes you get an insight that's startling and important and affects the decision, but you also get participative involvement so that there is buy-in and a recognition of how we got to that decision. It's not as if the boss went off in a corner and waved a magic wand and, bang, out came the decision."

协商式风格是指领导者在最终做出决策前，将问题提交给每位员工或员工群体，并询问他们的想法与意见。

促进式风格是指领导者向员工群体提出问题，并寻求一致的解决方案，同时确保领导者个人的意见权重不会超过其他任何人。

With a **delegative style,** the leader gives an individual employee or a group of employees the responsibility for making the decision within some set of specified boundary conditions. The leader plays no role in the deliberations unless asked, though he or she may offer encouragement and provide necessary resources behind the scenes. "I think the most difficult transition for anybody from being a worker bee to a manager is this issue of delegation," says Tachi Yamada, the president of the Bill and Melinda Gates Foundation's Global Health Program. "What do you give up? How can you have the team do what you would do yourself without your doing it? If you're a true micromanager and you basically stand over everybody and guide their hands to do everything, you don't have enough hours in the day to do what the whole team needs to do." Daniel Amos, CEO and chairman of Aflac, also believes strongly in a delegative style. He says, "My theory is that when you start telling people what to do, they no longer are responsible; you are. I'll give them my opinion and say; 'Look, this is my opinion, but if you choose that and you fail, you're not blaming it on me. It is your fault.' I think it makes them stronger."

授权式风格是指领导者赋予个体员工或员工群体在某些特定条件下做出决策的责任。

WHEN ARE THE STYLES MOST EFFECTIVE? Which decision-making style is best? As you may have guessed, there is no one decision-making style that's effective across all situations, and all styles have their pluses and minuses. There are many factors to consider when leaders choose a decision-making style. The most obvious consideration is the quality of the resulting decision, because making the correct decision is the ultimate means of judging the leader. However, leaders also have to consider whether employees will accept and commit to their decision. Research studies have repeatedly shown that allowing employees to participate in decision making increases their job satisfaction. Such participation also helps develop employees' own decision-making skills.

Of course, such participation has a downside for employees because it takes up time. Many employees view meetings as an interruption of their work. One recent study found that employees spend, on average, six hours a week in scheduled meetings and that time spent in meetings relates negatively to job satisfaction when employees don't depend on others in their jobs, focus on their own task accomplishment, and believe meetings are run ineffectively. Diane Bryant, CIO at Intel, argues that "You need people who are critical to making the decisions on the agenda, not people who are there only because they'll be impacted. At Intel, if we see someone who doesn't need to be there, people will say, 'Bob, I don't think we need you here. Thanks for coming.'" Similarly, executives at GM are trying to change the slow bureaucratic culture that has hampered the automaker for decades—the company is known for decisions having to be made by committee. Once, they even appointed a committee to take a look at how many committee meetings should be held!

How can leaders effectively manage their choice of decision-making styles? The **time-driven model of leadership** offers one potential guide. It suggests that the focus should shift away

领导时间驱动模型表明，关注的焦点应从独裁式、协商式、促进式、授权式的领导者转向独裁式、协商式、促进式、授权式的情境。

from autocratic, consultative, facilitative, and delegative *leaders* to autocratic, consultative, facilitative, and delegative *situations.* More specifically, the model suggests that seven factors combine to make some decision-making styles more effective in a given situation and other styles less effective. Those seven factors include:

- *Decision significance:* Is the decision significant to the success of the project or the organization?
- *Importance of commitment:* Is it important that employees "buy in" to the decision?
- *Leader expertise:* Does the leader have significant knowledge or expertise regarding the problem?
- *Likelihood of commitment:* How likely is it that employees will trust the leader's decision and commit to it?
- *Shared objectives:* Do employees share and support the same objectives, or do they have an agenda of their own?
- *Employee expertise:* Do the employees have significant knowledge or expertise regarding the problem?
- *Teamwork skills:* Do the employees have the ability to work together to solve the problem, or will they struggle with conflicts or inefficiencies?

Figure 12-3 illustrates how these seven factors can be used to determine the most effective decision-making style in a given situation. The figure asks whether the levels of each of the seven factors are high (H) or low (L). The figure functions like a funnel, moving from left to right, with each answer taking you closer to the recommended style (dashes mean that a given factor can be

FIGURE 12-3 The Time-Driven Model of Leadership

<table>
<tr><th></th><th>Decision Significance</th><th>Importance of Commitment</th><th>Leader Expertise</th><th>Likelihood of Commitment</th><th>Shared Objectives</th><th>Employee Expertise</th><th>Teamwork Skills</th><th></th><th></th></tr>
<tr><td rowspan="22">START HERE</td><td rowspan="18">H</td><td rowspan="13">H</td><td rowspan="5">H</td><td>H</td><td>-</td><td>-</td><td>-</td><td>Autocratic</td><td rowspan="22">END HERE</td></tr>
<tr><td rowspan="4">L</td><td rowspan="3">H</td><td rowspan="2">H</td><td>H</td><td>Delegative</td></tr>
<tr><td>L</td><td rowspan="3">Consultative</td></tr>
<tr><td>L</td><td>-</td></tr>
<tr><td>L</td><td>-</td><td>-</td></tr>
<tr><td rowspan="8">L</td><td rowspan="4">H</td><td rowspan="3">H</td><td rowspan="2">H</td><td>H</td><td>Facilitative</td></tr>
<tr><td>L</td><td rowspan="3">Consultative</td></tr>
<tr><td>L</td><td>-</td></tr>
<tr><td>L</td><td>-</td><td>-</td></tr>
<tr><td rowspan="4">L</td><td rowspan="3">H</td><td rowspan="2">H</td><td>H</td><td>Facilitative</td></tr>
<tr><td>L</td><td rowspan="3">Consultative</td></tr>
<tr><td>L</td><td>-</td></tr>
<tr><td>L</td><td>-</td><td>-</td></tr>
<tr><td rowspan="5">L</td><td>H</td><td>-</td><td>-</td><td>-</td><td>-</td><td>Autocratic</td></tr>
<tr><td rowspan="4">L</td><td rowspan="4">-</td><td rowspan="3">H</td><td rowspan="2">H</td><td>H</td><td>Facilitative</td></tr>
<tr><td>L</td><td rowspan="3">Consultative</td></tr>
<tr><td>L</td><td>-</td></tr>
<tr><td>L</td><td>-</td><td>-</td></tr>
<tr><td rowspan="4">L</td><td rowspan="3">H</td><td rowspan="3">-</td><td>H</td><td>-</td><td>-</td><td>-</td><td>Autocratic</td></tr>
<tr><td rowspan="2">L</td><td rowspan="2">-</td><td rowspan="2">-</td><td>H</td><td>Delegative</td></tr>
<tr><td>L</td><td>Facilitative</td></tr>
<tr><td>L</td><td>-</td><td>-</td><td>-</td><td>-</td><td>-</td><td>Autocratic</td></tr>
</table>

Source: Adapted from V.H. Vroom, "Leadership and the Decision-Making Process," *Organizational Dynamics* 28 (2000), pp. 82–94.

skipped for that combination). Although the model seems complex at first glance, the principles within it are straightforward. Autocratic styles are reserved for decisions that are insignificant or for which employee commitment is unimportant. The only exception is when the leader's expertise is high and the leader is trusted. An autocratic style in these situations should result in an accurate decision that makes the most efficient use of employees' time. Delegative styles should be reserved for circumstances in which employees have strong teamwork skills and are not likely to commit blindly to whatever decision the leader provides. Deciding between the remaining two styles—consultative and facilitative—is more nuanced and requires a more complete consideration of all seven factors.

For our earlier example of Sergio Marchionne, decision significance is high, importance of commitment is low, and leader expertise is high, so he adopts an autocratic decision style. However, for Jack Griffin, CEO of Time Inc., autocratic decision making didn't seem to go over too well. Griffin became known within the company for his "imperious" decision-making behavior. For example, he insisted that every magazine include a masthead with his name at the top (an extra page that cost the company about $5 million a year) almost right after hundreds of employees were laid off—a decision that used to be left up to individual editors. A source within the company was quoted as saying "Time Inc. has long operated on the collegial consensus approach and I don't think that was Jack's strength." With magazine publishing operating during such a precarious time, we would label decision significance as high, importance of commitment as high, and the leader not appearing to have expertise in the subject matter of the decisions. As a result, his autocratic style led to a rebellion by those working for him and his termination only six months after his appointment. A key point about Figure 12-3 is that unless a leader is an expert with regard to the focus of the decision, autocratic decisions are not the right style to choose.

Research tends to support many of the time-driven model's propositions, particularly when it uses practicing managers as participants. For example, one study asked managers to recall past decisions, the context surrounding those decisions, and the eventual successes (or failures) of their decisions. When managers used the decision-making styles recommended by the model, those decisions were rated as successful 68 percent of the time. When managers went against the model's prescriptions, their decisions were only rated as successful 22 percent of the time. It's also interesting to note that studies suggest that managers tend to choose the style recommended by the model only around 40 percent of the time and exhibit less variation in styles than the model suggests they should. In particular, managers seem to overuse the consultative style and underutilize autocratic and facilitative styles. Sheila Lirio Marcelo, the CEO of Care.com, uses a unique approach by actually letting her staff know what type of decisions will be made prior to each meeting. "We do Type 1, Type 2, Type 3 decisions," she said. "Type 1 decisions are the decision-maker's sole decision—dictatorial [autocratic]. Type 2: people can provide input, and then the person can still make the decision [consultative]. Type 3, it's consensus [facilitative]. It's a great way to efficiently solve a problem."

日常的领导行为
DAY-TO-DAY LEADERSHIP BEHAVIORS

Leaving aside how they go about making decisions, what do leaders *do* on a day-to-day basis? When you think about bosses that you've had, what behaviors did they tend to perform as part of their daily leadership responsibilities? A series of studies at Ohio State in the 1950s attempted to answer that question. Working under grants from the Office of Naval Research and the International Harvester Company, the studies began by generating a list of all the behaviors leaders engage in—around 1,800 in all. Those behaviors were trimmed down to 150 specific examples, then grouped into several categories, as shown in Table 12-3. The table reveals that many leaders spend their time engaging in a mix of initiating, organizing, producing, socializing, integrating, communicating, recognizing, and representing behaviors. Although eight categories are easier to remember than 1,800 behaviors, further analyses suggested that the categories in Table 14-2 really boil down to just two dimensions: initiating structure and consideration.

结构维度反映了领导者界定与结构化员工角色以实现目标的程度。

12.4
What two dimensions capture most of the day-to-day leadership behaviors in which leaders engage?

Initiating structure reflects the extent to which the leader defines and structures the roles of employees in pursuit of goal attainment. Leaders who are high on initiating structure play a more active role in directing group activities and prioritize planning, scheduling, and trying out new ideas. They might emphasize the importance of meeting deadlines, describe explicit standards of performance, ask employees to follow formalized procedures, and criticize poor work

TABLE 12-3 Day-to-Day Behaviors Performed by Leaders

BEHAVIOR	DESCRIPTION
Initiating Structure	
Initiation	Originating, facilitating, and sometimes resisting new ideas and practices
Organization	Defining and structuring work, clarifying leader versus member roles, coordinating employee tasks
Production	Setting goals and providing incentives for the effort and productivity of employees
Consideration	
Membership	Mixing with employees, stressing informal interactions, and exchanging personal services
Integration	Encouraging a pleasant atmosphere, reducing conflict, promoting individual adjustment to the group
Communication	Providing information to employees, seeking information from them, showing an awareness of matters that affect them
Recognition	Expressing approval or disapproval of the behaviors of employees
Representation	Acting on behalf of the group, defending the group, and advancing the interests of the group

Source: R.M. Stogdill, Manual for the Leader Behavior Description Questionnaire-Form XII, Bureau of Business Research, The Ohio State University, 1963.

when necessary. Millard Drexler, CEO of J. Crew (the New York–based clothing retailer) has a unique initiating structure approach as he belts out instructions, assigns tasks, discusses clothing trends, and talks about sales statistics and goals about a dozen times a day over loudspeakers in the main Manhattan office. If he isn't in the office (and he often isn't), he has his assistant patch him in through his cell phone.

关怀维度反映了领导者建立与员工相互信任、尊重员工想法及考虑员工感受为特点的工作关系的程度。

Consideration reflects the extent to which leaders create job relationships characterized by mutual trust, respect for employee ideas, and consideration of employee feelings. Leaders who are high on consideration create a climate of good rapport and strong, two-way communication and exhibit a deep concern for the welfare of employees. They might do personal favors for employees, take time to listen to their problems, "go to bat" for them when needed, and treat them as equals. Jeff Immelt, CEO of General Electric, attempts to do this with many of the officers in his company by hosting a sleepover a couple of times a month. Immelt says, "We spend Saturday morning just talking about their careers. Who they are, how they fit, how I see their strengths and weaknesses—stuff like that. The personal connection is something I may have taken for granted before that I don't want to ever take for granted again."

The Ohio State studies argued that initiating structure and consideration were (more or less) independent concepts, meaning that leaders could be high on both, low on both, or high on one and low on the other. That view differed from a series of studies conducted at the University of Michigan during the same time period. Those studies identified concepts similar to initiating structure and consideration, calling them production-centered (or task-oriented) and employee-centered (or relations-oriented) behaviors. However, the Michigan studies framed their task-oriented and relations-oriented concepts as two ends of one continuum, implying that leaders couldn't be high on both dimensions. In fact, a recent meta-analysis of 78 studies showed that initiating

Jeff Immelt, CEO of General Electric, exhibits consideration by holding "sleepovers" with his officers to get to know them better.

structure and consideration are only weakly related—knowing whether a leader engages in one brand of behavior says little about whether he or she engages in the other brand. To see how much initiating structure and consideration you engage in during leadership roles, see our **OB Assessments** feature.

After an initial wave of research on initiating structure and consideration, leadership experts began to doubt the usefulness of the two dimensions for predicting leadership effectiveness. More recent research has painted a more encouraging picture, however. A meta-analysis of 103 studies showed that initiating structure and consideration both had beneficial relationships with a number of outcomes. For example, consideration had a strong positive relationship with perceived leader effectiveness, employee motivation, and employee job satisfaction. It also had a moderate positive relationship with overall unit performance. For its part, initiating structure had a strong positive relationship with employee motivation and moderate positive relationships with perceived leader effectiveness, employee job satisfaction, and overall unit performance. One of the most amusing and upbeat CEOs in the country, Panda Express's Andrew Cherng, agrees that both are important to a leader's success. Cherng states, "Before, we used to be more task-based, but now, if you want to be a manager at Panda, you have to be committed to being positive, to continuous learning."

Although initiating structure and consideration tend to be beneficial across situations, there may be circumstances in which they become more or less important. The **life cycle theory of leadership** (sometimes also called the *situational model of leadership*) argues that the optimal combination of initiating structure and consideration depends on the readiness of the employees in the work unit. **Readiness** is broadly defined as the degree to which employees have the ability and the willingness to accomplish their specific tasks. As shown in Figure 12-4, the theory suggests that readiness varies across employees and can be expressed in terms of four important snapshots: R1–R4. To find the optimal combination of leader behaviors for a particular readiness snapshot, put your finger on the relevant R, then move it straight down to the recommended combination of behaviors.

领导生命周期理论（有时也称为“情境领导理论”）认为结构维度和关怀维度的最优组合取决于工作单位中员工的意愿。

广义的**意愿**是指员工有能力并且愿意完成具体任务的程度。

The description of the first two R's has varied over time and across different formulations of the theory. One formulation described the R's as similar to stages of group development. R1 refers to a group of employees who are working together for the first time and are eager to begin, but they lack the experience and confidence needed to perform their roles. Here the optimal combination of leader behaviors is **telling**—high initiating structure and low consideration—in which case the leader provides specific instructions and closely supervises performance. The lion's share of the leader's attention must be devoted to directing followers in this situation, because their goals and roles need to be clearly defined. In the R2 stage, the members have begun working together and, as typically happens, are finding that their work is more difficult than they had anticipated. As eagerness turns to dissatisfaction, the optimal combination of leader behaviors is **selling**—high initiating structure and high consideration—in which the leader supplements his or her directing with support and encouragement to protect the confidence levels of the employees.

告知（高结构维度和低关怀维度）是指领导者给员工提供具体的指导并密切监督绩效。

推销（高结构维度和高关怀维度）是指领导者以支持和鼓励的形式对员工提供补充指导，以维护员工的自信水平。

As employees gain more ability, guidance and direction by the leader become less necessary. At the R3 stage, employees have learned to work together well, though they still need support and collaboration from the leader to help them adjust to their more self-managed state of affairs. Here **participating**—low initiating structure and high consideration—becomes the optimal combination of leader behaviors. Finally, the optimal combination for the R4 readiness level is **delegating**—low initiating structure and low consideration—such that the leader turns responsibility for key behaviors over to the employees. Here the leader gives them the proverbial

参与（低结构维度和高关怀维度）是领导行为的最优组合。

授权（低结构维度和低关怀维度）是指领导者把关键行为的责任移交给员工。

OB ASSESSMENTS

INITIATING STRUCTURE AND CONSIDERATION

How do you act when you're in a leadership role? This assessment is designed to measure initiating structure and consideration. Please write a number next to each statement that reflects how frequently you engage in the behavior described. Then subtract your answers to the boldfaced questions from 6, with the difference being your new answer for that question. For example, if your original answer for question 16 was "4," your new answer is "2" (6 – 4). Then sum up your answers for each of the dimensions. (For more assessments relevant to this chapter, please visit http://connect.mcgraw-hill.com.)

1 NEVER	2 SELDOM	3 OCCASIONALLY	4 OFTEN	5 ALWAYS

1. I let group members know what is expected of them. _______
2. I encourage the use of uniform procedures. _______
3. I try out my ideas in the group. _______
4. I make my attitudes clear to the group. _______
5. I decide what shall be done and how it shall be done. _______
6. I assign group members to particular tasks. _______
7. I make sure that my part in the group is understood by the group members. _______
8. I schedule the work to be done. _______
9. I maintain definite standards of performance. _______
10. I ask group members to follow standard rules and regulations. _______
11. I am friendly and approachable. _______
12. I do little things to make it pleasant to be a member of the group. _______
13. I put suggestions made by the group into operation. _______
14. I treat all group members as equals. _______
15. I give advance notice of changes. _______
16. **I keep to myself.** _______
17. I look out for the personal welfare of group members. _______
18. I am willing to make changes. _______
19. **I refuse to explain my actions.** _______
20. **I act without consulting the group.** _______

SCORING AND INTERPRETATION:

Initiating Structure: Sum up items 1–10. _______

Consideration: Sum up items 11–20. _______

For initiating structure, scores of 38 or more are high. For consideration, scores of 40 or more are high.

Source: R.M. Stogdill, *Manual for the Leader Behavior Description Questionnaire–Form XII* (Columbus, OH: Bureau of Business Research, The Ohio State University, 1963).

FIGURE 12-4 The Life Cycle Theory of Leadership

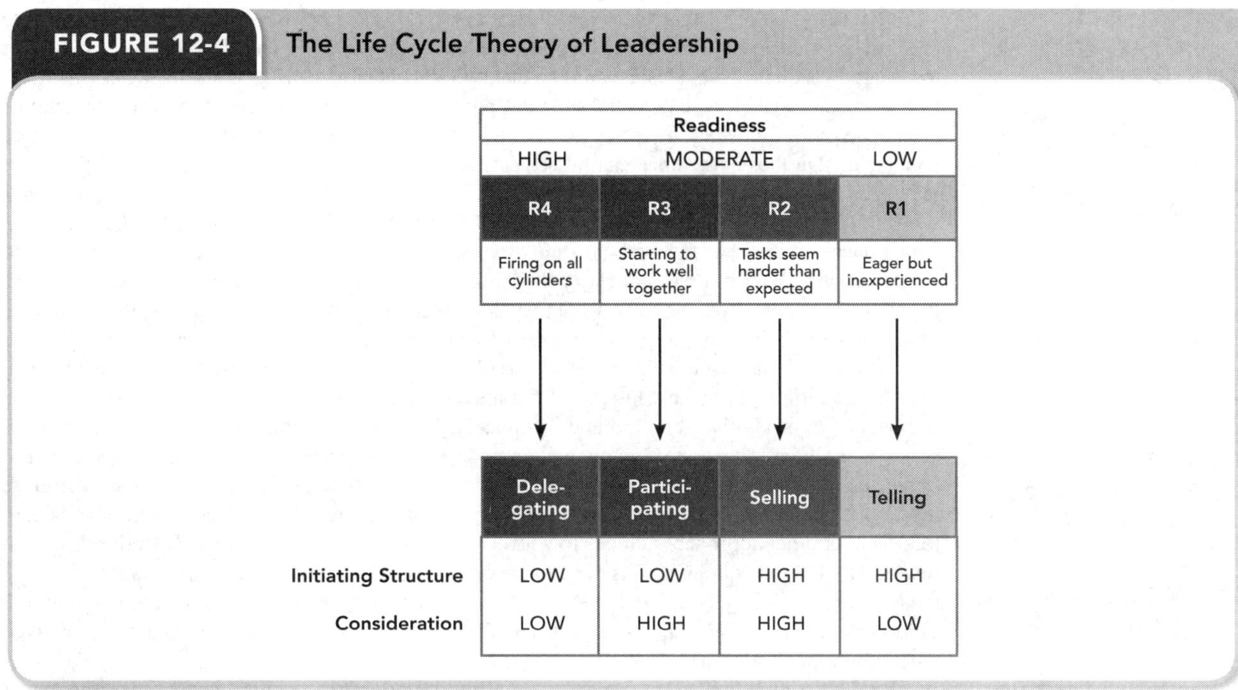

Source: Adapted from P. Hersey and K. Blanchard, "Revisiting the Life-Cycle Theory of Leadership." *Training and Development* January 1996, pp. 42–47.

ball and lets them run with it. All that's needed from the leader is some degree of observation and monitoring to make sure that the group's efforts stay on track.

Estimates suggest that the life cycle theory has been incorporated into leadership training programs at around 400 of the firms in the *Fortune* 500, with more than one million managers exposed to it annually. Unfortunately, the application of the theory has outpaced scientific testing of its propositions, and the shifting nature of its terminology and predictions has made scientific testing somewhat difficult. The research that has been conducted supports the theory's predictions only for low readiness situations, suggesting that telling and selling sorts of behaviors may be more effective when ability, motivation, or confidence are lacking. When readiness is higher, these tests suggest that leader behaviors simply matter less, regardless of their particular combinations. Tests also suggest that leaders only use the recommended combinations of behaviors between 14 and 37 percent of the time, likely because many leaders adhere to the same leadership philosophy regardless of the situation. It should also be noted that tests of the theory have been somewhat more supportive when conducted on an across-job, rather than within-job, basis. For example, research suggests that the performance of lower ranking university employees (e.g., maintenance workers, custodians, landscapers) depends more on initiating structure and less on consideration than the performance of higher ranking university employees (e.g., professors, instructors).

转化型领导行为
TRANSFORMATIONAL LEADERSHIP BEHAVIORS

By describing decision-making styles and day-to-day leader behaviors, we've covered a broad spectrum of what it is that leaders do. Still, something is missing. Take a small piece of scrap paper and jot down five people who are famous for their effective leadership. They can come from inside or outside the business world and can be either living people or historical figures. All that's important is that their name be practically synonymous with great leadership. Once you've compiled your list, take a look at the names. Do they appear on your list because they tend to use the right decision-making styles in the right situations and engage in effective levels of consideration and initiating structure? What about the case of Richard Branson? Do decision-making styles and day-to-day leadership behaviors explain his importance to the fortunes of Virgin?

转化型领导包括激发下属承诺对他们工作有意义的共同愿景，同时也发挥角色榜样的作用，帮助下属开发潜能并从不同的角度观察问题。

The missing piece of this leadership puzzle is what leaders do to motivate their employees to perform beyond expectations. **Transformational leadership** involves inspiring followers to commit to a shared vision that provides meaning to their work while also serving as a role model who helps followers develop their own potential and view problems from new perspectives. Transformational leaders heighten followers' awareness of the importance of certain outcomes while increasing their confidence that those outcomes can be achieved. What gets "transformed" is the way followers view their work, causing them to focus on the collective good more than just their own short-term self-interests and to perform beyond expectations as a result. Former President Dwight D. Eisenhower once noted, "Leadership is the ability to decide what is to be done, and then to get others to want to do it." Former President Harry S. Truman similarly observed, "A leader is a man who has the ability to get other people to do what they don't want to do, and like it." Both quotes capture a transformation in the way followers view their work and what motivates them on the job.

自由放任型领导表现为推迟重要行动、忽略责任、权力和影响力未得到有效利用。

交易型领导是指领导者依据下属的绩效来奖励或惩罚下属。

消极的例外管理是指领导者等待错误与过失发生后才采取必要的纠正行动。

积极的例外管理是指领导者积极地安排工作以监控错误和过失，并在必要的时候采取纠正行动。

权变奖励是指一种更积极和有效的交易型领导方式，领导与下属就需要做什么达成一致，并运用约定的或实际的报酬换取员工应有的绩效。

Transformational leadership is viewed as a more motivational approach to leadership than other managerial approaches. Figure 12-5 contrasts various approaches to leadership according to how active or passive they are and, ultimately, how effective they prove to be. The colored cubes in the figure represent five distinct approaches to motivating employees, and the depth of the cubes represent how much a leader prioritizes each of the approaches. The figure therefore represents an optimal leadership approach that prioritizes more effective and more active behaviors. That optimal approach includes low levels of **laissez-faire** (i.e., hands-off) **leadership,** represented by the red cube, which is the avoidance of leadership altogether. Important actions are delayed, responsibility is ignored, and power and influence go unutilized. One common measure of leadership reflects laissez-faire styles with this statement: "The leader avoids getting involved when important issues arise."

The three yellow cubes represent **transactional leadership,** which occurs when the leader rewards or disciplines the follower depending on the adequacy of the follower's performance. With **passive management-by-exception,** the leader waits around for mistakes and errors, then takes corrective action as necessary. After all, "if it ain't broke, don't fix it!" This approach is represented by statements like: "The leader takes no action until complaints are received." With **active management-by-exception,** the leader arranges to monitor mistakes and errors actively and again takes corrective action when required. This approach is represented by statements like: "The leader directs attention toward failures to meet standards." **Contingent reward** represents a more active and effective brand of transactional leadership, in which the leader attains follower agreement on what needs to be done using promised or actual rewards in exchange for adequate performance. Statements like "The leader makes clear what one can expect to receive when performance goals are achieved" exemplify contingent reward leadership.

Transactional leadership represents the "carrot-and-stick" approach to leadership, with management-by-exception providing the "sticks" and contingent reward supplying the "carrots." Of course, transactional leadership represents the dominant approach to motivating employees in

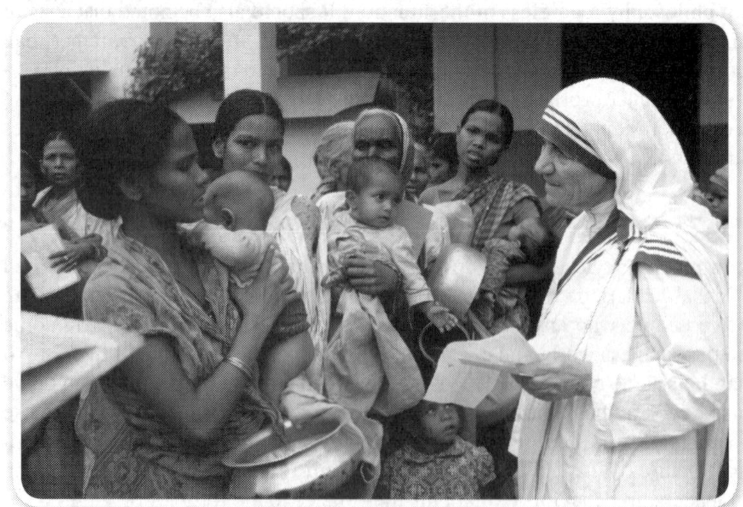

Mother Teresa's inspiring humanitarian work with India's sick and poor, and her founding of the influential Missionaries of Charity, became known around the world and suggest that she was a transformational leader. She was awarded the Nobel Peace Prize in 1979.

FIGURE 12-5 Laissez-Faire, Transactional, and Transformational Leadership

EFFECTIVE

Transformational

Transactional: Contingent Reward

Transactional: Active Management-by-Exception

PASSIVE

ACTIVE

Transactional: Passive Management-by-Exception

Laissez-Faire

INEFFECTIVE

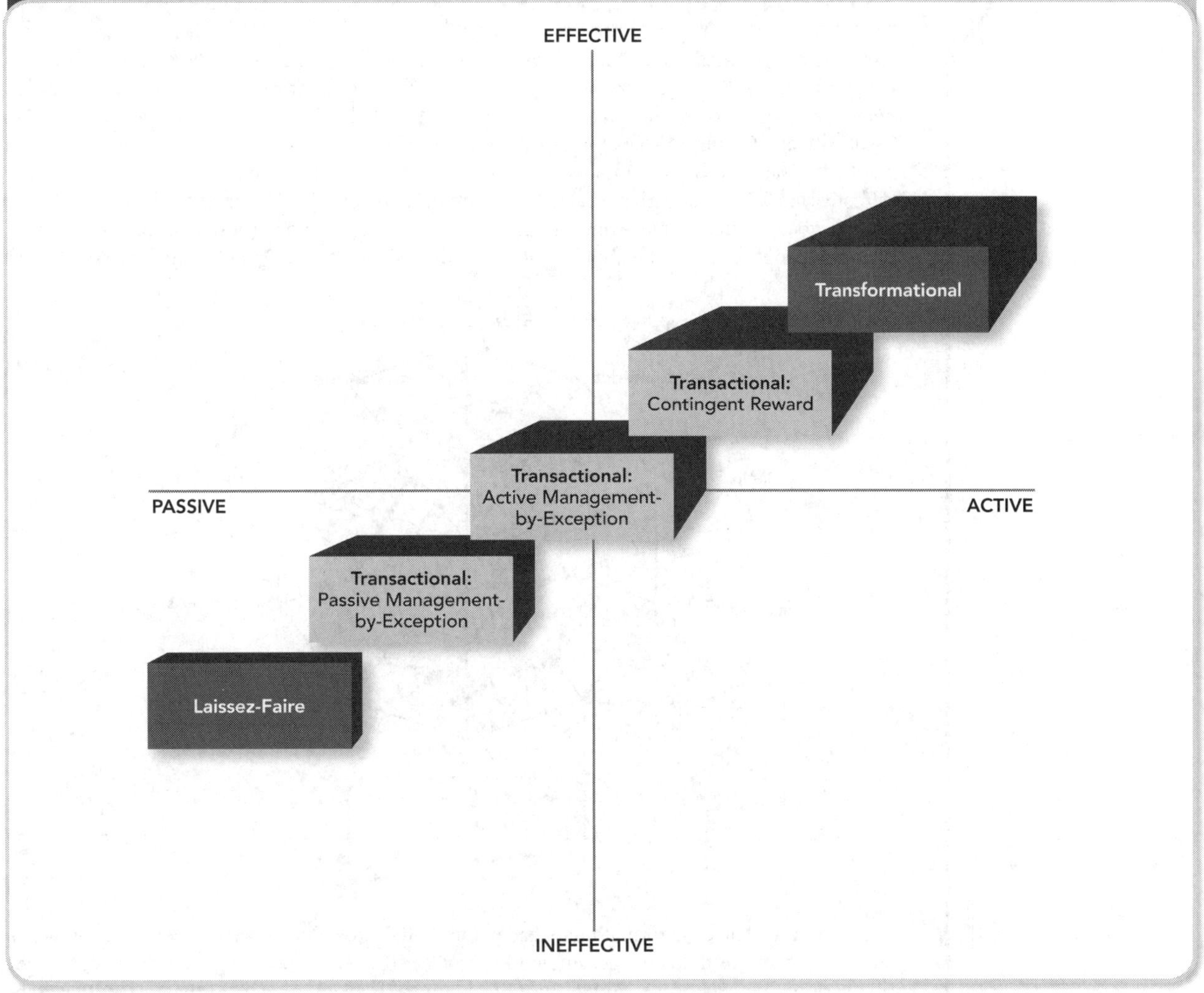

Source: Adapted from B.M. Bass and R.E. Riggio, *Transformational Leadership,* 2nd ed. (Mahwah, NJ: Lawrence Erlbaum Associates, 2006).

most organizations, and research suggests that it can be effective. A meta-analysis of 87 studies showed that contingent reward was strongly related to follower motivation and perceived leader effectiveness (see Chapter 6 on Motivation for more discussion of such issues). Active management-by-exception was only weakly related to follower motivation and perceived leader effectiveness, however, and passive management-by-exception seems actually to harm those outcomes. Such results support the progression shown in Figure 12-5, with contingent reward standing as the most effective approach under the transactional leadership umbrella.

Finally, the green cube represents transformational leadership—the most active and effective approach in Figure 12-5. How effective is transformational leadership? Well, we'll save that discussion for the "How Important Is Leadership?" section that concludes this chapter, but suffice it to say that transformational leadership has the strongest and most beneficial effects of any of the leadership variables described in this chapter. It's also the leadership approach that's most universally endorsed across cultures, as described in our **OB Internationally** feature. In addition, it probably captures the key qualities of the famous leaders we asked you to list a few paragraphs back. To understand why it's so powerful, we need to dig deeper into the specific kinds of actions and behaviors that leaders can utilize to become more transformational. It turns out

12.5
How does transformational leadership differ from transactional leadership, and which behaviors set it apart?

OB INTERNATIONALLY

Does the effectiveness of leader styles and behaviors vary across cultures? Answering that question is one of the objectives of *Project GLOBE*'s test of *culturally endorsed implicit leadership theory,* which argues that effective leadership is "in the eye of the beholder" (see Chapter 7 on Personality and Cultural Values for more discussion of such issues). To test the theory, researchers asked participants across cultures to rate a number of leader styles and behaviors using a 1 (very ineffective) to 7 (very effective) scale. The figure below shows how three of the styles and behaviors described in this chapter were rated across 10 different regions (note that the term "Anglo" represents people of English ethnicity, including the United States, Great Britain, and Australia).

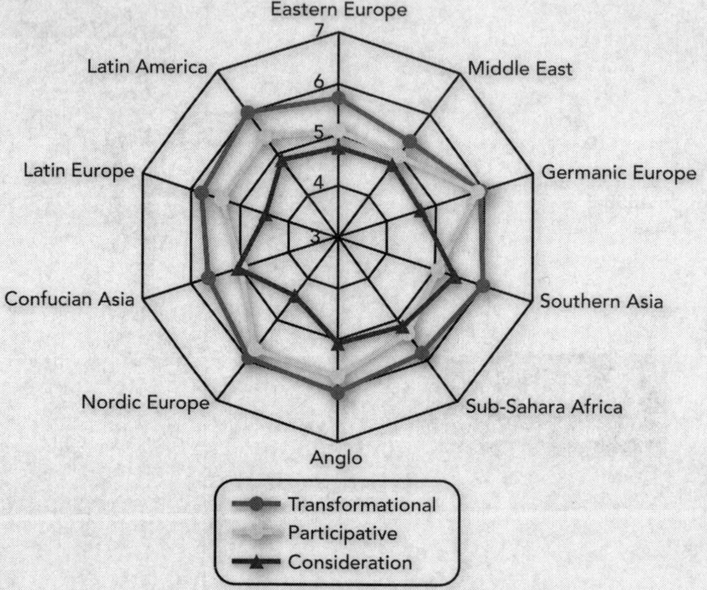

It turns out that transformational leadership is the most universally accepted approach to leadership of any of the concepts studied by Project GLOBE, receiving an average rating near 6 in every region except the Middle East. That appeal is likely explained by the fact that transformational leaders emphasize values like idealism and virtue that are endorsed in almost all countries. The figure also shows that a participative style is favorably viewed in most countries, though more variation is evident. Even more variation is seen with consideration behaviors, which are endorsed a bit less across the board but especially in Europe. Understanding these kinds of results can help organizations select and train managers who will fit the profile of an effective leader in a given region.

that the full spectrum of transformational leadership can be summarized using four dimensions: idealized influence, inspirational motivation, intellectual stimulation, and individualized consideration. Collectively, these four dimensions of transformational leadership are often called "the Four I's." For our discussion of transformational leadership, we'll use Steve Jobs, former CEO of Apple, who was widely recognized as one of the most transformational leaders in the corporate world, as a running example. Fortune named Jobs "CEO of the Decade" for the 2000s. Jobs battled various health problems over the last few years and took numerous medical leaves of absences from the company eventually causing him to resign as CEO. Steve Jobs died in late 2011.

理想化影响力是指领导者的行为能够赢得下属的钦佩、信任与尊重，引起下属的认同和效仿。

Idealized influence involves behaving in ways that earn the admiration, trust, and respect of followers, causing followers to want to identify with and emulate the leader. Idealized influence is represented by statements like: "The leader instills pride in me for being associated with him/her." Idealized influence is synonymous with *charisma*—a Greek word that means "divinely inspired gift"—which reflects a sense among followers that the leader possesses extraordinary qualities. Charisma is a word that was often associated with Steve Jobs. One observer noted that even though Jobs could be very difficult to work with, his remarkable charisma created a mysterious attraction that drew people to him, keeping them loyal to his collective sense of mission.

To some extent, discussions of charisma serve as echoes of the "great person" view of leadership that spawned the trait research described in Table 12-2. In fact, research suggests that there is a genetic component to charisma specifically and to transformational leadership more broadly. Studies on identical twins reared apart show that such twins have very similar charismatic profiles, despite their differing environments. Indeed, such research suggests that almost 60 percent of the variation in charismatic behavior can be explained by genes. One explanation for such findings is that genes influence the personality traits that give rise to charisma. For example, research suggests that extraversion, openness to experience, and agreeableness have significant effects on perceptions of leader charisma, and all three of those personality dimensions have a significant genetic component (see Chapter 7 on Personality and Cultural Values for more discussion of such issues).

Inspirational motivation involves behaving in ways that foster an enthusiasm for and commitment to a shared vision of the future. That vision is transmitted through a sort of "meaning-making" process in which the negative features of the status quo are emphasized while highlighting the positive features of the potential future. Inspirational motivation is represented by statements like: "The leader articulates a compelling vision of the future." At Apple, Steve Jobs was renowned for spinning a "reality distortion field" that reshaped employees' views of the current work environment. One Apple employee explained, "Steve has this power of vision that is almost frightening. When Steve believes in something, the power of that vision can literally sweep aside any objections, problems, or whatever. They just cease to exist."

鼓舞激励是指领导者的行为能为未来的共同愿景激发热情和承诺。

Intellectual stimulation involves behaving in ways that challenge followers to be innovative and creative by questioning assumptions and reframing old situations in new ways. Intellectual stimulation is represented by statements like: "The leader gets others to look at problems from many different angles." Intellectual stimulation was a staple of Jobs's tenure at Apple. He pushed for a different power supply on the Apple II so that the fan could be removed, preventing it from humming and churning like other computers of the time. Years later, he insisted on removing the floppy drive from the iMac because it seemed silly to transfer data one megabyte at a time, a decision that drew merciless criticism when the iMac debuted.

智力激发是指领导者通过质疑假设及重构旧情境来激发下属的创新性与创造性。

Individualized consideration involves behaving in ways that help followers achieve their potential through coaching, development, and mentoring. Not to be confused with the consideration behavior derived from the Ohio State studies, individualized consideration represents treating employees as unique individuals with specific needs, abilities, and aspirations that need to be tied into the unit's mission. Individualized consideration is represented by statements like: "The leader spends time teaching and coaching." Of the four facets of transformational leadership, Steve Jobs seemed lowest on individualized consideration. Employees who were not regarded as his equals were given a relatively short leash and sometimes faced an uncertain future in the company. In fact, some Apple employees resisted riding the elevator for fear of ending up trapped with Jobs for the ride between floors. As one observer describes it, by the time the doors open, you might have had your confidence undermined for weeks.

个性化关怀是指领导者通过教练、指导和开发的方式，帮助员工发挥自身潜能。

One interesting domain for examining transformational leadership issues is politics. Many of the most famous speeches given by U.S. presidents include a great deal of transformational content. Table 12-4 includes excerpts from speeches given by presidents that rank highly on transformational content based on scientific and historical study. One theme that's notable in the table is the presence of a crisis, as many of the presidents were attempting to steer the country through a difficult time in history (e.g., World War II, the Cold War, the Civil War). That's not a coincidence, in that times of crisis are particularly conducive to the emergence of transformational leadership. See this chapter's **OB on Screen** feature for a great example. Times of stress and turbulence cause people to long for charismatic leaders, and encouraging, confident, and idealistic visions resonate more deeply during such times. In addition, support for this suggestion comes from President George W. Bush's speeches before and after the tragedies on 9/11. Coding of his major speeches, public addresses, and radio addresses shows a significant increase in the transformational content of his rhetoric after the 9/11 attacks, including more focus on a

TABLE 12-4 Transformational Rhetoric among U.S. Presidents

PRESIDENT	TERM	REMARK	WHICH "I"?
Abraham Lincoln	1861–1865	"Fourscore and seven years ago our forefathers brought forth on this continent, a new nation, conceived in Liberty, and dedicated to the proposition that all men are created equal."	Idealized influence
Franklin Roosevelt	1933–1945	"First of all, let me assert my firm belief that the only thing we have to fear is fear itself—nameless, unreasoning, unjustified terror which paralyzes needed efforts to convert retreat into advance."	Inspirational motivation
John F. Kennedy	1961–1963	"And so, my fellow Americans . . . ask not what your country can do you for you—ask what you can do for your country. My fellow citizens of the world: Ask not what America will do for you, but what together we can do for the freedom of man."	Intellectual stimulation
Lyndon Johnson	1963–1969	"If future generations are to remember us more with gratitude than sorrow, we must achieve more than just the miracles of technology. We must also leave them a glimpse of the world as it was created, not just as it looked when we got through with it."	Idealized influence
Ronald Reagan	1981–1989	"General Secretary Gorbachev, if you seek peace, if you seek prosperity for the Soviet Union and Eastern Europe, if you seek liberalization: Come here to this gate! Mr. Gorbachev, open this gate! Mr. Gorbachev, tear down this wall!"	Idealized influence
Bill Clinton	1993–2001	"To realize the full possibilities of this economy, we must reach beyond our own borders, to shape the revolution that is tearing down barriers and building new networks among nations and individuals, and economies and cultures: globalization. It's the central reality of our time."	Intellectual stimulation

Sources: J.S. Mio, R.E. Riggio, S. Levin, and R. Reese, "Presidential Leadership and Charisma: The Effects of Metaphor," *Leadership Quarterly* 16 (2005), pp. 287–94; http://www.usa-patriotism.com/quotes/_list.htm.

collective mission and more articulation of a values-based vision. As future research is conducted, we're fairly confident that President Barack Obama's speeches will be described similarly, as many of his campaign and postelection speeches are high in transformational content. In fact, President Obama is known for being a very charismatic leader in terms of both the messages he delivers and the mannerisms that go along with them.

总结：为什么某些领导者比其他领导者更有效
SUMMARY: WHY ARE SOME LEADERS MORE EFFECTIVE THAN OTHERS?

So what explains why some leaders are more effective than others? As shown in Figure 12-6, answering that question requires an understanding of the particular styles that leaders use to make decisions and the behaviors they perform in their leadership role. In terms of decision-making styles, do they choose the most effective combination of leader and follower control in terms of the autocratic, consultative, facilitative, and delegative styles, particularly considering the importance of the decision and the expertise in the unit? In terms of day-to-day behaviors, do they engage in adequate levels of initiating structure and consideration? Finally, do they utilize

OB ON SCREEN

THE KING'S SPEECH

> *If I'm a King, where's my power? Can I form a government? Can I levy a tax? Declare a war? No. And yet I'm the seat of all authority, why? Because the Nation believes that when I speak, I speak for them . . . But I can't speak.*

With those words, King George VI (Colin Firth) expresses frustration at his seeming inability to deliver his first wartime speech to the nation due to a stuttering condition in *The King's Speech* (Dir.: Tom Hooper, The Weinstein Company, 2010). The King is preparing to deliver his first radio address—a speech that will be broadcast around the world immediately following England's declaration of war against Germany in 1939. Prior addresses to large crowds have been disastrous, with the King (then Prince Albert, Duke of York) developing an inability to speak and crowds being highly uncomfortable with his stammer. Helping him to overcome his speech issues is Lionel Logue (Geoffrey Rush), an Australian speech therapist with no real qualifications and very nontraditional and sometimes humorous methods. Lionel is somewhat pushed upon Prince Albert by his wife Elizabeth (Helena Bonham Carter).

Throughout the movie it is made clear that Prince Albert is perhaps not cut out to be the king. He doesn't possess some of the charismatic qualities of his older brother, Prince Edward (Guy Pearce), the self-confidence one might expect of a king, or the behaviors of someone who might lead others. However, through a strange sequence of events culminating in his brother's resignation from the post, he is thrust into the role and the people of Great Britain are looking to him to provide guidance and inspiration in the face of what will soon become World War II. Through much training and effort, King George VI rises to the occasion and becomes the transformational leader his nation needs him to be, providing a vision for the nation and inspiring every citizen to do their part in the war effort. Although he holds no formal power, he becomes known for his encouraging speeches and becomes a "symbol of the resistance" for many British citizens.

an effective combination of transactional leadership behaviors, such as contingent reward, and transformational leadership behaviors, such as idealized influence, inspirational motivation, intellectual stimulation, and individualized consideration?

领导有多重要

HOW IMPORTANT IS LEADERSHIP?

How important is leadership? As with some other topics in organizational behavior, that's a complicated question because "leadership" isn't just one thing. Instead, all of the styles and behaviors summarized in Figure 12-6 have their own unique importance. However, transformational

FIGURE 12-6 Why Are Some Leaders More Effective Than Others?

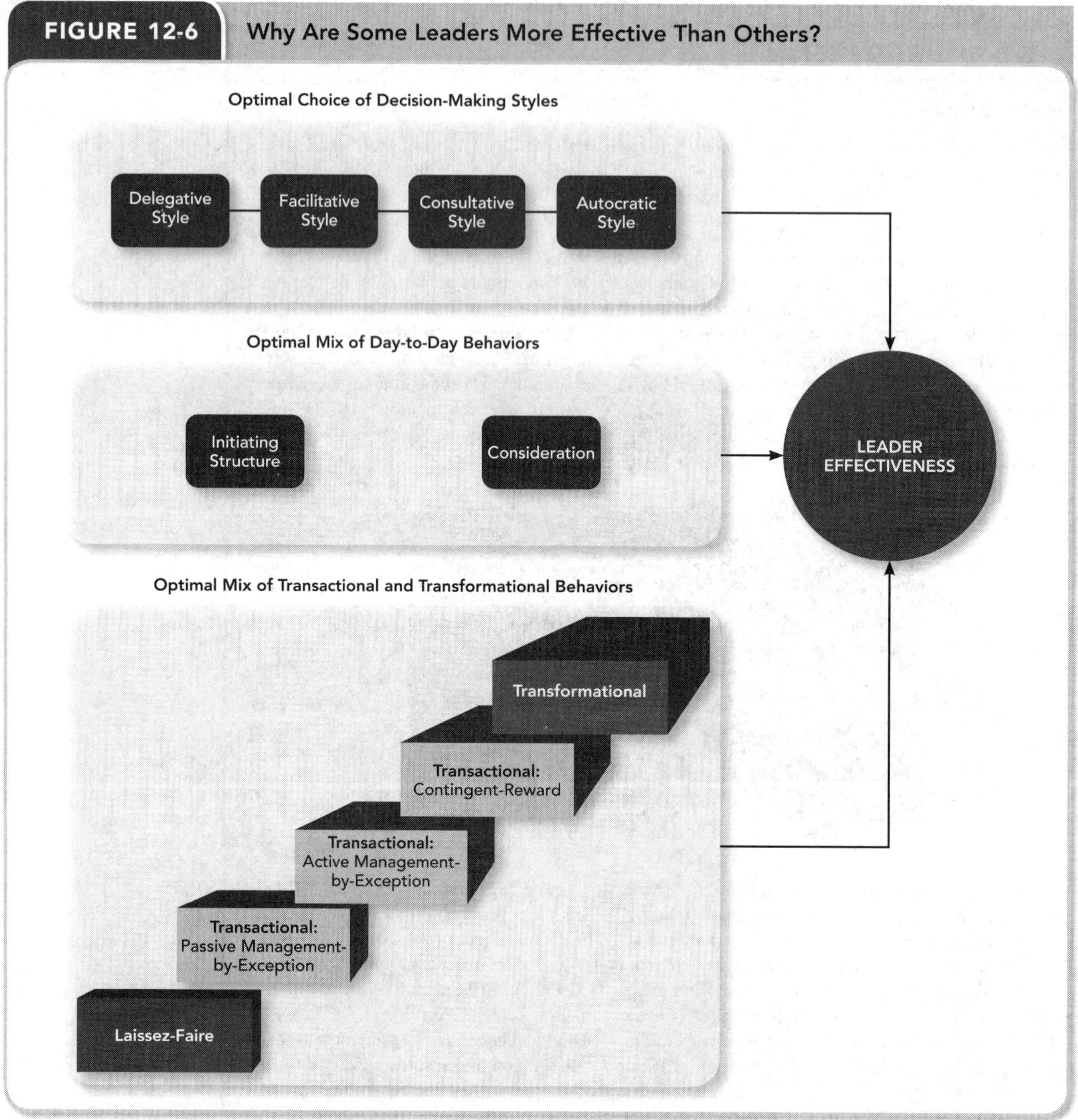

leadership stands apart from the rest to some extent, with particularly strong effects in organizations. For example, transformational leadership is more strongly related to unit-focused measures of leadership effectiveness, like the kind shown in the top panel of Table 12-1. Units led by a transformational leader tend to be more financially successful and bring higher-quality products and services to market at a faster rate. Transformational leadership is also more strongly related to dyad-focused measures of leader effectiveness, like the kind shown in the bottom panel of Table 12-1. Transformational leaders tend to foster leader–member exchange relationships that are of higher quality, marked by especially strong levels of mutual respect and obligation.

What if we focus specifically on the two outcomes in our integrative model of OB: performance and commitment? Figure 12-7 summarizes the research evidence linking transformational leadership to those two outcomes. The figure reveals that transformational leadership indeed affects the job performance of the employees who report to the leader. Employees with transformational leaders tend to have higher levels of task performance and engage in higher levels of citizenship behaviors. Why? One reason is that employees with transformational leaders have higher levels of *motivation* than other employees. They feel a stronger sense of psychological empowerment, feel more self-confident, and set more demanding work goals for themselves. They also *trust* the leader more, making them willing to exert extra effort even when that effort might not be immediately rewarded.

12.6

How does leadership affect job performance and organizational commitment?

Figure 12-7 also reveals that employees with transformational leaders tend to be more committed to their organization. They feel a stronger emotional bond with their organization and a stronger sense of obligation to remain present and engaged in their work. Why? One reason is that employees with transformational leaders have higher levels of *job satisfaction* than other employees. One study showed that transformational leaders can make employees feel that their jobs have more variety and significance, enhancing intrinsic satisfaction with the work itself. Other studies have shown that charismatic leaders express positive emotions more frequently and that those emotions are "caught" by employees through a sort of "emotional contagion" process. For example, followers of transformational leaders tend to feel more optimism and less frustration during their workday, which makes it a bit easier to stay committed to work.

Although leadership is very important to unit effectiveness and the performance and commitment of employees, there are contexts in which the importance of the leader can be reduced. The **substitutes for leadership model** suggests that certain characteristics of the situation can constrain the influence of the leader, making it more difficult for the leader to influence employee

领导替代模型认为，某些情境特性可以制约领导者的影响力，加大了领导者影响员工绩效的难度。

FIGURE 12-7 Effects of Transformational Leadership on Performance and Commitment

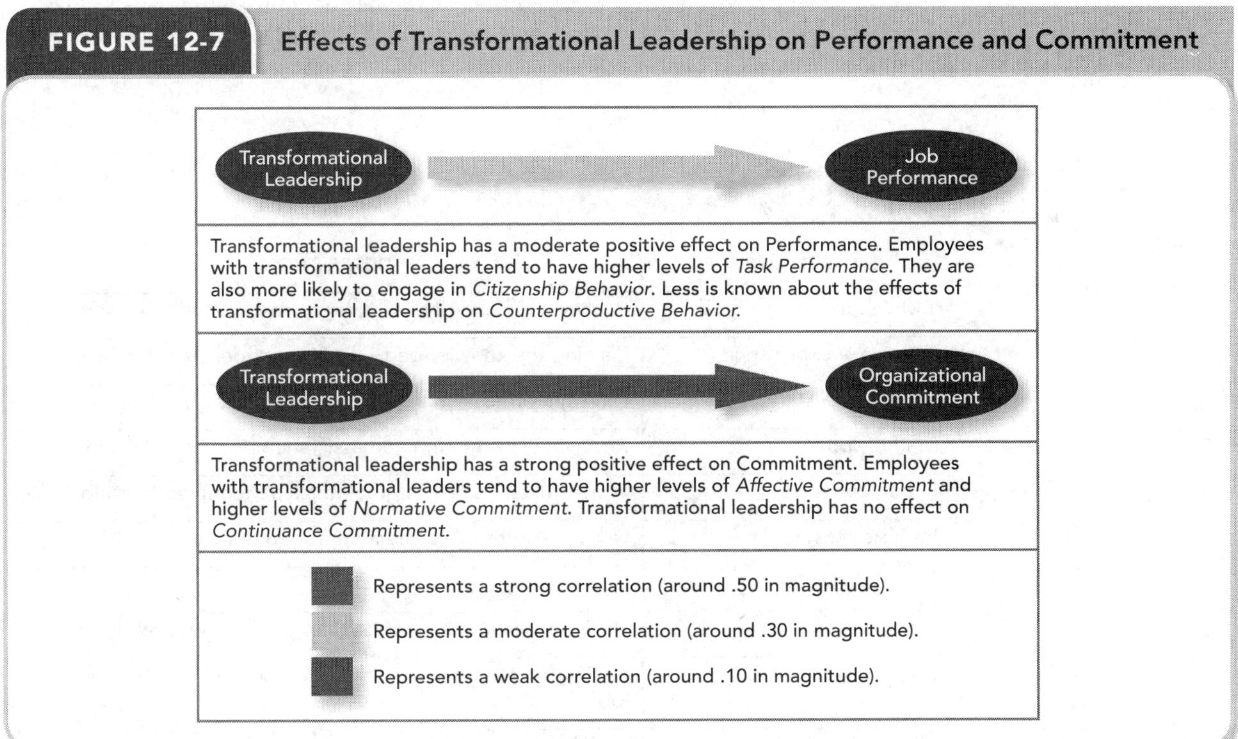

Sources: T.A. Judge and R.F. Piccolo, "Transformational and Transactional Leadership: A Meta-Analytic Test of Their Relative Validity," *Journal of Applied Psychology* 89 (2004), pp. 755–68; J.P. Meyer, D.J. Stanley, L. Herscovitch, and L. Topolnytsky, "Affective, Continuance, and Normative Commitment to the Organization: A Meta-Analysis of Antecedents, Correlates, and Consequences," *Journal of Vocational Behavior* 61 (2002), pp. 20–52; and P.M. Podsakoff, S.B. MacKenzie, J.B. Paine, and D.G. Bachrach, "Organizational Citizenship Behaviors: A Critical Review of the Theoretical and Empirical Literature and Suggestions for Future Research," *Journal of Management* 26 (2000), pp. 513–63.

替代因素会减弱领导者的重要性，同时直接有益于员工绩效。

抵消因素只减弱领导者的重要性，但本身对绩效没有有益的影响。

performance. Those situational characteristics come in two varieties, as shown in Table 12-5. **Substitutes** reduce the importance of the leader while simultaneously providing a direct benefit to employee performance. For example, a cohesive work group can provide its own sort of governing behaviors, making the leader less relevant, while providing its own source of motivation and job satisfaction. **Neutralizers,** in contrast, only reduce the importance of the leader; they themselves have no beneficial impact on performance. For example, spatial distance lessens the impact of a leader's behaviors and styles, but distance itself has no direct benefit for employee job performance.

The substitutes for leadership model offers a number of prescriptions for a better understanding of leadership in organizations. First, it can be used to explain why a leader who seemingly "does the right things" doesn't seem to be making any difference. It may be that the leader's work context possesses high levels of neutralizers and substitutes. Second, it can be used to explain what to do if an ineffective person is in a leadership role with no immediate replacement waiting in the wings. If the leader can't be removed, perhaps the organization can do things to make that leader more irrelevant. Studies of the substitutes for leadership model have been inconsistent in showing that substitutes and neutralizers actually make leaders less influential in the predicted manner. What is clearer is that the substitutes in Table 12-5 have beneficial effects on the job performance and organizational commitment of employees. In fact, the beneficial effects of the substitutes is sometimes even greater than the beneficial effects of the leader's own behaviors and styles. Some leadership experts even recommend that leaders set out to create high levels of the substitutes in their work units wherever possible, even if the units might ultimately wind up "running themselves."

应用：领导培训

APPLICATION: LEADERSHIP TRAINING

Given the importance of leadership, what can organizations do to maximize the effectiveness of their leaders? One method is to spend more time training them. One training analyst explains

TABLE 12-5 Leader Substitutes and Neutralizers

SUBSTITUTES	DESCRIPTION
Task feedback	Receiving feedback on performance from the task itself
Training & experience	Gaining the knowledge to act independently of the leader
Professionalism	Having a professional specialty that offers guidance
Staff support	Receiving information and assistance from outside staff
Group cohesion	Working in a close-knit and interdependent work group
Intrinsic satisfaction	Deriving personal satisfaction from one's work
NEUTRALIZERS	
Task stability	Having tasks with a clear, unchanging sequence of steps
Formalization	Having written policies and procedures that govern one's job
Inflexibility	Working in an organization that prioritizes rule adherence
Spatial distance	Being separated from one's leader by physical space

Source: Adapted from S. Kerr and J.M. Jermier, "Substitutes for Leadership: Their Meaning and Measurement," *Organizational Behavior and Human Performance* 22 (1978), pp. 375–403.

the increasing emphasis on leadership training this way: "The biggest problem that companies face today is an acute shortage of midlevel managers. They look around and just don't have enough qualified people." The same analyst notes that hiring leaders away from competitors isn't an option "because they probably don't have enough managers either."

Leadership training programs often focus on very specific issues, like conducting more accurate performance evaluations, being a more effective mentor, structuring creative problem solving, or gaining more cultural awareness and sensitivity. However, training programs can also focus on much of the content covered in this chapter. For example, content could focus on contextual considerations that alter the effectiveness of decision-making styles or particular leader behaviors, such as initiating structure and consideration. This is exactly what Campbell Soup Company is doing through its "CEO Institute"—a two-year program focused on personal leadership development. What about transformational leadership? Given how dependent charisma is on personality and genetic factors, is it possible that transformational leaders can only be born, not made? See our **OB at the Bookstore** feature for one answer to that question.

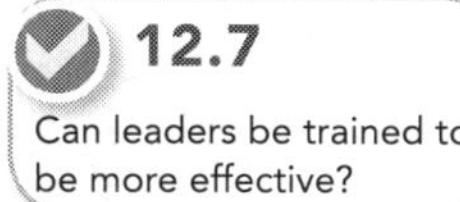

12.7
Can leaders be trained to be more effective?

OB AT THE BOOKSTORE

THE CORNER OFFICE: INDISPENSABLE AND UNEXPECTED LESSONS FROM CEOS ON HOW TO LEAD AND SUCCEED.

by Adam Bryant (New York, NY: Times Books, 2011).

> *People learn to lead through experience; there really are no shortcuts. But CEOs who have learned to lead can, like high-altitude sherpas, offer some guidance about how to handle the challenges along the way.*

With those words, Adam Bryant lays out his case for why we should pay attention to what CEOs have to say about success and leadership. Bryant writes a weekly column for *The New York Times* entitled "The Corner Office" in which he interviews a corporate executive about management, life-lessons, and leadership. His book attempts to summarize and consolidate the thoughts and opinions of 75 of these individuals collected over a two-year period. The book is divided into sections on succeeding, managing, and leading. The most prominent section of the book outlines the five key attributes that all of these leaders seemingly share. They include:

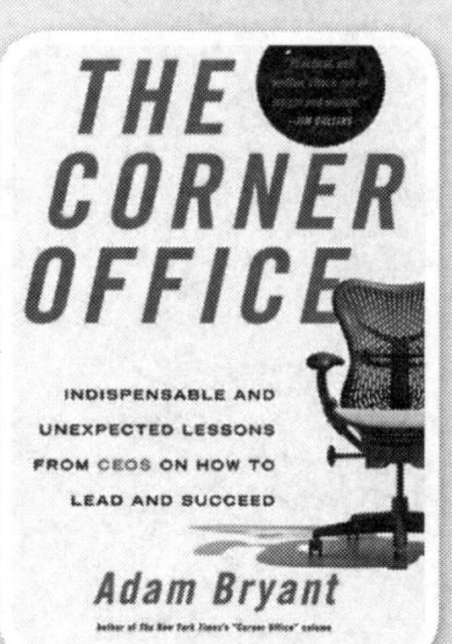

1. *Passionate Curiosity.* A mixture of passion for what one does and a curiosity about how to make things better.
2. *Battle-Hardened Confidence.* The experience of having handled adversity along with an attitude that one should solve one's own problems.
3. *Team-Smarts.* Understanding how teams work, the roles of each individual, and how to get the most out of a group.
4. *A Simple Mindset.* The ability to take seemingly complex phenomena and boil it down to simple and concise ideas that can be communicated easily.
5. *Fearlessness.* A willingness to shake things up and create change even when it doesn't appear to be needed—a propensity for risk-taking.

Although not exact duplicates, these five qualities have much in common with the "Four I's" of transformational leadership. More importantly, a major theme in the book is that none of these executives arrived at their position because they were born with these qualities. Indeed, most of the stories told by these CEOs were of the mistakes they made and how they had to "learn" to lead effectively by adapting over time through trial and error. Although the book is not really a step-by-step guide on how to become a better leader, it does provide the reader with a realization that through experience and training, we all can become better leaders.

It turns out that many training programs focus on transformational leadership content, and research suggests that those programs can be effective. One study of transformational leadership training occurred in one of the largest bank chains in Canada. Managers at all of the branches in one region were randomly assigned to either a transformational training group or a control group. The managers in the training group took part in a one-day training session that began by asking them to describe the best and worst leaders they had ever encountered. Where applicable, the behaviors mentioned as belonging to the best leaders were framed around transformational leadership. The transformational dimensions were then described in a lecture-style format. Participants set goals for how they could behave more transformationally and engaged in role-playing exercises to practice those behaviors. The managers then created specific action plans, with progress on those plans monitored during four "booster sessions" over the next month. The results of the study showed that managers who participated in the training were rated as more transformational afterward. More importantly, their employees reported higher levels of organizational commitment, and their branches enjoyed better performance in terms of personal loan sales and credit card sales.

PART

5

ORGANIZATIONAL MECHANISMS

组织机制

chapter 13

Organizational Structure

组织结构

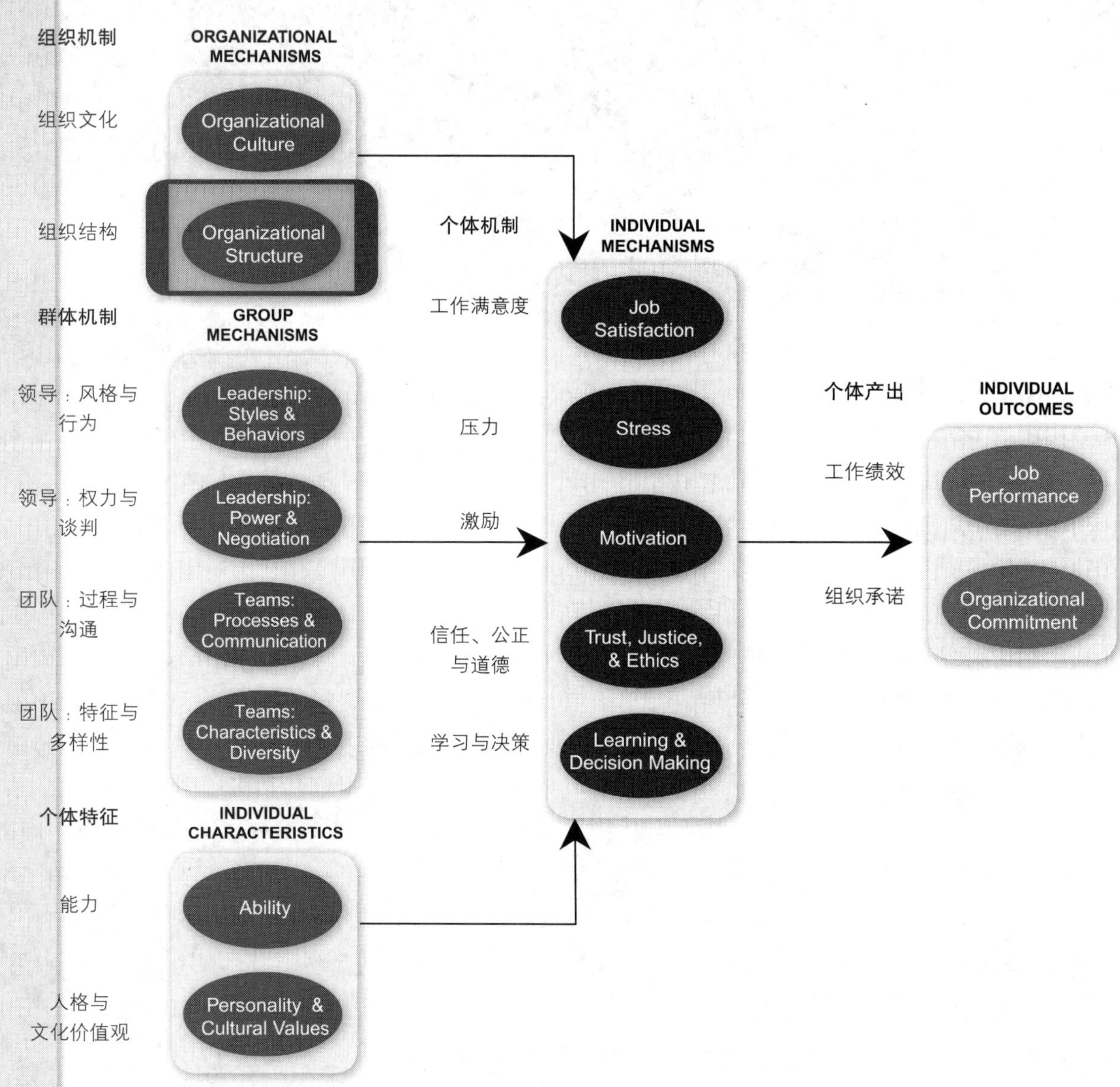

LEARNING GOALS

After reading this chapter, you should be able to answer the following questions:

13.1 What is an organization's structure, and what does it consist of?

13.2 What are the major elements of an organizational structure?

13.3 What is organizational design, and what factors does the organizational design process depend on?

13.4 What are some of the more common organizational forms that an organization might adopt for its structure?

13.5 When an organization makes changes to its structure, how does that restructuring affect job performance and organizational commitment?

13.6 What steps can organizations take to reduce the negative effects of restructuring efforts?

STARBUCKS

"I'd like an iced grande latte with nonfat milk to the bottom line only, ice to the top with super-stiff foam with a dome lid." How is that for a coffee order? Although it sounds a bit crazy, these types of orders come in all the time to each of Starbucks' 16,000 stores across 54 countries and every customer expects the order to be made exactly the same way they've had it before. Paradoxically, customers also want each Starbucks location to be unique to its local environment and for it to recognize them as individual customers. Needless to say, it is quite a challenge for Starbucks to be so highly standardized that their product remains the same, but flexible enough to make each store unique to its local clientele. How does Starbucks accomplish this? Part of the answer is through the company's organizational structure and how jobs and tasks are coordinated between their 200,000 partners (which is the term Starbucks uses for its employees).

Starbucks as a company struggled mightily during the late 2000s as its growth rate exceeded its ability to deliver an exceptional product. Howard Schultz, the company's founder and first CEO, had retired in 2000 and then came back in 2008 to try to refocus Starbucks on the core nature of its business. He did this first by making some structural changes at the top. One of his first steps was removing the position of COO so that all senior leaders reported directly to him—giving him more control and access to unfiltered information. He also created a new position of chief information officer (CIO), a role that used to report to the CFO. Starbucks was way behind in updating store technology—in 2008, the front of their stores was still running a point of sale system that operated on an old Microsoft DOS platform (Microsoft had stopped supporting the platform back in the mid-nineties). As Howard Schultz would put it, "In short, a Starbucks store was essentially the equivalent of a $1 million-a-year business, but an iPhone had more business application power than our store's technology."

Yet the larger problem still remained: how does a company deliver a standardized product through its operations and yet be willing to be flexible to its local customers? Starbucks partly accomplished this by changing to a matrix organizational structure. Employees not only report up through their traditional functional (what they do) hierarchy, they also report to regional executives who are tasked with customizing the Starbucks experience to local clientele. In the U.S. this means four geographic divisions including Western/Pacific, Northwest/Mountain, Southeast/Plains, and Northeast/Atlantic. By doing this, Starbucks executives place the focus of their employees on multiple dimensions that they feel are equally important.

组织结构
ORGANIZATIONAL STRUCTURE

As the Starbucks example illustrates, an organization's structure can have a significant impact on its financial performance and ability to manage its employees. The decisions that Howard Schultz has made regarding Starbucks' organizational structure will have an impact on how employees communicate and cooperate with one another, how power is distributed, and how individuals view their work environment. In fact, an organization's structure dictates more than you might think. We've spent a great deal of time in this book talking about how employee attitudes and behaviors are shaped by individual characteristics, such as personality and ability, and group mechanisms, such as teams and leaders. In this and the following chapter, we discuss how the organization as a whole affects employee attitudes and behavior.

13.1
What is an organization's structure, and what does it consist of?

组织结构正式规定了公司内部的工作和任务如何在个人与群体之间进行划分和协调。

Think about some of the jobs you've held in the past (or perhaps the job you hope to have after graduation). What types of employees did you interact with on a daily basis? Were they employees who performed the same tasks that you performed? Or maybe they didn't do exactly what you did, but did they serve the same customer? How many employees did your manager supervise? Was every decision you made scrutinized by your supervisor, or were you given a "long leash"? The answers to all of these questions are influenced by organizational structure. An **organizational structure** formally dictates how jobs and tasks are divided and coordinated between individuals and groups within the company. Organizational structures can be relatively simple when a company only has 5–20 employees but grow incredibly complex in the case of Starbucks' 200,000 partners.

为什么某些组织的结构与其他组织的有所不同

WHY DO SOME ORGANIZATIONS HAVE DIFFERENT STRUCTURES THAN OTHERS?

One way of getting a feel for an organization's structure is by looking at an organizational chart. An **organizational chart** is a drawing that represents every job in the organization and the formal reporting relationships between those jobs. It helps organizational members and outsiders understand and comprehend how work is structured within the company. Figure 13-1 illustrates two sample organizational charts. In a real chart, the boxes would be filled with actual names and job titles. As you can imagine, as companies grow larger, their organizational charts get more complex. Can you imagine drawing an organizational chart that included every one of Starbucks' 200,000 employees? Not only would that require a lot of boxes and a lot of paper, it would probably take a couple of months to put together (plus, as soon as someone left the organization, it would be time to update the chart!).

组织结构图是表示组织中的每种工作以及这些工作之间正式报告关系的一种图表。

组织结构的要素

ELEMENTS OF ORGANIZATIONAL STRUCTURE

The organizational charts described in this chapter are relatively simple and designed to illustrate specific points (if you want to see how complex some of these charts can get, do a search on the Internet for "organizational chart," and you'll begin to see how varied organizations can be in the way they design their company). Specifically, charts like those in Figure 13-1 can illustrate the five key elements of an organization's structure. Those five key elements, summarized in Table 13-1, describe how work tasks, authority relationships, and decision-making responsibilities are organized within the company. These elements will be discussed in the next several sections.

工作分工是组织中的任务被划分成独立的工作的方式。

13.2
What are the major elements of an organizational structure?

WORK SPECIALIZATION. **Work specialization** is the way in which tasks in an organization are divided into separate jobs. In some organizations, this categorization is referred to as a company's division of labor. How many tasks does any one employee perform? To some degree, work specialization is a never-ending trade-off among productivity, flexibility, and worker motivation. Take an assembly line worker at Ford as an example. Henry Ford was perhaps the earliest (and clearly most well-known) believer in high degrees of work specialization. He divided tasks among his manufacturing employees to such a degree that each employee might only perform one single task, over and over again, all day long. Having only one task to perform allowed those employees to be extremely productive at doing that one thing. It also meant that training new workers was much easier when replacements were needed.

However, there are trade-offs when organizations make jobs highly specialized. Highly specialized jobs can cause organizations to lose the ability associated with employees who can be flexible in what they do. By spending all their time performing specialized tasks well, employees

FIGURE 13-1 Two Sample Organizational Structures

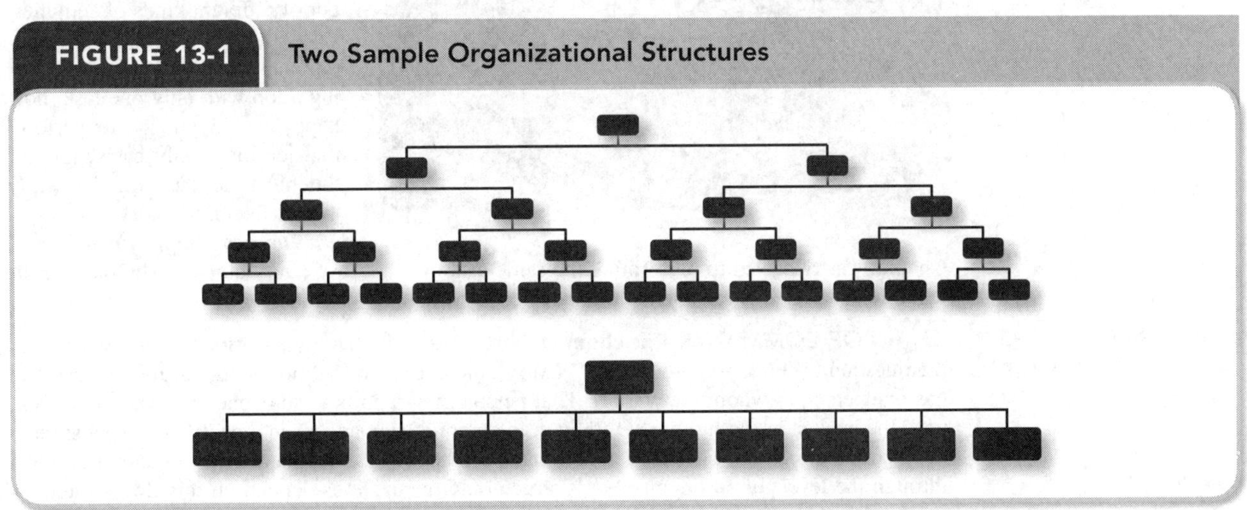

TABLE 13-1 Elements of Organizational Structure

ORGANIZATIONAL STRUCTURE DIMENSION	DEFINITION
Work Specialization	The degree to which tasks in an organization are divided into separate jobs.
Chain of Command	Answers the question of "who reports to whom?" and signifies formal authority relationships.
Span of Control	Represents how many employees each manager in the organization has responsibility for.
Centralization	Refers to where decisions are formally made in organizations.
Formalization	The degree to which rules and procedures are used to standardize behaviors and decisions in an organization.

fail to update or practice other skills. Accounting majors, for example, might specialize in taxes or auditing. Some larger companies might hire these graduates for their ability to do either auditing or tax—but not both. Other companies might be looking for an accountant who can perform either aspect well, depending on how they divide up accounting duties within their organization. Still other companies might want to hire "general managers" who understand accounting, finance, management, marketing, and operations as a part of their job. Thus, high levels of specialization may be acceptable in larger firms with more employees but can be problematic in smaller firms in which employees must be more flexible in their job duties. Aetna, the Hartford, Connecticut–based health insurer, publishes more than 1,300 different job titles, each of which has its own list of the competencies that employees in those jobs must perform.

Organizations may also struggle with employee job satisfaction when they make jobs highly specialized. If you recall from Chapter 4 on Job Satisfaction, we discussed five core characteristics of jobs that significantly affect satisfaction. One of those characteristics was variety, or the degree to which the job requires a number of different activities involving a number of different skills and talents. Employees tend to be more satisfied with jobs that require them to perform a number of different kinds of activities. Even though you might be very efficient and productive performing a job with only one task, how happy would you be to perform that job on a daily basis? One of the most famous films in early motion picture history was *Modern Times,* a film in which Charlie Chaplin was relegated to performing the same task over and over, very quickly. The movie ridiculed work specialization and the trend of treating employees as machines.

Modern Times (1932), starring Charlie Chaplin, ridiculed work specialization and the treating of employees as machines. Have things changed since then?

组织中的**指挥链**从根本上回答了“谁向谁汇报工作”的问题。

CHAIN OF COMMAND. The **chain of command** within an organization essentially answers the question "Who reports to whom?" Every employee in a traditional organizational structure has one person to whom they report. That person then reports to someone else, and on and on, until the buck stops with the CEO (though in a public company, even the CEO is responsible to the board of directors). The chain of command can be seen as the specific flow of authority down through the levels of an organization's structure. Organizations depend on this flow of authority to attain order, control, and predictable performance. Some newer organizational structures make this chain of command a bit more complex. It has become common to have positions that report to two or more different managers. For example, Intel placed two people apiece in charge of the two largest divisions of their organization. Questions have arisen as to how their duties will be split up and whether employees will know whom it is they report to.

SPAN OF CONTROL. A manager's **span of control** represents how many employees he or she is responsible for in the organization. The organizational charts in Figure 13-1 provide an illustration of the differences in span of control. In the top chart, each manager is responsible for leading two subordinates. In most instances, this level would be considered a narrow span of control. In the bottom chart, the manager is responsible for 10 employees. Typically, this number would be considered a wide span of control. Of course, the key question in many organizations is how many employees one manager can supervise effectively. Answering that question requires a better understanding of the benefits of narrow and wide spans of control.

管理跨度代表一个人在组织中负责多少员工。

Narrow spans of control allow managers to be much more hands-on with employees, giving them the opportunity to use directive leadership styles while developing close mentoring relationships with employees. A narrow span of control is especially important if the manager has substantially more skill or expertise than the subordinates. Early writings on management assumed that the narrower the span of control, the more productive employees would become. However, a narrow span of control requires organizations to hire many managers, which can significantly increase labor costs. Moreover, if the span of control becomes too narrow, employees can become resentful of their close supervision and long for more latitude in their day-to-day decision making. In fact, current research suggests that a moderate span of control is best for an organization's productivity. This relationship is illustrated in Figure 13-2. Note that organizational performance increases as span of control increases, but only up to the point that managers no longer have the ability to coordinate and supervise the large numbers of employees underneath them. Most organizations work hard to try to find the right balance, and this balance differs for every organization, depending on its unique circumstances. However, there is no question that spans of control in organizations have increased significantly in recent years. Organizations such as Coca-Cola have vice presidents with up to 90 employees reporting to them!

An organization's span of control affects how "tall" or "flat" its organizational chart becomes. For example, the top panel of Figure 13-1 depicts a tall structure with many hierarchical levels and a narrow span of control, whereas the bottom panel depicts a flat organization with few

FIGURE 13-2 Span of Control and Organizational Performance

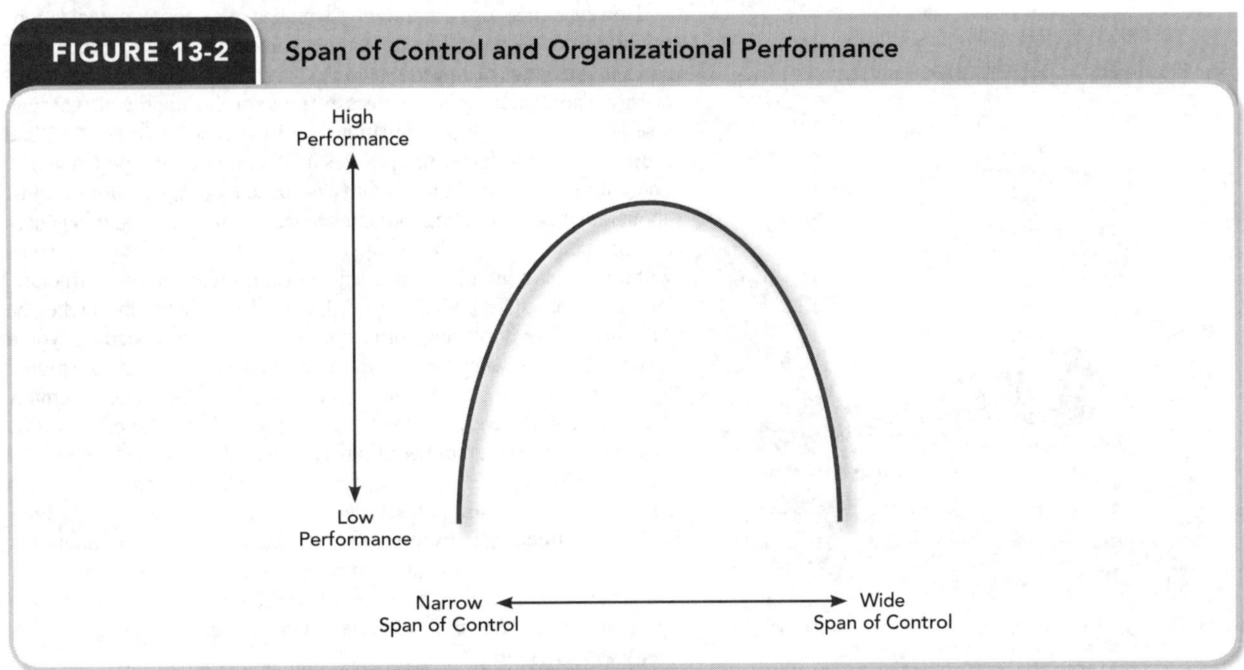

Source: Adapted from N.A. Theobald and S. Nicholson-Crotty, "The Many Faces of Span of Control: Organizational Structure Across Multiple Goals," *Administration and Society* 36 (2005), pp. 648–60.

levels and a wide span of control. Think about what happens when an organization becomes "taller." First, more layers of management means having to pay more management salaries. Second, communication in the organization becomes more complex as each new layer becomes one more point through which information must pass when traveling upward or downward. Third, the organization's ability to make decisions becomes slower, because approval for decisions has to be authorized at every step of the hierarchy.

Throughout the 1990s and the 2000s, organizations worked to become flatter to reduce the costs associated with multiple layers of management and increase their ability to adapt to their environment. Intel, for example, announced a reduction in its managerial ranks of 1,000 positions (or 1 percent of its 100,000 employees). A spokesperson from Intel announced that "This [layoff] is designed to improve costs and improve decision making and communications across the company." Putnam Investment Company also went through a flattening of its organization, reducing the workforce by 11 percent—including 25 of its 50 highest-paid executives. Putnam CEO Ed Haldeman noted, "To attract and retain the best people, it's necessary to provide them with the autonomy and independence to make decisions."

集权表示决策是在组织的哪一层正式制定的。

CENTRALIZATION. **Centralization** reflects where decisions are formally made in organizations. If only the top managers within a company have the authority to make final decisions, we would say that the organization has a highly "centralized" structure. In contrast, if decision-making authority is pushed down to lower-level employees and these employees feel empowered to make decisions on their own, an organization has a "decentralized" structure. Decentralization becomes necessary as a company grows larger. Sooner or later, the top management of an organization will not be able to make every single decision within the company. Centralized organizational structures tend to concentrate power and authority within a relatively tight group of individuals in the firm, because they're the ones who have formal authority over important decisions.

Many organizations are moving toward a more decentralized structure. A manager can't have 20 employees reporting to him or her if those employees aren't allowed to make some decisions on their own. Yahoo is a company that recently restructured to become more decentralized. Former CEO Carol Bartz was moved to observe, "Organizations can get in the way of innovation, because if people are all bound up, and if they don't know if they get to make the decision or somebody else, and if they do, what happens to them, and so on and so forth. There's a freeing when you organize around the fact that you're clearly in charge and go for it. It's really a fantastic group of people, and just cleaner lines and cleaner responsibility, and freedom to make mistakes, and have some fun."

当组织中使用很多具体的规则和程序来规范行为和决策时，这个组织就是高度**正规化**的。

However, it's also important to realize that some organizations might choose to centralize a few functions while leaving other decisions in the hands of lower-level managers. Arlington, VA–based AES energy manufacturing is a perfect example of this approach. Through a series of startups and acquisitions over the past 20 years, AES had grown to a size of 50,000 employees in 29 countries around the world. Each of its offices had the authority to make its own decisions on just about anything including human resources, finances, and business development. In fact, the company basically ran for over 20 years without rules, regulations, or even a formal organizational structure. Paul Hanrahan, CEO of AES, says that an executive told him when he was hired, "We don't have procedures, if we had a procedure, you'd assume we knew what we were doing when we wrote it, and we didn't. So figure it out and use your common sense." Still, the fact is that many decisions could have been made more efficiently by the organization as a whole. Due to a number of laws that have been passed (especially Sarbanes-Oxley), AES has been forced to centralize finance, business development, and human resources. As Hanrahan now says, "There's still a lot of freedom to experiment, to find better ways to do things, but we don't want people to come up with new ways to report income." Have the organizations where you've worked been largely centralized or decentralized? See our **OB Assessments** feature to find out.

"No, now all of our pillaging is done electronically from a centralized office."

Source: © Christopher Weyant, The New Yorker Collection, www.cartoonbank.com

FORMALIZATION. A company is high in **formalization** when there are many specific rules and procedures used to standardize behaviors and decisions. Although not something you can necessarily see on an organizational chart, the impact of formalization is felt throughout the organization. Rules and procedures are a necessary mechanism for control in every organization. Although the word *formalization* has a somewhat negative connotation, think about your reaction if every McDonald's made its french fries in different ways at each location. Or think about this: Would it bother you if every time you called Dell for technical support, you got an operator who treated you differently and gave you conflicting answers? Formalization is a necessary coordination mechanism that organizations rely on to get a standardized product or deliver a standardized service.

Alcoa's Michigan Casting Center, a leading automotive part supplier, was plagued by the fact that it could have two machine operators running the same machine on two different shifts and get up to a 50 percent performance difference in output and quality between the workers. The company conducted a study to identify the best practices for each machine in its plant. These best practices became standard operating procedures for each worker, and that formalization allowed the company to get a more predictable level of output. Companies such as W.L. Gore, the Newark, Delaware–based manufacturer of Gore-Tex, fall at the other extreme when it comes to formalization. Whereas most companies have titles for their jobs and job descriptions that specify the tasks each job is responsible for, Bill Gore (company founder) felt that such formalization would stifle communication and creativity. After one of his employees mentioned that she needed to put some kind of job title on a business card to hand out at an outside conference, Gore replied that she could put "supreme commander" on the card for all he cared. She liked the title so much that she followed through on his suggestion, and it became a running joke throughout the company.

ELEMENTS IN COMBINATION. You might have noticed that some elements of an organization's structure seem to go hand-in-hand with other elements. For example, wide spans of control tend to be associated with decentralization in decision making. A high level of work specialization tends to bring about a high level of formalization. Moreover, if you take a closer look at the elements, you might notice that many of the elements capture the struggle between efficiency and flexibility. **Mechanistic organizations** are efficient, rigid, predictable, and standardized organizations that thrive in stable environments. Mechanistic organizations are typified by a structure that relies on high levels of formalization, a rigid and hierarchical chain of command, high degrees of work specialization, centralization of decision making, and narrow spans of control. In contrast, **organic organizations** are flexible, adaptive, outward-focused organizations that thrive in dynamic environments. Organic organizations are typified by a structure that relies on low levels of formalization, weak or multiple chains of command, low levels of work specialization, and wide spans of control. Table 13-2 sums up the differences between the two types of organizations.

机械式组织是存在于稳定环境中的有效率的、僵化的、可预测的和标准化的组织。机械式组织的典型结构特点是正规化程度高、僵化和层级的指挥链、工作分工程度高、决策权集中化和管理跨度窄。

有机式组织是存在于动态环境中的灵活的、具有适应性的、专注于外部的组织。有机式组织的典型结构特点是正规化程度低、弱指挥链或多重指挥链、工作分工程度低和管理跨度宽。

TABLE 13-2 Characteristics of Mechanistic vs. Organic Structures

MECHANISTIC ORGANIZATIONS	ORGANIC ORGANIZATIONS
High degree of work specialization; employees are given a very narrow view of the tasks they are to perform.	Low degree of work specialization; employees are encouraged to take a broad view of the tasks they are to perform.
Very clear lines of authority; employees know exactly whom they report to.	Although there might be a specified chain of command, employees think more broadly in terms of where their responsibilities lie.
High levels of hierarchical control; employees are not encouraged to make decisions without their manager's consent.	Knowledge and expertise are decentralized; employees are encouraged to make their own decisions when appropriate.
Information is passed through vertical communication between an employee and his or her supervisor.	Lateral communication is encouraged, focusing on information and advice as opposed to orders.
Employees are encouraged to develop firm-specific knowledge and expertise within their area of specialization.	Employees are encouraged to develop knowledge and expertise outside of their specialization.

Source: Adapted from T. Burns and G.M. Stalker, G.M. *The Management of Innovation* (London: Tavistock, 1961).

OB ASSESSMENTS

CENTRALIZATION

Have you experienced life inside an organization with a highly centralized structure? This assessment is designed to measure two facets of what would be considered a centralized organizational structure. Those two facets are *hierarchy of authority,* which reflects the degree to which managers are needed to approve decisions, and *participation in decision making,* which reflects how involved rank-and-file employees are in day-to-day deliberations. Think about the last job you held (even if it was a part-time or summer job). Alternatively, think about a student group of yours that seems to have a definite "leader." Then answer each question using the response scale provided. (For more assessments relevant to this chapter, please visit http://connect.mcgraw-hill.com.)

1 STRONGLY DISAGREE	2 DISAGREE	3 UNCERTAIN	4 AGREE	5 STRONGLY AGREE

1. There can be little action here until a supervisor approves a decision. _______
2. A person who wants to make his or her own decisions would be quickly discouraged. _______
3. Even small matters have to be referred to someone higher up for a final answer. _______
4. I have to ask my boss before I do almost anything. _______
5. Any decision I make has to have my boss's approval. _______
6. I participate frequently in the decision to adopt new programs. _______
7. I participate frequently in the decision to adopt new policies and rules. _______
8. I usually participate in the decision to hire or adopt new group members. _______
9. I often participate in decisions that affect my working environment. _______

SCORING AND INTERPRETATION:

Hierarchy of Authority: Sum up items 1–5. _______

Participation in Decision Making: Sum up items 6–9. _______

A centralized structure would be one in which Hierarchy of Authority is high and Participation in Decision Making is low. If your score is above 20 for Hierarchy of Authority and below 8 for Participation in Decision Making, your organization (or student group) has a highly centralized structure.

Source: Adapted from M. Schminke, R. Cropanzano, and D.E. Rupp, "Organization Structure and Fairness Perceptions: The Moderating Effects of Organizational Level," *Organizational Behavior and Human Decision Processes* 89 (2002), pp. 881–905.

If you think about the differences between the two types, it probably wouldn't be too difficult to come up with a few companies that fall more toward one end of the continuum or the other. Where would you place Starbucks? Evidence indicates that a mechanistic or organic culture can have a significant effect on the types of employee practices a company adopts, such as selection, training, recruitment, compensation, and performance systems. In addition, organic structures are more likely to allow for transformational leadership to have a positive effect on employees. However, it's important to remember that few organizations are perfect examples of either extreme. Most fall somewhere near the middle, with certain areas within the organization having mechanistic qualities and others being more organic in nature. Microsoft is a good example as an organization that has many organic qualities, but even within its own walls it had teams that worked completely apart from each other while developing Windows Vista and when they came together, what each group had done was incompatible with the other—a mistake they tried to rectify during the creation of Windows 7. Although it's tempting to label mechanistic as "bad" and organic as "good," this perception is not necessarily true. Being mechanistic is the only way for many organizations to survive, and it can be a highly appropriate and fruitful way to structure work functions. To find out why that's the case, we need to explore why organizations develop the kinds of structures they do.

组织设计
ORGANIZATIONAL DESIGN

组织设计是设立、选择或者改变组织结构的过程。

 **13.3**

What is organizational design, and what factors does the organizational design process depend on?

Organizational design is the process of creating, selecting, or changing the structure of an organization. Ideally, organizations don't just "let" a structure develop on its own; they proactively design it to match their specific circumstances and needs. Research indeed shows this is how it works in most cases. However, some organizations aren't that proactive and find themselves with a structure that has unintentionally developed on its own, without any careful planning. Those organizations may then be forced to change their structure to become more effective. A number of factors should influence the process of organizational design. Those factors include the environment in which the organization does business, its corporate strategy and technology, and the size of the firm. However, for some firms in dire straits, changing the structure becomes a strategy in and of itself, often leading to very poor results. See this chapter's **OB at the Bookstore** for more.

商业环境由对组织设计产生影响的消费者、竞争者、供应商和公司外部的其他因素组成。

BUSINESS ENVIRONMENT. An organization's **business environment** consists of its customers, competitors, suppliers, distributors, and other factors external to the firm, all of which have an impact on organizational design. One of the biggest factors in an environment's effect on structure is whether the outside environment is stable or dynamic. Stable environments don't change frequently, and any changes that do occur happen very slowly. Stable environments allow organizations to focus on efficiency and require little change over time. In contrast, dynamic environments change on a frequent basis and require organizations to have structures that are more adaptive. Sony made a well-publicized corporate mistake when it failed to meet the needs of its changing business environment to match Apple's iPod. Because it took it so long to recognize and adapt to this environmental shift, Sony has struggled to be profitable. Some would argue that the world is changing so fast that the majority of companies can no longer keep up.

公司战略描述了组织的使命和目标以及组织如何利用其资产实现盈利的方式。

COMPANY STRATEGY. A **company strategy** describes an organization's objectives and goals and how it tries to capitalize on its assets to make money. Although the myriad of organizational strategies is too involved to discuss here, two common strategies revolve around being either a low-cost producer or a differentiator. Companies that focus on a low-cost producer strategy rely on selling products at the lowest possible cost. To do this well, they have to focus on being as efficient as they can be. Such companies are more likely to take a mechanistic approach to organizational design. Other companies might follow a differentiation strategy. Rather than focusing on supplying

Partially due to its organizational structure, Sony was unable to adjust to its changing business environment, allowing Apple to dominate the portable music player market with its innovative line of iPods.

OB AT THE BOOKSTORE

HOW THE MIGHTY FALL

by Jim Collins (New York: Harper Collins, 2009).

> *Reorganizations and restructurings can create a false sense that you're actually doing something productive. Companies are in the process of reorganizing themselves all the time; that's the nature of institutional evolution. But when you begin to respond to data and warning signs with reorganization as a primary strategy, you may well be in denial. It's a bit like responding to a severe heart condition or a cancer diagnosis by rearranging your living room.*

With those words, Jim Collins derides organizational design as a tool for fixing a failing company. Collins's *New York Times* bestseller takes a look at the question: What causes extremely successful companies to fail? He finds that failing companies typically follow a five-stage path to failure:

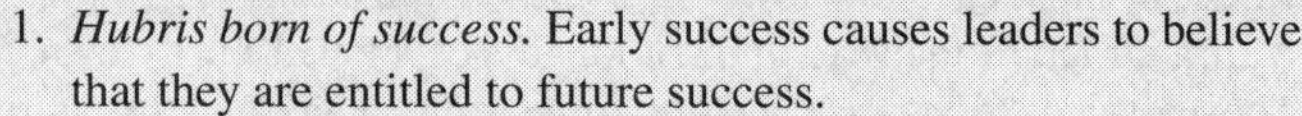

1. *Hubris born of success.* Early success causes leaders to believe that they are entitled to future success.
2. *Undisciplined pursuit of more.* Growing in directions away from the core business and faster than highly talented people can be hired to manage it.
3. *Denial of risk and peril.* While results are still strong, signs that things might not be going well are written off or ignored and blamed on unique one-time situations.
4. *Grasping for salvation.* Companies look for a "silver bullet" to try to turn things around.
5. *Capitulation to irrelevance or death.* Leaders throw in the towel when the hope of a turnaround is lost.

One consistent theme through the book, especially in Stages 3 and 4, is that companies seem to think a reorganization will help them avoid the inevitable or solve their problems. Collins lists numerous examples of companies that reorganize incessantly, hoping that by moving lines on an organizational chart, their business will turn around. His analysis suggests that there is no perfect organizational structure and that all structures have trade-offs. This revelation doesn't mean that restructuring is always bad, it's just that organizational design changes should happen only after a lot of thought, for the right reasons, and to solve real underlying problems in the organization, not just to make it look to outsiders or employees like something is being done.

a product or service at the lowest cost, these companies believe that people will pay more for a product that's unique in some way. It could be that their product has a higher level of quality or offers features that a low-cost product doesn't. A differentiation strategy often hinges on adjusting to changing environments quickly, which often makes an organic structure more appropriate.

技术是组织将投入转化为产出的方法。

TECHNOLOGY. An organization's **technology** is the method by which it transforms inputs into outputs. Very early on in the study of organizations, it was assumed that technology was the major determinant of an organization's structure. Since then, the picture has become less clear regarding the appropriate relationship between technology and structure. Although not completely conclusive, research suggests that the more routine a technology is, the more mechanistic a structure should be. In many ways, this suggestion makes perfect sense: If a company makes the exact same thing over and over, it should focus on creating that one thing as efficiently as possible by having high levels of specialization, formalization, and centralization. However, if technologies need to be changed or altered to suit the needs of various consumers, it follows that decisions would be more decentralized and the rules and procedures the organization relies on would need to be more flexible.

COMPANY SIZE. There is no question that there is a significant relationship between **company size,** or the total number of employees, and structure. As organizations become larger, they need to rely on some combination of specialization, formalization, and centralization to control their activities, thereby becoming more mechanistic in nature. When it comes to organizational performance, however, there is no definite answer as to when an organization's structure should be revised, or "how big is too big." As many organizations get bigger, they attempt to create smaller units within the firm to create a "feeling of smallness." W.L. Gore did just that by attempting to prevent any one location in the company from having more than 150 employees. Top management was convinced that a size of 150 would still allow all the employees to talk to one another in the hallways. However, even Gore hasn't been able to maintain that goal; the company has grown to encompass 7,300 employees in 45 locations.

常见的组织形式
COMMON ORGANIZATIONAL FORMS

Our discussion of organizational design described how an organization's business environment, strategy, technology, and size conspire to make some organizational structures more effective than others. Now we turn our attention to a logical next question: What structures do most organizations utilize? The sections that follow describe some of the most common organizational forms. As you read their descriptions, think about whether these forms would fall on the mechanistic or organic side of the structure continuum. You might also consider what kinds of design factors would lead an organization to choose that particular form.

13.4
What are some of the more common organizational forms that an organization might adopt for its structure?

SIMPLE STRUCTURES. **Simple structures** are perhaps the most common form of organizational design, primarily because there are more small organizations than large ones. In fact, more than 80 percent of employing organizations have fewer than 19 employees. Small accounting and law firms, family-owned grocery stores, individual-owned retail outlets, independent churches, and landscaping services are all organizations that are likely to use a simple structure. Figure 13-3 shows a simple structure for a manager-owned restaurant. The figure reveals that simple structures are just that: simple. Simple structures are generally used by extremely small organizations in which the manager, president, and owner are all the same person. A simple structure is a flat organization with one person as the central decision-making figure; it is not large enough to have a high degree of formalization and will only have very basic differences in work specialization.

简单结构或许是组织设计最常见的形式，主要是因为小型组织的数量比大型组织多得多。

A simple structure makes perfect sense for a small organization, because employees can come and go with no major ripple effects on the organization. However, as the business grows, the coordinating efforts on the part of the owner/manager become increasingly more complex. In the case of our restaurant, let's assume that the growth of the restaurant requires the owner to spend time doing lots of little things to manage the employees. Now the manager has lost the ability to spend time focusing on the actual business at hand. The manager then decides to add a supervisor to handle all of the day-to-day organizing of the restaurant. This arrangement works well until the owner decides to open a second restaurant that needs to have its own supervisor. Now let's assume that this second restaurant is much larger, leading the owner to decide to have separate

FIGURE 13-3 An Organizational Structure for a Small Restaurant

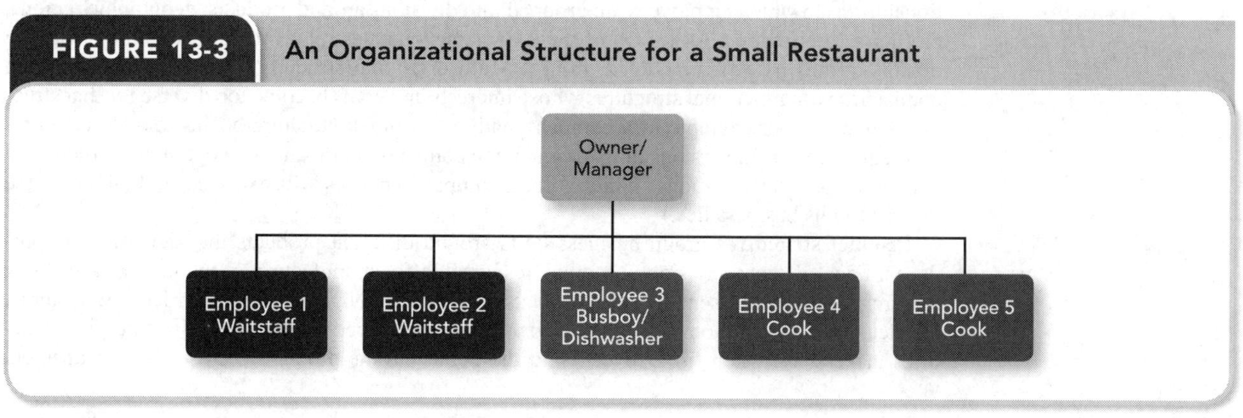

supervisors directly in charge of the wait staff and the kitchen. All of a sudden, our little restaurant has three layers of management!

官僚结构是表现出机械式组织的很多方面特征的组织形式。

职能结构是根据员工在组织中完成的职能不同而把他们进行组合的组织形式。

多分部制结构属于官僚组织形式，围绕产品、地理区域或顾客将员工组合为不同分部的组织形式。

产品结构是围绕公司生产的不同产品组合业务单位。

BUREAUCRATIC STRUCTURES. When you think of the word *bureaucracy,* what thoughts come to mind? Stuffy, boring, restrictive, formal, hard to change, and needlessly complex are some of the terms that have a tendency to be associated with bureaucracies. Those unflattering adjectives aside, chances are very good that you either currently work in a bureaucracy or will after you graduate. A **bureaucratic structure** is an organizational form that exhibits many of the facets of the mechanistic organization. Bureaucracies are designed for efficiency and rely on high levels of work specialization, formalization, centralization of authority, rigid and well-defined chains of command, and relatively narrow spans of control. As mentioned previously, as an organization's size increases, it's incredibly difficult not to develop some form of bureaucracy.

There are numerous types of bureaucratic structures on which we might focus. The most basic of these is the **functional structure.** As shown in Figure 13-4, a functional structure groups employees by the functions they perform for the organization. For example, employees with marketing expertise are grouped together, those with finance duties are grouped together, and so on. The success of the functional structure is based on the efficiency advantages that come with having a high degree of work specialization that's centrally coordinated. Managers have expertise in an area and interact with others with the same type of expertise to create the most efficient solutions for the company. As illustrated in our previous example of the fast-growing restaurant, many small companies naturally evolve into functionally based structures as they grow larger.

However, small companies experiencing rapid growth are not the only organizations to benefit from a functional structure. Macy's, the New York–based clothes store, is moving toward a more traditional functional structure. The 150-year-old retailer used to be organized around geographic regions, but has restructured to be more functionally based with buying, planning, and marketing now all operating out of one location in New York. Macy's hopes that the efficiencies generated by the change in structure will afford it enough cost savings to get a jump on its competitors like J.C. Penney and Kohl's. Indeed, Macy's believes the changes have saved the company $500 million over two years.

Functional structures are extremely efficient when the organization as a whole has a relatively narrow focus, fewer product lines or services, and a stable environment. The biggest weaknesses of a functional structure tend to revolve around the fact that individuals within each function get so wrapped up in their own goals and viewpoints that they lose sight of the bigger organizational picture. In other words, employees don't communicate as well across functions as they do within functions. The Sony example also highlights this danger, in that hardware engineers failed to communicate with software developers, which prevented the hardware and software people from seeing all the pieces of the puzzle. Even in the example directly above, Macy's CEO Terry Lundgren worries about the company's ability to cater to local tastes with a functional structure. To deal with this, he has assigned specific managers in each region to be aware of and responsible for unique local needs.

In contrast to functional structures, **multi-divisional structures** are bureaucratic organizational forms in which employees are grouped into divisions around products, geographic regions, or clients (see Figure 13-4). Each of these divisions operates relatively autonomously from the others and has its own functional groups. Multi-divisional structures generally develop from companies with functional structures whose interests and goals become too diverse for that structure to handle. For example, if a company with a functional structure begins to add customers that require localized versions of its product, the company might adopt a geographic structure to handle the product variations. Which form a company chooses will likely depend on where the diversity in its business lies.

Product structures group business units around different products that the company produces. Each of those divisions becomes responsible for manufacturing, marketing, and doing research and development for the products in its own division. Boeing, Procter & Gamble, Hewlett-Packard, and Sony are companies that have developed product structures. Product structures make sense when firms diversify to the point that the products they sell are so different

FIGURE 13-4 Functional and Multi-Divisional Structures

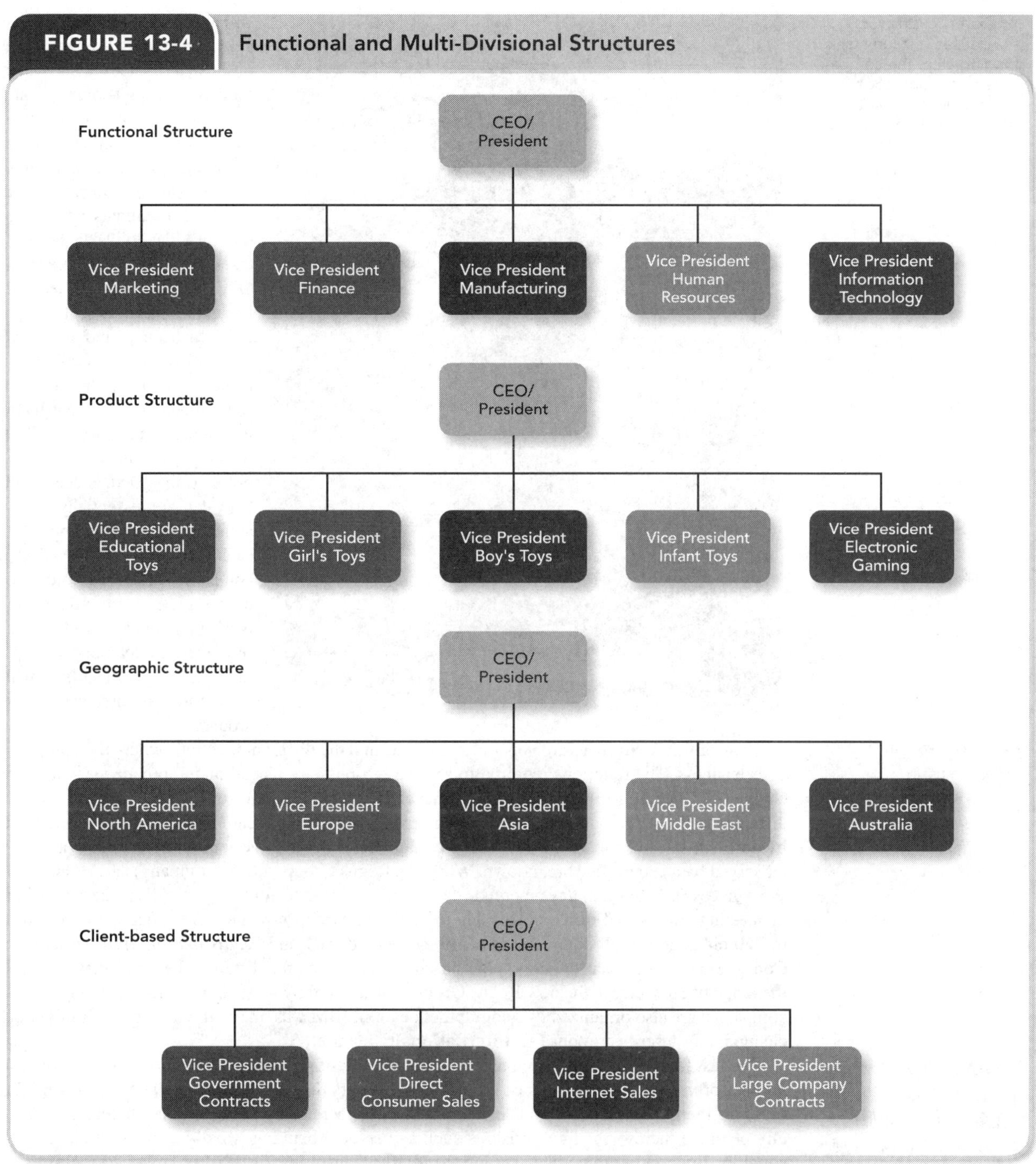

that managing them becomes overwhelming. Hewlett-Packard's organizational structure was recently changed to become more product-based. The company did this because its sales force (in a centralized functional structure) simply had way too many products to sell (from the largest servers to the smallest printers). Shifting the sales force into three different product-based divisions allowed the salespeople to concentrate on a core set of products, reinvigorating the Hewlett-Packard sales force.

Clarence Otis, CEO of Darden restaurants, is bringing all of the company's restaurants together in order to have them share information with one another.

However, there are downsides to a product structure. One of those downsides arises when the divisions don't communicate and they don't have the ability to learn from one another. Darden restaurants is, for the first time, bringing the headquarters for all of its restaurants under one roof in Orlando. Their hope is that it will allow managers from Olive Garden, Red Lobster, and Longhorn Steakhouse to learn from each other and focus on best practices. Not all companies want their divisions to share though—they want them to compete. Fiat-Chrysler CEO Sergio Marchionne reorganized so that Dodge, Jeep, and Chrysler are essentially operating as separate companies, each with its own CEO. These companies are being forced to compete with each other for marketing and development resources. Marchionne is hoping that the competition will help to turn all three car brands around.

地理结构一般是基于公司经营的不同区位。

Geographic structures are generally based around the different locations where the company does business. The functions required to serve a business are placed under a manager who is in charge of a specific location. Reasons for developing a geographic structure revolve around the different tastes of customers in different regions, the size of the locations that need to be covered by different salespeople, or the fact that the manufacturing and distribution of a product are better served by a geographic breakdown. When the Regus Group (a U.K. company) and HQ Global Workplaces (a U.S. company) merged, they came together to form the world's largest supplier of meeting spaces and office suites. The new Regus Group now has 750 office suite facilities in 350 cities across 60 countries. When they merged, HQ and Regus had different structures. Considering the necessarily geographic-based business (i.e., the distances between facilities and the range of customers), the new Regus Group is structured by geographic region. Many global companies are also organized by geographic location. IBM was one of the first, but that might be changing, as described in our **OB Internationally** feature.

客户结构是多分部制结构的最后一种形式。当组织有许多行为方式相似的大客户或者顾客群时，他们就可能围绕着服务顾客来组织业务。

One last form of multi-divisional structure is the **client structure.** When organizations have a number of very large customers or groups of customers that all act in a similar way, they might organize their businesses around serving those customers. For example, small banks traditionally organize themselves into divisions such as personal banking, small business banking, personal lending, and commercial lending. Similarly, consulting firms often organize themselves into divisions that are responsible for small business clients, large business clients, and federal clients. After spending its entire existence organized around a product structure (as are most technology companies), Dell recently adopted a client structure in order to give their top managers more responsibility and flexibility. The company is now structured around four customer groupings: consumers, corporations, small and mid-sized businesses, and government and educational buyers.

矩阵结构是一种较为复杂的组织设计，尝试同时利用两种类型的结构。

Matrix structures are more complex designs that try to take advantage of two types of structures at the same time. Companies such as Xerox, General Electric, and Dow Corning were

OB INTERNATIONALLY

Traditionally, IBM has structured its 200,000-employee organization along geographic lines. Some might argue that IBM was the company that pioneered the first multinational geographic structure by setting up mini-IBMs in countries around the globe. Each country in which IBM operated had its own workforce and management team that reacted to the clients for whom it provided services in that country. The structure made perfect sense in a world in which consultants needed to be on location with their clients when those customers were having software or computer issues. However, IBM's environmental factors are changing rapidly. Competitors, especially those coming out of India, are providing many of the same services for significantly less money.

To change along with its competitors and respond to the "flattening world," IBM is reorganizing its workforce by creating and utilizing what it calls "competency centers." These centers will group employees from around the world on the basis of the specific skill sets that they have to offer clients. Some workers will be grouped into one location that can service clients all over the world through the use of technology. In Boulder, Colorado, IBM employs 6,200 professionals as part of a "call center" that monitors clients' computing functions worldwide. If something goes wrong in one of IBM's 426 data centers, employees in Boulder will more than likely be the ones to handle it or send it to someone who can. Other IBM workers will be grouped by broader geographic locations so that they can still be in relatively close proximity to their customers. When these employees are needed by a client, IBM has a computer database that allows it to put together teams of highly specialized consultants by examining the skill sets listed on 70,000 IBM resumes.

Does this change in structure sound familiar to you? It should—though IBM is maintaining some of it geographical structure, its organizational structure is becoming more functional. As the world becomes flatter through technology, clients expect the best talent from around the world, not just the best talent that happens to be sitting in their city. These structural changes will allow IBM to give clients just that. For IBM, these are the necessary changes that come with being a global company. In fact, IBM has recently been called "the world's most complex organization." It's not just about structure though, according to IBM Senior Vice President Robert W. Moffat Jr.: "Globalization is more than that. Our customers need us to put the right skills in the right place at the right time."

among the first to adopt this type of structure. Figure 13-5 provides an example of a matrix structure. In this example, employees are distributed into teams or projects within the organization on the basis of both their functional expertise and the product that they happen to be working on. Thus, the matrix represents a combination of a functional structure and a product structure. There are two important points to understand about the matrix structure. First, the matrix allows an organization to put together very flexible teams based on the experiences and skills of their employees. This flexibility enables the organization to adjust much more quickly to the environment than a traditional bureaucratic structure would.

Second, the matrix gives each employee two chains of command, two groups with which to interact, and two sources of information to consider. This doubling of traditional structural elements can create high stress levels for employees if the demands of their functional grouping are at odds with the demands of their product- or client-based grouping. The situation can become particularly stressful if one of the two groupings has more power than the other. For example, it may be that the functional manager assigns employees to teams, conducts performance evaluations, and decides raises—making that manager more powerful than the product- or client-based manager. Although matrix structures have been around since the 1960s, the number of organizations using them is growing as teams become a more common form of organizing work. They have also become more common in global companies,

FIGURE 13-5 Matrix Structure

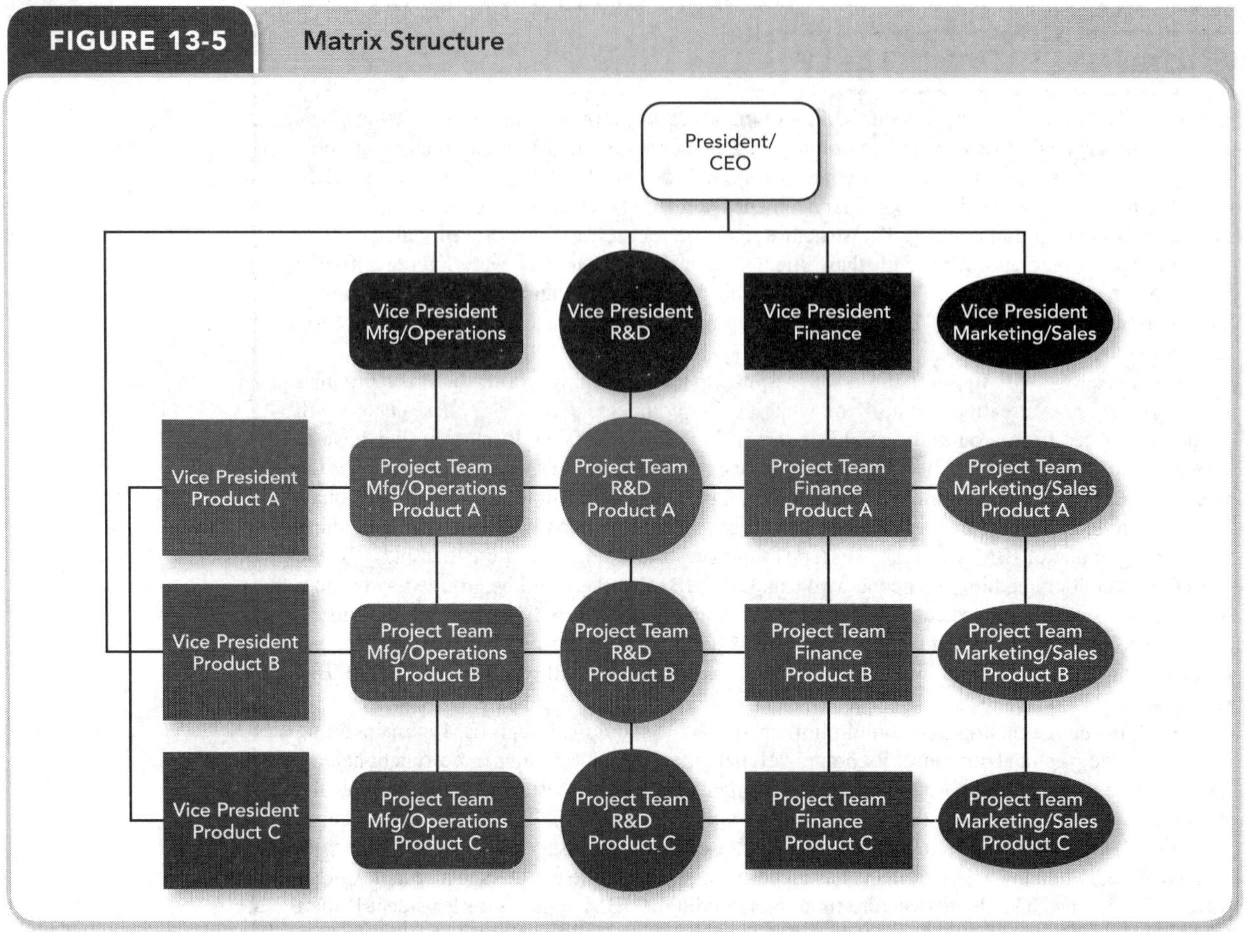

with the functional grouping balanced by a geographic grouping. In fact, numerous companies now have matrix structures with enough layers to be considered four- or five-dimensional. Bristol-Myers Squibb, the New York–based biopharmaceutical company, is heavily matrixed throughout the company. Jane Luciano, vice president of global learning and organizational development, explains, "We have the matrix every way it can be organized, including geographically, functionally, and on a product basis. Based on our size and in a highly regulated industry, the matrix helps us to gain control of issues as they travel around the globe and to leverage economies of scale."

总结：为什么某些组织的结构与其他组织的有所不同
SUMMARY: WHY DO SOME ORGANIZATIONS HAVE DIFFERENT STRUCTURES THAN OTHERS?

So why do some organizations have different structures? As shown in Figure 13-6, differences in the business environment, company strategy, technology, and firm size cause some organizations to be designed differently than others. These differences create variations in the five elements of organizational structure: work specialization, chain of command, span of control, centralization, and formalization. These elements then combine to form one of a number of common organizational forms, including: (1) a simple structure; (2) a bureaucratic structure, which may come in functional, product, geographic, or client forms; or (3) a matrix structure. Some of these forms are more mechanistic, whereas others are more organic. Taken together, these structures explain how work is organized within a given company.

FIGURE 13-6 Why Do Some Organizations Have Different Structures Than Others?

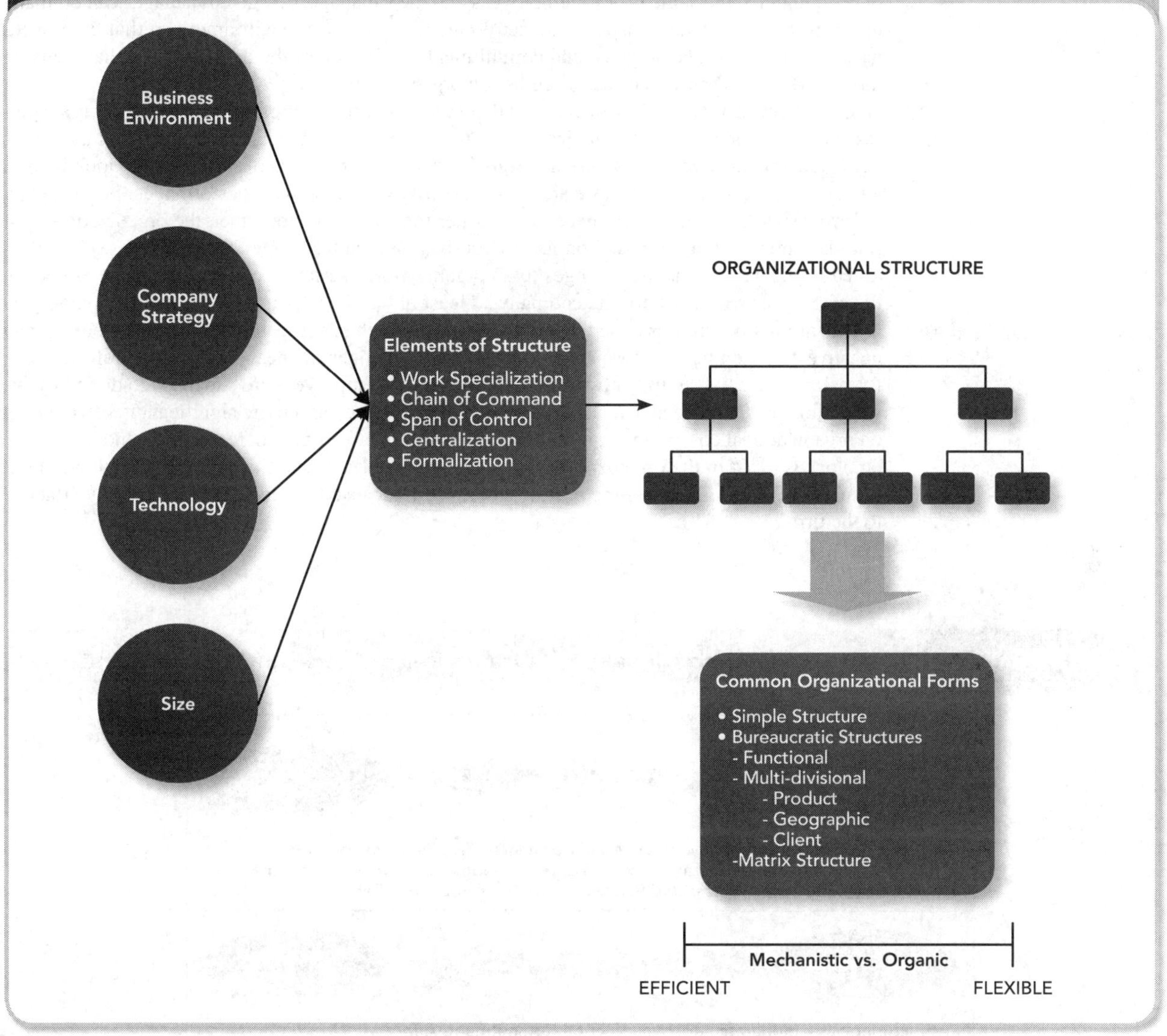

结构有多重要

HOW IMPORTANT IS STRUCTURE?

To some degree, an organization's structure provides the foundation for almost everything in organizational behavior. Think about some of the things that organizational structure affects: communication patterns between employees, the tasks an employee performs, the types of groups an organization uses, the freedom employees have to innovate and try new things, how power and influence are divided up in the company . . . we could go on and on. Picture the walls of a house. The occupants within those walls can decorate or personalize the structure as best they can. They can make it more attractive according to their individual preferences by adding and taking away furniture, but at the end of the day, they're still stuck with that structure. They

 **13.5**

When an organization makes changes to its structure, how does that restructuring affect job performance and organizational commitment?

have to work within the confines that the builder envisioned (unless they're willing to tear down walls or build new ones at considerable time, effort, and expense!). Organizational structures operate in much the same way for employees and their managers. A given manager can do many things to try to motivate, inspire, and set up an effective work environment so that employees have high levels of performance and commitment. At the end of the day, however, that manager must work within the structure created by the organization.

Given how many organizational forms there are, it's almost impossible to give an accurate representation of the impact of organizational structure on job performance. In fact, we might even say that an organization's structure determines what job performance is supposed to look like! In addition, the elements of structure are not necessarily good or bad for performance. For example, a narrow span of control is not necessarily better than a broad one; rather, the organization must find the optimal solution based on its environment and culture. One thing we can say, as illustrated in Figure 13-7, is that changes to an organization's structure can have negative effects on the employees who work for the company, at least in the short term. The process of changing an organization's structure is called **restructuring.** Research suggests that restructuring has a small negative effect on task performance, likely because changes in specialization, centralization, or formalization may lead to confusion about how exactly employees are supposed to do their jobs, which hinders *learning* and *decision making*. Restructuring has a more significant negative effect on organizational commitment, however. Restructuring efforts can increase *stress* and jeopardize employees' *trust* in the organization. There is some evidence that the end result is a lower level of affective commitment on the part of employees, because they feel less emotionally attached to the firm.

重构是指变革组织结构的过程。

FIGURE 13-7 Effects of Organizational Structure on Performance and Commitment

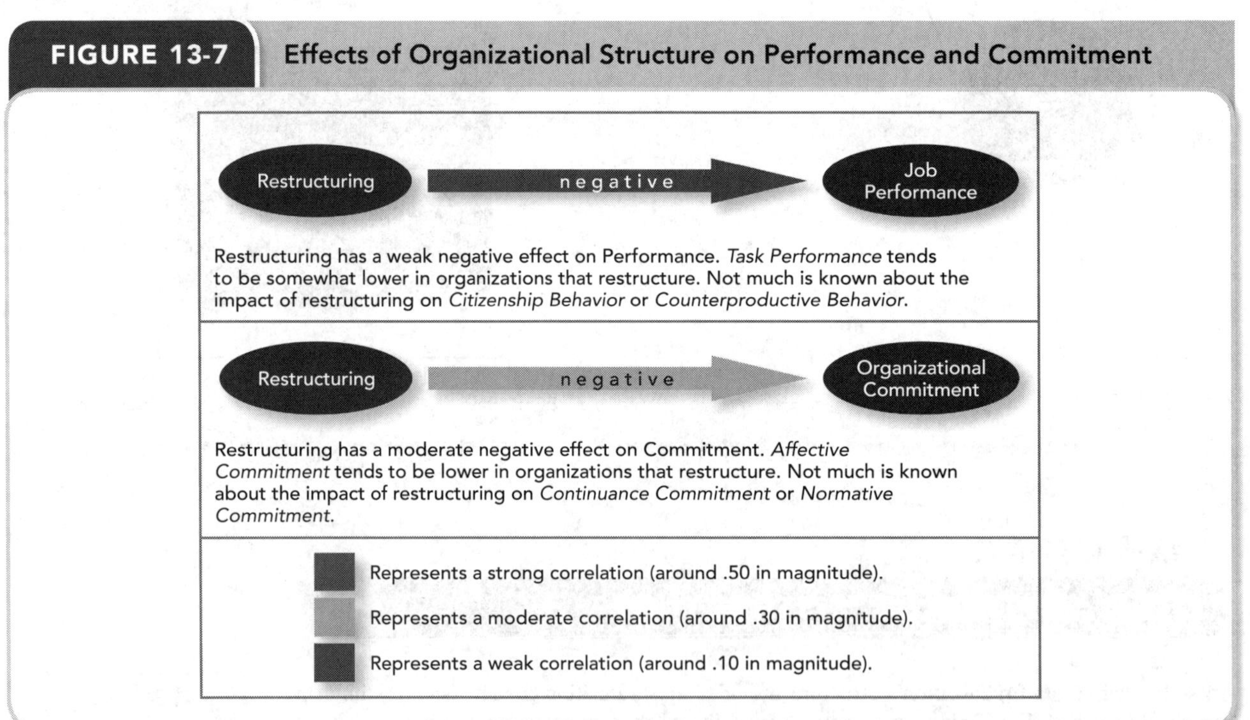

Sources: K.P. DeMeuse, M.L. Marks and G. Dai. "Organizational Downsizing, Mergers and Acquisitions, and Strategic Alliances: Using Theory and Research to Enhance Practice." In *APA Handbook of Industrial and Organizational Psychology,* Vol. 3, ed. S. Zedeck. Washington: APA (2011), pp. 729–68; C. Gopinath and T.E. Becker, "Communication, Procedural Justice, and Employee Attitudes: Relationships under Conditions of Divestiture," *Journal of Management* 26 (2000), pp. 63–83; and J. Brockner, G. Spreitzer, A. Mishra, W. Hockwarter, L. Pepper, and J. Weinberg, "Perceived Control as an Antidote to the Negative Effects of Layoffs on Survivors' Organizational Commitment and Job Performance," *Administrative Science Quarterly* 49 (2004), pp. 76–100.

应用：重构

APPLICATION: RESTRUCTURING

As you've read through our discussion of organizational structure, you may have noticed how important it is for organizations to adapt to their environment. The first step in adapting is recognizing the need to change. The second (and sometimes much more problematic) step is actually adapting through restructuring. Organizations attempt to restructure all the time—in fact, it's difficult to pick up a copy of *Businessweek* or *Fortune* without reading about some organization's restructuring initiatives. General Motors has undertaken a massive restructuring effort no less than eight times over the past 25 years! (And look where that got them. . .!) Most of the examples we put into this chapter pertain to organizations that were restructuring.

Restructuring efforts come in a variety of shapes and sizes. Organizations may change from a product-based structure to a functional structure, from a functional structure to a geographic-based structure, and on and on. However, the most common kind of restructuring in recent years has been a "flattening" of the organization. Why do so many organizations do this? Primarily to show investors that they are reducing costs to become more profitable. Think back to our discussion of tall and flat organizational hierarchies, in which we noted that taller organizations have more layers of management. Many restructuring efforts are designed to remove one or more of those layers to reduce costs. Of course, removing such layers doesn't just mean deleting boxes on an organizational chart; there are actual people within those boxes! Thus, efforts to flatten require organizations to lay off several of the managers within the company.

 13.6

What steps can organizations take to reduce the negative effects of restructuring efforts?

When employees get a sense that their company might be getting ready to restructure, it causes a great deal of stress because they become worried that they will be one of those to lose their jobs. When ex-CEO Carly Fiorina decided to restructure Hewlett-Packard, it caused widespread fear and panic among employees. For the 60 days prior to the actual restructuring announcement, work came to a standstill at the company—tales of high stress, low motivation, political battles, and power struggles abounded. It's estimated that Hewlett-Packard as a company lost an entire quarter's worth of productivity. Not a great way to run a business, especially when, not two years later, the new CEO essentially undid everything that had previously been restructured! He unmerged units that had been merged, decentralized the company where it had been centralized, and flattened the layers of management from 11 to 8 levels. For one example of how restructuring and layoffs can affect employees see this chapter's **OB on Screen.**

One of the ways in which managers can do their best to help a restructuring effort succeed is to help manage the layoff survivors (i.e., employees who remain with the company following a layoff). Many layoff survivors are known to experience a great deal of guilt and remorse following an organization's decision to remove some employees from the company. Researchers and practitioners recently have been trying to understand layoff survivors better, as well as how to help them adjust more quickly. One of the major problems for layoff survivors is the increased job demands placed on them. After all, that coworker or boss the employee had was doing *something*. Layoff survivors are generally burdened with having to pick up the leftover tasks that used to be done by somebody else. This burden creates a sense of uncertainty and stress. Research suggests that one of the best ways to help layoff survivors adjust is to do things that give them a stronger sense of control. Allowing survivors to have a voice in how to move forward or help set the plans about how to accomplish future goals are two ways managers can help employees feel more in control. In addition, honest and frequent communication with layoff survivors greatly helps reduce their feelings of uncertainty and stress. This communication is especially necessary when the organization is hiring at the same time it's firing. For instance, Boeing planned to cut 9,000 jobs in 2009, but in the same year, it had more than 1,500 current and anticipated job openings. Many other employers, such as Microsoft, AT&T, and Time Warner, have experienced something similar. This conflict sends mixed messages to those being laid off, as well as to the survivors. One sobering fact is that the survivors never know whether the restructuring will be a great idea, like Starbucks', that leads to success, or if it's simply a process of grasping at straws to avoid the ultimate demise of the company. For a restructuring to be truly successful, it requires more than simply changing lines on an organizational chart; it demands a different way of working for employees.

OB ON SCREEN

THE COMPANY MEN

What do you want me to do? Parrot back everything you say? I've always told you what I think, right or wrong, and this . . . is wrong.

With those words, Gene McClary (Tommy Lee Jones) makes a last-ditch plea to CEO James Sallinger (Craig T. Nelson) to avoid another round of layoffs in *The Company Men* (Dir.: John Wells, Weinstein Company, 2010). McClary (along with Sallinger) is one of the cofounders of Boston company GTX, currently second-in-command, and is in charge of the last vestige of heavy manufacturing (ship-building) in the company. Although the layoffs will likely raise the stock price and make him considerably wealthier, having his company release thousands of people from their jobs tears at him emotionally—eventually ruining a lifetime friendship and getting him fired as well. One scene in the movie depicts the process of deciding whom to layoff and McClary questioning the ethics of the company's choices even if they're legally defensible.

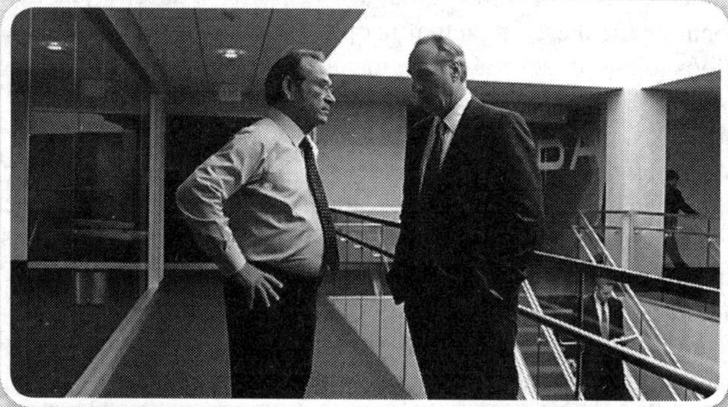

The movie's main storyline gives us a glimpse into the lives and tribulations of some of those who have been laid off, namely Bobby Walker (Ben Affleck) and Phil Woodward (Chris Cooper), and details the struggle of trying to find a new job through outplacement services (Bobby ends up working for his home-renovating brother-in-law (Kevin Costner) for a period of time). However, it also shows us employees that are left behind and the typical feelings they have during the restructuring process. We see employees feeling high levels of anxiety and stress given they don't know if they will have a job the next day or not. The first interactions Bobby Walker has with fellow employees after his exit interview are not statements of sympathy, but rather, "Have you heard anything about me?" questions. Following the restructuring, layoff survivors grapple with how they're going to get all the work done with fewer people around to do it. One employee asks McClary, "I'm already traveling two out of every four weeks, what am I supposed to tell my kids?" McClary's quick response is, "Tell them you're lucky enough to have a job."

chapter 14

Organizational Culture

组织文化

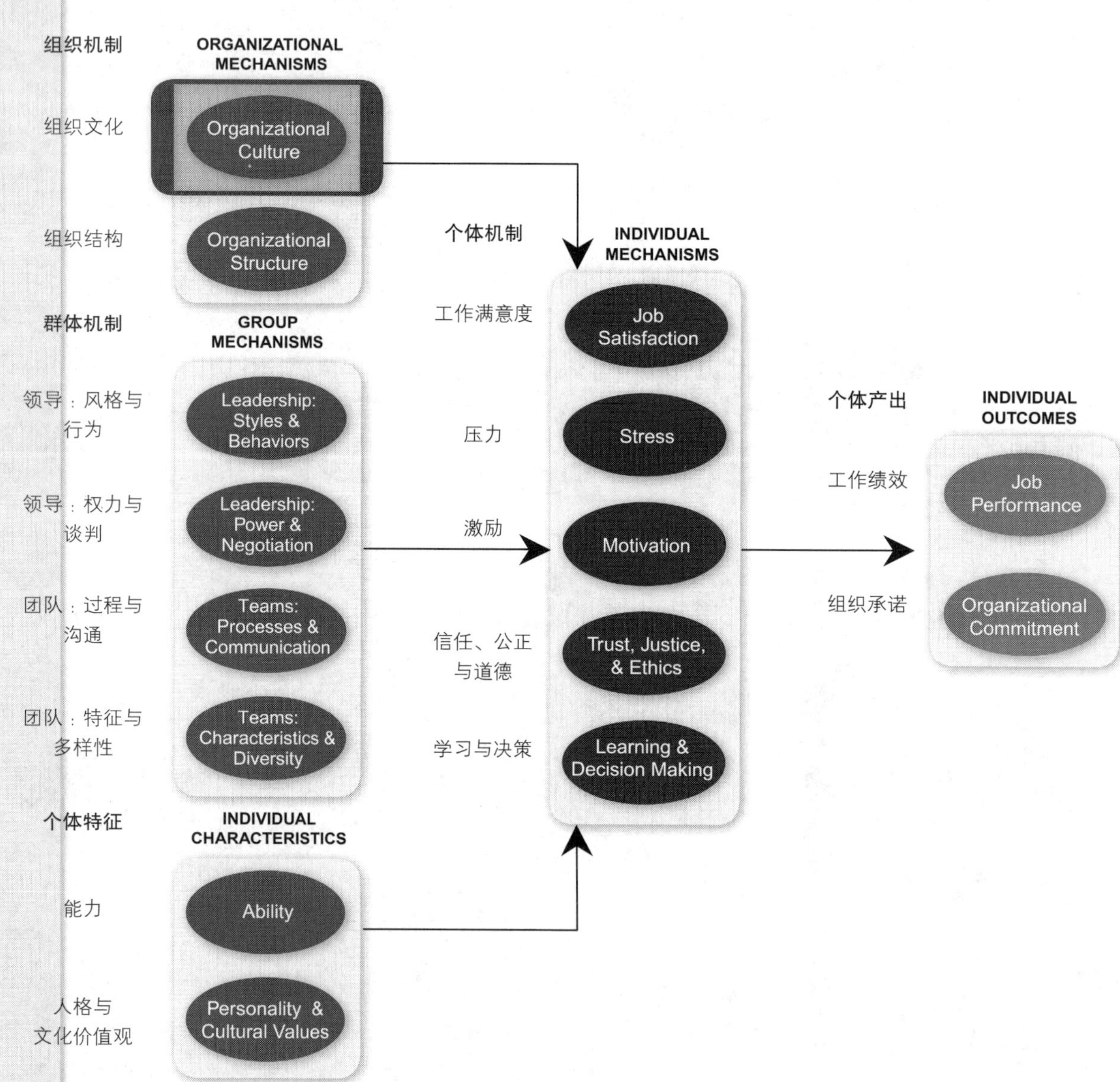

LEARNING GOALS

After reading this chapter, you should be able to answer the following questions:

14.1 What is organizational culture, and what are its components?

14.2 What general and specific types can be used to describe an organization's culture?

14.3 What makes a culture strong, and is it always good for an organization to have a strong culture?

14.4 How do organizations maintain their culture and how do they change it?

14.5 What is person–organization fit and how does it affect job performance and organizational commitment?

14.6 What steps can organizations take to make sure that newcomers will fit with their culture?

ZAPPOS

When you mention "organizational culture," Zappos.com, the Nevada–based online retailer might very well be the company that pops into many people's minds. Well-known for its quirky, fun-loving, happy culture, the company regularly finds itself ranked toward the top of almost every "best company to work for list" (they're number six on *Fortune*'s 2011 list). They aren't on that list for their pay—call-center operators start off at $11/hour with no bonuses or 401(k) contributions. CEO Tony Hseih believes that the best employees work mainly for the psychological gratification of helping others. When Hseih joined the company in 1999 he had two goals for the first 10 years. First, reach $1 billion in annual sales (they were $1.6 million at the time). Second, get on the list of best companies to work for. Zappos accomplished both by 2009.

How did they do that so quickly? Customer service? After all, Zappos is known for its free shipping, free returns, 365-day return policy, and 24-7 access to customer representatives. Zappos' call-center agents are known to talk with customers on the phone for hours at a time and they have complete freedom to do whatever they have to in order to make customers happy. Zappos does many things most online retailers don't—but these policies aren't things that other companies can't match. So what is it that sets them apart? Aaron Magness, Zappos' director of business development and brand marketing, says the company isn't focused on customer service, "It's focused on company culture, which leads to customer service. We don't talk about customer service; we allow it to happen on its own by having the right people."

CEO Tony Hsieh says, "At Zappos, we view culture as our number-one priority. About five years ago, we formalized the definition of our culture into ten core values. We wanted to come up with committable core values, meaning that we would actually be willing to hire and fire people based on those values, regardless of their individual job performance." Those core values include things like "Do more with less" and "Create fun and a little weirdness." The truth is that companies are flocking in from around the world just to see what makes Zappos tick. Due to the demand, Zappos is now holding two-day seminars on just that! One of the single biggest fans of the Zappos culture is Amazon.com's CEO Jeff Bezos. In fact, he loved it so much he bought it (for $1.2 billion in late 2009). Although there was a huge concern that Amazon's efficiency-oriented culture would ruin Zappos, the fact is that Zappos is being left completely alone. Bezos stated that the culture and brand "are huge assets that I value very much and I want to see those things continue."

组织文化

ORGANIZATIONAL CULTURE

In almost every chapter prior to this point, we have simply given you definitions of important topics. However, here are just about as many definitions of organizational culture as there are people who study it. In fact, research on organizational culture has produced well over 50 different definitions! It seems that the term *culture* means a great many things to a great many people. Definitions of culture have ranged from as broad as, "The way we do things around here" to as specific as . . . well, let's just suffice it to say that they can get complicated. Not surprisingly, the various definitions of organizational culture stem from how people have studied it. Sociologists study culture using a broad lens and anthropological research methods, like those applied to study tribes and civilizations. Psychologists tend to study culture and its effects on people using survey methods. In fact, many psychologists actually prefer the term *climate,* but for our purposes, we'll use the two terms interchangeably. In this chapter, we define **organizational culture** as the shared social knowledge within an organization regarding the rules, norms, and values that shape the attitudes and behaviors of its employees.

组织文化是组织内部共享的关于规则、规范和价值观的社会知识，这些知识塑造了员工的态度和行为。

This definition helps highlight a number of facets of organizational culture. First, culture is social knowledge among members of the organization. Employees learn about most important aspects of culture through other employees. This transfer of knowledge might be through explicit communication, simple observation, or other, less obvious methods. In addition, culture is shared knowledge, which means that members of the organization understand and have a degree of consensus regarding what the culture is. Second, culture tells employees what the rules, norms,

14.1
What is organizational culture, and what are its components?

'I don't know how it started, either. All I know is that it's part of our corporate culture.'

Source: © Mick Stevens, The New Yorker Collection, www.cartoonbank.com

and values are within the organization. What are the most important work outcomes to focus on? What behaviors are appropriate or inappropriate at work? How should a person act or dress while at work? Indeed, some cultures even go so far as to say how employees should act when they aren't at work. Third, organizational culture shapes and reinforces certain employee attitudes and behaviors by creating a system of control over employees. There is evidence that your individual goals and values will grow over time to match those of the organization for which you work. This development really isn't that hard to imagine, given how much time employees spend working inside an organization.

为什么某些组织的文化与其他组织的有所不同
WHY DO SOME ORGANIZATIONS HAVE DIFFERENT CULTURES THAN OTHERS?

One of the most common questions people ask when you tell them where you are employed is, "So, tell me . . . what's it like there?" The description you use in your response is likely to have a lot to do with what the organization's culture is all about. In calculating your response to the question, you might consider describing the kinds of people who work at your company. More than likely, you'll do your best to describe the work atmosphere on a regular day. Perhaps you'll painstakingly describe the facilities you work in or how you feel the employees are treated. You might even go so far as to describe what it is that defines "success" at your company. All of those answers give clues that help organizational outsiders understand what a company is actually like. To give you a feel for the full range of potential answers to the "what's it like there?" question, it's necessary to review the facets of culture in more detail.

文化成分
CULTURE COMPONENTS

There are three major components to any organization's culture: observable artifacts, espoused values, and basic underlying assumptions. You can understand the differences among these three components if you view culture like an onion, as in Figure 14-1. Some components of an organization's culture are readily apparent and observable, like the skin of an onion. However, other components are less observable to organizational outsiders or newcomers. Such outsiders can observe, interpret, and make conclusions based on what they see on the surface, but the inside remains a mystery until they can peel back the outside layers to gauge the values and assumptions that lie beneath. The sections that follow review the culture components in more detail.

FIGURE 14-1 The Three Components of Organizational Culture

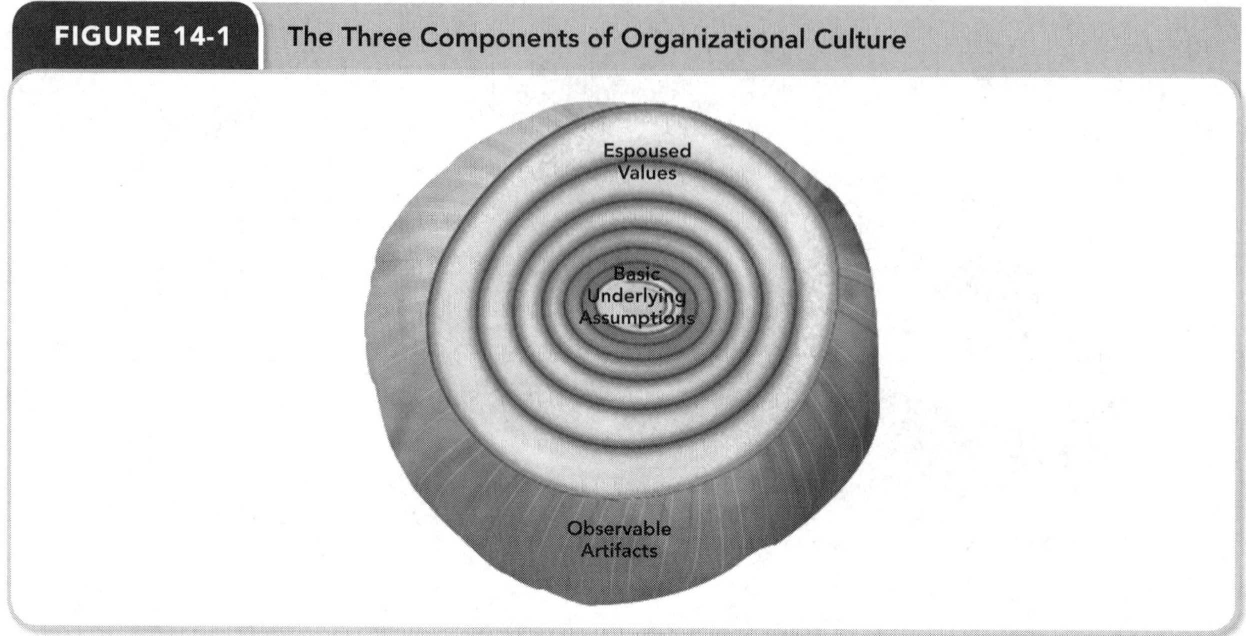

物化层是员工可以轻易看到或谈论的组织文化的表现形式。

OBSERVABLE ARTIFACTS. **Observable artifacts** are the manifestations of an organization's culture that employees can easily see or talk about. They supply the signals that employees interpret to gauge how they should act during the workday. Artifacts supply the primary means of transmitting an organization's culture to its workforce. It's difficult to overestimate the importance of artifacts, because they help show not only current employees but also potential employees, customers, shareholders, and investors what the organization is all about. There are six major types of artifacts: symbols, physical structures, language, stories, rituals, and ceremonies.

从公司标识到其官网上的图像，再到公司员工穿着的制服，**标志**在组织中随处可见。

Symbols can be found throughout an organization, from its corporate logo to the images it places on its website to the uniforms its employees wear. Think about what Nike's "swoosh" represents: speed, movement, velocity. What might that symbol convey about Nike's culture? Or consider Apple Computer's "apple" logo. That symbol brings to mind Newton's discovery of gravity under the apple tree, conveying the importance of innovation within Apple's culture. When you think of the words "dark suit, white shirt, tie," what company do you think of? For many, the symbol represents IBM because that summarizes the company's long-standing dress code. Even though that dress code hasn't been in place at IBM for 15 years, it still symbolizes a formal, bureaucratic, and professional culture.

物理结构也反映了很多文化的内容。如，办公室是开放的吗？高层管理者的工作是否在大楼的独立区域？

Physical structures also say a lot about a culture. Is the workplace open? Does top management work in a separate section of the building? Is the setting devoid of anything unique, or can employees express their personalities? Takanobu Ito, CEO of Honda Motor, sends a message about the company's culture in his office. Ito works at a plain wooden desk in room with a dozen other executives. John Childress, founding partner of The Principia Group, tells the story of a Ford executive he worked with whose entire office had burned down: "He'd been having terrible problems between departments. There were barriers that meant information wasn't flowing. He had to quickly rent new premises and all he could find was an open-plan building. The culture changed overnight because of the different ways of working." IDEO, a creative design firm, also has an open-office environment, though IDEO lets employees set up their offices however they like. When you walk around their work areas, you'll be walking underneath bicycles hanging over your head and crazy objects and toys in every direction.

语言反映了组织内部使用的行话、俚语和口号。

Language reflects the jargon, slang, and slogans used within the walls of an organization. Do you know what a CTR, CPC, or Crawler is? Chances are you don't. If you worked for Yahoo, however, those terms would be second nature to you: CTR stands for click-through rate, CPC stands for cost-per-click, and a Crawler is a computer program that gathers information from

The ability to set up your own work space, as at the design firm IDEO, is a hallmark of an open corporate culture. Would this environment suit your working style?

other websites. If you worked at Microsoft and got an e-mail from a software developer telling you that they were "licking the cookie," what would you think? For Microsoft employees, "licking the cookie" means that a person or group is announcing that they are working on a feature or product and it is now off-limits for others to work on. Home Depot maintains a "stack it high and watch it fly" slogan, which reflects its approach to sales. Yum Brands Inc., which owns Pizza Hut, Taco Bell, KFC, and other fast-food restaurants, expects employees to be "customer maniacs" —language that conveys its culture for customer interaction.

Stories consist of anecdotes, accounts, legends, and myths that are passed down from cohort to cohort within an organization. Telling stories can be a major mechanism through which leaders and employees describe what the company values or finds important. For example, Howard Schultz, CEO of Starbucks, tells the story of how (to improve quality) he forbade the common practice of resteaming milk. What this rule inadvertently created was the loss of millions of dollars of milk, as thousands of gallons of lukewarm liquid were poured down the drain. One of his store managers came up with a simple, brilliant suggestion: Put etched lines inside the steaming pitchers so baristas would know how much milk to pour for the drink size they were making, instead of just guessing. Paul Wiles, president/CEO of Novant Health in Winston-Salem, North Carolina, believes strongly in the power of storytelling to foster culture; he claims, "Talk about numbers, and people's eyes glaze over; talk about one child who died unnecessarily, and no one can walk away from that."

故事是由在组织内部口口相传的轶事、传说、传奇和神话组成。

Rituals are the daily or weekly planned routines that occur in an organization. Employees at New Belgium Brewing in Colorado, home of Fat Tire Ale, can enjoy a beer in the tasting room after their shift as well as get one free twelve-pack a week, conveying the importance of both employees and the company's product. At UPS, every driver and package handler attends a mandatory "three-minute meeting" with their managers to help with communication. The 180-second time limit helps enforce the importance of punctuality in the UPS culture. The Men's Wearhouse pays managers quarterly bonuses when theft (referred to as "shrink") is kept low. That ritual sends a message that "when workers steal from you, they are stealing from themselves and their colleagues." At Davita, the Denver–based kidney dialysis company, CEO Kent Thiry says, "We do songs. We do chants. We do call and response. Many kind of organizations in all cultures use these methods. Why? For positive energy. Some of our new executives say, 'That's really dumb' or 'That's really cheesy.' And two years later, they're leading it." At M5 networks, a New York–based seller of VoIP phone systems, over a third of the employees learn to play musical instruments in a rock band on company time. Dan Hoffman, CEO, says, "As adults, we tend to forget how to learn. The idea with the rock band program was to remind people how to learn."

仪式是组织内每天或每周有计划举行的例行活动。

典礼通常是以组织成员作为观众表演的正式活动。

Ceremonies are formal events, generally performed in front of an audience of organizational members. At Care.com, all workers are forced to move desks every year at the same time. CEO Sheila Marcelo assigns the seats. She says, "People don't have a choice where they sit. Part of the reason was to embrace change, to remove turfiness so that you're not just chatting with your friends and sitting with your friends. You sit with somebody else from a different team so you get to know their job. What are they doing? What are they saying on the phone? How do they tick? And it's getting to know different people so that we build a really big team. And we do that every year. And it's now actually become an exciting thing that people embrace." In the process of turning around the company, Continental Airlines held a ceremony to burn an employee-despised 800-page policy manual. Gordon Bethune, then-CEO of Continental, put together a task force that came up with a new 80-page manual. Other types of ceremonies revolve around celebrations for meeting quality goals, reaching a certain level of profitability, or launching a new product.

制度层是公司明确表达的信仰、经营理念与规范。

ESPOUSED VALUES. **Espoused values** are the beliefs, philosophies, and norms that a company explicitly states. Espoused values can range from published documents, such as a company's vision or mission statement, to verbal statements made to employees by executives and managers. Examples of some of Whole Foods Market's outward representations of espoused values can be found in Table 14-1. What does each of these statements tell you about Whole Foods and what it cares about?

It's certainly important to draw a distinction between espoused values and enacted values. It's one thing for a company to outwardly say something is important; it's another thing for employees to consistently act in ways that support those espoused values. When a company holds to its espoused values over time and regardless of the situations it operates in, the values become more believable both to employees and outsiders. However, in times of economic downturns, staying true to espoused values isn't always easy. Marriott International has been struggling in the most recent economic downturn, like many of its competitors in the lodging/travel business. It has been very tempting for the company to do everything it can to slash expenses, but its espoused value of always treating its people right prevents cuts that would harm employee benefits. J.W. "Bill" Marriott Jr., the company's chairperson and CEO, states, "If the employees are well taken care of, they'll take care of the customer and the customer will come back. That's basically the core value of the company." It is worth noting that not all companies are open in regards to their values. Trader Joe's, the Monrovia, CA–based grocery chain is known by its patrons as perhaps the coolest, local product-seeking, customer-oriented business in America. In opposition to Whole Foods, they are also perhaps one of the most secretive companies in the world when

TABLE 14-1 The Espoused Values of Whole Foods

Below is a list of the seven core values that Whole Foods believes lay the foundation for its organizational culture. The company believes that these values set it apart from competing organizations, show others why Whole Foods is a great place to work, and will always be the reasons for the company's existence regardless of how large it grows. More details about each value can be found on the company's website.

1. Selling the highest-quality natural and organic products available.
2. Satisfying and delighting our customers.
3. Supporting team member happiness and excellence.
4. Creating wealth through profits and growth.
5. Caring about our communities and our environment.
6. Creating ongoing win–win partnerships with our suppliers.
7. Promoting the health of our stakeholders through healthy-eating education.

Source: From Whole Foods Core Values, http://www.wholefoodsmarket.com/company/corevalues.php

it comes to their business practices. In fact, suppliers have to sign agreements that they won't disclose anything having to do with their business relationship with the store before they are allowed to supply products to them.

BASIC UNDERLYING ASSUMPTIONS. **Basic underlying assumptions** are the taken-for-granted beliefs and philosophies that are so ingrained that employees simply act on them rather than questioning the validity of their behavior in a given situation. These assumptions represent the deepest and least observable part of a culture and may not be consciously apparent, even to organizational veterans. Edgar Schein, one of the preeminent scholars on the topic of organizational culture, uses the example of safety in an engineering firm. He states, "In an occupation such as engineering, it would be inconceivable to deliberately design something that is unsafe; it is a taken-for-granted assumption that things should be safe." Whatever a company's underlying assumptions are, its hidden beliefs are those that are the most likely to dictate employee behavior and affect employee attitudes. They're also the aspects of an organizational culture that are the most long-lasting and difficult to change.

精神层是员工认为理所当然的信仰和经营理念，在员工中如此根深蒂固，以至于在给定的情形下，员工只是按照信仰和经营理念做事而不质疑他们行为的有效性。

一般文化类型
GENERAL CULTURE TYPES

If we can consider the combination of an organization's observable artifacts, espoused values, and underlying assumptions, we can begin to classify its culture along various dimensions. Of course, there are many different types of organizational cultures, just like there are many different types of personalities. Many researchers have tried to create general typologies that can be used to describe the culture of any organization. For instance, one popular general typology divides organizational culture along two dimensions: solidarity and sociability. Solidarity is the degree to which group members think and act alike, and sociability represents how friendly employees are to one another. Figure 14-2 shows how we might describe organizations that are either high or low on these dimensions. Organizations that are low on both dimensions have a **fragmented culture** in which employees are distant and disconnected from one another. Organizations that have cultures in which employees think alike but aren't friendly to one another can be considered **mercenary cultures.** These types of organizations are likely to be very political, "what's in it for me" environments. One example of a company with a history of being a mercenary culture can be found in this chapter's **OB at the Bookstore.** Cultures in which all employees are friendly to one another, but everyone thinks differently and does his or her own thing, are **networked cultures.** Many highly creative organizations have a networked culture. Organizations with friendly employees who all think alike are **communal cultures.** There is

在**散裂型文化**（社交性低和团结性低）中，员工彼此之间疏远又分离。

在**图利型文化**（社交性低和团结性高）中，员工彼此之间想法相同但是关系并不友好。

 **14.2**

What general and specific types can be used to describe an organization's culture?

在**网络型文化**（社交性高和团结性低）中，所有的员工彼此之间很友好，但每个人想法不同且各行其是。

在**共有型文化**（社交性高和团结性高）中，员工彼此友好且想法相同。

FIGURE 14-2 A Typology of Organizational Culture

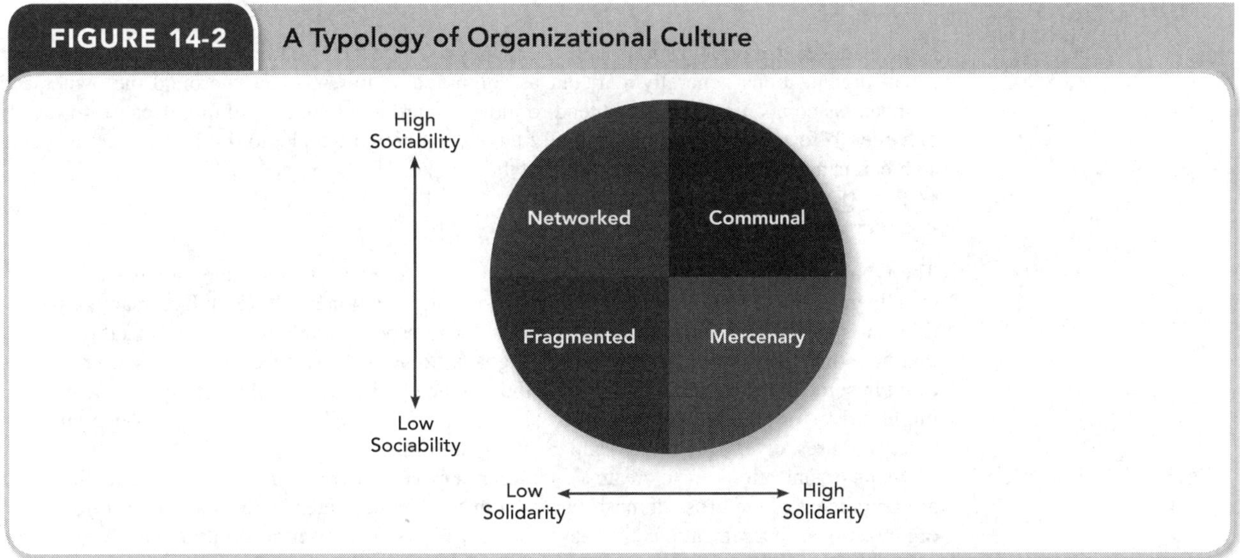

Source: Adapted from R. Goffee and G. Jones, *The Character of a Corporation* (New York: Harper Business, 1998).

OB AT THE BOOKSTORE

THOSE GUYS HAVE ALL THE FUN: INSIDE THE WORLD OF ESPN

by James Andrew Miller and Tom Shales (New York: Little, Brown and Company, 2011).

> *"ESPN is really a mentality, and unlike any other place I've ever seen. People are very competitive, and it starts at the beginning. As soon as you start out, you have to make it, either you're good enough or you don't have a job. Competitiveness and drive exist from the bottom up, and that's part of the culture. So people really care about what they're doing, and that makes for a very successful place."*

With those words, production assistant Michael Mandt describes what he felt the culture was like at ESPN. Written by James Andrew Miller and Tom Shales, the book is essentially an amalgamation of quotes from interviews with current and former ESPN employees, personalities, and owners. According to the authors, ESPN is "the most important part of the Disney empire, worth more than the entire National Football League, worth more than the NBA, MLB, and the NHL put together." When you pay your cable bill (and over 100 million of us do every month), $4 of it goes directly to ESPN. This book is the story of how the company originated (using $9,000 on a credit card) and was built into the influential behemoth it is today.

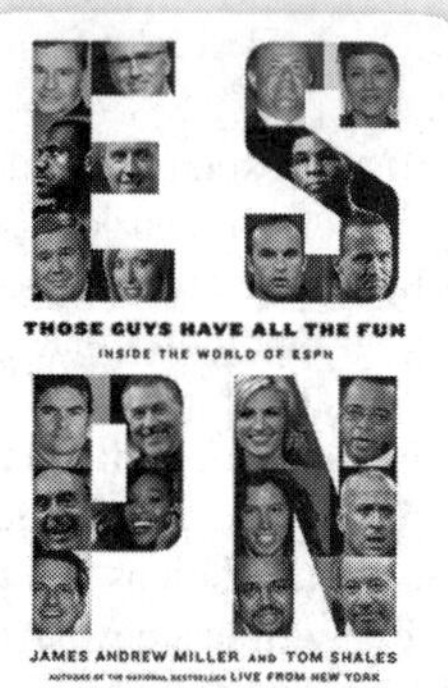

The book is relatively unique in that it gives readers the chance as it's to follow the culture of the company, being formed and then somewhat changed over time to where it is today. How it gets there is rarely a pretty process. The history of ESPN (as seen through the eyes of employees and outsiders) reads like a corporate soap opera with tales of competition, power, politics, and sexual harassment. However, one thing that remains constant throughout is a love for sports and the fact that the talent can never be more important than the brand (or you won't be around long—see Keith Olberman, Craig Kilborn, Dan Patrick). Although the passion for what they do is strong, it is clear that the mercenary culture grinds on employees over time. As sportscaster Jack Edwards states, "It was a very, very negative place to work. Don't believe the mascot promos. Life is not like that at SportsCenter."

some evidence that organizations have a tendency to move through the cultures as they get larger. Small organizations generally start out as communal cultures oriented around the owner and founder. As companies grow, they tend to move toward a networked culture, because solidarity is harder to foster when groups get really large. Although we like to think of culture as being stable, it can change, as we discuss later in this chapter.

特殊文化类型
SPECIFIC CULTURE TYPES

The typology in Figure 14-2 is general enough to be applied to almost any organization. However, there are obviously other ways to classify an organization's culture. In fact, many organizations attempt to manipulate observable artifacts and espoused values to create specific cultures that help them achieve their organizational goals. Some of these specific cultures are more relevant in some industries than in others. Although the number of specific cultures an organization might strive for are virtually endless, we focus on four examples: customer service cultures, safety cultures, diversity cultures, and creativity cultures.

顾客服务型文化主要关注服务质量。

Many organizations try to create a **customer service culture** focused on service quality. After all, 65 percent of the gross domestic product in the United States is generated by service-based organizations. Organizations that have successfully created a service culture have been shown to change employee attitudes and behaviors toward customers. These changes in attitudes and behaviors then manifest themselves in higher levels of customer satisfaction and sales.

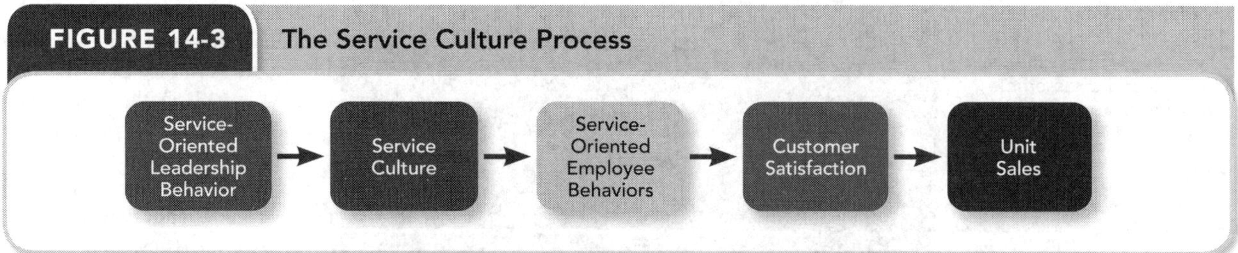

Source: Adapted from B. Schneider, M.G. Ehrhart, D.M. Mayer, J.L. Saltz, and K. Niles-Jolly, "Understanding Organization–Customer Links in Service Settings," *Academy of Management Journal* 48 (2005), pp. 1017–32.

Figure 14-3 illustrates the process of creating a service culture and the effects it has on company results. Numerous companies claim that the sole reason for their continued existence is their ability to create a service culture in their organization when it wasn't originally present. USAA, the Texas–based provider of financial services to military families, is perhaps the single best example of a customer service culture there is, having come in either first or second place for four years running in *Businessweek*'s Customer Service awards. As an example of the pains they go to in order to create that culture, USAA call center reps are required to spend close to six months in training before actually answering the phones so that they can understand the lives of their military customers. Companies might go out of their way to hire customer-oriented employees, but research also shows that a customer service culture can lead to even more customer-oriented behaviors on the part of their employees and a larger bottom-line profit as a result.

In the United States, there were over three million nonfatal workplace accidents and five thousand fatal ones in 2009. It's not uncommon for manufacturing or medical companies to go through a string of accidents or injuries that potentially harm their employees. For these organizations, creating a **safety culture** is of paramount importance. There is a clear difference between organizations in terms of the degree to which safe behaviors at work are viewed as expected and valued. A positive safety culture has been shown to reduce accidents and increase safety-based citizenship behaviors. A safety culture also reduces treatment errors in medical settings. General Electric instigated an investigation into some of its service centers that were suffering unacceptable levels of accidents and injuries. Plants that were having problems underwent a process to energize their safety cultures through a series of two-day meetings that identified safety problems and potential solutions. Although GE does not expect all of its problems to be fixed overnight, it's so satisfied with the new culture created at these plants that it's working on rolling out similar programs in all of its 67 service centers across the United States. As with many changes, it's very important that management's actions match its words. One study found that employees were highly cynical of a safety program when they perceived a mismatch between espoused and enacted safety values by management. Two recent meta-analyses provide clear evidence though that having a safety-oriented culture means higher levels of safety performance and fewer injuries and accidents for an organization.

安全文化主要关注员工的安全。

There are a number of reasons why an organization might want to foster a **diversity culture.** What images come to mind when you think of Denny's? Do you think of the Grand Slam breakfast, or do you think of race discrimination? Although the lawsuits that charged company discrimination against African Americans were settled back in 1994, the stigma of Denny's discrimination complaints still lingers. Since 1994, Denny's has maintained a position within the company of chief diversity officer, whose sole responsibility is to help create a culture of diversity. Denny's has since become a prime example of how to aggressively lead a charge toward a diversity culture. What used to be an all-white, all-male organization has tried to transform itself by hiring a large number of new minority managers and franchise owners, replacing half of the all-male board of directors with women, conducting diversity sensitivity training sessions, and performing a whole host of other symbolic actions. Many of the techniques used by Denny's are now recognized as key elements in successful corporate diversity initiatives. The Interpublic Group, a New York–based advertising giant (40,000 employees), has also been recognized for its diversity culture. Heide Gardner, chief diversity and inclusion officer says, "What I am learning is: Inclusion is pretty much the same everywhere. It's not just about making diversity counts but about making diversity count. And that holds true wherever you are." Diversity isn't just for big companies though; Teshmont Engineering Consultants, a

多元文化主要关注提升和利用员工的群体多元化。

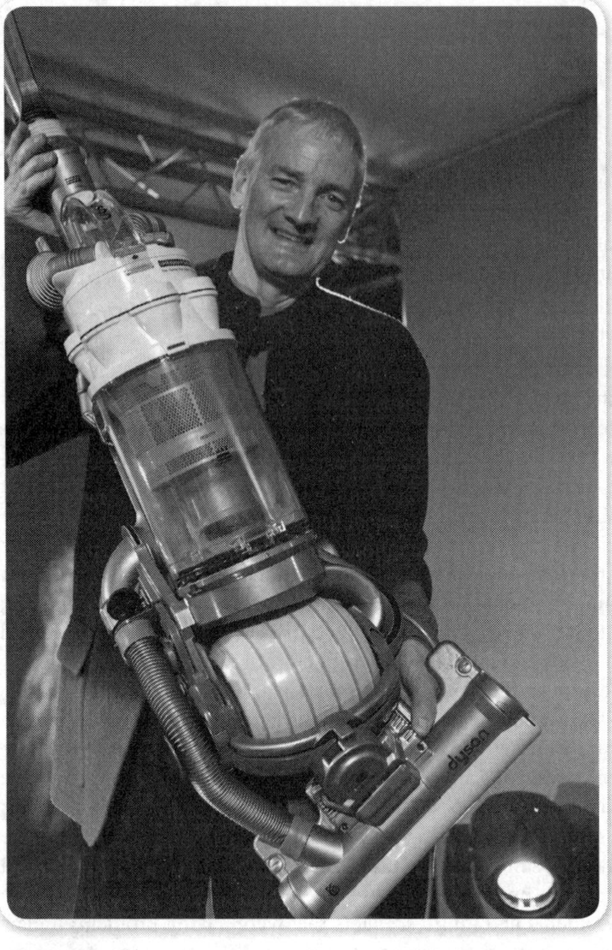

In order to foster a creativity culture, James Dyson (pictured) has engineers assemble and disassemble a Dyson vacuum cleaner their first day on the job.

创新文化主要关注培养创新氛围。

small (less than 100 employees) Canadian–based company, has a culture centered around diversity as well, with 31 different mother tongues spoken at the firm.

Given the importance of new ideas and innovation in many industries, it's understandable that some organizations focus on fostering a **creativity culture.** Creativity cultures affect both the quantity and quality of creative ideas within an organization. 3M believes that creativity comes from freedom and not control; workers in R&D are allowed to spend 15 percent of their time researching whatever they want. At Dyson, the extremely innovative U.K.–based appliances manufacturing company, CEO and founder James Dyson forbids the wearing of suits or ties as well as the writing of memos. He feels that workers will be more creative if they talk to each other about their ideas. New engineers are required to disassemble and reassemble a Dyson vacuum cleaner on their first day on the job. SAS, the business analytics software firm based in North Carolina, has a full-blown infant day care center, a Montessori school, and an after-school program to allow employees to spend more time thinking about creative solutions to problems and less time worrying about their kids. To see whether you've spent time working in a creativity culture, see our **OB Assessments** feature.

文化强度
CULTURE STRENGTH

 **14.3**

What makes a culture strong, and is it always good for an organization to have a strong culture?

文化强度是指员工认同组织中事情应该如何发生的方式，并且他们的后续行为与这些期望保持一致的程度。

Although most organizations seem to strive for one, not all companies have a culture that creates a sense of definite norms and appropriate behaviors for their employees. If you've worked for a company and can't identify whether it has a strong culture or not, it probably doesn't. A high level of **culture strength** exists when employees definitively agree about the way things are supposed to happen within the organization (high consensus) and when their subsequent behaviors are consistent with those expectations (high intensity). As shown in Figure 14-4, a strong culture serves to unite and direct employees. Weak cultures exist when employees disagree about the way things are supposed to be or what's expected of them, meaning that there is nothing to unite or direct their attitudes and actions.

Strong cultures take a long time to develop and are very difficult to change. Individuals working within strong cultures are typically very aware of it. However, this discussion brings us to an important point: "Strong" cultures are not always "good" cultures. Strong cultures guide employee attitudes and behaviors, but that doesn't always mean that they guide them toward the most successful organizational outcomes. Toyota ran into major problems when its notoriously secretive culture clashed with U.S. regulators who demanded that the company disclose safety threats. As such, it's useful to recognize some of the positive and negative aspects of having a strong organizational culture. Table 14-2 lists some of the advantages and disadvantages. You

OB ASSESSMENTS

CREATIVITY CULTURE

Have you experienced a creativity culture? This assessment is designed to measure two facets of that type of culture. Think of your current job, or the last job that you held (even if it was a part-time or summer job). If you haven't worked, think of a current or former student group that developed strong norms for how tasks should be done. Answer each question using the response scale provided. Then subtract your answers to the boldfaced questions from 6, with the difference being your new answer for that question. For example, if your original answer for question 7 was "4," your new answer is "2" (6 – 4). Then sum up your scores for the two facets. (For more assessments relevant to this chapter, please visit http://connect.mcgraw-hill.com.)

1 STRONGLY DISAGREE	2 DISAGREE	3 UNCERTAIN	4 AGREE	5 STRONGLY AGREE

1. New ideas are readily accepted here. _______
2. This company is quick to respond when changes need to be made. _______
3. Management here is quick to spot the need to do things differently. _______
4. This organization is very flexible; it can quickly change procedures to meet new conditions and solve problems as they arise. _______
5. People in this organization are always searching for new ways of looking at problems. _______
6. It is considered extremely important here to follow the rules. _______
7. **People can ignore formal procedures and rules if it helps to get the job done.** _______
8. Everything has to be done by the book. _______
9. **It is not necessary to follow procedures to the letter around here.** _______
10. **Nobody gets too upset if people break the rules around here.** _______

SCORING AND INTERPRETATION:

Innovation: Sum up items 1-5. _______

Formalization: Sum up items 6-10. _______

If your score is 22 or above for either facet, your organization or workgroup is high on that particular dimension. Creative cultures tend to be high on innovation and low on formalization. So if your score was 22 or above for innovation and 21 or below for formalization, then chances are you've experienced a strong creativity culture.

Source: From Malcolm G. Patterson, Michael A. West, Viv J. Shackleton, Jeremy F. Dawson, Rebecca Lawthom, Sally Maitlis, David L. Robinson, and Alison M. Wallace, "Validating the Organizational Climate Measure: Links to Managerial Practices, Productivity and Innovation," *Journal of Organizational Behavior,* Vol. 26, 2005, pp. 379–408. Reprinted with permission of John Wiley & Sons, Inc.

might have noticed that all of the advantages in the left-hand column of Table 14-2 allow the organization to become more efficient at whatever aspect of culture is strong within the organization. The right-hand column's disadvantages all lead toward an organization's inability to adapt.

In some cases, the culture of an organization is not really strong or weak. Instead, there might be **subcultures** that unite a smaller subset of the organization's employees. These subgroups may

亚文化是由组织中小部分的员工组成的文化。

FIGURE 14-4 Culture Strength and Subcultures

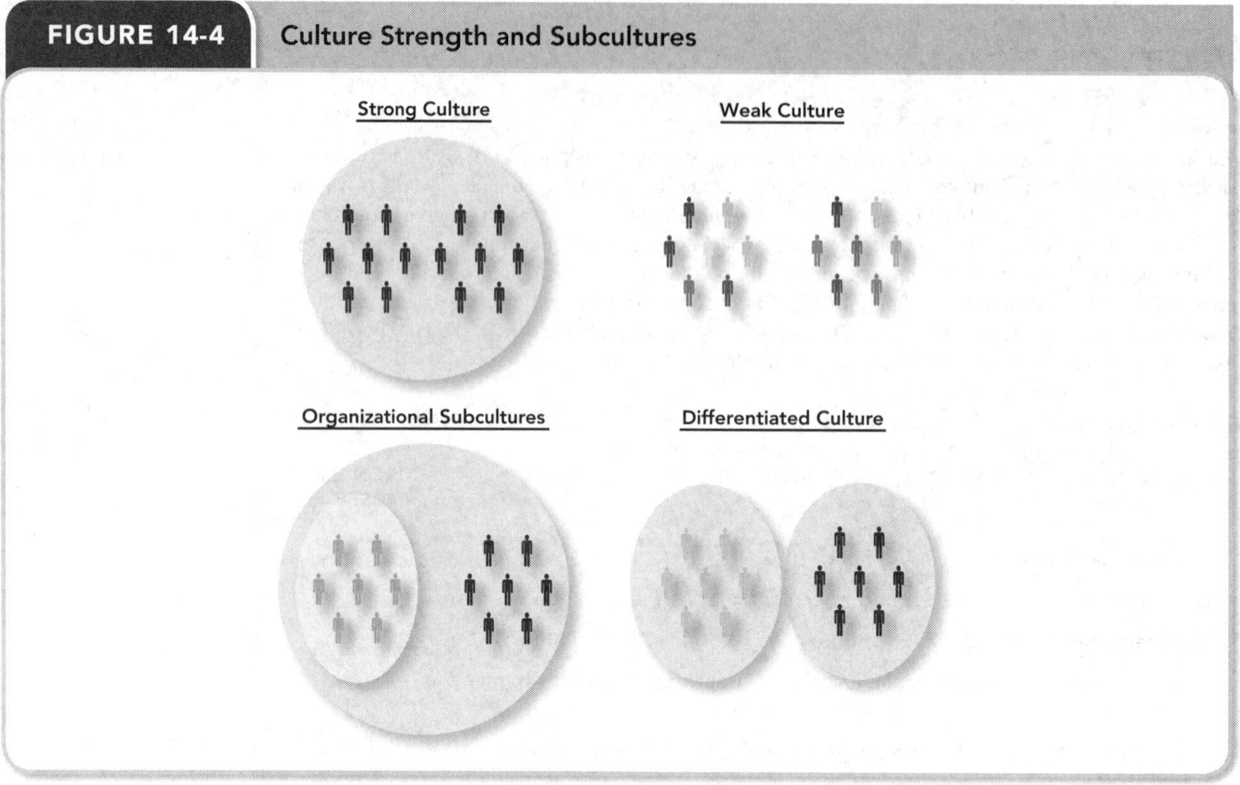

be created because there is a strong leader in one area of the company that engenders different norms and values or because different divisions in a company act independently and create their own cultures. As shown in Figure 14-4, subcultures exist when the overall organizational culture is supplemented by another culture governing a more specific set of employees. Subcultures are more likely to exist in large organizations than they are in small companies. Most organizations don't mind having subcultures, as long as they don't interfere with the values of the overall culture. In fact, subcultures can be very useful for organizations if there are certain areas of the organization that have different demands and needs for their employees. However, when their values don't match those of the larger organization, we call subcultures **countercultures.** Countercultures can sometimes serve a useful purpose by challenging the values of the overall organization or signifying the need for change. In extreme cases however, countercultures can split the

当亚文化的价值观与组织的价值观不匹配时，我们称亚文化为**反主流文化**。

TABLE 14-2 Pros and Cons of a Strong Culture

ADVANTAGES OF A STRONG CULTURE	DISADVANTAGES OF A STRONG CULTURE
Differentiates the organization from others	Makes merging with another organization more difficult
Allows employees to identify themselves with the organization	Attracts and retains similar kinds of employees, thereby limiting diversity of thought
Facilitates desired behaviors among employees	Can be "too much of a good thing" if it creates extreme behaviors among employees
Creates stability within the organization	Makes adapting to the environment more difficult

organization's culture right down the middle, resulting in the differentiated culture in Figure 14-4. See this chapter's **OB on Screen** for an example of a subculture within a larger culture.

维持组织文化 MAINTAINING AN ORGANIZATIONAL CULTURE

Clearly an organization's culture can be described in many ways, from espoused values and underlying assumptions, to general dimensions such as solidarity or sociability, to more specific types such as service cultures or safety cultures. No matter how we describe an organization's culture, however, that culture will be put to the test when an organization's founders and original employees begin to recruit and hire new members. If those new members don't fit the culture, then the culture may become weakened or differentiated. However, two processes can conspire to help keep cultures strong: attraction–selection–attrition and socialization.

14.4

How do organizations maintain their culture and how do they change it?

OB ON SCREEN

NEW IN TOWN

This will be an exciting utilization of new branding for capitalizing on a highly profitable demographic.

With those words, mid-level executive Lucy Hill (Renee Zellweger) tells a group of employees at a food processing plant in New Ulm, Minnesota (pop. 13,595), that change is coming in *New in Town* (Dir.: Jonas Elmer, Columbia Pictures, 2009). Her "fancy" words and corporate attitude don't go over well with the plant's employees—especially once they find out what that "change" really means. Lucy is a hard-driving Miami businesswoman in a large food conglomerate, accustomed to the "numbers mean everything" and "people are objects" culture that the corporate offices exude. Somewhat against her wishes (but willing to do whatever it takes to succeed), Lucy gets sent to Minnesota to downsize and run a small-town plant that is losing money. What she runs into is a section of the company that she can hardly believe exists. The small town plant is a completely different culture than what she's used to.

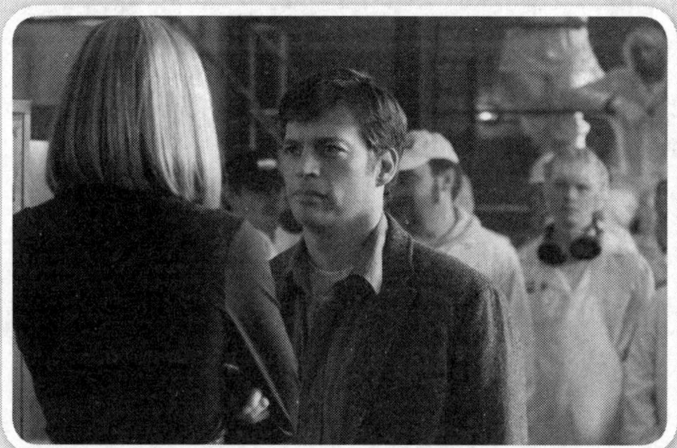

The first people she butts heads with are Stu Kopenhafer (J.K. Simmons) and the union representative, Ted Mitchell (Harry Connick, Jr.). Stu is a crusty old manager who likes things the way they are and has a high level of distrust toward corporate employees and outsiders in general. To say Stu is skeptical of Lucy's goals for the plant would be a huge understatement. Lucy's run-ins with Stu and Ted near the beginning of the movie help highlight the differences between the plant and the corporate atmosphere that Lucy knows so well. One of the central struggles Lucy faces thus pertains to deciding which of the two cultures actually provides a better fit for her. The New Ulm plant is a definite subculture within the overall company, but whether that subculture is useful to the organization, or instead really a counterculture, you'll have to decide for yourself.

吸引－选择－损耗框架（ASA 框架）认为，潜在的员工将会被吸引到组织文化与员工个性相匹配的组织，这意味着一些潜在的职位申请者会由于感知到缺乏这种匹配而不申请。另外，组织会根据申请者的个性是否与组织文化匹配来进行甄选，进一步淘汰潜在的“不适合者”。最后，那些仍然不能适应组织文化的人在工作时要么不快乐，要么没有效率，这会导致损耗（比如说自愿或非自愿的离职）。

ATTRACTION–SELECTION–ATTRITION (ASA). The **ASA framework** holds that potential employees will be attracted to organizations whose cultures match their own personality, meaning that some potential job applicants won't apply due to a perceived lack of fit. In addition, organizations will select candidates based on whether their personalities fit the culture, further weeding out potential "misfits." Finally, those people who still don't fit will either be unhappy or ineffective when working in the organization, which leads to attrition (i.e., voluntary or involuntary turnover).

Several companies can provide an example of ASA in action. FedEx has worked hard to create a culture of ethics. The executives at FedEx believe that a strong ethical culture will attract ethical employees who will then strengthen moral behavior at FedEx. Headhunters and corporate recruiters are well aware of the fact that employees who have lots of experience in certain types of cultures (i.e., places they "fit") will have a hard time adapting to other types of cultures. One type of culture they look out for specifically is high levels of bureaucracy—recruiters point to British Airways, General Mills, and Occidental Petroleum as prime examples of non-risk taking, bureaucratic cultures whose employees are rarely successful when they leave to go somewhere else. Of course, attraction and selection processes don't always align employees' personalities with organizational culture—one reason voluntary and involuntary turnover occurs in every organization.

社会化是员工学习社会知识，以使得他们理解和适应组织文化的主要过程。

SOCIALIZATION. In addition to taking advantage of attraction–selection–attrition, organizations also maintain an organizational culture by shaping and molding new employees. Starting a new job with a company is a stressful, complex, and challenging undertaking for both employees and organizations. In reality, no outsider can fully grasp or understand the culture of an organization simply by looking at artifacts visible from outside the company. A complete understanding of organizational culture is a process that happens over time. **Socialization** is the primary process by which employees learn the social knowledge that enables them to understand and adapt to the organization's culture. It's a process that begins before an employee starts work and doesn't end until an employee leaves the organization. What is it that an employee needs to learn and adapt to in order to be socialized into his or her new role within an organization? Most of the important information can be grouped into six dimensions, highlighted in Figure 14-5.

FIGURE 14-5 Dimensions Addressed in Most Socialization Efforts

Source: G.T. Chao, A.M. O'Leary-Kelly, S. Wolf, H.J. Klein, and P.D. Gardner, "Organizational Socialization: Its Content and Consequences," *Journal of Applied Psychology,* Vol. 79, 1994, pp. 730–43. Copyright © 1994 by the American Psychological Association. Adapted with permission. No further reproduction or distribution is permitted without written permission from the American Psychological Association.

Research shows that each of these six dimensions is an important area in the process of socialization. Each has unique contributions to job performance, organizational commitment, and person–organization fit.

Socialization happens in three relatively distinct stages. The **anticipatory stage** happens prior to an employee spending even one second on the job. It starts the moment a potential employee hears the name of the organization. When you see the company name Microsoft, what does it make you think about? What are the images that come to your mind? Anticipatory socialization begins as soon as a potential employee develops an image of what it must be like to work for a given company. The bulk of the information acquired during this stage occurs during the recruitment and selection processes that employees go through prior to joining an organization. Relevant information includes the way employees are treated during the recruitment process, the things that organizational insiders tell them about the organization, and any other information employees acquire about what the organization is like and what working there entails.

预期阶段发生在员工开始工作之前。它始于一名潜在员工听到组织名称的那一刻。

The **encounter stage** begins the day an employee starts work. There are some things about an organization and its culture that can only be learned once a person becomes an organizational insider. During this stage, new employees compare the information they acquired as outsiders during the anticipatory stage with what the organization is really like now that they're insiders. To the degree that the information in the two stages is similar, employees will have a smoother time adjusting to the organization. Problems occur when the two sets of information don't quite match. This mismatch of information is called **reality shock.** Reality shock is best exemplified by the employee who says something to the effect of, "Working at this company is not nearly what I expected it to be." Surveys suggest that as many as one-third of new employees leave an organization within the first 90 days as a result of unmet expectations. The goal of the organization's socialization efforts should be to minimize reality shock as much as possible. We'll describe some ways that organizations can do this effectively in our Application section that concludes this chapter.

碰撞阶段始于员工开始工作的那一天。一旦员工成为组织的内部人士，有关组织及其文化的知识只能通过学习来获得。

当两组信息不完全匹配时就出现了问题，这种信息的不匹配称为**现实冲击**。

The final stage of socialization is one of **understanding and adaptation.** During this stage, newcomers come to learn the content areas of socialization and internalize the norms and expected behaviors of the organization. The important part of this stage is change on the part of the employee. By looking back at the content areas of socialization in Figure 14-5, you can begin to picture what a perfectly socialized employee looks like. The employee has adopted the goals and values of the organization, understands what the organization has been through, and can converse with others in the organization using technical language and specific terms that only insiders would understand. In addition, the employee enjoys and gets along with other employees in the organization, knows who to go to in order to make things happen, and understands and can perform the key functions of his or her job. Talk about the perfect employee! Needless to say, that's quite a bit of information to gain—it's not a process that happens overnight. Some would say that this last stage of socialization never truly ends, as an organization's culture continues to change and evolve over time. However, organizations also know that the more quickly and effectively an employee is socialized, the sooner that employee becomes a productive worker within the organization.

社会化的最后一个阶段是**理解和适应阶段**。在这个阶段，新员工开始学习社会化的内容，并将规范及期望的行为内化。

It's important to note that the length of the socialization process varies depending on the characteristics of the employee, not just the company. For example, some employees might progress more rapidly through the stages because of the knowledge they possess, their ability to recognize cultural cues, or their adaptability to their environment. In fact, there is growing evidence that proactivity on the part of the employee being socialized has a significant effect on socialization outcomes. Some organizations might help their employees socialize more quickly because they have stronger cultures or cultures that are more easily understandable. The biggest difference though is that some organizations simply work harder at socializing their employees than others.

变革组织文化
CHANGING AN ORGANIZATIONAL CULTURE

Given all the effort it takes to create and maintain a culture, changing a culture once one has been established is perhaps even more difficult. In fact, estimates put the rate of successful major culture change at less than 20 percent. At eBay, CEO John Donahoe and chief technology officer Mark Carges are trying to change the culture to avoid the sense that every little decision must be an exercise in bureaucracy, with careful examination of all permutations of a possible outcome before acting. "Now we're actually going to put something out before we've got all the answers," claims Carges. Their goal is to get eBay's employees to think about technology differently—a major culture shift for the company and many of its analytically inclined employees. One way they're initiating this shift is by moving employees who traditionally would not interact together in the workplace, such as making business staffers and software developers sit next to one another. Changes like this can send a loud signal about what's going to be important in the future, even in the midst of massive change. In practice though, two other ways are more common methods to change a culture: changes in leadership and mergers or acquisitions.

CHANGES IN LEADERSHIP. There is perhaps no bigger driver of culture than the leaders and top executives of organizations. Just as the founders and originators of organizations set the tone and develop the culture of a new company, subsequent CEOs and presidents leave their mark on the culture. Many times, leaders are expected simply to sustain the culture that has already been created. At other times, leaders have to be a driving force for change as the environment around the organization shifts. This expectation is one of the biggest reasons organizations change their top leadership. For example, Nortel Networks hired two former Cisco executives into the roles of chief operating officer and chief technology officer. It is Nortel's hope that these executives will help bring some of Cisco's culture of aggressiveness to Nortel and thus allow it to compete more effectively in the high-technology industry environment.

MERGERS AND ACQUISITIONS. Merging two companies with two distinct cultures is a surefire way to change the culture in an organization. The problem is that there is just no way to know what the culture will look like after the merger takes place. What the new culture will resemble is a function of both the strength of the two cultures involved in the merger and how similar they are to each other. Ideally, a new culture would be created out of a compromise in which the best of both companies is represented by the new culture. There are many stories that have arisen from the mergers of companies with very different cultures: AOL/Time Warner, Exxon/Mobil, HP/Compaq, and RJR/Nabisco, to name a few. Unfortunately, very few of these stories are good ones. Mergers rarely result in the strong culture that managers hope will appear when they make the decision to merge. In fact, most merged companies operate under a differentiated culture for an extended period of time. Some of them never really adopt a new identity, and when they do, many of them are seen as failures by the outside world. This perception is especially true in global mergers, in which each of the companies not only has a different organizational culture but is from a different country as well, as our **OB Internationally** box details. Every now and then though, a merger happens in which the leadership focuses on culture from the start, such was the case with the merger of Delta and Northwest Airlines. Rather than risk creating a fragmented culture, Delta CEO Richard Anderson went to the extreme of changing the ID numbers on every employee's security badge, so that employees could not tell whether a colleague started with Delta or Northwest. According to Anderson, he wanted to avoid a situation in which "employees were constantly sizing up which side you were on."

Merging two different cultures has major effects on the attitudes and behaviors of organizational employees. Companies merge for many different strategic reasons, and though many managers and executives may realize its importance, whether the cultures will match is rarely the deciding criterion. Slightly less troublesome but still a major hurdle to overcome are acquisitions. In most instances, the company doing the acquiring has a dominant culture to which the other is expected to adapt. A recent example is the acquisition of Anheuser-Busch by the Belgian-based firm InBev. InBev and its CEO Carlos Brito are known for their heavy-handed, cost-cutting ways; Anheuser-Busch is known for its free-spending atmosphere, in which employees get free admission to the company's theme parks and two cases of free beer each month. One industry analyst joked that the Budweiser Clydesdales get better treatment than the average InBev employee. Another example comes from the acquisition of Mail Boxes Etc. by UPS. Strategically, the acquisition had many advantages that supposedly would allow UPS to compete better with FedEx and the U.S. Postal Service. However, the culture clash between the efficiency

OB INTERNATIONALLY

As mentioned previously, there is perhaps no more perilous journey for a company to take than merging with or acquiring another large firm. These problems are exacerbated when the two companies are from different countries. As few as 30 percent of international mergers and acquisitions create shareholder value. Nevertheless, 2010 set a record pace for global mergers and acquisitions. Why is this the case? Hopefully, we've illustrated the inherent difficulties of trying to merge two different cultures even when the organizations are in the same country. These cultural differences can be magnified when international culture plays a role as well. Chances are good that your experiences in college have shown you that different countries have different cultures, just like organizations. People who come from different countries tend to view the world differently and have different sets of values as well. For example, DaimlerChrysler bought a controlling stake in Mitsubishi Motors, thinking that a strong alliance between the two automotive companies would result in high levels of value for both. Unfortunately, the merger broke up, for reasons that have been attributed to the international culture differences between the two firms. The Japanese managers tended to avoid "unpleasant truths" and stay away from major change efforts—a tendency that DaimlerChrysler never confronted but also could not accept.

There are many stories of failed international mergers, and one of the greatest reasons for them is that corporations fail to recognize the impact that national culture differences (in addition to organizational culture differences) have on their ability to be successful. One such acquisition that doesn't intend to fall victim to this issue is the purchase of Volvo Car Corporation. (Sweden) from Ford by China's Geely Holding Group. Although the relationship started out extremely rocky, with Geely executives storming out of an initial meeting in Sweden because they felt they were being treated like they were stupid, the two companies seem to have reached some compromises. Volvo, somewhat against their more safe and family-friendly culture, is now producing some high-end luxury models to compete with Mercedes-Benz and BMW, which fit with Chinese desires. In addition, although Geely wanted to build three assembly plants in China to jump-start sales, they are following Volvo's more slow, quality approach at the behest of Volvo's CEO. For now, it seems that both CEOs are determined for each company to learn from the other.

and rigidness of UPS and the entrepreneurial spirit of Mail Boxes Etc. franchisees has caused UPS some major headaches. We've noted how difficult it is to get just one person to adapt to an established culture through the socialization process. Can you imagine how difficult it is to change an entire organization, all at one time?

One of the major reasons that one company purchases another is simply to acquire the technology that it has. In such cases, the acquired company usually is expected to change to fit the buyer's culture. However, a new approach being used by several companies, including Hewlett-Packard, Yahoo, and Cisco, is to buy companies with the intention of infusing their different culture into their own. Clorox, the Oakland, CA–based consumer products manufacturer, acquired Massachusetts–based personal care product maker Burt's Bees with the full knowledge of their environmentally friendly and socially responsible culture, which Clorox hoped would help them in their quest to be more environmentally focused as well. Although this process of "innovation via absorption" looks good on paper, it's very difficult, and companies need to think twice about changing the fundamental cultures they have built.

Clorox acquired Burt's Bees in the hopes of using their environmentally friendly culture to accentuate their own.

总结：为什么某些组织的文化与其他组织的有所不同
SUMMARY: WHY DO SOME ORGANIZATIONS HAVE DIFFERENT CULTURES THAN OTHERS?

So why do some organizations have different cultures than others? As shown in Figure 14-6, attraction–selection–attrition processes, socialization, changes in leadership, and mergers and acquisitions shape the three components of organizational culture: basic underlying assumptions, espoused values, and observable artifacts. Specific combinations of those culture components then give rise to both general and specific culture types. For example, cultures can be categorized on the basis of solidarity and sociability into fragmented, mercenary, communal, and networked types. Cultures can also be categorized into more specific types, such as customer service, safety, diversity, and creativity. Finally, those general and specific types can be further classified according to the strength of the culture. Taken together, these processes explain "what it's like" within the hallways of a given organization.

FIGURE 14-6 Why Do Some Organizations Have Different Cultures Than Others?

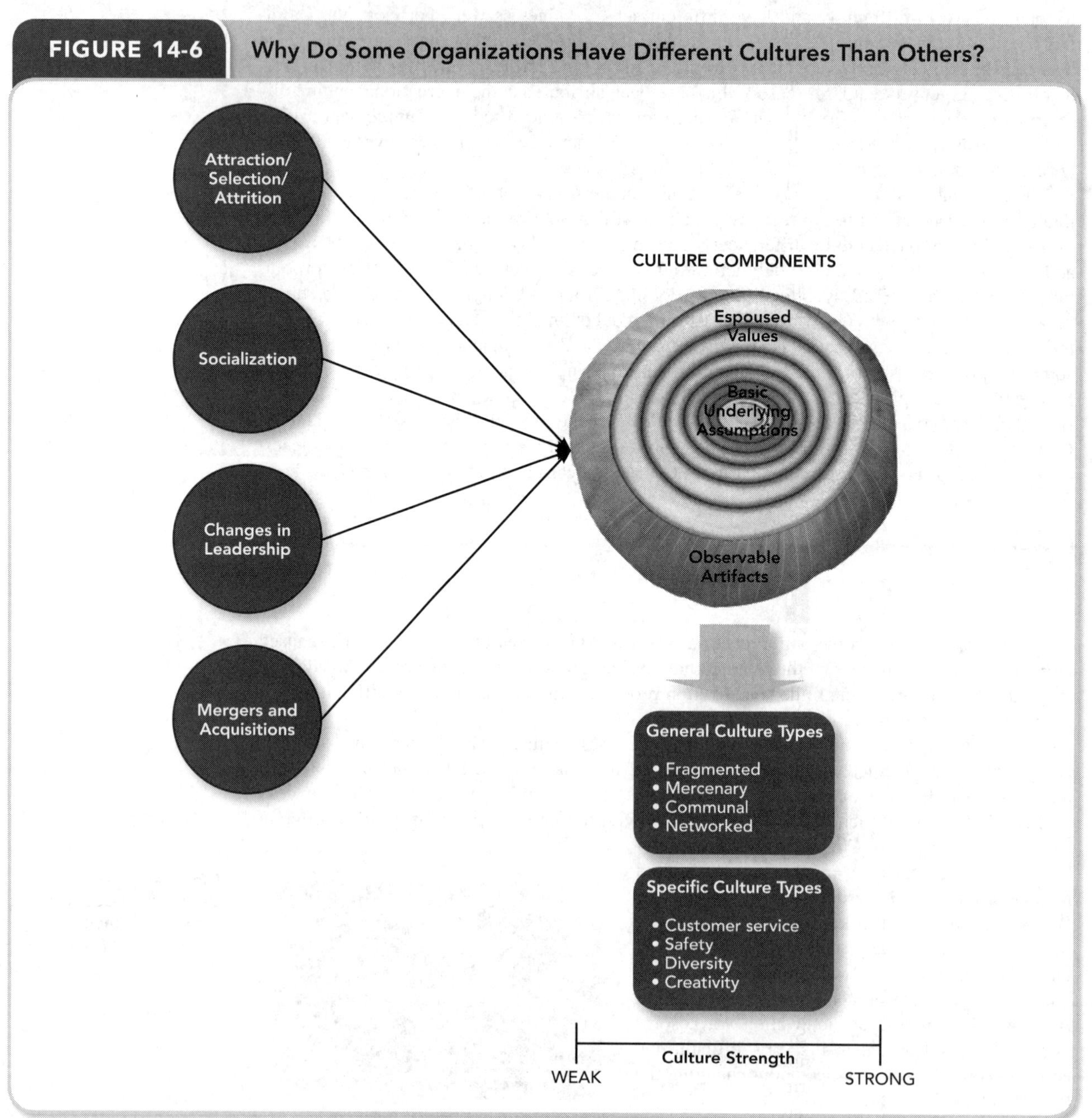

组织文化有多重要

HOW IMPORTANT IS ORGANIZATIONAL CULTURE?

Normally, this section is where we summarize the importance of organizational culture by describing how it affects job performance and organizational commitment—the two outcomes in our integrative model of OB. However (similar to organizational structure in Chapter 13), it's difficult to summarize the importance of culture in this way because there are so many different types and dimensions of the concept. Although there has been some support for distinct culture types having an effect on employee attitudes, high solidarity cultures, high sociability cultures, diversity cultures, creativity cultures, and so forth all have different effects on performance and commitment—effects that likely vary across different types of organizations and industries.

Regardless of the type of culture we're talking about, however, one concept remains important for any employee in any business: fit. Think for a moment about working for an organization whose culture doesn't match your own values. Maybe you work for an organization that produces a product that you don't believe in or that might be harmful to others, such as Philip Morris, Budweiser, or Harrah's casinos. Maybe your employer is an organization that expects you to perform questionable behaviors from an ethical standpoint or produces a product that's of poor quality. **Person–organization fit** is the degree to which a person's personality and values match the culture of an organization. Employees judge fit by thinking about the values they prioritize the most, then judging whether the organization shares those values. Table 14-3 provides a set of values that many people have used to judge fit. Which of these values would you say are the most important to you?

个人－组织匹配是指一个人的人格和价值观与组织文化相匹配的程度。

Two recent meta-analyses illustrate the importance of person–organization fit to employees. When employees feel that their values and personality match those of the organization, they experience higher levels of *job satisfaction* and feel less *stress* about their day-to-day tasks. They also feel higher levels of *trust* toward their managers. Taken together, those results illustrate why person–organization fit is so highly correlated with organizational commitment, one of the two outcomes in our integrative model of OB (see Figure 14-7). When employees feel they fit with their organization's culture, they're much more likely to develop an emotional attachment to the company. The effects of fit on job performance are weaker, however. In general, person–organization fit is more related to citizenship behaviors than to task performance. Employees who sense a good fit are therefore more likely to help their colleagues and "go the extra mile" to benefit the company.

 **14.5**

What is person–organization fit and how does it affect job performance and organizational commitment?

应用：管理社会化

APPLICATION: MANAGING SOCIALIZATION

Most organizations recognize the importance of having employees adapt to the culture of their organization quickly. Luckily, there are a number of actions that organizations can take to help their employees adapt from the first day they walk in the door. Table 14-4 highlights some of the different tactics organizations can use when socializing their employees. Note that companies can take two very different approaches to the socialization process. The left-hand column represents a view of socialization in which the goal of the process is to have newcomers adapt to the organization's culture. This view assumes that the organization has a strong culture and definite norms and values that it wants employees to adopt, which is not always the case. Some organizations don't have a strong culture that they want employees to adapt to, or they might be trying to change their culture and want new employees to come in and "shake things up." The socialization tactics listed in the right-hand column of Table 14-4 might be more appropriate in such circumstances. In addition to the socialization tactics listed in the table, there are three other major ways in which organizations routinely and effectively help speed up the socialization process of newcomers: realistic job previews, orientation programs, and mentoring.

真实工作预览主要运用在招募过程中的社会化预期阶段，是指通过提供正反两方面的工作信息，使潜在员工对于将要工作的组织形成准确的印象。

 **14.6**

What steps can organizations take to make sure that newcomers will fit with their culture?

REALISTIC JOB PREVIEWS. One of the most inexpensive and effective ways of reducing early turnover among new employees is through the use of **realistic job previews.** Realistic job previews (RJPs) occur during the anticipatory stage of socialization during the recruitment process. They involve making sure a potential employee has an accurate picture of what working

TABLE 14-3 Values Used to Judge Fit with a Culture

Flexibility	Adaptability
Stability	Predictability
Being innovative	Take advantage of opportunities
A willingness to experiment	Risk taking
Being careful	Autonomy
Being rule oriented	Being analytical
Paying attention to detail	Being precise
Being team oriented	Sharing information freely
Emphasizing a single culture	Being people oriented
Fairness	Respect for the individual's rights
Tolerance	Informality
Being easy going	Being calm
Being supportive	Being aggressive
Decisiveness	Action orientation
Taking initiative	Being reflective
Achievement orientation	Being demanding
Taking individual responsibility	High expectations for performance
Opportunities for growth	High pay for good performance
Security of employment	Offers praise for good performance
Low level of conflict	Confronting conflict directly
Developing friends at work	Fitting in
Working in collaboration with others	Enthusiasm for the job
Working long hours	Not being constrained by rules
Having an emphasis on quality	Being distinctive from others
Having a good reputation	Being socially responsible
Being results oriented	Having a clear guiding philosophy
Being competitive	Being highly organized

Source: C.A. O'Reilly, J.A. Chatman, and D.F. Caldwell, "People and Organizational Culture: A Profile Comparison Approach to Assessing Person–Organization Fit," *Academy of Management Journal,* Vol. 34, 1991, pp. 487–516. Copyright © 1991. Reproduced with permission of via Copyright Clearance Center.

for an organization is going to be like by highlighting both the positive *and* the negative aspects of the job. Although RJPs almost always occur prior to hiring, Cisco Systems has a unique program called "Cisco Choice" where their 2,500 new hires a year interview and hear presentations from managers in over 30 business units after they are hired. The new hires then get to choose where in the company they want to work. Cisco feels that by allowing new hires to pick

FIGURE 14-7 Effects of Person–Organization Fit on Performance and Commitment

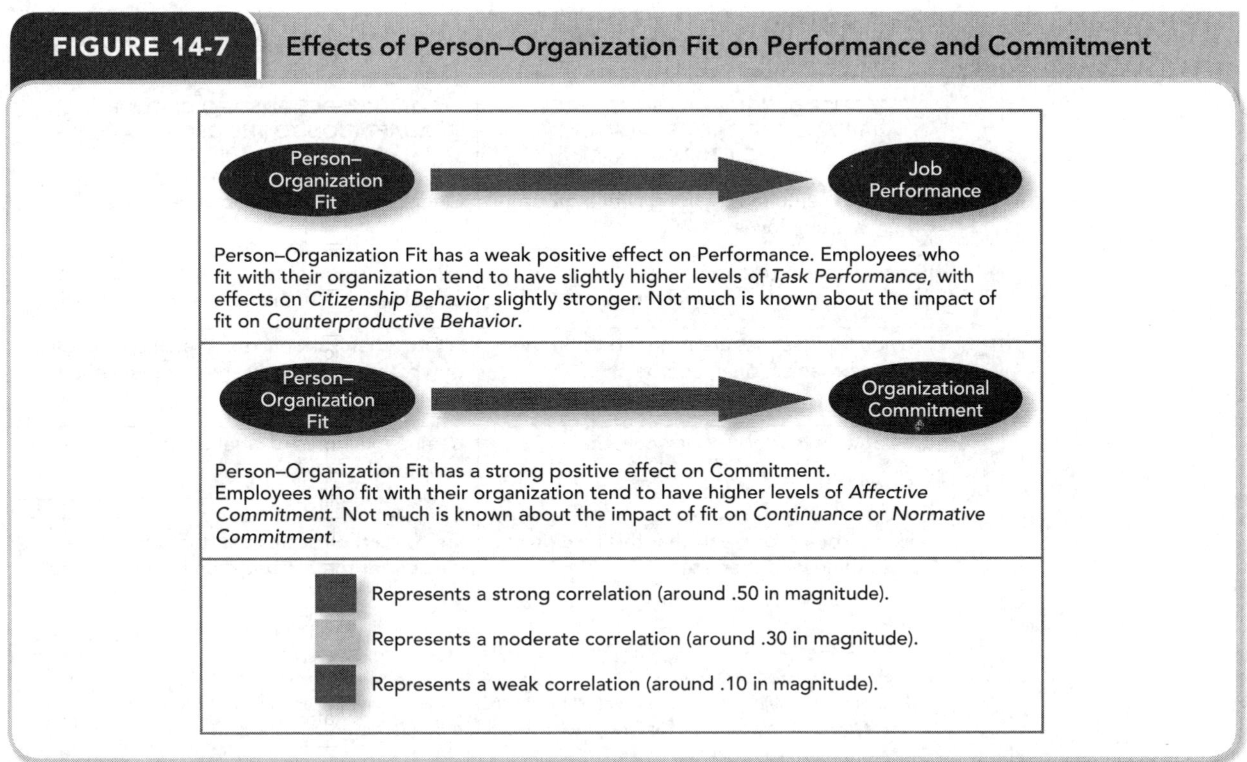

Sources: W. Arthur Jr., S.T. Bell, A.J. Villado, and D. Doverspike, "The Use of Person–Organization Fit in Employment-Related Decision Making: An Assessment of Its Criterion-Related Validity," *Journal of Applied Psychology* 91 (2007), pp. 786–801; and A.L. Kristof-Brown, R.D. Zimmerman, and E.C. Johnson, "Consequences of Individuals' Fit at Work: A Meta-Analysis of Person–Job, Person–Organization, Person–Group, and Person–Supervisor Fit," *Personnel Psychology* 58 (2005), pp. 281–342.

jobs based on their interest and skills, they are likely to work harder and stay with the company. It also lessens reality shock and shortens the encounter stage that normally accompanies initial employment. James Revis, after going through Cisco Choice as a new hire, sees benefits even beyond his choice of where to work, "Normally [new employees] just know what their department does and what their specific product is. When we collaborate, I already know what the other department does." Given Cisco's astounding 98 percent two-year retention rate, it's hard to argue with them.

ORIENTATION PROGRAMS. One effective way to start the socialization process is by having new employees attend some form of **newcomer orientation** session. Apparently most organizations agree, given that 64–93 percent of all organizations use some form of orientation training process. Not all orientation programs are alike however, and different types of orientation training can be more effective than others. Orientation programs have been shown to be effective transmitters of socialization content, such that those employees who complete orientation have higher levels of satisfaction, commitment, and performance than those who don't. Jet Blue CEO Dave Barger believes strongly in these sessions and shows it by having been to over 250 of them over the last decade. Barger tells his new hires, "The hard product—airplanes, leather seats, satellite TVs, bricks and mortar—as long as you have a checkbook, they can be replicated. It's the culture that can't be replicated. It's how we treat each other. Do we trust each other? Can we push back on each other? The human side of the equation is the most important part of what we're doing."

新员工开始社会化过程的一个有效方法是让新员工参加某种形式的**新人适应会议**。

MENTORING. One of the most popular pieces of advice given to college students as they begin their careers is that they need to find a mentor or coach within their organization. **Mentoring** is a process by which a junior-level employee (protégé) develops a deep and long-lasting relationship

指导是组织中初级员工(门徒)与高级员工(导师)建立一种深厚和持久关系的过程。

TABLE 14-4 Tactics Organizations Use to Socialize New Employees

TACTICS DESIGNED TO *ENCOURAGE* ADAPTATION TO THE ORGANIZATION'S CULTURE	TACTICS DESIGNED TO *DISCOURAGE* ADAPTATION TO THE ORGANIZATION'S CULTURE
Orient new employees along with a group of other new employees.	Orient new employees by themselves.
Put newcomers through orientation apart from current organizational members.	Allow newcomers to interact with current employees while they are being oriented.
Provide hurdles that are required to be met prior to organizational membership.	Allow organizational membership regardless of whether any specific requirements have been met.
Provide role models for newcomers.	Use no examples of what an employee is supposed to be like.
Constantly remind newcomers that they are now part of a group and that this new group helps define who they are.	Constantly affirm to newcomers that they are to be themselves and that they were chosen for the organization based on who they are.

Sources: Adapted from G.R. Jones, "Socialization Tactics, Self-Efficacy, and Newcomers' Adjustments to Organizations," *Academy of Management Journal* 29 (1986), pp. 262–79; and J. Van Maanen and E.H. Schein, "Toward a Theory of Organizational Socialization," *Research in Organizational Behavior* 1 (1979), pp. 209–64.

with a more senior-level employee (mentor) within the organization. The mentor can provide social knowledge, resources, and psychological support to the protégé both at the beginning of employment and as the protégé continues his or her career with the company. Mentoring has always existed in companies on an informal basis. However, as organizations continue to learn about the strong benefits of these relationships, they're more frequently instituting mentoring programs that formally match newcomers with mentors. In fact, nearly 76 percent of companies use mentoring in order to develop skills. Formal programs allow the company to provide consistent information, train mentors, and ensure that all newcomers have the opportunity to develop one of these fruitful relationships. Morgan Stanley started their program by having leaders develop a curriculum for what makes employees successful within the firm and then paired mentors and protégés who were expected to cover specific material. McGraw-Hill Education paired mentors and protégés based on what the protégé's goals were and who could best help them achieve those goals.